THE

HOLLYWOOD

STORY

Joel Finler was born in the Bronx, New York City, and grew up in Philadelphia and Washington D.C. Educated at Oberlin College in Ohio, University College London and in the film department of the Slade School of Art, he settled in London in the early 1960s. He worked as a writer and lecturer on the cinema and became film critic for *Time Out*. His first book, on the actor and silent film director Erich von Stroheim, was published in 1967. In the 1970s he gave up lecturing and reviewing to concentrate on writing, with a special interest in the history of the American cinema, while expanding his own archive and photo collection. His other books include *All-Time Movie Favourites* and *The Movie Directors Story*. Joel Finler has lived in north London for twenty-five years and has recently completed a book on Alfred Hitchcock's years in Hollywood. Current projects include a book on the history of Hollywood movie stills photography and on the history of colour in the cinema. His father, Bennett Finler, who helped with much of the research on *The Hollywood Story*, lives in Jerusalem and works in the library of the Jerusalem Cinémathèque. *The Hollywood Story* won the British Film Institute award as the outstanding film book of 1989.

THE
HOLLYWOOD
STORY

Joel W. Finler

Research assistance by
Bennett Finler

Mandarin

To the memory of Matilda Hay Finler (1906-1976)

A Mandarin Paperback
THE HOLLYWOOD STORY

First published in Great Britain 1988
by Octopus Books Limited
The edition published 1992
by Mandarin Paperbacks
Michelin House, 81 Fulham Road, London SW3 6RB

Mandarin is an imprint of the Octopus Publishing Group,
a division of Reed International Books Limited

Text © Joel W. Finler
Copyright © Octopus book Limited, 1988

A CIP catalogue record for this title
is available from the British Library

ISBN 0 7493 0637 8

Typeset by Falcon Typographic Art Ltd,
Edinburgh & London
Printed and bound in Great Britain
by Cox & Wyman Ltd, Reading, Berks

Contents

INTRODUCTION   7

PART 1 · THE HOLLYWOOD MOVIE INDUSTRY   11
HOLLYWOOD AND THE SILVER SCREEN   13
FROM ONE-REELERS TO CINEMASCOPE   26
MOVIES AND FINANCE   44
HOLLYWOOD MOVIEMAKERS   65
HONOURS AND AWARDS   83

PART 2 · THE MAJOR HOLLYWOOD STUDIOS   101
The Histories · The Releases · The Finances · The Stars
The Directors · The Creative Personnel
The Academy Awards
COLUMBIA   103
FOX   141
MGM   189
PARAMOUNT   237
RKO   287
UNITED ARTISTS   321
UNIVERSAL   357
WARNER BROS.   393

PART 3 · THE FACTS AND FIGURES   439
LEADING HOLLYWOOD CREATIVE PERSONNEL   441
BOX-OFFICE HITS   471
RELEASES – GENERAL STATISTICS   484
STUDIO REVENUES AND PROFITS   500
GENERAL FILM INDUSTRY AND TV STATISTICS   504
BIBLIOGRAPHY   512
INDEX   519

Introduction

In its classic form the Hollywood movie industry first took shape in the late 20s, dominated by a small number of companies. The five biggest were MGM, Paramount, Fox, Warner Bros. (which had taken over First National) and the newly formed RKO, followed by three smaller majors – Universal, Columbia and United Artists. Though there have been ups and downs for the individual companies – the three smaller studios began to challenge the top group in the 50s – these eight companies have occupied a commanding position from the silent era to the present day, with RKO as the only casualty. (It ceased production in 1957.) Though UA appears to be gone, as of 1991.

In discussing the origins and history of each studio, its releases, important stars, directors and other leading personnel, the main focus of the book is on the classic studio period from the silent era up to the 50s. The growth of filming in colour, however, is of special interest from the late 30s/early 40s to the 60s, overlapping with 3-D and widescreen which was first introduced in the 50s. The discussion of the financial development of each company concentrates on the classic era, but also comes up to date in including the box-office hits and flops from the 20s through the 80s, with special attention to the high-cost movies of recent years. Similarly, each studio's Oscar winners span the years from 1927 to 1990.

Since the general chapters in Part 1 and the studio facts and figures in Part 3 are arranged in a similar manner to the studio chapters, it is possible to read the book by tracing various main themes – the finances, the releases, and the careers of the stars and other personnel. Thus, the general section on the financial history of Hollywood in Part 1 serves as an introduction to the section on finances in each studio chapter, while Part 3 presents the basic financial data including revenue and profit figures in greater detail.

The format of the book and wide range of topics covered within a limited space means that it has proved impossible to discuss individual films at length. Some titles appear extremely prominent, such as *Gone With The Wind* (1939) which was a smash hit, a notable example of early filming in Technicolor and a big Oscar winner, while other equally interesting black-and-white movies of the same era may be mentioned only briefly. In the same way, a few key personalities appear to play a disproportionately large role within the studio system. Cecil B. DeMille, for instance, was not only one of the original founders of the Lasky Company and Paramount but, as producer and director, he also provided the studio with many of its most successful pictures – from the silent era right up to the Oscar-winning *The Greatest Show On Earth* (1952) and the extremely popular *The Ten Commandments* (1956) filmed in Paramount's own VistaVision process.

To accompany the text there is a large amount of supplementary information presented at the end of each section. And since the same pattern has been followed in every chapter, this makes it easier to compare the experiences of the different companies and better understand the similarities and differences between them. The listings of leading personnel which can be found in each studio chapter are based on feature film credits during the peak studio era from the 20s through the 50s.

However, although they rank amongst the most important contributors, scriptwriters do not fit easily into this format and have had to be treated slightly differently. Though tremendous numbers of writers were signed by the studios, few stayed on for long, and the system of screen credits was extremely unreliable. (It was normal practice to assign many writers to a major production, most of whom would not be credited.)

It is significant that many leading personnel remained for long periods at each studio. The cameramen and art directors, in particular, played an important role in establishing and maintaining the different studio styles. They also provided a stability and continuity over the years, especially at a studio like RKO where there were many management changes and where directors, too, came and went with great frequency. But there was also a negative side, as noted by the *American Cinematographer*: 'They (the studios) sign up the best directors of photography available – men who have made top reputations for individual skill and artistry. And, judged by the results on the screen, they seem to shackle these highly paid artists by insisting that all photography on the lot conform to rigid, if unwritten, regulations . . .' Similarly, the control over the 'look' of studio productions exercised by a few powerful supervising art directors, most notably Cedric Gibbons at MGM and, to a lesser extent, Hans Dreier at Paramount and Van Nest Polglase at RKO, must be taken into account in assessing the pictures which were filmed at these studios (although their power was mainly supervisory, and they worked directly on few of the pictures for which they are credited).

Though there have been major advances in film scholarship during recent years, the vast majority of books about the American cinema are written with little understanding of, or interest in, the workings of the studio system. (David Chierichetti's book on Hollywood costume design as it developed at each of the leading studios serves as a model for the kind of informed approach which is required.) The movie directors, for example, are all too often given credit for everything that appears on the screen. Yet, under the studio system a busy director such as Michael Curtiz had little time for pre-production work and the visual style of each film owes as much to leading Warners art director Anton Grot, and the cameramen, as to Curtiz himself. The filming of *Citizen Kane* in 1940 is one of the few, well-documented examples of how the studio system worked. Though director, co-writer and star Orson Welles brought with him his Mercury players and composer Bernard Herrmann – and drew on the talent of writer Herman Mankiewicz and cameraman Gregg Toland – he otherwise depended on contributions from a large number of leading RKO contract personnel, most notably unit art director Perry Ferguson (and not the more prominently credited Van Nest Polglase), special-effects experts Linwood Dunn and Vernon Walker, and make-up expert Maurice Seiderman, among others. Similarly, the production of MGM's *The Wizard Of Oz* (1939) was only made possible within the walls of a giant, well-equipped Hollywood studio with its large costume, music and art departments and contributions from many talented individuals such as Adrian (costumes) and Jack Dawn (make-up). Clearly, much work still remains to be done in revealing the true story of movie-making in Hollywood . . .

It's hard to believe that only four years have passed since this book was first written. So many changes have taken place in Hollywood during these years. Not only have a number of leading studios changed hands, but many of the smaller, independent companies, which were actively challenging the majors in the mid-80s, have folded or been taken over.

Of special interest, and new to Hollywood, has been the substantial foreign investment, beginning in 1985 with Rupert Murdoch's purchase of 20th Century-Fox. But a large number of spectacular deals took place within a brief span of time during 1989–90 in particular. Twenty-five years after a first series of takeovers and mergers when a number of the top studios became the film production and distribution arm of giant media conglomerates, big changes have been taking place in Hollywood once again.

Aside from Warner's merger with Time Inc and Italian magnate Giancarlo Parretti's purchase of MGM/UA, most attention has been devoted to the new Japanese involvement. Sony's purchase of Columbia and Tri-Star from the Coca-Cola Company and Matsushita's takeover of MCA and Universal appear to symbolize the awesome economic power exercised by Japan in the 80s and the extensive Japanese investments in the US in particular. But it is not at all certain what impact these changes of ownership will have on the Hollywood of the 90s. The generally accepted view is that the Japanese owners will continue to rely on the expertise of American producers and management and the proven box office appeal of American stars.

When this book was first being written, during 1986–87, there were more small and medium-sized independent film companies in the US than ever before. They accounted for a substantial proportion of the total film market, with some apparently poised to make the leap to major company status. Now, however, only four years later, most of them have either folded (such as De Laurentiis' DEG), been taken over (Cannon, Tri-Star) or are struggling to survive (Orion). Yet, of the seven major Hollywood studios going into the 60s, five are still going strong, thirty years later, joined by Disney – the big success story of the 80s with its Touchstone subsidiary producing a variety of adult features – while MGM/UA has recently been taken over and may yet recover some of its past glory. (Though MGM and UA were struggling throughout the 80s, as recently as 1988 there were signs of life as both had some major successes – MGM with *Moonstruck* and *A Fish Called Wanda*, UA with *Rain Man*.) The recent difficulties of Orion Pictures, for example, demonstrate the problems of a reasonably well-run and successful independent company. But when a big name studio gets in trouble, the chances are good that some major investor will be ready to step in.

Thus, the basic concept of this book appears as useful today as when it was first developed by me over ten years ago – that so much of the mainstream history of the American cinema, unlike that of any other country, can be seen through the development of a small number of giant studios which have effectively dominated the industry ever since the 20s. This provides the film historian with the opportunity to trace the history of the American cinema through these companies, But also, by juxtaposing them one can compare and contrast their parallel individual studio histories over a period of seventy years or more, thus gaining a new perspective on those many changes which have taken place.

The entire book has now been brought up to date through 1990, which neatly completes the 80s decade. Though the information contained in the book is essentially the same, most of the larger charts have had to be cut, while some new ones have been added. In addition, some of the material has been reorganized. For example, the listings of stars, directors and other leading personnel can now be found in the individual studio chapters, rather than at the back. The discussion of the various widescreen and 70mm processes introduced in the 50s and 60s has been extensively revised and corrected, based on newly available information. (Special thanks here to Grant Lobban.) Of special interest here is the new data on the early history of 35mm Panavision.

It is hoped that the book will continue to be as useful as when it first appeared four years ago. Corrections and suggestions from readers are always most welcome – please write to me c/o the publisher.

Joel W. Finler

Author's Acknowledgements

Special thanks to the many people who have contributed to this book, to David Burn, the original editor whose enthusiasm for the project was instrumental in getting the publishers interested, to Ann Lloyd who took on the daunting task of editing the book at short notice and never looked back. Also a special note of appreciation to copy-editor Robyn Karney whose support for the project was a great source of encouragement, to research assistants Hillel Tryster and Sally Hibbin, and to Tony Sloman, Bernard Happé, David Gordon and Julian Fox.

PART I

The Hollywood Movie Industry

Part I of *The Hollywood Story* explores the many different facets of Hollywood and the American movie industry from the silent era to the 80s. 'Hollywood and the Silver Screen' includes a brief history of a place called Hollywood, and how it came to be adopted as the main centre of movie making. It traces the progress of movie theatres – from nickelodeons to picture palaces, then on to drive-ins and the multiplexes of recent years. It also examines the way movie publicity campaigns and stunts have changed over the decades. 'From One-reelers to CinemaScope' studies the pattern of pictures produced by the eight leading studios with particular attention to the transition from silents to sound, the growth of colour filming and the introduction of the various wide-screen processes in the 50s and early 60s. 'Movies and Finance' includes a general financial history of the companies followed by a discussion of the costs and income from individual pictures – with reference to the notable hits and flops. The various people involved in movie-making, from producers, directors and stars to the main creative and technical personnel, are the subject of 'Hollywood Moviemakers', while 'Honours and Awards' presents a historical survey of the Oscars and other leading movie prizes.

Hollywood and
The Silver Screen

The growth of the cinema in the USA coincided with rapid industrial expansion and urban development which took place in the early decades of the 20th century. Cheap storefront nickelodeons soon gave way to purpose-built cinemas, then lavish picture palaces in the 20s, while production shifted from the East Coast to the never-never land of Hollywood where the movie colony flourished in relative luxury and isolation. Here the stars built their lavish mansions complete with tennis courts and swimming pools. Tinseltown continued to grow throughout the 20s, it survived the coming of sound and the impact of the Depression, and experienced a golden age during the 30s, the peak years of the giant studio movie factories. Decline finally set in during the postwar years when films were increasingly shot on location or abroad, away from the studios. And then, in the 50s, along came TV . . .

MOVIES IN AMERICA

The cinema first began to develop as a popular form of entertainment in the early 1900s in many countries simultaneously, most notably France, England and, especially, America, where the first primitive nickelodeons quickly multiplied. The simple and crudely made early motion pictures held a special appeal for the large number of immigrants, as well as for the native working classes. The transformation of the USA from a primarily rural population to a more urbanized and industrialized society, and the rapid growth of its large cities during the early decades of the century, provided a vast new market for this newest form of mass entertainment.

Social attitudes were changing, too, and the cinema exerted an influence on thinking through its treatment of moral and social themes which were introduced into many feature-length pictures in the 'teens and 20s. In attempting to break away from the vulgar origins of the movies, with their fairground and music-hall association, many of the early film-makers turned to uplifting subjects. They adapted literary and stage works for the screen, and adopted the middle-class values of the period which stressed the sanctity of home and family, embraced Christian values, and were strongly anti-trade union and heavily patriotic – particularly in response to America's involvement in World War I.

Around this time the USA emerged as the leading producer (and distributor) of popular movie fare for the worldwide market, a position it has continued to exploit successfully to the present day. Having grown steadily throughout the 'teens and 20s, the movie business had been transformed during this period from an assortment of small, competing companies into a highly developed and efficiently run industry dominated by a few giant corporations. The cinema flourished, and played an increasingly important role, at a time when American society was undergoing many important changes within a generally optimistic economic and political climate. Other growth industries included electricity, which became more widely available to factories and homes than ever before, and the automobile, which had a far-reaching impact on transport and on society generally. Also of special interest was the growth in mass-circulation newspapers and illustrated magazines, while the radio was emerging as a popular new entertainment medium along with new styles of popular music and jazz, and the beginnings of the recording industry – a clear indication that the introduction of sound to motion pictures could not be far off.

During the 20s there was a boom in the construction of cinemas and opulent movie palaces, and Hollywood soon grew into the main centre of production. The very name 'Hollywood' became shorthand for the American movie industry in general, but it was also readily associated in the public mind with the glamour and life-style of the stars, with the latest in high fashion, and the palatial mansions located in nearby Beverly Hills or along the Santa Monica beachfront.

News and gossip about the stars and their personal lives was eagerly devoured by fans all over the world. The actors and actresses were closely identified with the characters they played on the screen, and star worship sometimes reached mythic proportions, as reflected in the public's response to the early death of Rudolph Valentino in 1926. When a number of scandals in the early 20s (best-known of which was the Fatty Arbuckle case) threatened to cause a backlash from local censors and watch committees, with a risk of governmental censorship, a number of industry leaders banded together to form the MPPDA (the Motion Picture Producers and Distributors of America, later known as the MPAA, the Motion Picture Association of America). Former Postmaster-General Will H. Hays was selected to administer a code of self-censorship known as the 'Hays Code', as well as to represent the industry in its dealings with the public, the government and other organizations. (The Production Code was first adopted in 1930. Though the strict enforcement of its provisions only dated from 1934, it lasted for over 30 years, till 1966, then was replaced by a new ratings system from 1968.)

Sound, arriving in 1928–29, attracted moviegoers in larger numbers than ever, continuing that virtually unbroken growth which dated back to the start of the century. Though the impact of the Depression was delayed for a year or two, it had a devastating effect on many of the large movie companies. In spite of this, the 30s saw the peak period of producer and production-company control over the film-making process, with stars, directors and technical personnel signed to long-term contracts.

Though the studios recovered in the late 30s, the problems of the Depression were not finally solved until the outbreak of World War II and the boom in war-time moviegoing. But new difficulties immediately surfaced in the postwar years. The studios were troubled by union problems and strikes, followed by the 'Red scare' investigations which led to the notorious blacklist in the 50s. One of the sorriest episodes in the history of Hollywood, the blacklist came at a time when the film industry could ill afford to lose so many of its leading creative talents. At the same time, the government's Consent Decree of 1948 forced the large studios to sell off their movie theatres and give up their monopolistic practices.

The decline in moviegoing reflected the fact that people were turning to new interests and activities. A boom in car buying, for example, meant a new mobility and a greater choice for those no longer looking to the neighbourhood cinema for their regular weekly, or twice weekly, entertainment (though there was an increase in drive-in cinemas.) A similar growth in home building and in the sale of radios, record players and other home appliances indicated a new interest in home activities even before the arrival of television. The production of TV sets first climbed over the one million mark in 1949, and by 1950–52 the average was over six million sets produced each year. The number of households with TV was still under four million in 1950, but had grown up to over 20 million by 1953, accounting for 45% of all American households, and continued to increase at a rapid rate throughout the 50s. The nature of filmgoing changed from a regular, habitual activity to a more selective one, in which a visit to the cinema became something of an occasion.

The movie companies attempted to cater to this developing market by introducing larger screens and filling them with lavish, 'casts of thousands' movie spectacles, and by shooting more pictures in colour and in the various newly introduced technical processes. It worked for a time and the fall in audiences was briefly halted, but by the late 50s the studios were selling off their back lots and spreading into other areas of entertainment such as records, publishing, and especially TV production.

The decline continued through the 60s as the studios ran out of solutions and many were taken over by giant conglomerates. The prospect brightened somewhat in the 70s, continuing on into the 80s, but the outlook is currently as uncertain as ever. The latest catchwords are video and colourization, with the likelihood that high-definition TV (and video) will be here soon.

In 1987 Hollywood celebrated its 100th anniversary. The name lives on, and though the days of its glory are well in the past, the movie industry has shown a remarkable resilience over the years. It is probably not as bad as the famous scriptwriter Ben Hecht thought 30 years ago when he prophesied that 'Hollywood will be a tourist spot like Tombstone, Arizona, before the century's done'. But, then again, he may be right . . .

A Chronology of Early Hollywood, 1887–1920

1887 Harvey Henderson Wilcox registers his 120-acre ranch located in an area just northwest of Los Angeles. The new name of 'Hollywood' is supplied by his wife Daeida.

1902 Exhibitor Thomas Tally opens his Electric Theatre seating 200.

1903 The fast-growing village of Hollywood is incorporated as a municipality. Construction of a local landmark, the Hollywood Hotel.

1907 Director Francis Boggs arrives with a movie crew to film coastal locations for the Selig Polyscope production of *The Count Of Monte Cristo*.

1908 Colonel Selig begins construction of a movie studio in Edendale.

1909 The New York Motion Picture Company builds a studio in Edendale. It will later be occupied by Mack Sennett's Keystone Comedies (from 1912), and by Mascot Pictures, followed by Republic in the 30s.

1910 In January 1910 the Biograph Company sends its leading director, D. W. Griffith, with film company and crew to Southern California to make pictures for the first time. They will return again during the following two winters.
The residents of Hollywood vote to become a district of Los Angeles to secure their future water supplies. By this date the total population has grown to about 5,000.

1911 The Horsley brothers, owners of the Centaur Film Company of New Jersey, build the Nestor studio, the first movie studio in Hollywood, from a converted tavern and grocery store on the northwest corner of Sunset Boulevard and Gower St. (Later known as the Nestor/Christie studio.)
The New York Motion Picture Company acquires the rights to a large property four miles north of Santa Monica, at the entrance to Santa Ynez Canyon, and constructs a studio for filming Westerns under the supervision of producer-director Thomas Ince – The Miller 100 Bison Ranch, as it was called, later becomes popularly known as 'Inceville'.
Vitagraph locates a branch of its company in Santa Monica.

1912 The Lubin company studio is located in east Hollywood at the corner of Sunset Boulevard and Hoover St. (Later occupied by Kalem, 1913–17, Monogram and Allied Artists.)
The Universal Film Manufacturing Company opens its first West Coast studio on the southwest corner of Sunset and Gower, later the home of Century Comedies.
Charles Urban opens a studio for the production of Kinemacolor pictures at 4500 Sunset Boulevard, at the intersection with Hollywood Boulevard.

1913 Vitagraph moves its studios to east Hollywood.
The Selig Company establishes a studio on Mission Road in Eastlake Park, east Los Angeles.

The Jesse L. Lasky Feature Play Company sets up its first studio at the corner of Selma and Vine and in December begins filming *The Squaw Man*, the first feature-length Western made in Hollywood. The studio is enlarged after the merger with Famous Players in 1916, but is abandoned in 1927 after the company moves into its newly equipped studio at Melrose and Van Ness.

1914 Mutual-Triangle takes over the Kinemacolor studio and it is then used by D. W. Griffith during the period up to 1920. It becomes known as the Griffith Fine Arts Studio, and here he films his best known early features, *The Birth Of A Nation* (1915) and *Intolerance* (1916). The studio is later occupied by Tiffany (from 1927) and John Stahl Productions.

1915 Carl Laemmle opens his new Universal studios, located in Universal City in the San Fernando Valley.
As part of the new Triangle Film Corporation headed by Henry Aitken, producer Thomas Ince builds a new studio at Culver City. (Later occupied by the Goldwyn Company and by MGM, from 1924.)

1916 Harold Lloyd and Hal Roach open the Rolin Film Company studio in Culver City, later known as the Hal Roach studio.
Metro rents its first studio in Hollywood.
William Fox buys the Selig studio in Edendale.
Mutual opens the 'Lone Star' studio for Chaplin's use at 1025 Lillian Way.

1917 The Fox Film Corporation moves into a studio at Sunset Boulevard and Western Avenue.
Metro takes over Mutual's 'Lone Star' studio in Hollywood.
Charles and Sydney Chaplin acquire an estate at the southwest corner of Sunset and La Brea where the new Chaplin studio is completed the following year.

1918 Producer Louis B. Mayer arrives in California. His new production company occupies a section of the Selig studio for a time. Mayer then builds his own small studio on Mission Road the following year.

1919 Thomas Ince builds a studio with a Colonial style frontage at 9336 Washington Boulevard in Culver City. (Later occupied by Cecil B. DeMille, Pathé, Pathé/RKO and independent David O. Selznick, who filmed *Gone With The Wind* here in 1939.) The population of Hollywood has grown to 35,000. (It will reach 130,000 by 1925.)
Douglas Fairbanks leads the movie star exodus to Beverly Hills. He moves into an Edwardian style house called Greyhall where plans are hatched for the formation of United Artists and constructs the lavish 'Pickfair' on the adjoining acreage after his marriage to Mary Pickford.

HISTORY OF HOLLYWOOD

'It's a great place to live if you're an orange' quipped Fred Allen, while Oscar Levant, his co-star in Howard Hawks' *The Ransom Of Red Chief* (1952) was equally cynical: 'Strip the phoney tinsel off Hollywood and you'll find the real tinsel underneath.' Founded in 1887, the village of Hollywood just northwest of Los Angeles grew slowly at first. It was incorporated as a municipality in 1903 and first began to attract the interest of the early movie companies from the East from about 1907 to 1909. However, it was barely considered worthy of mention by the

1909 'Baedeker Guide to the USA': 'From Los Angeles to Santa Monica by Southern Pacific Railway – on the way we pass Hollywood, a suburb of charming homes . . .'

It has been suggested that the independent companies chose to film in Southern California in order to put as much distance as possible between them and the agents of the Motion Picture Patents Company who were attempting to enforce its monopoly on the various film-making patents. But many of the Trust members were also attracted to the place, among them Selig, Biograph and Vitagraph. All were quick to recognize the area's ideal climate and its exceptional variety of settings – deserts, mountains, villages, seaside and the large metropolis of Los Angeles were all within close proximity. In addition, labour costs were significantly lower than those in New York City, the other main centre of movie making. Extras were cheap to employ and the local population presented a useful mixture of different races and nationalities, including large Mexican and Oriental communities.

The extremely primitive and undeveloped state of the suburbs around Los Angeles at the time is difficult for us to appreciate today. As described by Kevin Brownlow in his book, 'Hollywood, The Pioneers', 'Sunset Boulevard snaked through the hills, following an old cattle trail, and petered out long before the coast. A bridle path ran down the centre, for the horse was the most sensible method of transport in Hollywood. Few of the roads were paved, and some of the studios provided hitching rails.'

The local residents were initially hostile to the movie people from the East, which accounted for the fact that there were more companies spread around the general area at first than in Hollywood proper. By the 20s, however, a large number of the mainly smaller studios could be found packed into a few square blocks bounded by Sunset Boulevard in the north, La Brea to the west, Melrose Avenue to the south, and Western Avenue in the east, while the most famous of those studios not located in Hollywood itself were Universal City in the San Fernando Valley to the north, the First National studios farther to the north in Burbank (later absorbed by Warner Bros.) and Culver City, seven miles to the south and the home of MGM. (Originally built by Thomas Ince, the studio was taken over by the Goldwyn Company, then inherited by MGM when Goldwyn merged with Metro.)

The concentration of filming activity in this region of Southern California continued on into the 30s for, with the coming of sound, the more free-wheeling shooting practices of the silent era were left behind and filming was confined to the actual studios (and their sound-proofed stages) more than ever before.

Throughout most of its history, Hollywood film-making took place within a very special world, that of a community dominated by movies and movie-making. Living in an extraordinary climate and placing emphasis on a glamorous lifestyle, Hollywood and its inhabitants were generally out of touch with the realities of everyday life, geographically distant from most of the US population, from the main centres of American culture, and from the businessmen and bankers on the East

Coast – a three-day train journey away. The studios were even relatively inaccessible to their own front offices located in New York City, where the money men and company heads were all too often aware of their powerlessness to control the movie-making activities of their own companies.

Movies about movie-making and about Hollywood have proved popular over the years and have reflected Tinseltown's fascination with its own image. These have ranged from large numbers of silent comedies including Chaplin's *The Masquerader* (1914) and *Behind The Screen* (1916), *Merton Of The Movies* (1924) and King Vidor's *Show People* (1927) starring Marion Davies, to more witty and perceptive treatments in *A Star Is Born* (1937) and writer-director Preston Sturges' *Sullivan's Travels* (1941). But, ironically, the most memorable selection of features was released in the early 50s at a time when the studios were just starting to fade away, and perhaps a sense of nostalgia was beginning to be felt. Billy Wilder's acerbic vision in *Sunset Boulevard* (1950) was followed by *The Bad And The Beautiful* and *Singin' In The Rain* (both released by MGM in 1952), while the effective musical remake of *A Star Is Born* (1954) was directed by George Cukor whose *What Price Hollywood?* (1932) had treated a similar theme many years before.

As late as 1948, director Frank Capra was extolling the virtues of getting away (from Hollywood) and suggested that 'it gives a producer or director a chance to get acquainted with the lives of other people – in Hollywood we learn about life only from each other's pictures.' In fact, the current trend was for more filming to take place on location, but change came only gradually. That same year, Joseph Losey, against his better judgement, found himself forced to shoot his first feature *The Boy With Green Hair* (1948) on the studio back lot in accordance with the current practice of the time, though he himself had grown up in a small American town and was well aware of what he was missing: 'That particular RKO small-town set was used many times before and many times after; it was, of course, very well done because a great deal of money was spent on it, but it was *any* American small town, and any small town is not like any other. It was much too generalised.'

By this date the decline of the old studios was already under way, most clearly symbolized by the fate of MGM. During the 50s many of the original founders of the studios retired or were replaced, and most of the studio back lots were sold off. MGM alone resisted for a time, but by the late 60s the decline of the once-proud giant and industry leader was apparent. It was made manifest by a sad event – a fabulous auction in May 1970 of thousands of famous movie props and costumes, which included Judy Garland's ruby-red slippers from *The Wizard Of Oz* (1939), Johnny Weissmuller's Tarzan loincloth, and Charlton Heston's chariot from the 1959 *Ben-Hur*.

In the early 70s, MGM sold its two largest back lots, totalling 100 acres, leaving only the original 44-acre studio, and in 1973 the company ceased distribution of its own, much-reduced output of features, at about the same time that Columbia gave up its long-established Gower Street studio and moved to Burbank where it shared studio facilities with Warner Bros. The MGM studio complex was finally sold to Lorimar-Telepictures in 1986 and MGM's own headquarters – after 62 years in Culver City – were relocated, together with 'Leo the Lion' whose famous sign had, for so long, dominated the skyline.

NICKELODEONS AND CINEMAS

The primitive early motion pictures depicting a dancing girl, a horse race, or brief scenes of everyday life, were widely seen for the first time in the mid-1890s in the peepshow arcades widely promoted by Edison under the name Kinetoscope. These arcades were soon replaced by tiny halls and converted shops where motion pictures were projected onto a screen. Known as nickelodeons because they charged audiences an entrance fee of five cents, they became extremely popular, and by 1907 it was estimated that there were about 3,000 in the USA alone, mainly concentrated in the larger cities. The rural areas had to make do with travelling film shows which could be presented in the local hall, and there was even an outdoor version of the nickelodeon called an 'Airdome'.

During these years the shows lasted only 15 to 20 minutes and were often supplemented by song slides or lectures. However, in response to popular demand, it was not long before the shows began to grow longer and the admission charge rose to ten cents, anticipating the changeover to feature-length pictures which took place in the middle and late 'teens. In addition, the filming of more serious subjects, including adaptations of plays and other literary works as presented by Adolph Zukor's Famous Players in Famous Plays, reflected an attempt to upgrade the image of the movies in general, distancing them from their lower-class associations as a cheap form of mass entertainment.

At about the same time there was a large increase in the number of purpose-built cinemas which replaced many of the old and ill-equipped nickelodeons. The peak years of cinema-building in the USA were between 1909 and 1921. During this period one architect alone, the Scottish-born Thomas Lamb, was responsible for 300 new cinemas beginning with the City Theatre on 5th Street, New York City (in 1909), and including one of the first of the new style of movie palaces, the Regent, which was constructed in Harlem in 1913. Yet another Lamb venue was the Capitol Theatre which came complete with carpeted floors, upholstered seats and uniformed ushers. It opened on Broadway in 1919 with seating for 5,300, and gained a new lease of life over 30 years later as a Cinerama showcase theatre. The Capitol was subsequently demolished, one of about 20 of New York's grandest cinemas which no longer survive. The Paramount (1926) formerly occupied the Paramount Building in Times Square. The building is still standing, but the 3,700-seat cinema has gone. Perhaps most lavish of all was the Roxy at 7th Avenue and 50th Street, designed by Chicago architect Walter Ahlschlager at a cost of $12 million with seating for 5,900. (It was demolished in 1961.) And the 6,200-seat Radio City Music Hall was built in 1932 by the celebrated Samuel 'Roxy' Rothafel in partnership with the

RKO Corporation. It had a spacious stage 144 feet wide and 80 feet deep, equipped for live entertainment, and boasted the latest in indirect auditorium lighting, including a 6¹/₂ ton main chandelier, 30 feet in diameter. An RKO movie, *The Animal Kingdom* starring Ann Harding and Leslie Howard, was selected for the grand opening in January 1933, followed, most notably, by the premiere of RKO's *King Kong* two months later. (No longer a cinema, Radio City is now in use for concerts and theatrical presentations.)

Luxurious showcase cinemas were constructed in all the large American cities and, on the West Coast, Grauman's famous Chinese Theatre opened in Hollywood with the premiere of Cecil B. DeMille's *The King Of Kings* in 1927. The boom in building continued throughout much of the 20s for, as Lewis Jacobs pointed out, 'expensive theatres in downtown districts were regarded as safe investments, since the country was experiencing a building and real-estate boom . . . In hundreds of towns the moving-picture theatre had become the outstanding building.'

By the late 20s, the number of cinemas had grown from about 15,000 in 1915 to over 20,000. It was a period characterized by intense competition among the largest film companies for control of the major first-run houses and affiliated chains. Initially the major battle was between Paramount and First National, but later Loew's (MGM), Fox, and then Warner Bros. joined the fray. (By the late 20s First National was the major loser).

The introduction of sound caused an immediate reduction in the number of buildings, for it proved uneconomic to convert many of the older and more dilapidated silent cinemas. Though the official figures still listed a total of 22,000 cinemas in 1931, a more accurate survey carried out by the Motion Picture Almanac found substantial duplication and inclusion of theatres which had been dismantled or demolished. Its corrected total showed less than 18,000 of which just under 15,000 were operational, and a further 3,200 (of 6,300) silent houses were 'closed but may reopen'. Of course, the realities of the Depression proved otherwise, and by 1935 the official figures gave a new total of just 15,300 cinemas in the USA.

The large first-run cinemas in the 20s had presented a typical programme of two to two-and-a-half hours, including the main feature, shorts, and a newsreel, plus a live show lasting 20–30 minutes. With the coming of sound, the live show (and pit orchestra) was easily replaced by screening one or two of the many musical and vaudeville shorts which were being churned out. During the Depression, the double feature became a standard item for attracting the customers and cinemas found that they could boost their falling revenues by pushing sales of popcorn, candy and soft drinks.

During the 30s and 40s the five giant companies, who were the leading cinema owners, further developed their system of centralized control over pricing, publicity, and releases aimed at maximizing income. The highest admission charges of $1 or more applied to the initial release of a new picture in first-run cinemas; and there was generally a gap of one to four weeks between the end of the first run and the start of showings at the second-run or neighbourhood theatres where admission could be as little as 15–20 cents.

In the early 40s, at the peak of their power, the five majors controlled or had interests in 17% of the cinemas in the USA (3,000 out of about 18,000 in 1945), as noted in the text of the 1948 Supreme Court decision regarding the government's Consent Decree, but also controlled an impressive 70% of the key first-run cinemas in the 92 largest American cities (those with populations exceeding 100,000) accounting for about 25% of total cinema seats. The different companies were strongest in different geographical areas of the country, with Loew's and RKO the leaders in New York-New Jersey, Paramount dominating the New England states and the South, Warners the mid-Atlantic region and Fox the Western states.

This situation was quickly changed, beginning in the late 40s, when the companies began to comply with the provisions of the Consent Decree which obligated them to dispose of their cinema holdings. Many cinemas were forced to close when audiences fell off badly in the late 40s and early 50s, but this fall in numbers was almost exactly balanced by a steady increase in the number of drive-in cinemas, capitalizing on the postwar boom in car sales. From only 300 in 1946, drive-ins totalled about 4,500 by the mid-50s and accounted for some 25% of the total of just over 18,000 cinemas.

The cinemas continued to struggle in the 60s. Around the time that their numbers had fallen to under 10,000, about half the total of the mid-40s, there was a new trend to make better use of space by converting a single large cinema into a multi-screen venue. This solution even saved a few of the famous old picture palaces such as the 3,900-seater Loew's Paradise, constructed in 1929 on the Grand Concourse in the Bronx. Though it was divided into four screens, its marble statuary and ersatz-cloud machines are still in place.

With the recovery of movie attendance in the mid-70s, the number of screens increased further. By 1977, though there were only about 10,000 four-wall cinemas, these accounted for about 13,000 'screens'. The numbers continued to grow in the 80s to well over 20,000 screens. This most recent, competitive boom in cinema building has been stimulated, at least in part, by a major investment from the giant companies which are, apparently, no longer barred from owning their own cinemas. In addition, there are a number of enterprising new companies endeavouring to bring back a touch of luxury and stylishness to the cinema buildings and lobbies even if the cinemas themselves are generally of the smaller, multiplex type. Thus, the general outlook for cinemas in the USA seems to have improved in recent years, in spite of the threat posed by increasing film-viewing on video at home.

MOVIE PUBLICITY

Publicity is almost as indispensable to the movie industry as film stock. It is the means by which the paying customers are lured into cinemas to provide a return on the film-maker's investment. In keeping with its fairground origins, the earliest publicity was simple and direct, for in those days the mere announcement that 'moving pictures' were to be shown was generally sufficient to attract a crowd.

Up to about 1910 posters were largely of the non-pictorial, information-sheet variety, but as films grew longer and increasingly relied upon stories as an attraction, so the posters advertising them emphasized their dramatic qualities. Around the year 1910, campaign sheets first began to be distributed to exhibitors. These advised them on the best ways of cashing in on their films, while weekly or monthly magazines were published by the leading companies. 'Any man can liven up his Theatre front by framed posters, which not only attract crowds, but tell those same crowds what they can see inside . . .' was the sound advice from *The Pathé Weekly Bulletin*, for example.

Events moved ahead rapidly. Carl Laemmle had initiated the star system virtually single-handed, though he was merely the first to bow to the public's wish to know more about its movie favourites. By 1912, stars were the dominant element in film publicity, as reflected in the posters of the period. Publicists were now regularly employed by all the companies, and a handful of future producers started in publicity, notably B.P. Schulberg at Rex and then Famous Players in the 'teens, and Hal B. Wallis with Warners in the 20s. Moviemaking in the USA had begun to be concentrated in a small, special town in Southern California called Hollywood. This made it relatively easy for the studios and their publicists to create a special movie-star mystique, elevating the screen idols to a grander status than that enjoyed by leading players of the theatre. In addition, provocative subject matter, most notably in Universal's *Traffic In Souls* (1913) and D. W. Griffith's *The Birth Of A Nation* (1915) caused controversy which in turn stirred up audience interest. By the 20s the public was becoming more sophisticated and new schemes had to be thought up. When Universal boss Carl Laemmle realized that he could not control the extravagance of his ace director, Erich von Stroheim, he determined to exploit the publicity value of the situation to the full. 'He's going to make you *hate him*! even if it takes a million dollars of our money to do it!' exclaimed the studio's house paper, *Moving Picture Weekly*.

But the most celebrated stunt was the erection of a giant electric sign on Broadway, regularly updated by the publicity department, which recorded the exceptional costs of Stroheim's *Foolish Wives* while it was being filmed in 1921. Special publicity campaigns continued unabated into the 30s. One which most successfully captured the public's imagination was producer David O. Selznick's search for the actress to play Scarlett O'Hara as part of the build-up to the filming and eventual release of *Gone With The Wind* in 1939.

The 30s was the peak decade of the studio and star systems and Hollywood publicity departments flourished accordingly, feeding the insatiable appetites of moviegoers all over the world for the latest news, gossip and personal details of the lives of their favourite screen idols. The largest studio, MGM, was run by the paternalistic but ruthless Louis B. Mayer who was closely involved with his publicity department, headed by Howard Strickling. As one of Mayer's most trusted aides, Strickling endeavoured to maintain the highest standards of studio policy throughout his long reign. He demonstrated a general concern with the welfare of all MGM contract players, and attempted to project a public image which was not too far removed from their true characters and lifestyles. (Strickling was especially hostile to the free-wheeling publicity gimmicks of less scrupulous publicists such as Selznick's Russell Birdwell.)

Careful grooming and handling of the stars was a characteristic of MGM, which also boasted one of the finest stills departments in Hollywood with leading photographers Clarence Sinclair Bull, Ruth Harriet Louise and George Hurrell under contract. This department was an essential tool in glamorizing and publicizing the leading female stars. In addition, an initial stills session was absolutely essential for any new arrival, both for testing the public's response to sample photos in magazines, newspapers and fan publications, and for consideration, along with a screen test, by studio executives in deciding whether or not to offer the newcomer a contract.

A closely related phenomenon in the 30s, the peak era of Hollywood glamour, was the fact that the leading ladies of MGM, Paramount and the other top studios had a tremendous influence on fashions around the world. Well-known examples include the craze for berets initiated by Garbo, Dietrich's fondness for wearing trousers and the strikingly different fuller make-up of their lips by Bette Davis and Joan Crawford, as well as Miss Crawford's famous padded-shoulder look. During World War II, in the interests of safety, Veronica Lake was forced to abandon her famous peek-a-boo hair style: large numbers of women working in factories risked catching their copycat hairdos in the machinery.

Movie advertising in newspapers, magazines and on the radio had been essential for publicizing the new releases ever since the 20s, but TV advertising has become especially popular during more recent years. Annual expenditure on TV ads topped the $175 million mark for the first time in 1979 and has continued to grow, accounting for about 30% of total advertising budgets. In the case of Fox's hit movie *Alien*, for example, the TV advertising budget topped the $3 million mark, while the studio claimed that its expenditure on newspaper ads, trailers, posters, publicity junkets and other promotional schemes in 1979 totalled about $16 million. This far exceeded its actual production cost of $11 million in making the picture and was the single most important factor in explaining why the movie failed to earn a profit on its initial release, though it had brought in worldwide rentals of $48 million in 1979. (By early 1980 *Alien* had finally made it into the black.) Indeed, it is a fact that it is not unusual today, for the marketing budget to exceed the cost of production.

Of special interest, too, are the recent efforts of movie companies to tap the vast potential of tie-in marketing of new pictures along with records, toys, and other accessories targeted at the large numbers of younger moviegoers. The most successful company in this area over the years has been the Disney organization which benefited from the great popularity of its cartoon characters, including Mickey Mouse and Donald Duck, all over the world. Recently, many more companies have been getting in on the act, especially in exploiting the rock music connection of such pictures as *Saturday Night Fever* (1977) and *Grease* (1978) while *ET. The Extra-Terrestrial* (1982) also presented a great marketing bonanza.

But, undoubtedly, the biggest story of movie merchandising during the 1970's and early 1980s has been that of George Lucas and his *Star Wars* trilogy. Sales of *Star Wars*-related goods, including a wide variety of candy, chewing gum and other snack foods, clothes, records, books, toys, gadgets and gimmicks, were estimated at around $1.5 billion per year worldwide at their peak levels in the early 80s, stimulated by TV showings of the original *Star Wars* (1977) and the cinema release of its two equally successful sequels. As a headline in *The Economist* magazine expressed it, 'May the sales force be with you.'

From One-Reelers
To Cinemascope

The feature-length picture was adopted by the leading studios and film-makers in the mid-teens, replacing the one-and two-reelers which had been the standard movie format in earlier years. The silent cinema flourished in the 20s – until the introduction of sound. This, followed by the onset of the Depression, led to changes in the types of pictures being made, and to the arrival of many new stars and directors. Production declined in the early 30s, but recovered soon after as the studios increased their output of all types of pictures, including the first features in three-strip Technicolor. But the number of colour films grew only slowly prior to the 50s when a new, cheaper Eastmancolor negative was introduced. At the same time the studios tried various new formats – the short-lived 3-D, then CinemaScope, which was replaced by Panavision in the 60s, and various 70mm processes which continued to be used in the 60s.

THE PATTERN OF RELEASES

The beginnings of the American cinema date from the early 1890s when the Kinetoscope viewing machine was first developed by the Edison company. The Kinetoscope was a coin-operated 'peep viewer' which played about 20 seconds of film on a continuous loop; it was introduced commercially in 1894, and by the end of the year Kinetoscope parlours were operating all over North America and Europe. Two years later pictures lasting up to a whole minute were being projected in converted halls for the first time, and this new form of presentation soon caught on and replaced the peep-show parlours.

The early movies depicted the most familiar and simple of moving images – a speeding train, a horse race, pedestrians and traffic passing along a city street. By the turn of the century the early film-makers had progressed to dramatizing scenes from real life, along with 'authentic' reconstructions of current, newsworthy events. Pictures listed in the 1901 Edison catalogue, for example, included *English Army In The*

Battlefield and *Boers Bringing In Prisoners* among the various scenes from the Boer War, while China, too, was in the news: *Boxer Massacres In Pekin (sic)* and *Scene In Legation Street, Pekin* were the eye-catching titles. Many popular vaudeville acts were recorded by the early cameras, along with a variety of leisure activities and sporting events. Little narrative skits were a popular item, but these were soon replaced by fully realized dramatic stories. The most successful (and best remembered) of all these early efforts was Edwin S. Porter's *The Great Train Robbery* (1903) which still holds up remarkably well when viewed today.

During the following years there was a rapid increase in the range and number of shorts being turned out by the many small companies in the USA. Though the subject matter continued to be derived mainly from American life, both contemporary and historical, the scenarios were becoming more complex and occasionally required the services of a writer who may have also been called upon to supply the titles. These titles were used more frequently and with greater sophistication from about 1909.

By the time that D.W. Griffith began directing one-reelers for Biograph in 1908, many of the basic techniques of the cinema had been discovered. However, Griffith is generally credited with developing a special style and craft in utilizing them which appealed to the general public, and to other contemporary film-makers who were strongly influenced by his work. Aside from his neglect of comedy, Griffith's Biograph shorts of 1908–12 present the best surviving examples of the kinds of pictures which were popular during these years. The emphasis was on action and drama with strong human-interest themes and included a fair number of Westerns and crime movies. They displayed a special fondness for the fast-moving chase climax and for the symbolic use of natural landscapes. Since his pictures were mostly set in America, he rarely required elaborate sets or costumes and could film quickly and cheaply. Though Griffith was tremendously prolific, completing 450 shorts between 1908 and 1913, his pictures and methods were much imitated at the time. (As director Allan Dwan recalled many years later, 'I just did what he did ... I'd see his pictures and go back and (re-) make them at my company').

The standard movie format up to 1912 was the one- or two-reel short running for 15–30 minutes on the screen. But after this date there was a gradual shift to four- or five-reelers. Movie audiences were immediately attracted to the features, in spite of the fact that so many of them suffered from weak acting and relatively unimaginative direction which was cruelly exposed by the new, longer format. At the same time a small group of leading directors – including Maurice Tourneur, Allan Dwan and relative newcomer Cecil B. DeMille – along with stars Mary Pickford and Douglas Fairbanks, were soon turning out quality features of all types. D.W. Griffith remained a dominating figure and extended the possibilities of the feature about as far as they could then go. His tremendously successful Civil War epic, the 12-reel *The Birth Of A Nation* (1914), was followed by the ambitious 14-reel *Intolerance* in which he experimented with intercutting four different stories set in four different eras of history. The picture was so long that Griffith was able to re-release the two most memorable episodes as separate short features. *The Fall Of Babylon* and *The Mother And The Law*, in 1919.

Though the feature-length pictures quickly replaced the two-reel short as the staple format of the mainstream commercial cinema, one-and two-reelers continued to be popular for many years and were especially suited to comedy. Top comedians, including Charlie Chaplin, Harold Lloyd and Buster Keaton, starred in shorts till well into the 20s, while such independent producers as Mack Sennett and Hal Roach were still turning them out in the 30s with W.C. Fields, the kids of Our Gang and, notably, Laurel and Hardy as the stars. In fact, all the major studios were involved in the production of shorts, using them, as with their B features, as a training ground for new directors and stars and for older players reaching the end of their careers. (Throughout the 30s and 40s the standard supporting programme in most cinemas included one or more shorts, a cartoon and a newsreel.)

The trend toward features was further reinforced by the policies of the leading studios during the late 'teens and early 20s. Paramount, the largest of all, churned out fairly short five-reel features in large numbers, releasing an annual average of 120 feature-length movies during 1917–22, but soon cut back to about half that number. Fox, too, reduced its total output around this time, aiming at, and achieving, a marked improvement in quality. But the formation and subsequent growth of many important new companies, including Warner Bros. and MGM, meant that the total numbers continued to grow throughout the last years of the silent era.

The modern movie industry took shape in the 20s, dominated by a small number of giant companies. At the same time, there were important changes in the way that movies were made within the studio system. Movie-making skills were becoming more specialized and the studios set up a variety of new departments to handle art direction, costume design and special effects. There were also important technical advances in lighting equipment and cameras, and an important change from orthochromatic to the more sensitive panchromatic film stock.

Each of the companies kept an eye on the activities of their competitors and when a new type of picture did particularly well for one studio the others would rush to follow suit. Thus, the success of Douglas Fairbanks and Rudolph Valentino in the early 20s led to a revival of interest in swashbucklers and costume roles. First National cast Richard Barthelmess in *The Fighting Blade* (1923) and Milton Sills as *The Sea Hawk* (1924), while Warner Bros. countered with John Barrymore as *Beau Brummell* (1924) and *Don Juan* (1926), and MGM cast John Gilbert in *Bardelys The Magnificent* (1926). Similarly, the success of Paramount's *The Covered Wagon* (1923) spawned a cycle of Western epics in the mid-20s, and MGM's first big smash-hit, *The Big Parade* (1925), stimulated a new interest in World War I movies both on the ground and in the air. Again, all the leading companies took part in a cycle which continued till well into the sound era. Fox enjoyed a big hit with *What Price Glory?* (1926) and its sequel, *The Cockeyed World* (1929). First National cast Richard Barthelmess as *The Patent Leather Kid* (1927), and Universal won the top Oscar with *All Quiet*

On The Western Front (1930), while Paramount took to the air with *Wings* (1927), another Oscar-winner, followed by United Artists' *Hell's Angels* which wasn't completed and released until 1930 – around the same time as Warners/ First National were standing by for take-off with *The Dawn Patrol*.

At the same time that the movie industry was developing as big business, the last memorable years of the silent era saw the release of many outstanding pictures from a cross section of leading silent directors, and reflected a strong European influence. From Fox came *Sunrise* (1927) directed by F.W. Murnau, while MGM released both the King Vidor masterpiece *The Crowd* and Victor Sjöström's *The Wind*, starring Lillian Gish, in 1928. That same year United Artists released the delightful *Sadie Thompson* starring Gloria Swanson and directed by (and co-starring) Raoul Walsh, while Paramount had the extravagant Erich von Stroheim's last silent masterpiece, *The Wedding March*, and Josef von Sternberg's atmospheric *The Docks Of New York* (both 1928). Even little Universal contributed a real surprise production in *Lonesome*, the last, outstanding silent feature from Hungarian director Paul Fejos (released with sound effects and some talkie sequences added). Unfortunately, none of these pictures did as well as they should, since audiences were no longer attracted to anything that didn't talk (though they showed up the inferior quality of many of the early talkies). And the companies hardly cared either, because they were already fully committed to sound by late 1928.

The general pattern and speed of the changeover to sound by the major studios can best be understood by looking closely at the different categories of feature released during the years 1928 and 1929. As one might expect, Warner Bros. was well in the lead in 1928, with 10 all-talking features and virtually all the rest of its pictures released with an accompanying soundtrack, either part-talkie or with sound effects and/or music. Fox came a distant second with over two-thirds of its pictures carrying a sound track in 1928, while, for MGM and Paramount, over 80% of their features were still silent. By the following year Fox had almost caught up with Warners in its conversion to all-talking movies. But most significant was the speed with which MGM and Paramount made the transition. Paramount, for example, had released only 11 sound features in 1928, none of them full talkies, but was 70% 'all-talkie' by the following year, while MGM lagged slightly behind with about 45% talkies.

The changes which took place in the sort of pictures being made in 1929–31 reflected not only the coming of sound and the arrival of many new talkie stars, but the impact of the great Depression and the important social changes taking place during these years. There was a move away from the European settings and characters of many 20s silents, while the very special, dream-like world of the silent cinema became a dim memory. The stylization and mimed performances of the silents gave way to a more naturalistic approach to characters and settings, acting styles underwent a radical change, and Hollywood turned its attention to American society, characters and institutions as never before.

Voices had to match their on-screen characters, as Norma Talmadge learned to her cost when she attempted to play *Dubarry, Woman Of Passion* (UA, 1930) with a strong Brooklyn twang. Other silent stars had similar problems with their voices, the best-known examples being those of John Gilbert and Clara Bow. In reality, they suffered more from the general change in the nature of stardom which was taking place during these years. The new breed of stars were generally tougher, more mature, and more in tune with the harsh realities of modern life than their silent, romantic counterparts. Lillian Gish felt insulted when studio boss Louis B. Mayer offered to create a scandal for her to help change her squeaky-clean image but unfortunately she made a poor choice for her talkie debut. She starred in an adaptation of Molnar's play 'The Swan', retitled *One Romantic Night* (UA, 1930), then joined the number of silent stars, many of whom had gotten their start in the 'teens and were now winding down their movie careers. Garbo, however, had the right idea when she made her talkie debut playing the title role in Eugene O'Neill's downbeat drama *Anna Christie* (MGM, 1930), and presented a surprisingly different image appropriate to the new era.

The romantic silent heroes were replaced by tough, down-to-earth men, typified by James Cagney, Edward G. Robinson and Paul Muni at Warner Bros., Clark Gable and Wallace Beery at MGM. There were also sophisticated and polished leading men who could handle dialogue with ease such as Ronald Colman, William Powell and Fredric March. And naturally there were no-nonsense, street-wise women to match. The era of the modern 30s woman had dawned, and with it the wisecracking ladies, led by Joan Blondell, Ginger Rogers and Jean Harlow, flourished alongside the versatile sophisticates and queens of melodrama – Bette Davis, Barbara Stanwyck, Joan Crawford.

Though many silents had been adapted from plays, the theatre was now more essential to Hollywood than ever before, for it was a ready source of new stars, directors and writers as well as new material. Plays, of course, provided ready-made dialogue, as well as plot and dramatic structure which could be readily accommodated within the four walls of a sound stage, with the appropriate exterior shots (or 'establishing shots') slotted in at various points in the narrative. Aside from the many comedies, musicals and dramas that one might expect, there were other subjects, such as the gangster film, which benefited from the stage connection. In fact, urban themes and all aspects of life in the big city as created on the studio back lots, held a special appeal. The glamorous and slightly naughty world of show biz, theatres and nightclubs, of show girls, gangsters, corrupt politicians and tabloid newspapers, became staple cinema fare. Movies still provided escapism, but escapism of a different sort. Movie-goers now identified with a new breed of gangster heroes, fast talking reporters and wisecracking chorus girls.

The very first 100% talkie, Warners' *Lights Of New York* (1928), linked gangster and show biz themes, as did Universal's lavish adaptation of *Broadway* the following year, which was derived from the George Abbott – Philip Dunning stage hit. At the same time, all the studios rushed to turn out stagey and generally unimaginative musicals which carried audiences along through the sheer vitality of their musical numbers and the novelty of sound. Many of the early musicals such as MGM's *The Broadway Melody* and Warners' *Gold Diggers Of Broadway* (both released in 1929) were smash-hits, but the law of diminishing returns soon set in. Audiences began to tire of the seemingly endless numbers of new musicals, and many of the later entries in the cycle, such as Universal's *King Of Jazz* (1930), flopped badly.

Among the early sound pictures of note there were play adaptations which focussed on important social issues such as *The Front Page* (UA, 1930) and *Five Star Final* (Warner Bros., 1931) with new stars from the stage Pat O'Brien and Edward G. Robinson respectively. Even the well-known Universal horror-movie cycle began with a theatre connection – *Dracula*, completed late in 1930, and the rather less stagey *Frankenstein* (1931) directed by a new arrival from the theatre, the talented James Whale. In addition, the numerous gangster plays which were popular on Broadway in the late 20s provided Hollywood with many of its new, tough-guy gangster stars. Edward G. ('Little Caesar') Robinson had first made his name as gangster Nick Scarsi in 'The Racket', and similarly Paul 'Scarface' Muni had established himself on the stage playing the gangster lead in 'Four Walls'. For Spencer Tracy his success in 'The Last Mile' led to his first feature, *Up The River* (1930), with a similar prison theme, followed by the racketeer lead in *Quick Millions* (1931) both filmed at Fox. James 'Public Enemy' Cagney had understudied Lee Tracy in 'Broadway', but his later portrayal of a petty murderer in 'Penny Arcade' led to a first movie role for him and his co-star Joan Blondell in the Hollywood version retitled *Sinner's Holiday* (Warner Bros., 1930). Clark Gable, too, first drew the attention of Hollywood when he played the lead in the West Coast production of 'The Last Mile' and was soon playing a variety of tough guy and gangster roles on his way to movie stardom.

The quantity of features released by the major companies had peaked in 1927, for the added cost of sound filming led to a subsequent falling off in numbers which was further reinforced by the decline in movie audiences due to the Depression. The worst year was 1932, and a recovery was already under way late in 1933. By 1934 the seven major studios (excluding United Artists) were already averaging 50 feature releases per year. They maintained this level up to 1941 – a booming era in movie production, if not in profits and box-office success – with the companies turning out vast numbers of pictures of all lengths and types. Musicals were popular, as were thrillers and crime movies, comedies and dramas. The B Western flourished during these years and the A Western made a comeback in the late 30s, at the same time that the studios were increasing their investment in high-quality costumers, historical dramas and action-adventure movies.

In addition, the studios had organized separate B units, headed by veteran producers such as Bryan Foy at Warners and Sol Wurtzel at Fox. The large numbers of cheaply made Bs were intended to balance out the few costly A movies. On the exhibition side, the companies attempted to attract audiences back into the cinemas with the highly popular double feature programme, which provided a full-length A supported by a B movie running for 70 minutes or less.

The peak period of production for Fox, Paramount and Warner Bros., was between 1937 and 1939. All three endeavoured to compete with MGM, the undisputed industry leader, while RKO pursued its own path of supplementing in-house productions by making distribution agreements with a variety of independent, or semi-independent, producers. Some indication of the relative importance of the B feature at each studio can be seen from the average running time of their 1938 releases. As one might expect, the MGM pictures had the longest average running time, of 87.9 minutes, reflecting the fact that the studio released relatively few Bs. Grouped together well behind MGM are the four largest competing majors, each of whom produced a fair number of quality features but also turned out many B movies. Paramount's average-length feature was 76.4 minutes, Fox's 75.3, Warners' 75.0, and RKO's 74.1. The two smaller majors, Columbia and Universal, turned out a larger proportion of Bs and relatively few A features; thus the average running time for their pictures was virtually identical at 66.4 minutes. United Artists alone occupied a special position near the top of the list as a distributor of prestige productions with an average running time of 87.6 minutes, while the bottom places were occupied by three Poverty Row studios – Grand National at 63.6 minutes, Republic at 63.1 and Monogram at 60 minutes exactly.

This peak era of film-making did not last for long. By 1940 the numbers of releases from the top five companies were falling and the decline accelerated rapidly in 1943–44 as they virtually gave up producing B movies. By 1944 their combined total of 138 features was only slightly over half that of five years before. (They had released 269 features in 1939.)

Since Columbia and Universal continued to supply the B-movie market throughout the early and mid-40s, in competition with the cheapie companies, they were releasing many more pictures each year than the Big Five. In the late 40s Columbia alone was still releasing large numbers of features under its autocratic boss, Harry Cohn, who stubbornly refused to reduce the company's output till well into the 50s.

Though there were irregular fluctuations in the number of features from the eight major companies in the 50s, the trend was clearly downward, reflecting the continuing decline in movie audiences. In the middle years of the decade the total had fallen back to about 230–240 per year as RKO wound down and finally ceased production, and in 1959 numbers fell below the 200 mark once again. There were also important changes in the types of pictures. The musical had boomed in the war years, celebrating traditional American values and often given a patriotic slant. There were fewer, but more lavish, musicals after the war at the same time that the A Western made a come-back which continued on through the 50s.

In the mid-40s the thriller, too, gained a new lease of life in the hands of a number of leading new (and not so new) directors. *Film noir*, as it is known today, provided the opportunity for dealing with contemporary social themes and for an unconventional treatment of characters and relationships within a commercially acceptable (and popular) format. The pictures were generally filmed quickly and inexpensively and included many of the most popular stars of the period, both established players and relative newcomers, from all the leading studios. Joan Crawford was *Mildred Pierce* (Warner Bros., 1945) and Rita Hayworth lit up the screen as *Gilda* (Columbia, 1946), while Lana Turner played opposite John Garfield in *The Postman Always Rings Twice* (MGM, 1946). Other popular pairings included Alan Ladd and Veronica Lake at Paramount in *The Blue Dahlia*, Humphrey Bogart and Lauren Bacall at Warners directed by Howard Hawks in *The Big Sleep*, and Cary Grant with Ingrid Bergman in Hitchcock's *Notorious* at RKO – all released in 1946.

But these few flourishing genres represented the last flowering of the Hollywood studio system. By the late 40s the leading companies were already running down their studio production facilities and reducing overheads, technical staff, and contract personnel including stars and directors. There was a trend toward balancing a smaller number of 'in-house' pictures with the release of a large number of independently produced features. Ironically, RKO, the studio which had been the first to develop this balanced approach in the 40s as a permanent feature of its releasing pattern, was also the only major studio which folded in the 50s. (There was nothing wrong with the policy – it was RKO's owner, Howard Hughes, who was responsible for the collapse.)

The other companies had followed the pattern set by RKO, but the pace of change varied widely from studio to studio. Though this changeover is generally considered to be a 50s phenomenon, Warner Bros. and Columbia were already moving in this direction by the late 40s. The Oscar-winning *All The King's Men* was a Robert Rossen Production released by Columbia in 1949, while Warners distributed the Hitchcock/Transatlantic productions *Rope* (1948) and *Under Capricorn* (1949), as well as *The Flame And The Arrow* (1950), the first feature from Burt Lancaster's own production company headed by producer Harold Hecht, and *A Streetcar Named Desire* (1951) which was a Charles K. Feldman/Elia Kazan production.

Columbia had a measure of success with independent producers (most notably Sam Spiegel), while a revitalized United Artists did best of all in the late 50s with its agreements to distribute features from leading independent producers, producer-directors and producer-stars. At the opposite extreme, Universal pursued its own policy, the last company still producing most of its own pictures from its own stars, directors and other personnel, shared between its TV and film-production arms. The other companies achieved varying degrees of success in mixing in-house with independent productions in the 50s, and by the 60s the Hollywood studio system of production and distribution was virtually finished. Since most of the independents moved freely between the different companies, it was now no longer as easy (or necessary) to differentiate between them.

COLOUR MOVIES

Movies in colour first began to be widely shown in the late 30s, filmed in the newly developed three-strip Technicolor process, and the term 'technicolor' gained wide currency as a metaphor for bright or strikingly colourful. In fact, colour had been a part of the moviegoing experience ever since the turn of the century when the shorts from French producers such as Méliès and the Pathé Company were tinted by hand or stencil. In the 'teens and 20s it became standard practice for all important features to be tinted or toned – sepia or yellow for day scenes, blue for night and the occasional use of other colours such as red or green when appropriate. In addition, there were various short-lived 'additive' colour processes such as Kinemacolor and Prizmacolor which required special colour filters on the projector apparatus and proved to be impractical. But it was not until the late 20s that the two-strip Technicolor process emerged as the clear favourite of the large Hollywood studios.

The Technicolor Corporation had been founded by Herbert Kalmus and Daniel Comstock in 1915 and had produced two early features, *The Gulf Between* (1917) and *The Toll Of The Sea* (1922). Beginning in 1923 with Cecil B. DeMille's *The Ten Commandments*, many of the best-known and most lavish productions of the 20s included Technicolor sequences – MGM's *Ben-Hur* and Universal's *The Phantom Of The Opera* (both released in 1925). And there were two full-length Techni-colored features, a Zane Grey Western from Paramount, *The Wanderer Of The Wasteland* (1924), and a Douglas Fairbanks swashbuckler, *The Black Pirate* (UA, 1926). But it was only in the late 20s that filming in two-strip Technicolor began to catch on. It was a period of technical innovation generally, and colour sequences were often used as a highlight of the most spectacular production numbers in the numerous early sound musicals such as Universal's *Broadway*, RKO's *Rio Rita*, Paramount's *Glorifying The American Girl* and MGM's *The Broadway Melody*, all released in 1929. When musicals fell out of favour, so did the two-strip Technicolor process. Warner Bros., which alone had filmed the largest number of colour features, including the highly successful *Gold Diggers Of Broadway* (1929), turned to the horror film for its last two – *Dr X* (1932) and *The Mystery Of The Wax Museum* (1933). By the time these were released, a new and improved colour system had already been introduced.

The three-strip Technicolor process represented a major advance over two-strip which had been unable to record the blue range of the spectrum. (The sea or sky, for example, invariably appeared in various shades of green.) An extra-wide, beam-splitter camera had been designed which could expose three negatives simultaneously, each recording one of the primary colours, and these were used, as with two-strip, to produce colour matrices or dye images which were suitable for making full colour prints.

Walt Disney was the first to use the new Technicolor in filming his cartoon shorts, notably the Oscar-winning *Flowers And Trees* (1932) and *The Three Little Pigs* (1933). Live-action filming in 1933–34 included a musical short, *La Cucaracha*, as well as sequences in a number of features, and the first full-length picture shot in three-strip Technicolor was *Becky Sharp*, produced by Pioneer Pictures in association with the Technicolor Corporation and released by RKO in 1935. But progress toward a wider adoption of colour was incredibly slow, in marked contrast to the speed with which the studios had converted to sound filming just a few years before. Most of the early pictures, comprising quite a diverse group, came from independent companies and producers.

Though it was a studio-bound costume picture, *Becky Sharp* was directed by Rouben Mamoulian with careful attention to, and effective use of, costumes, lighting and overall design within its controlled studio setting. The impact of the colour alone was quite stunning. In contrast, Walter Wanger opted for location filming of a backwoods story in his production of *The Trail Of The Lonesome Pine* (Paramount, 1936) and proved that the new Technicolor could be equally impressive in faithfully recording natural settings. Though both films were based on conventional (and uninspired) literary adaptations, between them they demonstrated the range of expressive possibilities of the new colour system – a system capable of considerable subtlety in colour reproduction as well as strong and dramatic colour effects when called for.

With *A Star Is Born* and *Nothing Sacred* (both released by UA in 1937) producer David O. Selznick proved that a romantic drama or screwball comedy set in contemporary America could equally well benefit from colour filming (though the Technicolor was employed with restraint). Based on well-written original screenplays, and with memorable performances from Janet Gaynor and Carole Lombard respectively and from Fredric March in both, these two pictures stand out as exceptional among the early colour productions. Most of the early colour features, including Selznick's own previous Technicolor production, *The Garden Of Allah* (1936) starring Marlene Dietrich, were based on feeble scripts in which the colour was the sole point of interest. Among the most forgettable of the early colour features were Fox's *Wings Of The Morning* (1937), the first Technicolor movie filmed in Ireland and Britain; *God's Country And The Woman* (1936) and *Valley Of The Giants* (1937) from Warner Bros., Walter Wanger's *Vogues of 1938, The Goldwyn Follies*, and Alexander Korda's production of *Over The Moon* in 1938 (these latter three all released by UA).

Technicolor filming was expensive, adding about 50% to the production cost of a feature, and audiences could not be attracted into the cinemas by colour alone. *Snow White And The Seven Dwarfs* (1937) and *Gone With The Wind* (1939) were tremendously successful, but they were unique productions and thus did little to boost the attractiveness of colour filming generally. There were a few other pictures of note released around this same time. Errol Flynn appeared in his most fondly remembered Technicolored role as Robin Hood in the best of the productions from Warner Bros. and Judy Garland was transported over the rainbow to the land of Oz, while the best of Korda's British features (for UA) were the pro-Empire, action-adventure movies at their best, as seen in *The Four Feathers* (1939) and the fantasy world of *The Thief Of Bagdad* (1940). But these were expensive pictures which only did fair business at the box-office on their initial release and failed to earn a profit.

Fox had a moderate success with *Kentucky*, followed by *Jesse James*, early in 1939, and embarked on the fullest programme of Technicolor features of all the studios during the following years. By concentrating on Westerns and more particularly, glossy musicals starring Alice Faye, Betty Grable, Carmen Miranda and Don Ameche, the studio set the tone for the 40s when the musical took over as the dominant colour genre, with Westerns placing a distant second and with the range of colour pictures surprisingly limited compared with earlier years. (Over 50% of the total of well over 200 Technicolored features were musicals, while about 15% were Westerns.)

The A Western made a comeback in the late 30s and included a number of colour productions from various studios, with Fox contributing more than its share and with many leading directors also involved. Henry King directed *Jesse James* and Michael Curtiz the large-scale *Dodge City* (Warner Bros., 1939) starring Errol Flynn, while a number of men were venturing into colour for the first time: Cecil B. DeMille contributed *North West Mounted Police* (Paramount, 1940) with Gary Cooper, and MGM, not to be outdone, backed King Vidor in his ambitious production of *Northwest Passage* (1940) starring Spencer Tracy (and intended as two full-length features, but the second was never completed). The two most underrated movies of the group both came from Fox: John Ford's entertaining *Drums Along The Mohawk* (1939), and Fritz Lang's relatively modest, but highly original and low-keyed approach to the Western in *The Return Of Frank James* (1940), both starring Henry Fonda.

In addition, Fox provided the opportunity for other directors to work in colour in the early 40s, among them Rouben Mamoulian with *Blood And Sand* (1940), his first Technicolor feature since *Becky Sharp*, as well as Ernst Lubitsch and Busby Berkeley, both new to colour filming. These examples are worth noting because they proved somewhat exceptional during a period when virtually all the leading directors and cameramen, and many of the top stars, preferred black-and-white. Colour filming continued to be held in low esteem for many years. A typical example of the attitude of most directors was that of John Ford who kept returning to black-and-white for many of his favourite projects throughout his later career up to the early 60s. 'For a good dramatic story I much prefer to work in black-and-white; you'll probably say I'm old fashioned, but black-and-white is real photography,' he asserted, while Fritz Lang complained that he couldn't get a street to look dirty when filming in Technicolor. And Joseph L. Mankiewicz claimed that 'I've never seen a good, serious dramatic movie in colour, except maybe *Gone With The Wind* . . . You can't get drama and make people real in colour.'

Many of the top stars, including Claudette Colbert and Joan Crawford, were concerned that they wouldn't photograph as well in colour, while Carole Lombard and Bette Davis were also reluctant to appear in Technicolor, particularly in view of the terrible scripts they were offered. (Miss Lombard had wisely turned down *Vogues Of 1938* and Miss Davis was suspended by Warners when she refused to appear in the equally dreadful *God's Country And The Woman*.) Neither Greta Garbo nor Norma Shearer ever starred in a colour feature before they retired from the screen, and both Katharine Hepburn and Barbara Stanwyck only appeared in their first colour movies in the 50s when colour was more widely accepted.

Black-and-white and colour existed side by side for many years up to the mid-60s and, for much of that period, one can detect a split between the serious dramatic stars and directors who worked mainly in monochrome in contrast to the lightweight comedies, costume pictures, and musicals in colour. Not only was black-and-white filming substantially cheaper, but there had been a number of important technical advances in the late 30s which made monochrome more attractive than ever – improved lenses, a lighter weight of camera, faster film stock, and a range of special-effects techniques were used imaginatively by the top directors (Welles, Ford, Hitchcock, Wyler) and cameramen (Gregg Toland, Arthur Miller, William Daniels). It was the last great era of black-and-white studio film-making, while the growth in colour was hampered by wartime shortages of film stock, limited access to the relatively small number of special Technicolor cameras, and a lack of the kind of imaginative use of colour or prestige colour successes which could help it to gain a wider acceptance. It is worth noting that no colour pictures won the top Oscar between 1939 and 1951, while the leading director working in colour in the 40s was not American but British, namely Michael Powell, who was responsible for such pictures as *The Life And Death Of Colonel Blimp* (1943), *Black Narcissus* (1947) and *The Red Shoes* (1948).

Technicolor stars of the 40s included Judy Garland, Dorothy Lamour and Maria Montez, along with a new group of redheads – Rita Hayworth, Maureen O'Hara and Danny Kaye. Following the standard practice of the period, Vincente Minnelli, the leading director of Technicolored musicals at MGM, continued to make all of his non-musical pictures in monochrome till well into the 50s. Thus, he disappointingly failed to provide a lead in demonstrating the expressive possibilities of filming dramatic subjects in colour. Similarly, though many Westerns had been filmed in colour since the late 30s, a surprisingly large number of the quality productions, including *The Oxbow Incident* (1943), *My Darling Clementine* (1946), *Red River* (1948), *Winchester '73* (1950) and *The Gunfighter* (1950), were shot in black-and-white.

The number of Technicolor releases was slow to rise during the 40s. Having averaged only 11 features per year, or about 4% of the total output from the eight leading studios, during 1938–42, the numbers increased to 25 per year (or 10%) by 1944–47 and had climbed to 15% or 40 features per year by the end of the decade. The years 1943–44 had marked a turning point as the smaller studios, Universal and Columbia, made their first ventures into Technicolor, while Sam Goldwyn produced the first of his many Danny Kaye musicals, and MGM developed a new interest in the colour musical and had its first big success with *Meet Me In St Louis* (1944). During the following years the MGM musicals represented the undoubted high point of colour movies from Hollywood and, in 1951, *An American In Paris* won the Oscar for Best Picture, followed by *Gigi* in 1958.

The long-overdue breakthrough for colour came in the early 50s and accelerated in 1953–54, reflecting the many changes which were taking place within the movie industry. Filming away from the studio by independent producers, directors and stars had increased, and many pictures were shot abroad to take advantage of lower overseas production costs – and picturesque locations. There were many features filmed in Africa, for example, such as *The African Queen* (1951), the first colour feature for its director, John Huston, as well as for its stars, Humphrey Bogart and Katharine Hepburn.

There had also been a modest increase in the number of pictures filmed with the cheaper colour processes such as Cinecolor – used especially for Westerns in the late 40s – followed by an improved SuperCinecolor and Ansco Color in the early 50s. But, beginning in about 1952, the Technicolor monopoly was seriously challenged for the first time by the less expensive single-strip Eastman Color which could be used in a standard 35 mm camera. By 1954 Technicolor was phasing out its bulky camera in favour of a single-strip or monopack system, too. Colour filming was encouraged by the large studios more than ever before, along with new widescreen techniques, as a means of attracting audiences and competing with black-and-white TV. The result was that the number of colour productions increased rapidly and accounted for a full 58% of the total feature releases from the eight leading studios in 1954–55. There were large numbers of Westerns and costume pictures of all types, especially Biblical epics, along with comedies and musicals. In addition, the list of leading directors who made their first colour features during these years is a long and impressive one that includes George Stevens, Nicholas Ray, Douglas Sirk, Anthony Mann and Robert Wise; for a few, their first in colour was also in a new widescreen process – George Cukor's *A Star Is Born* (1954) and Elia Kazan's *East Of Eden* (1955) were both in CinemaScope, while Fred Zinnemann filmed *Oklahoma!* (1955) in Todd-AO.

In some cases the Hollywood companies had put pressure on directors to film in colour and widescreen. When, however, it became apparent that movie audiences were decreasing again, the pressure came off, and by the late 50s many directors such as Billy Wilder, John Ford, Joseph Mankiewicz, Robert Wise and Elia Kazan returned to filming in the black-and-white which they preferred. The number of features in colour peaked in 1955, accounting for over 60% of the total, fell off in the late 50s, then made a slight recovery, averaging just under 50% during 1959–62. But it was apparent that the resumption of the trend toward a high proportion of colour was only a matter of time. The introduction of improved, faster colour film stock meant that shooting in colour had become easier and cheaper in relation to monochrome. The balance was finally tipped by the introduction of colour TV. Ironically, whereas colour and widescreen had developed in the 50s as a means of competing with TV, now the sale or leasing of movie rights to TV had become an important source of ancilliary income. Once colour TV was introduced in the USA and began to replace monochrome, a feature film in colour became of greater value than in black-and-white, and there was renewed pressure on directors to choose colour. The final move into total movie colour came in 1967–68 when over 20% of households in the US had purchased their first colour TV sets and the numbers were growing fast. A last memorable group of monochrome features released included *Who's Afraid Of Virginia Woolf?* and *The Fortune Cookie* in 1966 and *In Cold Blood* in 1967. Since horror, thriller and gangster pictures were among the last genres of movie still being filmed in monochrome in the 50s and 60s, it was not surprising to find that among those pictures which created the greatest impact on the screen were *Bonnie And Clyde*, *In The Heat Of The Night* and *Cool Hand Luke* in 1967, *Bullitt* and *Rosemary's Baby* in 1968 all filmed in colour.

A few directors returned to filming a few select features in black-and-white in the 70s and had a measure of success. Peter Bogdanovich began this with *The Last Picture Show* (1971) and *Paper Moon* (1973), followed by Woody Allen with *Manhattan* (1979), *Zelig* (1983) and *Broadway Danny Rose* (1984), and in *The Purple Rose of Cairo* (1985) he mixed colour with black-and-white sequences representing the 'film within a film'. In 1980 Martin Scorsese shot *Raging Bull*, the powerful and dramatic biopic of boxer Jake LaMotta in black and white, but by far the biggest black-and-white hit of the past thirty years was Mel Brooks' *Young Frankenstein* in 1974. However, the movies in black and white remain few and far between. Clearly, there had been a basic change in the attitudes of directors, cameramen and movie audiences over the years. With the widespread adoption of colour TV, for a substantial majority of the population colour was now taken for granted, and was further confirmed by the new popularity of video recorders and the availability of feature films on video, along with the growth of cable TV in the 80s, and the development of electronic, computerized systems of colourization of old monochrome pictures. Suddenly colourization had become big business, for the colourized version of feature films achieved consistently better viewing figures on TV and far out-sold the monochrome version in the video shops. TV and cable mogul Ted Turner spent a substantial sum in 1986, running into hundreds of millions of dollars, in purchasing the MGM/UA film and TV library with a view to colourizing the old pictures. In spite of the outraged reaction from most movie directors and critics, this is a trend it will be difficult to stop.

Thus, the final move into 100% colour had not been achieved in 1968 after all, but was taking place about 20 years later with the colourization of old features which represented the last logical step toward total colour. However, there is the consolation, for those opposed to this process, that original negatives and prints for cinema projection are not affected. This new development is confined entirely to video.

1952
▶ First MGM release in Anscocolor *The Wild North* (January)
▶ First Eastman Color and Warner Color releases
▶ First Cinerama presentation – *This Is Cinerama* (September)
▶ First 3-D release – *Bwana Devil* (UA, November)
1953
▶ Peak year of 3-D releases – 19 colour, 5 b/w
▶ First three CinemaScope releases beginning with *The Robe* (Fox, September)
1954
▶ 3-D filming abandoned by all major companies by the middle of the year
▶ First VistaVision release – *White Christmas* (Paramount, April)
▶ Release of last features to be shot with 3-strip Technicolor cameras
▶ First SuperScope releases – *Cattle Queen of Montana* (RKO, December) *Vera Cruz* (UA, December)
1955
▶ Fifties peak in number of colour releases (132) and as % of total (62%)
▶ Peak in number of CinemaScope releases (72, all in colour)
▶ First Todd-AO release – *Oklahoma* (Magna)
1956
▶ First b/w CinemaScope release – *Teenage Rebel* (Fox)
▶ Todd-AO production *Around The World in 80 Days* (UA), wins Best Picture Oscar
▶ Release of CinemaScope 55 productions: *Carousel* and *The King and I*
▶ First Technirama release – *The Monte Carlo Story* (Titanus/UA)
▶ Peak year in number of VistaVision releases – 19
1957
▶ Peak year for total number of RegalScope releases – 17
▶ First Camera 65 release – *Raintree Country* (MGM), a forerunner of Ultra Panavision 70
▶ First 35mm Panavision release – *Jailhouse Rock* (MGM)

3-D AND WIDESCREEN

In the early 50s, with movie attendance still falling, the large studios appeared slow to react. Though the new drive-in cinemas appealed to the car-owning public and more pictures were being filmed in colour, this had hardly slowed the decline. The companies attempted to reduce their overheads, cutting back on staff and releasing expensive stars from their contracts, but it was left to a small number of enterprising independent producers to show the way forward.

There had been various experiments in 3-D filming and in using formats larger than the standard 35mm in the 20s and 30s, but none of these had caught on. MGM had released a number of 3-D 'specials', called Audioscopiks, in its Pete Smith series of shorts. These were quite popular at the time, while the best-known of the early 70mm processes was Fox's short-lived Grandeur system, introduced in the late 20s. Now these early techniques were revived and refined in the early 50s, in some cases by the same men who had tried unsuccessfully to sell their ideas to the leading studios years previously. One such was Fred Waller who had introduced a multi-screen presentation called Vitarama at the 1939 New York World's Fair. With backing from a group of independent showmen that included Lowell Thomas, Merian C. Cooper and Mike Todd, Waller launched his new Cinerama in 1952. Making use of huge curved screen and stereophonic sound, *This Is Cinerama* was presented on a road-show basis in a number of the largest American cities and was a great success. It was followed, only a few months later, by *Bwana Devil*, a cheaply produced and independently released 3-D feature which advertised 'A Lion in Your Lap!' and created a sensation. (The brainchild of producer Milton Gunzburg and director Arch Oboler, it was quickly acquired for wider distribution by UA).

The unexpected success of these new pictures brought a rapid response from Hollywood. All the studios rushed to turn out their own 3-D pictures, but met with little success at the box-office. Warners did best with *House Of Wax* and *The Charge At Feather River* but, by mid-1954, 3-D was already on the way out. At the same time that Fox was making its contribution to the 3-D cycle with *Inferno* (1953), and *Gorilla At Large* (1954) starring Anne Bancroft, the studio turned its attention to another of the early widescreen systems. Originally devised by French inventor Henri Chrétien in 1928 and now renamed 'CinemaScope', this made use of a special, anamorphic lens which could squeeze a wide picture onto the standard size 35mm film which then could be unsqueezed by a matching lens on the projector. The resulting wide image, projected onto a large screen, gave a sense of added depth similar to 3-D – the adverts were quick to point out that 'You see it without glasses!' – along with the larger image and stereo sound such as that provided by Cinerama. CinemaScope had the advantage of novelty combined with practicality as it required only minimal adjustments to the cinemas and their projection systems, and could be filmed with a standard 35mm camera.

All of Fox's earliest CinemaScope releases were extremely popular, beginning with *The Robe* and *How To Marry A Millionaire* in 1953, and most of the other studios soon made use of the process. The number of features increased rapidly in 1954 and 1955, and the success of CinemaScope also influenced the types of pictures being produced. Directors were encouraged to think big and take on projects which made use of large casts and spectacular settings. Historical subjects, especially Biblical stories and tales set in ancient times, were much in favour following the success of *The Robe*. Thus, against his better judgement, Howard Hawks agreed to make his only CinemaScope picture, *Land Of The Pharaohs* (1955) for Warner Bros. Similarly, John Ford directed *The Long Grey Line* (Columbia, 1955) using the 'Scope process though he 'hated it'. Fritz Lang also reluctantly made *Moonfleet* in 'Scope that same year. (Playing the part of a film producer in Jean Luc Godard's *Le Mépris* a few years later, Lang disparagingly referred to CinemaScope as 'only good for funerals and snakes'.) And Robert Wise directed one of his least memorable pictures that same year – *Helen Of Troy*, starring Rossana Podesta. Not surprisingly, the studios soon realized that CinemaScope alone would not solve their problems. The number of features filmed in colour and CinemaScope declined after 1955, but this was at least partly balanced by the introduction of a black-and-white version of the process in 1956.

Only two of the leading studios had declined to join the general rush into CinemaScope. RKO had developed its own rival system known as SuperScope, while Paramount opted for a non-anamorphic process which it christened VistaVision. This made use of a special camera which exposed a larger negative area by running the 35mm film horizontally and achieved a sharpness of definition and superior quality image. Introduced one year later than CinemaScope with the hit musical *White Christmas* (1954), VistaVision also peaked a year later (in 1956) and was used less often in the late 50s when yet another similar process appeared under the name Technirama. This was a process developed by the Technicolor Corporation for making use of the excellent three-strip Technicolor cameras which had become obsolete after the introduction of the new Eastman, single-strip colour negative. These cameras were adapted to expose a 35mm colour negative running laterally (as with VistaVision) and a partially squeezed image (as with CinemaScope). The first Technirama picture, *The Monte Carlo Story* (1956) was soon followed by such productions of note as *The Big Country* and *The Vikings* (both 1958) and *Solomon And Sheba* (1959) – all distributed by UA. Other costume epics filmed in Technirama in the early 60s, for special 'roadshow' screening with 70mm prints, known as Super Technirama 70, included *Spartacus* (1960), *El Cid* and *King Of Kings* (both 1961), *55 Days At Peking* (1962), *The Leopard* (1963) and *Circus World* (1964). (With the exception of *Spartacus* and *The Leopard*, these were all Samuel Bronston productions filmed in Spain.) In general, Technirama was used more in Europe than in the US. Though introduced later than CinemaScope and VistaVision, Technirama too was eventually replaced by the new 35mm Panavision in the 60s.

In fact, the Panavision company had first developed its own 35mm lenses for MGM in 1957 at the same time that it was introducing a new 70mm process, too. Ironically, the term 'CinemaScope' had become so closely identified with the anamorphic, wide-screen format that all the early films using Panavision lenses were advertised as being in 'CinemaScope'. It was only in the 60s that pictures were announced as having been filmed 'in Panavision'. In fact, the first 35mm Panavision film had been MGM's *Jailhouse Rock* starring Elvis Presley (in black-and-white) in 1957, and the number of Panavision films, in both colour and black-and-white, grew rapidly during the following years. Vincente Minnelli at MGM was the first director of note to use the new 35mm Panavision lenses on such films as *Some Came Running* and *Bells Are Ringing* in 1958–59, while *The Apartment* (UA, 1960) was the first film shot in 35mm Panavision which won the Oscar for Best Picture.

In addition to these various 35mm systems, there was also a renewed interest in 70mm. Showman Mike Todd had been one of the first to recognize the shortcomings of the Cinerama three-camera process. He supported Dr Brian O'Brien of the American Optical Company in his efforts to develop a new improved single-camera system which was called Todd-AO. But when the first Todd-AO picture, the independently produced movie adaptation of Rodgers and Hammerstein's *Oklahoma* (Magna, 1955) failed to do justice to the new process, Todd set out to remedy this himself. His spectacularly successful version of Jules Verne's *Around The World In 80 Days* (UA, 1956) provided yet one more example of a relative outsider showing the way for the rest of the movie industry.

The Fox studio also experimented with a larger negative in order to achieve a better-quality image. But it dropped its newly introduced CinemaScope 55 after only two productions and adopted Todd-AO for most of its opulent movies of later years beginning with *South Pacific* (1958) and including *Cleopatra* (1963) and *Hello, Dolly!* (1969) among others. Not to be outdone by Fox, and Paramount with its VistaVision, MGM hired Robert Gottschalk of the Panavision Corporation to develop its own new 70mm process. First introduced as Camera 65 – the negative was 65mm wide – it was used on *Raintree County* (1957) and the remake of *Ben-Hur* in 1959. A variation on this same process continued to be widely used in the 60s, going by such names as Ultra Panavision and Super Panavision, while Panavision 70 was the term used for productions like *Dr Zhivago* (1965), filmed in anamorphic (35mm) Panavision and blown up to 70mm for roadshow screenings. (Of the total of about 40 70mm productions in the 60s, 20 were accounted for by Panavision, 10 were filmed in Todd-AO and the rest divided between Cinerama and a short-lived newcomer called Dimension-150.)

The 70mm filming in the 60s included many of the most expensive pictures of the decade. The very few top hits – including *The Sound Of Music* (1965) and *Airport* (1970) – were far outweighed by the spectacular flops such as *Mutiny On The Bounty* (1962), *Cleopatra* (1963), *The Greatest Story Ever Told* (1965), *Dr Dolittle* (1967) and *Star!* (1968). In addition, such high-cost productions as *Hello Dolly!* (1969) and *Ryan's Daughter* (1970) contributed to the industry's financial crisis of 1969–70 and were thus among the last of the large Hollywood studios' 70mm productions.

The improved quality of Panavision equipment, along with new colour film stock from Eastman, meant that by the late 60s it had become cheaper and more convenient to film in 35mm Panavision, then, 'print up' to 70mm from the 35mm fine-grain negative. Thus, virtually all the 70mm presentations at first-run cinemas in the USA during the 70s and 80s have been such 'blow-ups'. Today one can already look back with a certain degree of nostalgia at the 60s, and the many large-scale musicals and costume epics filmed with the giant Todd-AO and 70mm Panavision cameras.

Movies and Finance

The broad outlines of the financial development of the movie industry in the US are fairly well known and can be simply stated. The period from the mid-teens up to 1930 was one of rapid growth and broad-based expansion. All the companies were badly affected by the Depression in the early 30s but recovered during the second half of the decade. When moviegoing boomed during the war years profits shot up, but this was followed by a long and virtually continuous decline until the early 70s. The subsequent recovery was sparked off, and sustained, by a series of spectacular hits from new directors. Though the industry has remained on a more or less even keel during the 80s, the experience of individual companies has varied considerably. To date, Paramount and Universal have been the most consistently successful, while UA, MGM and Fox have experienced the most serious difficulties.

INTRODUCING MOVIE FINANCE

By its very nature film-making is a high-risk business and very competitive and, for much of its history, profits have been small in relation to the scale of financial investment and the risks involved. There is generally little understanding of how brief was the boom era of large audiences and exceptional profits. Moviegoers were attracted by the novelty of sound in 1929 and 1930, and returned to the cinemas in large numbers during World War II. Otherwise, the 40-year period from 1931 to 1971 was characterized by declining audiences and unpredictable profits. Though the standard view of the American movie industry dates the decline from 1946, with its peak profits, this is extremely misleading. The war period is quite atypical; profits were artificially high while the studios were operating far below their peak levels.

A large number of hits were concentrated into the years 1945–47, as had happened during the earlier boom that began with the introduction of sound in 1929–31. Otherwise there were few really big hits prior to the 50s. The most extraordinary of them all (and it is impossible to calculate the profits exactly) was the tremendous success of D. W. Griffith's *The Birth Of A Nation* in 1915, while Metro's *The Four Horsemen Of The Apocalypse* (1921) was the outstanding hit of the early 20s. Warners' Al Jolson vehicle, *The Singing Fool* (1928), was the top-grossing sound film until the release of Walt Disney's *Snow White And The Seven Dwarfs* (1937), but *Gone With The Wind* (1939) may still qualify as the highest-earning picture ever made if the figures are adjusted for inflation. Its cost of $4.25 million was exceptional for the period, but by the late 50s the multi-million dollar budget had become all too familiar and the box-office had failed to keep pace. There were a few big hits such as *Ben-Hur* (1959) and *The Ten Commandments* (1956), but numerous other expensive epics failed to cover their costs. This situation continued on through the 60s when many of the studios were involved in corporate mergers and diversified their activities into TV production, records and publishing.

A major turning point occurred between 1969 and 1971 when large numbers of expensive flops, resulting in huge losses, forced the companies to cut back on their investment in risky, high-cost productions. Soon, however, a modest recovery in box-office receipts and profits followed, as a new generation of young directors and producers – including Francis Ford Coppola, George Lucas and Steven Spielberg – led a Hollywood revival which carried the leading studios into the 80s in better shape. But of special interest in the mid-80s was the challenge to the majors' domination of the industry from a comparatively small group of new companies, led by Orion, Tri-Star and Disney's Touchstone.

FINANCIAL PROFILE OF THE INDUSTRY

The fledgling movie industry in the US started out as a diverse collection of small companies at the turn of the century. Though the leading producers and exhibitors had banded together to form the Motion Picture Patents Company in 1908, as late as 1910–12 they were still turning out one-reel shorts and, like drapery merchants, selling them by the foot or the yard, with little to differentiate them aside from the titles and company names – though Biograph with Griffith was an exception. It was left to a new group of more adventurous moguls to take the first steps toward transforming the industry. During the years 1912–14, when the power of the Trust was finally broken, such notable figures as Adolph Zukor, Carl Laemmle, Jesse Lasky and William Fox began making features, signing up stars and expanding generally.

The American film industry had become a worldwide force to be reckoned with even before the outbreak of World War I which severely affected the output of its competitors in Britain, France and other European countries. The pace of events in the USA was quite astonishing. In 1916 Adolph Zukor arranged a merger between his Famous Players and Lasky, then took over the Paramount distribution company, thus establishing a pattern of mergers and vertical expansion which would serve as a model for (and warning to) the rest of the industry.

Reacting to the threat posed by Paramount, a number of leading theatre owners joined together in 1917 to form the First National Exhibitors' Circuit and soon began to sign up leading stars such as Charlie Chaplin and Zukor's own Mary Pickford. Zukor fought back by developing such practices as block booking – designed to maximize the profitability of his pictures – and began acquiring his own cinemas as part of a continuing policy of expansion in this area which would seriously weaken First National in the mid-20s. Meanwhile, Fox and Universal studios continued to grow, UA was formed in 1919, and Loew's, the exhibition giant, took over Metro in 1920.

If anything, the competition got even tougher in the 20s. The major companies vied with each other to sign up the top stars, improve their production facilities and further strengthen their position as vertically integrated corporations by expanding their ownership of film exchanges and movie theatres.

By 1920 Paramount's annual profits had grown to an impressive $5 million. Though hit by the recession of 1922, the studio soon recovered strongly. Profits averaged over $5 million during 1924–26 and were growing. A similar cycle was experienced by the smaller Fox company whose profits, though healthy, were about half those of Paramount. In fact, the recession caused only a brief setback to the movie industry generally, and it continued to grow in strength in the mid-20s. The pace accelerated in the following years, with the most notable advances made by Loew's, Fox and a small new upstart, Warner Bros., who all challenged the supremacy of Paramount.

The strongest challenge of all was mounted by Loew's/Metro. The company had been roughly comparable in size to Fox in the early 20s, but was rapidly transformed by a merger with the Goldwyn and Mayer companies in 1924. By the following year the new Loew's/MGM was already releasing the first of its many hit movies and its 1926 profits matched those of Paramount.

Around this same time Warner Bros., followed by Fox, was beginning to experiment with sound. According to the 'Motion Picture Almanac' (the standard reference source for the industry) in 1931, these two companies, along with Paramount, led the industry with a massive investment of over $20 million each in new plant and equipment between 1925 and 1930, accounting for just over half of the industry-wide investment total of over $110 million. A great increase in outside investment in the film industry had occurred during these years, much of it connected with the changeover to sound and stimulated by the large increase in movie audiences. The findings of the 'Motion Picture Almanac' showed that from April 1928 to April 1931 the number of stockholders in Fox, Paramount and Warner Bros. increased from about 20,000 to 63,000.

Fox and Warners had their first success with sound in 1927 and by 1928 their profits were climbing rapidly. They continued growing in many directions simultaneously, including a major acquisition of movie theatres. William Fox attempted (but failed) to carry off the biggest coup of all by merging his studio with MGM to create a single giant corporation; Warner Bros. bought a major share in First National in 1928 as a first step toward a full takeover the following year; and David Sarnoff, head of the giant Radio Corporation of America (RCA), masterminded the formation of a major new movie company, RKO Radio, from a merger of the Film Booking Offices Of America (FBO) with the Keith-Albee-Orpheum theatre circuit – followed by a takeover of Pathé which was completed early in 1931.

The tremendous popularity of the early talkies had cushioned the film industry from the initial impact of the Depression, but by 1931 the novelty value of sound had worn off. Swinging from boom to bust in the space of a few years, the cyclical fluctuations of the movie business were seen at their most extreme in the early 30s, setting a pattern for later years. Total profits of over $50 million recorded by the eight leading studios in 1930, had turned into losses of $56 million by 1932. The cycle was made even more extreme by the extensive ownership of theatres. Though cinemas were a useful asset and contributed to profits in the good years, they could be a serious liability when movie audiences were meagre. (This was most apparent in the case of Paramount, which had the highest profits of all the leading companies during the peak years of 1929 and 1930 when it had few hit movies to its credit; but as it controlled over 1,000 theatres in the USA, it then suffered the worst losses of all when the Depression struck and was in the red to the tune of $21 million by 1932.)

As a result of the financial turmoil and period of transition which took place in the early 30s, the shape of the industry was more or less set for the next dozen years. MGM, the only company to stay in the black throughout the worst years, emerged as the industry leader, with Paramount, Fox and Warner Bros., all badly hurt by the Depression, as its main rivals (and RKO as the perpetual 'also-ran'). These three would catch up with MGM in the boom years of the mid-40s, but all would be badly hurt by declining audiences in the postwar years.

Of the three smaller majors and RKO the story was generally one of tiny or non-existent profits. Columbia did best of all and managed a steady if unspectacular rate of growth. Universal and Columbia only had a few good years in the 40s, but by the early 50s they, along with a newly reorganized United Artists (which had struggled through the 40s), were set to compete with the larger companies (minus their film theatres) on more equal terms than ever before. (RKO alone fell by the wayside having been virtually destroyed by its eccentric billionaire owner, Howard Hughes.)

Though it has never been clearly spelled out, it is apparent that the film industry as a whole never fully recovered from the problems experienced during the Depression years. The profits of most of the companies had partly recovered by 1935–37 but then declined again on being hit by the 1938 recession, and they continued to be uneven and unpredictably low (with the sole exception of MGM). Yet, throughout virtually the entire period from 1934 to 1941, production was at peak levels with each studio turning out about 50 A and B features per year. Profits remained low or nonexistent in spite of the fact that movie attendance had recovered from the worst years of the Depression, and that the companies owned their own theatres. Further, they were making use of various supposedly advantageous restrictive practices such as block booking, price fixing and discriminating against the small independent exhibitors – practices which would be outlawed by the government's Consent Decree in the 40s.

Apparently the classic Hollywood studio system of peak production and distribution was not, on the whole, a profitable one. Not only did it encourage overproduction, with too many features being released to earn well, but the high cost of quality pictures meant that many of the best and most popular features had a struggle to break even or earn a small profit. Most high-quality A features cost $1 million or more, and many of the best-known prestige productions were budgeted at between $1.5 and $2 million. Since this was the kind of rental figure that a hit picture could expect to earn in the USA around this time, it meant that many productions lost money.

This view of the system is further reinforced by developments which took place in the mid-40s, when the number of features released by the eight leading studios had declined by about one-third from their level in the late 30s – and those of the five largest companies had fallen even more. (They had largely given up producing B features around this time.) However, profits were setting new records, even exceeding the highest levels recorded in the early sound years of 1929 and 1930. Individual pictures were doing exceptional business, and were being held over on longer runs, with many of the top hits of the decade concentrated between 1945 and 1947. But it was a strange sort of 'boom', with production at its lowest level since the introduction of sound. To complete the cycle the number of releases rose slightly in the late 40s and early 50s while profits remained at low levels throughout these years after having declined rapidly in 1947–48.

One group of indexes which provide a further insight into developments during these years are those which measure the relationship between movie box-office receipts and both total consumer spending and expenditure on other recreation activities (as provided by the US Department of Commerce). They show that moviegoing was most popular in the early 30s and again during the war. The special attraction of the early talkies was followed by the Depression when, as a relatively cheap form of entertainment, the movies remained popular compared with other forms of entertainment. But when the decline set in in 1934, it was virtually continuous. Though there was a very brief recovery during the war when the choice of entertainment and opportunities for spending money were limited, by the later war years (1944–45) the indexes fell quickly as people found new ways to spend their money. Though, in absolute terms, the amount spent at the pictures remained high, there were already indications by 1946 that audiences were falling once again and that the wartime boom had been a very special phenomenon. This information also makes it clear how misleading is the standard view of the decline of the American movie industry in which the fall in movie audiences and company profits is regarded as a postwar development dating from 1947, ignoring the fact that many of the weaknesses and problems date back to the 30s.

Though all the studios were hurt by the postwar decline, the experiences of the individual companies varied considerably. Paramount, Fox and Warner Bros. continued to earn reasonable profits for a number of years, in contrast to MGM and RKO who experienced a swift drop in profits in 1947 and 1948. For MGM this marked the end of its many years as the most profitable studio in Hollywood, while the capricious style of management of RKO's new owner, Howard Hughes, led to a rapid running down of the studio in the early 50s. The year 1948 was also bad for Columbia, Universal and United Artists, but all three made a comeback in the 50s. UA was revived by a new management team and Universal benefited from a merger with Decca Records in 1952. Since they owned no movie theatres, these two companies were spared the problems experienced by the five larger companies who were forced to sell off their cinemas in accordance with the terms of the government's Consent Decree.

This divestiture process is generally regarded as one of the important factors contributing to the decline of the studios in the early 50s. It has been suggested, for example, that the general reduction in the number of features was due to the fact that the studios no longer needed to turn out enough pictures to fill their own cinemas throughout the year. However, the number of features released by the five largest companies actually increased slightly during the early 50s. The subsequent decline, it would seem, was related to other changes in the movie industry. From about 1954 on the majors were producing fewer but more expensive movies, filmed in colour and in the newly introduced CinemaScope or VistaVision processes, while the continuing fall in movie audiences in the late 50s was obviously the most important factor of all. It can, therefore, be argued that, from the studios' point of view, the enforced sale of their cinemas came at just the right time.

Many other important changes were happening during these years within the film industry, with new management taking over the running of a number of the companies. They expanded into other areas of entertainment such as recording, publishing and, especially, TV production, while reducing their film-making activities and their lists of expensive contract personnel. Most significantly, they came to depend more than ever before on deals with independent producers to provide a full programme of releases each year.

In an effort to attract audiences back into the cinema, many more pictures were filmed in colour and the new, mainly larger, screen processes which were introduced and widely promoted during the 1952–54 period. These were extremely successful for a time. Since the companies were producing fewer pictures with smaller overheads and with costs kept under control, income and profits rose in the mid-50s but once the novelty value wore off, audiences once more began to decline.

Profits had peaked in 1955 and fell off in the late 50s for virtually all the studios – aside from United Artists where a new management team had initiated a revival which continued throughout the decade. These new studio executives had taken full advantage of the fact that the company produced no pictures of its own but could devote all of its efforts to making the most favourable deals with the leading independents. It is difficult, because of the diversified nature of their income and other special transactions, to assess how badly the movie companies were doing during these years. Fox's financial difficulties during 1959–60, for example, were disguised by substantial income from the sale of the studio's back lot, while Warner Bros. continued to record small profits thanks to income from its TV productions and from the sale of its old movies to TV.

During these same years there had also been important changes in the international status of most of the companies. They had made a special effort to expand their activities outside the USA in both distribution and production. American pictures and stars had a worldwide appeal and the income from abroad helped to compensate for the falling box-office receipts at home. At the same time, the companies invested substantial sums in filming abroad, attracted by the lower wages (and other costs) along with picturesque or exotic locations. Italy and Spain in particular were often used for the filming of expensive epics in the 50s and early 60s, while the Hollywood companies made their largest investment in the British film industry during the 60s.

The 20-year period from the early 50s up to the early 70s marked a confusing, difficult and extended transition for the studios. The older, personal style of running the companies practised by the long-established moguls came to an end, and a new generation of studio heads was hired in the late 60s and early 70s. Many of them made the switch from talent agencies as part of the industry shake-up which took place during these years.

In fact, the companies had been unsuccessful in their efforts to halt the decline in movie audiences. Struggling to earn reasonable profits, they were vulnerable to possible takeover bids or mergers, yet they still retained some of that glamorous aura traditionally associated with Hollywood. Thus, they could be regarded as attractive and desirable acquisitions by corporations outside the entertainment industry as well as by those already involved in other areas of the media and show business, such as the giant MCA, headed by Lew Wasserman, which set its sights on Universal in the early 60s.

The MCA takeover of Universal was completed in 1962, the first of many such mergers in the 60s, continuing (and speeding up) the process of diversification which had been under way since the early 50s. At the same time, the control of many of the companies thus passed into the hands of a new breed of powerful media executive. In 1966 Paramount was taken over by Gulf + Western headed by Charles Bluhdorn; the Transamerica Corporation took over United Artists in 1967; and that same year Eliot Hyman's Seven Arts company merged with Warner Bros., then was taken over in turn in 1969 by Kinney National Services, headed by Stephen J. Ross.

Though Columbia, Fox and MGM remained independent companies, they, too, continued to diversify their activities so that the production and distribution of features became a smaller part of their activities.

Among the obvious benefits of the new system was the fact that the movie companies could draw on the extensive resources of the parent company to finance new pictures, while diversification meant that they were less vulnerable to the fluctuations of the notoriously volatile movie industry. The fall in Warner Bros.' film income from 1968 to 1970, for example, was partially cushioned by the growth in TV revenues, records and the music business. But the opposite situation could also develop, as Warners learned to its cost in 1983/84 when the large losses experienced by its Atari video-games subsidiary caused a major crisis in the company.

It should be stressed that the 60s mergers merely drew attention to the changing nature of the movie companies. Many writers have deplored the fact that the old-style moguls were replaced by hard-headed businessmen who were more concerned with making profits than making movies, as if this was a sudden change which took place to the detriment of Hollywood picture making. In fact, it was merely the culmination of a trend of many years during which the studios had lost their special individual character and had increasingly begun to rely on distribution deals with independent producers, directors and stars.

The crunch came in the late 60s and early 70s when a large number of expensive pictures flopped at the box-office and the combined losses of the leading companies were greater than at any period since the Depression years of 1931–32. Thus, the new system of conglomerate control had to face the first major test of its strength. Though none of the companies folded, there were many management changes, with the most serious reorganization taking place at MGM. Las Vegas financier Kirk Kerkorian took control, sold off studio assets, cut back on production, channelled new investment into the giant MGM Grand Hotel and gave up the studio's distribution arm in 1973.

These years marked the bottoming out of the 25-year decline in movie audiences. By 1974–75 admissions had recovered to just over one billion per year and have fluctuated slightly around this level ever since, with 1978–79 and 1982–84 as the peak years. Though industry-wide profits have generally held up well, with earnings from video sales in particular as yet another form of ancillary income in the 80s, the different companies have experienced considerable variations.

During the shake-up and rebalancing within the industry which took place during the critical years of the early 70s, Paramount, Universal and Warner Bros. emerged as the new leaders, with Columbia slightly slower to recover and Fox experiencing the most extreme ups and downs. United Artists continued to distribute many quality productions and earned reasonable, but not large, profits throughout the 70s.

As had been the case throughout the history of the American industry for about 60 years, the small number of major companies continued to dominate the movie market. Thus, as recently as the early 80s the six top studios (with MGM/UA functioning as a single distributor) accounted for almost 90% of the film-rental income from the North American market. However, there were new factors to be reckoned with: the continuing success of Orion Pictures (formed in 1978 by a breakaway group of top UA executives), the newly formed Tri-Star Pictures, and a major venture into adult features by the Disney company through its new Touchstone subsidiary. In addition, there was a major increase in the size and influence of the large number of other independent companies and a suggestion that this might mark the beginning of a shift in power away from the majors. But this challenge from the independents proved short-lived. Many of the top independents, along with the smaller companies, experienced serious problems in the late 80s and merged or folded, while Disney alone grew and prospered. Firmly established as a leading studio during 1987–90, Disney occupied the position of market leader for the first time ever, in 1988, with the spectacular success of *Who Framed Roger Rabbit* along with *Good Morning, Vietnam*, and repeated in 1990.

Aside from Disney, the six other majors accounted for only slightly over 60% of the American market during 1986–90, but appeared set to recover some lost ground in the 90s after a series of mergers and takeovers which has brought new investment into the movie industry from abroad and especially Japan. The merger of Time Inc with Warner Communications to form a giant media and entertainment conglomerate in 1989 was quickly followed by Sony's purchase of Columbia Pictures from Coca-Cola, while Giancarlo Parretti's Pathé Communications acquired MGM/UA from Kirk Kerkorian in 1990, and Matsushita's takeover of MCA and Universal took place later that same year. With so many changes of ownership and management having taken place during such a short period of time, it is impossible to predict what effect this may have on the Hollywood of the future.

Changing shares of the Movie Market (figures as % of total)

COMPANY	1939	1949	1956	1964	1972	1980	1986	1990
Columbia	7	8	9	15	9	14	9	5
Fox	17	21	18	8	9	16	8	14
MGM	22	22	17	17	6	7	4	3
United Artists	7	4	10	16	9			
Paramount	14	14	13	17	22	16	22	15
Universal	7	7	10	12	5	20	9	14
Warner Bros.	14	11	15	6	18	14	12	13
RKO	9	9	4					
Disney/Buena Vista	1	1	1	9	5	4	10	16
Others	4	3	3	1	16	9	25	20

MOVIE COSTS, BOX-OFFICE HITS AND FLOPS

Throughout the silent era, as pictures grew longer and film-making became more sophisticated, the costs of movie-making rose steadily. The development of new cameras, lighting equipment and other accessories meant an increase in the size of the regular crew, as well as in the number of specialized technicians required for each picture. Sets and costumes became more elaborate and greater care was taken in the choice of film locations. Most important of all, however, was the competition between the leading companies in their attempts to attract the top stars by offering them ever-higher salaries.

During the early period, 1908–1910, a quality one-reeler – the standard format of the period – could be produced for about $1,000–$1,500, but by the mid-teens a four- or five-reel feature meant an investment of $20,000–$30,000. Many of the smaller companies were wary of the higher costs and risks involved in feature-film production and kept expenditure as low as possible. Thus, Universal's *Traffic In Souls* (1913) and Fox's first feature, *Life's Shop Window* (1914), were each completed at a rock-bottom cost of $6,000. Since both movies were quite successful, they gave a welcome boost to their respective companies in their struggle to establish themselves within the fast-growing and constantly changing industry.

In these early days of feature-film production there was clearly plenty of scope for earning good profits, as Jesse Lasky and Cecil B. DeMille proved with their first picture, *The Squaw Man*, in 1914. Budgeted at $25,000, it cost about half as much again, but still proved popular and profitable enough to launch their new production company successfully.

D. W. Griffith spent the relatively lavish sum of $36,000, about twice the original budget, on his first feature, the four-reel *Judith Of Bethulia* in 1913, which probably lost money. But his wish to continue directing only features led to a dispute with the heads of Biograph. He left late in 1913 after over six years as the company's leading director, joining Reliance-Majestic where he turned out a number of features before plunging into the tremendously risky and ambitious (and independently produced) epic, *The Birth Of A Nation*. Twelve reels in length and completed at a cost of $100,000, an exceptional sum for that period, the picture was released early in 1915 and turned out to be one of the most profitable productions in the history of the cinema and the most successful silent feature ever, though Griffith himself saw only a fraction of the total profits. (Since it was distributed on a 'states rights' basis, it is difficult to find an accurate revenue figure, though reliable estimates suggest US revenues of $10 million or more. Louis B. Mayer's company, for example, made a $1 million profit from the New England franchise alone.) Unfortunately, Griffith lost most of the $400,000 that he invested in his remarkable follow-up picture, the now-classic *Intolerance* (1916), which flopped at the box-office.

Costs rose steadily in the late 'teens as the industry continued its rapid rate of expansion. By 1920 the average expenditure on a feature was estimated at $60,000 and was almost double that sum at the giant Paramount where A-feature 'specials' were budgeted in excess of $150,000. At Fox the average cost of a feature rose from $42,000 in 1916–18 to $67,000 in the early 20s, and continued rising – as did costs at the other leading studios which turned to producing better-quality and more expensive pictures. By the end of the silent era (1927–28) the average expenditure on a Fox feature had risen to $190,000 but was still substantially below that of MGM's $275,000.

The intense competition between the leading companies had first begun to take a clearer shape in the post-World War I years, with one or two large hits registering each year from 1919 up to the coming of sound. The important role played by the stars is immediately apparent. First National, for example, had many of the top stars and independent producers under contract and had its biggest success with Mary Pickford in *Daddy Long Legs* (1919), Charlie Chaplin's first feature *The Kid* (1921), and Norma Talmadge (*Smilin' Through*, 1922), while Paramount's hits were the multi-star vehicle, *The Miracle Man* (1919) with Betty Compson, Thomas Meighan, Elinor Fair and Lon Chaney, followed by two Rudolph Valentino vehicles – *The Sheik* (1921) and *Blood And Sand* (1922). A few scattered hits from the other studios included UA's first major success with D. W. Griffith's *Way Down East* (1920) starring Lillian Gish and Richard Barthelmess, and Metro's phenomenally successful *The Four Horsemen Of The Apocalypse* (1921), which was directed by Rex Ingram and made the name of Rudolph Valentino.

Both of these latter pictures had been completed for about $800,000, a generous sum for the period. But with costs on the rise, a $1 million budget soon became not uncommon. Erich von Stroheim's *Foolish Wives*, filmed for just over $1 million in 1921, was a special case at the economy-minded Universal. However, Douglas Fairbanks invested $1.5 million in his spectacular production of *Robin Hood* in 1922, and later that same year Paramount completed filming on *The Covered Wagon* for almost $800,000, the most lavish Western epic ever filmed up to that date and a favourite project of production chief Jesse Lasky. Cecil B. DeMille was not far behind with his version of *The Ten Commandments* (1923) which topped the $1.8 million mark.

Fortunately for Paramount and Douglas Fairbanks all these pictures (along with Doug's costly *The Thief Of Bagdad*, 1924) proved to be big money-earners. But other companies were not so lucky. Universal had lost about $250,000 on *Foolish Wives*, and D. W. Griffith's *Orphans Of the Storm*, also completed and released in 1922, cost just under $1 million and failed to break even. Similarly, the Cosmopolitan production of *When Knighthood Was In Flower* (1922) starring Marion Davies was financed by William Randolph Hearst, her newspaper-tycoon companion of many years, to the tune of $1.5 million with little chance of recovering that sum at the box-office. In 1923, shortly before merging into the newly formed MGM, the Goldwyn Company embarked on a lavish movie version of *Ben-Hur* in Italy. By the time the much-troubled production was completed under the new management of Irving Thalberg and Louis B. Mayer, the cost had risen to almost $4 million, far beyond the point where the picture could hope to break even, though it did perform extremely well at the box-office and helped to make a name for the new studio.

The arrival of MGM with a number of hits in its first full year of operation marked the commencement of a new attitude of competitiveness in
the Hollywood of the late 20s. Most surprising of all was the extent of
the success experienced by both Fox and Warner Bros. Having upgraded
its features generally, Fox enjoyed a string of hits beginning with *What
Price Glory?* (1926) and *Seventh Heaven* (1927), followed by many early
talkies and musicals such as *Sunny Side Up* (1929). However, slightly
ahead of Fox in adapting to sound was the then tiny Warner Bros. studio
which was given a tremendous boost by the great success of *The Jazz
Singer* (1927) – the first (part) talkie – and further helped by the even
more profitable follow-up movie in 1928, also starring Al Jolson, *The
Singing Fool*. (Though each cost only $500,000 the studio had already
invested over $3 million in its earlier experiments with sound.)

Virtually all the studios rushed to produce movie musicals in 1929.
MGM had a big hit with the first of the bunch, *The Broadway Melody*,
completed at a cost of under $400,000 – only slightly more than the
average for an early MGM talkie ($360,000), in comparison with a
$305,000 average at Fox. The introduction of sound added about 30% to
the budget generally but, with the box-office booming, even the smaller
studios were eager to get in on the act. Samuel Goldwyn spent $1.3
million on *Whoopee!*, the first of his Eddie Cantor vehicles, and earned
a substantial profit in spite of the fact that, by the time it was released late
in 1930, audiences had had a surfeit of musicals and box-office receipts
were beginning to fall off generally. Little Universal had followed up its
$1 million production of *Broadway* (1929) with the lavish *King Of Jazz*
(1930) – costing an extravagant $1.65 million – and ended up losing $1
million on this one picture. And the studio was also extremely unlucky
with its investment of $1.25 million in the remarkable Oscar-winning *All
Quiet On The Western Front* (1930) which barely succeeded in earning
a small profit.

The full impact of the Depression in the early 30s meant that budgets
actually fell for a time as the studios struggled to cut their costs and
remain solvent. MGM emerged then as the single most profitable
company, able to continue producing a high proportion of expensive
A features. Occupying the upper end of the market, MGM's average
budgets rose from $450,000 in the early 30s to $700,000 by the end
of the decade. It was rare for even an MGM feature to cost over $1
million in the early 30s, however, but by the later years most of the
studios had recovered from the worst effects of the Depression and
were competing in the production of quality pictures. But revenues were
slow to recover and profits remained generally small. Though production
standards were high, so too were production costs. A survey of the many
prestige pictures of the period shows that a surprisingly large proportion
of them lost money, while relatively few earned a good profit. Since many
of the top hits only attracted US rentals income of about $1.5 million in
the late 30s, once the cost of a picture had passed the $1 million mark,
its chances of earning a good profit became relatively slim, as happened
with C. B. DeMille's *The Crusades* (Paramount, 1935), for example.

A roughly similar pattern can be discerned at a number of the studios where the top stars and directors were allowed ever-higher budgets, and in many cases reached the point where their pictures could no longer be profitable. Thus, the interest of both Warner Bros. and Fox in producing more lavish pictures and attempting to compete with MGM, was severely limited by box-office considerations. Warners could do no better than break even on the first of its million-dollar productions, *A Midsummer Night's Dream* (1935) and *Anthony Adverse* (1936), then lost money on most of its high-cost movies in the late 30s, many of them starring Errol Flynn and/or filmed in Technicolor, including *The Prince And The Pauper* (1937), *The Private Lives of Elizabeth And Essex*, *Dodge City* and *Juarez*, all released in 1939. Even the superbly entertaining *The Adventures Of Robin Hood* (1938) cost a hefty $1.9 million and thus earned only a small profit. (Not surprisingly, Warner Bros. had virtually given up filming in Technicolor by late 1939.)

Similarly, production chief Darryl F. Zanuck at Fox had succeeded in reviving the studio during 1936–37 but encountered serious problems in the late 30s with his more expensive productions, many of them filmed in Technicolor. Of that group of well-known pictures which fell into the $1.5–$2 million cost range, and featured many of the studio's top stars, only *In Old Chicago* (1938) and *Drums Along The Mohawk* (1939) made a small profit, while *Suez* in 1938, *Stanley And Livingstone*, *The Rains Came* and *Swanee River* in 1939, *Little Old New York*, *The Blue Bird* and *Brigham Young* in 1940 all lost money as company profits plummeted.

In the case of RKO, however, the break-even point was much lower than for Fox or Warners. This meant that by the late 30s the cost of the Katharine Hepburn and Fred Astaire-Ginger Rogers pictures had risen to the point where they were no longer profitable to produce. Though the studio had spent less than $1 million on *Quality Street* (1937) and *Bringing Up Baby* (1938), and only slightly more on *Carefree* (1938) and *The Story Of Vernon And Irene Castle* (1939), they all lost money. But RKO did manage to just break even on its most expensive movie of the decade, the $1.9 million *Gunga Din* (1939), and even earned a small profit on *The Hunchback of Notre Dame* (1939), which cost only slightly less.

For the comparatively small Columbia, the cost of its Frank Capra features had risen to the point where the studio's star director no longer contributed to the company profits. Most expensive of all was the $2 million *Lost Horizon* (1937) which probably lost money, while *You Can't Take It With You* (1938) and *Mr Smith Goes To Washington* (1939) came in at about $1.5 million each and more or less broke even.

After joining United Artists in 1935, David O. Selznick soon learned the hard facts of life as an independent producer, as he attempted to make prestigious pictures that were also profitable. Of his five best-known features, released during 1936–38 and all costing over $1 million, he earned reasonable profits on the least expensive ($1.1 million) productions, *A Star Is Born* and *The Prisoner Of Zenda* (both 1937), broke even with *Nothing Sacred* (cost $1.3 million) and sustained losses on the most expensive – *The Garden Of Allah* (1936) and *The*

Adventures Of Tom Sawyer (1938), each filmed in Technicolor at a cost of about $1.5 million. Samuel Goldwyn, the other leading UA producer during these years, was somewhat more successful in keeping his costs down, partly by filming in black-and-white in preference to the more expensive Technicolor favoured by Selznick. But for Goldwyn, too, the story during these years was not much different. He made a profit on *Dead End* and *Stella Dallas*, completed in 1937 at about $1 million each, broke even on *The Hurricane* (1938) which cost rather more, and lost substantial sums after running over budget (final cost $1.4 million) on *The Adventures Of Marco Polo*, and the $2 million production of *The Goldwyn Follies* (both 1938).

Even at the giant MGM, which had the best distribution, the most effective publicity and earned the most consistent profits, many of the most expensive movies were money-losers during these years. They included the two lavish Norma Shearer vehicles, *Romeo and Juliet* (1936) and *Marie Antoinette* (1938) in which the studio invested about $2 million each, as well as *The Good Earth* (1938) and *The Wizard Of Oz* (1939), both of which climbed over the $2.5 million mark. (*The Wizard Of Oz*, of course, earned a substantial profit in later years, but lost money on its initial release.)

All in all, there were fewer smash-hit movies in the 30s than in any other decade. With virtually all the top grossers clustered in the $1.5–$2.7 million range, only two pictures topped the $3 million mark, as compared with eight in the 20s, and both were very special independent productions. Walt Disney took a big risk when he decided to invest $1.5 million in his first feature-length animated film, *Snow White And The Seven Dwarfs* (1937). It became the biggest hit of the sound era and the largest-grossing movie since *The Birth Of A Nation* – until the release of independent producer David O. Selznick's *Gone With The Wind* just two years later. Selznick was involved in every aspect of this lavish Technicolor production. At $4.25 million, with part of the money coming from distributor MGM, it just about surpassed MGM's own silent version of *Ben-Hur* as the most costly Hollywood movie up to that date, but also overtook *The Birth Of A Nation* as the biggest hit.

The general pattern of the late 30s – of relatively few big-grossing pictures and a profit squeeze for the more expensive productions – continued on into the early 40s. The only big success, topping the $6 million mark, during the 1940–42 years was the Jesse Lasky-Howard Hawks production of *Sergeant York* (Warner Bros., 1941) starring Gary Cooper. This all began to change, however, during 1942–43. Movie attendance was back at peak levels for the first time since the early 30s, with most of the biggest hits of the decade concentrated into the three-year period 1945–47. These years included the top successes from Fox (*Leave Her To Heaven*, 1945), MGM (*Meet Me In St Louis*, released late in 1944), RKO (*The Bells Of St Mary's*, 1945), Columbia (*The Jolson Story*, 1946) and Universal (*The Egg And I*, 1947), each bringing in rentals of over $5 million.

This was a concentrated period of peak profits and long cinema runs. Continuing the pattern of the late 30s, independent producers and producer-directors accounted for many of the biggest hits – five of the top seven for the decade – reflecting the increasingly important role which they played in Hollywood in the 40s. Sam Goldwyn had the biggest box-office success of his career and the top hit of the decade with *The Best Years Of Our Lives*, followed by David O. Selznick's lavish $5.3 million Western *Duel In The Sun* (both released in 1946). The other big money-earners were Cecil B. DeMille's *Samson And Delilah* (1949), along with *The Bells Of St Mary's* (1945) and *Going My Way* (1944), both from writer-producer-director Leo McCarey.

As in the 30s, many of the 40s hits were grouped together within a fairly narrow range, with over 70 movies earning rentals of between $4 and $5.7 million. But one important difference was the fact that, though costs were rising, they were not all that much higher than in the late 30s and profits were correspondingly greater. In addition, many of those pictures with a rental income of $2–$4 million and thus not included among the top box-office hits, were also quite profitable: these included such well-known titles as the enduring *Casablanca* (1943 – rentals of $3.7 million), *Gilda* (1946–$3.75 million) *The Big Sleep* (1946 – $3 million), *Crossfire* (1947 – $2.5 million), *Call Northside 777* (1948 – $2.7 million) and the Tracy-Hepburn *Adam's Rib* (1949 – $3 million).

When revenues and profits fell off badly in the late 40s the companies endeavoured to hold down costs as much as possible, reducing their overheads by cutting back on their lists of contract stars and contract personnel. Though the average cost of a feature had risen to about $1 million by the mid-40s, it remained at the same level for a number of years before it was boosted, once again, by the important technological changes taking place in the early 50s. But it should be noted that the rise in the average cost of a typical feature was only partly due to an increase in real costs, for it also reflected a shift away from B pictures to the more costly As. There was a long-overdue increase in the number of features filmed in colour, while the widely publicized introduction of such new processes as 3-D, Cinerama, CinemaScope and VistaVision helped to halt the decline in movie attendance, if only for a few years. An important change was also taking place in the pattern of movie hits, leading towards the kind of situation more familiar to us today. For the first time ever, many individual pictures achieved extraordinarily high rental figures and profits which, even taking into account a certain amount of inflation, would have been unheard of only a few years earlier. Whereas the top 40s hit *The Best Years Of Our Lives* (1946) chalked up rentals of $10.4 million, there were over a dozen movies topping the $12 million mark in the 50s. Among these the top ten presented a cross-section of the new techniques, including two each in CinemaScope, VistaVision and Todd-AO, and one each filmed in Cinerama, Technirama and Camera 65.

This trend also reflected a successful effort on the part of a number of the studios such as Fox (with CinemaScope) and Paramount (with VistaVision) to regain some of the ground lost to the independent producers. Thus, the top ten presented a mixture of studio productions such as *Ben-Hur* (MGM, 1959) filmed in Camera 65, *The Robe* (Fox,

1953) filmed in CinemaScope and *White Christmas* (Paramount, 1954) filmed in VistaVision, while independent hit pictures included Mike Todd's *Around The World In 80 Days* (UA, 1956) filmed in Todd-AO and the Sam Spiegel production of *The Bridge On The River Kwai* (Columbia, 1957) filmed in CinemaScope.

BREAKDOWN OF COSTS AND REVENUES – *STAR WARS*

(Fox 1977)	$	$
Date of Budget: 1976		
1. **Salaries and wages**		
Producers' fees and cast*	750,000*	
(includes George Lucas, $100,000)		
Production crew and personnel	2,100,000	
		2,850, 000
2. **Final script**		50,000
3. **Score and music**		100,000
4. **Transport and Tunisia location costs**		700,000
5. **Set construction and lighting**		1,600,000
6. **Special effects and models of spaceships and robots**		3,900,000
7. **Miscellaneous production costs**		800,000
Rental of studio, special-effect stages,		
dubbing theatre, offices: 300,000		
Costumes: 300,000		
Film stock and processing: 200,000		
8. **Cost of Insurance and financing**		1,000,000
Finance, loans, Fox's overhead and completion bond: 800,000		
Insurance: 200,000		
TOTAL COST		11,000,000
($1,000,000 over initial budget)		

Revenues as at 1980	$	$
Worldwide box-office receipts	510,000,000	
Exhibitors	(260,000,000)	
Rentals (including N. American rentals, $185.1m)	250,000,000	
Deduct		
Negative costs	11,000,000	
Prints and advertising	16,500,000	(102,500,000)
Fox distributors fee	75,000,000	
TOTAL PROFITS		147,500,000
Fox (60%)	88,500,000	
Producers (40%)		
(George Lucas, Gary Kurtz etc)	59,000,000	
(Producers' share includes percentage points of personnel:)		
Alec Guinness 2¼% of profits	3,318,750	
Mark Hamill	368,750	
Carrie Fisher ¼% of profits each	368,750	
Harrison Ford ⅔% of profits	1,000,000	
Set workers 1/20% of profits	73,750	
(or multiple thereof)		
Office workers 1/200% of profits	7,375	
(or multiples thereof)		
		147,500,000

*Additional payments to producers, cast and personnel in the form of percentage points in the profits – see Costs and Revenues
Source: David Pirie (ed) Anatomy of the Movies (Windward, 1981)

		$	$
BUDGET *CASABLANCA* (Warner Bros. 1942)			
Date of budget: June 2, 1942			
1	**Story cost**		20,000
1a	**Continuity and treatment**		
	W. Klein (Kline)	1,983	
	A. MacKenzie	2,150	
	J. Epstein	15,208	
	P. Epstein	15,208	
	H. Koch	4,200	
	L. (Lenore) Coffee	750	
	Secretaries	1,432	
	Script Changes	6,350	
			47,281
2	**Director** Michael Curtiz	73,400	
2a	**Producer** Hal Wallis	52,000	
3	**Assistant Directors** Lee Katz	9,837	
4	**Cameramen & Assistants** Arthur Edeson	10,873	
5a	**Cast Salaries**		
5b	**Contract talent**		
	Rick Humphrey Bogart	36,667	
	Martinez* Sydney Greenstreet 2 weeks @ 3750	7,500	
	Laszlo Paul Henreid	25,000	
	Yvonne Madeleine LeBeau 3$^{1}/2$ weeks @ 100 doubled	700	
		69,867	
5c	**Outside talent**		
	Ilsa Ingrid Bergman 8 weeks @ 3125	25,000	
	Renault Claude Rains 5$^{1}/2$ weeks @ 4000	22,000	
	Annina Joy Page 2 weeks @ 100	200	
	Strasser Conrad Veidt	25,000	
	Carl S. Z. Sakall 6$^{1}/2$ weeks @ 400	2,600	
	Sam Dooley Wilson 7 weeks @ 500	3,500	
	Sascha Leonid Kinskey 5$^{2}/3$ weeks @ 400	2,267	
	Ugarte Peter Lorre 1$^{1}/3$ weeks @ 1750	2,333	
	Abdul Dan Seymour 4 weeks @ 250	1,000	
	Heinze Ludvig Stossel 4 weeks @ 400	1,600	
	Berger John Qualen 1 week @ 400	400	
	Farrari 4 weeks @ 100	400	
	Tonelli Charles La Tour 4 weeks @ 75	300	
	Pickpocket Curt Bois 1 week @ 1000	1,000	
	Jan Helmut Dantine 2 weeks @ 400	800	
	Andreya Corinna Mura 4 weeks @ 500	2,000	
	Croupier Marcel Dalio 1$^{1}/3$ weeks @ 500	667	
	Headwaiter Martin Garralaga 2 weeks @ 150	300	
	Waiter Oliver Prickett 2$^{/1}/3$ weeks @ 150	350	
		91,717	
			161,584
6	**Talent** (extras, bits, etc.)		56,019
7	**Musicians** (arrangers, etc.)		28,000
	Score: Max Steiner		
	Music dir: Leo F. Forbstein		
8	**Property Labor**		10,150
9	**Construction of Sets**		18,000
10	**Stand-by Labor**		15,350
11	**Electricians**		20,755
12	**Striking**		7,000
12a	**Make-Up (Hairdressers, etc.)** Perc Westmore		9,100
13	**Art Department Salaries** Carl Jules Weyl		8,846
14	**Cutters' Salaries** Owen Marks		4,630
15	**Property Rental & Expense**		6,300
16	**Electrical Rental & Expense**		750

17	**Location Expense**	1,252
18	**Trick, Miniature etc.** Lawrence Butler, Willard van Enger	7,475
19	**Wardrobe Expense** Orry Kelly	22,320
20	**Negative Film**	8,000
22	**Developing & Printing**	10,500
25	**Camera Rental & Expense**	400
26	**Meals**	1,200
27	**Auto Rental Expense & Travel**	5,000
28	**Insurance**	2,800
29	**Miscellaneous Expense**	3,350
30	**Sound Expense**	2,200
31	**Trailer**	2,000
32	**Sound Operating Salaries**	8.000
34	**Stills**	850
34a	**Publicity**	3,000
	TOTAL DIRECT COST	638,222
35	**General studio overhead** @ 35%	223,822
40	**Depreciation** @ $2^{1}/_{2}$%	15,956
	GRAND TOTAL COST	878,000

*'Martinez' was changed to 'Farrari.'
NOTE: in job categories, only most senior name is given here
Source: Rudy Behlmer *Inside Warner Bros: 1935–1951* (New York: Viking 1985)

In the case of Fox the average picture cost in the 50s rose from $1.4 million at the beginning of the decade to just under $2 million for a typical feature shot in CinemaScope and colour in 1954–55. Though the studio invested the considerable sum of $5 million in its first CinemaScope movie, the smash-hit Biblical epic *The Robe*, it also recorded substantial profits from less expensive early 'Scope pictures such as *How To Marry A Millionaire* (1953) which cost $2.5 million, and *The Seven Year Itch* (1955) at $2 million. But there were large numbers of expensive flops, too, from all the studios in the late 50s and especially in the early 60s which proved that new technology alone could not solve the film industry's problems. This became even clearer in the 60s when most of the studios invested substantial sums in a variety of opulent productions, including many 70mm blockbusters costing $12 million or more. By 1961 the average cost of a Hollywood feature had risen to $2 million and it continued rising, to about $3 million by the end of the decade.

Universal just about broke even with its $12 million *Spartacus* (1960), but MGM spent around $20 million on its remake of *Mutiny On The Bounty* (1962) as did UA on *The Greatest Story Ever Told* (1965), and both companies lost heavily. Warner Bros. invested $17 million in the screen adaptation of *My Fair Lady* (1964) which failed to cover its costs at the box-office – nor did Fox's much-troubled production of *Cleopatra* (1963), finally completed at the staggering cost of $37 million. If anything, box-office success appeared more elusive and unpredictable than ever before.

Fox and Paramount came up with the two most spectacular successes of the decade – *The Sound Of Music* (1965) and *Love Story* (1970) respectively, as the spread between the top and bottom titles among the leading 80 hit movies continued to widen. (Whereas in the 40s the gap between *The Best Years Of Our Lives* and the many money-earners with rentals of $4 million was only $6.4 million, in the 50s the spread between *Ben-Hur* and the other hit titles was $30 million, and it jumped to over $60 million in the 60s.)

Though many of the companies had been reorganized, merged, or taken over by corporate conglomerates, there was little discernible difference in the pattern of production. They continued to invest in many high-risk, high-cost productions up to the end of the 60s when a series of box-office disasters finally brought to an end that cycle of excessive expenditure and dependence on blockbusters which can be traced back to the early 50s. Paramount lost heavily on such expensive movies as *Paint Your Wagon* (1969), *The Molly Maguires* (1970) and *Darling Lili* (1970). United Artists was brought low by *The Battle Of Britain* (1969) and *The Private Life Of Sherlock Holmes* (1970), MGM by *Ryan's Daughter* (1970), and Fox did worst of all with *Star!* (1968), *The Only Game In Town* (1969) and *Tora! Tora! Tora!* (1970) among others.

Of course, not every expensive movie lost money – popular films of quality such as MGM's *2001: A Space Odyssey* (1968) earned a large profit, as did Fox's *Patton* (1970), but these were the exception. At the same time, the surprise success of the Dennis Hopper-Peter Fonda movie *Easy Rider* in 1969, immediately followed by Paul Mazursky's *Bob & Carol & Ted & Alice* later that same year, along with the smash hits *M*A*S*H* and *Love Story* (both 1970), proved that it was not necessary to spend large sums of money to come up with big hits. These pictures also opened the way for a number of new young directors to be given their first opportunity with a major feature. Though many fell by the wayside, from among those who were successful there emerged a new group of producer-directors who would provide many of the top hit movies of the 70s and 80s. William Friedkin with *The French Connection* (Fox, 1971) and *The Exorcist* (Warner Bros., 1973) and Francis Ford Coppola, with the two Godfather pictures for Paramount, were followed by George Lucas, director of *American Graffiti* (Universal, 1972) and *Star Wars* (Fox, 1977), who then produced the equally successful *Star Wars* sequels, as well as the Indiana Jones movies for Paramount in the 80s. Finally, there was Steven Spielberg who directed *Jaws* (Universal, 1975), *Close Encounters Of The Third Kind* (Columbia, 1977), *E T, The Extra-Terrestrial* (Universal, 1982), *The Color Purple* (Warner Bros., 1985) and the three Indiana Jones pictures, and was executive producer on *Poltergeist* (MGM, 1982), also *Gremlins* (Warner Bros., 1984) and *Back to the Future* (Universal, 1985) and their sequels, and *Who Framed Roger Rabbit* (Disney/Buena Vista, 1988).

Not only were these relatively young men responsible for a large percentage of the biggest hits, but they also succeeded in dividing them between a number of different companies, thus ensuring that the benefits have been widely distributed. Thus, the top 20 hits, all with rentals of over $50 million in the 70s, were shared among the top Hollywood companies and reflected the relative success of each studio during these years: Universal had six, Paramount four, Fox and Columbia three each, Warner Bros. and United Artists two each.

In addition to the new producer-directors there were many highly successful independent producers in the 70s, some of them linked with a particular studio: Richard Zanuck and David Brown provided Universal with *The Sting* (1973), *Jaws* (1975) and *Jaws II* (1978), while Ray Stark played a similar role at Columbia with *Funny Girl* (1968), *The Way We Were* (1973) and *California Suite* (1978). But even the most dependable producers and directors were likely to suffer the occasional box-office disaster in the modern era of high-cost and high-risk productions. This happened to Steven Spielberg with his $27 million production of *1941* (1979), also Richard Zanuck-David Brown's *The Island* (1980), costing $22 million, to Ray Stark and the $40 million screen version of *Annie* (1982), George Lucas with his $34 million lemon called *Howard The Duck* (1986), and actor-producer Warren Beatty with the $40 million *Ishtar* (1987). But Michael Cimino's $40 million Western epic, *Heaven's Gate* (1980), lost the most money of all and occupies pride of place as the best-known flop of recent years.

Fuelled by inflation, costs had risen rapidly throughout most of the 70s. The average expenditure on a Hollywood feature was about $7 million by the end of the decade and this shot up to $12 million by the mid-80s. But the long, post-1946 decline in movie audiences had come to an end by the early 70s, and the rentals earned by the top hit pictures had risen accordingly, achieving some spectacular profits. Most of the trends established in the 70s have continued, with Paramount and Universal maintaining their position as the industry leaders and benefiting from the George Lucas-Steven Spielberg connection in particular. Paramount had the added benefit of the surprise Australian mega-hit, *Crocodile Dundee*, in 1986, and the extremely successful producer partnership of Don Simpson and Jerry Bruckheimer who came up with the Eddie Murphy vehicle *Beverly Hills Cop* (1984) and its sequel in 1987, as well as *Top Gun* (1986) and several others, and demonstrated a special talent for tapping the highly lucrative 'teen' market. But both Warners and Fox had their good years too. Warner Bros. was the industry leader in 1985 and 1989 boosted by the box office success of *Batman* and *Lethal Weapon* 2, while Fox's hits included *Home Alone* and *Die Hard* 2, both released in 1990.

The spread between the top and bottom grossers among the hit pictures also continued to grow between the 70s and 80s, while the rise in the average cost of a feature meant that the box-office take of many pictures failed to cover their costs. Film-making was as risky a business as ever. But the occasional unexpected and spectacular adult-movie success continued to emerge, such as *Tootsie* which starred Dustin Hoffman in 1982 and Oliver Stone's harrowing *Platoon* (1986).

The surprise success of a number of relatively modestly budgeted movies in 1990 and early 1991, including *Ghost*, *Pretty Woman*, *Home Alone* and the Oscar-winning *Dances with Wolves* caused some serious rethinking in Hollywood, at a time when many high-cost pictures were struggling to break even. The most dramatic example of a new reassessment of company policy for the 90s could be seen at Paramount. Here a celebrated court case, brought by writer and columnist Art Buchwald (who claimed that his story had been used, uncredited, for the Eddie Murphy movie, *Coming to America*) had revealed some of the more questionable accounting methods regularly used by the Hollywood studios. And this coincided with the failure of some of the studio's most expensive productions, such as *Days of Thunder*, while it had a smash hit with *Ghost*. Not surprisingly, Paramount decided that it could no longer afford the services of the high-priced actor Eddie Murphy and producers Simpson and Bruckheimer who had been the stars of the Paramount lot in the 80s. It will be interesting to see if the extravagant costs of the 80s will really be brought under control by Paramount and the other leading studios in the 90s.

Hollywood Moviemakers

Many leading figures first made their names in the 'teens when the American film industry was expanding rapidly. Adolph Zukor, William Fox, Jesse Lasky and Carl Laemmle were among the most enterprising of the early movie moguls, while the top directors of the period included Cecil B. DeMille, Maurice Tourneur and Allan Dwan along with D. W. Griffith, the most famous and respected of all. The growth of the major studios in the 20s created a great demand for creative technicians who were put under contract along with stars, directors and script writers. And the changeover to sound involved new skills – sound men, music directors, composers and writers of dialogue, while many new stars were signed up from the Broadway stage. Having maintained high levels of production and impressive technical standards for many years, the studio system was wound down in the postwar period.

CHANGING THE SHAPE OF THE INDUSTRY

In the 1890s the fledgling movie industry was dominated by a small group of inventors and entrepreneurs, founders of the early companies which bore their names such as Edison, Lubin and Selig. It was not until the early 1900s that the first movie directors began to make their mark. The best-known of these pioneers was Edwin S. Porter, who directed *The Great Train Robbery* (1903), but it was D. W. Griffith who emerged as the most famous figure, thanks to the quality of his work at Biograph between 1908 and 1912. In the early days of cinema, actors on the screen were anonymous players, generally held in low esteem by those who acted on the stage and regarded the movies merely as a means of earning some spare cash between stage appearances. By the mid-teens, however, the general quality of movie acting had improved considerably, and players were beginning to be billed on film credits and movie posters, while a few well-known faces such as Mary Pickford and Charlie Chaplin were already establishing worldwide reputations with fabulous salaries to match. The film star had arrived.

As the feature-length picture took over from the one and two-reeler, the various tasks involved in movie-making became progressively more specialized. The cameraman had been the one important technician in the early years: not only did he photograph the picture, devise the special effects and look after the props, but he often supervised the developing of the negative as well. He now acquired a full team of assistants. Great improvements were made in the quality of motion-picture lighting and photography, and it was not long before the props department was brought under the supervision of a proper art director and set designers. Costume designers took a little longer to arrive.

In the 20s the industry became increasingly dominated by a small number of giant companies headed by a few of the most competitive and enterprising moguls – most notably, Adolph Zukor, William Fox, Marcus Loew, Carl Laemmle and Louis B. Mayer. These studios had a major influence on the way that the movies were made. They signed up many of the leading stars and directors, as well as technical personnel who were assigned to newly organized, specialized departments. Though a number of the top stars and directors were able to preserve their independence during the 20s, releasing their pictures through United Artists, with the coming of sound the giant studios – led by MGM, Paramount and Warner Bros. – became more powerful than ever before.

The 30s was the peak decade for the studio and star systems, but it was a difficult period for directors, writers, and those stars who wished to have some control over their roles. The companies were turning out large numbers of pictures with their contracted personnel who were kept busy with regular studio assignments. Producer Richard Zanuck remembers that his father Darryl, vice-president in charge of production at 20th Century-Fox, had a big chart under the glass top of his desk, 'and it had everybody that was under contract there. All the producers, and the directors, and the writers and actors and actresses. And it was so simple . . . Casting meetings would take all of about ten minutes. Not only casting, but putting the whole picture together. He would say, "Well, we've got Julian Blaustein as producer, he's available next week. Put him with Hathaway, he'll direct. And we've got Tyrone Power, he's going to finish his picture, give him a week off." And that was the end of it.'

Though it produced some fine movies, the system was wasteful of talent. With the postwar decline of the studios, stars and directors regained independence. The 40s was a memorable decade for writer-directors and producer-directors, while the top cameramen took advantage of the new developments in cameras and film stock to achieve remarkable results.

The death or retirement of many of those leading moguls who had run the studios for 20 or 30 years left a gap which could never be filled. Similarly, many of the famous directors, stars and technicians who had played an important role in the cinema for a long period, were reaching the end of their careers. Thus, the large companies went through a long and difficult period of transition before experiencing a revival of sorts in the 70s with the help of a new generation of producers, stars, writers and, especially, directors.

THE MOGULS

The major Hollywood producers, popularly known as the 'movie moguls', played an essential role in the development of the early American cinema and were instrumental in establishing its dominating commercial position worldwide – which it has maintained to the present day.

The most important of the first producer-moguls associated with the early beginnings of the industry in the 1890s were Thomas Alva Edison, the famous inventor and entrepreneur, Sigmund Lubin and William N. Selig. Even before the pictures were projected in the primitive earliest cinemas known as nickelodeons, the Lubin Company, based in Philadelphia, was in competition with Edison in supplying short subjects to the peep-show arcades. This was around 1896–97, about the same time that J. Stuart Blackton, an actor, writer and director as well as an important producer in the early years, joined with Albert Smith and William Rock to form the Vitagraph Company, while the Selig Polyscope Company was just getting under way in Chicago.

A second important group of pioneer producers entered the still tiny, but growing industry about 10 years later. In 1907, George K. Spoor and G.M. 'Bronco Billy' Anderson (S and A) founded the Essanay Company in Chicago and soon began producing one-reel Westerns and slapstick comedies. And in New York City, Kalem (K-L-M) was set up by George Kleine, Samuel Long and Frank Marion and quickly expanded its activities to Florida and California.

All of these pioneer producers, along with Biograph and the French companies Pathé and Méliès, had joined together to form the Motion Picture Patents Company, a monopolistic trust designed to protect their interests against outside competition. However, the important new group of moguls who emerged in the early 'teens were an altogether new breed of entrepreneurs. They refused to be intimidated by the Trust, and reacted strongly against its restrictive practices. They were more willing to take risks, invest larger sums of money in picture-making, and venture into new areas. They signed up and promoted stars, and began moving into the production of feature-length movies. The best-known names among this new group were Carl Laemmle of IMP and then Universal, who led the battle against the Trust in the courts; Adolph Zukor of Famous Players, who masterminded a merger with the Jesse L. Lasky Company in 1916 to form Famous Players-Lasky (or Paramount Pictures), the giant company which was to dominate the industry for many years; and William Fox with his Fox Film Corporation.

When French, British, and other European movie companies were severely affected by World War I, these new American producers took advantage of the opportunity to open up worldwide markets for their pictures. At the same time virtually all the early pioneer companies in America – with Vitagraph the one notable exception – proved unable to meet the challenge and ceased production. The new group of moguls grew even more powerful in the 20s as their studios continued to expand. Marcus Loew, theatre-chain owner and the sole exhibitor-mogul among them, had extended his activities into production in 1920 when his Loew's Inc. took over the Metro Company, and he would play a major role in the formation of the giant MGM in 1924.

The new group of 20s moguls clearly differed from the previous generation: they gained their fame and their power less as businessmen and entrepreneurs and more through their direct involvement in movie production. The three best-known names were Harry Cohn, the founder (with his brother Jack) and production chief of Columbia Pictures, Jack Warner, the founder (with his brothers) and studio head of Warner Bros., and Louis B. Mayer who was involved in the formation of MGM and headed the studio. All three reigned throughout the studio era from the mid-20s to the 50s.

Following hard on their heels was an assorted collection of dynamic and creative younger producers who also got their start in the 20s. Irving Thalberg first served as assistant to Laemmle at Universal, then moved on to MGM where he made his name as vice-president in charge of production under Mayer; independent producer Joseph Schenck is best remembered for the 10 years that he spent as president of United Artists (1925–35); while B. P. Schulberg headed Paramount's West Coast studio from 1925 to 1932. All of these men had left their most creative years behind them by 1936, the year that Thalberg died, but two others remained major figures for rather longer. David O. Selznick, who started at Paramount under Schulberg in the late 20s, became production chief of RKO in the early 30s, then worked briefly as a producer at MGM (1933–35) before establishing himself as a leading independent producer responsible for such productions as *A Star Is Born* and *The Prisoner Of Zenda* (both 1937), *Gone With The Wind* (1939), *Duel In The Sun* (1946) and *A Farewell To Arms* (1957). And Darryl F. Zanuck rose from a lowly and prolific scriptwriter at Warner Bros. to producer, and then production chief, under Jack Warner in the early 30s, before leaving in 1933 to form his own, extremely successful company, 20th Century Productions, with Joseph Schenck of United Artists. Zanuck then merged with, and virtually took over, Fox in 1935, where he became production chief and studio boss of the new 20th Century-Fox. He held this position until 1956, returned to independent production for a time, and came back to serve as Fox's company president in the 60s.

Other lesser, but nonetheless important, moguls included Hal B. Wallis who stepped into Zanuck's shoes at Warner Bros. and served as production chief from 1933 to 1943, then became an independent producer, while Pandro S. Berman followed Selznick at RKO in the 30s. Walter Wanger and William Goetz were associated with a number of different studios in the 30s and 40s, and Samuel Goldwyn, the most important of the independents, started out with Lasky in the 'teens but is best remembered as one of the mainstays of United Artists from 1925 to 1940.

HOLLYWOOD DIRECTORS

Although the movie director today is generally widely regarded as the leading creative force behind the making of most pictures, this has not always been the case. The fluctuation in the power and prestige of the director represents a fascinating and revealing aspect of Hollywood's history over the years. In the early silent days the director most often functioned as a producer-director, taking charge of, and responsible for, all the elements that went into the completed movie. He not only instructed the actors in front of the camera, and often talked and gestured to them to encourage and influence their performances while filming was in progress, but he also organized the props, costumes and settings with the help of a number of assistants. In addition he would work closely with the writer of the film story or 'photoplay', then continue to make his own script adjustments during the course of shooting. And after filming was completed he would supervise the editing to achieve the final result.

In the interest of greater efficiency the assistants soon began to specialize and, by the 20s, the director on a major production had at his command a full crew of cameramen, art director, props men and editors, as well as costume designers, special-effects experts and others. In the early 20s the top directors achieved a special standing within the rapidly growing industry. Such leading producer-directors as Cecil B. DeMille at Paramount, Erich von Stroheim at Universal, Rex Ingram at Metro and D. W. Griffith, one of the original founders of United Artists with his own studio at Mamaroneck, New York, were among the most powerful, respected and best-known figures in the movie industry. But by the mid-20s, the tremendous growth and consolidation of the giant studios meant that the balance of power was beginning to shift in favour of the producer – and the studio, which was also the distributor and, in many cases, the exhibitor. Thus, it became increasingly difficult for the directors to preserve their independence.

From this period up to the late 40s, the peak years of the studio era, the directors, along with stars and technicians, were generally placed under contract by the studios. This meant that, on the whole, they now had little opportunity to initiate their own projects but were regularly assigned to productions by the studio and could be suspended without pay if they refused an assignment which they considered unsuitable. It also meant that they moved from picture to picture with relatively little control over script, casting or editing of the final cut. In practice, this pattern would vary according to the status of each individual director. A lowly contract hack assigned to B movies might be expected to turn out five or six formula Westerns, thrillers or comedies each year. But the top-rated directors such as Frank Capra (at Columbia), John Ford (Fox), Cecil B. DeMille (Paramount) or King Vidor (MGM) would only be expected to complete one – or perhaps two – pictures per year. They would be allowed the luxury of thorough preparation, collaborating with the scriptwriter (or writers) before filming commenced, and with the editor and composer afterwards, up to completion of the film in

COLUMBIA

1920	
Harry Cohn, Joe Brandt and Jack Cohn found CPC Sales Company	
1924	
CBC becomes Columbia, with Harry Cohn as production chief	
1932	
Harry Cohn buys out Brandt and becomes president as well as production chief	
1958	
Harry Cohn dies	

FOX

1915
William Fox founds Fox Film Corporation
1930
William Fox forced out of his own company
1935
Fox merges with 20th Century to form 20th Century-Fox, with Joseph Schenck as president and Darryl F. Zanuck as vice president in charge of production; Fox producer William Goetz promoted to vice president
1941
Schenck resigns as president
1943
Goetz leaves to found International UNIV 1946
1944
Schenck returns as producer
1952
Schenck finally leaves
1956
Zanuck resigns to become independent producer releasing through Fox
1962
Zanuck becomes president. Appoints son Richard vice president in charge of production
1969
Zanuck Sr becomes chairman and chief executive; Richard president
1970
Zanuck Sr fires son from presidency
1971
Darryl Zanuck resigns

LOEW'S/MGM

1910

Marcus Loew, Joseph Schenck and Nicholas Schenck found Loew's exhibition company

1917

Joseph Schenck leaves UA 1924

1920

Loew's acquires Metro as production and distribution arm

1924

Metro combined with Goldwyn Pictures (lacking Sam) and Louis B. Mayer Productions to form Metro-Goldwyn Mayer (MGM). Marcus Loew is president of Loew's/MGM (till 1927). Louis B. Mayer is studio head (till 1951). Irving G. Thalberg is production chief (till 1932, then producer till death in 1936)

1927

Nicholas Schenck becomes president (till 1955)

1929

Cecil B. DeMille is producer/director (till 1931) PAR 1932

1933

David O. Selznick is producer (till 1935) UA 1935

1940

Pandro S. Berman comes in from RKO as producer (till 1970)

1948

Dore Schary becomes vice president in charge of production

1951

Mayer resigns; Schary becomes head of studio (till 1956)

PARAMOUNT

1912

Adolph Zukor founds Famous Players

1913

Jesse L. Lasky, with Samuel Goldfish (later Goldwyn) and director Cecil B. DeMille, founds Jesse L. Lasky Feature Play Company

1916

The two companies merge as Famous Players-Lasky and acquire Paramount as a distribution arm. Zukor president of whole company - (President till 1936; then figurehead posts as chairman and chairman emeritus till 1976). Lasky vice president in charge of production (till 1932) Goldfish leaves the same year to co-found Goldwyn (till 1922) UA 1925. DeMille producer-director (till 1924)

1925

B.P. Schulberg appointed general manager of West Coast production (till 1932), with David O. Selznick as his assistant (1927-30). Selznick RKO 1930

1932

Lasky forced out. DeMille returns as producer-director (till 1956)

1935

Ernst Lubitsch made production chief (till 1936)

1936

William LeBaron made production chief (till 1941). Barney Balaban president (till 1964)

1944

Hal Wallis joins as independent producer (till 1969)

RKO

1928

RCA merges FBO with Keith-Albee-Orpheum theatre chain to found Radio-Keith-Orpheum (RKO): David Sarnoff of RCA is chairman of the board and William LeBaron is production chief (till 1931)

1931

David O. Selznick is production chief (till 1933) MGM 1933

1933

Merian C. Cooper vice president in charge of production (till 1935)

1935

Pandro S Berman becomes production chief (till 1940) MGM 1940

1937

Disney distributes through RKO (till 1954)

1941

Goldwyn distributes through RKO (till 1952)

1946

Dore Schary production chief (till 1948) MGM 1948

1948

Howard Hughes acquires control

1955

Hughes sells out

1957

Studio ceases production

UNITED ARTISTS

1919

Charles Chaplin, Douglas Fairbanks, D.W.Griffith and Mary Pickford found UA

1924

Griffith leaves, Joseph Schenck brought in as chairman of the board

1925

Sam Goldwyn joins as independent producer (till 1940) RKO 1941

1926

Joseph Schenck becomes president on death of Hiram Abrams (till 1935) FOX 1935

1931

Walt Disney distributes through UA (till 1936)

1933

Korda distributes British films through UA (till 1942; then 1951-56). Schenck, Zanuck and William Goetz found 20th Century Pictures, distributing through UA

1935

Schenck leaves with Zanuck and Goetz on merger of 20th Century with Fox FOX 1935

1937

Walter Wanger distributes through UA (till 1941). Selznick distributes through UA (till 1945)

1940

Goldwyn leaves RKO 1941

1951

Syndicate headed by Arthur Krim and Robert Benjamin buys 50% of the company, takes over management and rescues ailing company

(continued on next page)

1955
Chaplin sells out

1956
Mary Pickford sells out

1957
The company goes public

1967
Krim and Benjamin stay on following Transamerica takeover (till 1978)

UNIVERSAL

1912
Carl Laemmle Sr founds Universal

1915
Opens Universal City studio

1920
Appoints Irving Thalberg production chief (1923) MGM 1924

1929
Appoints Carl Laemmle Jr production chief

1936
Laemmle Sr sells company and Laemmle Jr is forced out

1946
Universal merges with Goetz's International (founded 1943) to form Universal-International, with Goetz as production chief (till 1952)

1952
Decca acquire company

1962
MCA, under Lew Wasserman, completes takeover (begun in 1959) by buying Decca and Universal too

WARNER BROS.

1923
Warner Bros. Pictures formed (Jack L. Warner, studio head: Harry Warner, president)

1928
Darryl Zanuck becomes production chief of Warner Bros. December: Hal Wallis production chief of First National, responsible to Jack Warner and Zanuck

1930
November: Zanuck takes over as production chief of combined Warner Bros./First National (till April) 1933 UA 1933

1933
Hal Wallis becomes production chief of Warner Bros. First National (till 1944) PAR 1944

1956
Harry and Albert Warner sell out but Jack stays on

1967
Jack leaves at merger with Seven Arts

1969
Warner Bros./Seven Arts Ltd taken over by Kinney National Service

more or less final form. In this way these directors were allowed a large measure of freedom within the studio system, retaining some degree of personal style and control over their pictures, although subject to certain constraints – staying within the agreed budget, for example, and having to work, for the most part, with the studio's own stars and technicians.

Of course, most of the Hollywood directors fell between these two extremes, but by the late 30s there were signs that directors generally were regaining some of the prestige that they had lost under the studio system. There was also a similar improvement in the status of leading scriptwriters around this time, and a number of them were allowed to try their hand at directing. The net result was that a strong line-up of established directors reaching their peak – among them John Ford, Howard Hawks, William Wyler, and recent British arrival Alfred Hitchcock – were joined by a new, younger generation of outstanding talents led by writer-directors Preston Sturges, Billy Wilder, John Huston and Joseph L. Mankiewicz, along with new-comers Orson Welles and Elia Kazan. Though officially still working within the studio system, these men were generally allowed a large degree of creative control. This trend toward greater independence continued on into the 50s when the contract system virtually came to an end.

During these years the film companies attempted to stem the decline in movie audiences by investing heavily in extravagant costume productions, musicals and epics. Established directors were offered expensive productions which were not always suited to their talents, but they found it difficult to resist the large fees and the tremendous resources at their disposal. Some talented directors clearly came unstuck on misconceived projects: the experienced Howard Hawks should have known better than to take on Land Of The Pharaohs (1955); similarly Robert Wise made a mistake with Helen Of Troy (1955) and, in the 60s, there was Lewis Milestone's remake of Mutiny On The Bounty (1962), Nicholas Ray's 55 Days At Peking and Joseph Mankiewicz with Cleopatra (both 1963), while George Stevens tackled The Greatest Story Ever Told (1965). An even clearer idea of the very mixed qualities of the period can be seen in the many directors who alternated between small-scale black-and-white pictures of quality and relatively impersonal block-busting spectaculars. Otto Preminger, for example, followed Anatomy Of A Murder (1959) with Exodus (1960); Stanley Kubrick moved from Paths Of Glory (1957) to the epic Spartacus (1960) and back again to black-and-white for Lolita (1962) and Dr Strangelove (1963); William Wyler switched from Ben-Hur (1959) to the intimate drama of The Children's Hour (1962); Robert Aldrich leaped from Sodom And Gomorrah (1962) to What Ever Happened To Baby Jane? (1963). Most 'schizophrenic' of all were Robert Wise and Stanley Kramer, both of whom zig-zagged between small black-and-white dramas and expensive wide-screen extravaganzas throughout the late 50s and early 60s. With the experiences of the directors, as always, tied to the fortunes of the various movie companies, the financial disasters of the late 60s brought the production of blockbusters to an end around the same time that many Hollywood veterans, such as John Ford, Howard Hawks, George Stevens and William Wyler, were reaching the end of their careers.

A number of new arrivals had first broken into pictures by way of the small screen in the late 50s and early 60s. They included Franklin Schaffner, John Frankenheimer, Delbert Mann and Martin Ritt; also the talented Arthur Penn, who had his biggest success with *Bonnie and Clyde* in 1967, and Sidney Lumet, the most prolific and successful of them all. Though they provided Hollywood with fresh blood, their influence proved comparatively small, and it was left to a new generation of talented young directors who had grown up with the cinema to breathe fresh life into Hollywood in the 70s. A virtual explosion of gifted directors – recalling that which had taken place in the 40s – was led by such talents as Francis Ford Coppola, William Friedkin, George Lucas, Martin Scorsese, Woody Allen and Steven Spielberg. Their influence has continued to be felt well into the 80s.

MOVIE STARS

The earliest American movie actors were hired on a freelance basis and appeared on the screen anonymously. During the years up to 1910 the leading producers, especially the members of the Motion Picture Patents Company, made a point of concealing the true identities of their stars, for they correctly surmised that the most popular among them would demand higher salaries and would be more difficult to control. But such a policy could not hope to succeed for long, for the public was eager to learn more about its screen favourites.

Producer Carl Laemmle was the first to break the mold and is generally credited with initiating the star system after poaching the Biograph Girl, Florence Lawrence, for his IMP Company and publicizing her true name. However, the two most popular screen idols in the midteens were Mary Pickford and comedian Charlie Chaplin. His unique genius as a performer quickly won him worldwide acclaim, while Miss Pickford's progress during the decade from 1909 to 1918 highlights the many changes which took place during these years and her own not inconsiderable role in them, which culminated in her becoming one of the founders of United Artists in 1919.

This was the small but high-quality company which allowed top stars such as Gloria Swanson and Norma Talmadge, as well as the star founders, to preserve their independence during the 20s when power was becoming increasingly concentrated in the hands of a select number of studio bosses. It is difficult today to imagine the scale of worldwide popularity of movie stars before the advent of radio and TV. There was a special magic about the silent stars which was lost with the introduction of sound – which coincided with the onset of the Depression and other important social changes.

The star system had evolved in the 20s, but flourished in the 30s. This was the peak era of Hollywood moviemaking when the studios became adept at discovering, grooming and exploiting their players in appropriate star vehicles. Each company was turning out a wide selection of pictures every year and typecasting was the order of the day. Promising newcomers were carefully schooled for stardom and were given the opportunity to appear in large numbers of features with experienced stars. Clark Gable at MGM and Cary Grant at Paramount, for example, were cast opposite many of the most glamorous women in Hollywood before emerging as established stars in their own right. But there was an obvious contradiction between the processing of newcomers to fit them into an identical mold, and the fact that the most successful stars had special qualities which could not be manufactured.

The standard studio contract lasted for seven years and provided for regular increases in salary, but rarely allowed the stars any choice in their assignments. If a contract player refused a script, he or she could be placed on suspension and this period added on to the term of the contract. In addition, stars could be loaned out to other studios at an immense profit. 'Your studio could trade you around like a ball player,' James Stewart recalled.

Though Hollywood turned out many memorable movies during these years, the system was tremendously wasteful of talent and many of the stars suffered and rebelled. Olivia de Havilland fought a court case and won a landmark decision in the early 40s that disallowed the studios from adding suspension time onto the contract period. The postwar decline of the studios led to a cutback in contract stars. This gave many of the top players a new freedom, and the opportunity to gain more control over their pictures by setting up their own production companies. Stars such as Burt Lancaster, John Wayne and Kirk Douglas made distribution agreements with a revitalized United Artists, for example, in the 50s, setting a pattern which has continued up to the present day. But the durability of so many 30s stars was a legacy of a vanished system, never likely to return.

CREATIVE PERSONNEL

Aside from the director, the person most essential to the making of pictures in the early years was the cameraman. His main job was to operate the equipment and make sure that the desired image was recorded. This meant hand-cranking the camera and controlling the lighting, the framing of shots and the focus for each scene. Primarily a technician, he could carry out repairs on the camera, which he generally owned and carried with him from picture to picture. But it was not long before these men had mastered a wide range of technical and trick effects which were accomplished within the camera. These ranged from soft focus, speeded-up action or slow motion, to multiple exposure, split-screen or glass shots, along with a standard repertoire of linking devices such as the fade, dissolve and iris in or out. In addition, when filming was completed the cameraman would generally work closely with the lab, supervising the development of the film negative.

By the late 'teens rapid advances had been made in motion picture photography. The primitive early studios and movie sets, which generally made use of open stages and were dependent on natural sunlight, began to be replaced by closed sets with a more sophisticated and controlled use of mainly artificial lighting. The leading cameramen were already demonstrating how much could be done artistically to enhance a movie story through the expressive use of lighting, composition and the development of a visual style which went far beyond the simple recording of images of the earlier years.

Design sketch for *Citizen Kane* (RKO, 1941) directed by Orson Welles, art director Perry Ferguson.

Prior to the 20s most pictures were filmed without an art director or designer as such. That function was loosely divided between the director, the cameraman and a property (or props) master. Thus, it is not surprising to find that D. W. Griffith played a major role in designing his own early pictures (though the spectacular *Intolerance*, 1916, had Walter L. Hall as art director), as did Erich von Stroheim before he discovered Richard Day and first employed him on *Foolish Wives* in 1921. Other visually sophisticated directors such as Maurice Tourneur and Cecil B. DeMille were among the very first to employ designers and were fortunate in developing close working relationships during the 'teens with two of the best. The gifted Ben Carré contributed to more than 30 Tourneur features from 1914 to

1920, some of them filmed at Paramount with such stars as Mary Pickford and Elsie Ferguson. DeMille's regular collaborator during this same period was Wilfred Buckland, who had made his name as one of the outstanding designers in the New York theatre. His close collaboration with cameraman Alvin Wyckoff on DeMille's *The Cheat* (1915) represents one of the most notable early examples of an expressive visual style: a controlled use of shadows, lighting, and decor to create an overall effect which contributed immensely to the impact of the story. One of the pioneering art directors of the era, Wilfred Buckland involved himself in every aspect of planning and shooting and played an important role in promoting and demonstrating the value of artificial versus natural lighting.

With the notable exception of Paramount, most of the studios were relatively slow to recognize the importance of the art director's contribution. This attitude changed in the 20s when the leading companies grew rapidly and expanded their lists of contract personnel of all types, with special attention to the camera and art departments. There was a general improvement in status at the same time that jobs became more specialized. The chief cameraman, for example, often referred to as the lighting cameraman or director of photography, found himself heading a crew consisting of camera operator, clapper loader and focus puller. Thus freed from the technical chores associated with the shooting, he was now able to devote himself to aesthetic and stylistic considerations in lighting the picture, working closely with the director and art director. In the 20s, leading cameramen such as John F. Seitz, Charles Rosher, Lee Garmes and James Wong Howe first began to develop the kind of clearly recognizable style associated with top cinematographers ever since.

Similarly, the position of the art director was boosted by the wide recognition of the work of William Cameron Menzies at UA in the 20s, and by the formation of MGM with Cedric Gibbons appointed to head the art department. As the most powerful and best-known designer in Hollywood, who exercized a tremendous influence over the look of MGM pictures for 30 years, the Modernist qualities of Gibbons' all-white, Art Deco sets had a tremendous worldwide impact, especially during the 30s when other studios, notably Paramount and RKO, followed suit. (A contrasting tradition of low-keyed design which had developed in Germany was also integrated into the Hollywood vocabulary quite early on, as seen in the work of the German-born Anton Grot and British-born Charles D. (Danny) Hall, among others).

Under the studio system, the supervising art directors such as Gibbons, Hans Dreier at Paramount and Van Nest Polglase at RKO rarely worked on individual pictures but oversaw the entire output of the studio. Unit art directors working on each picture were assisted by a full staff including sketch, scenic, and model artists, and would have the sets designed and under construction before a director had even been assigned to the production. The greater recognition given to cameramen and art directors coincided, ironically, with a diminished status for the contract director. Nevertheless, for the leading directors, the tradition of close collaboration with the cameraman and designer, first established in the 20s and later adopted as standard practice, has continued more or less unchanged up to the present day.

But it was not only cameramen and art directors whose contributions came to be valued. As the studios strove for greater efficiency, they recognized the necessity for technical expertise in other departments, and signed up large numbers of technical personnel in several different fields. Specialized departments were set up to take care of editing and special effects, costume design and make-up, and this trend was further reinforced by the coming of sound. In addition to newly-formed sound and music departments, the proliferation of musicals, from 1929 on, led to the signing of many leading songwriting teams from the Broadway stage. The introduction of sound had a major impact on all aspects of movie-making, affecting the work of camera-men and editors in particular, and it was necessary to recruit vast numbers of writers, many of whom had experience in the theatre and became more important to the film-making process than ever before – especially those who displayed a knack for writing convincing movie dialogue.

Of particular interest is the changed role of the editor. In the silent days, the editor had a large measure of freedom. He assembled the differ-ent individual shots or 'takes' to construct sequences, while establishing an overall rhythm and pace – faster for comedies or action pictures, more measured for drama – and took into account the need to insert title cards at various points. However, the addition of synchronized dialogue, sound effects and background music, all carefully planned out and then 'mixed' to achieve the final soundtrack exactly matched to the pictures, made the editing process much more complicated. Thus the editing staff involved on any feature-length production grew to include a number of assistants, sound editors, a mixer and a nega-tive cutter.

Many of the leading editors in the 20s were women. There was Dorothy Arzner at Paramount, Anne Bauchens, Cecil B. DeMille's editor for 30 years and the first woman to win a technical Oscar (for editing *North West Mounted Police* in 1940), and Margaret Booth, a top editor at MGM for over 40 years and for much of that period the studio's supervising editor. This tradition of important lady edi-tors has continued up to the present day, highlighting such impor-tant figures as Barbara McLean at Fox and, more recently, Verna Fields (Oscar winner for *Jaws* in 1975), Dede Allen, Marcia Lucas (co-editor of *Star Wars*, 1977) and Thelma Schoonmaker. But it also draws attention, by default, to the lack of women in other important areas of Hollywood film-making, aside from scriptwriting and costume design.

Having originally depended on the Western Costume Company to meet their basic costume needs in the 'teens, the leading studios began to set up their own departments in the 20s. By the end of the decade they were each employing a leading costume designer or two, supported by a full staff of sketch artists, wardrobe assistants and seamstresses.

Personnel Involved in the Filming of a
Major Hollywood Production - *Ghostbusters* (Columbia, 1984)

PRE-PRODUCTION

PRODUCTION DEPARTMENT
Executive Producer: Bernie Brillstein *(assembles the initial 'package' and raises the finance)*
Producer: Ivan Reitman
Associate Producers: Joe Medjuck, Michael C. Gross *(continuing responsibility for overall production, costs, and budget)*
Production Manager: John G. Wilson
+ Production Coordinator, Assistant Accountant, Secretaries (overseeing day-to-day details of production)

Script
Writers (original): Dan Aykroyd, Harold Ramis
Script Supervisor: Trish Kinney

Sets
Production Designer: John De Cuir *(establishes overall look of production, working closely with director of photography)*
Set Designer: George Eckert
Property Master: Jack E. Ackerman
Set Director: Marvin March
Construction Coordinator: Don Noble
Standby Painter: Paul Campanella

Costumes
Costume Designer: Theoni V. Aldredge
Costume Supervisor: Bruce Erickson
Costumers: Dayton Anderson, Peggy Thorin

Casting
Karen Rea

Publicity
Nancy Willen

Stills Photography
Gemma La Mana-Wills

SHOOTING THE PICTURE

MAIN STUDIO FILMING AT THE BURBANK STUDIOS

Cast
Bill Murray, Dan Aykroyd, Harold Ramis, Sigourney Weaver + *Featured Players.*
Minor Actors, Extras, Stand-ins, Stunt Men/Women etc.

Direction
Director: Ivan Reitman *(in charge of all creative aspects of filming)*
First Assistant Director: Gary Daigler
Second Assistant Director: Katterli Frauenfelder

Camera Crew
Director of Photography: Laszlo Kovacs ASC *(also known as 'lighting cameraman': responsible for 'ook' of film, with production designer)*
Camera Operator: Bob Stevens
First Assistant Cameraman: Joe Thibo *(focus puller)*
Second Assistant Cameraman: Paul Mindrup *(clapper/loader)*

Sound Crew
Sound Designers: Richard Beggs, Tom McCarthy Jr
+ Sound Mixers, Sound Boom, Cableman, etc.

Electrical Crew
Gaffer: Colin Campbell *(chief electrician)*
Best Boy: Robert Jason *(assistant electrician)*

Stage Crew
Key Grip: Gene Kearney *(stagehand foreman)*
Grip Best Boy: Bob Munoz *(his assistant)*

NEW YORK PRODUCTION UNIT FOR LOCATION FILMING
Full Crew
Headed by Production Manager, First Assistant Director and Director of Photography

SPECIAL EFFECTS UNIT
Visual Effects: Richard Edlund ASC
Special Effects Supervisor: Chuck Gaspar, Entertainment Effects Group, Los Angeles

POST-PRODUCTION

Editing
Editors: Sheldon Kahn ACE and David Blewitt
ACE + *Assistant Editors, Sound Editors*

Music
Score: Elmer Bernstein
'Ghostbusters' Theme Song: written and
performed by Ray Parker Jr (and various
additional songs from different sources) + *Scoring
Mixer, Orchestrators, Supervising Music Editor*

Film Titles
Main Titles: Pacific Title
Main Title Animation: R. Greenberg Assocs.

RELEASE DETAILS

15 weeks' shooting, completed principal
photography February 1984

Final cost: $32 million

N. American release date: 8 June 1984
Length: 105 minutes
N. American Rentals: $128 million
(through 1986)

**A COLUMBIA PICTURES PRESENTATION
A BLACK RHINO/BERNIE BRILLSTEIN
PRODUCTION
AN IVAN REITMAN FILM
Filmed in Panavision and Metrocolor with
Dolby Sound**

This chart provides some idea of the range and numbers of people involved in a major Hollywood feature through an abridged version of the credits for *Ghostbusters.* The full list included a main crew of 75, a New York unit of 23, and 88 people credited for the elaborate special effects - including model makers, designers and builders of mechanical props, matte and animation artists, sculptors, creature designers, electronics engineers, and many more.

Before long, Hollywood fashion was exerting a remarkable influence on women's dress all over the world. Leading figures who got their start in the 20s included Adrian at MGM, Vera West at Universal, Howard Greer and Travis Banton, joined by Edith Head, at Paramount and Mitchell Leisen at UA. (The talented Orry-Kelly did not arrive at Warner Bros. till the early 30s.)

Though most important silent features had been released with an accompanying score, the arrival of sound opened the way for developing a new type of background music. With the development of new techniques which allowed the mixing of different soundtracks, the score could be more subtly and precisely matched to the picture than ever before. In the late 20s and early 30s, some of the first of a new breed of music directors and composers arrived in Hollywood. Led by such names as Max Steiner and Alfred Newman, they were providing original scores of real quality by the mid-30s.

In addition to those creative personnel already mentioned there were pioneering technicians in other, less well-known areas of film-making who got their start in the 20s. A number of the first make-up departments were started by members of the remarkable Westmore family who divided up the various Hollywood studios between them and demonstrated the importance of a then comparatively new movie skill. They were much valued by the stars as well as by the companies which employed them.

Special effects had started out as an offshoot of cinematography, but a few early practitioners of the art made such remarkable advances in the 20s that they, too, were allowed to organize their own specialized departments. This field grew rapidly in the 30s as the repertoire of techniques expanded to include a more sophisticated use of mattes and other optical effects, miniatures and models, and back (or rear) projection. Leading names here were Farciot Edouart and Gordon Jennings at Paramount, John P. Fulton at Universal and A. Arnold Gillespie, the expert who worked closely with Cedric Gibbons at MGM for 30 years and also doubled as an art director. Of special interest was the work of Willis O'Brien who pioneered the development of stop-motion photography. Having been used so effectively in his feature length version of *The Lost World* (First National, 1925), O'Brien was finally given the opportunity to create his enduring masterpiece, *King Kong*, at RKO in 1933.

Honours and Awards

The Academy Awards – or Oscars, as they are generally called – are the best-known, longest-running and most widely publicized of all movie prizes, and they pack the biggest punch at the box-office. Oscars are often featured prominently in trailers and advertisements for the winning pictures, as well as in countless films about Hollywood from *A Star Is Born* (both 1937 and 1954 versions) and *California Suite* (1978), to a forgettable 1966 feature called, simply, *The Oscar*. The famous gold-plated statuette was designed by MGM's leading art director, Cedric Gibbons, and has become one of the most readily identifiable symbols of Tinseltown. 'Why, it looks just like my uncle Oscar', the Academy librarian Margaret Herrick was supposedly heard to exclaim on first seeing the award – but Bette Davis and columnist Sidney Skolsky also claim credit for the nickname.

OSCARS AND OTHER AWARDS

The annual Academy Awards ceremony is the most celebrated activity of the Hollywood-based and grandly named Academy of Motion Picture Arts and Sciences (or AMPAS) which was founded in 1927 and celebrated its 60th anniversary in 1987. Among the leading film industry figures associated with the setting up of AMPAS were producers Louis B. Mayer, Irving Thalberg and Harry Rapf from MGM, Joseph Schenck, Douglas Fairbanks and Mary Pickford of UA, the two best-known Warner brothers, Jack and Harry, Jesse L. Lasky, and Cecil B. DeMille.

There were also a few representatives of the creative branches – art director Cedric Gibbons, writers Carey Wilson, Bess Meredyth, Jeanie Macpherson, and Frank Woods, directors Raoul Walsh and Henry King, and actors Harold Lloyd and Richard Barthelmess.

Many important changes were taking place in Hollywood at that time. Warner Bros. was investing heavily in experiments with sound which would soon transform the industry, while movie audiences were growing steadily. The real power in the industry was becoming increasingly concentrated in a small number of vertically integrated companies but, at the same time, labour-relations problems were threatening to become a major headache for the giant studios. It has been suggested that the Academy was founded by the studio bosses, led by Louis B. Mayer, in order to forestall the unionization of the various talent groups – actors, writers, directors and technicians.

For a brief period AMPAS was in direct competition with Actors Equity for the right to represent the actors in their negotiations with the studios; and late in 1927 the Academy succeeded in negotiating the first actor-producer agreement within the industry. However, having won its battle with Equity in the 20s, AMPAS then jeopardized its position a few years later when it readily agreed to across-the-board pay cuts in an attempt to alleviate the effects of the Depression on the industry. Such a decision led many of the members to conclude that the Academy really was behaving like a 'company union' and did not have their best interests at heart.

In July 1933 a number of actors quit to form the Screen Actors Guild. They were given strong support by the Screen Writers Guild which had been founded in the 20s, but was newly reorganized to represent the writers in their current contract disputes with the studio bosses. (One of the most active members of the Writers Guild, Dudley Nichols, became the first person to refuse an Oscar, awarded to him in 1935 for scripting *The Informer*.) Then in 1936 a dozen directors also broke away from the Academy to form the Screen Directors Guild, later renamed the Directors Guild of America or DGA – which encompasses both films and television.

These various disputes, which seriously depleted the membership of the Academy, were finally resolved in 1937 when the organization wisely decided to withdraw from any further involvement in the highly sensitive area of labour relations.

As part of its activities in the less controversial area of education and research, the Academy's technicians' branch soon became involved in co-sponsoring a series of lectures and seminars on the newly introduced incandescent lighting and on the various problems of sound filming in 1928. Over the years the Academy has continued to make many contributions in this area, including the award of scholarships to film students and the sponsorship of such projects as the restoration of the Library of Congress paper-print collection of pre-1912 films which was undertaken in the early 50s.

The fact is that the annual Awards ceremony was not originally regarded as an important part of the Academy's activities and began as a relatively informal occasion. The first group of awards, for the 1927–28 season, was presented at a banquet in May 1929, held to celebrate the second anniversary of the Academy's formation. In that first year honours were restricted to silent films, a kind of last farewell to the silents which included a special award to Warner Bros, 'for producing *The Jazz Singer*, the pioneer outstanding talking picture which has revolutionized the industry,' while the second ceremony, for 1928–29, was dominated by the early talkies, with MGM's *The Broadway Melody* voted the Best Picture.

For the first two years the winners were decided through a somewhat undemocratic three-tier process. The 400 Academy members took part in the nominating only, with those 10 pictures receiving the largest number of votes in each category then referred to groups of judges who reduced the choice to three finalists. These were then submitted to a central board of judges which made the final decision on the winners. To be eligible a film must be shown in the Los Angeles area for at least a week in the relevant year which, for the first six ceremonies, ran from 1 August to 31 July before changing over to calendar years (from 1934).

Over the years, the voting procedures and number of categories included in the awards have undergone many adjustments. The change-over to sound meant that several awards, such as title writing, were dropped in the second year. Sound recording was soon added, along with short films and a section devoted to special technical or scientific achievements, followed (in 1934) by editing and scoring categories. From the 1929–30 ceremony until 1935 the entire Academy voted on the winners after nominees in each category had been selected by the members of that particular craft. The membership total peaked at about 600 quite early on, but declined in the 30s when the labour disputes led to mass resignations. Numbers fell to less than 100, but recovered in the late 30s and 40s. For a number of years (1937–45) nominations and voting were thrown open to some 15,000 members of the industry; then, from 1947 to 1956, nominations balloting was restricted to guild and union members (excluding screen extras) with the winners determined by the Academy. Ever since 1957, both the nominations and final votes have been confined to the approximately 4,000 Academy members.

The new categories added over the years have included special effects (in 1939), costume design (1948) and a foreign-language film award (in 1956), while the writing awards were reduced from three categories to two in 1957. With the virtual disappearance of black-and-white filming of major features, the separate categories for colour cinematography, art direction and costume design were eliminated in 1967. In addition, prior to 1946 the number of nominees in some categories tended to vary from year to year, but since this date nominations by members of the Academy have been limited to a maximum of five entries.

Though there are many other movie organizations which give out prizes each year, such as the New York Film Critics and the Hollywood Foreign Press Association, some of them modelled on the Oscars, none of them attempts to match the Academy in the range of its coverage. Over the years, in addition to the widely publicized Oscars for top pictures, stars, and directors, the Academy has given well-deserved recognition to many of the most creative technicians in Hollywood – and special awards to others who have made exceptional contributions to the movie industry which may not be included in the normal Oscar categories.

Among the most important of the other annual awards, those granted by the New York Film Critics since 1935 have presented an interesting comparison with the Oscars, generally opting for small black-and-white pictures of quality. Prior to 1946 the New York awards were limited to four leading categories only (picture, actor, actress, director), but a foreign-film award was added in 1946, screen writing in 1966, and supporting actor and actress in 1969. That year the separate awards for the best English-language and foreign films were dropped in favour of a single top prize. The result was that, for the next eight years, the New Yorkers' choice regularly differed from the Academy's. They opted for outstanding pictures from leading foreign directors or from American directors outside the mainstream – all of whom won the accompanying director's award. These included, for example, Bob Rafelson's *Five Easy Pieces* (1970), Stanley Kubrick's *A Clockwork Orange* (1971), Ingmar Bergman's *Cries And Whispers* (1972), Fellini's *Amarcord* (1974) and Robert Altman's *Nashville* (1975). In 1977 the New York Film Critics chose Woody Allen's Manhattan-based *Annie Hall* – as did the Academy – and ever since both groups have concurred more often than not.

The Golden Globe awards were first presented in 1943, voted by the 80 or so active members of the Hollywood Foreign Press Association, but they split their awards for best picture, actor and actress into two categories, making a useful distinction between drama and comedy or musical. Presented in a nationally televised ceremony early in February, six weeks or so prior to the Oscars, the Golden Globes provide a likely indication as to who will win the year's Academy Awards. There has been close agreement between the Golden Globe and the Oscars over the years, especially in the Best Picture category (taking into account the split awards.) The Golden Globes are often awarded to two strong Oscar contenders, for example *A Place In The Sun* (drama) and *An American In Paris* (musical/comedy) in 1951, *In The Heat Of The Night* and *The Graduate* in 1967, and Oliver Stone's *Platoon* honoured along with Woody Allen's *Hannah And Her Sisters* in 1986.

The categories covered by the Golden Globes have often changed over the years, and have included awards to Most Promising Newcomer, World Film Favourite and Best Film Promoting International Understanding, along with the honouring of outstanding work on TV – best dramatic and comedy series, best TV movie or mini-series, and best actor and actress in each of these, among others.

The Directors Guild of America began to present its annual awards in 1948/49. The five nominees are voted on by the entire membership, currently totalling about 8,000 directors (and assistant directors) working in films and TV, with the winner generally announced three or four weeks prior to the Oscar ceremony. (The Oscar nominees for directing are chosen by the relatively small number of Guild members, currently numbering about 230, who also belong to the Academy.) The Academy has only disagreed with the DGA award winner four times in 38 years – most recently in the case of Steven Spielberg, director of *The Color Purple* (1985), the only example ever of the DGA director not even earning an Oscar nomination. Thus, its award is generally a reliable guide as to who will win the Oscar in a given year. (In addition, the DGA has presented an annual award for TV directing since 1953, when Robert

Florey was the first winner for his Four-Star Playhouse production of *The Lost Voyage*.)

Other annual awards are voted by the National Society of Film Critics (founded in 1966) and the National Board of Review, which began compiling its selection of the best American and foreign movies of the year in 1930, then chose one best picture along with directing, acting and other awards in the 40s, while the Writers Guild of America began honouring the scriptwriters of American pictures, mainly within the categories of drama, comedy and musicals, along with a number of career-achievement awards, beginning in 1948.

With its large membership and long list of awards, the Academy's nominating and voting procedure is extended over a number of months in the new year, including special screenings of nominated pictures for Academy members in Los Angeles. (For example, the rules now require that all those members voting for the best foreign film must view all five nominated contenders.) This means that each year there is a gradual progression to the Oscar ceremony, beginning with the New York Critics awards (generally announced in late December), the Golden Globes in early February – around the same time that the DGA and Oscar nominees are announced – followed by the DGA winner (early March), and culminating in the nationally televised Academy Awards ceremony in late March or early April. Such a pattern means that the other awards avoid being overshadowed by the Oscars and even gain an added interest as a guide to where the Oscars may go. At the same time, Academy members have a period of time in which to catch those pictures they may not have seen and evaluate those many films released late in the year, for the Christmas season, as well as being able to take into account (and no doubt be influenced by) those awards made by other organizations which have already been announced.

THE BEST PICTURE AWARDS

The 60-year history of the Oscar reflects many of the changes which have taken place within the American film industry during that period: the variations in the popularity of different types of pictures along with shifting fashions in stars, directors, and others associated with them and – especially – the variable fortunes of the different studios. As one would expect from an organization which is so integral a part of the movie industry, the Academy tends to prefer the worthy and well-crafted picture which has achieved some measure of popular success to the extremely original or offbeat production. This has often meant going for the safe option, the movie adapted from an already successful novel or play, with adaptations outnumbering screen originals by over two to one. Thus, the Academy preferred *Cavalcade* to *I Am A Fugitive From A Chain Gang* in 1932/3, *How Green Was My Valley* to *Citizen Kane* in 1941, *My Fair Lady* over *Dr Strangelove* in 1964, *Rocky* over *Taxi Driver* in 1976 and *Kramer vs. Kramer* over *Apocalypse Now* in 1979. But there have been some surprising and worthwhile choices, too, including *All Quiet On The Western Front* (1929/30), *It Happened One Night*

(1934), *The Lost Weekend* (1945), *The Apartment* (1960) and *Annie Hall* (1977).

As the single most profitable and successful studio with the largest number of top stars, MGM was the dominant company throughout the early period up to 1942 and had by far the largest number of Oscar nominations and winners. But this dominance was not immediately apparent, for the Best Picture award was shared among six different studios in the first seven years. There was a welcome diversity in the types of pictures, too, although they were generally representative of the more popular genres of the period. Few of the companies, though, won with pictures which were typical of their output. The World War I epics *Wings* (Paramount, 1927) and *All Quiet On The Western Front* (1930) from the small Universal studio, as well as RKO's spectacular Western, *Cimarron* (1931), and the historical family saga, *Cavalcade* (1933), from Fox were all expensive prestige productions – so expensive that, in spite of winning the top Oscar and doing well at the box-office, they failed to earn a profit (with the sole exception of *Cavalcade*). Paramount and Universal would not receive another Best Picture Oscar for many years, while RKO never won it again.

Not surprisingly, the most profitable of the early winners came from MGM, the company which was most expert at blending quality with profitability, even through the worst years of the Depression. *The Broadway Melody* (1929) was one of the first and most popular of the early musicals, while *Grand Hotel* (1932) was an extremely efficiently produced multi-star vehicle.

The one genuinely small and inexpensive Oscar winner was *It Happened One Night* (1934) from tiny Columbia. But when MGM then won with the epic *Mutiny On The Bounty* (1935) followed by the spectacular musical biopic, *The Great Ziegfeld* (1936), the pattern of the Oscar winners was well on its way to being established. This was further confirmed by the pictures which earned the top accolade in the following years. Warners' two Oscar winners, *The Life of Emile Zola* (1937) and *Casablanca* (1943), were relatively modest A pictures, but Frank Capra's second comedy win for Columbia, *You Can't Take It With You* (1938), was on a much more elaborate scale than his first, with a budget many times larger and a starstudded cast worthy of MGM (indeed, James Stewart and Lionel Barrymore were on loan from MGM). *Gone With The Wind* (Selznick/MGM, 1939) was the longest, most expensive and elaborate production of the decade; similarly, *How Green Was My Valley* (Fox, 1941), *Rebecca* (Selznick/UA, 1940) and *Mrs Miniver* (MGM, 1942) were all well-crafted, classy adaptations of popular novels of the period, featuring major stars and highly successful at the box-office. (No less than nine of the winners up to 1942 were based on novels.) Rather than the diversity of the very first years, there was a leaning toward dramatic pictures with serious themes which has continued up to the present day, with relatively few comedies or musicals as winners and nothing in the way of Westerns, horror, fantasy or science fiction.

Though Paramount came up a winner with Leo McCarey's *Going*

My Way in 1944, this was the last comedy to gain the top award until Billy Wilder's *The Apartment* in 1960. But it was a younger and more serious Wilder who set the Oscar pattern for the rest of the 40s, a surprise winner with his treatment of alcoholism on the screen in *The Lost Weekend* (Paramount, 1945). It was a period when directors were becoming more important and enjoying an increasing degree of success both at the box-office and with the Academy, while turning their attention to adult social themes: the readjustment problems of returning war veterans in *The Best Years Of Our Lives* (directed by William Wyler for Goldwyn/RKO, 1946), antisemitism in *Gentleman's Agreement* (directed by Elia Kazan for Fox, 1947) and political idolatry and corruption in the Deep South in *All The King's Men* (directed by Robert Rossen for Columbia, 1949). The witty comedy-drama *All About Eve* (Fox, 1950) was the cinematic inspiration of writer-director Joseph L. Mankiewicz, while Laurence Olivier's *Hamlet* (1948) was the first British picture to win the top award, reflecting the quality of the best British productions in the 40s. Not surprisingly, this was the period when the Academy was most in agreement with the New York Film Critics who generally preferred smaller black-and-white movies to the expensive epics. The New Yorkers had chosen *The Informer* (1935) and *Mr Deeds Goes To Town* (1936) in preference to the MGM blockbusters selected by the Academy – *Mutiny On The Bounty* and *The Great Ziegfeld* respectively; they also gave the nod to Samuel Goldwyn's *Wuthering Heights* over *Gone With The Wind* in 1939.

Having once dominated the Oscars, the giant MGM studio then found itself out in the cold. Many of its best 40s productions, especially the musicals, were largely ignored by the Academy. (The delightful *Meet Me In St Louis*, 1944, for example, was only nominated in four minor categories and did not win any awards.) In addition the studio was somewhat lacking in notable directorial talent, while the overall size and influence of the large companies now counted for less than the quality of individual productions. It is ironic to note that the same 'snobbism' on the part of the Academy which accounted for MGM's success in the 30s and the relative neglect of the lively and fast-moving Warner Bros. product, for example, was turned against the MGM musicals in the 40s.

A belated recognition came in 1951 when *An American In Paris* won the top accolade and, again, with *Gigi* in 1958 during the period which was the most confused and schizophrenic in Hollywood and Academy history. The decline of the studios and the introduction of new technology was complicated by the Red-scare witchhunts and blacklisting which particularly affected writers, and ruined the careers of many leading directors, at a time when they were needed more than ever before. The winning pictures ranged from intimate black-and-white productions to the most lavish costume epics, frequently competing with one another in the nominations. In 1952 Cecil B. DeMille's *The Greatest Show On Earth* won over *High Noon; The Bridge On the River Kwai* succeeded against *Twelve Angry Men* and *Witness For The Prosecution* in 1957, while the epic *Ben-Hur* triumphed over *Room At The Top* and *Anatomy Of A Murder* in 1959. On the other hand, *Marty* was preferred to both *Mr Roberts* and *Picnic* in 1955, and *The Apartment* beat *Elmer Gantry* and *The Alamo* in 1960. The companies which did best during these years, and incidentally achieved major status for the first time – Columbia and United Artists – were successful with a wide variety of productions in both colour and black-and-white.

An important new development during these years was the notable increase in filming abroad, especially in the production of the most expensive blockbusters. Many of these needed to make use of foreign locations and could also benefit from the generally high standards of British and European technicians along with their cheaper labour costs. From 1956, when UA's *Around The World In Eighty Days* was the winner, till the late 60s the vast majority of the Best Picture nominees and winners were filmed either in part or entirely outside the USA. American-financed British productions were especially popular in the 60s and included four of the seven winners during 1962–68, the peak years of American investment in Britain, while a fifth, *The Sound of Music* (1965), was filmed in Austria. The biggest surprise of all was provided by the low-budget all-British production of *Tom Jones* (1963), backed by United Artists. More typical winners were the expensively produced *Lawrence Of Arabia* (1962) and *Oliver!* (1968), both financed by Columbia.

Continuing the pattern of the 50s, the winners were mostly divided between expensive blockbusters or musicals and smaller dramatic pictures or comedies. But in the late 60s a large number of expensive flops and a dramatic fall in income led most of the major companies to cut back on the filming of epics abroad. Leading the shift back to US-based production, there was an upgrading of the crime movie which had previously been regarded as an inferior, 'bread and butter' genre, generally confined to black-and-white prior to the mid-60s. Now such pictures were being filmed in colour and given larger budgets – though still modest in comparison with the costs of other types of features – with leading stars and directors. First of the new breed of Oscar winners was the thriller *In The Heat Of The Night* starring Rod Steiger and Sidney Poitier, which won out over *Bonnie And Clyde*, another highly successful crime movie, in 1967.

The trend became more apparent in the early 70s, however. In 1971 director William Friedkin won the top Oscar (and the directing award) with *The French Connection*, while the New York Film Critics bestowed their top prize on Stanley Kubrick's futuristic crime-drama *A Clockwork Orange*. Friedkin was the first Oscar winner from a new generation of young directors, but the most prominent of that group was Francis Ford Coppola, director and co-writer of the Oscar winning pictures *The Godfather* (1972) and *The Godfather Part II* (1974). Sandwiched between was a comedy-thriller, *The Sting* (1973), which beat out the horror-thriller *The Exorcist*, directed by Friedkin and winner of the Golden Globe award. Other leading Oscar nominees in the thriller genre included Roman Polanski's *Chinatown* and *The Conversation* (Francis Ford Coppola again) in 1974, also *Dog Day Afternoon* and the tremendously popular action-adventure thriller *Jaws* from director Steven Spielberg in 1975. The following year *Rocky* was a surprise winner over the political thriller *All The President's Men* (based on the true events of Watergate) and director Martin Scorsese's chillingly effective *Taxi Driver*. (Ironically, Warner Bros., the studio most readily associated with crime movies over the years, and the distributor of *Bonnie and Clyde*. *A Clockwork Orange, Klute, The Exorcist* and *All The President's Men* among others, failed to win a Best Picture Oscar during these years.)

More recently the Academy has returned to the mainstream pattern of earlier years, with the emphasis on worthy and successful movies and a special preference for human-interest drama. *Kramer vs. Kramer* (1979), *Ordinary People* (1980), *Terms of Endearment* (1983) *Out of Africa* (1985), *Rain Man* (1988) and *Driving Miss Daisy* (1989) were all of this type, while *The Deer Hunter* (1978) tried to be a little different, but was still more human-interest than war picture. Oliver Stone's *Platoon* (1986) was conventional, if more direct, in the treatment of its central theme, that of men under stress in Vietnam. In such company the Milos Forman winners, *One Flew Over The Cuckoo's Nest* (1975) and *Amadeus* (1984), appear positively offbeat. The only comedy winners since Billy Wilder's little masterpiece, *The Apartment* (1960), have been Tony Richardson's English period romp *Tom Jones* (1963) and Woody Allen's very personal and very entertaining *Annie Hall* (1977).

In 1990 *Dances with Wolves*, directed by and starring Kevin Costner, was the first Western winner in sixty years and the first ever winner with subtitles – for its authentic Indian (Lakota Sioux) dialogue.

There was a strong showing from British film-makers in the 80s with *Chariots of Fire* (1981) and *Gandhi* (1982), fitting into the pattern of popular but worthy subjects which have characterized recent winners. In addition, there were another half a dozen British productions nominated, while British producers and production companies have been responsible for co-producing four other recent winners beginning with *The Deer Hunter* (EMI, 1978) and including *Platoon* (Hemdale, 1986) *The Last Emperor* (Jeremy Thomas, 1987) and *Dances with Wolves* (Majestic Films, 1990)

AWARD-WINNING DIRECTORS

As with other aspects of change in Hollywood, the altered status of directors over the years is clearly reflected in the Oscars. It seems that the Best Director award, initially, was confined to the members of a select and exclusive club, and it is otherwise difficult to account for the fact that there were such a small number of winners, and virtually all of them from the largest studios. (Columbia's Frank Capra was the one obvious exception.) During the peak years of the studio era, up to the early 40s when virtually all directors were contract employees and somewhat confined in their status and creative independence, only eight directors in all won the top accolade from the Academy. In 1941 John Ford joined Frank Capra as a three-time winner, while two statuettes each had gone to Lewis Milestone, Frank Borzage and Frank Lloyd (an original founder member of the Academy and one of the original group of awards judges). Leo McCarey, Norman Taurog and Victor Fleming had each won once.

Among that distinguished group of men who were occasionally nominated but who never won were Ernst Lubitsch, Josef von Sternberg, King Vidor and Clarence Brown. These – and a second important group – received a token form of recognition when their productions were either nominated for Best Picture or named in the lesser scripting categories. Thus, in the case of Howard Hawks, the scripts for *The Criminal Code* and *The Dawn Patrol*, on which he collaborated uncredited, were both nominated in 1931, with the latter a winner. Similarly, the scripts of *Dr Jekyll And Mr Hyde* (1931) and *Fury* (1936) were both nominated, though their respective directors, Rouben Mamoulian and Fritz Lang, never were, and William A. Wellman won his only statuette for co-writing the original story of *A Star Is Born* (1937).

The years 1940–41, however, represented a definite turning point, with the directors of quality becoming more prominent than ever before. A clear indication of their new status and the extent to which they had become identified with the final product can be seen in the Best Picture and directing awards. Prior to 1941 the director of the winning picture rarely gained his own statuette. Indeed, only five directors of the 13 pictures also won, with two of the five accounted for by Frank Capra. But from 1941 on, it was extremely unusual for the director of the top picture not to win – this disparity only occurred eight times in 46 years.

Though John Ford won in both 1940 and 1941, the veritable explosion of directorial talent, which has never been matched before or since, was evident in the nominations and other awards and pointed the way to the future. William Wyler, for example, was also nominated in 1941 and won his first of three statuettes in 1942 for *Mrs Miniver*. Preston Sturges was nominated for the first time (and won) for scripting *The Great McGinty*, his first effort as writer-director in 1940. Alfred Hitchcock's first two American features were both nominated that year with *Rebecca* as the Best Picture winner, although Hitch failed to win for directing. In 1941 Howard Hawks and Orson Welles were nominated for the only time, with Welles winning as co-writer of *Citizen Kane*, while John Huston was nominated for scripting *The Maltese Falcon*, his first feature as writer-director. (The pictures of all three were also nominated.)

A number of these same men made their contribution to the war effort by successfully turning their talents to the documentary field in the 40s. Thus, among the first winners in the new documentary Oscar categories were John Ford for *The Battle of Midway* (1942), and *December 7th*, co-directed with Gregg Toland, in 1943, Frank Capra for *Prelude To War* (1942), and William Wyler for *The Fighting Lady* (1944) – while John Huston was nominated for *Report From The Aleutians* (1943).

Many of the talented new directors of the 40s, especially those associated with bringing more adult themes to the screen – such as Billy Wilder, Elia Kazan, John Huston and Joseph L. Mankiewicz –

continued to be nominated and win Oscars throughout the rest of the decade. In addition, the exceptional quality of the British cinema of the period led to first Academy recognitions for David Lean, Carol Reed and Laurence Olivier, though it was many years before a British director actually won.

In contrast to the new names of the 40s, the 50s and 60s represented a period of retrenchment when many of the same comments made with regard to the Best Pictures also apply. The nominees and winners were most often those who had mastered the skills of directing on a large scale and who were therefore associated with the most popular epics and extravagant musicals of the period. They were often familiar names from the smaller, black-and-white movies of the 30s and 40s: George Stevens (winner with *Giant*, 1956), David Lean, the first British winner with *The Bridge On The River Kwai* (1957), Vincente Minnelli (*Gigi*, 1958), William Wyler (*Ben-Hur*, 1959), Robert Wise with *West Side Story* (1961) and *The Sound Of Music* (1965). But the most important phenomenon in the 60s was the large number of British winners – David Lean again for *Lawrence Of Arabia* (1962), Tony Richardson, an unexpected success with *Tom Jones* (1963), Carol Reed for the musical *Oliver!* (1968) and even the British director of a highly successful American production – John Schlesinger for *Midnight Cowboy* (1969).

The cinema moves in cycles, and by the late 60s and 70s, with the failure of many expensive blockbusters, it was time for the younger directors of a new generation to be given their chance, as had happened in the 40s. Many of them were writer-directors such as Francis Ford Coppola and Woody Allen, also Michael Cimino, Robert Benton and Oliver Stone; others were simply solid, talented commercial directors, notably Mike Nichols, William Friedkin, Sydney Pollack and the Czech-born Milos Forman, as well as a number of surprisingly successful stars-turned-director, Robert Redford (*Ordinary People*, 1980), Warren Beatty (*Reds*, 1981), Richard Attenborough (*Gandhi*, 1982) and Kevin Costner (*Dances With Wolves*, 1990). On the whole, however, the Academy's choices continued to be relatively conservative and as predictable as the Best Picture winners.

The first foreign-language director that the Academy honoured was Jean Renoir. Though not nominated himself, in 1938 his picture *La Grande Illusion* was, a unique early example which was not matched for another 31 years until Costa-Gavras' *Z* in 1969. Foreign-language directors, mainly French and Italian, gained their first token recognition from the Academy in the 40s via the screenwriting categories and an honorary foreign film award which became competitive in 1956. Vittorio De Sica won two of the first honorary statuettes with *Shoeshine* (1947) and *Bicycle Thieves* (1949), while Roberto Rossellini (*Paisan*, 1949), Max Ophuls (*La Ronde*, 1951) and Jacques Tati (*Monsieur Hulot's Holiday*, 1955) were each nominated for their scripts. But it was Federico Fellini who emerged as the single most successful foreign director over the years, closely followed by Sweden's Ingmar Bergman. First nominated for scripting Roberto Rossellini's *Rome, Open City* in 1946, Fellini won the first two competitive foreign-language film Oscars for *La Strada*

(1956) and *Nights of Cabiria* (1957), followed by *8¹/₂* (1963), *Satyricon* (1970) and *Amarcord* (1975) and was the first foreigner included in the Best Director nominations, in 1961, resulting from the tremendous international success of *La Dolce Vita*. He was followed by many others, including Ingmar Bergman (for *Cries and Whispers*, 1973) and François Truffaut (*Day For Night*, 1974) and, indeed, a 'token' foreign director has since been nominated virtually every year up to 1976 when Lina Wertmuller was included for *Seven Beauties*, the only female director ever to be a nominee. But no foreigner has ever won the Oscar for a foreign language picture, whereas the New York Film Critics have given their top directing award to Ingmar Bergman, François Truffaut and Federico Fellini, honoured once each in the 70s when foreign cinema and foreign film-makers were enjoying a period of high regard in the USA.

STARS AND SUPPORTING PLAYERS

The Academy's acting awards have been the most hotly contested over the years and have led to many famous disputes and controversies. There was an outraged reaction in 1934, for example, when Bette Davis' name was not included in the list of nominees for her performance in *Of Human Bondage*, leading to what might be termed the 'compensation award' that she won the following year for a lesser picture, *Dangerous* (1935). Among many other stars who were honoured the year after they were expected to win were Spencer Tracy (in 1937), James Stewart (in 1940) and Joan Fontaine (in 1941).

Many newcomers have been boosted to stardom by winning a statuette relatively early in their careers. There have also been some unexpected cases of established character or supporting actors suddenly elevated by winning the top Oscar – for example, Lee Marvin for *Cat Ballou* (1965) and Gene Hackman for *The French Connection* (1971). It has even been alleged that there is a jinx attached to the Oscar. For example, the movie careers of Luise Rainer (in the late 30s) and Olivia de Havilland (in the early 50s) declined after they won two awards. But there are so few examples of this happening, in comparison with the large numbers who have benefited, that it is difficult to take this seriously.

A list of top stars who never won reveals some extraordinary omissions: Greta Garbo, Charlie Chaplin, Cary Grant, Barbara Stanwyck, Irene Dunne, Peter Sellers, Al Pacino, Rosalind Russell and Deborah Kerr. Edward G. Robinson was never even nominated, while James Dean received posthumous nominations for two pictures released after his early death. During more recent years Marlon Brando and George C. Scott have refused to accept their awards, while Vanessa Redgrave created a furore while accepting hers (for *Julia*) at the 1977 ceremony because she used the occasion to publicize her support for her pro-Palestinian and anti-Israeli political views.

Many of the characteristic qualities of the Oscar choices were established in the early years: the honouring of old-timers such as George Arliss or Marie Dressler near the end of distinguished careers; the preference for dramatic performances over comedy or musicals; the encouragement of relative newcomers such as Janet Gaynor (the first winner in 1927–28), a youthful Helen Hayes and Katharine Hepburn, among others.

In 1936 Luise Rainer won for her first American picture, *The Great Ziegfeld*, joined by supporting actress Gale Sondergaard who was honoured for *her* first picture, *Anthony Adverse*. The supporting categories had just been introduced that year, a long-overdue gesture at a time when the Hollywood studios overflowed with large numbers of outstanding supporting players and character actors. Among the winners in the early years were Hattie McDaniel, the first black to be honoured by the Academy, Jane Darwell, Mary Astor, Ethel Barrymore, Donald Crisp, and Walter Brennan who set a record which has never been equalled by taking the award three times in five years. Barry Fitzgerald set another record of sorts by being nominated as Best Actor and Best Supporting Actor for the same role, that of the elderly priest in *Going My Way* (1944). He won the latter, but the rules were then clarified to allow each performance inclusion in one category only. However, the distinction between lead and supporting roles has never been strictly observed. Maximilian Schell in *Judgement At Nuremburg* (1961), Lee Marvin in *Cat Ballou* (1965) and Marlon Brando as *The Godfather* all won the top award for comparatively small roles, while one of the strangest of all was the situation with *Hud* in 1963: Patricia Neal gained the top accolade in being named Best Actress for a part which was no larger than that of Melvyn Douglas in the same picture, for which he only won in the supporting category.

MGM had both the largest number of popular stars in its stable and the strongest influence within the Academy from the beginning. Thus, the studio dominated the lead acting awards up to the early 40s. This had a curious 'delayed action' effect on the awards in the 40s when many of the winners were (non-MGM) 30s stars whose recognition was long overdue. They included Olivia de Havilland, Paul Lukas, Loretta Young, Ray Milland and a surprisingly large number of major performers whose names all began with 'C' – James Cagney, Gary Cooper, Bing Crosby, Joan Crawford and Ronald Colman – all starring in non-MGM pictures.

The 50s was a more mixed period, especially for the men, with the awards divided between such relative newcomers as José Ferrer and Marlon Brando and stars as long established as Humphrey Bogart and David Niven, with the occasional surprises, such as Ernest Borgnine winning for *Marty* in 1955. On the distaff side, the newer stars proliferated. They included Judy Holliday, Shirley Booth, Grace Kelly and Joanne Woodward, with Audrey Hepburn and Anna Magnani winning for their first American films. A youthful Shirley MacLaine was first nominated in 1958 for *Some Came Running* and again for *The Apartment*: 'I lost to a tracheotomy', was her classic comment when Elizabeth Taylor, recently recovered from her near-fatal illness, walked off with the statuette for her performance in *Butterfield 8* (1960) – yet another example of the Academy's sentimental streak. Miss MacLaine had to wait another 23 years before she, too, became the sentimental favourite and gained her accolade for *Terms Of Endearment* (1983).

Similarly, Henry Fonda had to wait until 1981 and *On Golden Pond* for his gold-plated statuette – 41 years after his first nomination for his performance in *The Grapes Of Wrath* (1940). Paul Newman brought a new twist to the saga of the overdue Oscar: having been passed over for his much-acclaimed portrayal of pool player 'Fast' Eddie Felson in *The Hustler* (1961), he finally won when he returned to the same character, 25 years later, in *The Color Of Money* (1986).

As the Academy and its membership have grown older, so have many of the performers, who found themselves drifting naturally into character parts and supporting roles. This had become especially evident by the 70s, when nominees in the supporting categories included Fred Astaire and Lee Strasberg (both for the first time), Burgess Meredith, Alec Guinness and, in 1979, Mickey Rooney, just 41 years after he had been awarded an honorary juvenile statuette. Also among the elderly winners have been John Mills, Ben Johnson, producer-turned-actor John Houseman, George Burns, Melvyn Douglas and, most recently, John Gielgud, Peggy Ashcroft, Don Ameche and Jessica Tandy in 1989. Then too, Helen Hayes and Ingrid Bergman became the first veteran performers to carry off a supporting Oscar some 30–40 years after they had first won as Best Actress. Perhaps the most striking example of the old-versus-new syndrome was seen in 1973 when Sylvia Sidney was matched against three youngsters just beginning their movie careers – Linda Blair, Candy Clark and the eventual winner, nine-year-old Tatum O'Neal – the youngest-ever winner in any competitive Oscar category.

In spite of the quality of British acting on stage and screen, there have been only a handful of British Oscar-winning performances (in British films) over the years. The six Best Actor winners have been spread over 50 years, starting with the surprise success of Charles Laughton as Henry VIII in 1933. Next came Robert Donat in *Goodbye Mr Chips* (1939), Laurence Olivier as *Hamlet* (1948), Paul Scofield in *A Man For All Seasons* (1966) and Ben Kingsley as *Gandhi* (1982). For the actresses, the winning performances were concentrated into the years 1965 to 1973, the peak period of US investment in British cinema – Julie Christie in *Darling* (1965), Glenda Jackson in *Women In Love* (1970) and *A Touch Of Class* (1973) and Maggie Smith in *The Prime Of Miss Jean Brodie* (1968). (Miss Smith's later supporting Oscar came for a strangely appropriate role, playing the part of a movie actress who is nominated, but fails to win, a much-coveted statuette in *California Suite*, 1978.) Perhaps the British lack of success is best symbolized by the position of Richard Burton and Peter O'Toole heading the list of most-nominated actors who have never even received an honorary award, with six and seven nominations respectively.

Of course, the nominations themselves represent an important and useful form of recognition. Unfortunately, all the hype and publicity leading up to the awards ceremony has grown progressively more hysterical over the years, while the whole idea of a 'winner' from among a diverse group of performances has always been a bit dubious.

(At least in the case of the Golden Globes the performances are divided into separate dramatic and comedy/musical categories so as to match roles which are more obviously comparable.) Of interest here are the remarks of George C. Scott after he refused his Oscar for *Patton* (1970). Pointing out his objections, he said, '. . . that whole thing of someone better than somebody else . . . I've been nominated four times, and I've always been very proud of that. There's nothing wrong with that. It's the bullshit that starts from then on that's so awful.'

OTHER CREATIVE CATEGORIES

The various technical categories and other non-acting awards demonstrate a particularly interesting and important, if somewhat neglected, aspect of the annual Awards ceremony. Since no other organization extends its recognition to such a wide range of crafts and skills, this represents a uniquely useful role for the Academy in an area less subject to the kind of hype and ballyhoo which surrounds the voting for the top awards. Unfortunately, the Academy's good intentions are often spoilt by unwieldy or outdated nominating and voting procedures. The foreign-film nominees, for example, are each submitted as its official entry by the country concerned, whose selectors often tend to go for the safe choice rather than judging on artistic merit alone, and each country is limited to one submission per year. All cartoons, shorts and documentaries are shortlisted by producer or production company, but with no credit to directors. During the studio era credit (or joint credit) was frequently given to the head of the relevant studio department, though he might not have worked on the film in question at all. (This was most blatantly the case with the supervising art directors such as Van Nest Polglase at RKO, and Cedric Gibbons of MGM who was thus able to claim 11 Oscars and a large number of additional nominations.)

In the case of most of the technical categories, however, the nominations have served to draw attention to those many outstanding cameramen, designers, scriptwriters, composers and others who have made a major contribution over the years. The list of nominees reads like a veritable 'who's who' of leading movie personnel, and though the most creative effort has not always emerged as the winner, the nominations themselves represent a much-valued form of recognition.

The Academy's early efforts to broaden the scope of the awards in the 30s meant that new categories were being added virtually every year. In 1929/30 a sound recording Oscar was introduced, with MGM's Douglas Shearer as the first winner, while provision was made for specialized scientific or technical awards in 1930/31. The following year cartoons and live-action short subjects were included, honouring Walt Disney's *Flowers And Trees*, the first cartoon in Technicolor, along with the Laurel and Hardy short, *The Music Box*. Special honorary awards were initially introduced at the first ceremony to highlight the achievement of Warners' *The Jazz Singer*, and Charlie Chaplin's *The Circus*. After a gap of four years, Walt Disney's cartoon character Mickey Mouse was honoured, but these special Oscars only became a regular feature of the awards in

1934. That year a miniature statuette was presented to the extraordinarily successful and popular child star, Shirley Temple, while the pioneering director D.W. Griffith was honoured in 1935 and the newly introduced documentary series, *The March Of Time*, in 1936. These awards have been included virtually every year up to the present date, honouring a wide range of movie personalities, directors and stars ranging from Mack Sennett, Judy Garland, Fred Astaire and Greta Garbo to Broncho Billy Anderson, Buster Keaton, Yakima Canutt, Lillian Gish, Orson Welles, Jean Renoir and Howard Hawks, among others.

In 1934 it was also the turn of editing and film music – both best song and best score – reflecting the increasing importance of movie music generally, while assistant director and dance direction awards were introduced in 1932/33 and 1935 respectively. However, these two awards were dropped after 1937. The supporting actor and actress Oscars were a popular addition in 1936, and the death of Irving Thalberg led to the establishment of the Irving Thalberg Memorial Award in 1937 to honour the most creative Hollywood producers. (Darryl F. Zanuck was the first recipient.) Special effects were added in 1939, followed by a documentary category in 1941. A few short non-fiction subjects such as the British GPO Film Unit's *London Can Take It* (1940), co-directed by Humphrey Jennings and Harry Watt, had previously been included among the short subject nominations. The provision of this new category was a direct result of the war, which generated new respect for non-fiction movie-making at a time when many leading Hollywood film-makers, including Frank Capra and John Ford, were involved in shooting government-sponsored documentaries.

Costume-design awards (for black-and-white and colour) were be-latedly introduced in 1948 – too late to honour many of those talented costumiers of the 30s who had flourished when the worldwide influence of Hollywood fashion was at its peak. (The prolific Edith Head with eight Oscars and 34 nominations has been the most successful here.) The competitive foreign-film award was added in 1956, while an Oscar for make-up, beginning in 1981, has been the one notable recent addition reflecting the increasing complexity and sophistication of modern make-up techniques.

As with the major awards, the largest studios tended to dominate in the leading technical categories during the 30s and 40s. However, the generally high quality of the independent Sam Goldwyn's productions resulted in a large number of awards to the leading members of his technical team headed by cameraman Gregg Toland, art director Richard Day and editor Daniel Mandell.

Over the years the craft awards, especially cinematography and art direction, have mirrored the technical changes which have taken place within the film industry. The tremendous success of *Gone With The Wind* in 1939, for example, and the growth in colour filming, led to the introduction of separate black-and-white and colour categories in the 40s. Though this adjustment was perhaps premature, as the number of colour pictures did not increase significantly till the early 50s, it did help to draw attention to the greatly improved quality of British productions in the postwar years. (In 1947 *Great Expectations* and *Black Narcissus* swept the Oscars for cinematography and art direction in black-and-white and colour respectively and in 1948 Laurence Olivier's *Hamlet* won for black-and-white art direction and costumes, while Michael Powell and Emeric Pressburger's *The Red Shoes* was honoured for colour art direction and music scoring.) In the 50s and 60s the introduction of new processes – CinemaScope, VistaVision and various 70mm techniques – was reflected in the awards, though black-and-white continued to play an important role up to 1967 when the separate categories were dropped. (Black-and-white specialist James Wong Howe, for example, was more appreciated and honoured by the Academy, with two Oscars, during these years as a freelance cameraman than during his period as a studio contract employee.)

Though the Academy generally tried to steer clear of politics, the problem of blacklisting in the 50s could not easily be ignored. (A bizarre clue to the climate that existed at the time can be seen in the fact that a simplistically anti-Red feature from Warners, *I Was A Communist For The FBI* starring Frank Lovejoy, was nominated as a 'documentary' in 1951!) The Academy was slow to act, however, and only modified its rules to exclude anyone who was blacklisted from February 1957, affecting the Oscars for 1956 and 1957 before the ruling was rescinded. The writers were the largest group of victims, though the situation was full of curious twists. The script of *Friendly Persuasion* was nominated in 1956 without a name, but was declared ineligible once the blacklisted writer Michael Wilson was revealed as the author, even though he had previously won for co-scripting *A Place In The Sun* in 1951. That same year, one 'Robert Rich' captured the Best Original Story award for *The Brave One*. Years later it was discovered that this was a pseudonym for the blacklisted Dalton Trumbo. In 1957 novelist Pierre Boulle was named as the winner for adapting his book *The Bridge On The River Kwai* when, in fact, the script was co-written by the blacklisted pair Michael Wilson (again) and Carl Foreman. Finally, in 1958 the Oscar for Best Original Screenplay went to Harold Jacob Smith and 'Nathan E. Douglas', the latter really Ned Young, yet another writer on the blacklist.

The Academy's failure to credit the directors of shorts and documentaries means that some sleuthing is required in order to discover that such directors as Fred Zinnemann, Mark Sandrich, George Sidney, Don Siegel and, more recently, John Carpenter, had all won short-film Oscars before graduating to features. Walt Disney's animated shorts dominated the Oscars throughout the 30s, while MGM's Tom and Jerry and the UPA/Columbia cartoons did well in the 40s and early 50s. But the remarkable originality of the Warner Bros. team, headed by Tex Avery, Friz Freleng, Frank Tashlin and Chuck Jones, was rather neglected. When their cartoons *were* nominated, in accordance with standard Academy practice the only name mentioned was that of the universally disliked executive producer Eddie Selzer (the prototype for UPA's cartoon character Mr Magoo).

During more recent years the cartoons, along with the other shorts and documentaries, have become more international. Many statuettes have gone to the quality productions of the National Film Board of Canada (NFBC). One of these, Norman McLaren's remarkable *Neighbours*, made use of an animation technique known as 'pixillation' and won the best documentary (!) Oscar in 1952. Other documentaries honoured by the Academy include Peter Watkins' *The War Game* (1966), Mike Wadleigh's rock festival film *Woodstock* (1970), and Barbara Kopple's *Harlan County USA* (1976), while winners in the cartoon category have included the Yugoslav Dušan Vukotić and British animators Bob Godfrey, Richard Williams and Nick Park in 1990.

PART 2

The Major
Hollywood Studios

The chapters in Part 2 present an in-depth portrait of the eight leading studios – Columbia, Fox, MGM, Paramount, RKO, United Artists, Universal and Warner Bros. – from the silent era up to the 80s, drawing on a wide range of newly compiled information. Each studio takes up one complete chapter, and each chapter is divided into sub-sections that follow the pattern set by the chapters in Part I. However, all begin with a studio history (and chronology), and this includes an assessment of the colourful, larger-than-life movie moguls who founded and ran the different companies and determined studio policy with regard to stars, types of picture and size of budgets. Next comes a discussion of the different types of releases, with special attention to colour and widescreen productions and to those pictures which most clearly reflect each studio's special character. The financial section deals with company profits and losses over the years with reference to hits and flops and high-cost movies. The studio's best-known stars, directors and other creative personnel who contributed to the style, content and overall quality of the pictures have their own sections, and each chapter concludes with an analysis of each company's success (or lack of it) in winning Oscars and other top film awards.

COLUMBIA

The letter 'C' stands for Columbia; for CBC, the original name of the company; for Frank Capra, its leading director in the 30s; for comedy, the studio's most successful and popular type of movie; and for Coca-Cola, the giant soft-drinks company that swallowed Columbia in the 80s. Most significantly, it stands for the brothers Jack and Harry Cohn, co-founders and heads of the company from 1924 until the mid-50s – especially Harry Cohn, the brash, tough, New York street kid who ran the studio while brother Jack headed the New York office. Under their leadership Columbia grew from a tiny studio on Poverty Row to one of the leading Hollywood companies and has continued to be a major force in the industry up to the present day with a variety of successes in the 60s and 70s, such as *Lawrence Of Arabia* (1962) and *Kramer vs Kramer* (1979).

The Cohns and Joe Brandt all started out as employees of Carl Laemmle at Universal before they broke away to form their own company, CBC or Cohn-Brandt-Cohn, also known as 'Corned Beef and Cabbage'. The elder Cohn brother, Jack, had been the first to venture into movies, having begun working for Laemmle's IMP company as early as 1910, and continued at Universal as editor of the studio's one- and two-reel shorts. Among Jack's contributions to the early success of that company was Universal Weekly, one of the first ever newsreels, which he devised and initiated and worked on as producer and editor. He played a major role in overcoming Laemmle's opposition to feature-length pictures by setting up the studio's first feature, *Traffic In Souls* (1913), then editing it behind the boss's back. It was a great success, and shortly after its release Jack managed to find a job at Universal for his friend Joe Brandt. In 1918 his younger brother Harry was hired as well and served as Laemmle's secretary. After trying a number of jobs, Harry had most enjoyed working as a song plugger, which required a combination of salesmanship, charm and showmanship, not all that different from his later role as film-studio boss. Song plugging led to a brief involvement in producing musical shorts, his first taste of movie-making before he arrived at Universal.

The CBC Film Sales Company was initially set up by the three men to exploit an idea of Jack's to make a series of shorts called Screen Snapshots; both popular and cheap to produce, they would show the offscreen activities of the movie stars and help to publicize new pictures and stars. A second series, the Hall Room Boys, followed the exploits of a pair of New York bums, and starred the popular vaudeville team of Edward Flanagan and Neely Edwards. This was an idea adapted from a successful vaudeville act which had itself been adapted from a popular comic strip.

While Jack Cohn and Joe Brandt handled the business affairs of the new company in New York, Harry was the one who favoured the production side of the business. He set up shop in Hollywood among the small-time independent movie producers located at Gower Street and Sunset Boulevard in the block known as Poverty Row. He was forced to operate on a shoestring budget, and each time a picture was completed and sold, the money was used to produce new pictures. Gradually the company was able to increase its output to include Westerns, and also comedies featuring Billy West (a Chaplin imitator). By 1922 Harry Cohn was ready to produce his first feature: *More To Be Pitied Than Scorned*, costing $20,000, was a big success, and early in 1924 the lowly CBC became the rather more grandly named Columbia Pictures Corporation.

During the following years the company continued to expand. Having previously marketed its movies on a flat-fee, States-rights basis – selling them outright to local distributors – the company lost out when they did well and the local exhibitors pocketed the profits. By 1926, however, Columbia was ready to begin establishing itself as a major distributor, opening the first of many film exchanges which would eventually cover the USA and most foreign markets as well. That same year Harry purchased his own small studio on Gower Street, not far from the lot he was renting from another Poverty Row producer, and appointed Sam Briskin as his general manager.

The forward momentum of the company was such that virtually every year brought new developments of note in addition to the regular increase in income and profits. In 1927 Harry produced his most lavish picture to date, *The Blood Ship*, directed by George Seitz. Offered the project by aging star Hobart Bosworth, Cohn filled out the cast with Richard Arlen and Jacqueline Logan and turned it into a big success, the first Columbia movie to play the Roxy in New York. It was but one example of the studio's ability to capitalize on a good opportunity. With few stars of its own – and those mainly of the second rank, such as Elaine Hammerstein, William Haines and Jack Holt – Columbia often made use of stars on loan, or hired those on their way up or down.

Similarly, the studio had few directors under contract. In 1927 a young and enthusiastic, but none too experienced, director was signed up and immediately began turning out features at a rapid rate – seven in his first year – and at a typically rock bottom cost of about $20,000 each. He didn't mind the low salary of $1,000 per film, for he liked making pictures and appreciated the fact that Cohn had given him the opportunity to do so with a large degree of freedom (provided he stayed within his budgets). His name was Frank Capra, and he would contribute immeasurably to the rise of Columbia Pictures.

As a small, economy-minded outfit, the coming of sound presented special problems for Columbia, pushing up costs generally and requiring the studio to be re-equipped. By late 1928 Cohn had gained enough confidence in Capra to assign him to replace another director on the studio's most expensive movie to date, *Submarine*, on which sound effects were used for the first time. It paid off at the box-office and Capra became the studio's leading director.

Cameraman Joe Walker arrived in 1928 just in time to help solve some of the problems in filming the new talkies, while John Livadary was hired soon after and stayed on as the studio's leading sound engineer for almost three decades, with many awards to his credit.

The running conflict which developed between the head office in New York and the studio operation in California was similar to that at other studios in spite of the fact that Jack (company secretary and treasurer) and studio boss Harry were brothers. President Joe Brandt often had to mediate between them, while generally supporting Jack. Matters came to a head in 1931 when Joe and Jack failed in their attempt to depose the formidable Harry. Joe retired and his share in the company was purchased by Harry; Jack was promoted to executive vice-president, but Harry took over the presidency himself while, at the same time, continuing as the studio boss.

Under Harry's leadership Columbia continued the slow but steady growth which had characterized it since its foundation, and it was barely held back by the Depression that badly hurt most of the other companies. Though the studio turned out more movies in the 30s, these included a substantial number of 'bread-and-butter' pictures – programmers and B Westerns – with a mere handful of A pictures each year (at least one of which had to be a big success). The studio continued to operate out of the same Gower Street lot, though it was considerably enlarged as the company took over many of the adjoining buildings between Gower and Beachwood Drive, and acquired a 40-acre ranch in Burbank for location filming. As actress Louise Brooks recalled, 'There was an office set, a street where they ran cars up and down, a penthouse and a night club. You could make all of Cohn's pictures in those days on those four sets.'

The studio remained small enough to enable Cohn to monitor the progress of all current productions personally. Studio employees credited him with keeping track of the activities of everyone on the lot, especially all arrivals and departures. His attitude was that movie-making was a tough business, and he was concerned that those he hired should be tough and confident. As a means of protecting the studio's investment in personnel, he was continually testing and bullying all those who worked for him. 'And that way', as Capra recalled, 'many a sensitive artist went through that studio quite chewed up, but Cohn didn't care. If you had guts, he'd give you an opportunity. If you didn't, he didn't want you around, no matter what your reputation was.'

Cohn's behaviour made him one of the most feared and detested men in Hollywood and led to many famous disputes involving the studio's top directors and stars. Even Capra, who had battled successfully with Harry for years, finally left in 1939 to set up his own company. There was an acrimonious fight with director Charles Vidor which ended up in court. The delightful Jean Arthur couldn't handle Harry at all and spent more time on suspension than making pictures. Though he made an effort to treat Rita Hayworth, the studio's most valuable star, with great care, he alienated her, too, by his clumsy attempts to control her private life.

But for all his failings, Cohn was a committed film-maker who gave a lot of freedom to those writers and directors in whom he had confidence and, while frequently at war with Columbia's own contract stars, managed to borrow many of the stars he needed from other studios. In the 30s such leading Hollywood directors as Leo McCarey (*The Awful Truth*, 1937), George Cukor (*Holiday*, 1938) and Rouben Mamoulian (*Golden Boy*, 1939) came to Columbia on one-picture deals that worked out well. By the late 30s the studio had a large number of successful pictures to its credit in addition to those Capra productions such as *It Happened One Night* (1934) and

Mr Deeds Goes To Town (1936) which first brought it widespread recognition.

Having grown throughout the worst years of the Depression, the studio continued expanding in the 40s and had its biggest hits so far with *The Jolson Story* (1946) and *Jolson Sings Again* (1949). Columbia could claim to be one of the leading studios for the first time in its history with such Oscar-winning successes as *All The King's Men* (1949), *Born Yesterday* (1950), *From Here To Eternity* (1953) and *On The Waterfront* (1954). Since it owned no cinemas itself, the company had not been affected by the government's Consent Decree which had forced the top studios to sell off their film theatres. This had a levelling effect, with all the studios struggling to break even. Though revenues remained high, profits were small, but Columbia benefited from the fact that it had been one of the first major movie companies to venture into TV production with its highly profitable Screen Gems subsidiary – headed by Jack's son, Ralph Cohn.

In the early 50s Harry Cohn's disputes with the front office became more frequent than ever, and it was clear that the 'studio era' was coming to an end. Forced to reduce the number of pictures it produced, the studio cut back on contract personnel. The seemingly indestructible Harry had a cancer operation early in 1954, and was much affected by the death of Jack in 1956. It was as if the studio and Harry were running down at the same time. He died in February 1958, just as Columbia was recording its first-ever loss for the fiscal year 1957/58. The company would never be the same with him gone. They did try; Sam Briskin, Harry's old associate, was brought in to head the studio for a while. There was a continuity of management, however, as Columbia would still be run by men who had worked their way up over the years – men such as Abe Schneider and Leo Jaffe, who had started out in the accounting department in the early 30s, but they were front-office men rather than producers.

With the coming of the 60s, Columbia opted for a major investment in British filming and had a number of its biggest successes with British productions. These included *The Bridge On The River Kwai* (1957), *Lawrence Of Arabia* (1962), *A Man For All Seasons* (1966) and the musical *Oliver!* (1968) both adapted from the stage, and *Gandhi* (1982). A major turning point came in the early 70s when the studio suffered the worst losses in its history and was only saved from bankruptcy when Herbert Allen Jr bought control and brought in a new management team headed by Alan Hirschfield and David Begelman. With such hits as *Shampoo* (1975) and *Close Encounters Of The Third Kind* (1977) they succeeded in reviving the company, but Begelman left in 1978 after a highly publicized embezzlement scandal and was followed soon after by Hirschfield. Frank Price, the head of Universal television, was hired to head Columbia Pictures and he successfully led the company for a number of years with such smash hits as the Oscar-winning *Kramer vs Kramer* (1979), and *Tootsie* (1982) – both starring Dustin Hoffman – and then *Ghostbusters* and *The Karate Kid* in 1984. Though Price had stayed on after the purchase of the company by the giant Coca-Cola

Company early in 1982, Columbia did poorly in 1985/86 after his departure.

In a surprise move in the summer of 1986, the independent British producer David Puttnam was signed up to a three-and-a-half year contract as chairman of the company. He had plans to concentrate on producing relatively low- and medium-cost pictures of quality, but was forced out when Columbia merged with Tri-Star Pictures in 1987. However, Columbia and Tri-Star continued to operate separately, with Dawn Steel appointed as the new president of Columbia Pictures late in 1987, while Jeffrey Sagansky headed Tri-Star. The company received a welcome boost when the Jeremy Thomas/Bernardo Bertolucci production of *The Last Emperor* won the 1987 Oscar for Best Picture. But the new management team were slow to get results, and after less than two, rather uneven, years, Coca-Cola sold its interest in Columbia and Tri-Star to the Sony Corporation of Japan. It had, in fact, become increasingly apparent from the many changes of management and restructuring during the 80s that the Coca-Cola Company was not happy coping with the many problems involved in running a major film studio and welcomed the opportunity to get out, especially given the favourable deal it was able to negotiate with Sony. It will be interesting to see if Sony will demonstrate a greater commitment to Columbia in the 90s than Coca-Cola in the 80s. For the studio continued to struggle during the first years under Sony, leading to the resignation of joint-chief Jon Peters early in 1991 and leaving Peter Guber in sole charge as head of the studio.

Columbia Studio Chronology

1920   Harry and Jack Cohn with Joe Brandt form a tiny new company called CBC.

1924   The company is renamed Columbia Pictures.

1927   Director Frank Capra arrives at the studio.

1931   Joe Brandt leaves the company and Harry Cohn takes over the post of president in addition to production chief, while Jack is vice-president and chairman of the board of directors.

1934   The studio has a tremendous success with *It Happened One Night*, the first production to win Oscars in all four main categories.

1938   Columbia and Capra have another major hit and Oscar-winner with *You Can't Take It With You*.

1939   Capra leaves after directing *Mr Smith Goes To Washington*.

1946   Cohn takes a big risk with an expensive Technicolor musical, *The Jolson Story*. It is a smash hit and boosts the studio's profits to their highest level to date.

1949   The studio wins the Best Picture Oscar for *All The King's Men*.

1953   Another Best Picture Oscar for *From Here To Eternity*.

1954   *On The Waterfront* wins the Best Picture Oscar for producer Sam Spiegel, one of the independent producers who play an increasingly important role in the development of the studio.

1956   Jack Cohn dies.

1957   Spiegel wins again with *The Bridge On The River Kwai*.

1958   Harry Cohn dies and the studio falls into the red for the first time in its history.

1962   *Lawrence of Arabia* (producer Spiegel, director Lean) is the first of the studio's British winners of the Best Picture Oscar, followed by *A Man for All Seasons* (1966) and *Oliver!* (1968).

1968   Profits peak at $9.4 million, but decline during the following years.

1973   Columbia records its worst-ever annual loss – $50 million. A new management team is headed by Alan Hirschfield and David Begelman.

1977   Steven Spielberg provides Columbia's biggest hit of the decade with *Close Encounters Of The Third Kind*.

1978   Frank Price replaces Begelman as production chief.

1979   Columbia releases *Kramer vs Kramer*, its first American-produced Oscar winner in 25 years.

1982   The company is purchased by the giant Coca-Cola Company.

1986   David Puttnam is appointed chairman of the company, the first British producer to hold such a post in a major American studio.

1987   Columbia is merged with Tri-Star Pictures and Victor Kaufman, of Tri-Star, is promoted to head the new corporation, renamed Columbia Pictures Entertainment. David Puttnam resigns and Dawn Steel is hired as the next president of Columbia.

1989   The Sony Corporation, the Japanese electronics giant, purchases Columbia from Coca-Cola for $3.4 billion, then hires the producers Peter Guber and Jon Peters as the new studio heads.

1991   Jon Peters resigns to return to independent production. The name of the company is changed to Sony Pictures Entertainment, with Columbia and Tri-Star as its film production subsidiaries.

The Releases

The studio grew steadily during the early years, turning out mainly comedy shorts and cheap features. By the mid-30s Columbia was producing over 40 features per year and a larger number of A features. It had its first big successes with a series of lively and entertaining 'screwball' comedies including *It Happened One Night* (1934) and *The Awful Truth* (1937). With Rita Hayworth as its leading star, the studio produced a number of Technicolor musicals in the 40s beginning with *Cover Girl* (1944) and the smash hit *The Jolson Story* (1946). In the 50s it ventured into CinemaScope for such prestige productions as *Picnic* (1955) and *The Bridge On The River Kwai* (1957), while *Lawrence Of Arabia* (1962) was the studio's most successful 70mm production. Many of its most interesting pictures, however, continued to be made in black-and-white, from *On The Waterfront* (1954), which showcased Marlon Brando, to *Anatomy Of A Murder* (1959), *Dr Strangelove* (1963) and *The Last Picture Show* (1971).

Starting out as a producer of comedy shorts (as CBC), the company began releasing its first, cheaply made features in 1922. Columbia grew steadily throughout most of the 20s, turning out a stream of small-budget dramas, action pictures (often starring Jack Holt) and comedies. When Frank Capra arrived late in 1927 he began directing comedies such as *That Certain Thing* (starring Viola Dana) and *So This Is Love?*, both released early in 1928, then settled into a pattern of mixing comedy films with dramas (starring a young Barbara Stanwyck) and action pictures including *Flight* (1929) and *Dirigible* (1931) both starring Jack Holt and Ralph Graves.

After a slight falling off in 1929 due to the changeover to sound, the number of feature releases grew year by year, with the gradual introduction of a small number of A features into the studio's regular diet of low-cost programmers. Though Columbia lacked the resources to compete with the top studios in the production of lavish costumers and musicals in the 30s, it could turn out dramatic pictures of quality, and even better comedies. The company was weak on stars and directors and had to borrow them from other studios or sign them up on short-term deals; but there was a small group of top writers under contract (writers could be hired relatively cheaply) including Jules Furthman, Norman Krasna, Robert Riskin and Jo Swerling.

Dore Schary, later a leading Hollywood producer, has recalled his first experiences as a writer at Columbia in 1933 and his initial assignment as co-scriptwriter of *Fury Of The Jungle* starring Victor Jory. This was a characteristically cheap action movie of the period involving piranhas, snakes and other jungle creatures. Schary was appalled to learn that a small monkey was earning more per day than he got per week, but was impressed by the work of the studio's efficient and economy-minded technical staff who transformed Lake Malibu into a reasonable simulation of the Amazon River.

Schary did not remain at Columbia long enough to see the changes that took place during the following years. The studio recovered rapidly from the Depression slump of 1932 and 1933, and the number of releases rose from an average of 30 per year to an annual total of over 50. For the first time in the history of the company Harry Cohn achieved his goal of releasing one feature per week, a level which he maintained (and, indeed, exceeded) for about 15 years, from the late 30s through the early 50s. In his own, colourful words, 'Every Friday the front door opens and I spit a movie out into Gower Street . . . I want one good picture a year. That's my policy . . . and I won't let an exhibitor have it unless he takes the bread-and-butter product, the Boston Blackies, the Blondies, the low-budget Westerns and the rest of the junk we make. I like good pictures too, but to get one I have to shoot five or six, and to shoot five or six I have to keep the plant going with the programme pictures.'

After directing a number of dramatic pictures – for example *The Miracle Woman* (1931) and *American Madness* (1932) – leading director Frank Capra returned to his first love, comedy, with great success. *Lady For A Day* (1933) was the first Columbia production to gain an Oscar nomination as Best Picture, while other nominations went to Capra, scriptwriter Robert Riskin and star May Robson. This was followed by Columbia's real breakthrough movie, the spectacularly successful multiple Oscar-winning comedy *It Happened One Night*, filmed later that same year and released early in 1934.

Capra had shown the way, and Harry Cohn was quick to see the possibilities. With the years on Poverty Row an all too recent memory, and his own reputation as the toughest, most vulgar studio boss in Hollywood, a fact that no-one would argue with, he was eager to establish a new and more respectable image for the studio. For the next 10 years or so Columbia excelled at producing a new style of sophisticated, contemporary comedy and demonstrated that in this area, at least, it was one of the Hollywood leaders. Drawing on its own comedy writers, men such as Robert Riskin and Sidney Buchman, and a readily available stock of talented character actors including Walter Connolly, Roscoe Karns and Raymond Walburn, Columbia initially borrowed most of the stars and directors it needed from the other studios. Thus, the tiny company found itself in an unexpected role, revealing and exploiting the comedy talents of numerous top stars. The actresses, in particular, often appeared reluctant to star in *any* film produced by the tiny studio, but once persuaded to do so were more easily encouraged to let their hair down there.

The pattern was first established in 1933/34 with *It Happened One Night*, when the tough Clark Gable from MGM and the sophisticated Claudette Colbert from Paramount demonstrated previously unseen skills in light comedy and walked away with a pair of Oscars. Similarly, the beautiful blonde Carole Lombard (also on loan from Paramount) was a delightful revelation in the screwball clowning of *Twentieth Century*, egged on by director Howard Hawks and co-star John Barrymore. The painfully shy Jean Arthur had been in pictures for a dozen years, including a stint at Paramount, before she suddenly emerged as a mature comedienne with her appealing, husky voice and a special style all her own. John Ford, who had directed Miss Arthur's first picture, *Cameo Kirby*, at Fox 11 years earlier, gave her her big opportunity in late 1934. She played the sensible and warm-hearted heroine of *The Whole Town's Talking* with such vitality that she was immediately requested by Capra for *Mr Deeds Goes To Town* (1936) and starred in his last two Columbia features as well. The ladylike Irene Dunne first let her hair down at Columbia in *Theodora Goes Wild* (1936), paired with Melvyn Douglas, in a role which some of her friends claim is the closest to her true character. She followed it with the delightfully scatty *The Awful Truth* (1937), co-starred with Cary Grant, and with Ralph Bellamy in his favourite role as 'the other man'. Bellamy turned up again in *His Girl Friday* (1940) and was once again thwarted by Grant, but this time the girl was Rosalind Russell, given the best comedy part of her career by director Howard Hawks.

The list of Columbia's most memorable comedies between 1933 and 1943 is an impressive one. Along the way the studio had acquired its own special group of comedy stars led by Melvyn Douglas, Cary Grant, and Jean Arthur who reigned as the queen of the Columbia lot when she wasn't fighting with Harry Cohn. The classic era of Columbia comedy came to an end with *The More The Merrier* (1943), and both Miss Arthur and Cary Grant left the studio the following year.

Dramatic pictures of note during these years included Josef von Sternberg's version of *Crime and Punishment* (1935) starring Peter Lorre and Edward Arnold, and *Craig's Wife* (1936) from the play by George Kelly (Grace's uncle) with Rosalind Russell, helmed by Dorothy Arzner, the leading woman director in Hollywood. Rouben Mamoulian directed William Holden as *Golden Boy* (1939) from the Clifford Odets play, while Howard Hawks contributed a memorable action drama *Only Angels Have Wings* (1939) starring Cary Grant, who also topped the bill in producer-director Frank Lloyd's *The Howards of Virginia* (1940), a rare studio venture into costume drama, set during the American war of independence.

In addition to the features, the studio's comedy shorts had also flourished, beginning in 1934 when producer-director Jules White was hired to head the department and immediately initiated three long-running series. The Andy Clyde shorts were popular for 23 years, while Harry Langdon starred in a series which only ended with his death in 1944. Longest-running of all were the Three Stooges who continued to turn them out up to 1958. (One of their earliest efforts, *Men In Black* directed by comedy specialist Del Lord was even nominated for an Oscar in 1934.) Charley Chase joined Columbia in 1937 as producer, writer, star and occasional director (under the name of Charles Parrott), while the last of the classic comedians to arrive at the studio, Buster Keaton, made 10 comedy shorts during 1939–41.

Columbia produced many different shorts throughout the studio era, up to the late 50s, like the Screen Snapshots which had begun as the first CBC series in 1920. For a short period the company distributed the extremely popular Disney cartoons, but lost out when that independent-minded producer moved to UA in 1931. Charles Mintz provided Columbia with Krazy Kat, Scrappy and Color Rhapsody cartoons in the 30s followed by Fox & Crow in the 40s. But most interesting of all was Columbia's link with Steve Bosustow's inventive UPA cartoon studio from 1948 through the 50s. UPA/Columbia won Oscars for its two most popular characters, Gerald McBoing Boing in 1950 and Mr Magoo in 1954 and 1956.

Throughout the 30s and 40s the studio manufactured large numbers of cheap Westerns and other programmers, especially crime movies and thrillers. The first B Westerns, with Buck Jones and Tim McCoy as the leading stars, appeared in the early 30s; Charles Starrett took over in 1935 and carried on for the next 18 years until the 'oaters' were phased out in the early 50s. Gene Autry also rounded off his movie career at Columbia around this same time, then moved on to TV. When the studio purchased a 40-acre ranch in Burbank for location shooting in 1937, this further facilitated the filming of Westerns and the company's newest ventures into serials production. From 1937 through 1956 Columbia turned out over 60 serials and series. As with so many of its B picture series the main sources were the radio (*The Shadow*, 1940) and strip comics (*Terry And The Pirates*, 1940 and *Batman*, 1943). Like MGM with its Andy Hardy series, Columbia made use of its cheap programmers to provide a first taste of screen acting for its newest young stars. In grooming Rita Hayworth for stardom, for example, Columbia cast her in a number of B thrillers during 1937 and 1938, and both she and Glenn Ford made one appearance each in the popular Blondie series.

Of all the leading studios, Columbia had the least interest in movie musicals during the 30s, and had but one major musical success with *One Night Of Love*, starring Grace Moore, in 1934. But with Rita Hayworth and dancer Ann Miller under contract, the studio began to produce more musicals in the early 40s, with 1944 as the peak year. Many of them were low-budget quickies, and *Cover Girl* (1944) teaming Hayworth with Gene Kelly (on loan from MGM) was Columbia's single outstanding contribution to the 40s boom in Technicolored musicals. The studio also released three musical biopics of note featuring two of its new stars – Cornel Wilde was Chopin in *A Song To Remember* (1945) and Larry

Parks was Al Jolson in *The Jolson Story* (1946) and in its sequel *Jolson Sings Again* (1949). Parks and Wilde both featured prominently in the studio's occasional ventures into costume adventure with such titles as *Bandit Of Sherwood Forest* (1946) and *The Swordsman* (1947).

Having acquired a number of leading stars by the late 40s, the range of Columbia's A pictures began – for the first time in its history – to resemble the output from the other major studios. The studio offered Rita Hayworth musicals, Randolph Scott Westerns. comedies starring Judy Holliday and Jack Lemmon, thrillers and *films noirs* with Glenn Ford (who also appeared in actioners and occasional Westerns), as well as a range of dramatic pictures whose stars regularly included Broderick Crawford, William Holden and Humphrey Bogart.

But the important difference between Columbia and the other companies was Harry Cohn. He was still running the studio, and he liked to produce lots of movies. As the last studio continuing to release large numbers of programmers, shorts, and even serials well into the 50s, for a time Columbia was turning them out in larger numbers than any other company in Hollywood. But this could not go on indefinitely. By the middle 50s Harry Cohn was ill. The profit margins on the shorts and B pictures had become too slim to make them viable productions, and they were proving increasingly difficult to sell. (Cinema programming was changing and TV was becoming a tough competitor.) An era had come to an end.

In later years Columbia claimed its big successes with many kinds of pictures besides comedies (not forgetting its prestige British productions), but no other Hollywood mogul had so firmly put his personal stamp on the output of a single studio. With Harry Cohn gone, Columbia would never be the same again.

Colour and Widescreen

As one of the smaller Hollywood studios throughout its early history, Columbia was never a technical innovator. It was relatively slow to move into sound (in 1929), into colour filming in the mid-40s and CinemaScope in the mid-50s. The studio first became interested in Technicolor in 1943, at about the same time as Universal, when the movie business was booming and all the leading companies, even the smaller ones, began to shoot selective productions in colour.

Columbia's first effort, a virtually forgotten Western, *The Desperadoes* (1943), starred Randolph Scott, Glenn Ford and Evelyn Keyes, and was directed by Charles Vidor. As one of the studio's leading contract directors Vidor handled many of the Technicolor productions, most notably *Cover Girl*, filmed later that same year. This picture represented a real breakthrough for the studio and for its top star, Rita Hayworth. She had already made two colour movies of note at Fox and photographed beautifully in Technicolor, especially with her new reddish hair style. (Apparently, this new look was originated by make-up expert Perc Westmore at Warner Bros. for a black-and-white picture! – *The Strawberry Blonde* in 1940 – and was further refined by Columbia's leading hair stylist, Helen Hunt, who worked on most of the star's major films.)

The production serves as a good example of what Arthur Schwartz, the composer (and producer of the picture), referred to as Harry Cohn's 'instinct for quality'. According to him, no other studio boss in Hollywood would have succeeded so well in balancing the various elements in the picture and assembling the many top talents involved. Leading costume designers Travis Banton and Gwen Wakeling, who had previously worked with Rita on her Fox Technicolor films, were kept busy by *Cover Girl*'s contemporary fashion theme, balanced by a series of Gay Nineties flashbacks, that called for a variety of period costumes. Co-star Gene Kelly was borrowed from MGM with his young choreographer assistant, Stanley Donen, while scriptwriter Virginia Van Upp, cameraman Rudolph Maté and art director Cary Odell were among the personnel who first made their names at Columbia on this production. Harry Cohn uncharacteristically – and advantageously – overlooked the fact that the cost soared well over the initial budget of $1 million.

One indication of Columbia's new status during the following years was a series of Technicolor movies featuring the studio's top stars. Cornel Wilde played Chopin in *A Song To Remember* (1945) and the son of Robin Hood in *Bandit Of Sherwood Forest* (1946), Larry Parks starred in the smash-hit musical *The Jolson Story* (1946), while Rita was teamed with Parks in *Down To Earth* (1947) and with Glenn Ford in *The Loves Of Carmen* (1948). Around the same time Columbia also produced a number of Randolph Scott and Gene Autry Westerns filmed in the cheaper Cinecolor process which was most effectively used in shooting outdoor subjects.

The year 1948 saw a peak in colour releases, but the box-office results were not encouraging and, for the next few years, the studio's colour movies were mainly routine actioners and Westerns. The most prestigious pictures were all in black-and-white: *All The King's Men* (1949), *Born Yesterday* (1950), *On The Waterfront* (1954) and *From Here To Eternity* (1953) which was also the one smash hit of these years.

Columbia was quick to take advantage of the industry's new vogue for 3-D in 1953 and was just as quick to drop the process when film audiences ceased to respond; it took up CinemaScope two years later and had its first big hit in this process late in 1955 with *Picnic*. Though the company's interest in 'Scope and colour fell off in the late 50s, it scored a major success with *The Bridge On The River Kwai* (1957).

The studio was unlucky with most of its (relatively few) expensive 70mm productions. *Porgy And Bess*, a 1959 Sam Goldwyn production filmed in Todd-AO 70mm, and Richard Brooks' version of Conrad's *Lord Jim* (1965) were major disappointments. *Barabbas* (1962), in Technirama, more or less broke even and David Lean's *Lawrence Of Arabia* (produced by Sam Spiegel) in 1962 in Super Panavision 70 was the one outstanding success.

During a period when several of the big American companies appear to have been unsure of what policies they should adopt with regard to colour, many of Columbia's most interesting and popular films continued to be in black-and-white: *3:10 To Yuma* (1957), John Ford's

The Last Hurrah (1958), *The Goddess* (1958), *Middle Of The Night, Suddenly, Last Summer* and Otto Preminger's *Anatomy Of A Murder* (all 1959), Preminger's *Advise And Consent* (1963), and Stanley Kubrick's *Dr Strangelove* (1963). Richard Brooks' *In Cold Blood* (1967) was one of the last major American films in black-and-white in the 60s, but just four years later *The Last Picture Show* (BBS/Columbia) proved that black-and-white filming was not yet dead.

Widescreen and 3-D Releases 1953–69

Process	1953	1954	1955	1956	1957	1958	1959	1960	1961	1962	1963	1964	1965	1966	1967	1968	1969
CinemaScope			8	8	3	5	5	3									
Technirama						1		1	1	3		1					
Panavision							1	5	2	2	5	1	5	7	6	5	2
Techniscope												2	3	1	1	4	1
Large format (70mm)						1				1			1				1
3-D	5	4															

The Finances

The revenues and profits of tiny Columbia were small in the early years, but continued to grow steadily, year after year, with only a slight decline during the worst period of the Depression and a slight 'hiccup' in 1937–39. By the early 40s the company was in a good position to take advantage of the wartime boom. *The Jolson Story* (1946) was a huge hit, while *Gilda* the same year and *Jolson Sings Again* (1949) did very well. Revenues and profits fell during the postwar period when, having attained the size of a major studio, Columbia was forced to cope with some of the same problems faced by the other majors during the 50s and 60s. The company was, however, assisted by a strong and profitable TV subsidiary, but fell deep into the red in the early 70s. The recovery in later years was helped by the success of Spielberg's *Close Encounters Of The Third Kind* (1977). After such hits as *Kramer vs Kramer* (1979), *Tootsie* (1982) and *Ghostbusters* (1984), Columbia did poorly at the box office in the late 80s, though *Ghostbusters II* and *When Harry Met Sally* gave the company a much-needed lift in 1989 shortly before it was purchased by Sony.

The tiny CBC, renamed Columbia, grew steadily throughout the 20s, turning out a mixture of shorts and cheap features produced at a cost of about $20,000 each. It is not surprising to learn that the leading director at the economy-minded studio, Frank Capra, was a former chemical engineer, for he relied on his own ingenuity to solve many of the technical problems which arose in the course of filming and with the arrival of sound. He was assigned to Columbia's first movie with sound effects, *Submarine* in 1928, budgeted at a mere $150,000. Capra tells of how he and cameraman Joe Walker devised their own 'special effects' shots with the help of a little toy diver and submarine and a discarded aquarium that he found in the props department.

Harry Cohn's close personal involvement with all pictures filmed at the small studio meant that he was able to keep costs low and record small profits during the transition to sound filming, as well as during the worst years of the Depression (1932 and 1933) when revenue and profits declined slightly, but the company never went into the red. Though Columbia had no big hits, it earned a steady income from its many shorts and cheaply produced features, and even its few A pictures rarely cost them more than $200,000 to make.

The studio made a quick recovery in 1934 with two hit movies, Capra's *It Happened One Night* and *One Night Of Love* starring singer Grace Moore. Between them they had only cost $500,000 dollars, but they demonstrated to Cohn the advantage of producing a few, carefully selected features on larger budgets each year. He then allowed Capra a budget of $500,000 solely for *Mr Deeds Goes To Town* (1936) and once again the result justified his confidence. Unfortunately, the cost of Capra's last features – *Lost Horizon* (1937), *You Can't Take It With You* (1938) and *Mr Smith Goes To Washington* (1939) – escalated beyond the point where they were likely to remain profitable. Though all three were quite successful, with budgets averaging between $1.5 million and $2 million dollars, they attracted much prestige but little profit. This was reflected in the company's balance sheet for the period from mid-1937 through 1939. Revenues remained high compared to previous years, but profits were tiny. (Cohn continued to control the cost of other A features, however, so that *The Awful Truth* in 1937, cost only $600,000 and *His Girl Friday* was budgeted at $900,000.)

As the company resumed its growth in the early 40s, Cohn increased the number of A pictures and aimed to turn out a wider range of features. Columbia's hit movies included two Westerns (*Arizona*, 1940, and the Technicolor *The Desperadoes*, 1943), comedies led by *My Sister Eileen* (1942) and *The More The Merrier* (1943), and musicals featuring Cohn's biggest star discovery, Rita Hayworth – *You Were Never Lovelier* (1942) partnered by Fred Astaire and *Cover Girl* filmed in 1943 co-starring Gene Kelly.

A gambler at heart – he regularly lost large sums of his own money betting on horses – Harry Cohn realized the degree of risk involved in the production of expensive A features, and this caused continual friction with the more conservative-minded businessmen in the New York head office. At the same time he recognized that there was no future in B pictures which earned a small but steady profit year after year (but would soon be killed off by television). Thus, he took a tremendous risk in 1945 by investing almost $3 million on a musical biopic of Al Jolson starring Larry Parks. A quite conventional treatment bearing little relation to Jolson's real life, and a less original musical than *Cover Girl*, nevertheless it featured lots of songs recorded by Jolson himself. The film was a tremendous hit and helped to make the years 1946 and 1947 the most profitable in Columbia's early history.

Other big hits were the Technicolored *Bandit Of Sherwood Forest* starring Cornel Wilde, and *Gilda* presenting the ultimate image of Rita Hayworth as sophisticated sex symbol, partnered by Glenn Ford with

George Macready as the villain. Both were released early in 1946 just in time for a pin-up image of Rita as Gilda to appear on the Bikini A-bomb, detonated on 1 July 1946. (None of her later pictures were as successful at the box office, but the offbeat Orson Welles thriller, *The Lady From Shanghai*, 1948, filmed at a cost of $2 million, was the only real flop in which she starred.)

From this point on Columbia's prestige productions began appearing regularly on *Variety*'s annual list of top-grossing pictures in the US. For example, of 92 features recorded with rentals of $1.5 million or more in 1949, Columbia provided seven, including *Jolson Sings Again*, the sequel to *The Jolson Story*, which topped the list. (The most successful movie of 1949 was Cecil B. DeMille's *Samson And Delilah*, but it was released too late in the year to make the 1949 listings.) Others from Columbia included three starring Glenn Ford and two with Humphrey Bogart whose own Santana company released through Columbia. Unfortunately, the remarkable Oscar-winning drama, *All The King's Men* (1949) performed somewhat poorly at the box office with rentals of only $2.4 million – about half those of the Jolson picture.

Fiscal year 1949/50 was the best single year for the company during the difficult period from about mid-1947 to mid-1953. Revenues continued to grow only slowly and profits lagged far behind. The only consolation for Columbia was the fact that the other studios were experiencing similar or worse problems at the same time, and were forced to cut back on their staff and studio operations.

Columbia recovered some of the lost ground during 1953–55, benefiting from a few smash-hits and from production deals with a new generation of successful independent producers characteristic of the new Hollywood – men such as Stanley Kramer, Buddy Adler and Sam Spiegel. But though company profits briefly returned to the peak level of 1946/47, these no longer reflected film production alone, but were boosted by the highly profitable TV production arm, Screen Gems.

Total revenues continued to grow in the late 50s, but profit margins were tighter than ever. However, in contrast to MGM which had its most profitable movies concentrated in the years 1958 and 1959, Columbia at least had the advantage of *its* top hits being spread quite evenly through the 1953–63 period.

The studio suffered heavy losses in the fiscal year 1957/58 in spite of the income from the biggest hit of the decade, *The Bridge On The River Kwai*. (Although profits were impressive – it had only cost $3 million, with US rentals of $15 million and substantial income from abroad – they had to be split with producer Spiegel.)

Sam Spiegel's British productions certainly helped to keep the company alive during a difficult period. Columbia struggled along with only tiny profits throughout the early 60s and up to 1966. A major recovery late that year was sparked off by a series of British-made hits. Though the company had turned down *Dr No* (1962) and *Tom Jones* (1963), both subsequently backed by UA, Columbia had opened its own production office in England in 1965. A contrasting group of

British-made hits included *A Man For All Seasons* (1966), *To Sir With Love* and *Georgy Girl* (both 1967) and *Oliver!* (1968).

By the late 60s the situation had changed once again. With the discarding of the outdated Motion Picture Production Code and the arrival of a talented young generation of directors and stars, American movies gained a new appeal, partly at the expense of the British. The suddenness of the change can be seen particularly clearly at Columbia. Whereas the two big hits of 1968 – *Oliver!* and *Funny Girl* – had been glossy and expensive musical adaptations from veteran directors Sir Carol Reed and William Wyler respectively, the top hits in 1969 were the cheaply made *Easy Rider* and *Bob & Carol & Ted & Alice*. They presented a fresh look at contemporary American society through the eyes of two new young writer-directors, Dennis Hopper and Paul Mazursky, with new stars, too.

In 1970 the company was still breaking even with a few successful youth-oriented pictures such as *Five Easy Pieces* and *Getting Straight*, and *The Owl And The Pussycat*, a Barbra Streisand follow-up to *Funny Girl*. (Both were produced by Ray Stark.) But by 1971–74 the profits of the late 60s had vanished and Columbia found itself in real trouble. Aside from producer Ray Stark and his top star Streisand, who alone were keeping the company afloat with such hits as *The Way We Were* (1973), *For Pete's Sake* (1974) and *Funny Lady* (1975), and Peter Bogdanovich's surprisingly successful *The Last Picture Show* (1971), few of Columbia's pictures even managed to break even. *Cromwell* (1970) and the ill-judged remake of *Lost Horizon* (1973) were the major flops, while a large number of British movies failed badly, including *MacKenna's Gold* in 1969 and *A Severed Head*, *10 Rillington Place*, and *Nicholas And Alexandra*, all in 1971, thus bringing Columbia's British experiment to an abrupt end.

When Alan Hirschfield and David Begelman arrived to manage the company in 1973, the worst was behind them, and profits began to grow once again, aided by such hits as *Shampoo* and *Tommy* (both 1975), followed by *Murder By Death*, another Ray Stark production, and Martin Scorsese's *Taxi Driver* in 1976. But it was not till 1977 that the company was doing really well again and continued to do so under new studio boss Frank Price. Steven Spielberg's *Close Encounters Of The Third Kind* (1977) was the first for Columbia of a new type of spectacularly successful 'super hit' with rentals at over $50 million. Others in that category during the following years included the Oscar-winning *Kramer vs Kramer* (1979), *Tootsie* (1982) starring Dustin Hoffman and directed by Sydney Pollack (who had contributed a number of Columbia hits), also *The Karate Kid* (1984) which only fell slightly short of the $50 million mark, and led to an even more successful sequel, *The Karate Kid: Part II* in 1986, and the amazingly successful *Ghostbusters* directed by Ivan Reitman in 1984.

These movies and a few others helped Columbia to maintain its position as a leading studio for a time in the 80s. Purchased by Coca-Cola in 1982, the studio had been hurt by the departure of Frank Price soon after, but benefited from its partnership with CBS Television and Time-Life's

HBO (Cable TV network) in a new jointly owned production company called Tri-Star Pictures. In 1986 Columbia hired British producer David Puttnam as its new chairman, but he was given only a year and a half on the job before the company was reorganized yet again, and two years later Coca-Cola sold out to Sony. Not surprisingly, with all these changes in management, the studio fared poorly at the box office in the late 80s with only a tiny number of hits including *Ghostbusters II* and *When Harry Met Sally* (both 1989), while Tri-Star contributed *Look Who's Talking* and *Steel Magnolias* in 1989 followed by *Total Recall* (1990), from Carolco which also produced another Arnold Schwarzenegger hit, *Terminator 2: Judgment Day* in 1991.

Aside from its over-dependence on sequels, the studio suffered from the fact that many of its biggest hits were produced by small independent companies such as Carolco or Rob Reiner's Castle Rock – which supplied *When Harry Met Sally*, *Misery* (1990) and *City Slickers* (1991). This meant that any profits would have to be split accordingly. At the same time, during recent years Columbia has been associated with more than its share of spectacular flops including the $55 million *Ishtar* (1985), the Bill Cosby vehicle *Leonard Part 6* (1987) which cost $31 million, Terry Gilliam's *The Adventures of Baron Munchausen* and *Old Gringo* in 1988, Peter Bogdanovich's *Texasville* (1990) and most recently *Hudson Hawk* (1991) starring Bruce Willis.

Box Office Hits

title	(cost)	North American rentals
1932–40	(in million $)	(in million $)
Lost Horizon (1937)	(2.0)	1.5
You Can't Take It With You (1938)		1.5
Mr Smith Goes to Washington (1939)	(1.5)	1.5
Arizona (1940)		1.5
1941–50		
The Jolson Story (1946)	(2.8)	7.6
Jolson Sings Again (1949)		5.0
Born Yesterday (1950)		4.2
1951–60		
The Bridge on the River Kwai (1957)	(2.9)	15.0
From Here to Eternity (1953)	(2.0)	12.2
The Caine Mutiny (1954)	(2.4)	8.7
Suddenly Last Summer (1959)		6.4
Picnic (1955)		6.3
Anatomy of a Murder (1959)		5.5
The Eddie Duchin Story (1955)		5.3
1961–70		
Guess Who's Coming to Dinner? (1967)		25.5
Funny Girl (1968)	(10)	24.9
To Sir, With Love (1967)		19.1
Easy Rider (1969)	(0.4)	16.9
Oliver! (1968)	(10)	16.8
Lawrence of Arabia (1962)	(13)	16.7
Bob & Carol & Ted & Alice (1969)	(2.)	14.6
The Guns of Navarone (1961)	(7.)	13.0
A Man for all Seasons (1966)		12.8
Cactus Flower (1969)		11.9

title	(cost)	North American rentals
1932–40 cont'd	(in million $)	(in million $)
The Owl and the Pussycat (1970)		11.5
Casino Royale (1967)	(10)	10.2
Cat Ballou (1965)		9.3
Five Easy Pieces (1970)		8.9
The Professionals (1966)		8.8
1971–80		
Close Encounters of the Third Kind	(18)	77.0
Kramer vs Kramer (1979)	(8.)	61.7
Stir Crazy (1980)	(8.)	58.4
The Deep (1977)	(15)	31.3
The Electric Horseman (1979) (co-prod.)	(12)	31.3
California Suite (1978)		29.2
The Blue Lagoon (1980)	(8.)	28.5
The China Syndrome (1979)	(9.)	26.1
The Way We Were (1973)		25.0
1941 (1979) (co-prod.)	(27)	23.4
1981–90		
Ghostbusters (1984)	(32)	132.7
Tootsie (1982)	(25)	94.9
Ghostbusters II (1989)	(39)	60.5
The Karate Kid Part II (1986)	(18)	58.3
The Karate Kid (1984)	(9.)	43.1
When Harry Met Sally (1989)	(16)	41.8
Stripes (1981)	(10)	40.9
Annie (1982)	(50)	37.5
Flatliners (1990)	(18)	28.8
Gandhi (1982)	(22)	25.0
The Toy (1982)	(19)	24.4
La Bamba (1987)		24.3
The Big Chill (1983)	(12)	24.1
Misery (1990)		23.0

Tri-Star Pictures – Box Office Hits

1981–90		
Terminator 2: Judgment Day (1991)	(90)	100.0
Rambo: First Blood Part II (1985)	(25)	78.9
Look Who's Talking (1989)	(9.)	68.4
Total Recall (1989)	(50)	65.0
Steel Magnolias (1989)	(22)	40.0
Rambo III (1988)	(58)	28.0
The Natural (1984)	(28)	25.0

The Stars

The studio is best known for its small but select group of female stars ranging from Barbara Stanwyck, at the beginning of her career in the early 30s, up to Barbra Streisand during *her* early years as a star, 1968–75. Along the way there was the delightful Jean Arthur who could not cope with Harry Cohn and retired abruptly in the 40s, the stunning Rita Hayworth who qualified as Harry's greatest star discovery and, in the 50s, a pair of contrasting blondes: the lively, talented Judy Holliday and the beautiful, sultry Kim Novak. Columbia fared less well with its male stars. It had a share of Cary Grant's contract for a time, but its own discoveries did not emerge till after the war, notably with Larry Parks (briefly), Glenn Ford and William Holden. There were, too, the Westerners – including Buck Jones, followed by the long serving Charles Starrett plus Randolph Scott and Gene Autry.

In the early years Columbia had few stars under contract and those were mainly of the second rank. Its leading silent players were Jack Holt, Ralph Graves and Dorothy Revier, who all appeared in Frank Capra's *Submarine* (1928). Holt and Revier were reteamed the following year in the studio's first talkie, *The Donovan Affair*, again directed by Capra. The beautiful Miss Revier failed to make it in the talkies and finished out her contract at Columbia in 1930 paired with Holt for the last time in *Vengeance*, then co-starred with Buck Jones in *The Avengers*. (Later in the 30s she rejoined Buck for a few last Westerns at Universal.) Action star Jack Holt fared somewhat better. Father of RKO star Tim Holt and his actress sister Jennifer, he continued to star in Columbia's many B movies throughout the 30s.

The studio's first major star, Barbara Stanwyck, arrived with sound in 1929. Her early success was closely identified with Capra's emergence as Columbia's leading director during 1929–32 and with Harry Cohn's efforts to upgrade the studio's image. The superb Stanwyck's first starring part was in *Ladies Of Leisure* (filmed in 1929), but in the title role of the female evangelist in *The Miracle Woman* (1931) she demonstrated that she could carry an entire picture on her own. Then, in Capra's unusual and exotic film *The Bitter Tea Of General Yen* (1932), she broadened her range further as the American lady both attracted to and repelled by the ruthless Chinese warlord who holds her captive.

Charles Starrett took over from Buck Jones as the studio's leading B Western star in the mid 30s, and Columbia had a brief success starring singer Grace Moore in a few musicals, but the popularity of the comedies meant that comedy stars dominated the list of contract players. The studio continued to borrow many of the major stars it needed, and they were less reluctant to work at the tiny Columbia after the surprise success of *It Happened One Night* (1934) which gave a further boost to the careers of Claudette Colbert and Clark Gable. Edward G. Robinson was borrowed from Warner Bros. for *The Whole Town's Talking* late in 1934, Gary Cooper from Paramount for *Mr Deeds Goes To Town* in 1935, and James Stewart for Capra's last two features – all co-starred with Columbia's own Jean Arthur. One of the studio's greatest assets for a decade, Miss Arthur unfortunately retired at her peak in 1944, and there was no one to replace her until Judy Holliday appeared six years later.

Jean Arthur was joined by Ralph Bellamy and Melvyn Douglas in the mid 30s, while Irene Dunne spent a few years at the studio and Cary Grant became the top male star under a non-exclusive arrangement whereby his services were shared with RKO. His Columbia earnings in 1941 were $100,000 but, added to his income from RKO and Warner Bros. (where he starred in *Arsenic And Old Lace* for Frank Capra), reached a total of $350,000. In comparison, less busy stars such as Loretta Young and Rosalind Russell were earning $85,000 and $100,000 respectively, at Columbia, around the same time, while Fred Astaire's fee was $150,000 per picture. As the studio's leading star in 1938, Jean Arthur took home $140,000, while the young Rita Hayworth was costing the studio a mere $250 per week.

Harry Cohn always aspired to match the impressive array of stars at the large studios. He finally got his chance as a starmaker in the late 30s when he began grooming Rita Hayworth for stardom, along with William Holden, given his first break as *Golden Boy* (1939), and Glenn Ford. Aside from war service (Ford, Holden) or marriages (Rita), all three remained at Columbia till well into the 50s when the studio was running down. As Ford recalled, 'I was one of Harry's children. There were three of us – Bill Holden, Rita Hayworth and me. He took over our lives, decided what we'd eat, where we'd live, what cars we would drive . . . By some coincidence all our contracts ran out at (about) the same time . . .'

Rita Hayworth was the biggest name of the three and Cohn's most major discovery, but she starred in the fewest pictures and reached her peak during the war years 1944–46 when she was a favourite pin-up girl of the soldiers abroad. None of her later movies was as popular as *Cover Girl* (1944) and *Gilda* (1946), nor as bizarre as *The Lady From Shanghai* directed by her then husband, Orson Welles, late in 1946 but not released till early 1948. Thus, she was the only 40s superstar to feature in both Technicolored musicals and *film noir* thrillers.

Glenn Ford co-starred with her very effectively in *Gilda*, but was disastrously miscast (as Don José) in *The Loves Of Carmen* (1948). He joined her again in her comeback picture, after a gap of four years when she was married to Prince Aly Khan. The movie, *Affair In Trinidad* (1952), was not very satisfactory. A generally under-rated actor, Ford appeared in a wide range of movies for Columbia – Westerns, comedies and thrillers – but never had the same degree of success as Holden, whose career paralleled his own. Admittedly, Holden's contract was shared with Paramount where he made many of his best pictures. He was the only Columbia star to feature prominently on the Quigley Publications' exhibitors poll of top box-office stars. Included among the top ten for every year from 1954 through 1958, he attained the number one spot in 1956 between his two biggest hits at Columbia, *Picnic* (1955) and *The Bridge On The River Kwai* (1957). (Ford only began appearing on the list in the late 50s after he had left Columbia for MGM and he reached number one in 1958, ahead of Elizabeth Taylor, Jerry Lewis and even Marlon Brando).

A large number of other new stars surfaced at Columbia in the early 40s. The young Janet Blair had her first big success as *My Sister Eileen* (1942), co-starred with Rosalind Russell who became typecast as the studio's resident 'career woman'. Russell claims that she was given the same office set in most of her Columbia features along with the same cameraman, Joe Walker, and the same propman, named Blackie. 'Those parts went on and on. I played 23 different career women.'

Evelyn Keyes, however, was given a wider range of 'feminine' starring roles. Married for a time to Columbia director Charles Vidor, she is best remembered for her likeable performances in *Here Comes Mr Jordan* (1941) and *The Jolson Story* (1946). Brilliant tap dancer Ann Miller made a lively contribution to many of the studio's musicals in the 40s before she departed for greater glory at MGM. Having played in a variety of movies at the studio in the 40s, Larry Parks suddenly shot to stardom in *The Jolson Story*, then just as quickly disappeared from Hollywood after the successful sequel three years later, a left-wing victim of the HUAC investigations into communism in the early 50s. Anita Louise, who had started out as a child star in the silents, also landed at Columbia in the 40s. (Harry Cohn once rather cruelly remarked, 'We get them going up and coming down.') In her last role of note she played the beautiful blonde Lady Catherine in *Bandit Of Sherwood Forest* (1946) opposite Cornel Wilde, who briefly qualified as the studio's top Technicolor star with the popular biopic of Chopin, *A Song To Remember*, and *A Thousand And One Nights* (both 1945).

For Columbia's new style of glossy and lightweight Technicolored movies, padded out with lots of attractive chorus girls, Harry Cohn recruited a new selection of starlets to the studio including Jinx Falkenburg, Adele Jergens and Shelley Winters. In her entertaining autobiography Shelley describes how she was given the standard studio treatment by head of casting Max Arnow (exactly as it is portrayed on the screen in both the 1937 and 1954 versions of *A Star Is Born*). She was horrified by his professional assessment of her looks: 'The hair's too dark blonde and kinky, but we can straighten and bleach it. Forehead too low; we'll take care of that with electrolysis. Eyes slant the wrong way, eyelashes should take care of that. Nose too wide; we may have to operate . . .' 'Like hell you will.' He ignored me. 'Lips too thin; make-up will take care of that. Teeth crooked, caps needed. Shoulders too broad, bosom too flat, waist not narrow enough, hips too wide, legs knock-kneed, wobbly walk, and speech work needed.' Then make-up expert Fred Phillips went to work on her: 'I looked into the mirror, and a gorgeous platinum blonde stared back. It wasn't me, but she sure as hell looked sensational.'

Miss Winters was cast as a Windmill girl in *Tonight And Every Night* in 1944 and was promoted to one of six harem girls in *A Thousand And One Nights*. Since it was obvious that the studio did not know what to do with her and had no plans to give her better parts, she left soon after. (She fetched up at Universal where she was similarly treated and the dreadful roles far outnumbered the good ones.)

Character actor George Macready was the studio's resident 'heavy' and made an appropriately sinister contribution to *Gilda*. Randolph Scott starred in so many Westerns that he made it onto the list of top box-office stars in the early 50s. Humphrey Bogart and John Derek (in his first starring role) appeared in the 'noirish' social drama, *Knock On Any Door*, directed by Nicholas Ray, the first production from Bogart's newly formed, independent company, Santana, in 1948. Bogart continued to work (as an independent star) at Columbia for a number of years where his most memorable role was as the disturbed scriptwriter of *In A Lonely Place* (1950), again directed by Ray for Santana with Gloria Grahame co-starring.

The heavy-set, middle-aged Broderick Crawford suddenly emerged as a new, if unlikely, star at Columbia in 1949 and made his name in two roles that bore a distinct resemblance to Harry Cohn – as the charismatic but power-hungry Southern politician in *All The King's Men* (1949) and the uncouth but wealthy ex-junk dealer in *Born Yesterday* (1950), co-starred with the unique and delightful Judy Holliday. The resemblance to Cohn suggested by the character's name, Harry Brock, was not entirely accidental – according to writer Garson Kanin who had had many dealings with Cohn over the years. Kanin had co-scripted *The More The Merrier* (1943) for Jean Arthur and had written the original play *Born Yesterday* for her as well. When Holliday was brought in as a last minute replacement, she made the role her own. Her performance in the movie version, directed by George Cukor, brought back memories of the 30s when the studio had done so well with its comedies, and her other pictures at Columbia in the 50s helped to brighten a difficult period for the studio. Tragically, Miss Holliday died of cancer at the age of 43, but her comedies paved the way for new stars like Jack Lemmon and Kim Novak who appeared with her in *Phfft* (1954) and were themselves co-starred a few years later in *Bell, Book And Candle* (1958) and *The Notorious Landlady* (1962).

Columbia's most successful star of later years was Barbra Streisand, many of whose films were produced by Ray Stark beginning with *Funny Girl* in (1968).

STARS

Arlen, Richard 1936–37
Arthur, Jean 1933–36, 1938–40, 1942–44
Astor, Mary 1936
Autry, Gene 1947–53
Ball, Lucille 1934, 1949–51
Bartholomew, Freddie 1941
Baxter, Warner 1943–49
Bellamy, Ralph 1934–39
Bickford, Charles 1931–32
Blair, Janet 1941–46, 1948
Bogart, Humphrey (Santana) 1948–51
Borgnine, Ernest 1951–53
Brando, Marlon 1953–54
Britton, Barbara 1946–49
Brown, Joe E. 1938–41
Brynner, Yul 1960
Canova, Judy 1944–46
Carroll, Nancy 1934–35
Chadwick, Helene 1927–28
Chapman, Marguerite 1942–48
Cochran, Steve 1945
Conte, Richard 1956–60
Crabbe, Buster 1947, 1950–52
Crawford, Broderick 1949–52
Crawford, Joan 1955–57
Cummings, Constance 1931–32
Davis, Joan 1943–44
Denny, Reginald 1936–37
Derek, John 1948–53
Dix, Richard 1936–37, 1944–46
Douglas, Melvyn 1936–41
Drew, Ellen 1946–48
Dunne, Irene 1936–37, 1944
Farrell, Glenda 1942–44
Foch, Nina 1943–49
Ford, Glenn 1939–43, 1945–50, 1953–54
Grahame, Gloria 1953–54
Grant, Cary 1936–44
Graves, Ralph 1927–32
Haines, William 1925
Hale, Barbara 1949–52
Hammerstein, Elaine 1924–25
Haymes, Dick 1952–53

Hayworth, Rita 1937–48, 1951–53, 1956–59
Heflin, Van 1957–59
Hodiak, John 1953
Holden, William 1939–42, 1947–57
Holliday, Judy 1950–56
Holt, Jack 1927–41
Jones, Buck 1930–34, 1937–38
Jory, Victor 1934–36
Karloff, Boris 1940–41
Keaton, Buster 1939–41
Keyes, Evelyn 1940–50
Kovacs, Ernie 1957–61
Ladd, Alan (Warwick) 1953–54
Lake, Arthur 1938–50
Lemmon, Jack 1953–61, 1963
Lewis, Jerry 1966–68
Lindsay, Margaret 1940–43
Louise, Anita 1940–47
Macready, George 1944–47, 1949–50
Malone, Dorothy 1949–50
Marvin, Lee 1952–54, 1965–66
Mason, James 1964–69
Maynard, Ken 1935–36
McCoy, Tim 1931–35
Miller, Ann 1941–45
Mitchell, Thomas 1936–37, 1939
Montgomery, George 1951–55
Moore, Grace 1934–37
Morley, Karen 1946–47
Morris, Chester 1936–37, 1941–48
Morris, Wayne 1950
Muni, Paul 1944–45
Murphy, George 1934–35
Nolan, Lloyd 1935–36
Novak, Kim 1954–61
O'Brien, Pat 1932, 1940–42
Paige, Robert 1938–39
Parks, Larry 1941–50
Poitier, Sidney 1958–60
Power, Tyrone 1954–56
Quinn, Anthony 1951, 1961–62
Reed, Donna 1951–54, 1957–58
Revier, Dorothy 1925–30

Robertson, Cliff 1955, 1958–61
Russell, Rosalind 1942–46, 1949
Scott, Randolph 1949–57,
    (Ranown) 1957–59
Sondergaard, Gale 1942–43
Sothern, Ann 1934–36
Stanwyck, Barbara 1929–32
Starrett, Charles 1935–52
Steiger, Rod 1954–56
Stewart, James 1959–60

Totter, Audrey 1953
Trevor, Claire 1941–43
Wayne, John 1931
Weissmuller, Johnny 1948–55
Wilde, Cornel 1944–45
Willes, Jean 1949–52, 1954–55
William, Warren 1939–42
Winters, Shelley 1943–45
Wray, Fay 1933, 1936–37
Young, Loretta 1940–42

The Directors

Throughout its history Columbia had relatively few
leading directors under contract. Frank Capra was the
studio's star director in the 30s and independent director
Howard Hawks contributed four pictures of note, while
George Stevens was under contract in the early 40s.
Otherwise the studio depended on freelancers or loans
from other studios and was particularly fortunate in
this respect. At one time or another many top directors
including John Ford, George Cukor, Fritz Lang, Robert
Rossen, Fred Zinnemann and Elia Kazan worked for
Columbia on A pictures of note. During more recent years
British director David Lean contributed a memorable pair
of Oscar-winning hits – *The Bridge On The River Kwai*
and *Lawrence Of Arabia*, while Sydney Pollack directed a
number of popular movies in the 70s and early 80s.

Columbia had few top directors of its own during the early years, and
that situation hardly improved in the 40s and 50s when the studio grew
larger and more successful. However, the company was fortunate in
being able to borrow suitable directors or to sign them for one or two-
picture deals. The list of directors who spent some time at Columbia is
long and impressive, and the studio was doubly fortunate in that the visit-
ing man's only production often turned out to be particularly interesting
or successful. Examples include John Ford's *The Whole Town's Talking*
(1935), Leo McCarey's *The Awful Truth* (1937), Rouben Mamoulian's
Golden Boy (1939), Welles' *The Lady From Shanghai* (1948), Kazan's
On The Waterfront (1954) and Kubrick's *Dr Strangelove* (1963).

Indubitably, the studio's most important director was Frank Capra,
who arrived late in 1927. He began by turning out cheap but entertaining
comedies, then graduated to A features and soon established himself
as the top director, a position he held for the next 10 years. He first
emerged as a major talent in 1932 with the atmospheric *The Bitter Tea
Of General Yen*, and a topical Depression drama, *American Madness*.
His biggest success came with two comedies, *Lady For A Day* (1933)
and the Oscar-winning *It Happened One Night* (1934), thus initiating

Columbia's highly successful cycle of sophisticated comedies which flourished until the early 40s. Capra continued his string of hits with the highly acclaimed *Mr Deeds Goes To Town* (1936), *Lost Horizon* (1937), *You Can't Take It With You* (1938) and *Mr Smith Goes To Washington* (1939). By the time he left in 1939 he had made an invaluable contribution in raising the general standard at Columbia and earning prestige and respect for the studio.

The importance of independent director Howard Hawks is less well recognized, perhaps because his four pictures at Columbia in the 30s were a diverse group, separated by long gaps when he was working elsewhere. But each was a winner, beginning with *The Criminal Code* (1930) starring Walter Huston – probably the studio's best early sound film and its only important entry in the early 30s gangster cycle, as well as the first Columbia movie to be nominated for an Oscar (Best Screenplay). The hilarious screwball comedy *Twentieth Century* (1934), with Carole Lombard and John Barrymore, was released shortly after, and was even more outrageously crazy than *It Happened One Night*. Having helped to launch the cycle, Hawks capped it six years later with the real masterpiece of the genre, *His Girl Friday* (1940), his second in a row at Columbia with Cary Grant. Though *Only Angels Have Wings* (1939) was more of a serious action drama, reflecting Hawks' special talent for balancing drama and comedy, both films were notable for their Hawksian heroines, emancipated and outspoken, played by Rosalind Russell and Jean Arthur respectively.

Wary of Harry Cohn – 'I've heard that unpleasant things happen to directors at Columbia' – George Stevens agreed to make three films only when his contract guaranteed that he would not have to have any contact with Cohn. Best of the three was *The More The Merrier* (1943) with Jean Arthur. Most of the studio's contract directors in the 40s were less well known: men like Henry Levin, Alfred E. Green, action director Joseph H. Lewis, comedy specialist Alexander Hall who directed *Here Comes Mr Jordan* (1941), and Hungarian-born Charles Vidor who handled most of Rita Hayworth's starring vehicles during her peak years, 1943–48.

The pattern continued – of outstanding results from directors whose stay was brief but effective. Robert Rossen made the Oscar-winning *All The King's Men* (1949); George Cukor delivered three entertaining movies starring Judy Holliday, including *Born Yesterday* (1950); Fred Zinnemann contributed the sensitively directed *The Member Of The Wedding* (1952) and the highly successful *From Here To Eternity* (1953); and Fritz Lang offered a pair of tough thrillers teaming Glenn Ford with Gloria Grahame, *The Big Heat* (1953) and *Human Desire* (1954). Otto Preminger had a big hit with *Anatomy Of A Murder* (1959), as did Joseph Mankiewicz with Tennessee Williams' *Suddenly, Last Summer* (1959). But the biggest contribution made by a director around this time came from David Lean who, in partnership with producer Sam Spiegel, made *The Bridge On The River Kwai* (1957) and *Lawrence Of Arabia* (1962).

Veteran director John Huston showed a remarkable return to form in the early 70s which included two pictures for Columbia, the gritty *Fat City* (1972) and an adaptation of Kipling's offbeat adventure story, *The*

Man Who Would Be King (1975). Steven Spielberg gave a great boost to the studio's balance sheet with his popular and imaginative *Close Encounters Of The Third Kind* in 1977, but the most consistently successful Columbia director during recent years has been Sydney Pollack who has provided such hits as *The Way We Were* (1973), *The Electric Horseman* (1979), *Absence Of Malice* (1981), and *Tootsie* (1982) starring Dustin Hoffman, a comedy in the true Columbia tradition.

DIRECTORS

Aldrich, Robert 1955–56
Archainbaud, George 1929, 1952–53
Bacon, Lloyd 1949–50
Barton, Charles 1939–44
Boetticher, Budd 1944–45, 1957–60
Brahm, John 1937–40
Buzzell, Edward 1932–33, 1950
Capra, Frank 1927–39
Castle, William 1944–47, 1953–56, 1959–63
Cummings, Irving 1932, 1943–44
De Toth, André 1943–44
Dmytryk, Edward 1941–42, 1952–54
Douglas, Gordon 1948–50
Edwards, Blake 1951–56
English, John 1947–51
Fleischer, Richard 1971–72
Florey, Robert 1941
Foster, Norman 1949–50
Fuller, Samuel 1959–60
Gering, Marion 1936–38
Gordon, Michael 1943
Green, Alfred E. 1936–37, 1942–46
Hall, Alexander 1938–42, 1944–47
Hawks, Howard 1938–39
Karlson, Phil 1948, 1951–58
Kenton, Erle C. 1928–31, 1935–37
Kramer, Stanley 1965–67, 1970–73
Lachman, Harry 1936–38
Landers, Lew 1941–45, 1949–52

Lang, Fritz 1953–54
Lang, Walter 1927
Lederman, D. Ross 1931–34, 1936–38, 1940, 1945–48
Levin, Henry 1944–51
Lewis, Joseph H. 1939–40, 1946–49
Lloyd, Frank 1940–41
Mann, Daniel 1959–62
Maté, Rudolph 1947–48
Mazursky, Paul 1982–84
Nazarro, Ray 1945–52
Neill, Roy William 1930–36
Pollack, Sydney 1977–82
Quine, Richard 1948, 1951–60
Rafelson, Bob (BBS) 1968–72
Ratoff, Gregory 1940–43
Ray, Nicholas 1948–49
Rogell, Albert 1929, 1933–38
Rossen, Robert 1947, 1949–51
Ruggles, Wesley 1940–41
Salkow, Sidney 1940–43, 1947, 1952–53
Schertzinger, Victor 1933–36
Schoedsack, Ernest 1937
Sears, Fred 1949–58
Sherman, George 1945–48
Sidney, George 1956–63
Simon, S. Sylvan 1946–49
Sirk, Douglas 1948
Sternberg, Josef von 1935–36
Stevens, George 1940–42
Sturges, John 1946–49
Vidor, Charles 1939–41, 1943–48
Wallace, Richard 1942–43
Zinnemann, Fred 1952–53

The Creative Personnel

The studio's leading cameraman for many years was Joe Walker; he was joined by Burnett Guffey and Charles Lawton Jr in the 40s. Similarly, the art department, headed by Stephen Goosson, grew in size as Columbia increased its production of A features. Many of the studio's most successful pictures reflected the important contribution made by its many fine writers, including Robert Riskin (Capra's regular collaborator), and Sidney Buchman and Virginia Van Upp who graduated from writing to become executive producers. In addition, Columbia had two outstanding costume designers under contract – Robert Kalloch in the 30s and the famous Jean Louis in later years – who provided the movies they worked on with some much-appreciated glamour in selective productions.

Cameramen and Art Directors

As a tiny studio producing only a few A-feature pictures for most of its early years, Columbia had little need for the kind of extensive technical departments found at the major studios. Quite early on, Harry Cohn assembled a small but efficient team of film technicians headed by cameraman Joe Walker and supervising art director Stephen Goosson.

Joe Walker worked on many important productions, specializing in comedies and lighter pictures ranging from early Capra silents up to the Judy Holliday films in the early 50s. He was Oscar-nominated for his only Technicolor movie, *The Jolson Story* (1946), and it was fitting that he should have participated in what proved to be the studio's biggest 40s hit.

Other cameramen generally handled Columbia's darker pictures. The great James Wong Howe contributed to the gritty look of *The Criminal Code* (1930) and joked about the fact that he was nicknamed 'Low-Key Howe', while Joe August photographed *Man's Castle* (1933), the bittersweet Depression drama, for director Frank Borzage, and John Ford's *The Whole Town's Talking* in 1934.

Lucien Ballard was at Columbia when it was still a tiny studio, and recalls that he '. . . had a 40-week contract, with a twelve-week layoff. So as soon as my 40 weeks were up, I'd go across the street and shoot comedies with the short-subject unit. It was a great experience.' Only at Columbia could one have found a lighting cameraman engaged in photographing such major features as *Crime And Punishment* (1935) and *Craig's Wife* (1936) while, at the same time, doubling on comedy shorts.

When the studio began producing more A pictures and its first in Technicolor in the 40s, an important new group of cameramen was hired. The experienced Rudolph Maté served for a time as Rita Hayworth's favourite photographer, beginning with *Cover Girl* in 1943 which earned him an Oscar nomination, and including the stylish *Gilda* (1946). At about the same time Burnett Guffey first established himself as a master of black-and-white cinematography, and was assigned to many of the studio's most interesting *films noirs* from *My Name Is Julia Ross* (1945) and *Johnny O'Clock* (1947) to *The Reckless Moment* (1949) and a pair of Nicholas Ray-Humphrey Bogart films, as well as *All The King's Men* (1949), and *From Here To Eternity* (1953), which won him an Oscar. Last of the 40s arrivals of note was Charles Lawton Jr who developed into the studio's leading photographer of Westerns and outdoorsy subjects, collaborating with directors Delmer Daves and Budd Boetticher in particular, but also shooting many comedies and musicals for Richard Quine. He, like Guffey, remained with Columbia till well into the 60s.

Leading art director Stephen Goosson arrived in 1931 and was soon working with Capra on *American Madness* (1932) which had a spacious bank as its main setting. As critic Elliott Stein noted, 'The decor is an art deco Temple of Mammon – a super set cathedral – forest of grilles, clocks and columns: one of the most beautifully designed and lit films of the 30s'. Goosson's elaborate futuristic designs for Capra's *Lost Horizon* were too coldly impersonal and inappropriate, but nonetheless impressive enough to win him an Oscar. He remained at Columbia long enough to benefit from the general upgrading of the studio's output in the 40s, contributing to two of the most striking productions, *Gilda* (1946), and *The Lady From Shanghai* (1948) with its amazing fairground denouement.

The studio hired a number of new art directors in the 40s. Cary Odell and Rudolph Sternad divided most of the prestige productions between them for about 10 years till the mid-50s, when Sternad left to continue working for independent producer-director Stanley Kramer (who had previously released many of his films through Columbia). Robert Peterson, the third important new arrival, generally concentrated on the tougher and less glamorous black-and-white movies. Peterson fitted in superbly at Columbia with its tradition of low-cost but effective pictures. For over 20 years he lent his special talents to creating realistic settings – some sleazy, some sinister – for such movies as *The Big Heat* (1953) and *Human Desire* (1954), and Sam Fuller's *Underworld USA* (1961).

Other Departments

In spite of his tyrannical and unpredictable behaviour, Harry Cohn inspired loyalty in many of his studio employees and he in turn was loyal to them and appreciated their contribution to the success of his pictures. From the early 30s Columbia had many fine scriptwriters under contract, reflecting Cohn's own respect for writers and his acknowledgement of their value, especially to the comedies. Robert Riskin was Capra's regular collaborator, while Sidney Buchman, who scripted *Theodora Goes Wild* (1936), *Mr Smith Goes To Washington* (1939) and *Here Comes Mr Jordan* (1941) among others, was appointed assistant head of production in the early 40s. He functioned as Cohn's right hand man for many years till he was blacklisted and forced to resign in 1951. (Since Harry never concerned himself with the politics of those he employed, Columbia was hit particularly hard by the blacklist. Writers like John Howard Lawson and Carl Foreman were the prime targets; Foreman's name was carefully left off the credits of *The Bridge On The River Kwai* in 1957, but he was able to restart his career as a successful writer-producer for Columbia in England in the 60s.) Writer Virginia Van Upp worked on many of the Rita Hayworth movies, most notably *Cover Girl* (1944) and *Gilda* (1946), and was upgraded to producer status. She was even put in charge of running the studio under Cohn for a while, a unique position for a woman to hold in Hollywood at that time.

In such areas as sound recording, scoring and costume design Columbia was fortunate in being able to sign up a few key personnel who headed their respective departments for many years. John Livadary, an electrical engineer, sound expert and musician, arrived in 1930 and soon established himself as the head of the sound department, a post he was to hold for almost 30 years. Nominated innumerable times, he won not only Oscars, but special scientific awards from the Academy for his many technical innovations.

The distinguished musician Morris Stoloff was at the studio almost as long, was nominated many times and won Oscars for his scoring of *Cover Girl* (1944) and *The Jolson Story* (1946). He was still doing occasional pictures for Columbia in the early 60s, winning a last award for co-scoring *Song Without End* (1960) and serving as music director (without screen credit) on *Lawrence Of Arabia* (1962) with its Oscar-winning score by Maurice Jarre. In the mid-40s Stoloff was joined by Mischa Bakaleinikoff and George Duning who often collaborated closely with him and also stayed on till the early 60s.

Just two men were the stars of the studio's costume department from the early 30s till the late 50s (with a brief gap in the early 40s). Robert Kalloch designed the costumes during the peak comedy years and occasionally had a bit of fun with them. Most memorable of all is the image of Irene Dunne in *The Awful Truth* (1937), trying to preserve her dignity in a pair of lounging pyjamas which are at least a foot too long and a housecoat with a striking pattern of giant, op-art diamonds which appear to have a life of their own. Jean Louis arrived in 1944 and began designing for Rita Hayworth, most notably for *Gilda* (1946), featuring the famous strapless black satin gown and elbow-length gloves for the 'Put the Blame on Mame' number. He remained at Columbia till the late 50s designing costumes for all the studio's leading ladies.

Of all the leading technical personnel at Columbia, the editors lasted the longest. Gene Havlick, Viola Lawrence, William Lyon and Al Clark all spent upwards of 30 years at the studio. In his autobiography the editor (and later director) Robert Parrish gives a fascinating behind-the-scenes account of the problems which he and Al Clark faced in attempting to edit the many hours of remarkable footage filmed by Robert Rossen on *All The King's Men* (1949) – problems which they never did manage to solve satisfactorily. Nonetheless, the final result was a memorable, Oscar-winning picture.

CAMERAMEN

August, Joseph 1932–35
Ballard, Lucien 1935–39
Gaudio, Tony 1945–46
Guffey, Burnett 1944–66
Lawton, Charles, Jr. 1945–62

Maté, Rudolph 1943–47
McCord, Ted 1930
Planer, Franz 1938–45, 1949–50
Tetzlaff, Ted 1928–33
Walker, Joseph 1927–52

ART DIRECTORS

Banks, Lionel 1934, 1937–44
Boyle, Robert 1957–59
Goosson, Stephen 1931–40, 1944–48
Jewell, Edward C. 1930, 1943–45
Kirk, Charles M. 1928
Meehan, John 1951–53

Odell, Cary 1941–62
Peterson, Robert 1940–47, 1948–64
Polglase, Van Nest 1943–46
Remisoff, Nicolai 1943
Sternad, Rudolph 1940–53
Wiley, Harrison 1928–30
Wright, Joseph C. 1928.

COSTUME DESIGNERS

Banton, Travis 1943–44
Irene 1941–42
Kalloch, Robert 1932–40

Louis, Jean 1944–58
Mabry, Moss 1965–66, 1968–73
Travilla, William 1941–43

COMPOSERS AND MUSIC DIRECTORS

Antheil, George 1949–50
Bakaleinikoff, Mischa 1944–60
Duning, George 1945–61
Hollander, Frederick 1941
Raksin, David 1943

Roemheld, Heinz 1949–50
Silvers, Louis 1934–35
Skiles, Marlin 1944–48
Stoloff, Morris 1936–53
Tiomkin, Dimitri 1937–39

EDITORS

Bryant, Edwin 1951–63
Caldwell, Dwight 1936–41
Clark, Al 1934–62
Fantl, Dick 1936–50
Havlick, Gene 1929–57
Hilton, Arthur 1933–36
Lawrence, Viola 1931–60
Lyon, William 1936–66

Meyer, Otto 1933–45
Milford, Gene 1929–40
Nelson, Charles 1942–67
Stell, Aaron 1943–54
Sweeney, James 1936–50
Thoms, Jerome 1943–62
Wright, Maurice 1929–33

SCRIPTWRITERS

Anhalt, Edward 1947–52
Buchman, Sidney 1934–51
Foreman, Carl 1957–63
Kanin, Garson 1950–53
Nugent, Frank 1957–60
Paxton, John 1954–57

Riskin, Robert 1932–38
Swerling, Jo 1930–36
Taradash, Daniel 1952–58
Tashlin, Frank 1947–50
Van Upp, Virginia 1944–52

The Academy Awards

Columbia and its leading director, Frank Capra, had their first big Oscar success with *It Happened One Night* in 1934 and this gave a great boost to the tiny studio. Six of Capra's productions were nominated for Best Picture in the 30s, with two winners. (*You Can't Take It With You*, 1938, was the second.) Unfortunately, Columbia won few awards in the 40s after Capra's departure. However, the company continued to grow and prosper and was the most successful of all the studios during the 1949–57 years with four Best Picture winners and numerous other awards in the four main categories. In the 60s Columbia fared best with its British productions, notably *Lawrence Of Arabia* (1962) and *A Man For All Seasons* (1966), and has had one major success in recent years with the 1979 *Kramer vs Kramer*.

The big surprise at the Academy Awards ceremony for 1934 was the fact that, for the first time, Columbia walked off with the top honours. It is impossible to overestimate the significance of this event for the tiny studio. In fact, *It Happened One Night* was the first ever picture to 'sweep the board', winning the Oscar not only for the Best Picture, but also for its two leads, its director and its script. This marked an important turning point for the studio and for director Frank Capra, and demonstrated that there could be a positive side to all the hoopla associated with the awards ceremony. But the Academy was not merely being indulgent, for the movie was unquestionably the best of the dozen nominees.

Columbia had gained its first-ever nomination a few years earlier for the script of Howard Hawks' excellent gangster movie, *The Criminal Code* (1930), followed by a nomination in 1931/32 for *Mickey's Orphans*, one of the last of the Walt Disney cartoons distributed by the studio. (Ironically, it lost out to another Disney cartoon and his first in Technicolor, the imaginative *Flowers And Trees* distributed by United Artists which had replaced Columbia as the regular Disney distributor.) The following year (1932/33) Frank Capra's *Lady For A Day* gained four Oscar nominations including Best Picture and director. When the presenter exclaimed, 'Come and get it, Frank', Capra suffered the embarrassment of heading toward the stage before he realized that the winner was Frank Lloyd for his version of Noel Coward's *Cavalcade*.

In fact, Capra ended up as the Academy's most honoured director of the decade with three statuettes, for *It Happened One Night, Mr Deeds Goes To Town* (1936) and *You Can't Take It With You* (1938). He served for four years as Academy president, and had two winning pictures – *You Can't Take It With You* was the second – out of six nominated for Best Picture. His productions accounted for all of Columbia's major awards, including that of the New York Film Critics for *Mr Deeds Goes To Town*, with the single exception of Leo McCarey's Oscar for directing *The Awful Truth* (1937).

The studio performed relatively poorly in the 40s after the departure of Capra. It gained many nominations but few statuettes for the last entries in its cycle of popular comedy features which was just coming to an end during 1940–43. *Here Comes Mr Jordan* (1941), for example, received seven nominations, but the writers of the original story and script were the only winners. *The Talk Of The Town* (1942) also had seven nominations, mainly in the technical categories, while Rosalind Russell was nominated for her performance in *My Sister Eileen* that same year. Supporting actor Charles Coburn won for his crotchety but likeable old gent in *The More The Merrier* (1943), while director George Stevens was nominated but had to be satisfied with the New York Critics Award.

Strangely, from 1944 to 1948, Columbia was even less successful with the Oscars, yet this was the period when it was doing better financially than ever before in its history and had some of its biggest hits. At least the nominations drew attention to the contributions made by many of the studio's important and long-serving technical personnel such as composer Morris Stoloff and sound expert John Livadary; cameramen Joe Walker and Rudolph Maté; art directors Lionel Banks, Stephen Goosson, Cary Odell and Rudolph Sternad; and Jules White, producer and director of many of the studio's comedy shorts.

Harry Cohn's last years, 1949–57, marked a new maturity and prestige for the company that had struggled for so long to achieve major studio status. This was reflected in its awards success. During this nine-year period Columbia productions won the Best Picture Oscar four times along with other major awards. First off was *All The King's Men* (1949) from producer-director Robert Rossen; it also took the New York Critics Award, while its star Broderick Crawford became the only Columbia contract actor to win the Best Actor Oscar (and the New York Critics Award). The following year Judy Holliday was voted Best Actress for her role in *Born Yesterday* – the studio's only contract actress to win this honour. (Claudette Colbert won in 1934, on loan from Paramount, and the freelancing Katharine Hepburn won for *Guess Who's Coming To Dinner* in 1967.)

Memorable performances from Fredric March in *Death Of A Salesman* (1951) and Julie Harris as *The Member Of The Wedding* (1952) each gained a well-deserved nomination. Then, for two years running, the studio came up with Oscar-winning pictures which were among the most successful in the history of the Academy Awards. *From Here To Eternity* (1953) and *On The Waterfront* (1954) garnered eight Oscars each including Best Picture, director (Fred Zinnemann and Elia Kazan respectively), screenplay, cinematography and other technical and acting awards. *From Here To Eternity* is remembered for some unusual casting, with Montgomery Clift as the tough boxer who refuses to fight, Deborah Kerr as the captain's adulterous wife, Columbia contract star Donna Reed as the classy prostitute and Frank Sinatra as the vulnerable loser Maggio, while Burt Lancaster – more obvious – was the tough but sympathetic sergeant. All five were nominated, with Sinatra and Miss Reed winning. Similarly, *On The Waterfront* gained five acting nominations with two winners – Marlon Brando and Eva Marie Saint.

When Columbia won yet again in 1957 with *The Bridge On The River Kwai*, this was the first of the studio's many successes with its British productions during the next dozen years. *The Bridge On The River Kwai* (like *Lawrence Of Arabia* five years later) won seven awards, mainly in the technical categories, along with Best Picture and director (David Lean) and Best Actor (Alec Guinness).

In 1966 director Zinnemann brought home another success for Columbia with the all-British cast and crew of *A Man For All Seasons*. The picture won six Oscars in all, including Best Actor to Paul Scofield in the role of Sir Thomas More which he had created on the stage. Two years later another of Columbia's British productions, *Oliver!*, also won Oscars for Best Picture and director (the veteran Carol Reed) as well as four technical awards. And in the 80s Columbia distributed two British-produced winners of the top Oscar, *Gandhi* (1982) and *The Last Emperor* (1987).

The studio's main award successes from American-made films during the past 25 years have been Barbra Streisand's Oscar for her performance as Fanny Brice in *Funny Girl* (1968), the New York Film Critics awards to *Five Easy Pieces* (1970) (for Best Picture, director Bob Rafelson and supporting actress, Karen Black) and *Kramer vs Kramer* (1979), which won Oscars and New York Critics Awards for picture, actor Dustin Hoffman and supporting actress Meryl Streep, with a pair of statuettes for writer-director Robert Benton. Finally, Kathy Bates was a surprise choice as best actress for her eccentric role in the offbeat Rob Reiner movie, *Misery*, in 1990.

FOX

William Fox, the founder and owner, controlled the company throughout the early years – up to 1930. He was the only nickelodeon pioneer who was also an innovator in sound film, with his Fox Movietone. The merger with 20th Century in 1935 led to a new production chief, Darryl F. Zanuck, who dominated the studio for virtually 35 years. He hired and marketed such stars as Tyrone Power and Betty Grable in the 40s and Marilyn Monroe in the 50s, and succeeded in balancing popular colour movies with more serious black-and-white fare from the studio's leading directors – men such as John Ford, Elia Kazan and Joseph Mankiewicz. The studio promoted glossy CinemaScope productions in the 50s and 70mm blockbusters in the 60s. Since 1960, Fox has been on a dizzy course of smash hits and correspondingly disastrous flops.

The career of William Fox, one of the pioneering moguls of the early American film industry, parallels that of Carl Laemmle, the founder of Universal. Fox began by operating a penny arcade, then opened his first nickelodeon in New York in 1904, about two years before Laemmle did the same in Chicago. Both men were soon running their own chain of nickelodeons, expanding their operations as far as they could and devising imaginative ways to advertise their picture shows. Fox graduated from small, converted shop premises to the purpose-built construction of elaborate 'picture palaces' which began to attract a better class of clientele, at about the same time that the quality of his pictures was also improving. Again like Laemmle, Fox soon branched out into film distribution. (His new company was called the Greater New York Film Rental Company.) As ambitious and independent-minded entrepreneurs, neither Fox nor Laemmle was willing to kowtow to the demands of the newly formed (1908) and monopolistic Motion Picture Patents Company. They led the fight against the Trust, which was finally resolved (in their favour) in 1913.

In the meantime both men continued to expand their businesses and both made the move into producing their own pictures. In 1914 Fox started a new company with the unwieldy title of the Box Office Attractions Film Rental Company. His first short feature, *Life's Shop Window*, was a success. Produced at a cost of $6,000, it starred Clare Whitney and Stuart Holmes and was directed by Henry Behlmer. The production company operated on a shoestring basis initially. Fox was assisted by Winfield Sheehan, who had joined him a few years earlier during the fight with the Trust, while Fox's wife, Eve Leo, served as both title writer and story department.

Fox's first star discoveries in 1915 were William Farnum and the legendary Theda Bara, whose box-office sex appeal contributed greatly to the rapid growth of the company in the following years. Starting out with a small studio on Staten Island, then moving to New York, by 1916 the newly renamed Fox Film Corporation, was ready to follow Jesse Lasky, Laemmle and others to California. One immediate result of the move was a marked increase in Western programmers, and the company acquired the flamboyant Tom Mix in 1917 and the talented Buck Jones soon after.

As early as 1915 William Fox had signed up an interesting group of directors including Herbert Brenon, Raoul Walsh and J. Gordon Edwards (grandfather of director Blake Edwards). Edwards took over in 1916 as Theda Bara's leading director and handled all her subsequent pictures up to 1919, averaging five features per year. He was also responsible for one of the studio's most lavish movies of the early 20s, *The Queen of Sheba* (1921), starring Betty Blythe and including an exciting chariot race organized by Tom Mix. As Miss Blythe recalled years later, 'There were some terrific night scenes with hundreds of soldiers, and at least a hundred trained swimmers and stunt men. Bodies were flying through the air like popcorn.'

After nine years of virtually unbroken growth, and having far out-distanced Laemmle's Universal, the studio fell back in 1923 and 1924. However, faced with increasing competition from Paramount, First National and a new giant, MGM, the company succeeded in forging ahead once again on many fronts simultaneously. Under William's dynamic leadership, Fox acquired a major chain of theatres, began its first experiments with sound and embarked on a new programme of prestige productions.

Though the studio was weak on stars, it more than made up for it with a strong line-up of directors, mainly new arrivals at the studio, including Frank Borzage, Howard Hawks, John Ford, F. W. Murnau from Germany, and Raoul Walsh who returned to the studio as a leading action-adventure director after six years as a successful freelancer. A range of noteworthy pictures released by Fox during 1926–28, all from these five directors, combined quality with popular success: *What Price Glory?* and *Three Bad Men* in 1926, *Sunrise* and *Seventh Heaven* (both starring the popular Janet Gaynor) in 1927, *A Girl In Every Port, Four Devils* and *Four Sons* in 1928.

Profits grew steadily and the improved quality of the pictures encouraged the still-ambitious, egocentric and individualistic William Fox to make extensive new investments – in film theatres, in the new technology (developing the highly successful new Fox Movietone sound system and the Grandeur widescreen process within a new, fully equipped sound studio, constructed in Westwood in 1928) and in an attempted takeover of Loew's/MGM, one of its main rivals. In many respects Fox was well placed to strengthen its position in the industry during the tremendously competitive period between 1928 and 1930, and perhaps even establish itself as the leading company, but in 1929 an auto accident incapacitated William Fox for a number of months. This misfortune was followed by the stock-market crash and the threat of anti-trust action – attacking his monopolistic dealings – from the Justice Department, which meant that Fox's new movie empire was in danger of collapse, and he was forced to sell out his interests in the company. Harley Clarke, one of the leaders in ousting Fox, took over as president, while Winfield Sheehan (vice-president in charge of production at the Fox studio) and Sol Wurtzel (studio general manager) continued in their posts.

Under the new ownership Janet Gaynor's pictures continued to do well and the arrival of the popular Will Rogers in 1929 gave a major boost to the studio; but Fox still suffered from a lack of top star talent. The impact of the Depression in 1931 and 1932 led to the swift departure of Clarke. He was replaced by Sidney Kent, a far more suitable president. The theatrical arm of the company – Fox West Coast Theatres – was forced into receivership in 1933, but the film production side made a slow recovery during 1933–35. *Cavalcade* (1933), based on the Noel Coward play and featuring an all-British cast, was a big hit and won the Best Picture Oscar, while little Shirley Temple was just emerging as the studio's biggest box-office attraction of the 30s. However, Sidney Kent was dissatisfied with the way the studio was run. Negotiations early in 1935 led to a merger between Fox and the tiny, but highly successful 20th Century Pictures headed by Darryl Zanuck and Joseph Schenck. Their company had prospered during 1933 and 1934 and had been largely responsible for a modest revival in the fortunes of United Artists during these years. Zanuck, however, had been unhappy with his treatment at the hands of the UA partner-owners and agreed to replace Sheehan as Fox's new production chief, with Schenck as chairman of the board, William Goetz as vice-president and executive assistant to Zanuck, and Kent continuing as president. It was perhaps symbolic that the newly renamed 20th Century-Fox adopted the 20th Century logo with its beaming searchlights and fanfare music to introduce its pictures.

Zanuck immediately set to work reorganizing the production company. He cancelled a number of projects and instituted various economies in the running of the studio, while the construction of additional new sound stages and a major extension of the back lot meant that the main studio was better equipped than ever before.

An experienced film-maker who had started out as a scenario writer at Warner Bros., Zanuck prided himself on his ability to read a script and assess the potential of a project at its inception, and he supervised the editing and final cut of the pictures so as to achieve the best possible results. (His right-hand 'man' for 20 years was his ace cutter, Barbara McLean, whom he brought with him from 20th Century along with writer Nunnally Johnson, who served as an associate producer, and occasionally director, at Fox until 1959.)

Under Zanuck, the studio turned out on average over 50 features per year. He himself took charge of the 30 or so A features produced at the main Westwood studio, while Sol Wurtzel supervised the 25 Bs filmed at the company's old eight-acre lot on Western Avenue with associate producers Sol Lesser, Max Golden, and John Stone who handled the Charlie Chan series starring Warner Oland.

Aware of the studio's shortage of stars – the death of Will Rogers in 1935 left Shirley Temple as the only big name – Zanuck immediately set out to remedy the situation. In 1936 he signed up Don Ameche. ice-skating champion Sonja Henie, and his former 20th Century star, Loretta Young; he up-graded the image of Alice Faye who had been at Fox since 1933 without fulfilling her true potential; and at the urging of director Henry King he agreed to give young Tyrone Power his first big chance as the star of *Lloyds Of London*. In addition, he ventured into Technicolor for the first time with *Ramona* (1936), starring Don Ameche and Loretta Young and directed by Henry King, immediately followed by *Wings Of The Morning*, filmed in Ireland late that same year with Henry Fonda and Annabella.

With the main emphasis on drama, romance and musical comedy within an American setting, only a relatively small number of Fox pictures were at all memorable. But they *were* popular at the box office. Zanuck's formula had worked, and the studio recorded good profits for 1936–38. By now Zanuck felt more confident about upgrading the studio's output. This is reflected most clearly in the collaboration between Henry Fonda and director John Ford on a number of outstanding productions beginning in 1939 with *Young Mr Lincoln* and culminating in *The Grapes of Wrath* (1940).

A number of leading technicians were hired by Zanuck at this time to help boost the quality of Fox pictures. These included art directors Boris Leven, Wiard Ihnen and Richard Day, composer Alfred Newman, and cameraman Leon Shamroy. The year 1939 marked a major increase in Technicolor productions. Indeed, Fox took the lead in this area and produced more features in colour than any other Hollywood studio until 1947.

With the death of Sidney Kent in 1941, the temporary absence of Joseph Schenck, and Zanuck's period of war service, an important new figure appeared on the scene. Spyros P. Skouras, previously head of the theatre operation, was promoted to company president, a position he would hold for 20 years. Around this time Fox cut back on its production of B features and reduced the number of feature releases by about 40%. For its shorts, the original Fox studio, and then 20th Century-Fox, had depended on the independent Educational Pictures company – in spite of its staid name, a leading Hollywood producer of comedy shorts – as its main source of supply in the 30s. Producer Paul Terry had provided the studio's cartoons, known as Terrytoons, since the early 30s, but most popular of all were his 40s series devoted to Mighty Mouse, a pint-sized version of Superman, and Heckle and Jeckle, the talking magpies. In 1942 Fox acquired the distribution rights to the well-known March Of Time documentary news series. But the studio continued to have its greatest success with its Fox Movietone newsreels which had been established as a worldwide market leader ever since its innovative introduction of sound in 1927.

Throughout the early and middle 40s Fox enjoyed a new position as one of the industry's leading companies. A varied selection of serious dramatic pictures in black-and-white, such as Oscar-winning *How Green Was My Valley* (1941), the (serious) Western *The Oxbow Incident* (1943), the thriller *Laura* (1944) and the war drama *A Walk In The Sun* (1945) were balanced by musicals, costumers and action pictures in Technicolor: Fritz Lang's *The Return Of Frank James* (1940); *Blood And Sand* (1941) – a stylish remake of the 1922 movie; a swashbuckler, *The Black Swan* (1942); and Busby Berkeley's *The Gang's All Here* (1943). There was also a noteworthy pair of dramas in colour: *Wilson* (1944) and *Leave Her To Heaven* (1945).

But in the postwar years, particularly after the failure of his favourite project *Wilson*, Zanuck appeared to lose interest in colour. He turned his attention instead to topical contemporary subjects and social themes and to thrillers filmed on location and often based on true stories. To handle the pictures he built up his list of contract directors with the addition of important new names like Elia Kazan and Joseph Mankiewicz, along with more experienced veterans – notably Henry Hathaway and Henry King, the studio's longest serving director.

For a while the studio continued to do relatively better than most of its competitors both financially and at the Oscar ceremonies, but it finally began to suffer the effects of declining film audiences in the early 50s at about the same time that it was forced to sell off its film theatres. The introduction of CinemaScope in 1953 coincided with the emergence of Fox's superstar find of the decade, Marilyn Monroe, who thus qualified as the first CinemaScope star in such pictures as *How To Marry A Millionaire* (1953), *River Of No Return* (1954) and *The Seven Year Itch* (1955).

The new process and Miss Monroe proved a sufficiently successful combination to restore the company's fortunes, but couldn't compensate for the departure of such leading directors as Kazan, Mankiewicz and Hawks and an apparent decline in the prestige and quality of Fox productions. The continuing emphasis on 'Scope and colour gave the studio a somewhat glossy and superficial image and won it few major awards (in marked contrast to the years up to 1950). With the focus on romance and adventure set in foreign or exotic locations and most often adapted from popular novels, many of Fox's high-cost productions turned out to be less interesting than might have been expected given the nature of each 'package'. The studio obviously suffered from a shortage of creative writers and directors and from a lack of executive leadership, particularly after the departure of Zanuck in 1956. (He was followed by Buddy Adler as production chief.) The presence of top stars could boost the box-office value of pictures, but it could not save them.

When the studio began to lose money in the late 50s and the costs of *Cleopatra* escalated disastrously in 1961, Zanuck was recalled as company president (replacing Skouras). With the help of his son, Richard Zanuck, as production chief, he immediately set about reducing staff and overheads and scrapping unpromising projects as he had done when he had first arrived at the studio 27 years before. He managed to get *Cleopatra* completed and released, and the spectacular box-office success of *The Sound Of Music* (1965) helped to turn the studio around in the middle 60s. In fact, Fox has swung from one extreme to the other throughout the past 30 years in a manner unmatched by any other Hollywood studio. The 60s revival was cut short in 1969 and 1970 by a series of expensive flops which pushed the company deep in the red and led to the final departure of both Zanucks. In the 70s the tide turned again under a new management team headed by Dennis Stanfill (president and chairman of the board) and production chief Alan Ladd Jr, who took over in the mid-70s when the company was again shaky. Ladd backed George Lucas and *Star Wars* (1977), then left to form his own Ladd Company in 1979.

But throughout the 70s the company was stronger on hits than productions of real quality and won few awards or major Oscars. After the purchase of Fox by tycoon Marvin Davis, with Alan Hirschfield as studio boss and Sherry Lansing as the first woman in charge of production at a major Hollywood studio, the company had few hits and even fewer quality pictures. Miss Lansing left in December 1982, Hirschfield followed her a little over one year later, and early in 1985 Marvin Davis sold his interest in the company to newspaper tycoon Rupert Murdoch – after sustaining huge losses. Company chairman Barry Diller soon succeeded in turning the studio around and it began to make profits once again in the late 80s though results were uneven. A new studio chief, film-maker Joe Roth, was hired in 1989 to increase film production, and he got off to a good stant with the success of *Die Hard* 2 and especially the surprise smash hit, *Home Alone*, in 1990. However, much of Murdoch and Diller's energy during these years had gone into developing a new, fourth television network in the US known as Fox Broadcasting. But the success of the film and television operations was overshadowed by the huge burden of debt carried by Murdoch's parent company, News Corporation, which faced a slightly uncertain future, hit hard by the recession in the early 90s.

Fox Studio Chronology

1914   William Fox forms his own production and distribution company, the Box Office Attractions Film Rental Company.

1916   The growing company is renamed the Fox Film Corporation.

1917   Fox Film moves into its new Sunset studio in Hollywood and shifts its main production operation from the East to the West Coast.

1927   The studio is a pioneer in the introduction of sound filming with its Fox Movietone process.

1929   Fox does well at the first Academy Awards ceremony, winning awards for Best actress, director, cinematography, script, and artistic quality of production.

1930   William Fox is forced out of the company he founded.

1933   The studio wins the Best Picture Oscar for *Cavalcade*.

1935   Fox merges with the small but successful 20th Century Productions headed by Darryl F. Zanuck and Joseph Schenck. Zanuck replaces Winfield Sheehan as production chief of the new 20th Century-Fox.

1941   Spyros P. Skouras is promoted to president.

1947   *Gentleman's Agreement* wins the Best Picture Oscar.

1950   The studio wins the top award again for *All About Eve*.

1953   Fox releases *The Robe*, the first CinemaScope production; it is a big hit.

1956   Zanuck resigns to become an independent producer releasing his films through Fox. Buddy Adler succeeds him as production head.

1962   The company is in financial trouble and Zanuck is brought back as president, replacing Skouras. He appoints his producer son Richard Zanuck as vice-president in charge of production.

1965   *The Sound Of Music* is a smash hit and wins the Best Picture Oscar.

1971   Richard Zanuck is dismissed, followed soon after by his father. Executive Dennis C. Stanfill becomes the new head of the company.

1974   Stanfill brings in producer Alan Ladd Jr to head the studio.

1977   The company receives a tremendous boost from the box-office success of *Star Wars* from producer-director George Lucas.

1979   Ladd leaves to form his own independent company.

1980   The studio has another spectacular hit with *The Empire Strikes Back*, the first sequel to *Star Wars*.

1981   Oil magnate Marvin Davis purchases Fox.

1982–83   The Company falls into the red in spite of a number of big hits including *Porky's, The Verdict* and especially *Return of the Jedi* which boosts Fox to the number one spot at the box office with a 21% share of the North American rentals market in 1983.

1985   After experiencing huge losses Davis sells out to Australian newspaper-tycoon Rupert Murdoch. Barry Diller, hired by Davis in 1984, stays on as co-chairman and chief executive.

1989   Joe Roth hired as new production chief.

The Releases

Starting out as a producer in 1914, William Fox was releasing 70 features per year by 1917. During the 20s he cut back on the total quantity in favour of better-quality productions including prestige Westerns, dramas, and early sound musicals such as the highly popular *Sunny Side Up* (1929). The studio depended on musicals to help it recover from the Depression, but diversified more in the late 30s under Darryl F. Zanuck. Fox was the first major studio to embark on a substantial and continuing programme of Technicolor filming, beginning in 1938–39 with a mixture of Westerns, musicals and dramatic pictures reflecting Zanuck's special interest in American subjects and settings. After the box-office failure of *Wilson* (1944), he became less interested in colour, but turned to *films noirs* and social-problem pictures. In the early 50s the introduction of CinemaScope helped to revive the studio's fortunes with a variety of glossy dramas and costumers. During later years Fox filmed a number of its most lavish and expensive productions in the Todd-AO 70mm process.

After winning his battle with the Trust in 1913, William Fox soon began producing (and distributing) his own pictures for the first time. His personal preference, as reflected in his earliest productions, was for contemporary dramas such as *Life's Shop Window* (1914). As production expanded, William Fox was always looking for new, suitable scenarios to film, and stories were often provided by his wife, Eve Leo, who was an avid reader. 'She would tell him a story which she had been reading, and the next day, when he went to the studio, he would talk it off to a stenographer, or maybe tell it to the director and between them they would put it into continuity . . . For five years no one knew the work she was doing.' ('Upton Sinclair Presents William Fox').

Having released 39 features in 1914–15, the total rose to 51 in 1916, for by now the studio was covering a wide range of subjects in order to make best use of its stars' diverse talents. After the successful launching of Theda Bara, the studio continued to provide her with a suitable variety of exotic roles. William Farnum was cast in action pictures and the occasional Western. Valeska Suratt appeared in dramas such as *The Soul Of Broadway* (1915) and *The Straight Way* (1916); *A Daughter Of The Gods* (1916) was a costume picture set in ancient times and suited to the talents of Australian swimming star Annette Kellerman (whose life was brought to the screen by MGM as *Million Dollar Mermaid* in 1952, starring the aquabatic Esther Williams).

By 1917 the studio was releasing an impressive 70 pictures annually and it maintained this prolific rate for a number of years. In order to keep up this level of production, the company had transferred most of its film-making activities to the West Coast, and it continued to draw on many sources for its themes (no longer dependent on Mrs William Fox). In 1917, the year that Tom Mix was signed by Fox, variety was still the keynote to the studio's output. There were childhood fantasies, such as *Aladdin And His Wonderful Lamp* and *Jack And The Beanstalk*, co-directed by the brothers Franklin (Sidney and Chester) with Francis Carpenter as the star. There were the Theda Bara vehicles including *Camille* and *Madame Du Barry*, while William Farnum appeared in *The Scarlet Pimpernel* and *A Tale Of Two Cities*, competently handled by British director Frank Lloyd. Also in 1917, Raoul Walsh directed Farnum in *The Conqueror*, a biopic of Sam Houston, the legendary Texan leader, and directed his younger brother George Walsh – who was launching his career as a leading action star at Fox – in a number of features of note. Among them were *The Honor System*, a contemporary drama advocating penal reform, and a comedy-fantasy about the movies, *This Is The Life*. (George landed the plum title role in the Goldwyn Company's production of *Ben-Hur* a few years later, but when the company became part of the new MGM in 1924, he was replaced by Ramon Novarro.)

In the early 20s the studio cut back on the number of feature releases to about one a week, or 50 per year, and maintained this level up to the early 30s. And by the late 20s there was a general air of quality about Fox features and the company was producing its pictures at two different studios, the old lot on Western Avenue and a newly constructed Fox Movietone (sound) studio out at Westwood.

With such Western stars as Tom Mix and Buck Jones on the Fox lot, along with 'action' stars William Farnum, George Walsh, George O'Brien and Victor McLaglen, and a strong staff of tough, outdoorsy directors including John Ford, Raoul Walsh, W.S. 'Woody' Van Dyke and William Wellman, it's not surprising that Fox made a major contribution to the Western during this period. Fox had a closely related interest in other types of action and adventure movies, too, and an emphasis on American subjects, both contemporary and historical. This was further reinforced with the introduction of sound when American accents proved less acceptable on the screen in portraying foreign characters. (It's hard to imagine Janet Gaynor and Charles Farrell repeating their roles in a sound version of *Seventh Heaven*, for example, and in fact the remake in 1937 served as a vehicle for French actress Simone Simon who was briefly under contract at Fox.)

Evidence of a general upgrading in the quality of Fox productions could first be seen in two prestige Westerns from John Ford, *The Iron Horse* (1924) and *Three Bad Men* (1926), with a variety of romantic and dramatic pictures of note during the following years from new Fox directors – Murnau, Borzage and Walsh (the latter back at the studio after an absence). *Napoleon's Barber*, an imaginatively conceived John Ford short, and, even more, a Raoul Walsh Western, *In Old Arizona* (finished by Irving Cummings when Walsh was injured), demonstrated the most interesting possibilities for sound filming in 1928. (Both made use of Fox Movietone equipment originally developed for shooting early sound newsreels.) As Alexander Walker noted in 'The Shattered Silents',

'For the first time voices and natural sounds were blended naturally and inventively in a full-length feature set frequently out of doors ... The landscape's authenticity was matched by that of the outdoor sounds which added naturalness and variety to the mood and the characters ... It sounds simple today: in *its* day it was a revelation.'

Another Walsh Western was selected to demonstrate the qualities of the 70mm Grandeur process in 1930. *The Big Trail* starred a young John Wayne, but when it flopped it brought to an end Fox's special interest in the Western, though George O'Brien continued to star in 'B' Westerns in the early 30s. At the same time Fox, along with the other studios, had turned its attention to a new sound genre, the movie musical. The company had its biggest hit of the period with one of its first musicals, *Sunny Side Up* (1929), and tried out the Grandeur process, less successfully, with another, *Happy Days*, later that same year.

Once the initial appeal of the talkies wore off, Fox became one of the studios worst-affected by the Depression. The clearest indication that sound alone could not continue to attract large movie audiences could be seen in the failure of many musicals which were often little more than filmed stage shows. Thus, Fox cut back drastically on the number of musicals in 1931 and 1932, while the total number of releases also fell in 1932 and 1933 for the first time since the early 20s. A new attempt to economize in the production of features began late in 1931 when the studio was reorganized, with Winfield Sheehan in charge of the dozen or so A features and Sol Wurtzel handling the Bs. The pioneer producer Jesse Lasky, who had been forced out of Paramount, joined them at Fox for three years (1933–35), while other producers included Sol Lesser, who handled B Westerns, and John Stone, who was put in charge of the studio's longest-running and most successful B series, the Charlie Chan cycle. This had begun early in 1931 when the Swedish-born Warner Oland first appeared on the screen as the inscrutable Oriental detective – based in fact on a real-life Chinese-American detective named Chang Apana – in *Charlie Chan Carries On*. When Oland died in 1938 after appearing in 16 Chan movies, Sidney Toler carried on for four more years and 11 titles. (The life of Chan's Japanese rival, Mr Moto, played by Hungarian-born Peter Lorre, was cut short in 1939 after only three years due to the outbreak of World War II. He was replaced by a more appropriate *British* sleuth, the eminent Sherlock Holmes as portrayed by Basil Rathbone; the two best early entries in the series came from Fox, then it was taken over, updated and continued on through the 40s at Universal.)

A new type of more sophisticated musical arrived to give the genre a comeback in Hollywood in 1933–34 and Fox was quick to join in. The studio's new musical stars were Shirley Temple and Alice Faye, and for the rest of the 30s Fox turned out musicals and feature films with songs at such a rate that they averaged a fairly steady one-third of total releases. New production chief Darryl F. Zanuck not only continued to promote Misses Temple and Alice Faye, but added to the studio roster many new musical stars – such as Sonja Henie and Don Ameche and, in the early 40s, Betty Grable and Carmen Miranda.

In general, the musicals fitted in well with Zanuck's interest in American subjects and helped to bring the studio back into profit in the late 30s. But by 1938–39 Zanuck was ready to upgrade the studio's output, demonstrating a first real commitment to filming in colour and a special fondness for biopics – which cut across genres. At the same time he reduced the number of musicals, and most of those that they *did* make were filmed in Technicolor and were good 'bread and butter' pictures – reliable moneymakers throughout the 40s. Zanuck also turned to a long-overdue revival of the A Western, beginning with *Jesse James* late in 1938, followed by *Drums Along The Mohawk* (1939) and others in colour. Zanuck's interest in the Western continued throughout the 40s, while social themes were explored in many of the studio's best black-and-white pictures of the decade, beginning most notably with *The Grapes Of Wrath* (1940) and *The Oxbow Incident* (1943). Fox was also an industry leader in its production of sophisticated thrillers, and of *films noirs*, which were often topical and dealt with social issues – as in *The House On 92nd Street* (1945) or *Boomerang* (1946). (Most consistent of all the studios, Fox averaged a steady three per year of these during 1945–51.) Many of Fox's best pictures of the decade were concentrated in these key genres (thrillers, *films noirs* and social-problem films), handled by a solid line-up of directors that included veterans John Ford, Fritz Lang, Henry King and Henry Hathaway, as well as relative newcomers Elia Kazan, Joseph Mankiewicz and Otto Preminger.

In contrast to the 30s when Fox turned out large numbers of features of variable quality, production in the 40s was of a higher standard generally. Having produced an average of over 50 features per year in the late 30s, the number fell off in the early 40s, and there was a sharp cut-back in 1943. Wartime restrictions, and the loss of stars like Tyrone Power and Henry Fonda to the armed services, provided an opportune moment to give up making B features altogether and concentrate further on improving the quality of the A's. Though there were many fluctuations from year to year, the studio continued to maintain this new average level, of about 30-plus features per year, up to the early 60s.

By the early 50s there were once again changes in the type of picture produced by Fox, which moved into colour and then CinemaScope, and also lost many of its leading 40s directors. The emphasis was on movies which best fitted the large, wide screen. There were glossy contemporary dramas such as *Three Coins In The Fountain* (1954), *Love Is A Many Splendoured Thing* (1956) and *Peyton Place* (1957). There were, more noticeably, musicals, Westerns and, especially, costume spectacles – for instance *The Robe* (1953), *Desiree, Prince Valiant* (both 1954), *Demetrius And The Gladiators* and *The Egyptian* (all 1954). By the late 50s the studio had lost the special identity which had been so carefully developed under Zanuck in earlier years.

In the 60s Fox was the last company to put its faith in reviving the big colourful Hollywood musicals of the postwar years, but was soon discouraged by a number of expensive flops. The studio fared better with a newly upgraded genre – science fiction. They had tried the occasional venture into the fantastic and futuristic as early as *The Last Man On*

Earth (1924) and *Just Imagine* (1931), and again in the 50s when *The Day The Earth Stood Still* (1951) represented one of the most memorable, adult examples of the genre, but it was not till the late 60s that the studio began to enjoy SF successes. First was *Planet Of The Apes* (1967) and its sequels; next came *Star Wars* (1977) and *its* two sequels, and then *Alien* in 1978. After a gap of eight years Fox brought back Flight Officer Ripley (Sigourney Weaver), the only survivor from the original space crew, and had its biggest hit of 1986 with *Aliens*.

Widescreen and 3-D Releases 1953–69

Process	1953	1954	1955	1956	1957	1958	1959	1960	1961	1962	1963	1964	1965	1966	1967	1968	1969
CinemaScope	3	17	23	20	23	23	30	27	24	17	12ᵃ	10	8	6	2		
Panavision														3	8	9	9
RegalScope (b/w)			3	17	8	4											
Large format (70 mm)					2		1		1		1		3	1	1	1	2ᶜ
3-D	1	1															

a includes one Technirama
c includes one Techniscope

Colour and Widescreen

William Fox had a special interest in sound and briefly experimented with a new 70mm widescreen process (Grandeur), but generally neglected colour. (The two Grandeur productions were the all-star musical *Happy Days* filmed in 1929 and *The Big Trail*, starring John Wayne, in 1930). In contrast to the other leading studios who made use of the new two-strip Technicolor, particularly for musicals, during 1929–30, Fox filmed *Sunny Side Up* (1929) in Multicolor and used this short-lived process for sequences in a few other pictures. Again, when the improved three-strip Technicolor became available, the studio was initially slow to respond. Fox introduced Technicolor sequences for the first time into the Shirley Temple musical *The Little Colonel* (1935), and later that year Winfield Sheehan planned to shoot the studio's first colour feature, *Ramona*, with young Rita Hayworth in her debut starring role. However, when Zanuck took over he dropped her from the picture and failed to take up her option, a move he was to regret a few years later when she became the top star at Columbia.

Zanuck previously had been one of the first to take up Technicolor, late in 1933, using it for the final sequences of *The House Of Rothschild*, released by 20th Century-UA early in 1934. The subject of *Ramona*, a romantic drama set in Southern California in the 1870s, appealed to Zanuck for his first colour feature and he reallocated the lead roles to two of his new 20th Century-Fox stars, Loretta Young and Don Ameche. Zanuck kept the original director, Henry King, who remained the studio's leading contract director and handled many colour subjects during the following years. He shared Zanuck's special interest in Americana and liked to film on location away from the studio whenever possible.

Fox's second Technicolor feature, *Wings Of The Morning*, starred Henry Fonda and Annabella, and was filmed on location in Ireland and England late in 1936. Though the story was old-fashioned and the script feeble, it was redeemed by some stunning photography from Ray

Rennahan and Jack Cardiff. The horse-racing theme was continued back in the US with *Kentucky* (1938) – lovely Loretta Young again, plus an Oscar-winning performance from Walter Brennan.

By 1938 Technicolor filming was beginning to catch on in Hollywood. MGM produced its first feature, *Sweethearts*, while the four Warner Bros. releases included the lively and colourful (but expensive) *The Adventures Of Robin Hood*. Zanuck responded by increasing his investment in colour filming late in 1938, further encouraged by the box-office success of *Kentucky*.

In fact, it was Zanuck and Fox who demonstrated the strongest commitment of all the Hollywood studios to Technicolor during these early years, 1939–44, with a steady average of six features per year. Colour was especially suited to the kind of American subjects most favoured by Zanuck, including costumers, Westerns and musicals to promote his leading stars Faye, Grable and Gene Tierney, Power, Ameche and Fonda, and was particularly effective for location filming. (The first Technicolored hits had been outdoor subjects: *The Trail Of The Lonesome Pine* from Wanger/Paramount in 1936 and Fox's own *Kentucky*, followed by *Jesse James*, released early in 1939 and directed by Henry King.)

Taken as a group the studio's early Technicolor features present a wide-ranging historical, and especially *geographical*, coverage of the USA, making use of a great variety of settings, both location and studio-created, which in many cases were here presented on the screen in colour for the first time. There was the American War of Independence as experienced by settlers in the Mohawk Valley region of upstate New York, in *Drums Along The Mohawk* (1939); the varying fortunes of a travelling circus in western New York state in the 1840s, in *Chad Hanna* (1940); the life of composer Stephen Foster in Kentucky, Pittsburgh and New York City in the middle years of the century, in *Swanee River* (1939). There were post-Civil War Westerns such as *Jesse James* and *The Return Of Frank James* (1940) set in Missouri and points west; the construction of the *Western Union* telegraph from Omaha, Nebraska to Salt Lake City; California of the 1870s featured in *Ramona*, and the Gay Nineties in musicals such as *Hello Frisco, Hello* (1943) and *My Gal Sal* (1942). The same approach moved into the 20th century with *Wilson* (1944) set in Princeton, New Jersey and Washington; early California film-making in *Hollywood Cavalcade* (1939); and such contemporary subjects as *To The Shores of Tripoli* (1942), filmed at the Marine base at San Diego and *Leave Her To Heaven* (1945), set in New Mexico and Maine. This selection merely draws attention to some of the best-known examples.

To make audiences aware of the kind of settings they could expect to see portrayed in each picture, place names were often featured prominently in the movie titles – *Kentucky* and *Maryland* (1940), *Home In Indiana* (1944), *Moon Over Miami* (1941), *Greenwich Village* (1944) and *Coney Island* (1943), *Nob Hill* (1945) and *Springtime In The Rockies* (1942). This ploy included a few Latin-American subjects, manufactured in the interests of inter-American relations and to provide roles for the irrepressible Carmen Miranda. She first appeared in *Down Argentine Way* (1940), followed by *That Night In Rio* and *Weekend In Havana* (both 1941).

Though musicals predominated in making use of the bright, sharp colours favoured by Zanuck, the studio also utilized colour on a variety of other productions. They provided an opportunity for a number of leading directors to work in Technicolor for the first time. In the case of Ford, Lang and Busby Berkeley, they are so closely identified with the black-and-white cinema of the 30s that their rare early ventures into colour have been unfairly neglected. John Ford's *Drums Along The Mohawk*, for example, was a beautifully realized Western starring Henry Fonda and Claudette Colbert. A hit with audiences at the time, it has been overshadowed by the director's better-known monochrome pictures such as *Stagecoach* (1939 – for UA), *Young Mr Lincoln* (1939) and *The Grapes Of Wrath* (1940). Similarly, Fritz Lang's *The Return Of Frank James* (1940) made use of a variety of stunning locations and an effective low-keyed Technicolor (with much of the film taking place at night). Though very different from his other 30s pictures, Lang's approach reflected his special attraction to American culture and the true history of the West. By introducing a number of social themes in *The Return Of Frank James* – for example, championing the rights of the individual in opposition to the power of the railroad – he was one of the first to recognize the possibilities of a new type of adult Western three years before the better-known Fox picture, *The Oxbow Incident* (which also starred Henry Fonda).

If Ernst Lubitsch's first venture into colour with *Heaven Can Wait* (1943) was a lightweight and disappointing trifle, Busby Berkeley was at his most imaginative and inventive with *The Gang's All Here* (1943). In this he proved that he could astonish us just as well with colour (and Carmen Miranda) as he had with his better-known monochrome movies at Warner Bros. 10 years earlier. Rouben Mamoulian, who directed the first Technicolor feature, *Becky Sharp*, in 1935, had not had the chance to work in colour again until Zanuck gave him the opportunity to demonstrate his qualities as a colour stylist of the first rank with the remake of *Blood And Sand* (1941). Tyrone Power and Linda Darnell were the Fox stars, but for Rita Hayworth, back at Fox after a gap of five years (on loan from Columbia), the picture marked her first, striking appearance in colour and a major step forward in her rise to stardom in the 40s.

John Stahl, like Busby Berkeley, is most often identified with a 30s black-and-white genre, in his case the 'woman's picture'. Given his first chance to work in Technicolor at Fox, he proved the effectiveness of his approach with the entertainingly over-the-top *Leave Her To Heaven* (1945) starring Gene Tierney. The studio's biggest Technicolor hit of the 40s, it also gave cameraman Leon Shamroy the opportunity to demonstrate his expertise and win an Oscar for this rare contemporary subject in colour.

As part of his expanded programme of colour filming, Zanuck had built up the studio's staff of cameramen, art directors and, notably, costume designers who made a major contribution to the success of the productions. Unfortunately, Zanuck's favourite and most expensive Technicolor project, *Wilson* (1944), a biopic of the President directed by Henry King, proved too serious, sophisticated and pacifist in tone for wartime audiences seeking escapism. Though it won a number of Oscars, including cinematography (Shamroy again) and art direction (Wiard Ihnen), it flopped at the box-office and marked the virtual end of Zanuck's special interest in colour filming.

During the postwar years the studio had little success with big costume productions – *Forever Amber* and *Captain From Castile* (both 1947) among them – and was generally overshadowed by MGM in the colour stakes. But it continued to turn out Betty Grable musicals, and outdoor movies such as *Smoky* (1946), *Green Grass Of Wyoming* (1948) and *Sand* (1949) – all directed by Louis King, younger brother of Henry. Zanuck's name became associated more closely with new trends in black-and-white filming, such as a series of gritty thrillers shot on location and social-problem pictures. All the top Oscar winners and many of the hits continued to be in monochrome. A few last Technicolor productions of note in the early 50s included *Broken Arrow* (1950), one of the first movies to treat the Indian with respect; *The Snows Of Kilimanjaro* (1952), an adventure starring Gregory Peck, Susan Hayward and Ava Gardner; and Marilyn Monroe's first starring musical, *Gentlemen Prefer Blondes* (1953).

The continuing drop in film audiences in the early 50s meant that the movie companies began looking for new ways to attract people back into the cinemas. In response to the successful introduction of Cinerama in 1952, followed by the first 3-D movies, Fox turned to the anamorphic wide-image process first developed by French inventor Henri Chrétien in 1928. (With the use of a special 'anamorphic' lens, a widescreen image could be 'squeezed' onto the standard 35mm film, then unsqueezed by a matching lens attached to the projector.) Though the anamorphic system could not be patented, Fox succeeded in promoting and popularizing its trade name, 'CinemaScope', then adopted by a number of other studios.

In fact, with the release of its first highly popular and profitable CinemaScope productions in 1953, beginning with *The Robe* and *How To Marry A Millionaire*, Fox found itself once again playing an important role during the most intense period of technical innovation in Hollywood since the introduction of sound some 25 years earlier. Along with its introduction of CinemaScope, the studio also attempted to improve the quality of the sound by making use of four-track magnetic (stereo) sound in place of the optical sound tracks which were the norm. And the colour output increased. The number of Fox pictures in colour virtually doubled from 1952 to 1953, and shot up again in 1954 as the company took advantage of the newly developed and cheaper Eastman Color which it processed as its own new 'Deluxe' labs. At one point the studio announced that all future releases would be filmed in colour and CinemaScope, and fully three-quarters of the Fox pictures in 1954–55 were in colour, with most of these in 'Scope as well. But the initial enthusiasm waned as many of the pictures performed poorly at the box-office, reflecting the deficient quality of the scripting and direction of many of the studio's glossy 'Scope productions. Many leading directors and cameramen were still in favour of black-and-white, and the studio finally relented. *Teenage Rebel* in 1956 was the first of a number of productions filmed in the cheaper black-and-white CinemaScope and, of these, *The Diary Of Anne Frank* (1959), the British-produced *Sons And Lovers* (1960), and *The Hustler* (1961) all won Oscars for the quality of their black-and-white cinematography. In 1956 Fox also introduced black-and-white RegalScope for its cheapest productions, but in late 1959 this process was abandoned. This meant that from 1955 to 1962 the vast majority of Fox releases were in CinemaScope or RegalScope.

In the mid-50s most of the major studios began to experiment with filming in formats larger than the standard 35mm. Fox introduced 'CinemaScope 55' (using 55mm) with two of its prestige releases in 1956 – *Carousel* and *The King And I*, both musicals. That same year *Around The World In 80 Days*, filmed in Todd-AO, was the first 70mm movie to win the Best Picture Oscar. In the following years Fox adopted Todd-AO for its own 'super productions', especially musicals, including *South Pacific* (1958), *Can Can* (1960), *Cleopatra* (1963) and *The Sound Of Music* (1965). It finally abandoned the process in the late 60s after three expensive flops in a row – *Dr Dolittle* (1967), *Star!* (1968) and *Hello, Dolly!* (1969) – and the studio's last 70mm production, the highly successful *Patton* (1970), was shot in Dimension-150.

Fox, along with most other studios, gave up the cumbersome and expensive 70mm filming in the late 60s. Economics apart, the improvements in Eastman film stock and in 35mm Panavision meant that it could be blown up to 70mm with little loss in quality. Fox's CinemaScope productions had fallen to about 50% of the total during 1963–66, and around 1967–68, just 15 years after its first introduction, Fox finally abandoned it, following the other studios in switching to the better quality Panavision. As Leon Shamroy said 'I fought to get Panavision introduced on the Fox lot, and at last I won.'

The Finances

The early financial success of the Fox studio as a producer and distributor of motion pictures led to a marked growth of the company in the late 20s. Then, Fox extended its investment into film theatres, and into developing the Movietone sound system for use in its features and popular newsreels. But owner William Fox overextended himself in attempting a takeover of Loew's/MGM and was forced out of his own company. Badly affected by the Depression, the studio recovered in the late 30s and emerged in the 40s as one of the most profitable movie companies. The studio successfully exploited the new CinemaScope process in the 50s and recovered from a few bad years (1959–62) with a number of big hits including *The Sound Of Music* (1965). The cycle of ups and downs continued as the company suffered large losses in 1969–70, but it bounced back yet again in the 70s and had a tremendous success with *Star Wars* (1977) and its sequels. The company suffered huge losses in the 80s under new owner Marvin Davis, but has recently been showing signs of a recovery.

Moving into film production in 1914, Fox's Box Office Attractions Company turned out four features for a total cost of slightly over $50,000. By the following year the company was well established and had upped its output to 36 short features, nine of them starring Theda Bara, and earned a small profit. Under its new name, the Fox Film Corporation, revenues continued to grow during the following years. Profits remained relatively static from 1915–18, but started climbing in 1919 to reach a peak of $2.7 million in 1922. With film-making becoming more sophisticated, the average cost of a Fox feature rose from $43,000 in 1917–19 to almost $70,000 in 1920–22.

Though profits and revenues fell off in 1923–24, the company embarked on its most spectacular period of growth in the middle and late 20s. By 1929–30 revenues and profits (the latter averaging almost $10 million per year) were at record levels, boosted by a run of hit movies which matched the output from any of the other top Hollywood studios during these years. Three hits each from leading directors Raoul Walsh and Frank Borzage, including Walsh's *What Price Glory?* (1926), Borzage's *Seventh Heaven* (1927) and John Ford's *Four Sons* (1928) were all capped by the spectacular success of the Janet Gaynor vehicle, *Sunny Side Up*, in 1929.

In 1925 William Fox issued $6.6 million worth of common stock as a means of raising additional capital to expand the company's chain of film theatres. He also invested heavily in developing a viable sound-on-film system which proved in the long run to be more practical than Warner Bros.' sound-on-disc. Fox was extremely successful with his Movietone sound newsreels which began in 1927, and was not far behind Warner Bros. in the production of feature talkies.

At the same time that the company was growing to the point where it could begin to compete on equal terms with industry leaders Paramount and Loew's/MGM in the production of films and acquisition of film theatres, William Fox became involved in a most extraordinary financial entanglement. The death of Marcus Loew in 1927 made it possible for Fox to purchase Loew's major holding in Loew's/MGM and thus gain control of one of his top rivals. A merger between Fox and MGM would create a motion-picture giant which would dominate the industry.

Though Fox's substantial assets had never looked more solid, he had been extending himself in many directions simultaneously. Thus, he was financially vulnerable and needed to preserve a good relationship with his bankers and associates. He had been acquiring new movie theatres both in the USA and abroad (the British Gaumont chain), along with major investments in new sound films and equipment, and in a special new large-screen process – 'Grandeur'.

In fact, Fox's purchase of a controlling interest in Loew's/MGM set in motion a complicated and ultimately disastrous chain of events. The story of his downfall is told in elaborate detail in the book 'Upton Sinclair Presents William Fox' – as an example of the worst excesses of American capitalism before the reforms instituted under the New Deal a few years later. This story of greed and duplicity on the part of many of Fox's friends, partners and business associates also involved many of the country's top industrialists, bankers and lawyers – A T & T, Rockefeller, Halsey, Stuart and Co, and Charles Evans Hughes among others. The Justice Department of the Hoover administration, newly elected in November 1928, initially appeared to have no objection to Fox's acquisition, but then mysteriously changed its mind late in 1929. (Without condoning such behaviour, it must be pointed out, as Sinclair neglects to do, that Fox's plan to merge his company with MGM would appear to be a clear violation of the anti-trust laws against monopolistic companies, aside from its obvious impracticality. It really is difficult to envisage this merger ever taking place and makes one question the soundness of Fox's judgement; some of his problems he certainly brought upon himself.)

The result was that the merger was cancelled and Fox was forced out of his own company which he had built up so successfully over many years. When he departed in 1930 the studio was still flourishing, but, along with most of the other leading film companies, it was badly affected by the Depression in 1931–32 with losses amounting to over $20 million. The lack of strong management at the top did not help, and the studio just managed to struggle back into profit in 1933–34, thanks to such box-office hits as *State Fair* and the Oscar-winning *Cavalcade*, both in 1933, while 1934 and early 1935 saw the first of the highly popular Shirley Temple musicals and the last features starring Will Rogers, who died in an accident in 1935.

That year marked a major turning point for the company which merged with 20th Century Pictures headed by Darryl Zanuck and Joseph Schenck. Under Zanuck's leadership the studio, now known as 20th Century-Fox, recovered rapidly. Profits between 1936–38 averaged a healthy $7.9 million, an indication of the popularity of the studio's new stars led by Alice Faye, Tyrone Power and Don Ameche. They appeared together in a pair of hits, *In Old Chicago* (1937) and *Alexander's Ragtime Band* (1938), while Sonja Henie costarred with Ameche in *Happy Landing* (1938). There were many other hits, but profits fell off for a time and a loss in 1940 reflected some high-cost flops – including *Brigham Young* which starred Power, and a Technicolored Shirley Temple vehicle, *The Blue Bird*.

But the studio was well placed to take advantage of the wartime growth in filmgoing through its chain of film theatres, and the range and quality of its pictures in both colour and black-and-white. The monochrome *How Green Was My Valley* (1941) and the Technicolored *The Black Swan* (1942) were both popular, while the black-and-white *The Song of Bernadette* (1943) was a smash hit. Profits grew from $10.8 million in 1942–43 to $12.6 million in 1944–45 and a spectacular $22.6 million in 1946, benefiting from a popular run of Technicolored features – *State Fair, The Dolly Sisters* and *Leave Her To Heaven* in 1945, *Margie* and *Smoky* in 1946 and *Forever Amber* in 1947. Having outdistanced MGM (which was no longer the industry leader) for the first time in its history, Fox continued to do well in spite of the postwar decline. By 1948–49 profits had fallen back to $12.5 million but were more than twice those of MGM. A group of black-and-white releases led the way in 1949 – *Pinky, The Snake Pit, I Was A Male War Bride* and *Mr Belvedere Goes To College* were four of the eight top hits of the year and Fox also had 10 pictures among the top 30.

But by the early 50s Fox, too, was badly affected by the box-office decline. The studio sought (and found) a solution with the introduction of CinemaScope in 1953. The company achieved its biggest hit of the decade with *The Robe* (1953), the first CinemaScope production, but the true impact of the new process was seen the following year when profits leaped to $8 million. Of the year's 35 top hits, Fox could claim 11 – all of them in colour and CinemaScope.

Throughout the rest of the decade, even after the departure of Zanuck early in 1956, the studio continued to do reasonably well. Profits averaged $6–7 million per year and the emphasis was on glossy entertainment filmed in the new widescreen processes. The top hits included *The Seven*

Year Itch starring Marilyn Monroe and *The Tall Men*, both released in 1955 in CinemaScope, a pair of musicals – *The King And I* (1956) filmed in CinemaScope 55 and *South Pacific* (1958) in Todd-AO – and last but not least, *Peyton Place* (1957) in CinemaScope.

Things started to turn a little sour around 1959. According to the annual balance sheet, Fox earned a small profit in 1959, recorded a small loss in 1960 and was seriously in the red in 1961 and 1962 to the tune of $22.5 million and $39.8 million respectively. In reality, substantial 1959–60 losses were disguised by income of $43 million from the sale of 260 acres of the back lot to the Aluminum Company of America. The losses in 1961–62 reflected the escalating costs of *Cleopatra* which ended up costing $37 million – to date the most expensive picture ever made by an American studio (if inflation is taken into account) – and a $2 million write-off on *Something's Got To Give*, Marilyn Monroe's last picture which was abandoned in mid-production. (Fox's most bankable star in the 50s, she only completed one movie there after *Bus Stop* in 1956 – the disappointing *Let's Make Love*, 1959).

As one of the few major film companies which was not merged into a diversified conglomerate in the 60s, and thus continued to depend primarily on income from feature-film production, Fox was especially vulnerable to fluctuations in the movie industry – not least because the profits from its hits were often ploughed back into risky high-cost productions. Indeed, Fox went through the most extreme boom-and-bust cycles of any of the studios. From the red ink of the early 60s, there was a remarkable recovery from 1963–68, then spectacular losses in 1969–70, followed by yet another rapid revival in the early 70s.

In 1962 Darryl Zanuck was brought back to replace Spyros Skouras as company president, just in time to benefit from the release of his own $8.5 million production, *The Longest Day*. He also managed to get the much-troubled *Cleopatra* completed and released in 1963, and got the studio moving forward once again with a number of new projects, including the movie adaptation of *The Sound Of Music* (1965). Zanuck must be credited with having confidence in this project from the start, investing a substantial $8 million and filming in the expensive Todd-AO process.

Profits from its spectacular success were reinvested in a wide range of films as Zanuck demonstrated his confidence in the future of the industry with Fox as one of the industry leaders. But he was playing a risky game, with a large number of expensive productions. *The Sand Pebbles* (1966) cost $10 million and more or less broke even and an $18 million Italian-made version of *The Bible – In The Beginning* (1966) lost money, while the studio had dreadful flops with *Dr Dolittle* (1967) which cost $20 million, and the $14 million *Star!* (1968). However, such hits as *Valley Of The Dolls* and *Planet Of The Apes* (both 1967), along with a number of lesser successes, meant continued profits during 1966–68.

Then, in 1969, disaster struck. The studio recorded losses of over $100 million for 1969–70 as the few big hits, such as *Butch Cassidy And The Sundance Kid* (1969) and *M*A*S*H* (1970), were far outweighed by a large number of high-cost flops led by the lavish musical, *Hello Dolly!* (1969), the war movie, *Tora! Tora! Tora!* and a gambling romance, *The Only Game In Town* (both 1970). Zanuck was forced out, but with new management the company quickly bounced back, led by *The French Connection* (1971) and *The Poseidon Adventure* (1972). The studio continued to share in the general industry revival of the 70s with a series of big hits, topped by the phenomenon of *Star Wars* (1977) and its almost equally successful first sequel, *The Empire Strikes Back* (1980).

Unfortunately, bad management, a large number of box-office flops, and the failure to control the excessive costs of such pictures as *Rhinestone* (1984) and *Enemy Mine* (1985), meant that the company did badly in the early 80s when it was purchased for over $700 million by oil billionaire Marvin Davis. By late 1985 Davis had had enough and sold out to Australian media tycoon Rupert Murdoch. Fox then experienced a modest revival in the late 80s with such hits as *Alien* (1986), *Big* and *Die Hard* (both released in 1988) followed by *The War of the Roses* (1989) and moved into the 90s in relatively good shape with *Die Hard 2* and especially *Home Alone* (both 1990) and with *Alien* III coming soon.

Box Office Hits

title	cost	North American rentals
1914–31	(in $ millions)	(in $ millions)
Sunny Side Up (1929)	(.8)	3.3
The Cock-Eyed World (1929)	(.8)	2.7
What Price Glory? (1928)	(.8)	2.0
Seventh Heaven (1927)		1.8
Street Angel (1928)		1.7
Common Clay (1930)		1.7
Four Sons (1928)		1.5
Daddy Long Legs (1931)		1.5
The Man Who Came Back (1931)		1.4
In Old Arizona (1928)		1.3
The Red Dance (1928)		1.3
Merely Mary Ann (1931)		1.3
A Connecticut Yankee (1931)		1.3
1932–40		
State Fair (1933)	(.7)	1.8
Cavalcade (1933)	(1.5)	1.5
In Old Chicago (1937)	(1.7)	1.5
Kentucky (1938)	(1.0)	1.5
Alexander's Ragtime Band (1938)	(1.3)	1.5
Happy Landing (1938)		1.5
Jesse James (1939)	(1.2)	1.5
Drums Along The Mohawk (1939)	(1.5)	1.5
The Rains Came (1939)	(2.0)	1.5
1941–50		
Leave Her To Heaven (1945)		5.5
Forever Amber (1947)	(5.0)	5.0
The Razor's Edge (1946)	(3.5)	5.0
The Song of Bernadette (1943)	(2.3)	5.0
Cheaper By The Dozen (1950)	(1.7)	4.4
State Fair (1945)	(2.1)	4.1

title	cost	North American rentals
1914–31	(in $ millions)	(in $ millions)
Margie (1946)	(1.6)	4.1
Mother Wore Tights (1947)	(2.7)	4.1
I Was A Male War Bride (1949)	(3.3)	4.1
1951–60		
The Robe (1953)	(4.1)	17.5
South Pacific (1958)	(5.6)	16.3
Peyton Place (1957)	(2.2)	11.0
The King and I (1956)	(4.6)	8.5
How To Marry A Millionaire (1953)	(2.2)	7.3
The Snows of Kilimanjaro (1952)	(2.6)	6.5
The Seven Year Itch (1955)	(2.0)	6.0
The Tall Men (1955)	(3.1)	5.0
1961–70		
The Sound of Music (1965)	(8.0)	72.0
M*A*S*H (1970)	(3.0)	30.0
Butch Cassidy And The Sundance Kid (1969)	(6.0)	29.2
Patton (1970)	(13.)	27.0
Cleopatra (1963)	(40.)	26.0
The Valley Of The Dolls (1967)	(4.7)	20.0
The Longest Day (1962)	(8.0)	17.6
The Bible – In The Beginning (1966)	(17.)	15.0
Planet Of The Apes (1967)	(5.8)	15.0
Hello Dolly! (1970)	(22.)	15.0
Tora! Tora! Tora! (1970)	(25.5)	13.7
The Sand Pebbles (1966)	(12.1)	15.5
1971–80		
Star Wars (1977)	(10.5)	185.1
The Empire Strikes Back (1980)	(22.0)	134.2
Nine To Five (1980)	(10.)	57.9
Towering Inferno (1974) (co-prod)	(15.0)	50.0
The Poseidon Adventure (1972)	(5.0)	42.0
Alien (1979)	(10.8)	39.8
Young Frankensteing (1974)	(2.8)	38.8
Silver Streak (1976)	(6.2)	30.0
The Omen (1976)	(2.8)	28.4
The French Connection (1971)	(3.0)	26.3
1981–90		
Return of The Jedi (1983)	(32.5)	168.0
Home Alone (1990)	(18.0)	80.0
Die Hard 2 (1990)	(60.0)	66.5
The Karate Kid Part II (1986)		58.3
Porky's (1982)	(5.0)	54.0
Big (1988)	(20.0)	52.0
Aliens (1986)	(21.)	43.7
The War Of The Roses (1989)	(25.)	41.4
Cocoon (1985)	(17.5)	40.0
The Cannonball Run (1981)	(18.)	36.8
The Jewel Of The Nile (1985)	(25.)	36.5
Romancing The Stone (1984)	(9.5)	36.0
Die Hard (1988)	(28.)	36.0
Mr Mom (1983)		32.0
Predator (1987)	(25.)	31.0

The Stars

Theda Bara was the first star personality to be created by the studio publicity machinery, complete with made-up name and fictitious biography. She was William Fox's first big star during 1915–19 and the original 'vamp' of the silver screen. But Fox didn't repeat the 'fabricated star' experiment and his other early stars were more conventional types. The studio was particularly strong on adventure and Western stars like William Farnum, Tom Mix, Buck Jones, George O'Brien and Victor McLaglen, but petite Janet Gaynor emerged as the top star in the late 20s, most often teamed with Charles Farrell as the screen's most popular romantic couple. Though the studio developed a number of male leads – Will Rogers, Tyrone Power, Henry Fonda and Gregory Peck – they were no match for the ladies, led by Shirley Temple in the *30s*, Betty Grable in the 40s and Marilyn Monroe in the 50s.

William Fox and his publicity department added an important new twist to the star phenomenon in 1914. A few years after the rise to fame of Florence Lawrence and Mary Pickford (each formerly known simply as The Biograph Girl), Fox decided to launch the career of a previously unknown actress and successfully turned her into an overnight star sensation. She was Theda Bara, the first ever example of a star personality created entirely for the screen.

Fox's publicity machinery worked overtime, and Miss Bara was presented to the public as an entirely new type of wicked and sophisticated movie heroine. With a made-up name and a totally fabricated biography which represented her as the daughter of an Egyptian princess, she made her screen debut as the star of the immensely popular *A Fool There Was* (1915), and was dubbed the first 'vamp' of the movies.

The dark-eyed Theda was photographed in a variety of flamboyant costumes and posed with human skulls, snakes, and other props designed to reinforce the illusion that she was possessed of mystic powers and was the embodiment of evil. (Miss Bara was, in fact, the daughter of a Jewish tailor, born in Cincinatti, and her real name was Theodosia Goodman.)

With the emphasis on historical or exotic subjects like *Carmen* (1915, director Raoul Walsh), *Camille* and *Cleopatra* (both 1917) and *Salome* (1918), she appeared in more than 40 features between 1915 and 1919. Her popularity rose, as did her salary – from $75 a week to $4,000. Though her image soon became dated and her appeal was relatively shortlived, for a few years at least her pictures contributed immensely to the success of the studio.

Fox's other important star during these early years was William Farnum who became a fixture at the studio for nine years (1914–23), appearing in a variety of costume dramas, action pictures and Westerns. But it wasn't long before Fox had acquired a pair of top Western stars, Tom Mix and Buck Jones, who each remained for 10 years till the end of the silent era. Though Mix had already appeared in a large number of one – and two-reelers for William Selig's film company, it was at Fox that he emerged as a top star with a special style of his own. The emphasis was on fast-moving action and comedy with plenty of daring stunts, in contrast to the more restrained and naturalistic approach favoured by William S. Hart, the other top Western star of the period. Well-written and directed, and filmed on location far from the studio, Mix's features were so popular that he was put in charge of his own unit and given the full star treatment by an appreciative studio, while his salary rose from $350 per week to $7500 by the middle 20s.

George O'Brien got his start working on the Mix pictures and was soon starring on his own. He first made his name in a group of Westerns directed by John Ford during 1924–26, including the studio's first epic Western, *The Iron Horse* (1924), Fox's answer to Paramount's *The Covered Wagon* (1923). Another Ford star at Fox during the late 20s was large, gruff but likeable Victor McLaglen, who had his biggest success at Fox teamed with Edmund Lowe in *What Price Glory?* (1926) and its sequels; he then returned to the studio in 1937 as an unlikely co-star for Shirley Temple in Ford's *Wee Willie Winkie*.

But during the last years of the silent era it was the petite Janet Gaynor who emerged as the studio's top star, and her popularity carried over into the early 30s. Most often paired with Charles Farrell – they appeared in a dozen pictures together – she also played opposite Fox's other leading men, including Warner Baxter (*Daddy Long Legs*, 1931) and Will Rogers (*State Fair*, 1933). Starting out at a salary of $100 per week, she partnered George O'Brien in three of her earliest films in 1926, the last of which was Murnau's remarkable *Sunrise*, immediately followed by *Seventh Heaven* (1927) in which she was teamed with Farrell for the first time. Frank Borzage directed the latter, and was again behind the camera for *Street Angel* (1928). For her performance in these three pictures Miss Gaynor gained the first-ever Academy Award for Best Actress, awarded in 1929, and by 1930 she was earning $1500 per week. In the first annual *Motion Picture Herald* exhibitors' poll of top box-office stars she came second (behind MGM's Marie Dressler), with Charles Farrell fourth and Will Rogers ninth. She held down the number three spot in 1933 and 1934, and in 1935, her last year with Fox, her salary came to $170,000, but by this time she was well past her peak.

With the coming of sound, Fox, like the other Hollywood studios, was in the market for new acting talent. For a brief period in the early 30s the studio was noticeably stronger on the male side, with Warner Baxter, El Brendel, John Boles, James Dunn, Humphrey Bogart and Spencer Tracy under contract, while Warner Oland played the inscrutable Charlie Chan from 1932 through 1937. Unfortunately, the studio failed to make the best use of Tracy's talent and he did not begin to fulfil his potential until he arrived at MGM in 1935. It took even longer for Bogart to reach star status. Initially signed up at $750 per week as 'Fox's answer to Gable', he was dropped after appearing in five movies in 1930–31.

Will Rogers, however, was Fox's top male star from 1929 till his death in a plane crash in 1935 – rated number two at the box office in the Quigley poll in both 1933 and 1935 and number one in 1934. A unique entertainer and popular screen personality, Rogers worked well with John Ford who directed three of his films, and recalled that '. . . no writer could write for Will Rogers. Some of the lines he'd speak from the script, but most of the time he'd make up his own . . . He'd work it out beforehand and then just get in front of the camera and get the sense of the scene in his own inimitable way.'

Shirley Temple, another Fox star, took over the top box-office position from Will Rogers in 1935 and held it for four years (a record only surpassed by Bing Crosby in the 40s). After Rogers' death she was the studio's most valuable asset, the most popular child star in the history of the cinema. Her pictures were supervised by Zanuck who, typically, provided her with an interesting screen character. Rather than just a sweet little curly-haired girl who could sing and dance, she was most often portrayed as sensible, resourceful and outspoken, reacting naturally and spontaneously to people and situations, exposing the pomposity and hypocrisy of the adult world and helping her parents or guardian out of a tight spot. According to director Allan Dwan, 'She was always on the job and ready – knew all of her "words", as she called dialogue – and her songs and dances. So it was very simple working with her.' (She was awarded a special juvenile Oscar in 1934.)

Zanuck quickly built up the studio's list of contract stars in 1936 with such new names as Sonja Henie, Don Ameche, Loretta Young, and Tyrone Power who stayed on for 18 years. He appeared in a variety of popular pictures but was at his best in costume actioners like *The Mark Of Zorro* (1940) and *The Black Swan* (1942). He first made it on to the list of top box-office stars in 1938 in the number ten spot behind Alice Faye (ninth), Jane Withers, the studio's *other* leading juvenile star (eighth), ice skating queen Sonja Henie (third) and Shirley Temple at number one. This was Fox's best-ever showing. (Little Shirley topped the payroll, too, with earnings of $307,000 for 1938 compared with Loretta Young at $175,000, Tyrone Power $118,000 and Sonja Henie $112,000.)

An important new arrival was Henry Fonda who had appeared on the screen for the first time at Fox three years earlier. His special qualities as an actor, projecting a quiet power and sincerity in such roles as *Young Mr Lincoln* (1939) and Tom Joad in the powerful Depression drama, *The Grapes Of Wrath* (1940), fitted in well with Zanuck's attraction to

American themes, both contemporary and historical. And Fonda played an important role in the revival and maturing of the Western, starring in *Jesse James* (1939), *The Return Of Frank James* (1940), *The Oxbow Incident* (1943), one of the first of a new type of adult Western, and appeared as Wyatt Earp in John Ford's *My Darling Clementine* (1946), all at Fox.

In keeping with its status as one of the leading studios, Fox continued to acquire new stars throughout the 40s, beginning most notably in 1940 even before the stimulus provided by the booming war years. Additions to the studio roster in that year alone included Laird Cregar, Anne Baxter, Gene Tierney and Dana Andrews, while Betty Grable, Carmen Miranda and Charlotte Greenwood would feature prominently in the studio's glossy new-style Technicolor musicals. All three appeared in *Down Argentine Way* (1940), Miranda's first American movie in which Grable was a last-minute replacement for the indisposed Alice Faye.

Having started as a chorus girl at Fox over 11 years earlier at the age of 13, Betty Grable had gained experience at various studios as an extra, then featured player and star in minor pictures, and was under contract to Paramount for a few years. But she had never been given a real chance as a star. As she herself complained early in 1940 when she was appearing on Broadway: 'Hollywood has a way of letting you down . . . The only reason I'm in a Broadway show is that the films don't want me. It comes like something of a shock after you've worked in several studios and have been publicized around the country for years, suddenly to realize there are no new roles for you.' A hard-working professional with a pleasant personality, her 'peaches and cream' complexion and blonde hair showed up well in Technicolor, and she became a favourite forces' pin-up, famous for her shapely legs. She had appeared at just the right time for Fox, picking up in 1940 more or less where Shirley Temple had left off. (A link was provided by Charlotte Greenwood who played Shirley's mother in her *last* Fox movie, *Young People*, in 1940, then was cast as Betty's lively aunt in her *first* starring vehicle.) Averaging a steady two or three features per year for the next dozen years, mostly Technicolored musicals (aside from a one-year break in 1946), she was often costarred with John Payne, Dick Haymes, Victor Mature and Cesar Romero and made four pictures with song-and-dance man Dan Dailey. Betty first appeared on the list of top ten box-office stars in 1942 and was never off it for the next ten years, reaching the number one spot in 1943 and was number two in 1947–48 when her salary climbed to a peak of $325,000 per year.

The success of the studio in the 40s was reflected in a stronger and more diverse list of contract stars. New arrivals, many of whom were in the early stages of a promising career, included such dramatic performers as Richard Conte, Lee J. Cobb, Maureen O'Hara, Dorothy McGuire and young Peggy Ann Garner, along with comedy and musical stars Clifton Webb, June Haver and Jeanne Crain. In spite of the postwar decline in film audiences, the pace of new signings at Fox did not begin to slacken until the early 50s. For example, 1947 was a vintage year, with the arrival of Jean Peters, Richard Widmark, Thelma Ritter, and

Gregory Peck who registered eighth on the list of box-office stars that very year. Oscar-nominated for three of his first four roles at Fox, the combination of critical and box-office success meant that Peck soon displaced the durable Tyrone Power as the studio's top male star. (Power had never been nominated for an Oscar.) Peck became the favoured lead for director Henry King (who had originally discovered and promoted Power) and appeared in such King productions as *Twelve O'Clock High* (1949), *The Gunfighter* (1950), as well as *David And Bathsheba* (1951) and *The Snows Of Kilimanjaro* (1952) – co-starred with Susan Hayward in both.

In addition, 1947 marked the first screen appearance of Marilyn Monroe, whose bit part in *Scudda Hoo, Scudda Hay* shrunk even further in the cutting room. She was earning only $150 per week at the time, but her option was dropped by the studio and it was another two-and-a-half years before she returned to Fox. Even then it was a struggle for her to land the good parts which she felt she deserved, and she was convinced that Zanuck disliked her. Certainly Fox was slow to recognize her qualities as a singer and actress and reluctant to boost her salary or give her better parts. Thus, Monroe's years at Fox were marred by one dispute after another. At least her parts began to get larger in response to public demand, and by 1953 she had achieved full star status with the release of her first two starring pictures in Technicolor – *Niagara* and *Gentlemen Prefer Blondes* – and her first appearance on the top box-office list. But she was still earning only $1200 per week.

Later in 1953, Monroe was teamed with Lauren Bacall and Betty Grable in the studio's second CinemaScope production, *How To Marry A Millionaire*. Betty's career was winding down, and it was clear that a new blonde had taken over as queen of the Fox lot. In fact, Marilyn appears as the last link in that chain of top female stars which stretched over a period of 30 years of the studio era from 1926 to 1956, beginning with Janet Gaynor and carried on by Shirley Temple in the 30s and Grable in the 40s.

Marilyn was suspended both in late 1953 for her refusal to appear in *The Girl In Pink Tights* and early in 1955. The role which she turned down in *How To Be Very Very Popular* was taken by Sheree North, one of a number of sexy starlets whom the studio had hired in the middle-50s to keep Marilyn in line, testing them for, and occasionally giving them, parts which she refused to play. (Joan Collins, for example, got her first big break as the star of *The Girl In The Red Velvet Swing*, 1955, another role which Marilyn had rejected.) But it was Jayne Mansfield who most obviously developed her short-lived career as an (inferior) imitation of Miss Monroe. She had a special quality of her own, however, as seen most enjoyably in the glossy comedies of Frank Tashlin – *Will Success Spoil Rock Hunter?* (1957) and, especially, *The Girl Can't Help It* (1956), a cult classic for all rock 'n' roll fans.

Potentially the studio's greatest star asset, Marilyn Monroe only completed two films of worth at Fox in the nine years prior to her death in 1962 – *The Seven Year Itch* (1955), a delightful comedy directed by Billy Wilder, and *Bus Stop* (1956). (Both *Some Like It Hot*, 1959, and

The Misfits, 1961, were filmed for United Artists.) In addition to Marilyn and the Misses North, Collins and Mansfield, the studio also had Lee Remick and the Oscar-winning Joanne Woodward under contract in the late 50s, making it particularly strong on the distaff side. The 60s, too, continued to be dominated by the ladies, most notably by Elizabeth Taylor as *Cleopatra* (1963) and Julie Andrews in *The Sound Of Music* (1965), with Jacqueline Bisset and Raquel Welch as promising young discoveries. Thus, it was perhaps appropriate that the ladies should play a major role in the final downfall of Darryl (and Richard) Zanuck. The numerous box-office disasters included *Star!* (1968), a musical biopic of Gertrude Lawrence starring Julie Andrews, *Hello, Dolly!* (1969), lavishly adapted from the Broadway show with Barbra Streisand as Dolly, and *The Only Game In Town* (1969) with Elizabeth Taylor, co-starred with Warren Beatty, as a Las Vegas showgirl, and *Hello-Goodbye* (1970), a weak romantic comedy starring Zanuck's French girlfriend, Geneviève Gilles.

STARS

Adorée, Renée 1922
Albert, Eddie 1951, 1961–62
Ameche, Don 1936–44
Ames, Leon 1936–39
Andrews, Dana 1940–48
Ankers, Evelyn 1937
Astor, Mary 1928–29
Atwill, Lionel 1938–40
Ayres, Lew 1934–35
Bacall, Lauren 1953–54
Bancroft, Anne 1952–54
Bankhead, Tallulah 1943–44
Bara, Theda 1915–19
Bari, Lynn 1934–46
Barrymore, Ethel 1949–53
Baxter, Anne 1940–52
Baxter, Warner 1928–39
Bel Geddes, Barbara 1950
Bellamy, Ralph 1932
Bendix, William 1943–46
Bennett, Joan 1930–33, 1941, 1942–45
Bickford, Charles 1943–45
Blaine, Vivian 1942–46
Blythe, Betty 1933
Bogart, Humphrey 1930–31
Boles, John 1931–35
Bow, Clara 1932–33
Brady, Scott 1956–58
Brendel, El 1929–33, 1936–38
Brennan, Walter 1956–57

Brent, Evelyn 1924
Brent, George 1930–31
Brynner, Yul 1956
Burton, Richard 1952–55, 1962
Carey, MacDonald 1951–52
Carradine, John 1937–43
Carroll, Madeleine 1936
Cobb, Lee J. 1942–50, 1954–55
Coburn, Charles 1952–53
Collins, Joan 1955, 1957–60
Conte, Richard 1943–49
Conway, Tom 1947–48
Cortez, Ricardo 1939–41
Cotten, Joseph 1952–53
Crain, Jeanne 1943–53
Cregar, Laird 1940–44
Dailey, Dan 1947–54
Darnell, Linda 1939–51
Darwell, Jane 1934–41
Davis, Joan 1936–41
Del Rio, Dolores 1926–28
Derek, John 1954
Donlevy, Brian 1936–38
Douglas, Paul 1948–51
Dove, Billie 1924–25
Dunn, James 1931–35
Eilers, Sally 1931–33
Ewell, Tom 1955–56, 1961
Farnum, William 1915–23
Farrell, Charles 1926–32
Faye, Alice 1933–45

Fetchit, Stepin 1929, 1934–37
Fonda, Henry 1935, 1938–43,
   1958–59
Fontaine, Joan 1958–61
Foster, Preston 1942–44
Francis, Anne 1951–52
Garner, Peggy Ann 1942–47
Gaynor, Janet 1926–35
Gaynor, Mitzi 1950–54
Gilbert, John 1921–24
Gilmore, Virginia 1940–42
Grable, Betty 1940–53
Graves, Ralph 1926
Gray, Coleen 1947–48
Greene, Richard 1937–40
Greenwood, Charlotte 1940–46
Hall, James 1927
Hardwicke, Cedric 1943–45
Harrison, Rex 1946–48
Hasso, Signe 1945
Haver, June 1943–52
Havoc, June 1947–50
Haymes, Dick 1943–47
Hayward, Susan 1949–55
Hayworth, Rita 1935–36
Heflin, Van 1954
Henie, Sonia 1936–43
Hersholt, Jean 1936–38
Hodiak, John 1944–45
Holm, Celeste 1946–50
Hovick, Louise (Gypsy Rose Lee)
1937–38
Hunter, Jeffrey 1951–58
Huston, Walter 1945
Jean, Gloria 1955
Jolson, Al 1938–39
Jones, Buck 1918–27
Jones, Jennifer 1955–57
Jory, Victor 1933–34
Keaton, Buster 1939
Landi, Elissa 1930–33
La Plante, Laura 1921
Laurel, Stan & Hardy, Oliver 1941–44
Leslie, Joan 1940
Lorre, Peter 1936–39
Louise, Anita 1934
Lowe, Edmund 1924–27, 1929–32,
1934–35
Loy, Myrna 1930–31

Lugosi, Bela 1930
Lundigan, William 1949–53
Lyon, Ben 1932
MacDonald, Jeanette 1930–31
Malden, Karl 1944–50
Mansfield, Jayne 1956–58
Marvin, Lee 1954
Mason, James 1951, 1956–57
Mature, Victor 1941–42, 1946–48,
1950, 1953–54
McDowall, Roddy 1941–42, 1944,
1962
McGuire, Dorothy 1946–50
McLaglen, Victor 1926–32, 1935–38
Meighan, Thomas 1931
Menjou, Adolphe 1936
Merkel, Una 1931, 1950–51
Miranda, Carmen 1940–46
Mitchell, Thomas 1942–45
Mix, Tom 1917–28
Monroe, Marilyn 1950–56
Montgomery, George 1939–43,
   1946
Moorehead, Agnes 1954–55
Morley, Karen 1935
Muni, Paul 1929
Neal, Patricia 1951–52
Newman, Paul 1957–61
Nolan, Lloyd 1940–45, 1965–67
North, Sheree 1955–58
O'Brien, George 1924–35
O'Hara, Maureen 1941–43, 1945–49
O'Sullivan, Maureen 1930–31
Oakie, Jack 1940–43
Oland, Warner 1915, 1932–37
Payne, John 1940–42, 1945–47
Peck, Gregory 1947–49, 1951–52
Peters, Jean 1947–54
Power, Tyrone 1936–54
Presley, Elvis 1960
Price, Vincent 1940–46
Quinn, Anthony 1942–44, 1964–65
Rathbone, Basil 1939
Ray, Charles 1941–42
Raymond, Gene 1933–34
Remick, Lee 1957–60
Rennie, Michael 1950–57
Ritter, Thelma 1947–53
Ritz Brothers, The 1936–39

Robertson, Dale 1949–54
Rogers, Ginger 1952
Rogers, Will 1929–35
Roland, Gilbert 1934–36
Romero, Cesar 1937–49
Ryan, Robert 1955–56
Sanders, George 1936–38, 1942–43, 1947–50
Scott, Randolph 1938–41
Scott, Zachary 1951
Sheridan, Ann 1949–50
Shirley, Anne 1928–30
Sills, Milton 1930
Silvers, Phil 1941–45
Simmons, Jean 1953–54
Simon, Simone 1936–37
Sondergaard, Gale 1940
Starke, Pauline 1923–24
Stewart, James 1949–50
Stuart, Gloria 1935–39
Temple, Shirley 1934–40

Tierney, Gene 1940–55
Tracy, Lee 1929–30
Tracy, Spencer 1930–35
Trevor, Claire 1933–37
Twelvetrees, Helen 1929, 1933–34
Vallee, Rudy 1948–49
Vera-Ellen 1946
Wagner, Robert 1950–59
Walsh, George 1915–20
Wayne, John 1927–30
Webb, Clifton 1944–61
Welles, Orson 1957–58
White, Pearl 1920–22
Widmark, Richard 1947–54
Wilde, Cornel 1941–43, 1945–48
Withers, Jane 1934–42
Wood, Natalie 1945–49
Woodward, Joanne 1957–60
Young, Loretta 1934–39
Young, Roland 1939–40

The Directors

Throughout its history Fox generally had a solid line-up of directors under contract. John Ford and Henry Hathaway spent the better part of 20 years at the studio, and Henry King was there for 30 years. Others, such as Frank Borzage, Raoul Walsh, Howard Hawks, John Stahl, Allan Dwan, Elia Kazan, Otto Preminger and Joseph Mankiewicz, made their home at Fox for extended periods. Indeed, the studio's most successful years, roughly 1925–30 and 1939–50, are the periods when the contribution made by its directors is most evident. The departure of Kazan, Preminger and Mankiewicz to become independent producer-directors in the early 50s was a major blow from which the studio never recovered.

During the early years, the leading Fox directors were competent craftsmen. There was the young Raoul Walsh, Frank Lloyd, and J. Gordon Edwards who directed most of the Theda Bara movies. John Ford arrived in 1921 and regarded the studio as a step up from Universal where he had started, providing him with a better opportunity to extend his range beyond formula Westerns. Roland V. Lee arrived in 1922 and William Wellman got his first chance, directing Westerns, during 1923–24.

As the studio began to expand in the middle 20s important changes were taking place. Ford made a major breakthrough in 1924 with *The Iron Horse* which, in his words, started out as 'just a simple little story.' But it grew as filming progressed on location in Nevada, far from the studio bosses, 'and came out as a so-called "epic", the biggest picture Fox had ever made.'

New arrivals in 1925 included Frank Borzage, and Howard Hawks who had previous experience as a producer, scriptwriter and shorts director. Given his first crack at feature directing, Hawks had his biggest successes with *A Girl In Every Port*, filmed in 1927 with Victor McLaglen and Louise Brooks, and *Trent's Last Case*, his first talkie released early in 1929. Raoul Walsh returned in 1926, the same year that William Fox signed up his 'German genius', F. W. Murnau. The presence of this new group was soon reflected in the improved quality of Fox productions from which some big hits emerged.

Ford directed another memorable Western, *Three Bad Men* (1926), featuring a striking landrush sequence, then had a big hit with his World War I drama, *Four Sons*, filmed in 1927. Borzage had two big successes in a row with *Seventh Heaven* (1927) and *Street Angel* (1928), both starring Janet Gaynor and Charles Farrell, while in *The River* (1928) Farrell was teamed with Mary Duncan. All three films were visually striking, and intense, lyrical love stories typical of the director at his best.

Raoul Walsh was the most consistently successful at the box-office, beginning in 1926 with the World War I movie, *What Price Glory?*, followed by *The Red Dance* (1928) starring Dolores Del Rio and set against the background of the Russian revolution, reflecting Walsh's special affinity for action and adventure in exotic settings. He had big hits with his first talkies in 1929 – *In Old Arizona*, which he co-directed with Irving Cummings, having been injured during filming, and *The Cock-Eyed World*, a comedy adventure sequel to *What Price Glory?* scripted by Walsh himself and an even bigger hit.

Murnau, in contrast, made remarkable but uncommercial pictures, yet brought the studio great prestige, particularly with his expensive masterpiece *Sunrise*. Given *carte blanche* by Fox, he shot this film during 1926–27 within a controlled world which he had created on some of the most elaborate exterior sets ever constructed for an American production. At Lake Arrowhead he and his German art director built a rural village, together with the downtown area of a city and Luna Park fairground; and he used many effects characteristic of the German Expressionist cinema. He followed *Sunrise* with *Four Devils* (1928), a circus drama also starring the popular Janet Gaynor, then made *Our Daily Bread* which was taken away from him, shortened and released as a part-talkie in 1930 under the title *City Girl*.

Hawks and Murnau left in 1929 and by the end of 1932 Walsh and Borzage had also gone, while Ford was dividing his time between Fox and other studios – in particular RKO. In spite of the arrival in 1930 of Frank Lloyd, who directed the Oscar-winning *Cavalcade* in 1933, and Henry King, the list of directors included few major talents. Typical Fox directors of this period were H. Bruce Humberstone, Sidney Lanfield, and musical specialists David Butler, Irving Cummings and Walter Lang. Butler had been a Fox actor in the silent era before he switched to directing in 1927 and had his biggest hits with the Gaynor-Farrell vehicles *Sunny Side Up* (1929), then with Will Rogers as *A Connecticut Yankee* (1931) and a number of popular Shirley Temple movies.

John Ford continued to direct the occasional film of note at Fox throughout the 30s: *Pilgrimage* (1933) was a post-World War I human-interest drama; he made an unusual (post-Civil War) historical picture, *The Prisoner Of Shark Island* (1936) starring Warner Baxter; three Ford movies starred the remarkable Will Rogers with whom the director enjoyed a special rapport; and he cast Shirley Temple as *Wee Willie Winkie* in 1937. Ford's growth in stature as a director during 1939–41 coincided with a general upgrading of the Fox product. It was a real turning point for the studio when Zanuck began to assemble a contract list of quality directors – he badly needed these if he was to maintain Fox's position as a top studio in terms of acclaim and awards as well as profits. In the space of a few years he acquired the services of a fine selection of mainly well-established directors. Fritz Lang, Rouben Mamoulian and Henry Hathaway were all hired in 1940, followed by John Stahl in 1942, Lubitsch and Lewis Milestone in 1943 and Edmund Goulding in 1946. In addition, Zanuck gave a second chance to Otto Preminger who had directed a couple of minor films for the studio in the 30s, and signed up two promising new talents – Elia Kazan, who had made his name in the New York theatre, and Joseph Mankiewicz, already a veteran producer and screenwriter (though only in his mid-thirties) who was eager to try his hand at directing.

The general quality and range of pictures which emerged from this group was impressive and registered well with the critics and at the box-office. The contributions of Ford, Kazan and Mankiewicz in particular helped the studio to gain a major share of the Oscars, making up for earlier years. Ford directed Henry Fonda in a memorable group of pictures including *The Grapes Of Wrath* (1940), then helped Zanuck to win his first Best Picture Oscar with *How Green Was My Valley* (1941). Mamoulian concentrated on stylish costumers both in black-and-white, *The Mark Of Zorro* (1940), and colour, *Blood And Sand* (1942) starring Tyrone Power, Linda Darnell and Rita Hayworth. Preminger mixed thrillers such as *Laura* (1944) and *Where The Sidewalk Ends* (1950), both starring Dana Andrews and Gene Tierney, with drama and costume pictures. Milestone specialized in war subjects – *The Purple Heart* (1944) and *A Walk In The Sun* (1945) with Dana Andrews. Kazan concentrated on American themes past and present, with particular attention to contemporary social problems in *Gentleman's Agreement* (1947) and *Pinky* (1949), as well as such superior thrillers as *Panic In The Streets* (1950). Henry King covered the widest range, from religious (*The Song Of Bernadette*, 1943) to historical (*Wilson*, 1944) to war (*Twelve O'Clock High*, 1949) to Westerns (*The Gunfighter*, 1950). Henry Hathaway was best known for his thrillers with a social theme, often based on true stories and filmed on location – such as *The House On 92nd Street* (1945), *Kiss Of Death* (1947) and *Call Northside 777* (1948). Mankiewicz was at his best with witty and satirical dramas, notably *A Letter To Three Wives* (1949) and *All About Eve* (1950), on which he could exercise his talents as Fox's leading writer-director.

In the early 50s most of these leading Fox directors left the studio to freelance as independent producer-directors. One arrival of note was the veteran Howard Hawks, returning to the studio where he had started directing over 20 years before. He collaborated with Cary Grant on a couple of delightful screwball comedies, *I Was A Male War Bride* (1949) and *Monkey Business* (1952), and gave a major boost to Marilyn Monroe with a small part in the latter and a co-starring role with Jane Russell in the musical *Gentlemen Prefer Blondes* (1953).

A few other arrivals, mainly directors of the second rank – Jean Negulesco, Delmer Daves, Sam Fuller – could not make up for the departures, and the new emphasis on glossy entertainment in colour and CinemaScope contrasted unfavourably with the studio's harder-hitting black-and-white films of the 40s.

Mankiewicz returned to direct *Cleopatra* in the early 60s, and directors Robert Wise and Gene Kelly handled a number of Fox productions, mainly musicals. But the studio's last long-serving director in the 50s, and again in the late 60s, was Richard Fleischer, who finally came unstuck at the same time as the Zanucks with such bombs as *Che!* (1969) and *Tora! Tora! Tora!* (1970).

DIRECTORS

Archainbaud, George 1935
Bacon, Lloyd 1944–49, 1951–53
Blystone, John 1924–36
Borzage, Frank 1925–32
Brahm, John 1941–44
Butler, David 1927–38
Cline, Edward 1934–35
Conway, Jack 1924
Cummings, Irving 1926, 1928–31, 1933–36, 1938–43, 1945
Dassin, Jules 1949–50
Daves, Delmer 1950–53
del Ruth, Roy 1935–40
Dieterle, William 1933
Dillon, John Francis 1932–33
Dmytryk, Edward 1954–55, 1957–59
Donen, Stanley 1966–69
Dwan, Allan 1926–27, 1929, 1931–32, 1935–40, 1957
Fleischer, Richard 1955–61, 1966–69
Fleming, Victor 1930
Ford, John 1921–31, 1933–35, 1938–41
Forde, Eugene 1932–47
Foster, Norman 1936–41
Fuller, Samuel 1951–57
Garnett, Tay 1936–37
Gordon, Michael 1951
Goulding, Edmund 1946–58
Green, Alfred E. 1927–29
Hathaway, Henry 1940, 1942–56, 1958–60
Hawks, Howard 1925–29, 1952–53
Howard, William K 1921, 1928–33
Humberstone, H. Bruce 1935–48
Huston, John 1957–58
Kazan, Elia 1945, 1947–50, 1952–53
King, Henry 1930–61
Koster, Henry 1948–56

Lachman, Harry 1933–36, 1940–42
Lanfield, Sidney 1930–33, 1935–39
Lang, Fritz 1940–42
Lang, Walter 1937–61
Lee, Rowland V. 1922–27, 1932–34
Leeds, Herbert 1938–48
Levin, Henry 1952–53
Litvak, Anatole 1948, 1951, 1955–56
Lloyd, Frank 1917–19, 1931–34
Lubitsch, Ernst 1943–47
MacFadden, Hamilton 1930–34
Mamoulian, Rouben 1940–42
Mankiewicz, Joseph L. 1945–51
Marin, Edwin L. 1949
Marshall, George 1920–21, 1926–27, 1934–38
Mayo, Archie 1940–44
Mazursky, Paul 1974–80
McCarey, Leo 1930, 1957–61
Milestone, Lewis 1943–45, 1951–52
Murnau, F.W. 1926–29
Negulesco, Jean 1948–58
Neill, Roy William 1925–27
Newman, Joseph M. 1951–53
Pichel, Irving 1939–43
Preminger, Otto 1936–37, 1942–50
Ratoff, Gregory 1936–40, 1944–47
Ray, Nicholas 1956
Reis, Irving 1949
Ritt, Martin 1957–58, 1970–74
Robson, Mark 1957–62
St Clair, Malcolm 1933, 1936–40, 1943–45, 1948
Sale, Richard 1950–53
Santell, Alfred 1929–33
Schertzinger, Victor 1925–27
Schuster, Harold 1937, 1941–43
Seaton, George 1945–50

Sedgwick, Edward 1920–22
Seiter, William A. 1936–38
Stahl, John M. 1942–49
Sturges, Preston 1948–49
Tashlin, Frank 1955–62
Taurog, Norman 1936–37
Taylor, Sam 1931–32

Van Dyke, W.S. 1924–25
Walsh, Raoul 1915–20, 1926–32,
   1955–56, 1958–61
Wellman, William A. 1923–24
Werker, Alfred L. 1929–33,
   1937–39, 1941–42
Wise, Robert 1950–53, 1964–68

The Creative Personnel

George Schneiderman and Ernest Palmer were the studio's most reliable and prolific cameramen in the early years. From 1939 on, Arthur Miller proved that he was one of the best black-and-white specialists around, while Leon Shamroy became expert in Technicolor cinematography and went on to distinguish himself in CinemaScope and 70mm filming in later years.

William Darling was the mainstay of the small Fox art department. It was not until Zanuck took over in 1935 that the department began to grow and gained a new prestige. There was a steady stream of important new arrivals – distinguished supervising art director Richard Day was succeeded by Lyle Wheeler and, finally, Jack Martin Smith from the late 50s on.

Zanuck had a major influence in upgrading the studio's other specialized departments, including make-up and special effects. He also brought with him chief editor Barbara McLean and composer Alfred Newman, both of whom became fixtures at the studio for 20 years. Charles LeMaire was supervising costume designer from 1943 up to the late 50s and assembled an outstanding team of collaborators which was the equal of any other studio.

Cameramen and Art Directors

During the early period prior to 1939 the Fox studio was not particularly known for the quality of its cameramen who tended to be solid craftsmen rather than major creative talents. George Schneiderman, for example, spent almost 20 years with Fox beginning in 1919; he served as cameraman on many of John Ford's silents, then alternated with Joe August on Ford's early talkies. A few top men – James Wong Howe, Lee Garmes, Hal Mohr – worked at the studio in the early 30s but soon moved on.

For *Sunrise* (1927), a special production, director F.W. Murnau was not restricted to Fox personnel and he was allowed to make his own choice of cameraman. He selected two of the best, Charles Rosher and Karl Struss, and they won the first cinematography Oscar for their efforts. (Rosher recalled it as a 'very difficult film . . . For some scenes, such as the swamp sequence, the camera went in a complete circle. This created enormous lighting problems . . . It was a big undertaking; practically every shot was on the move.') Murnau, however, used a Fox cameraman, Ernest Palmer, for his more modest second feature, a circus drama, *Four Devils* (1928). Palmer became a fixture at the studio, staying on for almost 30 years through various changes of management, and making the transition from silents to sound, black-and-white to colour. Having gained his first Oscar nomination for the Murnau silent, he was last nominated for the Technicolored *Broken Arrow* in 1950.

The year 1939 marked a turning point for the studio. Most important was the arrival of Leon Shamroy, who would remain at Fox for 30 years and develop into the studio's leading colour specialist and top cinematography Oscar winner. Arthur Miller, like Shamroy, had been a lighting cameraman for many years without gaining much recognition. (Both had to wait a long time for their first Oscar nominations.) At Fox from 1932, Miller handled many of the Shirley Temple pictures, but only began to get better assignments from 1939 on. During the following years he worked with virtually all the studio's important new directors – Mamoulian, Lang, Stahl, Kazan and Mankiewicz – as well as Ford and King. Once given the opportunity, he rose to the challenge and emerged as one of Hollywood's leading black-and-white cameramen.

Both Shamroy and Miller were Oscar-nominated in 1940, marking the beginning of a decade in which the quality of Fox cinematography in both colour and black-and-white compared favourably with all the other major studios. Miller won his first statuette the following year for Ford's *How Green Was My Valley* in black-and-white at the same time that Ernest Palmer won his only Oscar for *Blood And Sand* in Technicolor, while Shamroy had to wait till the next year for *his* first for the Technicolored *The Black Swan*. Miller and Shamroy were nominated many more times and ended up with several Academy Awards each. The Fox camera department was also considerably strengthened by the arrival of Joe MacDonald, Joseph LaShelle (Oscar for *Laura* in 1944) and Milton Krasner, who lent distinction to the studio's many CinemaScope productions in the 50s, winning the first CinemaScope Oscar for *Three Coins In The Fountain* (1954).

It was Shamroy, however, as Fox's most prestigious cinematographer, who led the way into CinemaScope. Assigned to the very first production, *The Robe* (1953), he handled other early 'Scope productions such as *The Egyptian* (1954). He was then involved in the studio's later ventures into large format (70mm) filming with *The King And I* (1956) in the new CinemaScope 55 process and another musical, *South Pacific* (1958), Fox's first Todd-AO production. Shamroy won his last Oscar in 1963 for the Todd-AO lensing of *Cleopatra*, then rounded out his career at the studio with such pictures as *Planet Of The Apes* (1967) and *Justine* (1969).

The first production designer to make his name at Fox in the 20s was the Hungarian-born William Sandorhazi Darling who arrived in 1922 after one year with the American Film Company and one year with Louis B. Mayer. He soon established himself as the studio's chief art director, a position he maintained for a quarter of a century. During the course of his 25 years at Fox he collaborated on numerous John Ford productions and won an Oscar for his work on *Cavalcade* (1933), *The Song Of Bernadette* (1943), and *Anna And The King Of Siam* (1946) near the end of his long career. Aside from his contribution to these, and other expensive productions such as *Lloyds Of London* (1936) and *In Old Chicago* (1937), some of his most impressive designs were for small-scale pictures; he provided convincingly gloomy back street sets for *While Paris Sleeps* (1932) directed by Allan Dwan, and an unusual main setting for the *Zoo In Budapest* (1933), which took him back to his roots.

Many top designers only stayed briefly at the studio. Murnau brought in his German art director, Rochus Gliese, who was reponsible for the remarkable atmospheric look of *Sunrise* (1927), one of the landmarks of Hollywood production design in the late 20s. Ben Carré, the pioneering French art director who had designed pictures for Maurice Tourneur a decade earlier (1914–1920), arrived at Fox in 1928. He worked on five films for director Raoul Walsh, including the striking Russian settings for *The Red Dance* (1928), and collaborated with Darling and Harry Oliver on Murnau's *City Girl* in 1929. Oliver had made his name a couple of years earlier working with Frank Borzage. His imaginative Paris settings for *Seventh Heaven* (1927) had earned him an Oscar nomination, in competition with Gliese's designs for *Sunrise*, a fine reflection of the quality of the Fox art department in these years.

Similarly, Stephen Goosson was nominated for his extraordinary futuristic vision of 1980 New York created for the El Brendel musical, *Just Imagine* (1931), then left to become the leading designer and supervising art director at Columbia. But it was a cameraman, James Wong Howe, who claimed responsibility for the authentically claustrophobic shipboard feel of *Transatlantic* (1931). A master of naturalistic lighting, Howe insisted that the passage-ways should be narrow, with ceilings above, '. . . and I made him change the engine room as well so there were more foreground pieces, more perspective', he recalled. Thus Howe was really responsible for Gordon Wiles winning his Oscar for art direction.

When Zanuck took over in 1935 he immediately began to build up the art department, hiring Hans Peters, Rudolph Sternad and Mark-Lee Kirk. But it was only in the late 30s, as part of the general upgrading of the Fox output and a further expansion of the department, that it could claim to match any other Hollywood studio in the variety and quality of its design work. The Russian-born Boris Leven had arrived in 1938, followed by Richard Day, Wiard Ihnen and Joseph Wright in 1939. Nathan Juran and Maurice Ransford were hired in 1940, James Basevi in 1941 and Lyle Wheeler in 1944. Wheeler later took over as supervising art director for a dozen years after the departure of Day in the late 40s.

Because of Zanuck's early interest in colour, the Fox art department was the first to adapt to handling a range of Technicolor films as well as black-and-white. The veteran Darling, with Leven and Ransford, continued to concentrate on black-and-white. Leven was Oscar-nominated for *Alexander's Ragtime Band* (1938) and provided imaginative designs for *Tales Of Manhattan* (1942). Ransford worked on *Brigham Young* (1940), the low-keyed *Hangover Square* (1944) and was nominated for *The Foxes Of Harrow* (1947) and *Titanic* (1953). Day and Juran collaborated on the black-lot recreation of a Welsh mining village in *How Green Was My Valley* (1941 Oscar-winner) and the prestige production of *The Razor's Edge* (1946 Oscar nominee). In contrast, Joseph Wright supplied the bright, sharp colour designs for the popular musicals. He was Oscar-nominated for *Down Argentine Way* (1940) and Busby Berkeley's delightfully extravagant *The Gang's All Here* (1943) and won for *My Gal Sal* (1942), while some of the most stylish work in colour came from Ihnen, credited with *The Blue Bird* (1940) and co-credited on the Oscar-winning *Wilson* (1944). (He had designed the first two Technicolor features, for Pioneer Pictures, in 1935.)

A number of late arrivals of note, George Davis, John DeCuir and Jack Martin Smith, along with Wheeler and Leland Fuller, ensured that the studio would continue to maintain one of the most productive of studio art departments throughout the 50s, well able to cope with the many glossy costumers, musicals and other CinemaScope productions. Jack Martin Smith became the leading designer at Fox, continuing on into the early 70s, and was rejoined on major productions by a number of art department alumni: DeCuir returned to collaborate on the spectacular Oscar-winning designs for both *Cleopatra* (1963) and *Hello, Dolly!* (1969) as well as *The Agony And The Ecstasy* (1965). Boris Leven was brought back by director Robert Wise for his three Fox movies – *The Sound of Music* (1965), *The Sand Pebbles* (1966) and *Star!* (1968) – all nominated for their production design. And the veteran Richard Day came back too, for *The Valley Of The Dolls* (1967), and *Tora! Tora! Tora!* (1970) which earned him a last Oscar nomination just a year before his death.

Other Departments

When Darryl Zanuck arrived in 1935 he immediately set about reorganizing and upgrading the studio's various technical departments so that, in many cases, the most interesting and creative contributions by leading technicians, ranging from special-effects experts to costume designers, date from this period. Frequently, they set a standard of expertise which was upheld by later arrivals.

For example, Ern Westmore, one of the most gifted members of the well-known family of make-up experts, began working at Fox at this time, establishing a tradition which was carried on for a further 20 years or so by Ben Nye, while John Chambers won a special Oscar for his work in creating the remarkably life-like ape characters in the *Planet Of The Apes* (1967). Fred Sersen took charge of the special-effects department and provided the spectacular destruction sequences for *In*

Old Chicago (1937) and *Suez* (1938). Frequently nominated, Sersen won Oscars for *The Rains Came* (1939) in black-and-white, and the Technicolored *Crash Dive* (1943). His work was carried on in the 50s by Ray Kellogg and by technical wizard L.B. 'Bill' Abbott in later years on such blockbusters as *Dr Dolittle* (1967), *Tora! Tora! Tora!* (1970) and *The Poseidon Adventure* (1972), all three winning him Oscars.

As an accomplished editor himself, Zanuck supervised the editing of most Fox features, assisted by a staff of long-serving cutters headed by Barbara McLean who arrived with him from 20th Century. (After five previous nominations, she finally won her first Oscar for editing *Wilson* in 1944.) Others who were first hired during 1935–38 and spent virtually their entire careers at Fox were Nick De Maggio, Robert Simpson (Oscar-nominated for *The Grapes Of Wrath*, 1940), and James B.Clark (nominated for *How Green Was My Valley*, 1941); also Dorothy Spencer (1943–63) and Louis Loeffler (1927–61), while William Reynolds emerged as the studio's leading editor in the 60s and an Oscar winner for *The Sound Of Music* (1965), directed by another leading editor, Robert Wise.

Yet another important figure who was employed by Zanuck at 20th Century, then joined him at Fox, was the tremendously prolific and versatile composer and conductor Alfred Newman, a multiple Oscar winner who spent over 20 years at the studio, much of that period as musical director. Some of his achievements during those years include *Alexander's Ragtime Band* (1938), *With A Song In My Heart* (1952) and *Love Is A Many Splendored Thing* (1955). Newman was joined for a time in the 40s and 50s by such outstanding musical talents as David Raksin (evocative scores for *Laura*, 1944, and *Forever Amber*, 1947), Bernard Herrmann (*Anna And The King of Siam*, 1946), and Hugo Friedhofer, testifying to the quality of the music department particularly during the Zanuck years.

Similarly, costume designer Gwen Wakeling moved from 20th Century to Fox where she shared the A pictures with Royer, while Herschel handled the B's on the separate B lot. Charles LeMaire was hired in 1943 and immediately took charge of the department, serving for many years as supervising costume designer. To cope with the studio's diverse list of black-and-white and Technicolor productions, LeMaire assembled a stellar team of designers: Kay Nelson, René Hubert, Bonnie Cashin and Oleg Cassini. He continued to design for his favourite stars, while working closely with the members of his staff, checking sketches and often present at fittings. The department flourished throughout the 50s, kept active by the requirements of the studio's large number of period films, epics and musicals in colour and CinemaScope.

Fox's last star designer in the 60s was Irene Sharaff who worked on many of the big pictures of the period, was Oscar-nominated for the lavish musicals *Can-Can* (1960) and *Hello, Dolly!* (1969), and won for the stunning costumes she designed for *Cleopatra* (1963) in collaboration with Renie who had also been at Fox in the 50s.

CAMERAMEN

Andriot, Lucien 1928–31, 1936–44
August, Joseph 1923–32
Ballard, Lucien 1942–44, 1951–55
Barnes, George 1940–41
Brodine, Norbert 1943–49
Clarke, Charles 1928–33, 1938–61
De Vinna, Clyde 1943–45
Edeson, Arthur 1928–31
Garmes, Lee 1932–34
Glennon, Bert 1934–36, 1939
Howe, James Wong 1931–33
Krasner, Milton 1949–59
La Shelle, Joseph 1943–54
MacDonald, Joseph 1941–59

MacWilliams, Glen 1925–32, 1941–46
Marley, J. Peverell 1934–44
Maté, Rudolph 1935–36
Mescall, John 1938
Miller, Arthur 1932–50
Mohr, Hal 1932–34
Palmer, Ernest 1925–50
Planck, Robert 1933, 1937–39
Rosson, Hal 1929
Schneiderman, George 1919–35
Seitz, John 1931–36
Shamroy, Leon 1939–69
Valentine, Joseph 1924–30, 1934
Van Enger, Charles 1929–30

ART DIRECTORS

Basevi, James 1941–47
Carré, Ben 1928–35
Darling, William 1922–46
Davis, George 1947–56
Day, Richard 1939–47
DeCuir, John 1949–62
Fuller, Leland 1943–61
Goosson, Stephen 1930
Haas, Robert 1927–28
Herzbrun, Bernard 1937–39
Hogsett, Albert 1934–57
Ihnen, Wiard 1939–44
Juran, Nathan 1940–46
Kirk, Charles M. 1929–30
Kirk, Mark-Lee 1936–40, 1945–59

Leven, Boris 1938–47, 1951–52
Menzies, William Cameron 1931–33
Oliver, Harry 1927–30, 1932
Otterson, Jack 1934–35
Parker, Max 1933–35
Peters, Hans 1935–40
Ransford, Maurice 1940–61
Schulze, Jack 1929–32
Smith, Jack Martin 1954–73
Spencer, J. Russell 1943–52
Sternad, Rudolph 1936–40
Urban, Joseph 1930–31
Wheeler, Lyle 1944–60
Wright, Joseph C. 1929–33, 1939–53

COSTUME DESIGNERS

Banton, Travis 1939–41
Cashin, Bonnie 1943–49
Cassini, Oleg 1942–50
Cox, David 1931–32
Herschel 1936–43
Hubert, René 1931–35, 1943–50
Jeakins, Dorothy 1952–54
Kaufman, Rita 1933–34
Lambert, William 1933–36
LeMaire, Charles 1943–59
Luick, Earl 1942–43
Mabry, Moss 1963–68

Myron, Helen 1935–40
Nelson, Kay 1943–55
Palmer, Adele 1957–59
Renie 1950–54, 1957
Rose, Helen 1943
Royer 1933–39
Stevenson, Edward 1950–52
Travilla, William 1949–56
Tree, Dolly 1929–32
Wachner, Sophie 1925–31
Wakeling, Gwen 1935–42
Wood, Yvonne 1943–45

COMPOSERS AND MUSIC DIRECTORS

Amfitheatrof, Daniele 1949
Buttolph, David 1935–47
Friedhofer, Hugo 1930–36, 1943–44, 1952, 1954–59
Herrmann, Bernard 1944–47, 1951–56
Lange, Arthur 1933–38, 1942–43
Mockridge, Cyril J. 1935–61

Newman, Alfred 1938–59
Newman, Emil 1941–47
Newman, Lionel 1946–60
Raksin, David 1942, 1944–49
Rapee, Erno 1924–29, 1931
Rosen, Milton 1948
Silvers, Louis 1936–40

EDITORS

Allen, Fred 1935–43
Beetley, Samuel 1962–67
Bischoff, Robert 1933–35, 1939–42
Boemler, George 1961–62
Bretherton, David 1955–62
Clancey, Margaret 1927–35
Clark, James B. 1938–61
Colbert, Norman 1938–46
Curtiss, Ray 1943–44
De Gaetano, Al 1929–40
De Maggio, Nick 1935–53
Dietrich, Ralph 1928–36
Fowler, Hugh 1952–62
Fritch, Robert 1943–52
Gilmore, Stuart 1957–59
Goodkind, Saul 1948
Hull, Frank 1929–33

Jones, Harmon 1944–50
Loeffler, Louis 1927–61
McLean, Barbara 1935–54
McNeil, Allen 1935–43
Morley, James 1938
Morra, Irene 1928–38
Morse, Terrell 1951–53
Murray, Jack 1929–38
Nosler, Lloyd 1935–37
Reynolds, William 1947–60, 65–70
Schuster, Harold 1929–35
Simpson, Robert 1937–69
Spencer, Dorothy 1943–63
Thompson, Walter 1937–43
Troffey, Alex 1928–40
Weatherwax, Paul 1929–30
White, Merrill 1951–53

SCRIPTWRITERS

Axelrod, George 1955–56, 1965–68
Behrman, S.N. 1930–33
Boehm, Sydney 1954–60
Brackett, Charles 1950–59
Burke, Edwin 1929–35
Diamond, I.A.L. 1951–52
Dunne, Philip 1934–59
Ephron, Henry and Phoebe 1950–56
Furthman, Jules 1920–23, 1930–31
Johnson, Nunnally 1935–42, 1949–63
Lederer, Charles 1949–53

Levien, Sonya 1929–40
Mayes, Wendell 1956–58
Nichols, Dudley 1929–35
Raphaelson, Samson 1934–35
Reisch, Walter 1949–59
Rivkin, Allen 1935–39
Robinson, Casey 1949–54
Seaton, George 1941–50
Trotti, Lamar 1933–54
Tugend, Harry 1935–39

The Academy Awards

Over the years Fox has had its fair share of Academy Award successes, beginning at the very first ceremony (for 1927/28) when *Sunrise* and *Seventh Heaven* between them captured a major quota of the awards. Best Picture winners have been spaced over a 40-year period from *Cavalcade* (1932/33) to *The French Connection* (1971), and have included a variety of films along the way such as *How Green Was My Valley* (1941), *Gentleman's Agreement* (1947) and *All About Eve* (1950), the musical *The Sound Of Music* (1965), and the war movie *Patton* (1970). Fox was strong on directors, and its distinguished list of award winners includes Borzage, Murnau, Ford, Kazan and Mankiewicz, while the studio has won more than its share of technical honours especially for art direction and cinematography. Fox's stars, however, have generally been overlooked by the Academy.

F.W. Murnau's *Sunrise*, his first American picture, and the sensitively directed *Seventh Heaven*, from Frank Borzage, both starred Janet Gaynor and were released in 1927. These two films ensured Fox a fine start to the first year of the Academy Awards. Each won two statuettes – *Sunrise* for cinematography and 'artistic quality of production', *Seventh Heaven* for director and screenplay – and they shared credit (along with Borzage's *Street Angel*, 1928) for the Best Actress award won by Miss Gaynor. In the succeeding years Warner Baxter was voted Best Actor for *In Old Arizona* (1929) and Borzage gained his second Oscar for directing *Bad Girl* (1932).

At the Oscar ceremony for 1932/33, Fox's *Cavalcade* was a surprising choice as Best Picture from the 10 productions nominated, which included RKO's *Little Women* and Warner Bros.' *I Am A Fugitive From A Chain Gang*. Director Frank Lloyd and art director William Darling were also honoured in Fox's two strongest technical categories. The studio's supervising art director in the 30s, Darling would be nominated four more times and share in two more Oscars in later years, while Stephen Goosson had been nominated for the remarkable set designs of *Just Imagine* (1931). In fact, the problems experienced by the studio during the next years, which only gradually recovered under Zanuck, meant that Fox failed to win any Oscars in 1934–36 and only a handful of minor awards during 1937–39, including a supporting Oscar for Alice Brady (*In Old Chicago*, 1937) and one for supporting actor Walter Brennan (*Kentucky*, 1938).

Fox made a strong showing in 1940, a turning-point year preceding a memorable decade. In the years from 1941–1950 the studio won three Best Picture Oscars along with numerous other awards. And it was unlucky not to win in 1940, for John Ford's outstanding *The Grapes Of Wrath* which did receive the top award from the New York Film Critics. Ford himself won the directing Oscar and the New York Critics' directing award. Other Fox nominations in 1940 drew attention to top technical personnel – cameramen Arthur Miller and Leon Shamroy and art director Richard Day – while Alfred Newman got an Oscar for his *Tin Pan Alley* score to go with the one he had received two years earlier for *Alexander's Ragtime Band* (1938). (Two more Oscars in the 40s and four in the 50s made him by far the studio's top Oscar winner.)

In 1941 20th Century-Fox finally won its first Best Picture Oscar for *How Green Was My Valley*. Additional Oscars went to supporting actor Donald Crisp and director John Ford who won the New York Critics award, too, for the second year running. The studio continued to do well with the technical awards and dominated the cinematography and art-direction categories (in both colour and black-and-white) in 1941–46 when the multiple winners were cameraman Leon Shamroy (colour) and Arthur Miller (black-and-white), along with supervising art director Richard Day (colour *and* black-and-white).

Fox, however, experienced a notable lack of success with its stars. From 1930 through 1969 only five leads in Fox pictures won Oscars – Jennifer Jones for *The Song Of Bernadette* (1943), Joanne Woodward for *The Three Faces Of Eve* (1957), Yul Brynner in *The King And I* and Ingrid Bergman as *Anastasia* in 1956, and Maggie Smith in the British-produced *The Prime Of Miss Jean Brodie* (1969). In the case of the Oscar-nominated *The Grapes Of Wrath* and the Oscar-winning *All About Eve* (1950), Henry Fonda and Bette Davis had only nominations from the Academy. Miss Davis, however, won the New York Film Critics award – indeed, Fox stars tended to do better in New York than in LA. Other New York winners were Olivia de Havilland for *The Snake Pit* (1948) and Gregory Peck for *Twelve O'Clock High* (1949).

The studio fared better with its directors, most notably relative new-comers Elia Kazan and Joseph Mankiewicz. Kazan won the directing Oscar in 1947 for *Gentleman's Agreement*, the year's Best Picture in the eyes of both the Academy and the New York Critics. But as the studio's best decade drew to a close, it was Mankiewicz who led the way, with Oscars for directing and scripting both *A Letter To Three Wives* (1949) and *All About Eve* – which also garnered the Best Picture award from the Academy and the New York Film Critics in 1950.

After this run of successes, the following years were a let-down. Fox made its best showing in the technical categories, mostly related to its introduction of CinemaScope in 1953 – two special Oscars added to two for colour art direction and costume design for *The Robe*, the first CinemaScope production, and one for the colour cinematography of *Three Coins In The Fountain* (1954). The stylish accomplishments of the studio's art department continued to provide Fox with most of its Oscars through the 50s and 60s, with a total of seven awards shared among Lyle Wheeler, John DeCuir, George Davis, Jack Martin Smith and Harry Horner, and a further 24 nominations. The studio's only Best Picture and director Oscars during this period went to the popular musical, *The Sound Of Music*, and its director Robert Wise.

Fox's biggest success since *All About Eve* exactly 20 years earlier came with the ambitious World War II biopic, *Patton* (1970), which won a total of seven Oscars – including Best Actor George C. Scott, impressive in the title role (also recognized by the NY Critics), director Franklin Schaffner and scriptwriters Francis Coppola and Edmund North. (Scott, who disapproves of the Oscars, refused his.) The studio repeated with these same four categories the following year. The picture was a fast-moving thriller, *The French Connection* (1971), the lead actor was Gene Hackman, and the director a relative newcomer, William Friedkin.

More recently, the studio's successes have mainly been concentrated in the technical categories. *Star Wars*, for example, gained seven technical Oscars in 1977, while Bob Fosse's *All That Jazz* (1979) won four. Perhaps Fox's frustrating lack of major Oscars is best exemplified by *The Turning Point* which set a record in 1977 (matched in 1985 by Steven Spielberg's *The Color Purple*), when it gained 11 nominations without winning a single award.

The studio has had just three major Oscar winners in the past 20 years – veteran Art Carney was the surprise Best Actor winner for *Harry and Tonto* (1974) and Sally Field won for *Norma Rae* in 1979. But Michael Douglas was the studio's most prominent star asset in the 80s, as producer and co-star of *Romancing the Stone* (1984) and *The Jewel of the Nile* (1985) with Kathleen Turner and Danny De Vito who also joined him in *The War of the Roses* in 1989. He came up a winner in 1987 for his performance in Oliver Stone's *Wall Street*. Fox's other acting awards in the supporting categories included statuettes to the elderly producer turned actor, John Houseman, for *The Paper Chase* (1973), to Vanessa Redgrave and Jason Robards in *Julia* (1977) and to veteran Fox star turned character actor Don Ameche for *Cocoon* in 1985 – the first time he had ever been nominated for an Oscar.

MGM

Metro-Goldwyn-Mayer, the biggest and best-known Hollywood studio, was founded in 1924, marking the beginning of the 'studio era'. Headed by Louis B. Mayer and Irving Thalberg, MGM established itself as the top studio of the 30s, with the lion's share of leading stars under contract. But MGM failed to adjust to changes in the 40s. Hard hit by the postwar decline in film audiences and the departure of many of its top stars, it had to depend for its position at the box-office on its colourful musicals. The studio enjoyed one last big success with the remake of *Ben-Hur* in 1959, but has experienced many ups and downs (more of the latter) since then. During the 70s, MGM reduced its investment in movie-making but has recently attempted to regain some of its former prestige. To date, the effort has met with little success.

The most famous of all the Hollywood studios, MGM – as Metro-Goldwyn-Mayer is almost always known – came into being in 1924 with the merger of a number of smaller companies: Metro Pictures (already associated with Loew's Incorporated), Goldwyn Pictures and Louis B. Mayer Productions. The formation of Columbia and Warner Bros. and the arrival of Joseph Schenck to take charge of United Artists took place at just about this same time. Thus, 1924 is a logical choice of date to mark the true beginning of the studio era.

The seeds of MGM can be traced to the early activities of Marcus Loew. Back in 1904 he formed the People's Vaudeville Company with a chain of theatres which put on both one-reeler movies and live variety shows. By 1910 the company had expanded considerably and was renamed Loew's Consolidated Enterprises. Loew's associates at this time included Adolph Zukor, who left to start his own company; Joseph Schenck, who left in 1917, and Joe's brother Nicholas, who stayed on as Loew's right-hand man. The company continued to prosper, was reorganized under the name of Loew's Inc in 1919 and took over the ailing Metro Pictures Corporation the following year. Metro was a film production and distribution company formed in 1915; it provided Loew with the kind of production link he needed and a steady supply of movies for his own cinemas.

Metro's *The Four Horsemen Of The Apocalypse*, starring Rudolph Valentino and directed by Rex Ingram, was a tremendous hit in 1921, but none of its other productions were nearly as successful. Loew's problems with the company were solved early in 1924 when he had the idea of merging it with the Goldwyn Co. which was experiencing similar difficulties after the departure of producer Samuel Goldwyn. (Goldwyn had nothing to do with MGM, though it bore his name.) A further merger with Louis B. Mayer Productions then took place, and MGM was born. The new management team was headed by Louis B. Mayer and Irving Thalberg. Metro contributed a number of leading stars and directors to the new MGM, while the Goldwyn assets included an impressive studio at Culver City (originally built by producer Thomas Ince in 1915) along with additional stars, directors, a small chain of cinemas, and a roaring lion symbol which was adopted by the new company. Mayer also brought his own small group of stars and other personnel from his own little company which was absorbed into the new studio. Marcus Loew continued as the president of the parent company, Loew's Inc, until his death in 1927 when Nicholas Schenck took over this post. The Hollywood studio (headed by Mayer) was merely a film-production subsidiary and the real corporate power lay with the heads of the company (in this case, Loew and Schenck) in New York.

Mayer and Thalberg worked well together and quickly established MGM as one of the top Hollywood studios. The excellent selection of stars and technical personnel from the founding companies was bolstered by a continuing stream of new arrivals. No other studio could match MGM for the quality (and loyalty) of its stars and, even more, its top technicians, many of whom remained with the studio for over 30 years. They helped to establish and maintain a standard of technical excellence which the other studios found difficult to match and which was a tribute to Thalberg's special qualities as production chief. However, individual creativity was not valued highly at MGM if it could not be accommodated to the demands of the studio. Thus, the directors were the most obvious casualties of the system, and its lack of really first-rate directors was the studio's greatest weakness. Stroheim, Ingram, Stiller and Sjöström all left MGM, while many of those who stayed on were efficient craftsmen rather than real creative talents, and were most valued for their ability to handle the studio's top stars. At MGM the stars came first.

Thalberg worked closely with his producers – called at MGM 'production supervisors' – and writers, planning projects and working hard to get the script right, often before a director was even assigned. Once a picture was completed, no effort was spared to perfect it, through repeated preview screenings if necessary. Since B movies comprised only a small percentage (compared with other studios) of its output, MGM was able to maintain a uniformly high standard and a 'look' which hardly varied. As cameraman Harold (Hal) Rosson pointed out in a recent interview, 'Naturally you didn't have as much time to spend on one of the Dr Kildare films, but I remember Mr Mayer saying to me, "If it's an MGM film, it has to look like an MGM film," regardless of the fact that it was officially a B picture.'

Though the main emphasis was on quality star vehicles, with a tendency for many of the studio's pictures to look much alike (thus reflecting the powerful influence of supervising art director Cedric Gibbons), there were a fair number of surprises. Victor Sjöström and Lillian Gish left behind them a harrowing masterpiece, *The Wind* (1928), before they quit the studio. King Vidor filmed *The Crowd*, a downbeat story of city life in 1927, and an all-black musical, *Hallelujah*, two years later. Tod Browning's *Freaks* (1932) was the studio's most bizarre production ever, while the uncompromising but brilliant Fritz Lang managed to complete one tough drama, *Fury* (1936), with support from producer Joseph Mankiewicz.

MGM was slow to make the transition to sound due to the high costs involved, but once the decision was made the studio moved rapidly ahead and provided more than its share of talkie hits during the boom years of 1929 and 1930, led by *The Broadway Melody*. The arrival of sound further strengthened the hand of the production supervisors as each production was more closely tied to studio filming then ever before. But tensions had developed between Thalberg and

Mayer, further complicated by William Fox's brief period of owning a controlling interest in the company. The hard-working Thalberg felt that Mayer took more credit than he deserved for the success of MGM and succeeded in negotiating an increase in his annual bonus (based on studio profits), while Mayer's was reduced.

However, all this changed when Thalberg became seriously ill late in 1932 and took a long leave of absence from the studio. His nine-year reign as production chief was effectively at an end and, by the time he returned, Mayer had reorganized the studio, promoting production supervisors who had worked under Thalberg to full producer status and hiring his son-in-law, David O. Selznick. A versatile and talented producer, Selznick soon came to rival Thalberg – but not for long. In 1936 he left to form his own production company. Thalberg, too, had plans to become an independent producer and signed up a number of new stars under a personal contract which meant that they would stay with him if and when he left MGM. Not surprisingly, this was another source of conflict between him and Mayer.

Now firmly in control, Mayer elected to play the father figure and liked to think of MGM as one big happy family. Actor Robert Taylor, for one, was appreciative of this: 'Some writers have implied that Mayer was tyrannical and abusive, and a male prima donna who out-acted his actors. As I knew him, he was kind, fatherly, understanding and protective. He gave me picture assignments up to the level that my abilities could sustain, and was always there when I had problems.' Similarly, supervising editor Margaret Booth spent virtually her entire career at MGM: 'It was like home . . . It was really a great family studio. Everybody worked together'.

But in addition to his behind-the-scenes activities, Mayer was determined to prove that he could run the studio on his own, with a small group of trusted assistants headed by Eddie Mannix and Benny Thau, and so justify his position as the highest-paid executive in the USA. As the studio continued to prosper, Mayer aimed at expansion in many different areas. He encouraged the production of such lavish costume pictures and musicals as *Mutiny On The Bounty* (1935, produced by Thalberg), *A Tale Of Two Cities* (1935, producer Selznick) and *The Great Ziegfeld* (1936, producer Hunt Stromberg), while at the opposite extreme were the type of human-interest B movies, idealizing 'the American way of life' which appealed to him. In addition, the studio increased its production of shorts of all kinds such as the Fitzpatrick Traveltalks, the Pete Smith Specialties (comedies) and the Crime Does Not Pay one- and two-reelers. These served as a training ground for new young directors like Fred Zinnemann, Jacques Tourneur and George Sidney, all of whom later graduated to directing features. MGM also distributed Hal Roach's Our Gang and Laurel and Hardy shorts, while cartoons were produced by Hugh Harman and Rudolph Ising in the mid-30s, then by Fred Quimby and the team of William Hanna and Joseph Barbera whose Tom and Jerry cartoons won a number of Oscars in the 40s, along with the remarkably eccentric cartoon creations – for example, Droopy – of Tex Avery. Finally, MGM's successful newsreel, News Of The Day, was produced by newspaper magnate William Hearst's organization. (For many years Hearst's Cosmopolitan Productions, which mainly turned out pictures starring his talented mistress, Marion Davies, was based at MGM.)

In the late 40s – at its peak – MGM's Culver City studio complex had grown from its original 40 acres to 187 acres comprising six different lots. Standing exterior sets included a small lake and harbour, a miniature jungle, a railway station, a number of parks, and squares and streets designed in a variety of styles, both period and modern. In addition, the film laboratory could turn out 150 million feet of release prints per year.

In 1941 writer Dore Schary approached Mayer with a request to be allowed to direct a small-budget picture. 'Mayer never had much feeling for directors,' Schary recalls, and instead he was given the opportunity to serve as executive producer of the studio's small-budget movies costing about $250,000 each. After a number of modest successes, and one smash hit with *Lassie Come Home* (1943), Schary left to work for Selznick, then for RKO, before he was invited back in 1948 to fill Thalberg's old position as production chief, working in tandem with Mayer. MGM had prospered during the booming war years, but had just suffered a drastic fall in profits and many of its typical 'star vehicles' had begun to look distinctly old-fashioned. Schary was brought in to help remedy this, and he introduced a number of serious black-and-white projects into the studio's production schedule, including *Battleground* (1949), *The Next Voice You Hear* (1950) and *The Red Badge of Courage* (1951). But the studio had just been expanding its production of colour movies when he arrived, a trend which continued on into the 50s and was further reinforced by the adoption of CinemaScope. Thus, Schary's influence was only marginal, and the studio continued to be characterized by its glossy colour productions, even after the departure of Mayer in 1951. (Following a series of disputes with Schary, Mayer had delivered a rash ultimatum to company president Nick Schenck that either he (Mayer) or Schary would have to go, with the result that Mayer was relieved of his post after 27 years as head of MGM.) More than ever before, the studio suffered from a shortage of really first-class directors, a situation which was not remedied by Schary. And his failure to restore MGM's profitability meant that his days, too, were numbered, and he was dismissed in 1956 shortly after Schenck himself was 'released'.

The studio recorded the first loss in its history in 1957, but just managed to break even the following year thanks to the success of *Gigi*. MGM had one last taste of glory with the successful release of *Ben-Hur* in 1959, but a series of management changes reflected the fact that the company lacked the kind of positive leadership needed to restore its fortunes. In recalling his years at MGM and the problems he had with the management, writer-director Richard Brooks has pointed out how badly the situation deteriorated in the late 50s after the departure of Schary: 'They had fourteen guys sitting around a table, and one guy would say . . . "I didn't like the music in the sixth reel." And another would say . . . "My dentist hates it . . !"'

Forced by the government to sell off its profitable cinemas, the company diversified into other areas like music publishing, records and TV production. It also made an effort to regain its former prestige through an investment in various high-cost projects, generally filmed in 70mm in the 60s. But the hits hardly balanced the flops, and by 1973, shortly before it was due to celebrate its 50-year anniversary, MGM gave up distributing its own pictures and cut back severely on its production schedule. The company recalled its past glories with the release of *That's Entertainment* (1974) which included clips from many of the studio's most famous musicals.

MGM moved to increase its investment in new movies in 1979, and followed this by taking over United Artists to form a new company, MGM/UA Entertainment Company, in 1981. About a dozen years after Kirk Kerkorian had first acquired the company and sold off many of its assets, while allowing it to run down so badly, he apparently became interested in re-establishing the studio as a leading production company once again. But unfortunately, a poor choice of film projects (and of production chiefs) led to a large number of expensive flops and disappointments. Not surprisingly, there were frequent changes of management and even executive shuffles between the two companies. And Kerkorian re-emerged as a wheeler-dealer once again in the mid-80s, selling off parts of MGM and UA, both separately and together, and negotiating a variety of deals, many of which fell through, but some did take place.

The first major reshuffle took place during 1985–86 when cable and TV mogul Ted Turner purchased the entire company. Then Kerkorian bought back UA and finally Kerkorian/UA repurchased MGM minus the MGM film library and the Culver City lot and film lab which Turner sold separately to Lorimar Telepictures. And two years later Kerkorian was back in action negotiating with a variety of possible buyers ranging from Rupert Murdoch's News Corporation and Sony of Japan to Guber-Peters-Barris (in 1988) and the Australian broadcasting group Qintex in 1989. Then, finally, in 1990 he sold his interest in both film companies to Giancarlo Parretti's Pathé Communications, the new company now to be known as MGM/Pathé Communications.

Parretti was soon put under pressure by the massive debts he had incurred to finance his purchase of the company. And with doubts expressed regarding his competence to head a major Hollywood studio, the company's financial backers forced him to resign his posts as chairman and chief executive of MGM/Pathé in the spring of 1991. Alan Ladd Jr, who had previously been hired as Pathé production chief, and had briefly headed MGM under Kerkorian in the mid-80s, was now promoted to head the studio with the challenge of trying to revive the ailing company. (As the leading stock-holder, Parretti still retained his involvement in the company with a major stake in its future success.)

MGM Studio Chronology

1920   Loew's Inc. takes over Metro Pictures.
1921   *The Four Horsemen Of The Apocalypse* is a tremendous hit.

1924   Marcus Loew of Loew's Inc. arranges a merger of his Metro Pictures with the Goldwyn Company and then Louis B. Mayer Productions to form Metro-Goldwyn-Mayer. Loew takes the post of president with Mayer as studio chief and Irving Thalberg in charge of production. Loew's Inc. continues to function as the parent company with extensive holdings of film theatres, while MGM is the new film-production subsidiary.

1925   The new company gets off to a successful start with the release of *The Merry Widow*, followed by *The Big Parade* and *Ben-Hur*, in its first year.

1927   Marcus Loew dies and Nicholas Schenck takes over as president.

1929   The studio has its first big musical success with *The Broadway Melody*, which wins the Best Picture Oscar.

1932   *Grand Hotel* wins Best Picture Oscar.

1933   Thalberg is downgraded to producer status. David O. Selznick joins the studio as a producer.

1936   Death of producer Irving Thalberg.

1939   The studio releases *The Wizard Of Oz*, and *Gone With The Wind* produced by David O. Selznick, a multiple Oscar winner and tremendous box-office hit.

1942   *Mrs Miniver* wins Best Picture Oscar.

1948   Dore Schary is appointed production chief under studio head Mayer.

1951   Mayer resigns and Schary takes over. *An American in Paris* wins Best Picture Oscar.

1955   Nicholas Schenck retires from the presidency.

1956   Studio head Schary is dismissed.

1959   The studio has its last big success with *Ben-Hur* which wins a record –
total of 11 Oscars.

1969   Financier Kirk Kerkorian gains control of the studio.

1973   MGM ceases distribution and cuts back on production.

1981   Kerkorian purchases United Artists from the Transamerica Corporation to form the MGM/UA Entertainment Company.

1985/86 TV mogul Ted Turner buys both companies, then sells them back to Kerkorian, retaining the extensive film and TV libraries. During this time Alan Ladd Jr is made chief executive officer.

1988   Kerkorian attempts to restructure the studio once again, leading to the resignation of MGM/UA chairman Lee Rich and MGM chairman Alan Ladd Jr.

1990   The studio is purchased by Italian financier Giancarlo Parretti's Pathé company and is now known as MGM/Pathé Communications.

1991   Heavily in debt, Parretti is forced to step down as chairman and chief executive, with Alan Ladd Jr appointed as the new studio boss.

The Releases

MGM's high-quality dramas, comedies and crime films were designed to show off its substantial roster of stars in the early years. When the company recovered from the Depression and prospered, it turned to lavish costumers and musicals such as *Mutiny On The Bounty* (1935), *San Francisco* and *The Great Ziegfeld* (both 1936). Rather than cheap Westerns and horror movies, studio boss Mayer was attracted to family movies and uplifting hospital stories as developed in the popular (and profitable) Andy Hardy and Dr Kildare series. MGM first ventured into Technicolor in 1938 and is best remembered for early features such as *The Wizard Of Oz* and *Gone With The Wind*, both released in 1939. The studio had its greatest successes in the 40s and later years with a series of imaginative colour musicals; in the 50s these were most often filmed in CinemaScope. The company also made use of the other large-format processes: Camera 65, for *Ben-Hur* (1959); three-screen Cinerama, for *How The West Was Won* (1962); and super Panavision 70 for many other epics. But the failure of David Lean's *Ryan's Daughter* (1970) marked the end of MGM's interest in 70mm filming.

From the very first years of MGM's existence it was apparent that Mayer and Thalberg had a clear idea of the flavour of picture they wanted to make at their new studio. Aiming to reach the widest possible audience, they established a basic pattern which remained surprisingly unchanged for the next 20 years or so. In total numbers, too, the studio's output remained remarkably stable. Though feature releases peaked at 48 per year during 1927–29 and again during 1936–41, the average for the entire 1925–42 period was 46 per year.

The majority of MGM movies fell into three general groupings, later to be joined by a fourth, the screen musical. Contemporary dramas often starred Garbo, Norma Shearer or Joan Crawford; comedies featured Buster Keaton or Marion Davies in the early years, Marie Dressler and the Marx Bros later on; crime movies or thrillers were often dominated by the formidable Lon Chaney in the silents, but focused on Clark Gable, Wallace Beery or Robert Taylor in the 30s and early 40s. These were the studio's high-quality 'bread and butter' pictures, turned out year after year. In spite of changes in style, the appearance of new stars, and the coming of sound (and then colour), these were recognizably the same categories which continued strong up to the early 50s. (In contrast to the sophisticated comedies of the 30s, for example, a particular type of undergraduate comedy was a staple item during the relatively carefree flapper era prior to the Wall Street crash of 1929; designed for such young stars as William Haines, Marion Davies or Johnny Mack Brown, they bore such titles as *Brown Of Harvard*, 1926, or *The Fair Co-Ed*, 1927.)

Produced relatively inexpensively, such pictures earned the studio a steady profit, but rarely did exceptional business as compared with the far smaller number of big-budget movies, epic historical and period films such as *Ben-Hur* (1925), *Mutiny On The Bounty* (1935), *San Francisco* (1936) and, of course, *Gone With The Wind* (1939). These included some of the studio's biggest hits and Oscar winners.

At the opposite extreme, and reflecting a standard policy of all the major studios of releasing a suitably varied range of subjects each year, MGM turned out its share of more routine fare. Westerns, family and sports films were especially popular during the silent era, in accord with the mood of the times. The studio produced an average of five Westerns per year during 1926–30. The series starring Tim McCoy was thoughtful and well-made, according to critic William Everson who notes that 'MGM was never on very familiar ground with non-"A" pictures.' The few A Westerns of note included *The Trail Of '98* directed by Clarence Brown in 1927 and *The Wind* (1928) starring Lillian Gish. Similarly, the studio had little interest in the horror film, but had inherited (from Louis B. Mayer Productions) one of the top stars of the genre in Lon Chaney. Thus, he and his favourite director, Tod Browning, accounted for most of the studio's small, but far from negligible, horror list with such pictures as *The Monster* (1925) and *London After Midnight* (1927), and Browning in addition directing the now cult movie *Freaks* (1932).

The show-biz or backstage theme, already popular before the coming of sound, was effectively taken over by the movie musical. The Western died out during the early 30s after the failure of a number of prestige productions from MGM and other companies. MGM's entry was *Billy The Kid* (1930) from King Vidor, starring Johnny Mack Brown. There was a similar reaction against the excesses of the musical boom of 1929 and 1930 which had provided MGM, and a number of the other companies, with their first big talkie successes. Most notable for MGM were the Oscar-winning *The Broadway Melody*, and *The Hollywood Revue of 1929* (both 1929). The musical soon made a comeback, however, and became established as MGM's most popular and enduring creative contribution.

Thalberg's illness and absence from the studio early in 1933 meant that Mayer began to exercise a greater personal control over MGM's output. A slight decline in the number of serious dramatic pictures was balanced by the musical revival, led by a singer who was to become one of Mayer's favourite stars. Jeanette MacDonald had arrived at MGM towards the end of 1933 and quickly appeared in three pictures in succession: *The Cat And The Fiddle* (1934) with Ramon Novarro was followed by *The Merry Widow* (1934) co-starring Maurice Chevalier and directed by Ernst Lubitsch, and then she was teamed with Nelson Eddy for the first time in the operetta *Naughty Marietta* (1935). Another new arrival, the rapid-fire dancer Eleanor Powell, starred in a number of musicals beginning in 1935, and in 1936 the studio hit the jackpot with *The Great Ziegfeld*.

In addition, MGM's rapid recovery from the Depression was reflected in a small but steady output of lavish costumers divided among such leading producers as Thalberg, David O. Selznick, and Bernard Hyman during 1934–37 in particular. But, most interesting of all, one can trace a specific line of development set in motion by Mayer's special interest in family movies, wedded to his wish to encourage a number of new juvenile stars. In 1935 Clarence Brown directed an affectionate adaptation of Eugene O'Neill's *Ah, Wilderness*, while young Jackie Cooper starred as *O'Shaughnessy's Boy* and, as a follow-up, was teamed with Mickey Rooney and Freddie Bartholomew in *The Devil Is A Sissy* (1936). Most important of all was *A Family Affair* (1936), for it turned out to be the first entry in a family series which was to develop into the studio's most popular of the 30s, revolving around the Hardy family with the versatile Mickey Rooney as Andy Hardy.

Mayer was personally touched by the simple and unaffected qualities that these cheaply made (and highly profitable) movies expressed about American small-town life and American values. He is alleged to have passed the word along to the director and writers working on the series, 'Don't try to make these films any better. Just keep them the way they are.'

Delighted with their success, Mayer asked the Hardy unit to explore possible ideas for a new series. The result was a cycle of hospital stories with a wide audience appeal that provided a suitable role for the now wheelchair-bound Lionel Barrymore. Beginning with *Young Dr Kildare* in 1938, this popular series continued on into the mid-40s with over a dozen entries.

Meanwhile the Hardy movies allowed for guest appearances by the studio's juvenile roster which included Ann Rutherford, Lana Turner and, notably, Judy Garland. She had first been teamed with Rooney in a racetrack film, *Thoroughbreds Don't Cry* (1937), and producer Arthur Freed saw them as the ideal combination for his new musical adaptation of Rodgers and Hart's *Babes In Arms* (1939). With its theme of talented youngsters putting on their own show and a small town family setting, it clearly recalled the Hardy series whose regular writer, Kay van Riper, was brought in to co-author the script. The tremendously successful series of musicals which grew out of this initial idea provided Arthur Freed, who set up the famous Freed unit, with his first big hits and put Garland well on her way to becoming MGM's leading musical star.

For seventeen peak years (1939–55) MGM turned out six or seven musicals per year, virtually all in colour from 1943 on and including many of the studio's greatest successes of this era. They were relatively unaffected by the fluctuations (mainly falls) experienced in other genres – by 1946–48 the annual total of 26 releases was about half that of the immediate pre-war years (1939–41). Comedies and thrillers were at their height, featuring established stars such as Garbo and Shearer (both now reaching the end of their MGM careers), William Powell and Myrna Loy (who continued to star in a popular series of films that followed on from their excellent comedy-thriller *The Thin Man*, 1934), and new stars Lana Turner and Van Heflin. A brief revival of interest in the Western had developed during 1939–42, highlighted by such quality Technicolor productions as *Northwest Passage* (1940) and *Billy The Kid* (1941), but it was cut short when such stars as Taylor, Beery and Spencer Tracy were moved into war pictures, and others including Gable and James Stewart, were lost to the armed services.

The number of crime pictures was down too, but thrillers, Westerns and war movies revived in 1949 and 1950 under new production chief Dore Schary. In contrast to Mayer, Schary had a special affection for uncompromisingly tough material such as *Border Incident* (1949) directed by Anthony Mann; *Battleground* and *Intruder In The Dust* from director Clarence Brown (both 1949); the thriller *The Asphalt Jungle* (1950) and the Civil War drama, *The Red Badge Of Courage* (1951), both directed by John Huston. But these were the exceptions. The studio still suffered from a shortage of top-rank directors, and it was impossible to disguise the fact that the vast majority of MGM's glossy star vehicles were beginning to appear distinctly old-fashioned and predictable.

Boosted by a surge in Technicolor productions, the number of releases recovered to a highly respectable 40 per year through 1949–51. But the studio had been over-optimistic in believing that the move into colour would restore its fortunes, and the sudden drop in MGM activity that followed, to a new low of 23 releases per year in 1954, was drastic and more or less irreversible. In spite of a modest recovery a few years later and again in the early 60s, the underlying trend was clearly downward. Forced to separate the production and exhibition sides of the business, MGM was no longer bound to turn out a set number of movies each year to supply its own cinemas. Pictures were more elaborate and expensive than ever before, filmed in colour and often in CinemaScope or Panavision from 1954 on, though there continued to be a select group of gritty black-and-white pictures of note from *Julius Caesar* (1953) and *The Blackboard Jungle* (1955) up to *The Night Of The Iguana* (1964), *The Americanization Of Emily* (1964) and *The Hill* (1965). Nonetheless, the company's continued emphasis on glossy but superficial entertainment was reflected in the disproportionately large number of costly musicals and costume epics. Many of these were flops, including *Kismet* and *The Prodigal* (both 1955), a remake of *Mutiny On The Bounty* and *The Wonderful World Of The Brothers Grimm* (both 1962).

MGM continued to churn out a variety of forgettable movies during the 60s and early 70s before a severe cutback in production reduced the once proud studio to a Hollywood also-ran. Ironically, its biggest successes during this era resulted from ventures into science fiction and thrillers. SF was best represented by Kubrick's innovative *2001: A Space Odyssey* (1968) scripted by Arthur C. Clarke, *Westworld* (1973), *Futureworld* (1974), and *Soylent Green* (1973) featuring Edward G. Robinson in his last role. Notable thrillers included Antonioni's *Blow-Up* and John Boorman's *Point Blank* (both released in 1967), the tough blaxploitation movie *Shaft* (1971) and Antonioni's *The Passenger* (1974) with Jack Nicholson.

The few films of note in the early 80s included the lavish musical *Pennies From Heaven* (1981), the Blake Edwards/Julie Andrews comedy, *Victor/Victoria*, and writer-director Barry Levinson's directorial debut film *Diner* in 1982, also two unusual early Mel Gibson features, *The Year Of Living Dangerously* with Sigourney Weaver in 1983 and *Mrs Soffel* (1984) with Diane Keaton. And the studio had its last good year under Kerkorian in 1988 with the release of *A Fish Called Wanda* and *Moonstruck*.

Colour and Widescreen

MGM expressed only a mild interest in filming in the early two-strip Technicolor during the 20s. A few colour sequences appeared in some of its best-known pictures, beginning with the epic *Ben-Hur* in 1925. And in 1928 the studio agreed to distribute *The Viking*, its first full-length Technicolor feature and a rare early example of an independent production (from the Technicolor Corporation) distributed under the MGM banner.

The studio had a tremendous success with *The Broadway Melody* followed by *The Hollywood Revue Of 1929*, both with colour sequences, and this naturally led on to the production of a full-length two-strip Technicolor musical later that year, *The Rogue Song* starring Lawrence Tibbett. However, by the time it was released in 1930, the market was glutted with musicals and MGM didn't repeat the experiment.

Late in 1933 MGM was one of the first studios to film in the new improved three-strip Technicolor process, used for the final sequence of the Jeanette MacDonald-Ramon Novarro musical, *The Cat And The Fiddle*. But again the company was reluctant to proceed further, although MGM was the most successful Hollywood studio during the 30s. Over the following years it released a number of colour shorts: in 1936, for example, there was *La Fiesta De Santa Barbara* and also entries in James Fitzpatrick's Traveltalks series. But it was the other aspiring majors – Fox, Paramount, Warner Bros. – who were using colour. They were doing so largely as a means of competing with MGM for status, in spite of the added cost and the fact that most of the Technicolor pictures were not profitable. MGM's attitude, on the other hand, was that its movies were profitable in black-and-white, so why go to the added trouble, expense and risk of colour? Thus, MGM didn't release its first Technicolor feature, the MacDonald-Eddy musical *Sweethearts*, until December 1938, exactly three-and-a-half years after the first Technicolor feature, *Becky Sharp* distributed by RKO.

MGM's second colour feature, *The Wizard Of Oz* (1939), was also the initial project developed by the newly formed musical unit headed by novice producer Arthur Freed in 1938. One of the most troubled productions in the history of the studio, the completed movie did well at the box-office, but not well enough to recoup the exceptional costs of $2.8 million. In marked contrast, Freed's second picture, *Babes In Arms*, starring Judy Garland and Mickey Rooney in black-and-white, was completed at a fraction of the cost of *The Wizard of Oz*, was more popular with audiences on its initial release and earned the studio a tidy profit. Not surprisingly, Freed spent the next few years producing musicals in black-and-white!

The studio's generally negative attitude toward colour meant that movie audiences had few opportunities to see their favourite MGM stars on the screen in colour. Norma Shearer's sole colour appearance before her retirement in 1942 came in a two-strip Technicolor sequence in *The Hollywood Revue of 1929*, while Joan Crawford starred in another picture with colour sequences only, *Ice Follies Of 1939*. So when Crawford returned to the studio 14 years later and MGM promoted her in *Torch Song* (1953) with the slogan 'For the FIRST TIME you'll see her in TECHNICOLOR' – it wasn't entirely accurate.

Eleanor Powell and Mickey Rooney had to wait until 1943 for their first appearance in colour, in *Thousands Cheer*, while Greta Garbo never made it on to the colour screen. As recalled by her favourite cameraman, William Daniels, 'The saddest thing in my career is that I was never able to photograph her in colour. I begged the studio. I felt I had to get those incredible blue eyes in colour, but they said no. The process at the time was cumbersome and expensive, and her pictures were already making money. I still feel sad about it.'

Perhaps most revealing of all was the fact that late in 1938, as filming was about to begin on *Gone With The Wind*, the MGM bosses were pressuring producer David Selznick to shoot in black-and-white. As he wrote in a letter to one of his associates, 'MGM, our partners in the enterprise, are still far from being sold on colour as an economic proposition . . . I have spent hours with Eddie Mannix recently in the presence of the entire MGM executive staff, debating the value of colour by comparison with its extra cost . . .'

Of course, *Gone With The Wind* turned out to be a landmark in colour film-making, reaching a far wider US and international audience than any previous colour film, and demonstrating the possibilities of an artistic and imaginative use of the process. Selznick took full advantage of his previous experience – the picture was his fifth in colour – and made use of the newly improved and faster Technicolor stock which required less lighting. It greatly enhanced the artistic possibilities by allowing a subtler grading of, and emphasis on, softer pastel colours and the use of shadows, with an improved colour rendition generally and especially at the green end of the spectrum.

Selznick assembled a highly skilled and experienced team of collaborators, most of whom had worked on previous colour productions, including art director Lyle Wheeler, costume designer Walter Plunkett, cameraman Ray Rennahan, and the distinguished production designer

William Cameron Menzies who played a major role in pre-planning the colour and design of the entire picture. The picture, not surprisingly, won colour Oscars for cinematography and art direction, with a special award to Menzies 'for outstanding achievement in the use of colour for the enhancement of dramatic mood in the production of *Gone With The Wind*'.

It is ironical that MGM, due to its association with *Gone With The Wind* and the ever-popular *The Wizard Of Oz*, is so often linked with Technicolor when, as we have noted, it was in fact the slowest of the Hollywood majors to move into colour filming.

But the studio couldn't hold out forever. The turning point came during the flourishing war years as part of a general, industry-wide move into colour. (Universal, for example, released its first Technicolor feature in December 1942 and Columbia followed soon after.) Having produced only seven Technicolor features during the 1938–42 period, MGM suddenly added 10 more in the space of two years, 1943–44. Aside from the musicals, this group included the popular *Lassie Come Home* (1943), starring a young Elizabeth Taylor, while a remarkable (and underrated) drama about the steel industry, *An American Romance* (1944), brought to an end King Vidor's long stint at the studio. (The film was not a hit, but he had done better with the studio's most ambitious Technicolor Western in 1939, *Northwest Passage*, starring Spencer Tracy.) The major revelation and biggest success, however, was *Meet Me In St Louis* (1944), the first colour picture from the talented Vincente Minnelli who emerged as the studio's leading colour stylist. (Unfortunately, he continued to shoot all his non-musical pictures in black-and-white until the mid-50s.)

The studio, with producer Arthur Freed, continued to turn out popular Technicolor musicals of the highest quality, including such memorable hits as *Ziegfeld Follies* (1946) (Minnelli again), as well as *Anchors Aweigh* (1945) and *The Harvey Girls* (1946), both directed by George Sidney. Dramatic pictures included *National Velvet* (1944), and *The Yearling* (1946) which won Oscars for colour cinematography and art direction. In fact, the rapid growth in MGM's colour output was only made possible by a new generation of outstanding technical personnel – cameramen, art directors and costume designers – who had joined the studio during the early 40s, along with a few talented old-timers, such as cameraman Charles Rosher and supervising art director Cedric Gibbons, who had made a successful transition from black-and-white to colour film-making.

Widescreen and 3-D Releases 1953–69

Process	1953	1954	1955	1956	1957	1958	1959	1960	1961	1962	1963	1964	1965	1966	1967	1968	1969
CinemaScope	1	7	18	12	15	13	2			2	1	1		1			
Technirama						1	1		1								
Panavision					1	2	9	11	7	10	12	10	14	12	10	15	9
VistaVision			2				1										
Large format (70mm)					1		1				3			1		2	
3–D		2															

note one large format (70mm) release in 1970

By 1948 the studio was releasing about a dozen colour features per year, and musicals were balanced by a larger number of other types of pictures. That year, for example, MGM released *Three Godfathers* (a John Ford Western), and a delightful version of *The Three Musketeers* starring Gene Kelly in addition to such memorable musicals as *The Pirate* (director Minnelli), *Summer Holiday* (director Rouben Mamoulian) and *Easter Parade*. Whereas most dramatic films continued to be shot in black-and-white during the 40s, including many of the biggest hits and all the top Oscar winners, by the end of the decade the studios had increased their colour filming in an attempt to recapture declining audiences. Colour was promoted more than ever before as a special attraction for moviegoers, and MGM led the way. Hard-hit by falling revenues, the company saw its glossy and colourful new movies as a natural continuation of a long tradition of producing high-quality family entertainment under studio boss Mayer, and a means of maintaining its share of a diminishing market.

Appropriately enough, MGM won the Best Picture Oscar in 1951 with *An American In Paris* (directed by Vincente Minnelli), the first major acknowledgement by the Academy of the quality of the studio's colour musicals and the first colour picture to win the top award since *Gone With The Wind* 12 years earlier.

As filming in colour grew, the search for new subjects and settings led to an increase in costume dramas and historical spectacle, and the trend toward more shooting on natural locations and abroad developed during the early 50s. MGM helped initiate a number of new colour cycles. *Quo Vadis?* (1951) was one of the first of many Biblical epics, while a pair of remakes, *King Solomon's Mines* (1950) and *Mogambo* (1953), contributed to a new African cycle; a knighthood series was sparked off by the highly successful *Ivanhoe*, filmed in Britain in 1952, followed by *Knights Of The Round Table* (1953). In fact, the next major increase in MGM's colour filming in 1953–54 coincided with, and was closely related to, a new technological revolution in Hollywood. If MGM had been slow to adapt to sound and colour, by the 50s and 60s when the company was no longer so financially secure, it was more receptive to the latest technical innovations.

Along with the other studios, MGM moved quickly in and out of 3-D filming in 1953 when it became apparent that this was merely a passing fad. (*Arena* and *Kiss Me Kate* were the only 3-D feature releases from MGM.) That same year, the studio was attracted by the apparent commercial potential of CinemaScope, a process which lent itself to filming the kind of entertaining, high-quality productions in colour that MGM was already turning out. Now MGM rushed to follow in the footsteps of 20th Century-Fox, and its first CinemaScope release, *Knights Of The Round Table*, opened only a few months after Fox's *The Robe* late in 1953. At the same time the studio began using the new improved Eastman Color, which it called Metrocolor, and Anscocolor (beginning with *The Wild North* in 1952), but dropped

Anscocolor after 1954 with the sole exception of Minnelli's *Lust For Life* (1956).

Being the studio's leading director, Minnelli was more or less forced to adopt CinemaScope for all of his pictures, beginning with *Brigadoon* in 1954. A visually inventive and sophisticated director who already liked to make use of crane shots and longish takes, he did not find it difficult to adapt to the new format, but was never entirely happy with it. As he recalled, years later, 'I never did like CinemaScope very much: it's not so much that it's wider as that there's less on the top and bottom. I don't think it's the right composition for pictures.'

By 1955, the peak year, fully three-quarters of MGM's (drastically reduced number of) releases were filmed in CinemaScope and Metrocolor. But for audiences the novelty value had worn off by then, and the number of 'Scope pictures fell back to about 50% of MGM productions, maintaining this same level for the next 10 years or so. MGM, however, was the first studio to shoot its 'Scope films with the new 35mm anamorphic lenses developed by the Panavision company. Beginning in 1957 with the Elvis Presley movie, *Jailhouse Rock*, MGM began changing over to 35mm Panavision during the following years and by 1960 was filming mainly in Panavision. (Early Panavision movies of note included *Torpedo Run* (1958), Oscar nominated for its special effects, also *Some Came Running* (1958) and *Bells Are Ringing*, filmed in 1959, both from director Vincente Minnelli.)

The studio was also one of the first to become seriously interested in the possibilities of filming on a larger-format film stock (rather than the standard 35mm gauge), especially after seeing the success of the three-screen Cinerama presentations and UA's *Around The World In 80 Days* (1956) filmed in Todd-AO (70mm). (MGM had experimented briefly with a widescreen process called 'Realife' in 1930, but had dropped it after only two productions, *The Great Meadow* and King Vidor's *Billy The Kid*.) Thus, in 1956 MGM joined with the Panavision company to develop a new process called Camera 65 which made use of a 65mm negative and was first used in a lavish $5 million production of *Raintree County* (1957), a Civil War subject reminiscent of *Gone With The Wind*. Unfortunately, it failed to make much impact at the box-office, but the studio was more successful with its second attempt – *Ben-Hur* (1959) was MGM's biggest 50s hit and Oscar winner. (MGM's Douglas Shearer along with Robert Gottschalk and John Moore of Panavision Inc. were awarded a special technical Oscar for developing the Camera 65 system.)

Encouraged by this success, MGM experimented with various of the new, larger formats in the early 60s. The studio backed producer Samuel Bronston in his production of *King Of Kings* (1961), directed by Nicholas Ray in Spain in the new Technirama, then embarked on a lavish remake of *Mutiny On The Bounty* (1962), filmed in Ultra Panavision 70 (the new name for Camera 65). At the same time MGM joined with the Cinerama Corporation to co-produce the first two narrative pictures shot in the multi-screen Cinerama process.

The MGM balance sheet tells the rest of the story – *How The West*

Was Won (1962) in Cinerama proved to be the only one of the four to break even, and the company's profits tumbled in 1962 and 1963. Ironically, MGM had its biggest success of the decade with *Dr Zhivago* (1965) which was filmed in 35mm Panavision, then blown up to 70mm with little loss of quality. Clearly the days of expensive filming with bulky 70mm equipment were numbered, though MGM continued to favour Super Panavision (70mm) for a few last selective productions. *Grand Prix* (1966) featured some remarkable racing sequences and multiple image effects devised by Saul Bass, while producer-director Stanley Kubrick took full advantage of his only opportunity to film in 70mm, providing some stunning, Oscar-winning special effects for his *2001: A Space Odyssey* (1968). However, *Ice Station Zebra* (also 1968) was a less than memorable action-adventure movie, while David Lean's production of *Ryan's Daughter* (1970) did poorly at the box office and brought MGM's investment in 70mm filming to an abrupt end.

The Finances

MGM got off to a terrific start with three big hits in its first year – *The Merry Widow*, *The Big Parade* and *Ben-Hur*, all released in 1925. The studio succeeded in turning out quality pictures year after year and soon developed into the most profitable Hollywood studio, never falling into the red, even in the worst years of the Depression. By the mid-40s, however, the other majors were doing so well that they caught up with MGM. The studio was particularly hard-hit by declining audiences in the postwar years and managed relatively few hits in the 50s and 60s. The company further cut back in the 70s and was merged with United Artists in 1981, then sold to Giancarlo Parretti's Pathé Communications in 1990.

A highly profitable and successful company from the very first year of its formation, Loew's/MGM grew and prospered throughout the boom years of the late 20s. Already in 1924 Mayer and Thalberg had to cope with numerous complex productions including several projects inherited from the founder companies. Highest priority of all was the much-troubled Goldwyn Company production of *Ben-Hur* which was currently filming in Italy and presented the greatest challenge to the success of the new studio.

Demonstrating for the first time his ruthless but effective approach to film-making, which would transform MGM into the leading Hollywood studio within the space of a few years, Louis B. Mayer had the guts to suspend the filming of *Ben-Hur* temporarily. He then restarted it with a new director (Fred Niblo), star (Ramon Navarro) and pair of scriptwriters (Carey Wilson and Bess Meredyth), and the picture was finally completed back in California. It ended up as the most expensive movie ever made up to that date, costing $4 million. (The average cost of an MGM feature in 1924 was around $160,000.) *Ben-Hur* was a big box-office hit and lent distinction to MGM, even though it lost money; Mayer and Thalberg had succeeded in turning a potential disaster into a triumph.

At the other end of the spectrum was King Vidor's *The Big Parade*, a World War I picture filmed from the personal view of an 'average man'. Originally budgeted at about $200,000, apparently Thalberg was so impressed by a rough-cut version of the movie that he urged Vidor to go back and shoot additional war footage to boost its 'production values'. The final cost was $380,000 (only $245,000 according to Vidor) but in either case earned the studio about $3.5 million – the most profitable movie in the first 20 years of the studio, until *Meet Me In St Louis* in 1944 (excluding Selznick's *Gone With The Wind*).

The third of MGM's early hits (though actually released first) was a quality production of *The Merry Widow* which cost just under $600,000 and brought in a profit of approximately $750,000 at the box-office. Thalberg demonstrated that it was possible to control the alleged extravagance of director Erich von Stroheim, but Stroheim left MGM soon after.

Certainly there was a great incentive for Mayer and Thalberg to maximize the studio's profits since, as part of the initial agreement, they were each paid a small percentage of profits in addition to their regular salaries.

The years 1928–29, which marked the changeover to sound, coincided with the most extraordinary episode in the studio's history, the takeover of Loew's/MGM by William Fox as part of a planned merger of the two companies into the biggest film corporation in the USA. As one of the first to exploit the move to sound with his Fox Movietone, Fox was in a strong financial position and had taken advantage of the fact that Marcus Loew's one-third interest in Loew's/MGM had come up for sale after his death in 1927. Abetted by the company's new president, Nicholas Schenck, Fox succeeded in his takeover bid, but the practical effect on the activities of the company were nil. Fox was seriously injured in an auto accident early in 1929, then was hit hard by the stock market crash later that year and was also confronted by a governmental anti-trust suit which forced him to sell off his interest in Loew's/MGM before he took control. (Schenck's role in aiding Fox, not surprisingly, soured relations between him and the MGM studio heads.)

At about the same time as these financial manoeuvres in the east, the studio in Culver City was just completing its changeover to sound filming. Though slow to take up the challenge of sound, MGM was able to make up lost ground, drawing on the skills and resourcefulness of its production staff and the financial backing of the (quite profitable) parent company. MGM produced many of the top hits of the period including *The Broadway Melody* and *The Hollywood Revue Of 1929*, followed by *Min And Bill* (Marie Dressler and Wallace Beery), *Anna Christie* (Garbo Talks!) and *Trader Horn*, all in 1930. The company's profits and revenues had grown steadily throughout the late 20s, and by 1930, the peak year, had reached an impressive $15 million and $130 million respectively.

Of all the studios, MGM was least badly hit by the Depression and continued to record profits, albeit small, even during the worst years of 1931 and 1933. Whereas the other majors had over-extended themselves and were deeply in debt due to their purchases of film theatres, MGM had maintained a relatively small number of key venues. These were efficiently organized and well run, and the studio's quality pictures at reasonable cost were easily marketed by its highly trained sales force in the USA, as well as by its extensive foreign-sales network. The company was able to take full advantage of the current practice of block booking, whereby movies were sold to exhibitors sight unseen on the strength of their titles and stars; the high standards set by MGM meant that cinema managers could depend on the quality and box-office appeal of the product. The studio's sales expertise meant that, as long as costs were kept under control, the vast majority of MGM films would earn a steady income.

The average cost of an A feature doubled from just over $400,000 in the early 30s to $800,000 by the end of the decade as the studio recovered from the Depression and invested in a large number of expensive productions. Whereas in the early 30s it was rare for any MGM movie to cost $1 million, by 1935 there were a number of million-dollar productions including *Anna Karenina, China Seas* and *David Copperfield*, while *Mutiny On the Bounty* cost almost $2 million, but all four showed a profit. The studio had more than its share of top hits in the 30s, led by *Grand Hotel* (1932) and *San Francisco* (1936), and a share in the most profitable movie of them all, *Gone With The Wind* (1939), produced by David Selznick at a cost of over $4 million, but distributed by MGM – which acquired the full rights from him in the 40s.

From a low point of $4.3 million in 1933, the company's profits recovered quickly and averaged $9 million per year during 1934–40, then rose further during World War II; revenues grew steadily to a peak of $165 million in the exceptional year of 1946 when profits hit a record $18 million. But major changes had taken place during the wartime boom. Suddenly MGM was overtaken by the other majors and was no longer the single leading studio, as it had been since about 1930. Not that MGM had done at all badly, but the flourishing film business meant that the other majors, with interests in a larger number of theatres, had grown even more spectacularly.

MGM suffered badly from the rapid postwar decline in audiences. The loss of its overseas markets during the war hadn't mattered too much when business was booming at home, but the company failed to regain its foreign position after the war, and that hurt. Annual profits, eroded by inflation, averaged a miserable $5.5 million per year from 1948–56, less than any previous year with the single exception of 1933, the worst year of the Depression. Due to its poor performance, Loew's/MGM was allowed to delay its reorganization of film production and exhibition into separate companies in accordance with the government's anti-trust Consent Decree. When the company finally completed its 'divorcement' early in 1959, it was the last to do so.

MGM only managed to place one picture among the top 20 hits of the 40s and early 50s, and that was the high-cost *Quo Vadis?* (1951). The studio's most successful movies during this period were the Technicolor musicals, but these were expensive to produce and thus yielded only modest returns. The high-powered Freed unit had done exceptionally well with its early black-and-white musicals starring Judy Garland. *Babes In Arms* (1939), *Strike Up The Band* (1940), *Little Nellie Kelly* (1940), *Babes On Broadway* (1941) and *For Me And My Gal* (1942) had all cost less than $1 million and brought in rentals of $3 million or more, thus earning a profit of over $2 million each. Nonetheless, a few early Technicolor musicals were inexpensive. Most remarkable of all was *Meet Me In St Louis* which cost slightly over $1 million and earned rentals of $6.5 million. But later hit musicals produced by Freed such as *The Harvey Girls, Ziegfeld Follies* and *Till The Clouds Roll By* (all 1946) cost $3 million each, while *Yolanda And The Thief* (1945) and *Summer Holiday* (1948) both lost money. Most disastrous of all was *The Pirate* (1948), which lost the company well over $1 million. Other major lossmakers during the early 50s were *Plymouth Adventure* (1952) and *Jupiter's Darling* (1955), both in the red to the tune of almost $2 million, while the most profitable musicals were concentrated into the years 1950 and 1951 (*Annie Get Your Gun, Show Boat* and *An American In Paris*).

In the late 50s the company briefly recovered its position and its profits, sparked by *Gigi* and *Cat On A Hot Tin Roof* in 1958, Hitchcock's *North By Northwest* (1959) and, best of all, the extravagant remake of *Ben-Hur* in 1959. But the company promptly lost many millions on another remake, *Mutiny On The Bounty* (1962) which ended up costing about $20 million.

Though the good years outnumbered the bad during 1962–71, the company's losses were greater than its profits – a 'good' year meant a small profit, while a bad year could mean disastrous losses. Thus, MGM recorded its top profit, of $14 million in 1967, but lost over $40 million in the slump of 1969 and 1970. Top hits were *How The West Was Won* (1962), *Dr Zhivago* (1965), *The Dirty Dozen* (1967) and *2001: A Space Odyssey* (1968), while the studio lost heavily on the $6 million *Zabriskie Point* (1969), and *Ryan's Daughter* (1970) cost $14 million.

A series of management changes in the 60s ended when Las Vegas financier Kirk Kerkorian took over the company in 1969. He made it profitable in the early 70s by selling off the valuable back lots, auctioning off old props and costumes, cutting back on film production and investing heavily in a new subsidiary, MGM Grand Hotels. In 1973 the company cut back even further, releasing an average of only four to five pictures per year for the remainder of the 70s, and gave up distributing its own films. (MGM movies were distributed through UA.)

By 1979 the company was ready to move back into moviemaking. It was restructured to separate the filmed entertainment from the hotel and casino operations and David Begelman was brought in as head of production. Unfortunately, the studio invested in a number of expensive losers, including *The Formula* (1980) which starred Marlon Brando and cost $15 million; a film version of Dennis Potter's *Pennies From Heaven* (1981), an entertaining but offbeat musical which cost $22 million and deserved to do better at the box office; *Yes Giorgio* (1982), a far-too-costly ($18 million) vehicle for tenor Luciano Pavarotti; and Natalie Wood's last movie, *Brainstorm* (1983), which was completed after her death at a cost of $20 million. On the plus side MGM had big hits with the Steven Spielberg production of *Poltergeist* (1982), and *War Games* (1983), and was boosted by the two latest James Bond pictures from UA in 1983 and 1985. For MGM had actually taken over UA, having purchased the company from Transamerica in 1981.

During 1978–81 MGM profits averaged about $20 million per year, although in 1979 special revenues from the TV licensing of *Gone With The Wind* pushed profits up to almost $30 million. After the takeover of UA, profits of the joint company climbed to a peak of $42 million in 1983, then fell back in 1984, and the company was deep in the red by 1985. Since then the company has struggled from one crisis to another as owner Kirk Kerkorian has been more interested in making deals than producing pictures. MGM had a big hit with *Moonstruck* in 1988, but otherwise it was the UA half of the partnership which contributed a handful of winners. The predictable success of UA's latest James Bond releases along with *Rocky 3* and *4* was far outweighed by the one surprise smash hit, *Rain Man* (1988). Entering the 90s under a new owner, the outlook for the company was not very good.

Box Office Hits

TITLE	(in $ million) cost	North Amer rentals
1914–31		
The Four Horsemen Of The Apocalypse (METRO) (1921)	(0.8)	4.5
Ben-Hur (1925)	(4.0)	4.0
The Big Parade (1925)	(0.4)	3.5
The Broadway Melody (1929)	(0.4)	3.0
Min And Bill (1930)	(0.3)	2.0
Anna Christie (1930)	(0.4)	1.5
The Champ (1931)	(0.4)	1.5
The Merry Widow (1925)	(0.6)	1.5
The Hollywood Review of 1929 (1929)	(0.4)	1.0
Trader Horn (1931)	(1.3)	1.0
1932–40		
Gone With The Wind (Selznick) (1939)	(4.2)	31.0
San Francisco (1936)	(1.3)	2.7
Grand Hotel (1932)	(0.7)	2.3
Emma (1932)		2.0
Mutiny On The Bounty (1935)	(1.9)	2.0
The Great Ziegfeld (1936)	(2.2)	2.0
Saratoga (1937)		2.0
Tarzan The Ape Man (1932)	(0.6)	1.5
Dancing Lady (1933)	(0.9)	1.5
Queen Christina (1933)	(1.1)	1.5
Tugboat Annie (1933)	(0.6)	1.5
China Seas (1935)	(1.1)	1.5
David Copperfield (1935)	(1.1)	1.5
Libeled Lady (1936)	(0.6)	1.5
Camille (1937)	(1.5)	1.5
The Good Earth (1937)	2.8)	1.5
Boys Town (1938)		1.5
Sweethearts (1938)		1.5
Test Pilot (1938)		1.5
Babes in Arms (1939)	(0.8)	1.5
The Wizard Of Oz (1939)	(2.7)	1.5

Northwest Passage (1940)		1.5
Strange Cargo (1940)		1.5
Strike Up The Band (1940)	(0.8)	1.5

1941–50

Meet Me In St Louis (1944)	(1.7)	5.2
The Yearling (1946)	(4.0)	5.2
Mrs Miniver (1942)		5.0
Green Dolphin Street (1947)		5.0
King Solomon's Mines (1950)		4.8
Battleground (1949)	(1.8)	4.7
Annie Get Your Gun (1950)	(3.8)	4.7
The Green Years (1946)		4.6
Random Harvest (1942)	(1.5)	4.5
Anchors Aweigh (1945)		4.5
Thrill Of A Romance (1945)		4.5
The Valley Of Decision (1945)		4.5
Easy To Wed (1946)		4.5
Till The Clouds Roll By (1946)	(2.8)	4.5
Easter Parade (1948)	(2.5)	4.5
The Harvey Girls (1946)	(2.5)	4.4
The Hucksters (1947)		4.4
Adventure (1945)		4.3
Thirty Seconds Over Tokyo (1944)	(2.5)	4.2
Weekend At The Waldorf (1945)		4.2
The Three Musketeers (1948)		4.2
Father Of The Bride (1950)		4.2
A Guy Named Joe (1943)		4.1
National Velvet (1944)	(1.5)	4.1
Cass Timberlane (1947)		4.1
Homecoming (1948)		4.1
Holiday in Mexico (1946)		4.0
Ziegfeld Follies	(3.2)	4.0
The Postman Always Rings Twice (1946)		4.0
The Stratton Story (1949)		4.0

1951–60

Ben-Hur (1959)	(15.0)	36.7
Quo Vadis? (1952)	(7.0)	10.5
Cat On A Hot Tin Roof (1958)		7.8
Guys And Dolls (1956) (co-prod)	(5.5)	6.9
Gigi (1958)	(3.3)	6.7
Ivanhoe (1952)		6.0
I'll Cry Tomorrow (1955)		6.0
Raintree County (1957)	(5.0)	6.0
North By Northwest (1959)	(4.3)	6.0
Butterfield 8 (1960)		6.0
High Society (1956)		5.8
The Teahouse Of The August Moon (1956)		5.7
Seven Brides For Seven Brothers (1954)		5.6
Please Don't Eat The Daisies (1960)		5.3
Show Boat (1951)		5.2
The Blackboard Jungle (1955)		5.2

1961–70

Dr Zhivago (1965)	(15.0)	43.0
2001: A Space Odyssey (1968)	(11.0)	21.5
The Dirty Dozen (1967)		20.1
Ryan's Daughter (1970)	(14.0)	13.4
How The West Was Won (1962)	(14.0)	12.2
Mutiny On The Bounty (1962)	(20.0)	9.8
Grand Prix (1966)		9.3

title	cost	North American rentals
1971–80	(in $ millions)	(in $ millions)
The Goodbye Girl (co-prod) (1977)	(3.5)	41.7
Coma (1978)		14.6
Network (co-prod) (1976)		13.7
The Champ (1979)		12.6
That's Entertainment (1974)		12.0
1981–90		
Poltergeist (1982)		38.2
Moonstruck (1987)	(14.0)	34.4
A Fish Called Wanda (1988)		29.8
Willow (1988)	(35.0)	28.0

The Stars

'More stars than there are in heaven' was the slogan coined by the MGM publicity department, and the studio's glittering line-up of beautiful women and handsome men, many of them also good actors, contributed immeasurably to its success. From its very beginnings in 1924, and throughout the following decades, the name Metro-Goldwyn-Mayer was closely identified with the Hollywood star system at its peak. The glamorous 30s of Garbo, Crawford, Shearer, Harlow and Gable gave way to the 40s of Tracy and Hepburn, Garson and Pidgeon, William Powell and Myrna Loy; and the famous series of musicals which brought Judy Garland, Mickey Rooney and others to the public. By the 50s the studio was in decline and most of the top stars had left or retired. Although the decade saw more arrivals, MGM was no longer the Hollywood dream factory.

In 1924 when Mayer and Thalberg set out to develop MGM into the leading Hollywood studio, they knew that a roster of top stars was the essential ingredient. Happily, the new company had already inherited a varied and useful group of faces and talents: Lon Chaney, Norma Shearer, John Gilbert and Marion Davies came from the Mayer and Goldwyn companies, while Buster Keaton, Ramon Novarro, Alice Terry and Mae Murray had all been at Metro.

During the years that followed, the studio demonstrated a remarkable ability to acquire or create new stars, thus easily withstanding the casualties of sound, such as John Gilbert, and accommodating the demands of expanding genres, such as the movie musical in the 40s. The sheer size of MGM, its abundant resources, and the large number of high-quality pictures it released every year, meant that each star was offered a scale of opportunity not available at most of the other, smaller studios.

Thus, from the mid-20s to the early 50s, there was a seemingly endless number of new arrivals at Culver City. A young Swedish actress named Greta Garbo was signed by Mayer in 1925. Magically paired with John Gilbert who, for a time, became her lover in truth as well as in fiction, Garbo lit up the screen in *Flesh And The Devil* (1927) followed by

Love (1927), a reworking of Tolstoy's 'Anna Karenina'. Joan Crawford, a relatively unknown young actress, joined MGM in 1925 and gradually worked her way up to star status by 1928 when she appeared as a flapper in *Our Dancing Daughters*. She thus qualifies as the studio's first major star discovery.

Some of the older, experienced actors added to the MGM roster included the remarkable Lillian Gish, as well as Lionel Barrymore and Marie Dressler, both of whom had solid backgrounds in the theatre which proved invaluable with the coming of sound. MGM was perhaps more fortunate in this respect than the other studios, as many of its stars easily made the transition from silents to sound. There was, of course, the well-known failure of John Gilbert, but his decline (like that of Ramon Novarro) was due less to his inability to adapt to sound than to a change in the attitudes of film audiences. The romantic hero of the silents was replaced by a tougher, he-man image. This new fashion boosted the careers of both plug-ugly Wallace Beery and uniquely handsome Clark Gable, the latter soon to become the studio's top male star.

MGM signed comparatively few stage actors – Robert Montgomery in 1929, Alfred Lunt and Lynn Fontanne who appeared in a film version of their stage hit, *The Guardsman* in 1931, and Helen Hayes and Franchot Tone in 1932. Yet MGM stars dominated the Best Actor and Best Actress Academy awards throughout the early years of the sound era from 1929 through 1932.

Clearly the MGM stars were well served by a studio geared to turning out a large number of 'star vehicles' of the highest quality year after year. Contract directors and fine cameramen aimed to enhance the stars, to bring out their best qualities, aided by many of the most creative technicians found in Hollywood. Cedric Gibbons, the head of the art department, and Adrian, the premier costume designer, represented the ultimate in Hollywood glamour, and were ably assisted by the studio's extensive make-up, hairdressing and stills photography departments. In addition, Irving Thalberg had a vast army of writers under contract, many of them women, including Frances Marion, Anita Loos, and his sister, Sylvia Thalberg. During the early 30s, Thalberg instituted the practice of assigning a number of different writers to work independently on the same story. This ensured that the studio's expensive stars would never remain idle due to the lack of a suitable script.

MGM added new names to its already impressive list throughout the decade, consolidating its position as the most powerful of all the studios. Thalberg was continually looking for new ways to exploit his valuable human assets. He promoted such multi-star vehicles as *Dinner At Eight* (1932), *Rasputin And The Empress* (1933), which brought the three Barrymores together on screen and, most successful of all, *Grand Hotel* which won the Best Picture Oscar in 1932. Similarly, many of the stars were promoted in pairs. Wallace Beery was teamed with Marie Dressler during the early 30s. Jean Harlow arrived in 1932 and soon achieved superstar status in *Red-Headed Woman*, followed by *Red Dust* (both 1932) in which her wise-cracking and sexually provocative behaviour was well matched by Gable's no-nonsense manliness. This was the first of many they made together, including *Saratoga*, Harlow's last before her tragic death in 1937. As the leading male attraction in a studio so rich in female talent, Gable had the opportunity of playing opposite a wide variety of glamorous co-stars. He appeared in a number of pictures with both Norma Shearer and Myrna Loy, for example, but was most often paired with Harlow and Joan Crawford during the 30s and Lana Turner in the 40s.

Johnny Weissmuller and Maureen O'Sullivan were signed to play Tarzan and Jane in 1932. This popular cycle of movies continued off and on for 10 years, until Weissmuller left to continue the series at RKO. *The Thin Man*, based on the book by Dashiell Hammett, turned out a surprise hit in 1934, teaming the debonair William Powell (as amateur detective Nick Charles) with Myrna Loy (as his loyal but long-suffering wife) and led to a highly successful series of Thin Man pictures. The following year Jeanette MacDonald and Nelson Eddy co-starred in *Naughty Marietta*, the first of their eight musicals together.

Garbo, however, stood alone and apart from the rest of the studio's hard-working stars, averaging less than one picture per year after 1932. In order to keep her happy MGM signed Fredric March to play Vronsky opposite her *Anna Karenina* in 1935, paid an extremely high price to get Charles Boyer on loan from producer Walter Wanger for *Conquest* (1936), and borrowed Melvyn Douglas from Columbia for her most delightful 30s comedy, *Ninotchka* (1939), scripted by Billy Wilder and Charles Brackett and directed by Ernst Lubitsch (all on loan from Paramount). *Camille* (1937), however, was the luminous Swede's best costume picture of the decade, in spite of the fact that her MGM co-stars were the somewhat unlikely 'father-and-son' pairing of Lionel Barrymore and the young Robert Taylor (who had arrived at MGM in 1934).

The pace of new arrivals during the 30s never seemed to slacken. In 1935 alone these included James Stewart, Spencer Tracy, signed by Thalberg when he was released from his Fox contract, and the Marx Bros who had left Paramount the year before. There were a number of new musical stars, too. The vivacious, long-legged dancer Eleanor Powell first appeared in *Broadway Melody of 1936*, while the young and multi-talented Judy Garland was cast in some musical shorts; she didn't appear in an MGM feature until 1937.

Later additions included Margaret Sullavan, Hedy Lamarr and Greer Garson, all in 1938, followed by Katharine Hepburn in 1940, Van Heflin in 1941 and a young Elizabeth Taylor in 1943. The early 40s, in fact, marked a major turning point in MGM history. At the same time that many of the leading dramatic stars either retired (Garbo and Shearer) or moved to other studios (Crawford to Warner Bros., Johnny Weissmuller and his loincloth to RKO) or joined the armed forces (Robert Montgomery, Gable and Stewart), MGM was embarking on its most ambitious programme of quality musicals.

Thus, not only was there a major turnover in the MGM star line-up, but it was now more heavily weighted with musical stars than ever before. The studio's already useful list of musical-comedy performers became even more impressive with the addition of such names as Gene Kelly, Frank Sinatra and Fred Astaire, Lena Horne and Esther Williams, Cyd Charisse and Jane Powell. The pattern continued into the 50s and, although the studio began to cut back on its star commitments, a last group of new arrivals notably included Howard Keel, Debbie Reynolds and Leslie Caron.

The Quigley Publications annual exhibitors' polls generally rated MGM stars highly in the 30s and 40s, though these surveys were unreliable and imprecise as an indicator of star popularity. Marie Dressler headed the poll in 1932 and 1933 – her salary had risen from $1500 per week in 1927 to $5000 in 1930, while the top ten stars of the early 30s also included Beery, Crawford and Shearer. Garbo obviously appeared in too few pictures in later years to make any impact on the poll and can only be found on the list in the first year, 1932. (Having begun at $350 per week, her salary had shot up to $5000 by 1927.)

Robert Taylor and Myrna Loy occasionally made the list between 1936 and 1940, but Gable, Rooney and Tracy can be found near the top. (Gable had started out at $350 per week in 1931, but had climbed to $2500 by 1933.) This same threesome continued strong in the early 40s, but appeared lower down. Interestingly, the top MGM name from 1941–45 was Greer Garson, while other stars on the annual lists from 1945 to 1950 included Judy Garland, Margaret O'Brien and Esther Williams, reflecting the popularity of the MGM musicals. (Annual earnings of MGM's top stars in the early 40s were: Spencer Tracy $225,000, Crawford $195,000 and Garland $95,000; in 1941 Katharine Hepburn was paid $190,000, Jeanette MacDonald $300,000 and Mickey Rooney $160,000.)

In the 50s MGM still had more than its share of Hollywood's most beautiful women under contract. A roster which included Elizabeth Taylor, Deborah Kerr, Ava Gardner, Lana Turner, Cyd Charisse and (briefly) Grace Kelly suggests that MGM could still claim to be Hollywood's most glamorous studio.

During the peak studio years Mayer and Thalberg's talent for exploiting their stars developed in a very special way and included a large measure of involvement in their personal lives. This represented a natural extension of the kind of controls and provisions found in the standard star contract of the period, for the bosses were obviously concerned with protecting their valuable investment. The studio had an awesome reputation regarding the control and treatment of its stars. 'We were really like slaves,' recalled Ann Rutherford who spent five years at the studio (1937–42). 'You were chattels of the studios, they could buy and sell you.'

In 1928 Lillian Gish had been surprised and shocked when Irving Thalberg offered to arrange a scandal for her as a means of increasing her popularity with film audiences by destroying her rather too 'pristine' public image. At the other extreme it was Louis B. Mayer who was first summoned to the scene of producer Paul Bern's suicide (in 1932) even before the police, and used all of his considerable influence behind the scenes. He was thus able to limit the publicity damage to Bern's wife, Jean

Harlow, who was just emerging as one of the studio's major box-office attractions.

In fact, it was Mayer who, in spite of stiff competition from the other Hollywood moguls, stood out as the undisputed master of controlling his stars. He regarded them as part of his MGM family and loved to strike a kind of fatherly pose as advisor, confidant or disciplinarian, depending on what role he felt would best serve the interests of the studio. According to Bosley Crowther's biography, 'His adroitness in manipulating Joan Crawford and her manifold wishes and complaints by flattery, threats, and entreaties was famous around the studio. He would solemnly counsel and cajole her; if need be, he would cry a little bit, then drop a few hints of his disfavour and what the consequences might be. It took a long time for Miss Crawford to get wise to him and then to summon up the courage to tell him where he could go.'

Similarly, Mayer's influence over the young Judy Garland, which he transmitted through her domineering mother, provides a fascinating, and ultimately unhappy, example of the relationship which he developed with some of his stars and the kind of power he could exercise over their personal lives. When he firmly opposed psychiatric treatment for Miss Garland, this led to a major row with her close friend, writer-producer Joseph Mankiewicz, and the departure of Mankiewicz from MGM in 1942 after eight years with the studio.

Mayer would make use of any possible trick or ploy to keep his stars working and ready even to accept parts they didn't like. He could turn on the charm to get his way, but when this failed he would resort to threats or violence or tears. Joseph Mankiewicz recalled that 'when someone like Myrna Loy decided to rebel, this was something Mayer himself had to stop.' As witnessed by Mankiewicz in his office, Mayer's face suddenly turned deathly grey and he collapsed. Miss Loy was terribly upset and had to convince him that she *really* wanted to play the part, and not just out of sympathy for him. But once she had left, Mayer jumped up from the couch where he had been lying, ready to carry on as if nothing had happened. 'I couldn't believe my eyes, this performance he gave.' Though he never appeared on the screen, perhaps it was really Louis B. Mayer who was the studio's greatest star.

STARS

Adorée, Renée (Mayer/Metro) 1923, 1924–30

Allyson, June 1943–53

Ames, Leon 1945–50

Angeli, Pier 1951–53, 1957

Arden, Eve 1939–40

Arnold, Edward 1933–34, 1941–50

Astaire, Fred 1944–45, 1948–53

Astor, Mary 1943–44, 1947–49

Atwill, Lionel 1934–35

Ayres, Lew 1938–42

Ball, Lucille 1943–46

Barrymore, Ethel 1949–53

Barrymore, John 1932–33, 1936

Barrymore, Lionel 1926–52

Bartholomew, Freddie 1935–38

Beery, Wallace 1930–48

Bennett, Constance (Roach) 1937–38

Bennett, Enid (Metro) 1923, 1924

Benny, Jack 1929, 1935

Bickford, Charles 1930

Blondell, Joan 1956–57

Blyth, Ann 1953–57

Boardman, Eleanor (Goldwyn) 1922–24, 1924–28, 1930–31
Boland, Mary 1939–40
Bolger, Ray 1935–39
Borgnine, Ernest 1967–68
Bremer, Lucille 1944–46
Brown, Johnny Mack 1927–31
Bruce, Virginia 1931–32, 1935–36, 1938–39
Brynner, Yul 1957–58
Burke, Billie 1934–35, 1937–40
Bushman, Francis X. 1925
Cabot, Bruce 1936
Calhern, Louis 1949–56
Carey, Harry, Sr. 1926–27
Caron, Leslie 1951–58
Chaney, Lon, Sr. 1924–30
Charisse, Cyd 1946–58
Chevalier, Maurice 1956–58
Cobb, Lee J. 1957–58
Coburn, Charles 1938–40
Colman, Ronald 1942–44
Conway, Tom 1940–42
Coogan, Jackie (Metro) 1923, 1924–27
Cooper, Jackie 1932–36
Crawford, Joan 1925–42
Cronyn, Hume 1943–47
Crosby, Bing 1956–57
Dahl, Arlene 1948–51
Dailey, Dan 1940–42
Davies, Marion (Cosmopolitan) 1924–34
Day, Laraine 1939–42
Dee, Sandra 1957–58
De Haven, Gloria 1940–50
Denny, Reginald 1930–31
Donlevy, Brian 1947–48
Douglas, Melvyn 1938–42
Dressler, Marie 1927–33
Dunne, Irene 1943
Durante, Jimmy 1931–34, 1944–47
Dvorak, Ann 1929–31
Eddy, Nelson 1933–41
Eilers, Sally 1930–31
Ferrer, Mel 1952–53
Foch, Nina 1951–53
Forbes, Ralph 1927–28, 1933–34, 1936

Ford, Glenn 1954–62
Ford, Harrison (Cosmopolitan) 1924–25
Foster, Preston 1945
Francis, Anne 1954–57
Gable, Clark 1930–42, 1945–54
Garbo, Greta 1926–41
Gardner, Ava 1942–56
Garland, Judy 1937–50
Garrett, Betty 1948–49
Garson, Greer 1939–54
Gifford, Frances 1943–48
Gilbert, John 1924–33
Gish, Lillian (Inspiration/Metro) 1923–24, 1925–28
Grahame, Gloria 1944–47
Granger, Farley 1952
Granger, Stewart 1950–57
Granville, Bonita 1940–41
Grayson, Kathryn 1941–53
Greer, Jane 1952
Grey, Virginia 1936–42
Hagen, Jean 1949–53
Haines, William (Goldwyn) 1922–23, 1924–31
Harding, Ann 1950–51
Harlow, Jean 1932–37
Harvey, Laurence 1960–64
Hasso, Signe 1942–45
Hayes, Helen 1933–35
Heflin, Van 1941–49
Hepburn, Katharine 1940–49
Hersholt, Jean 1931–35
Heston, Charlton 1958–59
Hodiak, John 1943–44, 1946–51
Holm, Celeste 1955–56
Holmes, Phillips 1932–33
Horne, Lena 1942–49
Hunt, Marsha 1939–45
Hunter, Ian 1939–41
Hussey, Ruth 1937–42
Huston, Walter 1932–33
Johnson, Van 1942–54
Jones, Allan 1935–37
Keaton, Buster (Schenck/Metro) 1920–21 & 1923–24, 1924–26, 1928–32, 1949
Keel, Howard 1950–55
Kelly, Gene 1942–57

Kelly, Grace 1955–56
Kendall, Kay 1955–58
Kerr, Deborah 1947–53
Kerry, Norman 1927
Lamarr, Hedy 1939–43
Landi, Elissa 1936
Langdon, Harry (Roach) 1929–30
Lansbury, Angela 1944–49, 1951–52,
   1961–62
Lanza, Mario 1949–53
Lassie 1943–50
Laurel, Stan & Hardy, Oliver (Roach)
   1928–38
Lawford, Peter 1942–52
Leigh, Janet 1947–53
Love, Bessie 1928–30
Lowe, Edmund 1936
Loy, Myrna 1932–41
Lundigan, William 1941–44
MacDonald, Jeanette 1934–42
MacLaine, Shirley 1958
MacMahon, Aline 1935, 1944–47
Main, Marjorie 1938–42, 1944, 1946,
   1950–51, 1953–54
Marshall, Herbert 1934
Marx Brothers, The 1935–41
Mason, James 1957–58
Maxwell, Marilyn 1942–47
McAvoy, May 1924
McCoy, Tim 1926–29
McCrea, Joel 1929, 1949–50
McGuire, Dorothy 1951
Menjou, Adolphe 1930–31, 1950–51
Merkel, Una 1932–39
Milland, Ray 1930–31
Miller, Ann 1948–56
Mitchell, Thomas 1945–47
Montalban, Ricardo 1947–53
Montgomery, Robert 1929–40
Moorehead, Agnes 1944–49,
   1952–53
Moran, Polly 1925–32
Moreno, Antonio 1926
Morgan, Dennis 1936–37
Morgan, Frank 1933, 1935–49
Morley, Karen 1931–33
Morris, Chester 1935–36
Murphy, George 1937, 1940,
   1946–51

Murray, Mae (Metro) 1921–23,
   1924–26
Nagel, Conrad 1924–27, 1929–30,
   1932
Newman, Paul 1955–56
Novarro, Ramon (Metro) 1921–23,
   1924–34
O'Brien, Margaret 1941–49
O'Brien, Virginia 1940–47
O'Connor, Donald 1952
O'Sullivan, Maureen 1932–41
Oliver, Edna May 1934–37
Paige, Janis 1959–62
Parker, Eleanor 1951–55
Patrick, Gail 1940–41
Pidgeon, Walter 1937–56
Poitier, Sidney 1956–57
Powell, Dick 1949–50
Powell, Eleanor 1935–43
Powell, Jane 1946–54
Powell, William 1934–46
Presley, Elvis 1963, 1964, 1967–68
Prevost, Marie 1930–31
Rainer, Luise 1935–38
Rathbone, Basil 1929–30, 1934–36
Ray, Charles 1925–26
Reed, Donna 1941–46
Reynolds, Debbie 1950–56
Rooney, Mickey 1934–48
Russell, Rosalind 1934–39, 1941
Rutherford, Ann 1937–42
Saint, Eva Marie 1957–59, 1961,
   1964–66
Sakall, S.Z. 1951–53
Sanders, George 1954–55
Shearer, Norma 1924–42
Simmons, Jean 1956–57
Sinatra, Frank 1945–49, 1955–56
Skelton, Red 1940–53
Smith, Kent 1958
Sondergaard, Gale 1938
Sothern, Ann 1939–47
Stanwyck, Barbara 1950–52
Starke, Pauline 1926–27
Stewart, James 1935–40
Stockwell, Dean 1945–47, 1949–50
Stone, Lewis 1929–52
Sullavan, Margaret 1938–40
Tamiroff, Akim 1933–34

Taylor, Elizabeth 1943–54
Taylor, Robert 1934–43, 1946–58
Taylor, Rod 1955–57, 1959–60,
  1963–64
Terry, Alice (Metro) 1920–23,
  1924–27
Tone, Franchot 1933–39
Totter, Audrey 1944–47
Tracy, Lee 1933
Tracy, Spencer 1935–53
Turner, Lana 1938–55
Veidt, Conrad 1940–42

Velez, Lupe 1931–32
Vera-Ellen 1948–51
Walker, Robert 1943–47, 1950
Weissmuller, Johnny 1931–41
Whitmore, James 1949–53
William, Warren 1937
Williams, Esther 1942–54
Winters, Shelley 1953
Wynn, Keenan 1942–55
Young, Gig 1951–53
Young, Robert 1931–42
Young, Roland 1929–31, 1940–41

A Sample of Star Activity at MGM's Culver City Studio
During a Typical Week in 1941

Stars	Film Title and Director	Type of Feature
Nelson Eddy, Rise Stevens	*The Chocolate Soldier* dir Roy del Ruth	musical – pre-recording songs on Stage 1
Katharine Hepburn, Spencer Tracy	*Woman Of The Year* dir George Stevens	comedy – rehearsal (on Stage 3)
Lana Turner, Robert Taylor	*Johnny Eager* dir Mervyn LeRoy	crime movie – filming first scene on Stage 4
Walter Pidgeon, Rosalind Russell	*Miss Achilles Heel* dir Norman Taurog	comedy – filming on Stage 10
William Powell, Myrna Loy	*Shadow Of The Thin Man* dir W S Van Dyke	comedy thriller – filming on Stage 16
Johnny Weissmuller	*Tarzan's Secret Treasure* dir Richard Thorpe	action-adventure – filming on Stage 12
Greta Garbo, John Alton	*Two-Faced Woman* dir George Cukor	comedy – filming 'Chica Choca Rhumba' on Stage 18
Hedy Lamarr, Charles Coburn, Robt Young	*H.M. Pulham Esq* dir King Vidor	drama – filming on Stage 22
Edward G Robinson	*Unholy Partners* dir Mervyn LeRoy	crime – filming airplane takeoff on Stage 30
Norma Shearer	*We Were Dancing* dir Robt Z Leonard	comedy – dancing lessons in Rehearsal Hall A
Eleanor Powell	*I'll Take Manilla* dir Edward Buzzell	tap dancing routine in Rehearsal Hall B
Judy Garland, Mickey Rooney	*Babes On Broadway* dir Busby Berkeley	musical – filming in Rehearsal Hall B
Wallace Beery, Marjorie Main	*Steel Cavalry* dir S Sylvan Simon	Western – filming exteriors on Lot 2

The Directors

With stars being especially favoured at MGM, the studio had few directors of the first rank under contract besides King Vidor, George Cukor and, later, Vincente Minnelli. The company pioneered a concept of efficient studio film-making under a system of tight producer control, leaving little room for the expression of individual creative qualities. Directors were there to serve, not to make their mark. Studio policy in this regard hardly changed over the years. Even by the 50s Dore Schary, who replaced Mayer as production chief, failed to recognize the importance of attracting top directors – and at a time when they were desperately needed. This attitude was MGM's Achilles' heel, and contributed to the decline of the once-proud industry leader.

From their previous production experience, Mayer and Thalberg already had a clear idea of the kind of role they expected directors to play in their new studio. They set out to build up a staff of solid, reliable and efficient men who could be depended on to stick closely to their scripts and budgets. At MGM the stars came first, and directors were valued for their ability to draw the best possible performances from those stars while working as part of a high-quality production team, as well as being expected to display flexibility in handling a broad spectrum of subjects.

Mayer and Thalberg were perhaps a little suspicious of the director who specialized in a particular type of film as this was often wedded to personal stylistic qualities which they felt would detract from the overall studio feel. Thus many of the directors at MGM were more or less interchangeable. It was not unusual for two (or more) directors to work on a film with only one credited. (Thalberg loved to make full use of the preview system whereby movies were tried out before randomly selected audiences and many adjustments made before the film was edited into its final form.)

At MGM the directors were under the control of the studio's production supervisors, including Bernie Hyman, Hunt Stromberg, Albert Lewin and Laurence Weingarten, who worked directly under Thalberg prior to 1933 and as producers under Mayer in later years. In addition,

Thalberg's own creative involvement in a project generally made itself felt at the script stage rather than during the actual shooting. He had large numbers of scriptwriters under contract and often had different writers taking turns on the same film; he liked to see each script knocked into final shape before a director was even assigned to the film. In this way the power of the director was curtailed by the studio set-up.

For those directors who fitted in well with the MGM approach the studio presented a congenial and prestigious film-making environment. Thus, Robert Z. Leonard, Jack Conway, Sidney Franklin, W. S. Van Dyke and Sam Wood all arrived at MGM during the 20s and spent virtually their entire careers at the studio. On the other hand, the more individualistic creative types didn't last long. A 'sorting out' of directors took place quite early on as the new studio bosses sought to establish their authority, which led to a number of disputes and departures.

Rex Ingram, the ace director at Metro who had been responsible for the studio's biggest hit, *The Four Horsemen Of The Apocalypse* (1921), and for other major successes such as *The Prisoner Of Zenda* (1922) and *Scaramouche* (1923), refused to have anything to do with the new studio. He made a special arrangement to work as an independent producer-director in Europe, releasing his pictures through MGM. It proved an unsatisfactory arrangement and only lasted a few years.

The brilliant Erich von Stroheim, unused to coping with temperamental stars, was forced to cast Mae Murray as *The Merry Widow* (1925). His determination to impose his own special quality on the picture led to rows with Miss Murray and with Thalberg, but the result was quite extraordinary, nevertheless. She gave the best performance of her career, while the picture became the new studio's first big box-office hit. It more than made up for the losses suffered on Stroheim's previous movie, the remarkable, naturalistic *Greed* (1924) which he had directed for the Goldwyn Company but which was released in a badly mutilated form by MGM. Clearly his view of the cinema did not match that of the new bosses of MGM and he left. There were other casualties. Marshall Neilan was forced to alter the tragic ending of his version of *Tess Of The D'Urbervilles* (1924) starring his wife, Blanche Sweet, and he too had departed by the end of 1925. Swedish director Mauritz Stiller failed to complete a single picture for the studio. He had a bitter row with Thalberg over the filming of *The Temptress* (1926), starring his protegée Greta Garbo, and was replaced by director Fred Niblo. Stiller's fellow Swede, Victor Sjöström, worked successfully at MGM for a few years, but relations were soured when the studio bosses insisted on changing the ending of his most memorable American film, *The Wind* (1928). It featured an astonishing performance from Lillian Gish who never worked for the studio again.

Of all those specially talented directors at MGM during the early years, the only survivors of note were King Vidor and Clarence Brown. Vidor delivered a tremendous hit with *The Big Parade* (1925), but had been talked out of his percentage contract by the wily Mayer and had lost a fortune. In part compensation he was given a reasonable measure of freedom to film more personal projects between his studio assignments, which resulted in *The Crowd*, his last memorable silent, in 1927 and *Hallelujah*, an all-black early sound musical in 1929. Less experimental by nature, Clarence Brown rather established himself as the studio's most stylish director, much sought after by the top stars, and was a particular favourite of Garbo's. They made six pictures together, beginning with *Flesh And The Devil* in 1927.

New arrivals of note during the early 30s were Victor Fleming, a fine director of action and dramatic movies who became a favourite with Gable and Tracy, and George Cukor, who came to MGM from RKO in 1933 along with producer David Selznick. Cukor soon established himself as the studio's top 'women's director'. Ironically, it was Fleming who replaced Cukor as the director of Selznick's production of *Gone With The Wind* (1939), the most successful movie ever distributed by MGM, and was the only MGM director to win an Oscar in the 30s.

The vast majority of new directors, however, were less interesting but efficient craftsmen, of the type most favoured by Mayer and Thalberg. New arrivals who found a congenial home at MGM during the 30s and 40s included George Seitz, Edward Buzzell, Norman Taurog, George Sidney and Roy Rowland, all of whom remained with the studio for over 10 years, while Richard Thorpe stayed on for almost 30 years.

The studio's new emphasis on musicals during the 40s, however, led to the hiring of innovative directors, notably Busby Berkeley (from Warner Bros.) and Vincente Minnelli (from Broadway). Others who emerged from the Freed unit were dancer-choreographer Gene Kelly and choreographers Stanley Donen and Charles Walters, all of whom easily made the transition to directing as part of a close-knit team effort. However, Berkeley's eccentric personal style and an unfortunate tendency to run over budget was not tolerated for long at MGM, and he spent the last years of his career demoted back to the role of choreographer only.

The attitude of the studio bosses to their directors never changed. Even the talented Minnelli, MGM's leading director of the 40s and 50s, was expected to help out (uncredited) on troubled productions such as *The Seventh Sin* (1957), while there were bad cuts and changes made behind his back to some of his own pictures, including the award-winning *Gigi* (1958) and *Two Weeks In Another Town* (1962).

To Louis B. Mayer the producer was far more important to the studio than any director. Good producers were hard to find, while he hired and fired directors every day. Thus, he couldn't understand why a successful producer (and writer) like Joseph Mankiewicz wanted to direct, and never gave him a chance to do so at MGM; or how Mervyn LeRoy could willingly take a cut in salary when he no longer wished to serve as producer on other directors' movies and returned to full-time directing. (LeRoy had been lured away from Warner Bros. in 1937 with the offer of a spectacular salary to produce *and* direct at MGM.)

In fact, the nature of Hollywood film-making had been changing during the 40s. There was a shift away from the studio-dominated product to accommodate a more personal approach to filming – exemplified by the work of an outstanding new group of directors, all at studios other than MGM. Among them were Orson Welles (RKO), Preston Sturges and Billy Wilder (Paramount), and John Huston (Warner Bros.). Undoubtedly the decline of MGM was due in part to its lack of top directors, a lack which was felt even more in the 50s when the studio could no longer depend on its musicals alone to attract the shrinking movie audiences. Though Dore Schary was brought in as production chief in 1948 and took over from Mayer in 1951, he was a former writer and producer himself and his attitude to directors was not all that different from Mayer's. As he wrote in his autobiography, 'In the years I was at Metro the chief architects of the film scripts we made were the writer and the producer. It was no studied attempt to denigrate the director but rather an effort to develop a closer relationship between the writer, the producer, and the director once he was assigned ... We had neither the time nor the funds to hand over a script to a director who might then decide to junk it and invent a new one ...' Not surprisingly Schary failed to attract the kind of directorial talent which the studio so badly needed. Clearly, one of the most damaging yet least recognized factors accounting for the decline of MGM was its attitude to and treatment of these vitally important creative people.

DIRECTORS

Beaumont, Harry 1928–34, 1944–48
Bell, Monta 1924–28
Berkeley, Busby 1939–42
Bernhardt, Curtis 1949, 1952–56
Boleslawski, Richard 1933–34, 1937
Borzage, Frank 1937–42
Brabin, Charles 1929–34
Brooks, Richard 1950–58
Brown, Clarence 1926–52
Browning, Tod 1925–29, 1932–34
Bucquet, Harold S. 1938–45
Buzzell, Edward 1938–49
Cline, Edward 1924–25
Conway, Jack 1925–48
Cukor, George 1933–37, 1939–44, 1949–50, 1952–53
Dassin, Jules 1942–46
del Ruth, Roy 1936–37, 1941–44
DeMille, Cecil B. 1929–31
de Mille, William 1929–30
Dieterle, William 1942–44
Donen, Stanley 1949–55
Fitzmaurice, George 1931–32, 1936–38
Fleming, Victor 1932–45

Foster, Norman 1952
Frank, Melvin (with Norman Panama) 1950–52
Franklin, Sidney 1926–37
Garnett, Tay 1943–45, 1950
Goldbeck, Willis 1942–47
Goulding, Edmund 1925–28, 1932–35
Hawks, Howard 1932–33
Hill, George W. 1925–32
Hiller, Arthur 1963–66
Howard, William K. 1934–35
Huston, John 1950–51
Ingram, Rex (Metro) 1920–23, 1924–27
Kelly, Gene 1949–58
Koster, Henry 1944–47
Lang, Fritz 1935–36
Leonard, Robert Z. (Metro) 1921–24, 1924–55
LeRoy, Mervyn 1939–45, 1948–54
Lewis, Joseph H. 1950, 1952–53
Lloyd, Frank 1935
Lubitsch, Ernst 1934, 1939
Mann, Anthony 1949–51

Mann, Daniel 1959–62
Marin, Edwin L. 1934–41
Marton, Andrew 1946, 1950–54
McLeod, Norman Z. 1940–43
Minnelli, Vincente 1943–63
Neilan, Marshall (Metro)
    1922–23, 1924–25
Niblo, Fred (Metro) 1923–24,
    1924–31
Potter, H.C. 1939–40
Robertson, John Stuart 1927,
    1929
Rowland, Roy 1943–51, 1954–58
Ruben, J. Walter 1935–38
Ruggles, Wesley 1942–44
Russell, Ken 1971–72
Saville, Victor 1946–51
Sedgwick, Edward 1926–32
Seitz, George 1933–44
Sidney, George 1941–54
Simon, S. Sylvan 1938–46
Sjöström, Victor (Goldwyn)
    1923, 1924–30

Stahl, John M. 1926–27
Stiller, Mauritz 1926
Stone, Andrew L. 1955–62
Stroheim, Erich von (Goldwyn)
    1923–24, 1924–25
Sturges, John 1949–55
Tashlin, Frank 1965–66
Taurog, Norman 1938–51
Thiele, Wilhelm 1937–40
Thorpe, Richard 1935–63
Tourneur, Jacques 1939–40
Van Dyke, W.S. 1927–42
Vidor, Charles 1953–55
Vidor, King (Goldwyn) 1923–24,
    1924–30, 1938–44
Walters, Charles 1947–64
Weis, Don 1951–53
Wellman, William A. 1936,
    1949–52
Wilcox, Fred M. 1943–56
Wise, Robert 1953–57
Wood, Sam 1927–39, 1949
Zinnemann, Fred 1942–48

The Creative Personnel

MGM's pictures were known for their sharp, clean look, characterized by a remarkable polish and technical virtuosity. From the atmospheric location photography and exotic back-lot jungles of Clyde de Vinna to the stylish and sophisticated studio filming of William Daniels, no matter what the subject, the MGM quality shone through. At its peak during the 30s and early 40s, the house style was maintained by a key group of excellent cameramen, many of whom spent 20 or 30 years at the studio.

The MGM art department was formidable. For over 30 years it was under the control of Cedric Gibbons, Hollywood's most famous and influential art director, who is also credited with having designed the Oscar statuette. The legendary Adrian was in charge of costume design and, when he left, other superb designers followed in his footsteps. The editing department was composed of very skilful people and, musically, if MGM lacked the very best in the 30s, they came into their own in the 40s with the rise of the screen musical. Douglas Shearer was the noted head of the sound department for three decades, and the studio also boasted top-flight experts in hairstyling and make-up.

Cameramen and Art Directors

The newly formed MGM was fortunate in inheriting an excellent group of established cameramen along with its first stars and directors. Oliver Marsh arrived from Metro with director Robert Z. Leonard, while William Daniels had developed into Erich von Stroheim's favourite cameraman at Universal, then at the Goldwyn Company, and naturally joined him to film *The Merry Widow* at MGM in 1925. Daniels stayed on to become a favourite cameraman of Garbo and Shearer. Clyde de Vinna was one of the many cameramen on the epic *Ben-Hur* (1925) who became a close collaborator with fast-working director W. S. 'Woody' Van Dyke at MGM during 1926–33. John Arnold came from Metro and immediately established himself as a fixture at MGM with his effective black-and-white filming of *The Big Parade* in 1925. He coped well with the problems of early sound filming in shooting *The Broadway Melody* late in 1928 which reflected his attraction to technical challenges, and he gave up shooting pictures in order to head the studio's camera department soon after. (Arnold actually invented an early version of the portable camera blimp – the sound-proof case which encloses the camera – and received a special technical Oscar in 1939 for one of his many innovations, a newly improved MGM camera crane.)

All of these men remained at MGM till the early 40s – Arnold headed the camera department for almost 30 years from 1929 to 1956 – providing a solid and reliable core of cameramen who shot a wide variety of pictures. Clyde de Vinna was one of the few who specialized for a time in outdoor subjects such as *California* (1927), *Trader Horn* (1931), and the first MGM Tarzan movies, and won the studio's first Oscar for cinematography for *White Shadows In The South Seas* (1929). The camera team was further strengthened by a select handful of new arrivals in the early 30s – Hal Rosson, Charles Rosher, Ray June, George Folsey and Joseph Ruttenberg. The brilliant German cinematographer, Karl Freund, arrived at the studio in 1936 and stayed for over 10 years, rounding out his already long and distinguished career with MGM and winning an Oscar for *The Good Earth* (1937).

All of these new men, too, remained at the studio for 20 years or more (with the exception of Freund) and helped to maintain MGM's reputation as the leading exponent of high-quality black-and-white studio photography during the 30s, working closely with the art department headed by Cedric Gibbons, and setting standards of excellence for the rest of the film industry. They also provided a stylistic continuity in the changeover to colour which took place during the late 40s and early 50s, and more or less determined that characteristically glossy MGM 'look' for much of the studio's history. As Hal Rosson recalled years later, 'All studios prided themselves on their work, and I was fortunate enough to be at MGM when they had an unbelievable number of actors and actresses and half a dozen cameramen who were considered the finest in their profession . . . Nothing was released until it was right . . . and maybe the MGM pictures did have a "look" that other studios did not have that was due to the photography . . .'

Unfortunately, the photographing of MGM pictures did eventually tend to become somewhat predictable and unimaginative, reflected in the fact that the studio's cameramen actually won relatively few Oscars. But this comment hardly applies to the seemingly ageless Robert Surtees who arrived at MGM in the 40s and demonstrated a tremendous adaptability. He was first Oscar-nominated for *Thirty Seconds Over Tokyo* in 1944 and was still gaining Oscar nominations over 30 years later. High points of his MGM career were Oscars for *King Solomon's Mines* (1950) filmed in Technicolor, for Minnelli's *The Bad And The Beautiful* (1952) in black-and-white, and for his contribution to the studio's last big success, the remake of *Ben-Hur* (1959), stunningly filmed in colour and in the large-screen Camera 65 process.

For over 30 years the MGM art department was run by one man, the distinguished Cedric Gibbons, who was perhaps the best-known and most influential art director in the history of the American cinema. Although he designed only a small percentage of films himself, Gibbons exerted a large degree of control over the visual qualities of most MGM productions. As the studio's 'supervising art director' his name appeared on the credits of virtually every MGM feature from 1924 to 1956. He was not only responsible for the studio's impressive staff of art directors, designers and sketch artists, but also supervised props, costumes, and process and special-effects photography. (One of his leading associates, A. Arnold Gillespie, headed the MGM special-effects department for almost 30 years; their association began with a close collaboration on *Ben-Hur* in 1924, and Gillespie was still around to work on the remake 34 years later.) Though still a young man (just turned 31) when MGM was formed, Gibbons already had many years of experience behind him at the Edison and Goldwyn studios. He assembled an outstanding team of designers at MGM in the 20s, many of whom later made their names at other studios, among them Van Nest Polglase (supervising art director at RKO in the 30s), James Basevi, Ben Carré, and Robert Day (Goldwyn's leading art director in the 30s, then supervising art director at Fox in the 40s).

Gibbons provided the MGM pictures with a special visual quality which evolved over the years, along with the changes in the pattern of studio productions. He was especially attracted to the Art Deco look and large white sets which can be seen in many of the studio's early comedies, musicals and dramatic pictures – for example *Our Blushing Brides* (1930), *Grand Hotel* (1932) and *The Merry Widow* (1934).

The opulent costume pictures and musicals of the late 30s allowed the art department more scope than ever before and it was strengthened by the addition of many talented new designers: William Horning, unit art director on *Conquest* (1937) and *Marie Antoinette* (1938), and Gibbons' right hand man for over 20 years; Preston Ames who came into his own working closely with Vincente Minnelli on his colour productions in the 50s; Paul Groesse, unit art director on *Pride And Prejudice* (1940), *Little Women* (1949) and *The Brothers Karamazov* (1958); Gabriel Scognamillo, Urie McCleary and Hans Peters were also there. The list is a long one, and all of them stayed on at the studio for 20 years or more, providing a continuity during the changeover from black-and-white to colour. Jack Martin Smith's years at MGM (1939–54) coincided exactly with the flourishing period of the MGM musical, and he became a staple collaborator within the Arthur Freed unit.

The influence of Gibbons undoubtedly contributed to the glory of MGM during the peak studio era, but he was a conservative figure, resistant to change in later years, and a heart attack in 1946 severely reduced his supervisory activity. Film director Mitchell Leisen, himself a former art director, expressed it quite succinctly when he complained of Gibbons' interference with the design of *Young Man With Ideas* (1952): 'The distinct Metro style was set up by Gibbons. Whether it fitted the story or not, he was going to have his sets paramount . . . He was God out there. He wanted it a certain way, that was the MGM style, and that's what you got'.

Other Departments

MGM's strong line-up of technical experts extended to every branch of film-making activity. Adrian, for example, was the most famous and respected costume designer in Hollywood in the 30s. He excelled in dressing the studio's large number of top female stars, working closely with Garbo, Crawford and Shearer in particular. His preference for strongly contrasting blacks and whites matched well with Cedric Gibbons' fondness for elaborate white sets and a general emphasis on stunning visual effects and glamour not always in keeping with the dramatic qualities of the stories. The best example of the worldwide influence of Hollywood fashion was the padded-shoulder look which Adrian provided for Joan Crawford (beginning in 1932 with *Letty Lynton*).

A tremendously inventive and prolific designer, Adrian flourished during the black-and-white era of the 30s but was no less imaginative when given the opportunity to work in colour, as demonstrated by his delightfully fantastic costumes for *The Wizard Of Oz* (1939). In fact, the big changeover in MGM's costume department came in the early 40s when the departure of Adrian coincided with a number of notable new arrivals including Irene (Cedric Gibbons' sister-in-law), Helen Rose, and Irene Sharaff who contributed to the look of the studio's new colour pictures and especially the musicals. But it was left to Walter Plunkett to carry on the tradition of MGM glamour into the 50s. He handled most of the studio's big films throughout this decade, but is best remembered today for creating the lavish costumes (including the green ball-dress) for *Gone With The Wind* in 1939.

The best-known of MGM's many outstanding editors was Margaret Booth, who spent over 40 years at the studio and served as supervising editor from 1939 through 1968. The studio's dependence on repeated previewings to help get the final version of each picture right may have diminished the power of its directors, but it certainly increased the influence of the editors who were required to attend previews and play a major role in the subsequent recutting and re-editing. As Miss Booth recalled, 'Sometimes we previewed five times if it was a picture that we felt was in trouble, or was not very good . . . If people laughed at something that we felt was dramatic, we knew we were in trouble and we would have to fix that.'

If MGM was lacking in star composers of the calibre of Max Steiner, winner of many Oscars, or Erich Wolfgang Korngold during the 30s, the studio's music department nonetheless came into its own with its expanded production of lavish screen musicals in the 40s. Herbert Stothart, MGM's leading composer, won the studio's first Oscar for a musical score for his work on *The Wizard of Oz*. Most important of all, producer Arthur Freed assembled an outstanding team of collaborators headed by Lennie Hayton, Roger Edens, Saul Chaplin, Conrad Salinger, and a young André Previn who arrived in 1949, the same year that composer and conductor Johnny Green became the new head of MGM's music department.

Other leading personnel who spent many years at MGM (all of them were numbered among the most respected professionals in Hollywood in their chosen fields of endeavour) included famous resident hair stylist Sydney Guilaroff, and Jack Dawn, the studio's leading make-up expert during the 30s and 40s, whose most remarkable achievement was his highly original make-up for the characters in *The Wizard Of Oz*. Douglas Shearer, brother of Norma, started the MGM sound department in 1928 which he headed for 30 years; in addition to his many important technical contributions, he is credited with creating the famous Tarzan yell with a voice track embellished electronically and run backwards.

CAMERAMEN

Alton, John 1949–52
Arnold, John (Metro) 1917–24, 1924–28, 1929–56 (head of camera dept)
Barnes, George (Metro) 1924–25, 1932
Brodine, Norbert 1930–33
Clarke, Charles 1933–37
Daniels, William 1925–43
De Vinna, Clyde 1924–42
Folsey, George 1933–59
Freund, Karl 1936–38, 1940–47
Howe, James Wong 1933–36
June, Ray 1933–53
Krasner, Milton 1959–66

Lawton, Charles, Jr. 1936–43
Marley, J. Peverell 1929–30
Marsh, Oliver (Metro) 1922–23, 1924–41
Mellor, William 1950–54
Planck, Robert 1940–56
Rosher, Charles 1930, 1934, 1942–54
Rosson, Hal 1930–34, 1936–53
Ruttenberg, Joseph 1934–63
Sartov, Hendrick 1925–28
Seitz, John 1937–40
Sharp, Henry 1926–30
Stradling, Harry, Sr. 1942–49
Surtees, Robert 1943–62

ART DIRECTORS

Ames, Preston 1936–70
Basevi, James 1925–29, 1936, 1950–52
Carfagno, Edward 1943–70
Carré, Ben 1924–26, 1939–44
Cathcart, Daniel 1936–58
Davis, George 1959–70
Day, Richard 1924–29
Duell, Randall 1938–57
Ferrari, William 1943–53, 1960–2
Gibbons, Cedric 1924–56
Gillespie, A. Arnold 1924–63
Goosson, Stephen 1943
Groesse, Paul 1937–59
Hope, Frederic 1926–37
Horning, William A. 1934–59
Leisen, Mitchell 1929–31

Lonergan, Arthur 1951–56
McCleary, Urie 1937–68
Oliver, Harry 1934, 1937
Peters, Hans 1944–62
Polglase, Van Nest 1929–31
Pye, Merrill 1925–68
Ree, Max 1926
Scognamillo, Gabriel 1934–42, 1949–53
Smith, Jack Martin 1939–54
Toluboff, Alexander 1926–34
Urban, Joseph (Cosmopolitan) 1924–25
Wheeler, Lyle 1942–44
Willis, Edwin B. (Goldwyn) 1919–24, 1924–57
Wright, Joseph C. 1925–26, 1934–39

COSTUME DESIGNERS

Adrian 1928–42
Cox, David 1927–30
Dean, Kay 1944–45
Herschel 1951–54
Hubert, René 1927–31
Irene 1942–49
Kalloch, Robert 1941–43
Keyes, Marion Herwood
  1944–46

Plunkett, Walter 1947–65
Rose, Helen 1943–67
Sharaff, Irene 1943–45
Shoup, Howard 1942–46
Steele, Gile 1938–44
Tree, Dolly 1932–42
Valles 1938–50
Wachner, Sophie (Goldwyn)
  1922–23, 1924

COMPOSERS AND MUSIC DIRECTORS

Amfitheatrof, Daniele 1942–43
Axt, William 1925–29, 1932–39
Bassman, George 1943–47
Deutsch, Adolph 1948–56
Green, Johnny 1942–48, 1949–58
Hayton, Lennie 1942–53
Kaper, Bronislau 1935–62
Previn, André 1949–58
Raksin, David 1950–52
Rozsa, Miklos 1949–57

Salinger, Conrad 1943–46,
  1951–54
Shilkret, Nathaniel 1943–46
Silvers, Louis 1933
Snell, David 1937–48
Stoll, George 1937–66
Stothart, Herbert 1933–50
Tiomkin, Dimitri 1935
Ward, Edward 1935–40
Waxman, Franz 1936–42

EDITORS

Akst, Albert 1941–56
Bauchens, Anne 1929–31
Berman, Henry 1962–70
Boemler, George 1927–56
Booth, Margaret 1926–68
  (supervising ed. 1939–68)
Dunning, John 1947–60
Fazan, Adrienne 1937–64
Gray, William 1929–37
Hamilton, William 1927–29
Held, Tom 1928–38
Hively, George 1926–32, 1943–45
Hull, Frank 1924–26, 1933–49
Kern, Hal 1933–34
Kern, Robert (Mayer/Metro)
  1923–25, 1934–52
Komer, Harry 1938–56
Kress, Harold 1939–63
Lewis, Ben 1924–67
McSweeney, John 1952–68

Morra, Irene (Coogan) 1924
Nervig, Conrad 1926–54
Newcom, James 1933–36, 1949–52
Nosler, Lloyd (Mayer/Metro)
  1923–24, 1924–26
Ruggiero, Gene 1946–61
Santillo, Frank 1956–66
Sewell, Blanche 1925–49
Smith, Frederick 1936–43
Steinkamp, Fredric 1959–67
Sullivan, Frank 1925–47
Vernon, Elmo 1937–43
Warburton, Irvine 1943–53
Webster, Ferris 1939–59
White, George 1943–53
Whytock, Grant (Metro) 1921–23,
  1924–30
Winters, Ralph 1941–63
Wrangell, Basil 1925–33, 1935–37
Wynn, Hugh 1924–35

SCRIPTWRITERS

Behrman, S.N. 1933–37, 1939–41

Butler, Hugo 1937–43

Coffee, Lenore 1929–36

Farnum, Dorothy 1924–29

Goodrich, Francis (with
Albert Hackett) 1933–39, 1948–55

Gordon, Ruth (with
Garson Kanin) 1949–53

Jennings, Talbot 1935–40

Kingsley, Dorothy 1943–54

Krasna, Norman 1935–38

Lederer, Charles 1938–42

Lennart, Isobel 1942–57

Levien, Sonya 1934–55

Loos, Anita 1932–42

Ludwig, William 1938–57

MacArthur, Charles 1930–32

Mahin, John Lee 1932–41, 1950–53

Mankiewicz, Herman J. 1933–40

Marion, Frances 1925–36

Mathis, June 1924–25

Meehan, John 1929–38

Meredyth, Bess 1924–25, 1929–33

Murfin, Jane 1938–44

Parker, Dorothy, 1936–38

Reisch, Walter 1938–39, 1942–44

Rivkin, Allen 1949–53

Schary, Dore 1937–41

Stallings, Lawrence 1934–39

Stewart, Donald Ogden 1932–35, 1940–42

Sullivan, C. Gardner 1931–32

Thalberg, Sylvia 1927–33

Trumbo, Dalton 1943–45

Vajda, Ernest 1931–38

Viertel, Salka 1933–37

West, Claudine 1929–34, 1937–44

Wilson, Carey 1924–39

Young, Waldemar 1924–29

The Academy Awards

As the leading studio in Hollywood, MGM took the lion's share of Academy Awards during the peak studio era up to 1942, noticeably – and perhaps not surprisingly – dominating in the acting categories. Oscar winners ranged from Marie Dressler, Norma Shearer and Wallace Beery to Spencer Tracy, Luise Rainer and Greer Garson, but also reflected the power and influence of MGM within the Academy. The studio fared less well in later years, however, gaining its last Best Picture Oscars for *An American In Paris* (1951) and *Gigi* (1958), a tribute to the high standards set by the studio's colour musicals and, finally, for the remake of *Ben-Hur* in 1959.

MGM had a special connection with the Oscars or Academy Awards from their very beginnings in 1927/28, for a number of leading figures at the studio were among the original group of founder members of the Academy: executives Louis B. Mayer, Irving Thalberg and Harry Rapf; directors John Stahl and Fred Niblo; writers Bess Meredyth and Carey Wilson; supervising art director Cedric Gibbons, who designed the Oscar statuette.

MGM's Oscar nominees and winners over the years have presented a reasonably accurate reflection of the studio's strengths and weaknesses. During the peak studio years 1928–42 when MGM was the industry leader, its total of five Best Picture winners and a share in a sixth, David Selznick's independently produced *Gone With The Wind*, could not be matched by any other studio. And it dominated the Best Actor and Best Actress categories as well. But in the following period, 1943–60, MGM was obviously a company in decline and won only three Best Picture awards, while from 1961 through 1986 it failed to capture any major awards at all.

In the early years the studio succeeded best with its dramatic pictures, though a few select comedies and musicals gained awards, too. MGM won its first Best Picture Oscar for *The Broadway Melody* (1929), while Norma Shearer in *The Divorcee* (1930), Lionel Barrymore in *A Free Soul* (1931), Wallace Beery in *The Champ* (1931) and Helen Hayes in *The Sin Of Madelon Claudet* (1932) all won Oscars for their performances. Other acting nominations during the early years of sound included two each for Garbo and Shearer, followed by a second Best Picture award for the studio's multi-star drama *Grand Hotel* (1932).

When MGM began to produce more expensive costumers and musicals in the middle and late 30s, this was reflected in its next big Oscar successes – *Mutiny On The Bounty* (1935), *The Great Ziegfeld* (1936) and a share in *Gone With The Wind* (1939). Both Luise Rainer and Spencer Tracy set a record which has never since been equalled, of winning the best acting award two years running. Norma Shearer was nominated for a trio of costume roles and Garbo, too, received her last nominations, for *Camille* (1937) and *Ninotchka* (1939). Incredibly, Garbo never won an Oscar but was twice given the best actress accolade by the New York Film Critics (for *Anna Karenina*, 1935, and *Camille*) and received a belated honorary Oscar in 1954. Similarly, Margaret Sullavan never won an Oscar but was selected as best actress by the New York Film Critics for her performance in *Three Comrades* (1938).

The studio's occasional comedy successes included Academy Awards for Marie Dressler in *Min And Bill* (1930), and James Stewart in *The Philadelphia Story* (1940); Judy Garland received a special (juvenile) Oscar in 1939 as did the Andy Hardy series in 1942, 'for representing the American way of life', and England's Robert Donat won the Best Actor award in 1939 for *Goodbye Mr Chips* (filmed in Britain).

MGM's Academy Award success with *Mrs Miniver* in 1942 topped all previous movies from the studio (excluding *Gone With The Wind*). It carried off six of the prized statuettes, including the Best Actress award to Greer Garson for her moving performance in the title role. (She had been nominated twice before and would receive three more in 1943–45, six nominations within the space of seven years.) In addition, Van Heflin won for Best Supporting Actor in *Johnny Eager* and the Irving G. Thalberg Memorial Award went to Sidney Franklin who had produced the two Garson movies, *Mrs Miniver* and the Oscar-nominated *Random Harvest* (also starring Greer Garson, teamed with Ronald Colman). This special award had been initiated by the Academy in 1937, the year after Thalberg's death, to honour Hollywood's most consistently creative producers; it was awarded to MGM producers Arthur Freed (1951), Laurence Weingarten (1973), Mervyn LeRoy (1975) and Pandro S. Berman (1976).

Though the studio did extremely well in 1942, this year marked the end of MGM's early domination of the awards, coinciding with the retirement or departure of a number of older stars and a major expansion in the production of colour films. From this point on the studio's major awards were few and far between. A somewhat belated recognition of the special quality of the MGM colour musicals came in the 50s when the Best Picture Oscar was awarded to *An American In Paris* (1951) and to *Gigi* (1958), both directed by Vincente Minnelli who also received his personal Oscar for directing *Gigi*. This marked the only occasion when an MGM director had actually received an Oscar for directing an MGM movie. Clarence Brown had been nominated six times, King Vidor four times (at MGM) and received an honorary award in 1978. Victor Fleming had, of course, won for directing David Selznick's *Gone*

With The Wind, while the independent director William Wyler won for two MGM movies, *Mrs Miniver* and *Ben-Hur* (1959). This latter marked the studio's last big Oscar success, setting a record by winning 11 in all, with a number of them going to MGM personnel – cameraman Robert Surtees, art directors William Horning and Edward Carfagno, composer Miklos Rozsa and special-effects expert A. Arnold Gillespie.

MGM had always done well with the technical and craft awards, reflecting the quality of their studio personnel. Joseph Farnum and Frances Marion were among the first writers honoured by the Academy; the studio's art directors and costumiers won a number of Oscars; cameramen Joseph Ruttenberg and Robert Surtees won three each, and sound expert Douglas Shearer received 14 nominations and five Oscars along with seven technical awards. In 1977 Margaret Booth was awarded a special Oscar for her 62 years as a distinguished film editor.

The high standard of MGM's short films and cartoons during the 30s and 40s resulted in the studio gaining more than its share of Oscar nominations and winners in these categories. Young directors David Miller, George Sidney and Fred Zinnemann were credited with Award-winning shorts early in their careers, and most successful of all were William Hanna and Joseph Barbera. They won seven Oscars for their popular Tom and Jerry cartoons between 1943 and 1952, beginning with *Yankee Doodle Mouse* (1943).

MGM's only major award in the 60s, more sentimental than earned, went to Elizabeth Taylor for her performance as a high-class call-girl in *Butterfield 8* in 1960, the year that she almost died. During more recent years the studio's few awards of note have continued to be mainly in the various acting categories. In the 70s MGM shared in three top acting awards – to Peter Finch and Faye Dunaway for their performances in *Network* (1976) a virulent attack on television's excesses, co-produced by MGM with UA, and to Richard Dreyfuss for *The Goodbye Girl* (1977), another MGM co-production, with Warner Bros. But the studio's biggest Oscar success since *Ben Hur* came in 1987 with *Moonstruck*, nominated for Best Picture and director (Norman Jewison) with statuettes going to Cher (actress), Olympia Dukakis (supporting actress) and scriptwriter John Patrick Shanley.

PARAMOUNT

In 1916 Adolph Zukor merged his Famous Players Film Company with Jesse Lasky's, and then took over the Paramount distribution company — from which the corporation eventually took its name. Paramount grew rapidly and soon became the USA's largest and most successful movie company. Though the studio made a quick and successful transition to sound, it was badly affected by the decline in movie audiences in 1931 and 1932. Barney Balaban took over as president in 1936 as the studio recovered strongly from the Depression and forged ahead in the 40s. However, in 1949 it was forced to sell off its film theatres, and was only moderately successful in the 50s. Financial difficulties in the 60s led to a takeover by the giant Gulf + Western conglomerate in 1966. In recent years Paramount has had more than its share of Oscar winners and hits.

The beginnings of Paramount can be traced back to the early activities of Adolph Zukor, a Hungarian immigrant who developed his initial interest in the fledgling movie industry shortly after the turn of the century. He invested in his first penny arcade in New York in 1903, around the same time as William Fox and, like Fox, he opened his first nickelodeon a year or so later. Next, he experimented with a chain of theatres presenting Hale's Tours: the audience was seated in a tiny hall shaped like a railroad coach and, as a series of travel pictures appeared on the screen, there were whistles and bells and rocking effects to simulate a rail journey. Zukor found that his customers soon tired of this type of presentation, although they were interested in the moving pictures and kept returning to see each new show. Thus, he switched back to nickelodeons, then tried combining vaudeville with movies and joined fellow entrepreneur Marcus Loew, serving as treasurer of Loew's company which operated a large chain of movie theatres.

After a few years Zukor left to start up on his own once again. His new idea was to produce (and exhibit) feature-length pictures adapted from stage plays. 'Famous Players in Famous Plays' was the motto of his newly formed Famous Players Film Company in 1912. Among his associates at this time were Broadway producer Daniel Frohman, pioneering movie director Edwin S. Porter and young B. P. Schulberg who would develop into a leading producer and studio chief at Paramount in the 20s.

Zukor had a big success with his first release in 1912, a four-reel French production of *Queen Elizabeth* starring the celebrated actress Sarah Bernhardt. Though it was a slow-moving, stage-bound production, Miss Bernhardt's name alone was sufficient to give the movie a special 'respectability' and contribute to a wider acceptance of feature-length pictures in the USA. Zukor followed it with his own productions of *The Count Of Monte Cristo* starring James O'Neill (father of playwright Eugene O'Neill), *The Prisoner Of Zenda* with James K. Hackett and *His Neighbor's Wife* with the famous Lillie Langtry. All three were directed by Porter and released in 1913, but were not even good examples of filmed theatre. Porter had made his name 10 years earlier with such pictures as *The Great Train Robbery* and had not kept up with advances in film-making since then. In addition, he was not adept at working with actors. He filmed with a fixed camera, using extremely artificial-looking sets, while the celebrated stage stars themselves were all well past their prime and unaware of the more naturalistic requirements of acting on screen.

Zukor's modest success with these initial ventures thus reflects the extent to which audiences at the time were attracted to the novelty of feature-length movies. Fortunately for Zukor, he had signed Mary Pickford at the same time, not because he recognized her talents as a film actress – she had been Griffith's leading star at Biograph a few years earlier – but because she was currently appearing on stage in 'A Good Little Devil' which he wanted to film. She alone emerged as his leading star and ensured the survival of his new company.

Having been forced to apply for special permission from the Motion Picture Patents Company to screen his Bernhardt film, Zukor supported Carl Laemmle and William Fox in their successful challenge to the Trust in the courts. As the power of the Trust and its members waned during the following years, Zukor was quick to recognize and take advantage of the new possibilities thus opened up by a relatively unrestricted movie market. He had already been involved in the industry for 10 years, but with a limited degree of success. Now, for the first time, he was able to demonstrate where his true talents lay. For a period of about 20 years, from 1913 to 1932, he established himself as a dominating figure in the movie industry.

No other movie mogul was as shrewd, enterprising, aggressive, and occasionally ruthless, in building up a motion-picture empire. Not only did Zukor push rapidly ahead in signing new stars and expanding production, but he perfected such dubious systems as 'block booking', which forced exhibitors to take the company's poorer-quality movies in order to get the popular Mary Pickfords. He arranged mergers and takeovers as he built Famous Players, then Famous Players-Lasky and Paramount into the leading company in the industry, a vertically integrated corporation involved in production, exhibition and distribution with an influence that was worldwide. In fact, such was the far-reaching impact of Zukor's activities that many of the important developments in the industry, such as the setting up of First National in 1917 and of United Artists in 1919, were a direct response to, and an attempt to counteract, the growing power of Zukor and his giant company.

Zukor's first studio was a converted warehouse on West 26th St in New York where his first pictures were filmed during 1912 and 1913, while late in 1913 another tiny new production company was just getting started. Founded by Jesse Lasky, Samuel Goldwyn and Cecil B. DeMille it was able to raise just enough capital to finance one feature, a Western costing about $20,000 which could be filmed mainly on location. Though director DeMille and star Dustin Farnum ended up in California and way over budget, the completed movie, *The Squaw Man*, was a big hit when it opened in February 1914. About one month later Zukor, too, had his first big hit with Mary Pickford as *Tess Of The Storm Country*, while later that year W. W. Hodkinson formed Paramount Pictures as a distribution company to handle the new features from Zukor's Famous Players and the Jesse L. Lasky Feature Play Co along with those of a number of smaller producers.

In his autobiography, 'The Public Is Never Wrong', Zukor matter-of-factly states: 'In a series of talks, Lasky, Goldwyn, DeMille and I had decided that a combination of our forces was advantageous.' The new company (formed in 1916) was called Famous Players-Lasky with Goldwyn as chairman of the board, DeMille as director-general, Lasky vice-president in charge of production and Zukor as president. Goldwyn never fitted well into the new set-up and soon left to form his own production company with the Selwyn brothers. Zukor lost no time in consolidating his power. He soon took over Paramount, the distribution company, ousting Hodkinson, and welded Famous Players-Lasky and Paramount (together with a few smaller companies) into the largest movie corporation in the USA – henceforth here called Paramount.

Zukor was soon signing up new stars, among them Fatty Arbuckle, William S. Hart and Douglas Fairbanks, and he upped the rate of production to over 100 features per year. In maintaining this high level of output for a number of years, the emphasis was on quantity rather than quality, with few major directors under contract aside from DeMille. Maurice Tourneur and Marshall Neilan spent some time at the studio and each directed Mary Pickford features during 1916–18, for she insisted on the best collaborators that Paramount could offer. (She left in 1918 when First National offered her complete artistic control over her pictures and a large salary increase.)

In fighting the growing power and influence of First National, Zukor arranged a $10 million line of credit and embarked on an ambitious programme of film-theatre purchases in 1919, culminating a number of years later in the acquisition of the Balaban and Katz chain which dominated the Chicago area. It became the cornerstone of Paramount's efficiently run and extensive Publix theatre subsidiary which continued to expand in the late 20s.

At the same time the studio began to pay more attention to improving the quality of its features and strengthening its list of contract stars and directors. Having lost early stars such as Pickford, John Barrymore and Marguerite Clark, as well as Douglas Fairbanks, it was Gloria Swanson who emerged as the leading female star in the early 20s. Valentino arrived in 1921 and had smash hits with *The Sheik* (1921) and *Blood And Sand* (1922), and the studio did even better with its epic Western, *The Covered Wagon* and DeMille's *The Ten Commandments*, both released in 1923.

Though profits averaged an impressive $5 million per year throughout the early 20s, Zukor was sensitive to the new challenge to Paramount's leadership posed by the formation of MGM in 1924. On the East Coast Walter Wanger was brought in and served for a time as chief of the Long Island studio with William LeBaron as associate producer during 1924–27. Zukor also realized that he needed a strong new studio boss in Hollywood to work under Lasky and, in 1925, he brought back B. P. Schulberg, his former head of publicity. Schulberg had left Paramount in the late 'teens and became a leading producer, best known for discovering and promoting Clara Bow. It was clear, too, that the company had outgrown its original Hollywood studio on Sunset and Vine, and in 1926 it moved into a larger and better-equipped studio complex on Marathon Street, shortly before Schulberg was put in charge.

Schulberg's record during the following years was an impressive one. He hired new directors of the stature of Josef von Sternberg,

Ernst Lubitsch, Rouben Mamoulian, and William Wellman whose first major production, *Wings* (1927), won the first-ever Best Picture Oscar. Schulberg also played a major role in the smooth transition to sound filming, with a useful contribution from his efficient young assistant, David O. Selznick, of whom more would be heard. Though initially reluctant to make the changeover to sound filming, once the company decided to do so in 1928, it accomplished the most rapid conversion of any Hollywood studio. Thus, a full 75% of Paramount's 1929 releases were 100% talkies.

There was a major changeover in stars, too. Paramount led all the other companies in its raid on the Broadway stage, making good use of its conveniently located Astoria, Long Island, studio (which had opened in 1920) for tests, shorts and a few features. *The Hole In The Wall* starring Claudette Colbert (with Edward G. Robinson) and the Marx Bros' first movie, *The Cocoanuts*, were both filmed there by new director Robert Florey in 1928–29. Other important new talkie stars who were signed up by the studio at around this time were Fredric March, Sylvia Sidney, Marlene Dietrich, Ruth Chatterton, Maurice Chevalier and Jack Oakie.

As profits climbed to peak levels during 1929 and 1930, the company continued to expand, acquiring new film theatres, setting up a new music division, investing in the CBS radio network – and generally ignoring the deepening Depression which had not yet affected the movie industry. In the process, however, Paramount's debts grew alarmingly, and when movie attendance began to fall off in 1931 the company found itself in serious trouble.

In 1932 Jesse Lasky was forced out of the empire he had helped to found and was followed soon after by Schulberg, while Zukor lost much of his power and was 'kicked upstairs' to the post of chairman of the board. In spite of its efforts at cost cutting, the company was unable to meet its debts and was forced to file for bankruptcy early in 1933. A pair of smash hits from Mae West undoubtedly helped Paramount to survive, and a plan for the reorganization of the company was approved in 1935. The following year Barney Balaban, an experienced executive from the exhibition side and one of the heads of the Balaban and Katz chain, was appointed president. He was to hold this post for almost 30 years, up to the mid-60s.

Manny Cohen was the studio's executive in charge of production during 1933 and 1934, followed by Ernst Lubitsch in 1935 and William LeBaron in 1936. (Lubitsch soon returned to the role which suited him better, that of a premier producer-director.) Y. Frank Freeman was brought in as vice-president in charge of production and studio head in 1936. He worked with LeBaron initially, then with producer-songwriter B.G. 'Buddy' DeSylva during 1941–44 followed by Harry Ginsburg in the late 40s. Freeman stayed on till the late 50s, almost as long as Balaban, and between them they controlled the company for over 20 years.

Paramount's recovery continued during the late 30s and early 40s with popular epics and Westerns from Cecil B. DeMille, and with musicals, comedies, and the very profitable series of Road movies starring Bing Crosby, Bob Hope and Dorothy Lamour. Balancing the creative contributions made by leading writer-directors Preston Sturges and Billy Wilder with more commercial productions, Paramount managed to re-establish itself as one of the leading studios for the first time since the early 30s – over a dozen years earlier. The studio won the Best Picture Oscar two years running – for Leo McCarey's *Going My Way* (1944) and Billy Wilder's *The Lost Weekend* (1945) – and recorded the most spectacular profits in its history in 1946 and 1947, reflecting the success of its theatres and popularity of its movies.

As the prime target of the government's Consent Decree, Paramount was forced to divest itself of its film theatres in the late 40s at a time when movie revenues were falling, and experienced a drastic decline in profits. The studio had some success in the 50s with established directors like William Wyler, George Stevens and Alfred Hitchcock who joined the ever-reliable Wilder and DeMille, while new star discoveries included Dean Martin and Jerry Lewis, Audrey Hepburn, Anthony Perkins and Elvis Presley.

In an attempt to stem the decline in movie audiences. Paramount experimented briefly with 3-D in 1953, then responded to Fox's successful introduction of CinemaScope with the launching of its own, superior VistaVision process in 1954. The first production was a Bing Crosby-Danny Kaye musical, *White Christmas*, a big hit, as was DeMille's last spectacular production, *The Ten Commandments* (1956). But other VistaVision pictures did less well; the process was expensive and the cameras cumbersome and it was phased out in the late 50s.

Though Paramount carried out some early experiments with 'theatre television' – stage acts and sporting events recorded with TV cameras and presented in film theatres in the 40s – the studio was slow to move into the profitable area of TV production. Profits remained small but reasonably steady throughout the 50s, maintained in part through selling off some of the company's assets. However, continuing financial difficulties in the early 60s, together with a decline in production and fall in the company's share price, made it vulnerable to a takeover bid. In 1966 Paramount was merged with Gulf + Western Industries headed by Charles Bluhdorn – one of the many mergers which were to transform the movie industry in the 60s.

Balaban and Zukor were retained in honorary positions while Robert Evans, a virtually unknown young producer (and former movie actor), was brought in as the new vice-president in charge of production. Under Bluhdorn's management Paramount boosted film production and substantially increased its investment in TV production. The studio did reasonably well in the late 60s, and managed to avoid the serious problems and huge losses experienced by most of the other majors in the early 70s. Evans had spectacular and unexpected successes with *Love Story* (1970), and with two Francis Coppola productions, *The Godfather* (1972) and *The Godfather: Part II* (1974).

After the departure of Evans in 1975 to become an independent producer (releasing his pictures through Paramount), the company continued to do well under chief executive officer Barry Diller and, more recently, under Frank Mancuso who moved up from vice-president in charge of distribution to chairman of Paramount Pictures. Ned Tanen, who had previously made his name at Universal in the 70s, took over as the new president of Paramount from 1984 to 1988. He continued the successful formula of hit movies established in the early 80s with the emphasis on exciting action-adventure pictures typically starring Eddie Murphy or Harrison Ford.

A newly slimmed-down Paramount entered the 90s in reasonably sound financial shape and with a new company name, Paramount Communications, having dropped the conglomerate name, Gulf+Western, which dated back to the 60s and had been parodied by Mel Brooks as 'Engulf and Devour' in his *Silent Movie*. The company planned to concentrate more on its entertainment and leisure activities, having sold off its substantial financial services group, The Associates, in 1989, and thus cushioned from the 1990–91 recession by a substantial amount of cash from this $1.8 billion sale.

As part of this new look, producer Stanley Jaffe was appointed as the company's new president early in 1991. As an independent producer he had provided Paramount with one of its biggest hits in *Fatal Attraction* in 1987. Although the studio had accounted for more than its share of top hits during recent years, when the high production and promotion costs are taken into account, a different picture emerges. Clearly Paramount, more than any other Hollywood studio, has paid a high price for its success. Whereas revenues have continued to rise, profits peaked in 1987, fell back in 1988–89, and declined further in 1990. It will be interesting to see if Jaffe can provide the new leadership which the company needs to put it back on course in the 1990s.

Paramount Studio Chronology

1912   Adolph Zukor releases *Queen Elizabeth* and forms his Famous Players Film Company.

1913   Jesse Lasky, Samuel Goldwyn and Cecil B. DeMille go into partnership to set up the Jesse L. Lasky Feature Play Company.

1914   Lasky releases his first production, *The Squaw Man*, co-directed by DeMille and Oscar Apfel. W.W. Hodkinson forms a new distribution company called Paramount Pictures.

1916   Zukor arranges a merger between his Famous Players and the Lasky company, to form his Famous Players-Lasky Corporation, then takes control of Paramount soon after. Zukor takes the post of president with Lasky as vice-president and DeMille as director-general. Goldwyn leaves the company.

1919   Zukor raises a $10 million line of credit from Wall Street to finance a major acquisition of film theatres.

1920   A new East Coast studio is completed at Astoria, Long Island.

1923   *The Covered Wagon* and *The Ten Commandments* are smash hits.

1925   The company name is changed from Famous Players-Lasky to Paramount-Famous-Lasky, with the newly enlarged Publix theatres as a subsidiary.

1926   A new, expanded Hollywood studio is completed on Marathon Street.

1927/28 *Wings* wins the first Academy Award for Best Picture and Emil Jannings is honoured as Best Actor.

1930 Reflecting the important role played by the company's theatres and its executives, Barney Balaban and Sam Katz, the company name is changed, yet again, to the Paramount-Publix Corporation.

1932 Jesse Lasky is forced out of the company, followed soon after by production chief B.P. Schulberg. Zukor, too, loses much of his power.

1933 Unable to handle its huge debts, Paramount-Publix files for bankruptcy.

1935 The reorganized company emerges from receivership and is now called Paramount Pictures Inc.

1936 Barney Balaban is appointed as the new president with Y.Frank Freeman as production chief and Zukor regains some control as the new chairman of the board.

1944 *Going My Way* is the studio's first sound film to win the Best Picture Oscar and carries off seven statuettes in all.

1946 The studio declares record profits of $39 million.

1949 The company is forced by the Government's Consent Decree to sell off its film theatres in the US.

1954 The studio introduces its new VistaVision process with *White Christmas*.

1956 Cecil B.DeMille has the biggest hit of his career with his last picture, *The Ten Commandments*.

1966 The company is taken over by the Gulf + Western conglomerate headed by Charles Bluhdorn. Robert Evans is appointed vice-president in charge of production.

1971 Frank Yablans is hired as president of Paramount.

1972 Francis Coppola's hit, *The Godfather*, wins the Oscar for Best Picture.

1974 Coppola repeats his success with *The Godfather Part II*. Barry Diller brought in as chairman.

1975 Frank Yablans leaves followed by Robert Evans.

1983 Death of Charles Bluhdorn, succeeded by Martin S. Davis as new head of Gulf + Western.

1984 Barry Diller leaves for Fox, replaced by Frank Mancuso with Ned Tanen as president.

1987 The studio celebrates its 75th anniversary.

1988 Ned Tanen resigns.

1989 The parent company is renamed Paramount Communications after selling off its financial services group, The Associates, in order to concentrate on films and television and other entertainment and publishing activities.

1991 Producer Stanley Jaffe is named President and chief operating officer, followed almost immediately by the resignation of Frank Mancuso.
Brandon Tartikoff is appointed as the new chairman of Paramount Pictures.

The Releases

From 1917 through the early 20s Paramount turned out an enormous number of features of all types. A reduction in quantity in the 20s allowed a larger investment in individual pictures of special interest. Cecil B. DeMille had successes with a series of marital comedies and his epic *The Ten Commandments* (1923), while there were actioners of note with *Beau Geste* and *Old Ironsides* (both 1926) and the World War I movie *Wings* (1927). In later years, the studio was best known for its Westerns, comedies and musicals – indeed, Paramount had a long Western tradition, beginning with *The Squaw Man* (1914), and continuing through the sound era with Gary Cooper as their star. Comedies in the 30s starred the Marx Brothers, Mae West and W. C. Fields, and often included musical numbers, thus providing a link with the many musicals starring Bing Crosby, Bob Hope and Dorothy Lamour. Paramount produced a few features in the early two-strip Technicolor in the 20s, but was slow to develop an interest in colour in the 30s, though it had a big hit with its first production, *The Trail Of The Lonesome Pine* (1936). All of DeMille's movies were in Technicolor from 1940 on, and there were some colour musicals, but the number of colour pictures only increased substantially in the 50s, boosted by the studio's own, high-quality widescreen process, VistaVision, in 1954.

A merger between Famous Players and Lasky in 1916 which marked the real launching of the studio also led to a rapid increase in production. By the following year Paramount was releasing about 120 features per year, though many of them were five-reelers, only about 65–75 minutes long, and the studio continued operating at this pace up to 1922.

There were large numbers of comedies, and dramatic pictures of all kinds, geared to the studio's reservoir of contract stars. Action and adventure comedies starred Douglas Fairbanks or Jack Pickford; there were romantic comedies for Mary Pickford, Billie Burke and Vivian Martin; outdoorsy dramas with a mining, lumbering or Western theme starred Wallace Reid, who also appeared in many romantic dramas along with Fannie Ward, Pauline Frederick, Sessue Hayakawa, Thomas Meighan, and many others. There were costume pictures, too, and a few thrillers; and Westerns most often starred William S. Hart, while there was the occasional topical feature dealing with a social theme of interest. Among the numerous two- and three-reelers were the lively and fast-moving comedies that Fatty Arbuckle wrote, directed and starred in, many of them featuring the young Buster Keaton, here getting his first taste of the movies during 1917–19 (with a break for war service).

In fact, Paramount had been quick to take advantage of the patriotic sentiment building up in the USA early in 1917, and had anticipated the country's entry into the war with a typically flag-waving DeMille super-production, *The Little American*, starring Mary Pickford. By the time of America's involvement in the fighting in 1918, the studio was releasing such virulently anti-German efforts as *The Claws Of The Hun* with Charles Ray and *The Hun Within*. In addition, it took out a full-page advert in 'Photoplay': 'Industries That Are Winning The War' read the headline, while the text went on to make the bold claim that Paramount and Artcraft pictures turned the movie screen into a 'weapon of victory'.

Though the studio continued profitably turning out large numbers of movies, the front office was not insensitive to changes in audience taste and knew that it was important to produce at least a small number of genuine 'specials' each year. Even before the war was over the Paramount bosses were urging DeMille to try something new – to 'get away from the spectacle stuff for one or two pictures' and turn instead to the modern era 'with plenty of clothes, rich sets and action'.

The result was *Old Wives For New* (1918), the first of a new type of modern comedy. And later that year DeMille signed up the very star he needed to make this kind of picture really click with movie audiences – young Gloria Swanson. They made six pictures together during 1918–21, including *Male And Female* (1919) adapted from J. M. Barrie's play, 'The Admirable Crichton', and *The Affairs Of Anatol* (1921) from Schnitzler, all having in common a witty and sophisticated approach to the treatment of contemporary marital relations. They were popular with audiences and extremely influential at the time.

The studio began to cut back on its vast numbers of features around 1923, the year of *The Covered Wagon* and *The Ten Commandments*, both of which demonstrated the advantages of producing fewer and better pictures. 'Fewer' in fact still meant about 60 features per year, the level of production which Paramount maintained from 1923 through 1937. Thus, young producer David O. Selznick, who arrived at the studio in the late 20s, was both appalled and impressed by B. P. Schulberg's ability to turn out such a large number of pictures each year on a virtual assembly-line basis. Inevitably, most of them were formula movies to fit one or another of the studio's many stars: comedies with Bebe Daniels, Raymond Griffith, Harold Lloyd or W. C. Fields; Westerns and adventure movies for Gary Cooper, Jack Holt, Wallace Beery, Richard Dix or Richard Arlen; dramas tailored to Gloria Swanson, Pola Negri or Emil Jannings; and a fair number of films treating topical contemporary subjects (such as flappers, jazz babies, sports and show biz,) were popular and often featured the vivacious Clara Bow. Additionally, the use of a college campus setting frequently provided a good excuse to fill out the cast with the studio's newest young stars and starlets.

As one of the largest Hollywood studios, it was not surprising that Paramount produced a few expensive, large-scale epics such as *Beau Geste* (1926) starring Ronald Colman, *Old Ironsides* (1926) and *The Rough Riders* (1927). But with its spectacular production of *Wings* (also 1927) the studio sparked off a whole new cycle of World War I flying pictures. Similarly, *Underworld* (1927), directed by the young Josef von Sternberg and scripted by Ben Hecht, was the first really modern gangster film. The studio was quick to see the possibilities it had opened up with this new genre and quickly followed with *The City Gone Wild* (1927) and *The Racket* (1928), while Sternberg weighed in with *The Drag Net* (1928), starring William Powell, and *Thunderbolt* (1929), his first sound film. But none of these efforts was as successful as *Underworld*, however, and the studio lost interest. Thus, it was left to Warner Bros. to make the genre its own in the early 30s.

The studio's special interest in the Western dated back to the very first Lasky-DeMille productions in 1914 – *The Squaw Man* and *The Virginian*, both starring Dustin Farnum, followed by *The Call Of The North*. It was Jesse Lasky who was most sympathetic to the idea of turning *The Covered Wagon*, directed by James Cruze in 1922, into the first epic Western. Its spectacular success led to *North of '36* (1924), *The Pony Express* (1925), which Cruze again directed, while Richard Dix starred in both *The Vanishing American* (1925) and *Redskin* in 1928. Finally, the sound remake of *The Virginian* (1929) was designed to capitalize on Gary Cooper's growing popularity.

Even Paramount briefly gave up on the A Western in the early 30s. A new director (Henry Hathaway) and a new star (Randolph Scott) first made their names on a group of low-cost productions in 1932–33. Though the return of the A Western was still a few years off, again it was Paramount which would lead the way. Mae West ventured out west as *Belle Of the Nineties* (1934) followed by the splendid Charles Laughton in *Ruggles Of Red Gap* (1935), both comedy Westerns directed by Leo McCarey, and William Boyd (Hopalong Cassidy) arrived in 1935.

But the big breakthrough came during 1936–37 with such productions as *The Texas Rangers* (1936), produced and directed by King Vidor, and *Wells Fargo* (1937), starring Joel McCrea, along with a pair of musical Westerns: Bing Crosby was just emerging as a leading star and was cast in *Rhythm On The Range* (1936), while the following year brought Rouben Mamoulian's *High, Wide And Handsome* starring Irene Dunne, Randolph Scott and Dorothy Lamour. At the same time DeMille, who had returned to Paramount in 1932, decided to forgo his preference for costumers for a time and renew his early links with the Western instead. *The Plainsman* (1936), starring Gary Cooper, was the first of four prestige Westerns that DeMille filmed between 1936 and 1946. He dramatized the railroad theme in *Union Pacific* (1938), while both *North West Mounted Police* (1940) and *Unconquered* in 1946 were in Technicolor, Cooper again starring.

Among its substantial output in the 30s, Paramount turned out other types of pictures, too – a few thrillers of note such as *The Glass Key* starring George Raft and *Four Hours To Kill* with Richard Barthelmess (both 1935); dramas included *A Farewell To Arms* (1932) and *Make Way For Tomorrow* (1937); and there were lots of comedies from Ernst Lubitsch, Leo McCarey, the Marx Bros, Mae West and W. C. Fields. There were a few memorable costume epics in the early 30s: DeMille kept his budgets low in filming *The Sign Of The Cross* (1932) and *Cleopatra* (1934) with Claudette Colbert, and Henry Hathaway directed Gary Cooper in the exciting *Lives Of A Bengal Lancer* in 1934. As the company recovered from its financial difficulties, however, it made a determined effort to keep up with the other leading studios in the production of more lavish costume and action movies. *The Crusades* (DeMille again) appeared in 1935 followed by *The General Died At Dawn* (1936) and, as the pace began to pick up, *Souls At Sea* (1937). The ubiquitous Cecil B. directed *The Buccaneer* in 1937 and *Union Pacific* in 1938; Ronald Colman starred as François Villon in *If I Were King*; Henry Fonda fought it out with George Raft in *Spawn Of The North* (both in 1938); the three Geste brothers were played by Gary Cooper, Ray Milland and Robert Preston (with a young Susan Hayward providing the romantic interest), for the 1939 remake of *Beau Geste*.

But most important of all was the music. Paramount was second only to Warner Bros. in the large number of musicals which it produced during the early years of sound, 1928–30, at both its Hollywood and Long Island studios. (Such future Paramount stars as Jack Benny, George Burns and Gracie Allen, and Charlie Ruggles first appeared in musical shorts filmed at Astoria.) At the same time the company set up a new musical division and signed up numerous songwriters, while making a major investment in radio as well. (For a brief period in the early 30s Paramount owned 50% of the CBS radio network.)

During the course of the 30s the studio turned out more musicals, musical shorts, and features with songs than any other company, involving the majority of their leading directors and stars. Ernst Lubitsch and Rouben Mamoulian both started at Paramount by directing musicals and returned to the genre periodically throughout their careers. Similarly, many of the Sternberg-Dietrich pictures included important song numbers, as did all the Marx Bros and Mae West features, reflecting the close links between the studio's many comedies and its musicals, while songs were introduced into numerous other non-musical features, too. The pattern was first established most impressively in 1929 with Lubitsch's stunning first talkie, *The Love Parade*, starring Maurice Chevalier and Jeanette MacDonald, and Mamoulian's memorable directorial debut with *Applause* starring Helen Morgan, both released at just about the time that Josef von Sternberg and Marlene Dietrich were filming *The Blue Angel* in Berlin.

The list of Paramount musical stars was impressive, unmatched by any other studio in the 30s, though MGM came to dominate the genre in the 40s. Bing Crosby, Maurice Chevalier, Jeanette MacDonald, Jack Oakie and Dorothy Lamour headed the list, followed by Charles 'Buddy' Rogers, George Raft, Betty Grable, Bob Hope, Martha Raye, opera singer Gladys Swarthout, a young Mary Martin, and many players who are all but forgotten today such as Carl Brisson and radio stars Joe Penner and Kate Smith. (Having invested heavily in radio in the early 30s, Paramount did more than any other studio to exploit the link between movies and radio, signing up numerous radio stars and dramatizing the link on the screen with its popular series of Big Broadcast films.)

The total of musicals and features with songs accounted for a remarkable 40–50% of releases throughout the 30s and 40s. Thus, many of the studio's dramatic and comedy stars found themselves involved in the odd musical. Carole Lombard, for example, was cast opposite George Raft in *Bolero* (1934) and *Rumba* (1935), while Claudette Colbert and Miriam Hopkins got to sing a duet in *The Smiling Lieutenant* (1931); and Miss Colbert demonstrated that this was no fluke when she played the title role in *Torch Singer* (1933). In her autobiography, Dorothy Lamour tells how she was halfway through filming her first feature, *The Jungle Princess* (1936), when the producers suddenly remembered that she was a singer and rushed to find a suitable number for her. Needless to say, she was provided with at least one song in all her early features.

The studio turned out so many musicals that it never felt the need to depend on a particular star or musical team as Fox did with Shirley Temple, RKO with Astaire and Rogers or Universal with Deanna Durbin. Jeanette MacDonald was paired with Chevalier in three early musicals, but this hardly compared with her later experience at MGM – a studio which made a more determined effort to exploit her partnership with Nelson Eddy. It was not till the early 40s that Paramount came closest to a musical series with its Road movies. Not surprisingly, Paramount was the only studio headed for a time by a director of musicals and comedies (Ernst Lubitsch), then by a songwriter-turned-producer (B.G. 'Buddy' DeSylva).

Paramount's output of about 60 features per year in the 30s was divided equally between A pictures and a wide variety of B's – cheap musicals, dramas, thrillers, Zane Grey Westerns and the Hopalong Cassidy series. The number of releases fell in the late 30s and was down to 45 per year by 1940–42, 31 in 1943–44, and levelled off at a very low average of 25 per year during 1945–53. The studio gave up producing Bs in the 40s and cut back on its tremendous numbers of shorts and cartoons in the early 50s. (For many years the cartoons had been produced by Dave and Max Fleischer, whose Betty Boop series was very popular in the pre-Hays Code days of the early 30s followed by Popeye The Sailor.) In addition, for 30 years the company distributed Paramount News, 'The Eyes and Ears of the World', one of the most successful and popular of movie newsreels.

Paramount continued in the 40s with more or less the same mixture as before, and many of the same stars – for example Gary Cooper, Ray Milland and Dorothy Lamour, as well as Hope and Crosby who carried on till the mid-50s. The overall quality of the studio's (drastically reduced) output was boosted by contributions from the cream of writer-directors – Billy Wilder, Preston Sturges and Leo McCarey. Along with contract director Mitchell Leisen, all had been with Paramount in the 30s. Wilder in particular contributed to the blacker side of the movie spectrum as the studio produced its share of *films noirs* featuring new stars such as Alan Ladd, paired in three thrillers with Veronica Lake, and William Bendix, along with the mature but still stunning and gutsy Barbara Stanwyck.

The ever-dependable DeMille helped to spark off a new 50s trend in Biblical spectaculars with the success of his *Samson And Delilah* (1949), but the departure of many stars and directors and the move into colour meant that Paramount, along with other leading studios, lost its special identity in the 50s. It did, however, stand out for a time, through its refusal to rush into CinemaScope or SuperScope or any other Scope, concentrating instead on developing its own, superior VistaVision process.

Colour and Widescreen

Under Jesse Lasky's leadership, Paramount demonstrated a willingness to try out various new techniques in the 20s. The studio used the new two-strip Technicolor in a number of its features during 1923–30 and was the first Hollywood major to produce a full-length Technicolor feature, *Wanderer Of The Wasteland* (1924) starring Jack Holt and Billie Dove. In addition, the studio tried out an early widescreen system called Magnascope for projecting such epics as *North of '36* (1924) and *Old Ironsides* (1926) onto a large screen, and a short-lived 56mm Magnifilm process for filming *We're In The Navy Now*, also in 1926.

In the silent era it was often the case that directors filmed with two cameras side by side, one for the US negative and the other for the foreign prints. Thus, it is not surprising to learn how the first Technicolor sequences ever filmed for a major feature came about. As DeMille recalled in his autobiography, the Technicolor company had simply approached him with the request that they be allowed to set up their camera alongside his black-and-white ones and shoot the Biblical scenes for *The Ten Commandments* (1923) in colour. He could then pay for and make use of the footage if he liked the results; otherwise the experiment would cost him nothing.

The experiment was a success, and led to the inclusion of Technicolor sequences in numerous productions from Paramount and the other leading companies. A full-length feature in colour was still another matter but, late in 1923, following the successful release of *The Covered Wagon* and *The Ten Commandments*, Lasky agreed to give it a try. A Zane Grey Western with its outdoor locations was chosen as the most suitable subject, but various technical problems in filming, the high cost of prints, and difficulties in projecting the film, *Wanderer*

Of The Wasteland, meant that Paramount abandoned the idea for the next five years.

Taking a leaf from the DeMille book, director Allan Dwan had some fun with a dream sequence in the Gloria Swanson comedy, *Stage Struck* (1925), in which the heroine imagines herself as Salome and Dwan improvised some multi-coloured lighting effects for the Technicolor camera. Similarly, a colour sequence in *Red Hair*, filmed in 1927, proved that Clara Bow really was a redhead. Director Erich von Stroheim had been attracted to the possible symbolic uses of colour and had experimented with hand tinting in *Greed* in 1923. In filming *The Wedding March* in 1926 he was one of the first to employ vivid and striking colours to dramatic effect, using them in the Corpus Christi Day sequence. But by the time the picture was released, in October 1928, not only was colour more common, but it was forced to compete with the early part-talkies and made little impact.

Another Western, *Redskin*, was originally selected as Paramount's second Technicolor feature in 1928, but when the cost of filming rose unexpectedly, it was decided that only the Indian sequences would be in colour, with the white man's world in black-and-white. The result was a particularly expressive use of colour contrasted with black-and-white (or toned amber) a decade before *The Wizard Of Oz* tried something similar.

Paramount's early interest in colour peaked with the changeover to sound and a new vogue for movie musicals in 1929–30. Technicolor sequences appeared in *Dance Of Life* and *Glorifying The American Girl* (both 1929), also in the all-star extravaganza of *Paramount On Parade* released early in 1930. Two 1930 musicals – *Follow Thru* and *The Vagabond King* – were filmed entirely in colour, which inspired some suitably 'colourful' prose on the part of Paramount's advertising copy writers: 'Blazing with gorgeous Technicolor throughout . . . With Broadway's favorite romantic stars, Dennis King and Jeanette MacDonald . . . Only Paramount with matchless resources and unrivaled manpower could unfold before your eyes this glittering panorama of song, color and romance . . .' But the studio's interest in colour filming came to an abrupt end with the demise of the early sound musical, and was slow to revive in the mid-30s when the improved, three-strip Technicolor first appeared.

The other major studios began experimenting with Technicolor inserts by 1933–34, but Walter Wanger only produced Paramount's first feature, *The Trail Of The Lonesome Pine*, late in 1935. In contrast to the more controlled, studio-bound filming of musicals and costume pieces such as *Becky Sharp* (Pioneer/RKO, 1935), Paramount went more for the outdoor approach and had a big hit. Though an old-fashioned subject that had previously been filmed as a silent, *The Trail Of The Lonesome Pine* was lifted by its cast (including Sylvia Sidney and Henry Fonda) and is still remembered as the first Technicolor feature shot mainly on exterior locations.

In spite of its success Paramount was slow to follow up and, when it did so, concentrated on a particular range of subjects – involving jungles, forests, desert islands and dramas on the high seas – which differentiated it from all the other studios. Not surprisingly, Dorothy Lamour was the top star. Dressed only in the familiar sarong which became her trademark, she did valiant service for Paramount in one Technicolored South Sea extravaganza after another, beginning with *Her Jungle Love* (1938) paired with Ray Milland, followed by *Typhoon* (1940), *Aloma Of The South Seas* (1941) and *Beyond The Blue Horizon* (1942). (Universal's exotic colour movies starring Maria Montez clearly owed a debt to Miss Lamour.)

Ray Milland took to the South Seas in *Ebb Tide* (1937), and the Caribbean with DeMille in *Reap The Wild Wind* (1942); and when the studio produced the first horror-fantasy in Technicolor (*Dr Cyclops*, 1940), it was set deep in the heart of the South American jungle (with remarkable special effects by Farciot Edouart). DeMille had first begun filming in the new Technicolor in 1940 with *North West Mounted Police*, and most of the picture was set deep in the Canadian forests of the West. Gary Cooper was the star. He was also paired with Ingrid Bergman who had never looked more lovely on the screen – it was her first colour film – in *For Whom The Bell Tolls* (1943). It was a big hit and Coop, who went on to star in two more DeMille colour epics, could claim to be the studio's top Technicolor star.

Shepherd Of the Hills (1941) and *The Forest Rangers* (1942) yet again made use of forest settings in the tradition of *The Trail Of The Lonesome Pine*. But 1942–43 was a turning point as many of the studios upped their output of features in colour. For Paramount this marked the end of its early, 'outdoorsy' phase and placed new emphasis on glossy Technicolored musicals, coinciding with a similar increase in musicals from MGM. *Happy Go Lucky*, released by Paramount late in 1942, gave a whole slew of musical stars their first opportunity to light up the screen in glorious Technicolor – Mary Martin, Betty Hutton, Dick Powell, Rudy Vallee, Eddie Bracken. And Bing Crosby, just emerging as the studio's top star, made his long-overdue colour debut in *Dixie* (1943), cast opposite Dorothy Lamour in her sixth colour feature and here given a chance to exchange her sarong for a 19th-century hoop skirt. Similarly, Ginger Rogers starred as the *Lady In The Dark* (1944), an extraordinarily elaborate and dreadfully kitschy musical, best remembered for some bizarre dream sequences and a strikingly designed red and gold dress with a skirt section that was decorated with mink and parted down the middle. The same director, Mitchell Leisen, fared somewhat better with the costume adventure, *Frenchman's Creek*, also filmed in 1943, but not released for a year. The athletic Joan Fontaine made a passable lady swashbuckler, but the film was effectively stolen by the villainous Basil Rathbone. (It won the Oscar for colour art direction.)

However, both pictures were quite expensive and lost money so, in spite of the fact that profits were growing, Paramount refused to increase its colour output and thus lagged behind its main rivals, MGM and Fox. It continued to maintain a more or less steady level of three features per year throughout the decade, along with a number of two-reel musical shorts in Technicolor, and even experimented with a few Randolph Scott

Westerns filmed in the cheaper Cinecolor process. The biggest colour hits were the Bing Crosby-Fred Astaire musical *Blue Skies* (1946), the Bob Hope-Jane Russell comedy *The Paleface* (1948), and two from DeMille, *Unconquered* (1947) and *Samson And Delilah* (1949).

When the studio finally increased its production of Technicolor features in the 50s, the emphasis was mainly on Westerns and actioners starring Alan Ladd, Charlton Heston, John Payne and Rhonda Fleming, minor Bing Crosby or Betty Hutton musicals, and Bob Hope comedies. Several directors of the calibre of Billy Wilder, William Wyler and George Stevens preferred black-and-white, and many of Paramount's most interesting and successful pictures continued to be filmed in black-and-white: *A Place In The Sun*, *Ace In The Hole* and *Detective Story* (all 1951), *Roman Holiday* (1953) and *Sabrina* (1954), both starring Audrey Hepburn, and *The Country Girl* (1954). But, even prior to the introduction of Paramount's own VistaVision process, there were a few notable Technicolor successes – DeMille's Oscar-winning *The Greatest Show On Earth* (1951), *Shane* (1953), a Western and the first colour feature from producer-director George Stevens, and *Rear Window* (1954), the first of a memorable group of Hitchcock thrillers.

Widescreen and 3-D Releases 1953–69

Process	1953	1954	1955	1956	1957	1958	1959	1960	1961	1962	1963	1964	1965	1966	1967	1968	1969
Technirama						1		1	1		1						
Panavision									5	3	2	2	6	5	4	8	5
Techniscope												5	6	7	8	7	2
VistaVision		2	14	15	15	14	9	3	1								
Large format (70mm)												1					
3-D	4	1															

Like all the leading companies, Paramount was involved in the changes which were taking place during 1953 and 1954. The studio experimented briefly with 3-D filming, releasing four features in 1953. Then it responded to Fox's success with CinemaScope by introducing its own widescreen VistaVision process in 1954. The proportion of features in colour continued to rise and, around this time, achieved a level of about 75% of the total. Some idea of the rapid pace of developments can be seen in the experience of Dean Martin and Jerry Lewis, the studio's top comedy team. They were still making their movies in black-and-white early in 1953, but later that year shot their first feature in colour and 3-D (*Money From Home*) and by mid-1954 were already filming *Three Ring Circus*, one of the very first VistaVision productions.

The VistaVision system used a special camera in which the 35mm film ran horizontally (rather than vertically), thus exposing an area about twice the size of a normal 35mm (or 35mm CinemaScope) frame. The larger negative produced a sharper image on the final print and was also capable of recording greater depth of field than CinemaScope or other anamorphic processes. (Paramount was the only major studio which totally avoided filming in 'Scope in the 50s.)

First introduced by the smash-hit Bing Crosby-Danny Kaye musical *White Christmas* in April 1954, and projected onto a giant screen measuring 30 by 55 feet, VistaVision proved to be equally effective in filming both large-scale action pictures and costume epics such as *Strategic Air Command* (1955), *War And Peace* and *The Ten Commandments* (both 1956), as well as more intimate black-and-white movies such as *Wild Is The Wind* (1957) and *The Matchmaker* (1958). In fact, the process was so good that Paramount won the Oscars for both colour and black-and-white cinematography in the first full year of its use, 1955, with Hitchcock's *To Catch A Thief* (photographed by Robert Burks) and *The Rose Tattoo* (shot by black-and-white specialist James Wong Howe). And the studio's technical department was awarded a special Oscar in 1956 for developing the VistaVision camera.

Paramount's other VistaVision pictures of note included the delightful Fred Astaire–Audrey Hepburn musical *Funny Face* and *Gunfight At The OK Corral* (both 1957), also Hitchcock's *Vertigo* (1958). In addition, the process was borrowed by other studios – by Warner Bros. for John Ford's stunning 1956 Western, *The Searchers*, and by MGM that same year for its star-studded musical, *High Society*. (Bing Crosby's first picture as a freelancer at the end of his long years at Paramount.) When Hitchcock filmed *North By Northwest* for MGM in 1959, he brought his favourite VistaVision camera (and cameraman Robert Burks) along with him.

During the peak years of 1955–57 the vast majority of Paramount features were photographed in VistaVision, but interest in the process declined in 1958–59 and by 1960 it had been virtually abandoned, aside from a few last releases such as Marlon Brando's much troubled but extraordinary Western, *One-Eyed Jacks* (1961). It had always been a costly process, since the camera was bulky and heavy, and very similar results could be achieved more cheaply with the improved film stocks and Panavision anamorphic equipment. Paramount switched over to filming a number of its pictures in Panavision in the early 60s, and James Wong Howe won another Oscar for his lighting of *Hud* in 1963, filmed in black-and-white Panavision. Paramount also made use of Techniscope and Technirama on a few of its productions, but never developed much of an interest in 70mm filming. The company distributed the last two epics from Spanish-based producer Samuel Bronston, *The Fall Of The Roman Empire* (1964 – filmed in ultraPanavision 70) and *Circus World* (1964 – shot in Super Technirama 70). Both flopped badly.

During more recent years the excellent VistaVision camera has been brought back by George Lucas and Steven Spielberg and adapted for use in shooting the special effects for such pictures as Lucas's *Star Wars* (Fox, 1977) and Paramount's Indiana Jones series in the 80s, produced by Lucas and directed by Spielberg.

The Finances

Paramount was the biggest and most profitable American film company for many years. Profits rose during the 20s, boosted by hits that included *The Sheik* (1921), *The Covered Wagon* (1923), *Beau Geste* (1926) and several DeMille pictures, and by income from the chain of Publix movie theatres. Profits peaked in 1930, and the collapse which followed led to bankruptcy and a reorganization of the company. Paramount recovered in the late 30s and did spectacularly well in the boom years of the 40s, but was badly affected by the government's Consent Decree which forced it to sell off its lucrative cinemas. Profits remained low during the 50s and early 60s, and the studio was taken over by the Gulf + Western conglomerate in 1966. Hit hard by the slump of 1969–70, Paramount made a quick recovery, helped by *Love Story* (1970) and *The Godfather* (1972), and continued to do well financially in the following years with more than its share of 'mega-hits' including Steven Spielberg's Indiana Jones pictures, *Beverly Hills Cop* 1 and 2, *Top Gun* (1986), and most recently *Ghost* (1990).

By turning out large numbers of pictures, distributing them efficiently and keeping costs low, Paramount was able to earn good profits throughout its early history. The average cost of a feature was less than $100,000 in the late 'teens, rising to about $150,000 in the early 20s.

Of special interest is the experience of Cecil B. DeMille, the studio's leading director. He is generally identified with the opulent productions of his later years but the majority of his silent features were produced quite economically, including numerous Westerns and comedies which kept well within the budget limits set by the front office. A lavish costume epic such as *Joan The Woman*, one of the first movies filmed after the merger of Famous Players and Lasky in 1916, was an exception. It came in at $300,000, but earned a small profit. More typical was DeMille's 1918 remake of *The Squaw Man* for $50,000, only slightly more than the original, his first feature which cost about $40,000. DeMille's modern comedies, for example, *Old Wives For New* and *Don't Change Your Husband* (both 1918) fell into the $65–75,000 range, while *Why Change Your Wife?* (1920) cost about $130,000.

In spite of his care in controlling the cost of his pictures, it was inevitable that DeMille would occasionally find himself in dispute with the front office – as represented by Zukor – while production chief Jesse Lasky was caught between the two. When his contract came up for renewal in 1920, DeMille made it clear that he felt he was underpaid and that he should be allowed to share more in the company's financial success, especially in view of the extent of his contribution: only two of his 37 movies had flopped at the box-office. Zukor, for his part, was not only concerned at the high cost of some of the pictures, but at the added expense of maintaining DeMille's own permanent staff and production unit. In the event his salary was upped to $6500 a week, while his general movie budget was set at $290,000, about twice that of Paramount's other A features, with a 50% share in net profits and the possibility of larger budgets for the occasional epic. In other words, between the big stories that he most wanted to make, DeMille would produce 'smaller commercial pictures for a lower financial outlay and, it was hoped, quicker returns'.

In fact, the dispute between DeMille and Zukor was not really resolved, but simmered beneath the surface until the director was mid-way into filming his most ambitious production yet, *The Ten Commandments*, in 1923. As costs mounted to the million-dollar mark, Zukor expressed alarm, for *Adam's Rib* (1923), DeMille's previous film, had cost $400,000 and had been one of the director's rare flops. DeMille responded by calling his bluff, offering to buy the picture from Paramount for $1 million, and Zukor was forced to back down. The completed *Ten Commandments* ended up costing a hefty $1.4 million but proved to be DeMille's biggest hit up to that date and earned a substantial profit. (He stayed on at Paramount for another year, but left early in 1925.)

During 1920–23 Paramount's profits averaged an impressive $4.5 million per year, and in the mid-20s they increased to $5.5 million as the studio continued to turn out successful movies and released a number of hits.

Rudolph Valentino was signed up in 1921 and promptly provided the studio with a big smash in his first feature, *The Sheik*, establishing his image as the great screen lover. His fourth at Paramount, *Blood And Sand* (1922), was also among the studio's biggest box-office successes.

But Paramount's major money earner of the decade, and of the studio's entire early history, was a Western, *The Covered Wagon* (1923), directed by James Cruze. Though the rights to the original novel had been purchased as the basis for another routine production, Jesse Lasky wanted to turn it into something a bit special. Budgeted initially at $500,000, the final film cost almost $800,000, an unheard of sum for a Western, but it created such an impact when it was first released that it stimulated a new interest in the 'epic Western'. (Fox countered with *The Iron Horse*, directed by John Ford the following year, while Paramount's own sequel was called *North of '36*, and William S. Hart produced *Tumbleweeds* for UA in 1925.)

If the success of *The Ten Commandments* and *The Covered Wagon* suggested that it was profitable to invest more heavily in prestige productions, Paramount's experience in the late 20s proved just the opposite, with virtually all its high-cost pictures performing badly. The biggest loss-makers were *Old Ironsides* (1926) directed by James Cruze at a cost of $1.5 million, and *The Sorrows Of Satan* (1926), a $1 million project that DeMille had wanted to direct, but which was given to D. W. Griffith instead, leading to DeMille's departure from Paramount.

There was also Erich von Stroheim's *The Wedding March* which had grown in length during the shooting (in 1926–27), with the cost rising to $1.1 million. By the time the film was taken away from him, re-edited (badly), and released late in 1928, it was forced to compete with the first of the talkies and flopped badly. At a cost of $2 million *Wings* (1927) was the studio's most expensive movie of the decade, and though it did well it was not good enough to earn a profit. (The Best Picture Oscar was not awarded to it till 1929, too late to help with the initial release.) Only *Beau Geste* (1926) starring Ronald Colman, was a big enough hit to earn a good profit on its $1 million cost.

However, in spite of the lack of any major hits, Paramount's profits continued to grow throughout the late 20s, rising from $5.6 million in 1926 to a peak of $18.4 million in 1930. This reflects the profitability of the company's chain of movie theatres, and its ability to earn small but steady profits from its large number of features through efficient marketing and distribution.

When the collapse came in 1931–33 Paramount was hit hardest of all. The company lost $21 million in 1932 and, unable to meet the debts accumulated during its years of rapid expansion, was adjudicated bankrupt. The studio released its two most profitable pictures of the decade in 1933, *She Done Him Wrong* and *I'm No Angel*, written by and starring Mae West. Produced at a rock-bottom cost of $200,000 each, they undoubtedly helped Paramount through the worst patch in its history, though the profits were swallowed up by a company awash in red ink.

By 1935 a reorganized Paramount had struggled back into profit for the first time since the collapse, and by 1936–37 it was well on the road to recovery, aided by the box-office success of *The Trail Of The Lonesome Pine* (1936), the studio's first in Technicolor, along with popular Westerns, including *The Plainsman* (1936) from DeMille, who had returned to the studio in 1932, and *Wells Fargo* (1937), and musicals: *The Big Broadcast of 1937* and *Waikiki Wedding* (1937) starring Bing Crosby. Though profits fell back in 1938–39 as the entire industry suffered a slight hiccup in its recovery from the Depression, Paramount was poised to re-establish itself once again as one of the industry leaders.

Paramount's profits were high in the early 40s and rose even higher. From a solid $6.3 million in 1940, they climbed to over $15 million in 1945, then shot up to a spectacular $39.2 million in 1946, far surpassing those of every other studio, including MGM which had been the industry leader ever since the early 30s. Paramount's cinemas were doing peak business and releasing smash-hit movies year after year: *Reap The Wild Wind* (1942), *For Whom The Bell Tolls* (1943), *The Lost Weekend* (1945), and a large number of comedies and musicals starring Bing Crosby, the most popular star of the decade.

Though profits were still averaging $25 million in 1947–48, there was an abrupt fall in 1949 when Paramount, the main target of the government's Consent Decree, was forced to sell off its highly lucrative film theatres. The company bounced back in 1950 helped, yet again, by the ever reliable DeMille whose *Samson And Delilah*, released late in 1949, proved to be the studio's top hit of the 40s.

In fact, the studio was able to maintain a small but steady level of profit throughout the 50s. It was releasing successful pictures from many of the top producer-directors in Hollywood. Leading the way, of course, was DeMille with the Oscar-winning *The Greatest Show On Earth* (1952) and his last movie, the spectacularly successful *The Ten Commandments* (1956), which earned substantial profits in spite of the fact that it had cost all of $13 million – Paramount's most expensive production up to that date. DeMille was joined by George Stevens, whose *Shane* (1953) was one of the most popular Westerns ever made, and Alfred Hitchcock, who contributed *Rear Window* (1954) and the offbeat, cheaply produced black-and-white chiller *Psycho* (1960), the most profitable picture of his entire career.

Profits continued at comparatively low levels throughout the early 60s, when there was a notable lack of box-office success. Though the company had a big hit with a glossy adaptation of Harold Robbins' best-seller, *The Carpetbaggers*, in 1964, its release coincided with the disastrous reception for *The Fall of The Roman Empire*, which toppled the empire of producer Samuel Bronston in Spain and marked the virtual end of Barney Balaban's long reign at Paramount. (At a cost of $20 million and with only tiny receipts, the film was one of the biggest flops of all time, virtually matching UA's *Heaven's Gate* 16 years later, if inflation is taken into account.)

Benefiting from its profitable TV production subsidiary and a number of solid hits such as *The Odd Couple*, *Rosemary's Baby* and *Romeo And Juliet* (all released in 1968), Paramount performed reasonably well in the late 60s after its merger with the giant Gulf + Western conglomerate. Of course, it had its share of costly flops during the difficult 1969–70 period: 1970 in particular was a dreadful year when income from the $20 million *Paint Your Wagon*, the $22 million *Darling Lili* and the $11 million production of *The Molly Maguires* failed to cover their costs. Fortunately, the studio enjoyed an unexpected bonanza with *Love Story* released later that same year, followed by the Oscar-winning *The Godfather* (1972) which helped to restore its fortunes.

Paramount continued to do well throughout the rest of the decade, but the big breakthrough came in 1978. Spectacular earnings from *Saturday Night Fever* and *Grease*, both starring John Travolta, and the Warren Beatty comedy *Heaven Can Wait* boosted operating income over the

$80 million mark for the first time, and it rose to a peak of $116 million in 1979.

Most impressive of all in the 80s have been the three Indiana Jones pictures, while the series of *Star Trek* features have also done well, trading on the popularity of its oft-revived, cult TV series of the 60s along with a newly introduced TV series as well. The producing partnership of Don Simpson and Jerry Bruckheimer contributed *Flashdance* (1983) and *Footloose* (1984) as well as *Beverly Hills Cop* and its sequel, starring Eddie Murphy, and *Top Gun* (1986) with Tom Cruise. And the studio's long list of hits included other Eddie Murphy vehicles such as *Coming To America* (1988), *Trading Places* (1983) and *48 HRS* (1982). But a celebrated court case during 1990–91 concerning *Coming To America* exposed some of the studio's dubious accounting practices, at the same time that expensive productions such as *Days Of Thunder* and *Another 48 HRS* were doing less well at the box office than expected, while a much more moderately priced picture, *Ghost*, proved to be the studio's big, surprise hit of the year. Bringing to an end its generous production arrangements with Simpson, Bruckheimer and Murphy, Paramount then hoped to develop a new, cost-conscious look for the 90s, attempting to keep budgets under control better that it had done previously.

Box Office Hits

TITLE	Cost	North American rentals
1914–32	(in $ millions)	(in $ millions)
The Covered Wagon (1923)	(0.8)	3.5
The Ten Commandments (1923)	(1.6)	2.5
The Sheik (1921)		1.5
Beau Geste (1926)	(0.9)	1.5
Blood And Sand (1922)		1.3
Dr Jekyll And Mr Hyde (1931)		1.3
The Miracle Man (1919)		1.0
1932–40		
I'm No Angel (1933)	(0.3)	2.3
She Done Him Wrong (1933)	(0.2)	2.2
The Crusades (1935)		1.7
The Trail Of The Lonesome Pine (1936)	(0.6)	1.6
Wells Fargo (1937)		1.5
Buck Benny Rides Again (1940)		1.5
Northwest Mounted Police (1940)		1.5
1941–50		
Samson And Delilah (1949)	(3.0)	9.0
Going My Way (1944)	(1.0)	6.5
For Whom The Bell Tolls (1943)	(2.7)	6.3
Welcome Stranger (1947)		6.1
Blue Skies (1946)	(3.0)	5.7
Unconquered (1947)		5.3
Road To Utopia (1944)		4.5
Road To Rio (1947)		4.5
The Paleface (1948)		4.5
Two Years Before The Mast (1946)		4.4
The Lost Weekend (1945)	(1.1)	4.3
Reap The Wild Wind (1942)		4.0
The Emperor Waltz (1948)		4.0

1951–60

The Ten Commandments (1956)	(13.0)	34.2
The Greatest Show On Earth (1952)		12.8
White Christmas (1954)		12.0
Psycho (1960)	(0.8)	9.1
Shane (1953)		8.0
The Country Girl (1954)		6.5
War And Peace (1956)	(5.5)	6.3
Strategic Air Command (1955)		6.0
Rear Window (1954)	(2.0)	5.3

1961–70

Love Story (1970)	(3.0)	50.0
The Odd Couple (1968)		20.0
The Carpetbaggers (1964)		15.5
Rosemary's Baby (1968)	(2.3)	15.0
Romeo And Juliet (1968)	(1.5)	14.5
Paint Your Wagon (1969)	(20.0)	14.5
True Grit (1969)		14.3
Catch-22 (1970)	(10.0)	12.3
Goodbye Columbus (1969)	(1.5)	10.5
Barefoot In The Park (1967)		9.0

1971–80

Grease (1978)	(6.0)	96.3
The Godfather (1972)	(6.0)	86.3
Saturday Night Fever (1977)	(3.2)	74.1
Star Trek: The Motion Picture	(42.0)	56.0
Heaven Can Wait (1978)		49.4
Airplane (1980)	(3.5)	40.6
King Kong (co-prod) (1976)	(24.0)	36.9
The Godfather Part II (1974)	(13.0)	30.7
Up In Smoke (1978)		28.3
Foul Play (1978)		27.5
The Bad News Bears (1976)		24.9
Popeye (co-prod) (1980)	(20.0)	24.6
Urban Cowboy (1980)		23.8
Ordinary People (1980)		23.1
The Longest Yard (1974)		23.0

1981–90

Raiders Of The Lost Ark (1981)	(22.)	115.6
Indiana Jones And The Last Crusade (1989)	(36.)	115.5
Indiana Jones And The Temple Of Doom (1984)	(27.)	109.0
Beverly Hills Cop (1984)	(14.)	108.0
Ghost (1990)	(22.)	94.0
Beverly Hills Cop II (1987)	(28.)	80.9
Top Gun (1986)	(14)	79.4
Crocodile Dundee (1986)	(6.0)	70.2
Fatal Attraction (1987)	(14.)	70.0
Coming To America (1988)	(40.)	63.1
The Hunt For Red October (1990)	(35.)	58.5
Crocodile Dundee II (1988)	(15.)	57.3
Star Trek IV: The Voyage Home (1986)	(23.)	56.8
An Officer And A Gentleman (1982)	(7.5)	55.2
Terms Of Endearment (1983)		50.3
Trading Places (1983)		40.6
Another 48 HRS (1990)	(40.)	40.1
Star Trek II: The Wrath of Khan (1982)		40.0
Days Of Thunder (1990)	(40.)	40.0
The Golden Child (1986)	(25.)	39.7
Star Trek III: The Search For Spock (1984)	(16.)	39.0

The Untouchables (1987)	(30.)	36.9
Flashdance (1983)		36.2
The Naked Gun (1988)	(14.5)	34.4
Footloose (1984)		34.0

Coming to America: A Statement of Participation (as of early 1990), or How An Apparent Hit Ended Up Losing Money

---

	$ (millions)	($ millions)
GROSS RENTALS		
U.S. rentals	63.1	
(from gross receipts of 125.3)		
Foreign rentals	43.7	
(from gross receipts of 138.3)		
Canada and U.K. rentals	14.9	121.7
NON-THEATRICAL INCOME		
Pay television: U.S.	13	
Canada	.4	
Soundtrack record	.7	
Book publishing deal	.1	
other	.1	14.3
TOTAL GROSS RECEIPTS		136.0
Less Distribution Fees to		
Paramount		42.3
30% of North American receipts, 35% of U.K., 40% of other foreign)		
BALANCE		93.7
LESS DISTRIBUTION EXPENSES		
Advertising: in the U.S.	15.8	
foreign	8.3	
		24.1
Other distribution expenses		12.2
Cost of prints: 2,000 U.S. prints	3.2	
foreign prints	2.2	
shipping and insurance	.6	
dubbing costs	.5	6.5
Miscellaneous costs		
taxes	1.3	
unions, pensions, etc	1.7	
MPAA dues	1	
'censoring' prints	.1	4.1
TOTAL DISTRIBUTION EXPENSE		46.9
NET RECEIPTS		46.8
LESS:		
Interest on negative cost		6.4
Direct negative cost		40.0
Gross participation payments to		
Eddie Murphy and John Landis		11.0
Studio overhead (15% of 51)		7.5
TOTAL COSTS		64.9
NET PROFITS (LOSS)		(18.1)

The Stars

Paramount played a major role in developing and exploiting the star system in the early years. Mary Pickford was the studio's first 'superstar' in the 'teens, followed by a similarly youthful Gloria Swanson. Paramount's other leading silent stars included Westerner William S. Hart, romantic idol Rudolph Valentino and 20s flapper Clara Bow, as well as comedian Fatty Arbuckle and handsome leading man Wallace Reid, both of whose careers ended in scandal. With the coming of sound the studio was very successful in signing up a varied selection of newcomers from the theatre, including Claudette Colbert, Fredric March, Sylvia Sidney, Marlene Dietrich and the Marx Bros. Around this time Gary Cooper began to establish himself as a leading man, followed by Cary Grant, Ray Milland and Fred MacMurray. Most of the important arrivals in the 30s were musical or comedy stars such as Mae West, Bob Hope, Dorothy Lamour and, especially, Bing Crosby, the most successful and longest-lasting Paramount star of all.

Tough guys Alan Ladd and William Bendix emerged in the 40s, followed by Charlton Heston and Audrey Hepburn in the 50s, along with two Hitchcock favourites, Grace Kelly and James Stewart. But the comedy team of Dean Martin and Jerry Lewis were the most popular of all for a time.

When he first planned to set up his own film production company in 1912, Adolph Zukor recognized the importance of stars to the success of the new enterprise. 'Famous Players in Famous Plays' was the motto, but he made a serious mistake: the established stage stars who appeared in his early pictures were in many cases well past their prime and looked even older on film. In addition, they were exponents of a theatrical style of acting which was unsuitable for the screen. Fortunately, Zukor's group of stage players included John Barrymore and Marguerite Clark who adapted well to the new medium, and the highly successful Mary Pickford who was already an experienced movie actress.

The 20-year-old Miss Pickford soon emerged as the studio's top star, whose pictures were consistently the most popular and helped the company to survive. Signed up in 1913 at a salary of $500 per week, within a year it was doubled to $1000 and by the end of 1914 it had doubled again. It did not take long for Mary and her shrewd mother to discover that Zukor was using her movies to help sell his other, less appealing features. In 1916 Charlie Chaplin, the only star whose drawing power could rival her own, signed with Mutual at $10,000 per week, and Miss Pickford was quick to point out to Zukor that he was still making two-reelers while she was appearing in features. As a result, Zukor was forced to match the Chaplin salary, and the Mary Pickford Motion Picture Company was set up with the profits to be split fifty-fifty between the star and her boss. Also, a special new releasing company called Artcraft would handle her movies, along with other Paramount 'specials', to set them apart from the run-of-the-mill product.

Under the terms of this new arrangement, Pickford was able to exercise a greater degree of control over her pictures than any other star of the period aside from Chaplin. She worked with only the best Paramount directors and appeared in no more than five features per year. (In 1915 she had made eight.) By the age of 23, Mary Pickford had established herself as the most powerful woman in the motion-picture industry. She was not only a talented actress and comedienne, whose performances in such pictures as *The Poor Little Rich Girl* and *Rebecca Of Sunnybrook Farm* (both 1917) have stood the test of time surprisingly well, but a smart businesswoman and an intelligent producer who collaborated closely on all aspects of her productions. (This became even more apparent after she left Paramount, late in 1918, for First National, where she gained complete artistic control over her films, before moving on to help found and run UA from 1919 onwards.)

When Zukor merged with Lasky in 1916, he immediately gained a number of new leading players including Wallace Reid, Thomas Meighan and opera star Geraldine Farrar. The rapidly expanding company began signing up many more stars to populate its extremely large number of releases. In 1917 alone the new arrivals included Douglas Fairbanks, Fatty Arbuckle, Elsie Ferguson and William S. Hart, while the departure of Mary Pickford in 1918 coincided with the signing of the petite Gloria Swanson. She soon emerged as the studio's new top female star and the favourite actress of Cecil B. DeMille. (They would make six features together while she was receiving the ridiculously low salary of $150 per week, increased to $250; only when she threatened to leave was it finally increased to $2500 in 1921, reflecting her true worth to the company.) A major coup in 1921 was the signing of Rudolph Valentino, who was dissatisfied with his treatment at Metro and went on to make a number of his most popular movies for Paramount.

As the single largest studio, and with many leading players under contract, Paramount took a major role in developing and exploiting the star system, but also suffered some serious setbacks. The studio was involved in all three of the major scandals that rocked the Hollywood community in 1921–22, cost Paramount three of its stars and one director, and led to the appointment of Will Hays as head of the MPPDA (the Motion Picture Producers and Distributors of America) to help improve the image of the film industry. (Later known as the 'Hays Office', it began in the 30s to administer the notorious Production Code of film censorship rules.)

The most infamous scandal was the Fatty Arbuckle case. He was accused of causing the death of a young actress, in mysterious circumstances, during the course of a wild party in 1921. Though Arbuckle was eventually acquitted, his career was ruined and the high-living style of many stars was exposed to public scrutiny for the first time. (Jesse Lasky initially insisted that Paramount would continue to release Arbuckle's pictures, but was forced to back down due to pressure in Hollywood and from the public at large.)

Late in 1922 the news broke that Wallace Reid, the tall, handsome, all-American leading man at Paramount, was a drug addict. He died in a private sanatorium early in 1923 aged only 32. But strangest of all was the unsolved murder of leading Paramount director William Desmond Taylor. Just ten years before MGM was forced to cope with the suicide of producer Paul Bern, husband of top star Jean Harlow, Paramount demonstrated the tremendous power wielded by the major studios. It provided MGM with a valuable lesson on how to stage a cover-up. The Paramount representatives were on the scene before the police, successfully concealing Taylor's homosexuality, and planting evidence that he was a promiscuous ladies man – a far more acceptable type of 'scandal'. Mary Miles Minter, the studio's teenage star, and comedienne Mabel Normand were both found to have been with Taylor and their film careers were finished. (A recent book, based on the 60s investigation of the case by veteran director King Vidor, concluded that Taylor was shot by Miss Minter's domineering mother.)

Confronted by the new MGM studio with its impressive line-up of stars in 1924, Paramount initially failed to meet the challenge, acquiring few major new names of its own, and even losing some. William S. Hart, near the end of his career, went over to UA in 1925 and Gloria Swanson soon followed. But these departures were balanced by the fact that B. P. Schulberg had brought Clara Bow with him to Paramount. She became tremendously popular, personifying the young flapper of the 20s on the screen in such pictures as *It* (1927) and *The Wild Party* (1929). In addition, the studio signed up leading independent comedy star Harold Lloyd in 1926. The celebrated German actor Emil Jannings arrived in 1927, as did a young, inexperienced Gary Cooper, who was signed up at about $175 per week and would develop into one of the studio's top star assets during the 30s.

The pace of arrivals and departures accelerated during the following years. With the move into sound, Paramount experienced a major turnover in stars unmatched by any other studio. (At MGM, its main rival, most of the top stars made the transition to the talkies with little difficulty.) Among the first of Paramount's silent stars to leave (in 1928) were Pola Negri, Thomas Meighan, and Louise Brooks who wrote about this era many years later. According to her, the studio bosses saw this as 'a splendid opportunity for breaking contracts, cutting salaries and taming stars'. (Emil Jannings, whose heavy German accent was a liability, left in 1930, followed by Clara Bow who was never able to break away from her 20s flapper image.)

But whether or not Miss Brooks was correct, the fact is that the studio did very well indeed. The list of new star acquisitions during 1928–31 is certainly an impressive one. Many of them were signed up from the Broadway theatre and provided Paramount with perhaps the strongest line-up of contract players in its history. It was well balanced, too, between men and women, dramatic stars, and musical and comedy talents, with the glamorous and sophisticated counterpointed by the more 'natural', down-to-earth personalities.

Plagued by financial troubles throughout most of the 30s, the studio depended on its stars more than ever before (or since) to give a much-needed lift to productions which were otherwise rather ordinary. Many of the better pictures were the product of successful star-director partnerships: Lubitsch with Maurice Chevalier and Jeanette MacDonald in the early 30s, Mitchell Leisen with Fred MacMurray or Ray Milland in later years, and Josef von Sternberg with Marlene Dietrich. Whereas MGM, the most affluent and profitable studio, *chose* to concentrate on its star vehicles in the 30s, Paramount had to rely increasingly on its stars from necessity. MGM glamour could be regarded as icing on the cake, but Paramount required the most attractive and opulently costumed stars to help give its pictures a more expensive 'look'. Travis Banton and Edith Head were all in favour and turned the Paramount ladies – Carole Lombard, Claudette Colbert, Kay Francis, Marlene Dietrich – into the most glamorous stars in Hollywood during the 30s.

Not surprisingly, the star-director combination of Dietrich and Sternberg fitted in well at Paramount for a number of years. He was a master at making his pictures look more lavish and expensive than they actually were, while Travis Banton was encouraged to be as imaginative, inventive and even outrageous in his costume designs as he could possibly wish, with the slim, attractive and highly disciplined Marlene as the object of his and Sternberg's creative efforts.

With the appearance of Mae West in 1932 Banton was given a different sort of challenge. As the writer of her own scripts, she followed in the line of independent-minded Paramount ladies such as Pickford and Swanson, producer-stars who refused to be dictated to by the studio. Mae, for example, insisted on making a film version of her play, 'Diamond Lil', in spite of the opposition of the executives who did not think that the Gay Nineties setting would appeal to young moviegoers. But they were very wrong. Miss West brought something original and new to the screen with her witty and colourful style of writing, full of sexual innuendo and double entendres which were to arouse the wrath of the movie censors, and through her lively performances and suitably exaggerated appearance. She was most often gowned in tight-fitting dresses to set off her hourglass figure, with plenty of jewellery, feathers, and huge hats to complete the overall effect.

Mae West was the first Paramount star to make the Quigley Publications' list of top ten box-office stars, in 1933–34, and the following year she was the highest paid woman in the USA with earnings of $481,000. (Her salary fell off rapidly in later years, however, as her popularity declined.) Other Paramount stars who appeared on the list in the 30s were Claudette Colbert (who averaged about $300,000 per year), Gary Cooper, and Bing Crosby who would feature more prominently in the 40s.

When Mae West joined the Marx Bros, W. C. Fields and Jack Oakie in the early 30s, along with George Burns and Gracie Allen, Paramount could reasonably have claimed to display the top line-up of comedy stars ever assembled at a single studio. But whereas all of these were veteran performers, the vast majority of the studio's new acquisitions of note were young players, of whom a remarkably large number went on to have long and productive movie careers. New leading men kept appearing year after year – George Raft and Cary Grant in 1931, followed by Randolph Scott (1932), Ray Milland and Buster Crabbe (1933) and Fred MacMurray in 1934. Then it was the turn of the ladies: Madeleine Carroll and Frances Farmer in 1935, Dorothy Lamour in 1936 followed by Paulette Goddard and Susan Hayward 1939, Veronica Lake in 1940 and Betty Hutton in 1941. Both William Holden and Sterling Hayden made a few early appearances in 1940–41, but only developed into important stars in the late 40s after their war service.

Certainly, a steady stream of new young hopefuls helped to keep the studio's wages bill low. Whereas Misses Lamour and Hayward both started out at $200 per week, Alan Ladd was signed in 1942 at $300 and Veronica Lake was pleased when she received a raise to $350 in 1941. Among the already-established stars, Bob Hope was earning $204,000 that same year as compared with $302,000 for Crosby, and an impressive $390,000 went to the long-serving Claudette Colbert who spent 16 years in all at Paramount.

The departure of a number of the studio's mature but elegant ladies – Dietrich, Lombard and Mae West – along with costumier Travis Banton in 1937–38 marked the end of the most glamorous era in Paramount history. The changing face of the studio was perhaps best symbolized by the arrival of young Dorothy Lamour who shot to stardom in her very first picture, cast opposite Ray Milland in *The Jungle Princess* (1936) and dressed only in a sarong, albeit designed by Edith Head. She was fortunate to be teamed with two of the most popular stars of the period, Bob Hope and Bing Crosby, with whom she appeared separately as well as rounding out the threesome in the highly successful series of Road movies, beginning with *Road To Singapore* in 1939. These were typical of the kind of lightweight escapist fare produced by Paramount in the 40s which shot both Hope and Crosby to a regular place in the annual list of top ten leading box-office stars.

Paramount had made little or no impact on this list in the 30s, but it was a different story from 1941 on. Both men were ranked high throughout most of the decade, and when they started to slip, it was another comedy double act from Paramount which replaced them – the popular Dean Martin and Jerry Lewis, who were placed second in 1951, 1953 and 1954, and came first in 1952.

But it was Bing Crosby who stood alone as the longest-serving and most successful star in Paramount history. Having arrived at the studio in 1931, his career really peaked during the 40s when he appeared in a spectacular run of smash-hit movies, beginning with the Oscar-winning *Going My Way* (1944) mid-way through his 26-year stretch at Paramount. Best known for his musicals and comedies and as a singer, Crosby was generally underrated as an actor because his relaxed, natural and easy-going style was deceptive, but in later pictures, notably *The Country Girl* (1954), he proved that he could handle more serious roles. Crosby starred in five of Paramount's top ten hits in the 40s and was voted the industry's number one box-office star for five years running, 1944–48, a record which has never been matched. (Shirley Temple at her peak came the closest, holding down the top spot for four years in a row from 1935 to 1938.)

Paramount had a few tougher stars under contract, too, most notably William Bendix, and Alan Ladd who was briefly teamed with the petite Veronica Lake, of the 'peek-a-boo' hair style, in a series of *films noirs* and also appeared in a number of action roles. Barbara Stanwyck made a memorable appearance as an archetypal shady lady of *film noir* in Billy Wilder's classic, *Double Indemnity* (1944), making a fool of Fred MacMurray, and stayed on at Paramount in a series of meaty Hal Wallis productions beginning with *The Strange Love Of Martha Ivers* (1946) which introduced Kirk Douglas to the screen. But the most remarkable appearance of the 40s came at the end of the decade. Gloria Swanson, still in great shape, was back at Paramount for the first time in 23 years, and even briefly reunited on screen with director Cecil B. DeMille playing himself in Billy Wilder's acerbic look at Hollywood in *Sunset Boulevard* (1950).

The studio continued to display a number of major star successes in the 50s, mainly with such newcomers as Audrey Hepburn, who had the benefit of working with William Wyler and Billy Wilder on her first two American productions, while Grace Kelly was a particular favourite of Alfred Hitchcock. Anthony Perkins spent three years at Paramount in the mid-50s, but is best remembered for his chilling performance in Hitchcock's *Psycho* (1960). Charlton Heston starred in DeMille's last two features. His Moses in *The Ten Commandments* (1956) was the first of those larger-than-life epic-historical roles with which he became associated, mostly away from Paramount, though he did star in *The Buccaneer* (1958) for the studio.

The leading Hitchcock star during the director's years at Paramount was James Stewart who appeared in two masterpieces, *Rear Window* (1954) and *Vertigo* (1958), along with other hits including *The Greatest Show On Earth* (1951) and *Strategic Air Command* (1955). Veteran producer Hal Wallis brought Paramount more profits than prestige with his Dean Martin-Jerry Lewis comedies in the early 50s and his mainly forgettable Elvis Presley vehicles in later years. Shirley MacLaine, however, was a rather more interesting Wallis star who appeared in Paramount pictures, on and off, for almost 30 years before winning her Oscar in 1984 for *Terms Of Endearment*.

Other leading stars who made an important contribution to Paramount in recent years included John Wayne in the 60s, and Robert Redford in the 60s and 70s, who finally won an Oscar in 1980, not for acting, but for directing *Ordinary People*. Many of the new generation of male stars have appeared in Paramount pictures: Al Pacino, Jack Nicholson, Robert De Niro and John Travolta starred in three of the studio's biggest hits, while the top box-office draws in the 80s were Harrison Ford (as Indiana Jones) and new discovery Eddie Murphy.

STARS

Albert, Eddie 1952–55
Andrews, Dana 1964–65
Arbuckle, Fatty 1917–21
Arlen, Richard 1925–34
Arnold, Edward 1933–34, 1937
Arthur, Jean 1928–31
Astor, Mary 1923–24
Ayres, Lew 1936–37
Bancroft, George 1925–36
Bankhead, Tallulah 1931–32
Barrie, Wendy 1935
Barrymore, John (Famous Players)
  1914–16, 1916–20, 1937–38
Barrymore, Lionel 1922
Baxter, Warner 1921, 1924–27
Beery, Wallace 1925–29
Bel Geddes, Barbara 1959
Bendix, William 1942–43, 1946–47, 1949
Bennett, Enid 1918–20
Bennett, Joan 1934–36
Benny, Jack 1935–40
Bickford, Charles 1933, 1936–37
Blue, Monte (Artcraft) 1917–18, 1918–20
Bogart, Humphrey 1955
Boland, Mary 1931–36, 1938–39
Booth, Shirley (Wallis) 1952–53, 1958
Bow, Clara 1925–31
Boyd, William 1920–22, 1930–31, 1935–41
Bracken, Eddie 1940–46
Brady, Scott (Lyles) 1967

Brendel, El 1926–27
Brent, Evelyn 1926–30, 1936–37
Brian, Mary 1925–30, 1935–36
Britton, Barbara 1941–45
Bronson, Betty 1922–27
Brook, Clive 1926–32
Brooks, Louise 1925–28
Bruce, Virginia 1929–30
Burke, Billie 1917–21
Burns, George & Allen, Gracie 1932–38
Cameron, Rod 1940–43
Canova, Judy 1937
Carey, MacDonald 1942–50
Carradine, John 1932–33
Carroll, Madeleine 1935–36, 1938–41
Carroll, Nancy 1928–33
Carson, Jack 1940
Caulfield, Joan 1945–49
Chaney, Lon, Sir. 1919
Chatterton, Ruth 1928–31
Chevalier, Maurice 1929–33
Clark, Marguerite (Famous Players) 1914–16, 1916–20
Clift, Montgomery 1949–51
Colbert, Claudette 1928–35, 1937–39, 1941–43
Colman, Ronald 1938–39
Compson, Betty 1921–25
Coogan, Jackie 1930–31
Cooper, Gary 1927–40, 1942–44
Cortez, Ricardo 1923–27

Crabbe, Buster 1933–39
Crawford, Broderick 1938–39
Crosby, Bing 1931–55
Dahl, Arlene 1952–53
Dana, Viola 1924
Daniels, Bebe 1919–28
Darwell, Jane 1930–32
Davies, Marion 1919–22
De Carlo, Yvonne 1942–44
Dee, Frances 1930–33, 1937–38
de Havilland, Olivia 1946
Dempster, Carol (Griffith) 1918–19,
   1925–26
Denny, Reginald 1937–39
Derek, John 1956–59
Dietrich, Marlene 1929–35, 1947
Dix, Richard 1923–29, 1940–41
Donlevy, Brian 1941–42, 1945–46,
   (Lyles) 1966–68
Douglas, Kirk 1951
Dove, Billie 1924–25
Drew, Ellen 1936–42
Errol, Leon 1930–34
Fairbanks, Douglas, Sr. 1917–19
Fairbanks, Douglas, Jr. 1923–25,
   1939–40
Farmer, Frances 1935–38, 1941
Ferguson, Elsie 1917–22
Fields, W. C. 1925–28, 1931–37
Fitzgerald, Barry 1944–51
Fleming, Rhonda 1948–51, 1957
Foch, Nina 1955
Fonda, Henry 1935–36
Fontaine, Joan 1950–51
Ford, Harrison 1918–19, 1922, 1925
Foster, Preston 1929–31, 1939–40
Foster, Susanna 1939–42
Francis, Kay 1929–31
Frederick, Pauline (Famous Players)
   1915–16, 1916–19
Freeman, Mona 1943–44, 1947–52
Gable, Clark 1958–59
Gaynor, Mitzi 1955–57
Gifford, Frances 1941–42
Gilbert, John 1920
Gish, Dorothy 1918–21
Gish, Lillian (Griffith/Artcraft)
   1918–19
Goddard, Paulette 1939–48

Goudal, Jetta 1924–25
Grable, Betty 1937–39
Grant, Cary 1931–36
Graves, Ralph 1919
Hall, James 1926–30
Harlow, Jean 1928–29
Hart, William S. (Hart) 1917–24
Harvey, Laurence (Wallis) 1960–64
Havoc, June 1949
Hayden, Sterling 1940–41, 1946–51
Hayward, Susan 1939–42
Heflin, Van 1959–60
Hendrix, Wanda 1946–49
Hepburn, Audrey 1952–56
Heston, Charlton 1950–56
Holden, William 1939–42, 1947–57
Holmes, Phillips 1928–32
Holt, Jack 1917–26, 1928
Hope, Bob 1937–57
Hopkins, Miriam 1930–34, 1949–50
Horton, Edward Everett 1923–25,
   1932–33, 1937
Hunt, Marsha 1935–37
Hussey, Ruth 1949–51
Huston, Walter 1929
Hutton, Betty 1941–52
Jannings, Emil 1927–30
Jones, Allan 1939
Joy, Leatrice 1921–24
Joyce, Alice 1925–26
Karns, Roscoe 1927–28, 1932–38
Kaye, Danny 1953–55
Keaton, Buster (Comicque) 1917–19
Kelly, Grace 1954–55
Kerry, Norman 1920–22
Keyes, Evelyn 1937–39
Ladd, Alan 1942–53
Lake, Veronica 1940–48
Lamarr, Hedy 1949–51
Lamour, Dorothy 1936–47, 1951–52
Lancaster, Burt 1955–56
Landi, Elissa 1934
La Rocque, Rod 1923–25
Laughton, Charles 1931–34
Lee, Lila 1918–23
Lewis, Jerry 1949–65
Lloyd, Harold 1926–32
Lombard, Carole 1930–37
Loren, Sophia 1957–60

Love, Bessie 1925
Lowe, Edmund 1932–33
Lukas, Paul 1928–32
Lund, John 1945–51
Lupino, Ida 1933–36
Lynn, Diana 1942–47, 1949–50
MacDonald, Jeanette 1929–30, 1932
MacLaine, Shirley 1955, 1958
MacMurray, Fred 1934–44
Macready, George 1948
Main, Marjorie 1932–34
March, Fredric 1928–33
Marshall, Herbert 1932–33
Martin, Dean 1949–56
Martin, Mary 1939–43
Marvin, Lee 1961–62
Marx Brothers, The 1929–33
McAvoy, May 1921–23
McCoy, Tim 1922–24
McCrea, Joel 1941–45
McLaglen, Victor 1933–34
Meighan, Thomas (Lasky) 1915–16,
  1916–28
Menjou, Adolphe 1921–29
Milland, Ray 1933–48
Minter, Mary Miles 1919–22
Moore, Constance 1940–41
Moreno, Antonio 1923–24
Morgan, Dennis 1938
Morgan, Frank 1930
Morley, Karen 1937
Morris, Chester 1942–43
Murray, Mae 1916–17, 1920
Nagel, Conrad 1920–23
Naldi, Nita 1920–25
Negri, Pola 1923–28
Nolan, Lloyd 1936–39
O'Brien, George 1923
O'Connor, Donald 1938–39,
  1955–56
Oakie, Jack 1928–36
Oland, Warner 1929–31
Oliver, Edna May 1923–25
Paige, Robert 1939–40
Patrick, Gail 1932–39
Perkins, Anthony 1956–58

Pickford, Mary (Famous Players)
  1913–16, 1916–18
Pitts, ZaSu 1917, 1922, 1927–28,
  1930, 1934
Powell, Dick 1940, 1942–43
Powell, William 1924–31
Presley, Elvis 1957–60, 1962–63
Preston, Robert 1938–42, 1947
Quinn, Anthony 1936–40, 1957–60
Raft, George 1931–38
Ray, Charles 1918–20
Raye, Martha 1936–39
Reagan, Ronald 1951
Reid, Wallace (Lasky) 1915–16,
  1916–22
Ritter, Thelma 1954–55
Roberts, Theodore (Lasky) 1915–16,
  1916–26
Rogers, Charles 'Buddy' 1926–30
Rogers, Ginger 1930, 1942–43
Ruggles, Charlie 1929–37, 1939–40
Russell, Gail 1942–48
Ryan, Robert 1940
Scott, Lizabeth 1945–47, 1949–50
Scott, Randolph 1932–38
Sheridan, Ann 1934–35
Sidney, Sylvia 1930–35, 1938
Sills, Milton 1920–22
Skipworth, Alison 1932–34
Sondergaard, Gale 1939
Stanwyck, Barbara 1938–40,
  1945–46, 1948–50
Stewart, James 1953–54
Swanson, Gloria 1918–26
Sweet, Blanche (Lasky) 1915–16,
  1916–17
Tamiroff, Akim 1935–43
Terry, Alice 1919
Tone, Franchot 1943–44
Tracy, Lee 1934–35
Valentino, Rudolph 1921–25
Vallee, Rudy 1942
West, Mae 1932–37
William, Warren 1936–37
Wray, Fay 1927–31
Young, Roland 1931–34

The Directors

Cecil B. DeMille was the studio's premier director from the earliest years when he was one of the original founders of the Lasky Company and served as director-general. He continued to be extremely active well into the 50s when he was still producing such hit movies as *The Greatest Show On Earth* (1951) and *The Ten Commandments* (1956). Paramount had many directors under contract in the 'teens, but the quality improved noticeably in the 20s when veterans such as Herbert Brenon and Allan Dwan were joined by a fine selection of newcomers including Victor Fleming, William Wellman, Josef von Sternberg and Dorothy Arzner. The late 20s and the coming of sound brought the studio important new talents Ernst Lubitsch and Rouben Mamoulian, followed in the 30s by Leo McCarey, and Mitchell Leisen who stayed on for almost 20 years as Paramount's most dependable contract director. A brilliant pair of writer-directors, Preston Sturges and Billy Wilder, made their mark in the 40s, and the studio was fortunate to sign a number of top men at the peak of their careers – William Wyler, George Stevens and, notably, Alfred Hitchcock.

When Famous Players merged with Lasky in 1916, the new company inherited a useful selection of directors – Sidney Olcott, who had directed Mary Pickford in *Madame Butterfly* and *Poor Little Peppina* in 1915, and J. Searle Dawley, one of the first directors to be signed by Adolph Zukor in 1913; also George Melford, who would later direct Valentino in *The Sheik* (1921), and William Desmond Taylor whose best pictures – including *Tom Sawyer* (1917) starring Jack Pickford, and *Captain Kidd Jr* (1919) with Jack's sister Mary – are less remembered today than the circumstances surrounding his violent death. There were two Famous Players actors, Marshall Neilan and Donald Crisp, who would turn to directing with some success, and the successful playwright and theatre director, William de Mille, who was initially reluctant to follow his younger brother Cecil into the movies, but soon demonstrated an understanding of the medium as both writer and director. He is best remembered for directing Thomas Meighan as *Conrad In Quest Of His Youth* (1920) and Lois Wilson as *Miss Lulu Bett* (1921).

Undoubtedly the most important director in the early years was Cecil B. DeMille. Not only was he one of the original founders of the Lasky Company, and director-general of the newly merged studio, but as an extremely active director he continued to provide many very popular and profitable pictures year after year. Sensitive to the look of his movies, he employed some of the best cameramen and art directors, and was one of the first Hollywood directors to recognize the importance of the designer's function, which led to the setting up of a proper art department at the studio fairly early on.

The 1916 merger sparked off plans for a major increase in output and the hiring of many new directors, and the studio attracted some experienced men. Maurice Tourneur was selected by Mary Pickford to handle *The Pride Of The Clan* and *The Poor Little Rich Girl* in 1916, and Allan Dwan returned to Paramount to direct a series of Douglas Fairbanks movies in 1917–18, having previously turned out early four and five-reelers for Famous Players in 1914–15 starring Miss Pickford.

Both Fred Niblo and George Fitzmaurice established themselves as leading directors at Paramount around this time, but are better known now for their later work at MGM. The company also gave an opportunity to new directors James Cruze (1918) and Sam Wood (1919) who would develop into important figures in the 20s. Cruze handled a number of Paramount's biggest and most expensive productions, including the hit *The Covered Wagon* (1923), and *Old Ironsides* (1927), a flop; while Wood was assigned to a series of Gloria Swanson features between 1921 and 1923 after having served as DeMille's assistant director. In addition, there was a large number of minor but interesting talents, the bulk of whose work is lost and who are virtually forgotten today – men such as Joseph Henabery, Robert Vignola, Irvin Willat, and John S. Robertson who is particularly recalled for the 1920 John Barrymore version of *Dr Jekyll And Mr Hyde*.

When the studio cut back on its vast output in 1922–23 and moved toward producing fewer but better-quality features, this meant an upgrading of directors. Throughout the decade there was a steady stream of new arrivals of note, along with a few key promotions of other studio personnel, such as cameraman Victor Fleming. He got his first chance to direct in 1922 and was soon turning out a variety of quality features, including *Mantrap* (1926) with Clara Bow, *The Way Of All Flesh* (1927) with Emil Jannings, and the early sound Western which made Gary Cooper's name, *The Virginian* (1929). The British-born Herbert Brenon arrived in 1923, bringing with him a special flair for British subjects: *Peter Pan* (1924), *A Kiss For Cinderella* (1925), and *Beau Geste* (1926). Allan Dwan returned to the studio yet again and became Gloria Swanson's favourite director for a time, working at Paramount's Long Island studio which Miss Swanson preferred to the cultural wasteland of Hollywood.

Writer Frank Tuttle was promoted in 1924 and spent almost 20 years as a reliable contract director, his work ranging from William Powell thrillers to Bing Crosby musicals. In 1925 the studio signed comedy specialists Gregory La Cava and Malcolm St Clair, and began distributing a highly original series of documentary adventures from Ernest Schoedsack and Merian C. Cooper, including *Grass* (1926) and *Chang* (1927). A young William Wellman arrived in 1926 and won his spurs the following year with the World War I flying picture *Wings*.

It was under the Schulberg-Lasky regime that Paramount first developed the unique style associated with the studio during its peak creative years. In 1927 Dorothy Arzner was promoted from top editor to director (after she threatened to leave) and Josef von Sternberg was hired, followed in quick succession by Robert Florey, Rouben Mamoulian and Ernst Lubitsch. With the departure of many silent stars and directors and the arrival of a new group, many with a particularly European sensibility and sophistication, a transformation was taking place.

The Paramount movies of this era have a special quality which differentiates them from those of the other studios and must be credited, primarily, to their many outstanding directors. At MGM, for example, there tended to be a lack of conviction about many pictures, though they were more lavishly produced, for the directors were generally regarded as one element in the total package. By contrast, directors at Paramount such as Lubitsch, Mamoulian, Sternberg, Leisen and DeMille were masters at integrating style and content, and were more likely to be involved in a project early on rather than assigned to it at an advanced stage. Similarly, the need to work within fairly tight budgets was a positive virtue, leading to a closer collaboration between director, cameraman and designers.

There was a characteristic warmth and luminous quality to the Paramount movies which fitted their exotic or period milieus and witty, intelligent scripts. No other studio was so successful in conjuring up such a wide variety of characters and settings. Lubitsch's films, for example, were frequently set in Paris, and he is alleged to have remarked that given a choice, he preferred Paris, Paramount to Paris, France. Most remarkable of all were the imaginative settings and imagined visions of China, Morocco, Spain and the Russia of Catherine the Great created for Sternberg's pictures starring Marlene Dietrich, with the director himself involved in all aspects of the design and photography.

In the 30s a large number of comedy specialists were signed – Norman McLeod, Wesley Ruggles, Norman Taurog and Alexander Hall among others – but Leo McCarey was the most successful of all. In quick succession during 1933–36 he directed the Marx Bros, W. C. Fields with Burns and Allen (in *Six Of A Kind*, 1934), Mae West, Charles Laughton in *Ruggles Of Red Gap* (1935) and Harold Lloyd, but made his biggest contribution when he wrote and co-scripted *Going My Way* (1944), one of the biggest successes in Paramount history.

Paramount employed a handful of the best writers in the business during the 30s. There was Jules Furthman, who scripted many of the Sternberg films, and comedy writers such as Samson Raphaelson who provided Lubitsch with many witty scripts, while a young Joseph L. Mankiewicz wrote comedies for Jack Oakie at the beginning of his long and distinguished career. Two of the best, Preston Sturges and Billy Wilder, emerged in the early 40s as the studio's leading writer-directors. Sturges' remarkable output was concentrated into the years 1940–43, when he satirized many aspects of American culture, while Wilder developed his own perceptive observation of the blacker side of American life as seen in *The Lost Weekend* (1945), *Sunset Boulevard* (1950) and *Ace In The Hole* (1951). Another writer-turned-director, John Farrow, specialized in action pictures, the studio's 40s equivalent to director Henry Hathaway in the 30s.

During the 40s and 50s Paramount had many directors handling its large numbers of musicals and comedies: Mark Sandrich, George Marshall and Hal Walker, also McLeod and Taurog who returned for a time, writer-director Melvin Frank, and Frank Tashlin who specialized in Dean Martin-Jerry Lewis comedies, then carried on with Lewis alone. But though these movies were popular and profitable, the studio gained its greatest prestige from more serious productions which included those of producer-directors William Wyler (*The Heiress*, 1949; *Detective Story*, 1951; *The Desperate Hours*, 1955); George Stevens (*A Place In The Sun*, 1951; *Shane*, 1953); George Seaton (*The Country Girl*, 1954). Paramount had inherited the services of Wyler and Stevens (along with Frank Capra) on the collapse of the short-lived, independent company, Liberty Films, and was fortunate in signing up another veteran, Alfred Hitchcock, at the peak of his career. He made six pictures for Paramount, including such masterpieces as *Rear Window* (1954), *Vertigo* (1958) and *Psycho* (1960), which were among the few highlights of the studio's output in these later years.

DIRECTORS

Archainbaud, George 1936–40	**DeMille, Cecil B.** (Lasky)
Arzner, Dorothy 1927–32	1913–16, 1916–25, 1932–56
Barton, Charles 1934–38	**de Mille, William** (Lasky)
Beaudine, William 1932–34	1915–16, 1916–25
Bell, Monta 1929–31	**Dieterle, William** 1948–53
Borzage, Frank 1920–22	**Dmytryk, Edward** 1939–40
Bretherton, Howard 1935–36	**Dwan, Allan** 1917–18, 1923–26
Brown, Harry Joe 1932–33	**Farrow, John** 1942–49
Capra, Frank 1949–51	**Fitzmaurice, George** 1919–23
Clemens, William 1941–42	**Fleming, Victor** 1922–29
Cline, Edward 1931–32, 1935–36	**Florey, Robert** 1928–29, 1935–40
Cromwell, John 1929–32	**Foster, Lewis R.** 1949–53
Cruze, James 1918–27	**Frank, Melvin** (with **Norman Panama**) 1954–59
Cukor, George 1930–31	**Garnett, Tay** 1947–48
Curtiz, Michael 1954–56	**Gering, Marion** 1931–36
d'Abbadie d'Arrast, Harry 1927–28, 1930	**Goulding, Edmund** 1929–31

Griffith, D.W. (Artcraft) 1917–19, 1926
Hall, Alexander 1932–37
Hathaway, Henry 1932–38
Hecht, Ben (with Charles MacArthur) 1934–36
Heisler, Stuart 1940–42
Hiller, Arthur 1970–71
Hitchcock, Alfred 1954–60
Howard, William K. 1924–25, 1935–36
Humberstone, H. Bruce 1932–33
Kenton, Erle C. 1933–34
La Cava, Gregory 1925–28
Lachman, Harry 1932
Lanfield, Sidney 1942–47
Lee, Rowland V. 1928–31
Leisen, Mitchell 1933–51
Lloyd, Frank 1926–27, 1937–39
Lubitsch, Ernst 1928–33, 1935–37
Mamoulian, Rouben 1929–33
Mann, Daniel 1952–55, 1962–65
Marshall, George 1942–50, 1952–54
Maté, Rudolf 1950–51
McCarey, Leo 1933–37
McDonald, Frank 1943–44
McLeod, Norman Z. 1930–36, 1947–51
Milestone, Lewis 1935–36
Neilan, Marshall 1916–18
Neumann, Kurt 1938–40
Niblo, Fred 1918–21
Nugent, Elliott 1934–35, 1938–41, 1947
Pichel, Irving 1944–46
Roberts, Stephen 1932–33
Robertson, John Stuart 1919–22

Ruggles, Wesley 1932–39
St Clair, Malcolm 1925–28
Sandrich, Mark 1939–44
Santell, Alfred 1938–42
Schertzinger, Victor 1928–30, 1940–41
Schoedsack, Ernest 1925–31
Seaton, George 1952–61
Seiter, William 1932, 1936
Selander, Lesley 1937–41
Siodmak, Robert 1941–42
Sternberg, Josef von 1927–35
Stevens, George 1950–52
Stiller, Mauritz 1927–28
Stone, Andrew L. 1938–41
Sturges, Preston 1940–43
Sutherland, A. Edward 1925–31, 1933, 1935–37
Tashlin, Frank 1955–64
Taurog, Norman 1930–36, 1952–56
Tuttle, Frank 1924–38, 1942–44
Vidor, Charles 1936–37
Vidor, King 1935–36
Walker, Hal 1945–52
Walker, Stuart 1931–33
Wallace, Richard 1928–32, 1936–37
Walsh, Raoul 1925–26, 1935–36, 1938–39
Weber, Lois 1920–21
Wellman, William A. 1926–30, 1938–41
Werker, Alfred L. 1928, 1934–35
Wilder, Billy 1942–54
Wood, Sam 1919–26
Wyler, William 1949–55
Young, Harold 1935–36

The Creative Personnel

As the largest and most prolific company in the early years, Paramount employed many young cameramen, art directors, and others who would later become important figures in the film industry. Paramount was one of the first studios to hire designers, costumiers and effects experts on a regular basis. The 30s represented the high point of close creative collaboration, with the presence of many top female stars inspiring the cameramen and designers to produce a body of memorable work. Over the years the studio employed leading figures in many different creative fields. There was a particularly strong selection of cameramen beginning with Alvin Wyckoff in the 'teens, followed by Karl Struss, Charles Lang, Lee Garmes and John Seitz. Top art directors were Wilfred Buckland in the early period and the formidable figure of Hans Dreier from 1923 through 1950. Between them, Travis Banton and Edith Head provided stylish costumes for over 40 years, while Farciot Edouart, Gordon Jennings and John P. Fulton handled the special effects and Victor Young wrote scores for high-quality productions. Among the best-known editors were Dorothy Arzner, Edward Dmytryk and William Hornbeck.

Cameramen and Art Directors

During the course of its long history Paramount employed many of the top American cameramen. On the very first Lasky Company productions, Alvin Wyckoff collaborated with DeMille and art director Wilfred Buckland to achieve some of the most remarkable early examples of atmospheric lighting effects, known as 'Lasky lighting', on such pictures as *The Cheat* (1915). DeMille also gave opportunities to Karl Struss who joined Wyckoff in the early 20s, and a young Peverell Marley who worked on *The Ten Commandments* (1923). When DeMille left Paramount in 1925, Marley went with him.

Another young cameraman, Arthur Miller, joined Paramount for a time, along with director George Fitzmaurice. Employed mainly in New York, they started out at the 56th Street studio in 1919, but soon moved to the new, larger and better-equipped Astoria studio which opened in 1920, then shot two of their pictures abroad in 1921, both starring Anna Q. Nilsson. *Three Live Ghosts* was filmed in London, making use of Paramount's Islington studio where Alfred Hitchcock was employed as art director.

A teen-aged James Wong Howe first joined the studio around 1917 as an assistant and slate boy for Alvin Wyckoff, then graduated to camera operator and full cameraman by 1922 when his ingenuity caught the eye of Mary Miles Minter. He briefly became her favourite lighting cameraman, working on her last features in 1922, then spent the next few years working with directors Herbert Brenon and Victor Fleming. An early example of his imaginative approach can be seen in the Brenon-directed *Peter Pan* (1924) where he created the character of Tinkerbell on screen with a tiny light bulb. Howe left Paramount in 1927, but returned as a freelance in the 50s and won Oscars for his photography on *The Rose Tattoo* (1955) in black-and-white VistaVision and *Hud* (1963) in black-and-white Panavision.

Karl Brown, who had served his apprenticeship as a teenager with D. W. Griffith (and has written a fine book about his early experiences), arrived at Paramount in 1920 where he worked with Joseph Henabery, then teamed up with James Cruze. He shot such pictures as *The Covered Wagon* (1923) and *The Pony Express* (1925), then directed one remarkable outdoor feature of his own, *Stark Love*, filmed in the mountain country of North Carolina in 1926.

Lee Garmes also followed the familiar pattern of breaking into movies as a prop boy and assistant cameraman. Garmes got his big break filming comedy shorts in the early 20s for director Malcolm St Clair who brought him to Paramount in 1925, but only established himself as a top cameraman when he returned to Paramount in the early 30s and contributed to the studio's great period of black-and-white film making. He collaborated closely with Sternberg on a number of the most stunning of the Dietrich films, while Struss also returned to Paramount and DeMille in the 30s, and filmed many of Mae West's pictures, too.

Charles Lang was another who joined Paramount in the late 20s. Lang, Harry Fischbeck and Victor Milner became staple figures at the studio for about 20 years, while Hal Rosson, who had begun at Metro in the 'teens, first made his name at Paramount in the 20s. He shot many of the Allan Dwan–Gloria Swanson movies and worked with Sternberg, most notably on the richly low-keyed *The Docks Of New York* (1928), set in the smoky dives and along the waterfront at night.

The early 30s was the great era of Paramount's most atmospheric and impressive black-and-white film making, and the studio effectively dominated the Oscars for cinematography. The many nominations and awards during the 1929–35 years included Oscars to Lee Garmes for *Shanghai Express* (1932), to Charles Lang for *A Farewell To Arms* (1932) and to Victor Milner for his contribution to DeMille's *Cleopatra* (1934).

Other important arrivals in the 30s were Leo Tover and William Mellor, followed by Daniel Fapp, John Seitz and Lionel Lindon in the early 40s. All specialized in black-and-white in their Paramount days, but later worked in colour. Seitz in particular was the studio's outstanding exponent of mood photography, and collaborated memorably with Billy Wilder on such powerful pictures as *The Lost Weekend* (1945) and *Sunset Boulevard* (1950).

Known mainly for its monochrome photography, Paramount never developed a strong line in colour, and as late as the 60s was gaining most of its Oscars and nominations for black-and-white. During more recent years the most distinguished pictures have been characterized by their subdued use of colour, mainly for dramas and thrillers such as *The Molly Maguires* (1970) – James Wong Howe again, both Godfather movies, *Chinatown* (1974), *The Day Of The Locust* (1975), *Looking For Mr Goodbar* (1977) and *Ragtime* (1981). The last four were all Oscar-nominated, the winners being *Days Of Heaven* (1978), and Warren Beatty's *Reds*, photographed by Vittorio Storaro (1981).

Paramount was the first major American company to develop a special interest in the design of its pictures. Recognizing the important contribution which an art director could make, the studio set up a proper art department and began employing designers, and in this respect played an innovative and influential role quite early on. A number of the men who worked at Paramount in the 'teens would develop into leading figures at other studios in the 30s and 40s – Van Nest Polglase at RKO, Robert Haas at Warner Bros., Ben Carré and Wiard Ihnen at Fox and, from the mid-20s, William Cameron Menzies at United Artists.

The initial credit goes to Jesse Lasky and Cecil B. DeMille who both came to films from the theatre and immediately signed up Wilfred Buckland, the well-known theatre designer, in 1914, apparently at the suggestion of C.B.'s mother. Buckland made rapid progress in adapting his ideas to the requirements of the movie camera. More than a mere set designer, he is generally credited with having introduced controlled interior lighting to picture-making and was one of the first to dress his sets with real furniture. In the words of Lasky, 'as the first bona fide art director in the industry, and the first to build architectural settings for films, Buckland widened the scope of pictures tremendously by throwing off the scenic limitations of the stage.'

The French-born Ben Carré had already designed films for Gaumont when he arrived in the USA, and soon began a fruitful collaboration with Maurice Tourneur, one of the most pictorial-minded of silent directors. Working first at the Peerless Studios in Fort Lee, New Jersey, they continued at Paramount in the late 'teens with features starring Mary Pickford and Elsie Ferguson. In 1919 the Paramount art department on the East Coast was properly established by Wiard Ihnen and Robert Haas, and office assistant Van Nest Polglase was promoted to assistant art director, while another young designer, William Cameron Menzies, soon joined this remarkable group. Menzies got his big break collaborating with Ihnen, director George Fitzmaurice and cameraman

Arthur Miller on two features that starred Elsie Ferguson before he moved on to join First National.

Meanwhile, back on the West Coast, Buckland, concerned that his work was not adequately appreciated, was reaching the end of his years with DeMille who soon turned to others to design his films. Mitchell Leisen, aged 20, was hired to design the Babylonian costumes and collaborate on *Male And Female* (1919), then developed into DeMille's leading designer in the mid-20s. And between Buckland and Leisen, came Paul Iribe whose most brilliant contribution can be seen in *The Ten Commandments* (1923).

But most important of all was the arrival late in 1923 of the German designer Hans Dreier, who was to spend almost 30 years at the studio. He served as supervising art director for much of that period, and exerted an influence over the look of Paramount movies comparable to that of Cedric Gibbons at MGM. Far less dictatorial than Gibbons, however, Dreier encouraged his designers to develop their own style rather than making them conform to a set pattern. Much liked by his associates, he attracted a large number of outstanding talents to Paramount and kept the studio in the forefront of design excellence throughout the 30s and 40s.

Dreier himself designed all the Sternberg and Lubitsch productions during 1927–32, easily alternating between the moodily atmospheric demands of the one and the lighter-weight fantasies of the other. Once he took over as department head, there was a sudden upsurge in the number of talented new arrivals. Among them were Ernest Fegté, Robert Usher and Earl Hedrick who all stayed on for a decade or more, while both Roland Anderson and John Goodman were upgraded to full art-director status. (Originally hired as a sketch artist in the 20s, Anderson remained at the studio till the late 60s.)

Two important new designers in the 40s were Hal Pereira, who took over from Dreier as supervising art director in 1950 and carried on for 18 years, and Henry Bumstead, who did some of his best work for Hitchcock in the 50s on *The Man Who Knew Too Much* (1956) and *Vertigo* (1958). During more recent years Paramount benefited from two outstanding members of the newer generation of production designers: Richard Sylbert contributed to the look of *Catch-22* (1970), and to Polanski's *Rosemary's Baby* (1968) and *Chinatown* (1974), while Dean Tavoulouris worked with Francis Coppola on both *Godfather* pictures and *The Conversation*, and won an Oscar for *The Godfather, Part II*.

Other Departments

As the largest studio in the 'teens and early 20s, Paramount began hiring a wide range of technical specialists. Roy Pomeroy, for example, was an early 'effects' innovator who devised the parting of the Red Sea for *The Ten Commandments* (1923) and was the only winner of a shortlived Oscar category called 'engineering effects' for his work on *Wings* (1927). Another pioneering technical specialist at Paramount in the 20s was Farciot Edouart who headed the special-effects department for many years. He was joined by Gordon Jennings and together they won Oscars for *Spawn Of The North* (1938), *I Wanted Wings* (1941) and *Reap The Wild Wind* (1942). When Jennings died suddenly in 1953, he was replaced by the equally talented John P. Fulton who had made his name at Universal in the 30s.

Quite early on DeMille became aware of the commercial appeal of the costumes in his pictures. 'I want clothes that will make people gasp when they see them,' he instructed the wardrobe department. In 1918 he had hired the studio's first costume designer, Claire West. She was assisted on *Male And Female* (1919) by Mitchell Leisen and by Howard Greer on *The Ten Commandments* (1923). Paramount's costume department set the tone for the rest of the Hollywood studios from about 1923–24 when, in addition to Greer, both Travis Banton and Edith Head took up their posts. Though the distinguished Miss Head began as a sketch artist and assistant to Greer and Banton, by the time of Greer's departure in 1927 she was ready to start designing on her own account. Today, of course, hers is the best-known name of all the costumiers, for she survived the longest, won the most Oscars and nominations, and after 40-plus years at Paramount, continued working at Universal until the late 70s.

Travis Banton, however, was the star designer during Paramount's most glamorous years when the studio had more than its share of stunning ladies under contract. As David Chierichetti has noted, 'his costumes for the great beauties of the 20s were just warming up exercises for Banton whose chief fame rests on his uniquely elegant designs of the 30s.' His costumes for Marlene Dietrich, Claudette Colbert, Carole Lombard and Mae West in particular contributed immeasurably to the studio's golden era which had reached its end by the time the designer left in 1938.

Best known of Paramount's editors were Dorothy Arzner and Edward Dmytryk, both of whom later graduated to directing. Miss Arzner had first made her mark contributing to a pair of the studio's most successful early productions, *Blood And Sand* (1922) and *The Covered Wagon* (1923), then emerged in the late 20s as the leading lady director in Hollywood at about the same time that Dmytryk was beginning his career as an editor. In fact, the studio acquired its strongest line-up of editors in the 30s at the very time when the number of features was beginning to fall. Ellsworth Hoagland, Doane Harrison, Everett Douglas, Arthur Schmidt, Archie Marshek and Alma Macrorie all averaged 20 years or more at Paramount, accruing a large number of Oscar nominations to their credit.

The studio's pre-eminent composer was the talented Victor Young, who scored many of the studio's most lavish dramatic productions from the late 30s through the early 50s. But Young's contribution was overshadowed in the 50s: first by a memorable pair of Oscar-winning scores by Franz Waxman (for *Sunset Boulevard* and *A Place In The Sun*, both 1951); then by the teaming of Bernard Herrmann and Alfred Hitchcock in one of the most remarkable collaborations between composer and director in the history of the cinema, beginning with *The Trouble With Harry* (1955), and including most notably *Vertigo* (1958) and *Psycho*

(1960) in which Herrmann's powerful, individual approach was most in evidence.

CAMERAMEN

Ballard, Lucien 1930, 1935
Barnes, George 1919–21
Bitzer, Billy (Artcraft) 1917–19, 1926
Brown, Karl 1920–25
Fapp, Daniel 1941–58
Fischbeck, Harry 1924–40
Folsey, George 1929–32
Garmes, Lee 1925–26, 1931–32, 1934–35
Glennon, Bert 1922–28, 1932
Greene, W. Howard 1940–41
Griggs, Loyal 1951–62
Harlan, Russell 1937–49
Howe, James Wong 1922–26
Krasner, Milton 1933–34
Lang, Charles B. 1929–52

Laszlo, Ernest 1944–47
Lindon, Lionel 1943–49, 1951–55
Marley, J. Peverell 1923–24
Mellor, William 1934–42
Mescall, John 1941–42
Miller, Arthur 1919–23
Milner, Victor 1925–44
Rennahan, Ray 1945–53
Rosher, Charles 1916–18
Rosson, Hal 1920–25, 1927–29
Seitz, John 1941–52
Shamroy, Leon 1933–37
Sharp, Henry 1932–40, 1944
Struss, Karl 1920–21, 1931–45
Tetzlaff, Ted 1935–41
Tover, Leo 1933–43, 1947–49
Wyckoff, Alvin (Lasky) 1914–16, 1916–26

ART DIRECTORS

Anderson, Roland 1932–69
Berger, Ralph 1941–44
Buckland, Wilfred (Lasky) 1914–16, 1916–20
Bumstead, Henry 1948–60
Carré, Ben 1917–19
Clatworthy, Robert, 1938, 1947–48
D'Agostino, Albert 1936–8
Douglas, Haldane 1941–47
Dreier, Hans 1923–50
Fegté, Ernst 1925, 1933–45
Goodman, John B. 1932–39
Haas, Robert 1919–21
Hedrick, Earl 1932–57
Herzbrun, Bernard 1926–37
Ihnen, Wiard 1919–20, 1928–34, 1936–38

Iribe, Paul 1921–24
Johnson, Joseph McMillan **1952–60**
Keller, Walter E. 1925–26
Kirk, Charles M. 1926
Leisen, Mitchell 1919–21, 1932–33
Lonergan, Arthur 1961–65
Meehan, John 1935–50
Menzies, William Cameron 1919
Odell, Robert A. 1930–40
Oliver, Harry 1933
Pereira, Hal 1941–68
Polglase, Van Nest 1919–28
Toluboff, Alexander (Wanger) 1935–36
Urban, Joseph (Cosmopolitan) 1920–22
Usher, Robert 1933–44

COSTUME DESIGNERS

Banton, Travis 1924–38
Dodson, Mary Kay 1944–51
Du Bois, Raoul Pene 1941–45
Greer, Howard 1923–27

Head, Edith 1927–67
Hubert, René 1924–26
Leisen, Mitchell 1919–21
Steele, Gile 1946–49

Visart, Natalie (DeMille) 1934–39,
    1942–44

Wakeling, Gwen (DeMille) 1947–49
West, Claire 1919–23

COMPOSERS AND MUSIC DIRECTORS

Carbonara, Gerard 1936–43
Dolan, Robert Emmett 1942–52
Harling, W. Franke 1931–33
Hollander, Frederick 1935–40
Laszlo, Alexander 1944–45

Lilley, Joseph J. 1943–57
Rozsa, Miklos 1943–44
Shuken, Leo 1937–44
Young, Victor 1936–37, 1940–49

EDITORS

Arzner, Dorothy 1921–26
Bauchens, Anne 1918–25, 1932–56
Bennett, Hugh 1933–41
Bischoff, Robert 1936–38
Blangsted, Folmar 1929–35
Bracht, Frank 1948–70
Curtiss, Ray 1936–37
Dmytryk, Edward 1930–39
Douglas, Everett 1935–59
Gilmore, Stuart 1937–45
Harrison, Doane 1935–53,
    (supervising ed.) 1950s
Heisler, Stuart 1935–36
Hoagland, Ellsworth 1933–55
Hornbeck, William 1949–53
Johnson, Stanley 1951–52, 1960–63
Kern, Hal 1961–63
Lovering, Otho 1928–36

Low, Warren (supervising ed.)
    1946–70
Macrorie, Alma 1937–62
Marshek, Archie 1937–67
Reynolds, William 1936–40
Schmidt, Arthur 1936–54, (Jerry
    Lewis) 1961–65
Shea, William 1928–47
Smith, Howard 1944–62
Smith, James 1935–41
Spencer, Dorothy (Wanger) 1936
Stone, LeRoy 1935–49
Swink, Robert 1951–55
Tomasini, George 1947–58
Warren, Eda 1927–58
Weatherwax, Paul 1935–44
White, Merrill 1928–32
Ziegler, William 1941–43

SCRIPTWRITERS

Akins, Zoe 1930–31
Bennett, Charles 1941–47
Binyon, Claude 1932–46
Boehm, Sydney 1950–52
Brackett, Charles 1932–50
Buchman, Sidney 1931–33
Butler, Frank 1935–48
Frank, Melvin (with Norman Panama)
    1941–46
Furthman, Jules 1925–30, 1931–32
Hayes, John Michael 1953–59
Hecht, Ben 1933–35
Hoffenstein, Samuel 1931–36
Lasky Jr, Jesse 1938–49
Levien, Sonya 1922–24
MacArthur, Charles (with Ben Hecht)

    1934–35
Macpherson, Jeannie 1915–24
Mainwaring, Daniel 1945–46, 1950
Mankiewicz, Herman J. 1926–32
Mankiewicz, Joseph L. 1929–33
Marion, Frances 1917–19
Mayer, Edwin Justus 1932–38
Panama, Norman (with Melvin Frank)
    1941–46, 1954–59
Perelman S.J. 1931–33
Raphaelson, Samson 1930–37
Rose, Jack 1946–49, 1953–63
Robinson, Casey 1933–34
Saunders, John Monk 1925–28
Sturges, Preston 1937–43
Sullivan, C. Gardner 1918–19,

1937–40
Tashlin, Frank 1945–48
Vajda, Ernest 1925–31

Wilder, Billy 1936–54
Young, Waldemar 1930, 1932–36

The Academy Awards

Throughout much of its long history Paramount fared surprisingly badly with the Academy Awards and experienced long gaps between its top winners. After taking the very first Best Picture Oscar with *Wings* (1927), the studio had to wait almost 20 years for its second, and hardly won a single major award during the 30s when it was producing some of the most imaginative pictures in Hollywood. Paramount finally gained its first statuette for Best Picture in the sound era with *Going My Way* (1944), immediately followed by *The Lost Weekend* (1945). DeMille's *The Greatest Show On Earth* was honoured in 1952, but there was another long wait until the early 70s before the studio began to do better. Between 1972 and 1983 it garnered four Best Picture winners, along with numerous other awards. Francis Ford Coppola directed and co-scripted two of the winning films, *The Godfather* (1972), and its sequel *The Godfather, Part II* (1974).

The studio scored a big success at the first Academy Awards ceremony covering the 1927/28 period. Not only did *Wings* (1927) win for Best Picture, but four of the five nominees came from Paramount, including *The Way Of All Flesh* (1927) and *The Last Command* (1928), both starring the studio's German import, Emil Jannings, who was named Best Actor. But it would be another 16 years before Paramount would win its second top award, and throughout most of that intervening period it was surprisingly unsuccessful in the Oscar stakes.

During the early years, however, the studio garnered a fair number of nominations, most often attracting attention by the quality of the Ernst Lubitsch and Josef von Sternberg films in particular.

Paramount Best Picture nominations in the early 30s were for *Skippy* (1931), two from Lubitsch (*The Smiling Lieutenant*, 1931, and *One Hour With You*, 1932), *A Farewell To Arms* (1932), and Mae West's tremendously successful first starring feature, *She Done Him Wrong* (1933). Paramount's only major Oscars throughout the entire decade went to Norman Taurog for directing *Skippy* and to Fredric March for his astonishing performance as *Dr Jekyll And Mr Hyde* (1931). For five years, 1936 through 1940, the studio did not have a single nominee in the Best Picture category, in spite of the fact that there were 10 films nominated in each year.

A few Paramount stars were honoured for their performances in off-beat comedy roles, but on loan-out to other studios. Claudette Colbert, for example, won an Oscar for *It Happened One Night* (1934) at Columbia. Paramount director Leo McCarey won the 1937 directing Oscar for *The Awful Truth* at Columbia, while the top Paramount combination of scriptwriters Billy Wilder and Charles Brackett, with director Ernst Lubitsch, came up with their best production of the late 30s on loan out to MGM. Their *Ninotchka* was nominated for Best Picture and screenplay in 1939.

Preston Sturges, the first Paramount writer-director to establish himself in the early 40s, won his only Oscar for scripting *The Great McGinty* (1940) and was followed by McCarey and Wilder who provided the studio with its (long overdue) first Best Picture Oscars in the sound era. With its entertaining blend of lightweight drama, comedy, a bit of music and a social message, McCarey's *Going My Way* (1944) was ideal wartime entertainment with a perfect pair of roles for its two stars, Barry Fitzgerald and Bing Crosby. The most honoured picture in Paramount's history, *Going My Way* won seven Oscars, including Best Picture, actor (Crosby), supporting actor (Fitzgerald) and screenplay, while McCarey won for directing, and for writing the original story. It was also named for best picture and director of the year by the New York Film Critics, but with Fitzgerald as best actor.

Altogether, 1944 was a great year for the studio. There were nominations for two of Preston Sturges' most witty and original screenplays, and seven nominations for Billy Wilder's brilliant *Double Indemnity*, adapted by him and Raymond Chandler from the James M. Cain novel. Wilder only had to wait till the following year for his extremely effective, downbeat study of an alcoholic, *The Lost Weekend*, to sweep the top awards from the Academy and the New York Film Critics – Best Picture, actor (Ray Milland rising to the challenge of the best role in his long career) and director (Wilder), with a fourth Oscar for the Wilder-Brackett screenplay.

Unfortunately, the studio performed poorly in the late 40s. *The Heiress* in 1949, with a total of eight nominations including Best Picture, marked the beginning of a regular pattern from 1949 to 1956 when the studio won few major awards but at least had one important contender and one Best Picture nominee every year. Between them the nine pictures (there were two in 1953) gained a total of 71 nominations and won 25 Oscars, but only six were in the major categories – with an additional pair from other pictures. William Holden in *Stalag 17* (1953) won the only Best Actor award between Ray Milland (in 1945) and John Wayne in *True Grit* (1969). The studio was most successful with its actresses, beginning with Olivia de Havilland's triumph in *The Heiress* (1949), followed by Shirley Booth in *Come Back Little Sheba* (1952), Grace Kelly in *The*

Country Girl (1954) and Anna Magnani in *The Rose Tattoo* (1955). The only Best Picture award went to *The Greatest Show On Earth* in 1952, one of Cecil B. DeMille's least memorable productions.

If Paramount's showing in the Oscars during these years was somewhat disappointing, it was even weaker in the years immediately before (1946–48) and after (1957–63) when the studio failed to get a single Best Picture nomination and managed to win just two major Oscars, both for actresses again – Olivia de Havilland for *To Each His Own* (1946) and Patricia Neal for *Hud* (1963). During 1964–68 Paramount did best with its European pictures such as *Becket* (1964) and *Alfie* (1966), reflecting its short-lived involvement in British production in the mid-60s; also Zeffirelli's *Romeo And Juliet* (1968). All three were nominated for Best Picture.

Paramount made its strongest-ever showing in the awards during the years from 1972 through 1983, with four Best Picture winners – *The Godfather* (1972), *The Godfather, Part II* (1974), *Ordinary People* (1980) and *Terms Of Endearment* (1983) – and many nominees, including *Nashville* which won the 1975 New York Critics awards for best picture and director Robert Altman. The studio captured a wide range of other Oscars including Best Actor to Marlon Brando for his portrayal of the Godfather and Jack Lemmon in *Save The Tiger* (1973), Best Actress to Shirley MacLaine for *Terms Of Endearment* and a number of supporting actor and actress statuettes. There was the usual selection of Oscars in the more minor and technical categories, reflecting the high standards at Paramount. Directing Oscars went to Francis Coppola who was responsible for both Godfather films, as well as a third nominee, *The Conversation* (1974); and to three newcomers – Robert Redford for *Ordinary People*, his first movie as a director, Warren Beatty for *Reds* (1981), his first feature as solo director, and James L. Brooks, also making his debut on the large screen with *Terms Of Endearment*, after gaining his early experience with TV.

Paramount gained its fair share of Oscar nominations and awards in the late 80s. Winners among the new generation of young actresses included Marlee Matlin for *Children Of A Lesser God* (1986), Jodie Foster for *The Accused* (1988) and the comedienne Whoopi Goldberg, supporting actress in *Ghost* (1990), the first black actress to win an Oscar since Hattie McDaniel in *Gone With The Wind*, while Sean Connery was honoured for his supporting performance in *The Untouchables* in 1987.

RKO

RKO was the one Hollywood studio that came into being as a direct result of the sound revolution. The prime mover behind the formation of the company was the giant Radio Corporation of America. When FBO was merged with the Keith-Albee-Orpheum theatre circuit in 1928, followed by a takeover of Pathé less than three years later, the result was a major production-distribution-exhibition operation which qualified RKO as one of a handful of top Hollywood studios.

Though the company produced memorable pictures, including *King Kong* (1933), the Astaire-Rogers musicals and *Citizen Kane* (1941), it never really lived up to its potential because of many changes in management and a troubled financial history. Then in 1948 RKO was purchased by the eccentric Howard Hughes who ran down the studio before selling it in 1955.

The 'pre-history' of RKO begins in 1921 when a small, British-owned company called Robertson-Cole decided to expand its production of feature films by building a small studio in Hollywood. The company was reorganized the following year and renamed Film Booking Offices of America (or FBO), functioning as a distributor and minor movie producer. The American financier Joseph P. Kennedy (father of the future President) bought a controlling interest in 1926. With the advent of the talkies RCA (Radio Corporation of America), headed by David Sarnoff, was looking for a means of exploiting its sound patents and expertise and purchased the FBO studio in 1928.

Later that year a merger with the Keith-Albee-Orpheum theatre chain was the final step in the creation of the major new production-distribution-exhibition company known as the Radio-Keith-Orpheum Corporation or RKO for short. With David Sarnoff as chairman of the board of directors, Hiram Brown as corporate president, Joseph Schnitzer as president of the RKO studio and William LeBaron as production chief, the new studio was soon producing and releasing its first talkies in 1929.

Lacking any really top stars or directors, the new company concentrated on musicals, which were very much in vogue at the time, and achieved its first big hits in this field, notably with *Rio Rita* (1929), as well as with a handful of comedies. Having begun life at an opportune time, RKO owed its early success more to chance than to the quality of its pictures, and the studio was obviously vulnerable to the effects of the Depression which hit the film industry hard in 1931–32. (Late in 1930 RKO had over-extended itself by taking over the Pathé studio and exchange.)

David O. Selznick replaced LeBaron as production chief in 1931 and immediately began hiring new stars (Katharine Hepburn, Fred Astaire), directors (George Cukor, John Cromwell) and potential producer talent (Merian C. Cooper, Kenneth Macgowan) with a view to improving the quality of RKO productions, while attempting to reduce costs at the same time. ('We had a very small budget for a very large number of films, so what I decided to do was to make the smaller pictures even smaller in order to save money on those for a few big films.') He also integrated the RKO and Pathé operations into a single production entity.

The first of many executive shuffles took place in 1932 when president Brown and studio head Schnitzer were replaced by Merlin Aylesworth and B.B. Kahane respectively. Unfortunately, it wasn't long before the new president began to tangle with Selznick, who insisted on the right to continue running the studio with a completely free hand. This dispute early in 1933 coincided with Irving Thalberg's illness and absence from MGM so that, when Selznick resigned and left RKO, he was immediately hired by Louis B. Mayer. It is tempting to speculate on how well RKO would have fared with Selznick at the helm for a decade or more. The parallel situation would be Darryl F. Zanuck's experience as the successful head of 20th Century-Fox from 1935 on. In any case, RKO never found anyone to replace him. Selznick's two leading producers, Merian C. Cooper and Pandro S. Berman, each headed the studio at one time or another during the following years, but both preferred to produce their own pictures (Cooper is best remembered for *King Kong*, 1933, while Berman produced most of the Astaire-Rogers musicals). B.B. Kahane, too, filled in for a time as studio boss and contributed to the development of the unit-producer system whereby each individual producer would be responsible for a number of productions each year. But the studio's recovery from the effects of the Depression was slow.

Perhaps encouraged by the improved quality and box-office success of RKO movies in 1935, which included *Top Hat, The Informer* and *Alice Adams*, Floyd Odlum and his Atlas Corporation bought a major share in the studio, thus initiating a new era in RKO management. (Odlum would increase his stake in the studio and continue to be a major force behind the scenes for the next twelve and a half years before selling out to Howard Hughes in 1948.) Leo Spitz became the new president in 1935 (replacing Aylesworth), Samuel Briskin replaced Kahane, and a number of new producers were signed up. But this new team was not really up to much. First to go was Briskin (in October 1937), followed by Spitz one year later when George Schaefer took over as the studio's fourth president in 10 years.

Schaefer lasted for almost four years in the job and thus had an opportunity to boost the quality of RKO productions while making basic changes in the way the studio operated. He was not content to leave the running of the studio to Pandro Berman, who had been persuaded to take up the post of production chief for a second time. His involvement in all creative matters, and his decision to sign up many independent production companies without consulting Berman, was a source of some friction between the two men. It led to Berman's departure at the end of 1939 just as the quality of the studio's output began to show a marked improvement. Releases of note in 1939 included *Gunga Din, The Story of Vernon And Irene Castle* (the last Astaire-Rogers musical at RKO), *Love Affair, Bachelor Mother* and *The Hunchback Of Notre Dame*.

In spite of all the changes which took place in management, producers and directors, the technical personnel at the studio remained surprisingly unaffected. As editor-director Mark Robson noted, 'RKO was a very good studio technically . . . All the department heads were exceptional. These men seemed to weather the storm from one regime to another, whereas at other studios when there was a change at the top, people could be let go.' (Of course, management changes happened so often that additional major changes in personnel would have been immensely disruptive to the functioning of the studio.)

The positive side of all the management changes was that a generally freer atmosphere resulted at the studio, which was appreciated by many of the directors. As recalled by John Cromwell who spent three different periods at RKO, 'They seemed to have a policy of trying to make everyone happy and contented as the best way to produce a picture ... In that respect it was very pleasant to be there. There wasn't any (studio) "politics".' And of special interest was John Ford's experience in filming *The Informer* early in 1935. He was allowed to go ahead provided he stayed within a tiny budget of a little over $200,000. 'But they wouldn't let me work on the lot – they sent me across the street to a dusty old stage, which was great because I was alone and they didn't bother me. They wouldn't build us any real sets though – the city of Dublin was just painted canvas.'

George Schaefer's policy of signing independents (rather than relying on in-house unit producers) in the early 40s meant that 15 of 53 releases in 1940 and 13 of 46 in 1941 were either independently made or co-produced by RKO. This proportion fell off after Schaefer's departure but the approach was an element of continuing importance in the RKO operation which distinguished it from the other studios in the 40s. It came to be more the norm with the decline of Hollywood in the 50s when many leading producers, directors and stars went independent and set up their own production companies. In this respect RKO actually led the way for the other studios.

Though the number of independent productions varied from year to year and the agreements with the leading independents like Disney (from 1937), Goldwyn (from 1941) and Selznick's Vanguard Films (1945–47) received the most publicity, there was a wide range of pictures involved. The many suppliers of programmers, for example, included Jack William Votion Productions which specialized in Lum and Abner comedies, Nat Holt who produced Westerns, and Sol Lesser's Principal Artists Productions which, in spite of the high-falutin' name, kept RKO well supplied with Tarzan flicks. In this way, RKO was able to keep its publicity and distribution arms and its film theatres working at top gear. Also, the company clearly gained added prestige from its long-running association with Disney and Goldwyn, though the agreement with Goldwyn was so favourable to the producer that RKO's financial benefit was minimal. There was an added irony here in the fact that RKO's reliance on independent producers in the 40s provided a foretaste of things to come. When Howard Hughes was running down the studio in the 50s, he came to rely increasingly on independents to maintain the minimum level of releases necessary to preserve the appearance of a functioning film company.

Though this system allowed the studio to limit its costs and its risks (while earning less profits), those risks could still be substantial, as the highly publicized example of Orson Welles and his Mercury Productions proved to Schaefer. Though the loss on *Citizen Kane* (1941) was tiny, and entirely due to the vicious influence of the Hearst press, and *The Magnificent Ambersons* (1942) lost less money than several other RKO productions, Schaefer was forced to resign in mid-1942. He was succeeded by an entirely new team headed by N. Peter Rathvon as corporate president, Ned Depinet, president of the studio, and Charles Koerner as production chief, but the real power lay with Floyd Odlum who bought out the RCA and Rockefeller interests in RKO and took the post of chairman of the board.

Benefiting from the war boom, the studio flourished for almost four years. Then Koerner's death, in February 1946, left a serious gap which was filled by Rathvon until Dore Schary was hired in January 1947. But Schary's reign was brief. In spite of a few major successes such as *Crossfire* (1947), the studio was on the skids again and falling rapidly into the red. In 1948 Odlum sold out to multimillionaire Howard Hughes, whose eccentric and irresponsible behaviour was the despair of those men who tried to run the studio for him during the following years. Schary quickly recognized the impossibility of dealing with Hughes and departed for MGM. He was replaced by Sid Rogell who lasted two years till he, too, was replaced, by Samuel Bischoff in 1950. That same year Jerry Wald and Norman Krasna, more optimistic than realistic, made a co-production deal with Hughes to make 60 features over the next five and a half years. But by the time they left in 1952, they had completed . . . just four. In the meantime Bischoff had departed and Hughes made a deal to unload the studio. The deal fell through.

In spite of it all, 1952 was a remarkable year by any standards, though most RKO pictures were supplied by independent producers. The year's releases included a Howard Hawks Western, *The Big Sky*, two from Fritz Lang – *Rancho Notorious* and *Clash By Night* – and the last (and best) of the Danny Kaye-Goldwyn musicals, *Hans Christian Andersen*. Then there was *Macao*, credited to Josef von Sternberg but largely re-shot by Nicholas Ray, who also directed *The Lusty Men* (the last of the Wald-Krasna productions), and an above-average group of thrillers including Otto Preminger's *Angel Face, Sudden Fear* starring Joan Crawford, and *The Narrow Margin* directed by Richard Fleischer. (Note that by this late date most RKO productions were still being filmed in black-and-white. Of this list, for example, only the Lang Western and the Kaye musical were in colour.)

James Grainger served as Hughes' last company president, from 1953 until the second (and definitive) sale to General Teleradio in 1955. The new owners failed miserably in their efforts to revive the studio in 1956, turning out a group of pictures which flopped badly. By early 1957 RKO was finished as a film production company.

RKO Studio Chronology

1928   The Radio-Keith-Orpheum Corporation (or RKO) formed in October from a merger between FBO and the Keith-Albee-Orpheum circuit, masterminded by David Sarnoff, head of RCA.

1929   William LeBaron appointed as production chief.

1931   The takeover of the Pathé exchange and studio is completed in January. David O. Selznick hired as vice-president in charge of production, replacing LeBaron.

1933   Selznick leaves for MGM. Producer Merian C. Cooper appointed as new production chief, with Pandro S. Berman as his assistant. *King Kong* released; also first pairing of Fred Astaire and Ginger Rogers in *Flying Down To Rio*. Due to serious financial difficulties, the company is put into receivership.

1935   Floyd B. Odlum buys a major share in the studio. Leo Spitz is appointed president with Sam Briskin as the new production chief. Cooper leaves, then becomes co-founder of Pioneer Pictures (releasing through RKO), while Berman stays on as production supervisor. *Becky Sharp* – first Technicolor feature (from Pioneer Pictures).

1938   George Schaefer hired as president and Berman becomes vice-president in charge of production.

1940   J.J. Nolan replaces Berman. The company emerges from receivership.

1941   *Citizen Kane*, a Mercury Production directed by and starring Orson Welles, was released through RKO.

1942   Floyd Odlum buys a controlling interest in the studio. George Schaefer is dismissed. Charles Koerner is hired as production chief with N. Peter Rathvon as president and Odlum chairman of the board.

1945   *The Bells Of St Mary's*, the studio's biggest-ever hit.

1946   Most profitable year in studio history. Goldwyn's production of *The Best Years Of Our Lives* wins the Oscar for Best Picture.

1947   Dore Schary hired to replace Koerner, who had died suddenly in 1946.

1948   Howard Hughes buys a controlling interest in the company from Odlum. Schary departs for MGM.

1955   Hughes sells the company to Thomas F. O'Neil's General Teleradio Corporation, a subsidiary of General Tire and Rubber Company.

1957   O'Neil sells the TV rights to over 700 old films to the C & C Cola Company for $15 million. Later that year the RKO studio is converted to TV production.

1958   The studio property is purchased by Desilu Productions, the TV production company owned by ex-RKO star Lucille Ball and her husband Desi Arnaz.

The Releases

The studio had its first successes with a routine selection of musicals and comedies, then turned increasingly to 'women's pictures' in the early 30s. A revival of the A musical was sparked off by the success of the Astaire–Rogers cycle, and in the late 30s RKO produced a number of lavish costume pictures of which *Gunga Din* and *The Hunchback of Notre Dame* (in 1939) were the most successful. War themes were introduced into the wide range of RKO features, but the most important development in the 40s was the studio's success with a new stylized approach to black-and-white filming, beginning in 1940 with *Citizen Kane*. RKO's special interest in low-cost but effective *films noirs* continued on into the 50s with pictures directed by Nicholas Ray and Fritz Lang.

RKO is remembered for its black-and-white filming, but distributed many independently produced colour productions during the 30s and 40s. These included cartoon features and shorts from Disney, Danny Kaye musicals from Goldwyn, and the first full Technicolor feature, *Becky Sharp*, from Pioneer Pictures in 1935. Slow to shoot its own features in colour, the studio experimented briefly with 3-D and both SuperScope and CinemaScope in the 50s, but with little success.

RKO's first releases in 1929–1930 were a fairly unimaginative mixture of drama, musicals and comedies, perhaps reflecting the fact that the studio lacked a supply of top stars and directors. Bebe Daniels starred in the studio's first big success, *Rio Rita* (1929), which included a few Technicolor sequences, and she was immediately rushed into three more musicals the following year before the musical bubble burst. Her co-stars, the comedy team of Wheeler & Woolsey, survived longer and appeared in a regular two movies per year from 1930 through 1937.

RKO increased its output in 1931 to almost 50 features with nary a musical among them, boosted by the takeover of Pathé which had strengthened its roster of female contract stars. This was roughly the level of releases that RKO would maintain over the next 13 years, helped by some independently produced and British-made pictures. During the early 30s the studio churned out seemingly endless numbers of inexpensive domestic dramas, romantic weepies and marital comedies, mostly adapted from plays, and drawing on a quality stock company which included Helen Twelvetrees, Betty Compson, Ann Harding, Constance Bennett, Mary Astor and Irene Dunne. RKO became known for its women's pictures – even the titles are strongly evocative and summon up an era. In 1931 alone there was *A Woman Of Experience* (Twelvetrees), *Born To Love* (Bennett), *Devotion* (Harding), *Smart Woman* and *Behind Office Doors* (both Astor), *The Lady Refuses* and *Three Who Loved* (both Compson), and two Dunnes, *Bachelor Apartment* and *Consolation Marriage*. Also in that year Dorothy Mackaill starred in *Kept Husbands* and Esther Ralston, Laura La Plante and Patsy Ruth Miller appeared in *Lonely Wives*.

The distinctly feminine tone of RKO was reinforced by the arrival of the unique Katharine Hepburn in 1932, and spilled over into other genres such as the Western. Irene Dunne starred in *Cimarron* (1931), while Barbara Stanwyck was *Annie Oakley* in 1935 and, nearly 20 years later, Jane Russell appeared as *Montana Belle* (1952). In truth the studio demonstrated a special penchant for biopics on the distaff side over the years. Miss Hepburn led the way as an aviatrix in *Christopher Strong* (1933) and as *Mary Of Scotland* (1936), while Rosalind Russell starred in the true story of Australian nurse *Sister Kenny* (1946), and Irene Dunne returned to RKO in 1948 to play the title role in *I Remember Mama*, also based on a true story. That same year RKO released the Wanger production of *Joan Of Arc* starring Ingrid Bergman.

Forced to concentrate mainly on low-cost features for a number of years while emerging from the Depression in the mid-30s, the studio was able to establish a more useful annual balance between a small number of prestige pictures and the larger number (and variety) of programmers and cheap Westerns. The A musical made a comeback too, stimulated by the tremendous success of the Astaire–Rogers cycle (two movies per year from 1934 through 1937), and attracted the interest of many of America's best songwriters. As producer Pandro S. Berman is fond of pointing out, 'Never in the history of Hollywood has anybody done what I did . . . to hire the Gershwins, Irving Berlin, Jerome Kern and Cole Porter, one after the other . . . They all wanted to write for Fred Astaire.'

RKO's long-running series of Western programmers began in 1931 with Tom Keene who came from Pathé and appeared in a dozen oaters between 1931 and 1933. George O'Brien was in the saddle from 1936 to 1940, but Tim Holt outlasted them all. He rode the range in 46 Westerns between 1938 and 1952 when he hung up his spurs for the last time.

Aside from the flow of cheap Westerns, RKO favoured low-budget series utilizing many of their contract character players. Edna May Oliver and James Gleason were teamed as schoolmarm sleuth Hildegard Withers and Inspector Piper in a series of films between 1932 and 1935.

Helen Broderick took over from Oliver in 1936, followed by ZaSu Pitts (1936–37). From 1938 George Sanders played The Saint five times before taking on another Leslie Charteris hero, The Falcon. In the fourth Falcon, Sanders' brother, Tom Conway, replaced him (in 1942), continuing in the role for another six years.

Jean Hersholt played the fatherly Dr Christian in six movies between 1939 and 1941; Lupe Velez and Leon Errol clashed with each other in eight Mexican Spitfire flicks (1940–43), and the comic-book detective Dick Tracy made an appearance four times in 1946 and 1947, impersonated by Morgan Conway and Ralph Byrd (twice each). Plump character actor Guy Kibbee had his own six-picture series as Scattergood, a country philosopher, while Johnny Weissmuller arrived from MGM to continue his Tarzan series until 1948 when Lex Barker, and then Gordon Scott, took over the apeman role for producer Sol Lesser. RKO also successfully teamed Victor Moore with Helen Broderick, and Gene Raymond with Ann Sothern, five times each in minor comedies and musicals.

The mid-30s revival for RKO, as for a number of the other major studios including MGM and Warner Bros., was marked by a selective move into quality costume pictures, most often derived from literary sources. The studio wisely limited itself to one or two such productions per year, for these blockbusters turned out to be regular money-losers at the box-office. For RKO the cycle was initiated by Schoedsack and Cooper's *The Last Days Of Pompeii* (1935). John Ford followed with two dramas in 1936 – *Mary Of Scotland* and *The Plough And The Stars* – while George Stevens directed Katharine Hepburn in *Quality Street* (1937). The biggest loss of all was chalked up by *The Toast Of New York* that same year, but the studio more or less broke even with *Gunga Din* (1939), directed by Stevens, and made a profit on *The Hunchback Of Notre Dame* (1939) starring Charles Laughton. They were back in the red, however, with *Abe Lincoln In Illinois* (1940), *All That Money Can Buy* (1941) and Orson Welles' *The Magnificent Ambersons* (1942). Unfortunately, RKO's shaky financial state made it difficult for the studio to write off its losses on such pictures – the price it had to pay for maintaining its position as a leading Hollywood studio. (By contrast with MGM, for example.)

The number of releases from RKO (and the other studios) fell off during the war years due to wartime restrictions, as well as the loss of stars and other personnel to the armed services. From 1944 through to 1952 the studio released an annual average of 34 films, about a dozen a year down on the previous decade.

Steering away from expensive war movies, RKO concentrated on the social aspects of the war at home and abroad instead, and introduced war themes into many of its series pictures, for example *A Date With The Falcon* and *The Falcon's Brother*, as well as into such musicals as *Seven Days Leave*, and comedies: Kay Kyser starred in *My Favourite Spy*, while Cary Grant and Ginger Rogers were teamed by Leo McCarey in *Once Upon A Honeymoon*. In fact, all these pictures were released in 1942, the year when RKO began to fight the war in earnest. The

French resistance and the Nazi occupation of France were dramatized in *Joan Of Paris* (1942) and Jean Renoir's *This Land Is Mine* (1944), while Tarzan was defeating some nasty Nazis in deepest Africa in *Tarzan Triumphs* (1943), and Russian guerillas led by Gregory Peck battled heroically against the Nazi invaders in *Days Of Glory* (1944). The studio developed a special interest in hard-hitting exposés of the repressive life experienced in the Axis countries, turning the spotlight on Nazi Germany in *Hitler's Children* (1943) and *The Master Race* (1944) and treating militaristic Japan in *Behind The Rising Sun* (1943). Back on the home front the studio had hits with *Government Girl* (Olivia de Havilland) and *Tender Comrade* (Ginger Rogers) in 1943. Largely self-explanatory were such titles as *The Navy Comes Through* (1942), *Bombardier* (1943) and *Back To Bataan* (1945) starring John Wayne, while *The First Yank Into Tokyo* was Tom Neal (1945).

By 1946 the war was left far behind. A detailed breakdown for this year, the most profitable in RKO history, shows the kind of mixture of in-house and independent features (other than war pictures, notable for their absence) which the company distributed in the mid-to late 40s. The listing reflects RKO's comparative lack of interest in quality Westerns and musicals and (not unrelated) its reluctance to increase filming in colour. RKO's two Technicolor features were both produced independently – *Make Mine Music*, a cartoon subject from Disney, and *The Kid From Brooklyn*, one of a handful of Goldwyn-produced Danny Kaye musicals in Technicolor, one per year, distributed by RKO during 1944–48. But of special interest is the large number of thrillers: eight of RKO's 17 in-house features, plus the first feature directed by Orson Welles since leaving RKO, *The Stranger* (an International Pictures production); and two notable co-productions with Selznick's Vanguard Films – Hitchcock's *Notorious* starring Cary Grant and Ingrid Bergman, and *The Spiral Staircase* with Dorothy McGuire, directed by Robert Siodmak. Not unrelated was the last of RKO producer Val Lewton's horror productions, and a number of downbeat dramatic pictures, all in black-and-white, of course, and reflecting RKO's special preference for low-keyed monochrome features in the 40s.

Ironically, at a time when Hollywood studio filming was in decline and the other major film companies were losing the special character that had differentiated them in the 30s and early 40s, RKO alone managed to retain an individual quality in many of its pictures through its emphasis on small, tough, inexpensively produced black-and-white dramas, horror films, and – especially – thrillers, which effectively set the tone for the studio's last dozen or so years.

Indeed, RKO played a key role in helping to launch a new style in 1940. Director Orson Welles and cameraman Gregg Toland had worked closely together on *Citizen Kane* (1941). They collaborated to make special use of expressionistic and moody, sparsely illuminated lighting effects, unusual, low camera angles, wide-angle lenses and a new type of stylized and imaginative filming which was to have a major influence for years to come. At the very same time director Boris Ingster and RKO cameraman Nicholas Musuraca had just completed *The*

Stranger On The Third Floor, another landmark in the introduction of expressionistic themes and lighting effects into the American 40s thriller. (Indeed, this film is often singled out as being the very first example of 40s *film noir*.)

The apparent link between *Citizen Kane* and *film noir* was confirmed by Welles' subsequent involvement in *Journey Into Fear* in 1942 (the last Mercury Production for RKO), followed by *The Stranger* and *The Lady From Shanghai* (which he directed for Columbia in 1946). And 1942 also marked the beginning of Val Lewton's cycle of low-budget horror thrillers which had a lot in common with the studio's *films noirs* both visually and thematically.

However, the *film noir* cycle at RKO did not get fully under way until early in 1944 when the filming of *Murder My Sweet*, director Edward Dmytryk's suitably moody and stylized treatment of Raymond Chandler's 'Farewell, My Lovely', coincided almost exactly with Fritz Lang's *The Woman In The Window*, starring Edward G. Robinson and Joan Bennett. During the following years the RKO studio strengthened its claim to be seen as the main Hollywood exponent of *film noir*. Memorable examples were Hitchcock's *Notorious*, Edward Dmytryk's *Crossfire* (1947), which introduced a strong social theme into its thriller framework, Nicholas Ray's first feature, *They Live By Night*, and Robert Wise's tough boxing movie *The Set-Up*, both released in 1949 along with the fantasy thriller *Mighty Joe Young* with Oscar-winning special effects from Willis O'Brien. (The last-named recalled, but did not come close to matching, RKO and O'Brien's first great ape movie 16 years earlier, *King Kong*).

The fantasy thriller was developed to near perfection by producer Howard Hawks in 1951 with *The Thing From Another World*, while RKO's last truly memorable year, 1952, was made so by an outstanding group of thrillers including *Clash By Night, On Dangerous Ground* and *Angel Face*. In fact, the final decline in the number of RKO releases was already under way. By 1954–55 the studio was releasing only 15 films per year, less than half the 1952 total. Most of RKO's last releases are best forgotten, but among them was a final pair of *films noirs* from the veteran director Fritz Lang, *While The City Sleeps* and *Beyond A Reasonable Doubt*, both released in 1956.

Colour and Widescreen

Although best known for its black-and-white pictures, RKO was marginally involved in a number of the earliest ventures into three-strip Technicolor (live action) filming through its production chief, Merian C. Cooper. In 1933 he played an important role in the formation of Pioneer Pictures, an independent company financed by the wealthy industrialist John Hay Whitney and set up for the express purpose of producing Technicolor movies for release by RKO.

The first project was a musical short, *La Cucaracha*, designed to show off the new process. Set in and around a Mexican cafe at night, the film included some nicely muted lighting effects, but mainly concentrated on the singing and dancing and colourful costumes of the performers in the cafe. It won an Oscar for the best comedy short of 1934, and later that year Pioneer embarked on its first Technicolor feature, *Becky Sharp*, based on a play version of Thackeray's 'Vanity Fair'. Director Rouben Mamoulian turned the film into a remarkable, if studio-bound, demonstration of the possibilities of controlled colour filming. Virtually every sequence was conceived and filmed with colour in mind, but in other respects the picture looked rather old-fashioned and failed to become anything much more than a filmed play. It did poorly at the box-office, while the final Pioneering feature, *The Dancing Pirate* (1936), was a disaster and brought an abrupt end to RKO's early involvement with colour. (Pioneer's commitment to shoot additional features in colour was taken over by independent producer David O. Selznick who then released them through United Artists.)

RKO did release the many Disney cartoon shorts and features in colour, beginning with *Snow White* in 1937, but no other live-action features until 1944 with *Up In Arms* – the first of the Sam Goldwyn–Danny Kaye Technicolored musicals. And in 1945 RKO finally produced its own first colour feature, the last of the major Hollywood studios to do so. *The Spanish Main* was a smash hit and quite profitable in spite of the high cost. It starred Paul Henreid with Maureen O'Hara, a lively and strikingly attractive redhead who was emerging as one of the leading Technicolor stars of the 40s. (Miss O'Hara was immediately cast in RKO's less successful follow-up, *Sinbad The Sailor*, opposite Douglas Fairbanks Jr. in 1946)

The studio had always been reluctant to venture into colour filming due to the costs involved. As early as 1933 Merian C. Cooper had hoped to film *Flying Down To Rio* in Technicolor, but had been turned down flat, and a colour sequence in the musical *Carefree* (1938) had similarly been rejected. As recalled by Hermes Pan, 'the studio was talking about having a surprise effect, so that when Fred (Astaire) sang, "I used to be colour blind, but now there's gold in your hair and blue in your eyes" and so forth, suddenly we would have a colour sequence. But something happened at the time. Cost or something prevented it, but it would have been a great idea.'

In view of its reluctance to film in colour, RKO made some strange choices during the 40s, including an ambitious Orson Welles production called *It's All True*, begun in 1942 but never completed, and the first feature from the relatively inexperienced director Joseph Losey, who was given a $1 million budget for *The Boy With Green Hair* in 1948. Costing far more than it could ever recoup at the box-office, at least it didn't lose as much money as the Technicolor *Tycoon* the previous year.

Under Howard Hughes the studio continued reluctant to work in colour and 'Scope in the mid-50s, though it was more quickly into 3-D filming in 1953–54, the most famous example being Jane Russell cavorting in 3-D in *The French Line* (1954). She also starred in *Underwater*, the picture which introduced the studio's new SuperScope process early in 1955. But the generally poor quality of most of the RKO releases was such that the increased use of colour and 'Scope from 1954 on was of little help in boosting box-office receipts or in prolonging the life of a studio whose days were obviously numbered.

Widescreen and 3-D Releases 1953–57

Process	1953	1954	1955	1956	1957
SuperScope		1	9	3	1
CinemaScope				2	
3-D	3	2			

Box Office Hits

TITLE	Cost	North Amer rentals
1914–31	(in $ million)	(in $ million)
Rio Rita (1929)		2.0
Syncopation (1929)		1.3
Cimarron (1930)	(1.4)	1.0
Check and Double Check (1931)		1.0
1932–40		
Snow White And The Seven Dwarfs (Disney) (1937)	(1.5)	8.0
Little Women (1933)	(0.4)	2.3
The Hunchback Of Notre Dame (1939)	(1.8)	1.5
Kitty Foyle (1940)		1.5
Top Hat (1935)	(0.6)	1.5
1941–50		
The Best Years Of Our Lives (Goldwyn) (1946)	(2.1)	10.4
The Bells Of St Mary's (1945)		8.0
Notorious (1946)	(2.4)	4.8
The Bachelor And The Bobby-Soxer (1947)		4.5
Cinderella (Disney) (1950)		4.3
Joan of Arc (Wanger) (1948)	(5.0)	4.1
The Kid From Brooklyn (Goldwyn) (1946)		4.0
1951–60		
Hans Christian Andersen (Goldwyn)	(4.0)	6.0
Peter Pan (Disney) (1953)		6.0
The Conqueror (1956)	(6.0)	4.5
The French Line (1954)		2.9
Flying Leathernecks (1951)		2.6
Alice In Wonderland (Disney) (1951)	(5.0)	2.4
The Blue Veil (1951)		2.2
Underwater (1955)		2.2

The Finances

Experiencing many financial ups and downs, RKO suffered from a lack of continuity in studio management and always struggled to earn profits. It was unlucky with many of its most interesting productions and brought home relatively few hits during the 30s. Those which contributed most to the studio balance sheet were led by *Little Women* (1933), *King Kong* (1933) and *The Hunchback of Notre Dame* (1939). The studio's only consistently profitable movies were the Astaire–Rogers musicals. Benefiting from the wartime boom, RKO saw its greatest financial success during 1943–46. But it was all downhill from then on. The studio fell badly into the red in the late 40s and continued to decline under the wayward management of the eccentric Howard Hughes in the 50s.

Throughout its history RKO was the least profitable of the five major studios. As the one new company originally set up to take advantage of the coming of sound, it got off to an excellent start in 1929–30, benefiting from the boom years of the early sound era. But it was hit hard by the Depression in 1931–32 and finances continued to suffer throughout most of the 30s.

The studio had its first success at the box-office in the second half of 1929 with three musical hits in a row. Betty Compson starred as *Street Girl*, then Bebe Daniels, co-starring with John Boles, was *Rio Rita*. This was a smash-hit adaptation of the Florenz Ziegfeld show, the rights of which had been acquired for the substantial sum of $85,000. Finally, Rudy Vallee co-starred with Marie Dressler as *The Vagabond Lover*.

Comedy teams Amos 'n' Andy and Wheeler & Woolsey provided the studio with a few of the all-too-rare hits of 1930 and 1931, while *Cimarron* (1931), RKO's most expensive production of the early 30s was one of the few winners of the Best Picture Oscar actually to lose money at the box-office. Starring Richard Dix, it cost $1.4 million and lost about $500,000; Dix's follow-up movie, *The Conquerors*, fell flat in 1932, the studio's worst year.

Over $10 million in the red, RKO was put into equity receivership early in 1933 with the Irving Trust Company as court-appointed receiver and trustee. (The company didn't emerge from receivership until January 1940.) This was in spite of the heroic efforts of studio boss David O. Selznick who had been hired in 1931. He had succeeded in reorganizing the studio and integrating the RKO and Pathé operations into a single functioning whole. He also claimed to have lopped almost $6 million off the total film-making budget, reduced from $16 million in the 1931/32 season to $10.2 million in 1932/33, with the average cost of an RKO feature cut from $350,000 to $230,000. To pay for a very special project such as *King Kong*, Selznick was forced to shave some money off the budgets of a number of other pictures. Eventually completed at a cost of almost $700,000, *King Kong* was a great success in 1933. Along with two Katharine Hepburn pictures, *Morning Glory* and *Little Women*, it helped the studio to reduce its losses.

During the following years RKO made slow but steady progress in reducing its deficit. Unfortunately, the trend was a far from consistent one, with hits and flops tending to balance each other out. A pattern can be discerned whereby many of the studio's most distinguished stars and directors, who had started out strongly, tended to fade badly just as their pictures were becoming progressively more expensive and less profitable. This happened with Katharine Hepburn and Wheeler & Woolsey, with directors John Ford, Ernest B. Schoedsack and George Stevens, and even with the Astaire–Rogers musicals.

Thus Katharine Hepburn's early films and Schoedsack's *King Kong* helped RKO recover from the Depression, but Hepburn soon began to lose her box-office appeal, though her movies were among RKO's most expensive product. *The Little Minister*, at $650,000, was the studio's costliest production of 1934, and just about broke even; *Sylvia Scarlett* (1936), *Quality Street* (1937) and *Bringing Up Baby* (1938) lost about $300,000 each. Similarly, director John Ford began strongly with *The Lost Patrol* (1934) and *The Informer* (1935), to balance out a pair of Schoedsack flops (*She* and *The Last Days of Pompeii*). But in 1936 Ford's last two RKO productions fared badly, thereby negating the benefits of two Astaire–Rogers hits. Finally, director George Stevens started out well in 1935–36 but had two flops in 1937, offset by the last Astaire–Rogers success, *Shall We Dance*.

The studio had just managed to record a small profit during 1936–37, but was back in the red once again during the reign of its new president, George Schaefer. Again, as in 1931–32, the slump was industry-wide, and there is a strong suggestion that the fluctuation in profits had less to do with management policies than with the ups and downs of the film industry in general. Even the Astaire–Rogers musicals which had grown more expensive (and less profitable) finally reached the point where they were losing money. Other loss-making A pictures in 1938 included *Joy Of Living* starring Irene Dunne, and the Marx Bros in *Room Service*, while *In Name Only* and *Love Affair* each made only a tiny profit. *Gunga Din* (1939) directed by Stevens, the studio's most expensive production of the 30s at just under $2 million, just about broke even, while the studio had hits in 1939 with *The Hunchback Of Notre Dame* and *Bachelor Mother*; the latter was Ginger Rogers' first really big hit without Astaire, reflecting her new status as the studio's top star attraction.

RKO began to recover once again in the early 40s, experiencing the most profitable years in its history as it benefited from the wartime boom of 1943–46; then, with the postwar decline in film audiences, it fell badly into the red. As the weakest of the large studios, lacking in strength and continuity of leadership, RKO was the most vulnerable to film-industry fluctuations. The studio had neither the exceptional pulling power of top stars, nor the kind of success in selling its pictures (which went with it) as demonstrated, for example, by MGM, which could thus buck the trends in the rest of the industry.

Since the period when Charles Koerner was in charge of the studio, 1943–46, was so profitable, it has been argued that his policies were responsible – in contrast to those of George Schaefer who had hired Orson Welles and is generally linked with the studio's loss-making quality productions. 'Koerner again changed studio gears,' according to film historian Douglas Gomery, 'fully abandoning the idea of prestige films in favour of lower-budget money-makers.' However, there is little evidence to support this view. From about 1935 on, the RKO production line-up generally included 10 or 12 A pictures balanced by 25 or so programmers and half-a-dozen Westerns. (The 1939–40 season, for example, included 12 A pictures budgeted at about $800,000 each, six low-cost movies at $200,000, 20 B's at $125,000 and six Westerns at $85,000.) The pattern continued through the mid-40s.

Thus, the big RKO hits in 1943 presented a familiar mixture of A pictures – Cary Grant as *Mr Lucky* (profit $1.6 million), the moderately budgeted *Government Girl* which starred Olivia de Havilland, and the low-cost *Hitler's Children* and *Behind The Rising Sun*, both directed by Edward Dmytryk and earning profits of $1.5 million each. A profit, albeit smaller, was also credited to Val Lewton's first horror-film production, *Cat People*, released late in 1942.

By tapping topical wartime themes the two Dmytryk movies achieved a spectacular and unexpected success, but for the rest of Koerner's reign it was mainly the A pictures which figured most prominently on the RKO balance sheet. The best-known flops included *Days Of Glory* (1944) – Gregory Peck's first movie, which cost just under $1 million; *None But The Lonely Heart* (1944) with Cary Grant and Ethel Barrymore; a Pat O'Brien comedy, *Man Alive* (1945), and Rosalind Russell as *Sister Kenny* (1946), a picture which lost $660,000 or slightly *more* than *The Magnificent Ambersons* (1942) for which George Schaefer had been heavily criticized. These were more than balanced, however, by a number of big hits such as *The Bells Of St Mary's* (1945), the most profitable production in RKO history, the Technicolored costume adventure movie *The Spanish Main* (1945) and Hitchcock's *Notorious* (1946). (Note that much attention had been paid to the fascinating series of low-cost horror films produced by Val Lewton during 1942–45, but their importance and profitability to the studio was really minimal in relation to the large profits earned in these years.)

With film audiences at peak levels and all the studios experiencing their best profits ever, it is difficult to estimate how much credit is due to Koerner for turning the company around. His death early in 1946 meant that his leadership was never really put to the test. Certainly RKO's vulnerability to a general decline in audiences was never more evident than during the postwar years. Profits dropped off from their peak of $12 million in 1946 to $5 million in 1947, and by 1948 the company was struggling to break even.

New production chief Dore Schary who had arrived in 1946 had one big personal success with *Crossfire* (1947), a thriller with a strong social theme, directed by Edward Dmytryk. But Schary was fighting a losing battle. Frank Capra's *It's A Wonderful Life* (1946) lost $500,000; the $3 million colour production of *Tycoon* (1947) starring John Wayne lost $1 million; and *Mourning Becomes Electra* (1947), directed by Dudley Nichols, chalked up a new record RKO loss of $2.3 million.

To Floyd Odlum of the Atlas Corporation, who owned a controlling interest in the studio, this appeared an opportune time to get out. He accepted an offer from multi-millionaire Howard Hughes, who had dabbled in films as a producer and director since the 20s. Hughes reassured Dore Schary that he would have a free hand to continue running the studio as before. The reality proved otherwise, and Schary soon departed.

In accordance with the government's Consent Decree, Hughes immediately began negotiations to sell off RKO's film theatres and thus realize a quick profit. In other respects, however, he ran the studio as though he had little interest in whether it earned a profit or not. RKO operated in the red more or less throughout Hughes' tenure. Reliable financial data is difficult to come by in the 50s, though the studio may have broken even in one year, 1951, when it enjoyed one last unexpected hit with *The Blue Veil* starring Jane Wyman.

Howard Hughes finally sold RKO to General Teleradio, a subsidiary of the General Tire and Rubber Company, after a previous sale in 1952 had fallen through. Though the new company, RKO Teleradio, had serious plans to revitalize the studio, most of its films flopped so badly that by early 1958 it was finished as a film production company and sold the studio. The buyers were Desilu, owned by former RKO star Lucille Ball and her husband, Desi Arnaz, who used the studio for the production of the very long-running hit series, 'I Love Lucy'.

For Box Office Hits see page 299.

The Stars

RKO began with a reasonable line-up of female stars
led by Bebe Daniels, Constance Bennett, Ann Harding
and Irene Dunne, but suffered from a shortage of men.
Katharine Hepburn was signed up in 1932, the studio's
biggest star discovery. The inspired teaming of Fred
Astaire and Ginger Rogers led to a highly popular series
of musicals, while Miss Rogers soon developed into a
top draw on her own, as did Lucille Ball. Among the
numerous top stars who spent some time at RKO were
Barbara Stanwyck, Cary Grant and Charles Laughton,
while Tim Holt was the resident B-Western star for 15
years, and John Wayne extended his range during his
RKO phase. In the 40s and early 50s RKO developed
a new group of star names headed by Robert Mitchum,
Robert Ryan, Jane Greer and Jane Russell, who all
appeared in the studio's many tough dramas and thrillers.

Throughout its history RKO suffered from a shortage of really first-rate
stars and thus a lack of drawing power at the box-office. There was a
tremendous rate of turnover of stars at the studio, perhaps related to
the frequent changes of management. The problem actually took various
forms. The studio had difficulties in keeping its top stars happy and they
were often attracted by better offers from rival studios. In addition, RKO
had many promising newcomers under contract who failed to develop
their full potential until after they left. Finally, a number of stars arrived
at RKO after they had passed their peak, but were still valuable to a
studio so short of star talent.

RKO quickly built up its roster of female stars during the early years.
Ann Harding and Constance Bennett were inherited from Pathé, while
silent stars Betty Compson, Bebe Daniels and Dolores Del Rio all spent
some time at the studio in the early 30s, but never regained the kind of
popularity in the talkies that they had previously experienced. (Bebe
Daniels did have one major success, starring in the studio's first smash
hit, *Rio Rita* in 1929.)

Myrna Loy arrived from Warner Bros. but soon moved on to MGM where she achieved true star status for the first time. Mary Astor stayed for two years, but turned down a starring contract as she preferred the variety of roles offered to her as a leading supporting player. Similarly, Fay Wray's stay at RKO was relatively short, but she is fondly remembered for her two sexy, scary, adventure roles: opposite Joel McCrea in *The Most Dangerous Game* (1932) and pursued through the same jungle setting by the formidable *King Kong* in 1933.

RKO was more fortunate with Ann Harding and Irene Dunne, both of whom remained with them for a number of years, as did Katharine Hepburn who arrived in 1932. All were mainstays of the type of 'woman's picture' in which the studio specialized during the 30s, and which also reflected their shortage of male talent. The few top male stars were led by the experienced Richard Dix, who was Oscar-nominated for his performance in *Cimarron* (1931), and a relative newcomer to movies, Joel McCrea. But as might be expected with RKO, Dix's best years were already behind him, while McCrea's were yet to come after he had left the studio for Goldwyn and Paramount.

During his short reign as production chief, David Selznick recognized the need to provide the studio with new star talent. His first outstanding discovery was Katharine Hepburn, who quickly developed into RKO's leading female star. Her first major role, a convincing portrayal of an aviatrix in *Christopher Strong*, was quickly followed by an Oscar-winning performance in *Morning Glory*. She was then cast as Jo in a sensitive and memorable adaptation of *Little Women*, RKO's biggest box-office hit of the decade, directed by George Cukor.

All three Hepburn pictures were released in 1933, and that same year Fred Astaire, also signed by Selznick, made his first screen appearances. Though loaned out to MGM for a cameo debut in *Dancing Lady*, he was soon paired with RKO contract star Ginger Rogers in *Flying Down To Rio*, before they co-starred in a series of musicals which proved to be the highlight of RKO's output in the 30s. As Astaire himself recalled, 'I came out to Hollywood because I was anxious to see what the movie thing was all about ... I didn't want a partner particularly but I ran into the ideal kind of girl to work with ...'

In fact, Astaire and Rogers together were the only RKO artists ever to appear on the Quigley Publications annual list of top box-office stars. They made the list three years running, from 1935–37, at the same time that Hepburn's appeal was beginning to wane and she was unfairly labelled 'box-office poison'. Neither Astaire nor Hepburn actually remained at RKO very long – only six years each – in relation to their extensive careers. Studio production chief Pandro S. Berman still remembers the problems he had in keeping the Astaire-Rogers partnership going; 'Most of my efforts were devoted to getting Fred to work with Ginger in *The Gay Divorcee* and to getting him to work with her again in *Roberta* and that went on throughout the whole series ... He never got over the feeling that he was being forced into being a member of a team, which was the last thing in the world that he wanted.'

The Astaire-Rogers musicals also provided opportunities for new young hopefuls, including Betty Grable, who had a small role in *The Gay Divorcee*, and Lucille Ball who landed her first bit part in *Roberta* in 1934. ('We were hiring models for the fashion show,' Berman recalls, 'and put her under a contract at about $50 a week.') Quick to take advantage of the success of her partnership with Astaire, Ginger was soon starring in comedies (and the occasional drama) on her own, taking over from Katharine Hepburn as the studio's top attraction in the late 30s and winning an Oscar for the dramatic *Kitty Foyle* in 1940.

Lucille Ball gradually worked her way up from bit parts and supporting roles to full star status and established herself as a leading comedienne, but few other young RKO contract players managed to do as well. Joan Fontaine, Van Heflin, Jack Carson, Ann Miller and Betty Grable all spent a number of years at the studio in the 30s without much luck, and all got their breaks elsewhere. MGM was especially successful in exploiting ex-RKO players in the 40s. (The MGM line-up included Van Heflin, Frank Sinatra, Ann Miller, Lucille Ball and Agnes Moorehead, while both Fred Astaire and Katharine Hepburn restarted their careers there after a short break.)

RKO was forced to borrow stars for many of its major productions. Well-known examples include Bette Davis, loaned by Warner Bros. for *Of Human Bondage* (1934), and Randolph Scott from Paramount, who starred in *Roberta* and *She* in 1935; Joan Fontaine made *Suspicion* (1941) on loan from David O. Selznick who also lent RKO the services of Ingrid Bergman for *The Bells of St Mary's* (1945) and *Notorious* (1946), along with director Alfred Hitchcock who was also under contract to Selznick. But it was obviously impossible for RKO to borrow all the stars it needed and the studio did succeed in attracting big names as well, even if their stay was relatively short, as often proved to be the case.

Barbara Stanwyck arrived in 1935 and Cary Grant, initially on loan from Paramount, began to work regularly at RKO from 1937 (alternating with Columbia) for over 10 years. Tim Holt's first RKO movies date from 1938, and the following year he established himself as the studio's leading star of Western programmers, succeeding George O'Brien. He played a few dramatic roles, too, most notably as the son in *The Magnificent Ambersons* (1942). Charles Laughton and Maureen O'Hara starred in an impressive production of *The Hunchback of Notre Dame* in 1939 and stayed on for a time, while the sublime Carole Lombard arrived that same year to play in a number of pictures which didn't turn out all that well. Best of the lot was *In Name Only* (1939) with Cary Grant and Kay Francis, but *They Knew What They Wanted* (1940), in which she co-starred with Laughton, was a big disappointment. A major event at RKO in 1940 was the arrival of Orson Welles with his Mercury Theatre stock company, all new to the screen, including Joseph Cotten and Agnes Moorehead. But they all moved on to other studios after only three RKO productions in which they had given some memorable performances.

A group of experienced stars whose best years were behind them helped to fill out the RKO roster for a number of years, among them Kay Francis, during 1939–40, and Johnny Weissmuller who brought his Tarzan loincloth with him from MGM. Robert Young joined the studio in 1945, and a teenage Shirley Temple arrived in 1946 but had clearly lost the charisma which had made her the top child star of the 30s. Having played the young romantic lead in innumerable 30s musicals at Warner Bros., Dick Powell demonstrated a surprising new hardboiled quality in such RKO thrillers as *Murder My Sweet* (1944) and *Cornered* (1945), while tough guy George Raft continued in the same vein, starring in a couple of the studio's biggest hits of the mid-40s, *Johnny Angel* (1945) and *Nocturne* (1946).

RKO had developed a tougher new look around this time, brought to life on the screen by a useful new selection of stars. A tough bunch of men led by Robert Mitchum, Robert Ryan and William Bendix was matched by no-nonsense ladies of the ilk of Gloria Grahame, Jane Greer, Ida Lupino and Jane Russell. But the deceptively lethargic-looking Mitchum was the hardest-working actor of the lot. ('I don't bother the studio and it doesn't bother me. Somebody hands me a script, I look at it and ask, "When do I start?") Mitchum appeared with iron-jawed Kirk Douglas and Jane Greer in *Out Of The Past* (1947), was pitted against Robert Ryan in both *Crossfire* (1947) and *The Racket* (1951), and was matched with Bendix in *The Big Steal* (1949) and *Macao* (1952). As he recalls, 'I played with a lot of girls like Jane Russell and Jane Greer who were the favourite dolls of the studio boss. So I had to be good, or else I'd be fired.'

Finally, near the end of RKO's studio life, its producers were turning out lots of cheap action pictures, thrillers and Westerns which offered roles to experienced stars who, in most cases, were also nearing the end of their studio careers – Linda Darnell, Rhonda Fleming, and Dana Andrews who made two thrillers with Fritz Lang in 1956; actions stars – including John Payne, and enterprising Ronald Reagan who virtually wrapped up his movie career at RKO with *Cattle Queen Of Montana* (1954), co-starring Barbara Stanwyck, and in the title role of *Tennessee's Partner* (1955), both directed by the veteran Allan Dwan.

STARS

Albert, Eddie 1943
Andrews, Dana (Goldwyn) 1940–43 & 1949–51, 1956
Astaire, Fred 1933–38
Astor, Mary 1930–32
Ball, Lucille 1935–42
Barrie, Wendy 1938–42
Bartholomew, Freddie 1940
Bel Geddes, Barbara 1947–48
Bellamy, Ralph 1933–34
Bendix, William 1951–53
Bennett, Constance (Pathé) 1929–31, 1932–33
Bergman, Ingrid 1945–46
Bolger, Ray 1941

Brent, George 1944–45
Brown, Joe E. 1937
Burke, Billie 1932–34
Cabot, Bruce 1932–34
Carson, Jack 1937–38
Cochran, Steve (Goldwyn) 1945–48
Colbert, Claudette 1945
Colman, Ronald 1940–41
Compson, Betty 1931
Conway, Tom 1942–46
Cooper, Gary (Goldwyn) 1941–42
Cortez, Ricardo 1931–32
Cotten, Joseph 1940–42
Daniels, Bebe 1929–30
Darnell, Linda 1952–54

Darwell, Jane 1942–43
Davis, Joan 1945–49
Day, Laraine 1938, 1943–49
Dee, Frances 1933–34
Del Rio, Dolores 1931–33
Denny, Reginald 1933–34
Dix, Richard 1929–35, 1938, 1940
Douglas, Kirk 1947
Douglas, Melvyn 1934–35
Dunne, Irene 1930–34, 37–38
Duryea, Dan (Goldwyn) 1941–42, 1954
Errol, Leon 1937–42, 1945
Fairbanks, Douglas, Jr. 1937–38
Fitzgerald, Barry 1938–39
Fleming, Rhonda 1955–56
Fontaine, Joan 1936–38
Foster, Preston 1934–38
Francis, Kay 1939–40
Grable, Betty 1933–36
Grahame, Gloria 1948–49
Granger, Farley (Goldwyn) 1947–52
Grant, Cary 1936–44, 1946–48
Greer, Jane 1944–50
Hale, Barbara 1943–48
Harding, Ann (Pathé) 1929–30, 1931–35
Hardwicke, Cedric 1939–41
Havoc, June 1941–42
Heflin, Van 1936–37
Hepburn, Katharine 1932–37
Hersholt, Jean 1939–41
Holt, Tim 1938–52
Karloff, Boris 1930–31, 1944–46
Kaye, Danny (Goldwyn) 1943–48
La Rocque, Rod 1939–40
Laughton, Charles 1939–42
Lombard, Carole 1939–40
Louise, Anita 1931
Loy, Myrna 1932
Lukas, Paul 1944–45
Lupino, Ida 1951–52
Marshall, Herbert 1936–37
Mayo, Virginia (Goldwyn) 1943–48
McCrea, Joel 1930–33
McGuire, Dorothy 1945–46
Menjou, Adolphe 1939–41
Miller, Ann 1937–38
Mitchum, Robert 1946–53

Mix, Tom (FBO) 1928–29
Moorehead, Agnes 1940–43
Morris, Chester 1937–38
Murphy, George 1941–42, 1944
Niven, David (Goldwyn) 1947–48
O'Brien, George 1936–40
O'Brien, Pat 1942–49
O'Hara, Maureen 1939–43, 1945–46
Oakie, Jack 1936–38
Oberon, Merle 1947
Oliver, Edna May 1930–33
Payne, John 1954–56
Pitts, ZaSu 1932, 1934
Powell, Dick 1944–45, 1952–55
Quinn, Anthony 1945–47
Raft, George 1945–49
Rains, Claude 1949–50
Raymond, Gene 1935–37, 1940
Reagan, Ronald 1954–55
Rogers, Ginger 1933–43
Russell, Jane 1950–54
Russell, Rosalind 1946–48
Ryan, Robert 1943–44, 1946–52
Sanders, George 1939–41
Scott, Randolph 1944–45
Sherman, Lowell 1930
Shirley, Anne 1934–44
Simmons, Jean 1952–53
Simon, Simone 1941–42, 1944
Sinatra, Frank 1943–44
Smith, Kent 1942–49
Stanwyck, Barbara 1935–38
Steiger, Rod 1956–57
Stroheim, Erich von 1931
Temple, Shirley 1946–48
Tracy, Lee 1936–40
Trevor, Claire 1944–46
Twelvetrees, Helen (Pathé) 1930–32
Vallee, Rudy 1945–47
Velez, Lupe 1939–43
Vera-Ellen (Goldwyn) 1944–45
Wayne, John 1943–51
Weissmuller, Johnny 1942–47
Welles, Orson 1940–42
Wray, Fay 1933
Wright, Teresa (Goldwyn) 1941–42, 1946
Young, Loretta 1945–48
Young, Robert 1945–47

The Directors

Where directors were concerned, RKO was an excellent studio that recognized their creative importance, and encouraged individuality. As with the stars, the turnover rate was high, but the studio's history boasts an impressive list of quality names from Leo McCarey through John Ford to Hitchcock and Fritz Lang. Opportunities were generously given to untried or fledgling talents, too. Thus, George Cukor first made his mark at RKO in the early 30s, writer Garson Kanin made some pictures at the end of the decade, and the early 40s saw the legendary directorial debut of Orson Welles. The company also permitted editors, cameramen, and makers of shorts to graduate to director status, thus promoting some leading feature film men such as Robert Wise and Joseph Losey. In the studio's declining years in the 50s, the roster of directors saw several veterans close their Hollywood careers with pictures for RKO.

RKO was a good studio for directors. Though there was a high turnover, as with the stars, the list of leading American directors who worked at the studio is a long and impressive one. A particularly open-minded attitude and a willingness to take chances on new talent meant that a large number of directors got their first break at RKO. A less strict categorization of talent than that found at other studios, giant MGM for example, meant that leading writers, actors and editors were allowed to switch to directing. Mark Robson, who spent more than a dozen years at RKO as assistant editor, editor and then director, recalls the management attitude at the time: 'As directors were considered extremely important, deals were made for the services of the best – Leo McCarey, John Ford, Gregory La Cava, George Stevens, John Cromwell, Tay Garnett and William Dieterle.' And Alfred Hitchcock made two important pictures for the studio in the 40s, *Suspicion* (1941) and *Notorious* (1946).

To a certain extent the history of RKO is reflected in its directors. The studio started out with a comparatively weak line-up, a situation which was quickly remedied by David Selznick. Thus, RKO could begin to be taken seriously as a studio in 1932 with the signing of a new group headed by George Cukor, Ernest B. Schoedsack and John Cromwell. All were relatively new to their profession, and were given their best opportunity by the new studio. They responded with a group of pictures which were among RKO's most interesting and successful of the following years including *Little Women* and *King Kong* (both 1933) and *Of Human Bondage* (1934). One of Mark Sandrich's RKO shorts won an Oscar in 1933 and he immediately advanced to features, specializing in musicals and the Astaire-Rogers cycle in particular. The pace of new arrivals hardly seemed to slacken: John Ford and George Stevens were signed up in 1934 and each delivered a surprise hit – *The Informer* and *Alice Adams* respectively, both nominated for Best Picture Oscars in 1935, with Ford the only one from RKO ever to win a directing Oscar.

Unfortunately, few of these men stayed for long, generally departing after one (or two) serious box-office flops, as happened to Schoedsack in 1935 and Ford in 1936. George Stevens lasted the longest, remaining at RKO until 1940, and leaving after the failure of *Vigil In The Night*.

Gregory La Cava and Howard Hawks were hired in 1937 to direct *Stage Door* and *Bringing Up Baby* respectively, while writer Garson Kanin arrived the following year and immediately made it clear to Pandro Berman, 'the perfectly congenial head of the studio', that he wished to break in as a director. Teaming up with writer Dalton Trumbo, he was allowed to direct *A Man To Remember* (1938) provided that he could shoot it quickly (in 18 days) and cheaply. It ended up costing under $100,000, less than the normal B feature, and launched Kanin on a brief directing career which included two of RKO's top hits of the period, *Bachelor Mother* (1939) and *My Favorite Wife* (1940).

There had never been such an explosion of new directorial talent as took place at RKO during the 40s, led appropriately enough, by Orson Welles. The studio made him an extremely favourable offer to direct a project of his own choosing and the remarkable result was *Citizen Kane* (1941). This was followed by *The Magnificent Ambersons* (1942) which, unfortunately, was taken away from him and completed by editor Robert Wise.

Relatively new directors Jacques Tourneur, Edward Dmytryk (a former editor) and cameraman Ted Tetzlaff were all given their first opportunity to develop their talent at RKO; editors Robert Wise and Mark Robson who had worked on *Citizen Kane* and *The Magnificent Ambersons* were given *their* first chance to direct as part of Val Lewton's close-knit horror-film unit. Richard Fleischer and Joseph Losey made the move from shorts to features after the war while, for a brief period, actress Ida Lupino became one of the few lady directors in Hollywood.

Last, but not least, Nicholas Ray made his memorable feature debut with *They Live By Night*, the first of the films he directed at RKO during 1947–52, including *Macao* which he completed (uncredited) in 1951. The movie was officially credited to Josef von Sternberg, one of many directors who more or less brought their studio careers to a close at RKO in the 50s. Others included Mitchell Leisen, Allan Dwan and Fritz Lang.

DIRECTORS

Archainbaud, George 1930–34, 1950
Auer, John 1943–47
Bacon, Lloyd 1953–54
Clemens, William 1943
Cline, Edward 1937–39
Cromwell, John 1933–35, 1939–40, 1950–51
Cukor, George 1932–33
Dieterle, William 1939, 1941–42
Dmytryk, Edward 1942–47
Douglas, Gordon 1943–48
Dwan, Allan 1954–55
Farrow, John 1939–40
Fleischer, Richard 1946–51
Ford, John 1934–36, 1947–49
Foster, Norman 1943, 1948
Fuller, Samuel 1957–58
Garnett, Tay 1932
Godfrey, Peter 1941–42
Hawks, Howard 1950–52
Hitchcock, Alfred 1941
Kanin, Garson 1938–41
Kenton, Erle C. 1939–41
La Cava, Gregory 1930–33, 1937–40
Landers, Lew 1936–39, 1947
Lang, Fritz 1951–52, 1955–56
Lee, Rowland V. 1937–38
Litvak, Anatole 1945–47
Lupino, Ida 1950–53
Mann, Anthony 1945–46
Marin, Edwin L. 1944–45
McCarey, Leo 1939, 1942, 1945, 1948
McLeod, Norman Z. (Goldwyn) 1946–47
Milestone, Lewis 1940–41

Neumann, Kurt 1936–37, 1945–47
Nugent, Elliott 1933–34
Pichel, Irving 1932–35
Potter, H.C. 1947–48
Rawlins, John 1947–48
Ray, Nicholas 1948–49, 1951–52
Reis, Irving 1940–48
Roberts, Stephen 1934–36
Robertson, John Stuart 1933–35
Robson, Mark 1943–46, (Goldwyn) 1949–50
Rogell, Albert (Pathé) 1931
Ruben, J. Walter 1931–34
Ruggles, Wesley 1931–32
Sandrich, Mark 1933–38
Santley, Joseph 1936–38
Schertzinger, Victor 1931
Schoedsack, Ernest 1932–35
Seiter, William 1931–34
Selander, Lesley 1948–52
Sherman, Lowell 1930–31
Siegel, Donald 1949, 1952
Stevens, George 1934–39
Stevenson, Robert 1942–43, 1949–52
Sutherland, A. Edward 1942
Tashlin, Frank 1953–54
Tetzlaff, Ted 1947–50
Thiele, Wilhelm 1943
Tourneur, Jacques 1942–49
Vidor, Charles 1935
Wallace, Richard 1943–44, 1947
Welles, Orson 1940–42
Wise, Robert 1943–49
Wood, Sam 1940, 1944–45

The Creative Personnel

If RKO was a little weak in the camera department (in spite of having a couple of leading cameramen under contract), the studio more than made up for it with one of the most outstanding art departments in Hollywood, headed by Van Nest Polglase. RKO depended on the expertise of Gregg Toland (on loan from Goldwyn) for the stunning photography of *Citizen Kane* (1941), but the studio's own art directors were responsible for the design of this and all other major productions. These ranged from the strikingly original look of the Astaire – Rogers musicals to the 40s horror films and thrillers, as well as to the impressive, imaginatively designed period productions such as *The Hunchback Of Notre Dame* (1939) and *The Magnificent Ambersons* (1942).

The music department was fortunate in acquiring Max Steiner during the early sound years, and he had a string of excellent successors, including the distinctively gifted composer Bernard Herrmann in the 40s. The technical departments at RKO were well-served by some skilled editors, including future directors Robert Wise and Mark Robson, and such expert costume designers as the well-known Walter Plunkett in the earlier years, Edward Stevenson in the 40s and, finally, Michael Woulfe.

Cameramen and Art Directors

RKO had relatively few top cameramen under contract besides Russell Metty (1934–44), Robert de Grasse (1935–49), George Barnes (1942–48) and the talented Nicholas Musuraca who remained a fixture at the studio for virtually its entire life (1929–1954). A specialist in low-keyed black-and-white photography, he contributed significantly to RKO's successful exploitation of the horror-film and thriller genres in the 40s. The most famous cameraman to work at RKO, however, was Gregg Toland whose contribution to the filming of *Citizen Kane* in 1940 is rightly recognized as one of the landmarks in the development of Hollywood studio cinematography. (Under contract to Samuel Goldwyn for much of his career, Toland worked on a number of pictures which were notable for their fine black-and-white photography, including *The Little Foxes*, 1941, and *The Best Years Of Our Lives*, 1946, both distributed by RKO.)

In filming *Citizen Kane* Toland took advantage of new technical advances – faster film stock, improved lighting equipment and specially coated wide-angle lenses. In addition, the production proved to be a model of close collaboration between cameraman, director (Orson Welles) and art director (Perry Ferguson). As noted by Toland, 'The photographic approach to *Citizen Kane* was planned and considered long before the first camera turned. That is unconventional in Hollywood where most cinematographers learn of their next assignments only a few days before the scheduled shooting starts.'

Though Toland was specially brought in (at his own request) to photograph *Citizen Kane*, as was Stanley Cortez for *The Magnificent Ambersons* (1942), the outstanding production design work on both films was accomplished by members of RKO's own art department. In this area RKO could match up to any studio in Hollywood. Perry Ferguson demonstrated a remarkable flair and ingenuity, working within a relatively tight budget on *Citizen Kane*. ('It was he who devised important scenes merely by using a hunk of cornice, a fireplace in the background and a foreground chair. By using such props and Gregg's depth-of-focus lens, Orson could create the illusion of a huge set,' as recalled by head grip Ralph Hoge.) Mark Lee Kirk's achievement in capturing an authentic period atmosphere for *The Magnificent Ambersons* also earned a well-deserved Oscar nomination.

During the classic era of black-and-white studio film-making of the 30s and 40s, RKO's design department, headed by Van Nest Polglase up to 1941 when he was replaced by Albert D'Agostino, represented one of the studio's greatest strengths. As with Cedric Gibbons at MGM, Polglase's name appears on many movies that he didn't work on, but he can be credited with a major role in establishing and maintaining an overall 'look' to RKO's pictures in the 30s. Given a relatively free hand in designing the settings for the highly successful Astaire-Rogers musicals, he and his leading unit art director, Carroll Clark, excelled themselves. Their elegant and spacious all-white interiors and Art Deco designs have never been equalled.

Though *King Kong* (1933) was a special case – the look of the film owed more to special-effects wizard Willis O'Brien than to the RKO art department – the studio's designers can be credited with a remarkable and varied range of productions. They were particularly strong on period movies which ranged from the cheaply produced *The Informer* (1935) to the more lavish *Mary Of Scotland* (1936) and the especially imaginative *The Hunchback Of Notre Dame* (1939).

Van Nest Polglase may be the name most readily connected with the RKO look, but it was the equally important Carroll Clark who spanned the full history of the studio, linking Astaire and Rogers with the last black-and-white thrillers of Fritz Lang in 1955–56 and designing the studio's relatively small number of lavish Technicolor productions, such as *The Spanish Main* (1945) and *Sinbad The Sailor* (1947), along the way.

Other Departments

RKO started out with a strong line-up of technical personnel with many technicians inherited from the Pathé and FBO companies, among them editor Archie Marshek, costume designer Walter Plunkett and lighting cameraman Nicholas Musuraca. In addition, composer Max Steiner was signed up by studio boss William LeBaron and arrived in Hollywood in 1929. First assigned to orchestrate the music for *Rio Rita* (1929), he was soon providing splendid scores for pictures such as *Cimarron* (1931), *King Kong* (1933), and *The Lost Patrol* (1934) which earned the first of his many Oscar nominations. (He won the following year for *The Informer*.)

Widely regarded as the most influential Hollywood composer of the early sound era, Steiner is credited with formulating and applying many of the basic principles of motion-picture scoring. He demonstrated a special genius for integrating his music with the action on screen at a time when most music soundtracks were still in a relatively undeveloped state. Tremendously prolific, he worked on 111 pictures (his own estimate) during his years at RKO from 1929 through to 1935. 'No one really escaped his influence in those days, certainly not I', states Roy Webb who took over from Steiner as the leading composer at RKO. Webb remained at RKO until 1952 as the studio's musical director, joined in the 40s by Constantin Bakaleinikoff, and by Bernard Herrmann who was brought to Hollywood by Orson Welles and won an Oscar for scoring *All That Money Can Buy* (1941).

Another fine artist who contributed to many of RKO's best musicals was dancer and choreographer Hermes Pan. Particularly remembered for his long and fruitful collaboration with Fred Astaire, he was – offscreen – Astaire's real dance partner. Apart from working out routines with Astaire when Rogers was busy with her non-musical films, his are the feet that are heard, dubbed over Ginger's, on the films' soundtracks. He had Oscar nominations in 1935 for the 'Piccolino' and 'Top Hat' routines in *Top Hat* and in 1936 for 'Bojangles' in *Swing Time*, and won an Award for the 'Fun House' number in *A Damsel In Distress* (1937).

Among those many collaborators who first made their names working with Welles were two members of RKO's editing staff, Robert Wise and Mark Robson, both of whom graduated to directing at RKO quite soon after. Wise still refers to the ingenious breakfast sequence showing the decline of the Kane's marriage through a series of dissolves, flash pans and wipes as an example of the kind of creative contribution that an editor can make to the final look of a film. Though the general approach to *Citizen Kane* had been planned in advance, 'it was in the cutting room where it was finally worked out the way it got in the picture . . . The actual rhythm of that whole marvellous sequence, with special assistance from composer Herrmann who also collaborated closely on the final remarkable result.'

RKO's costume department started off in good shape in 1928 with Max Ree, who doubled as an art director, and Walter Plunkett who was to develop into one of the leading costume designers in Hollywood. He made his name at RKO during the 30s, dressing all the studio's major female stars, working on virtually all the Katharine Hepburn pictures and demonstrating a special flair for costume movies. Edward Stevenson arrived in 1936 and became the studio's top costume designer for a dozen years after the departure of Plunkett (who eventually joined MGM). Versatile and prolific, he handled virtually all the studio's A pictures in the 40s, ranging from thrillers and musicals to costumers, in both colour and black-and-white. Last of RKO's big three was Michael Woulfe, RKO's chief costume designer through the entire Hughes era (1949–56), who continued on at the studio after Hughes sold out and remained for 10 years with Desilu Productions designing costumes for Lucille Ball and the 'I Love Lucy' TV show up to his death in 1968, thus becoming the last remaining survivor of the RKO studio.

CAMERAMEN

Alton, John 1940
Andriot, Lucien 1932, 1934–35
August, Joseph 1935–41
Ballard, Lucien 1947–48
Barnes, George 1942–48
Brodine, Norbert (Pathé) 1929
De Grasse, Robert 1935–49
Glennon, Bert 1933
Krasner, Milton 1945–46, 1949
Maté, Rudolph 1942
McCord, Ted (Pathé) 1931–32
Mescall, John (Pathé) 1927–30

Metty, Russell 1934–44
Miller, Arthur (Pathé) 1928–32
Milner, Victor 1945
Mohr, Hal (Pathé) 1931–32
Musuraca, Nicholas (FBO) 1926–28, 1928–54
Rosher, Charles 1932–33
Ruttenberg, Joseph 1933
Stradling Jr, Harry 1940–41
Toland, Gregg 1940–46
Tover, Leo 1929–32

ART DIRECTORS

Basevi, James (Argosy) 1948–50
Berger, Ralph 1944–51
Boyle, Robert 1946–47
Clark, Carroll (Pathé) 1930–31, 1932–56
D'Agostino, Albert 1933–34, 1940–58
Day, Richard (Goldwyn) 1949–51
Fegté, Ernst (Goldwyn) 1944–45
Ferguson, Perry 1933–41, (Goldwyn) 1942–48
Goosson, Stephen (Goldwyn) 1941
Herman, Alfred 1933–52
Herzbrun, Bernard 1939–42

Ihnen, Wiard (Pioneer) 1935–36, 1945–46
Jenkins, George (Goldwyn) 1946–49
Keller, Walter E. 1942–54
Kirk, Charles M. 1933–37
Kirk, Mark-Lee 1940–43
Okey, Jack 1943–53
Oliver, Harry 1935–37
Peters, Hans 1943
Polglase, Van Nest 1932–42, (Bogeaus) 1954–56
Ree, Max 1929–31
Schulze, Jack 1937

COSTUME DESIGNERS

Greer, Howard 1932–33, 1938
King, Muriel 1936, 1944
Newman, Bernard 1934–36
Plunkett, Walter 1929–39
Ree, Max 1929–32
Renie 1936–49

Sharaff, Irene (Goldwyn) 1946–48
Stevenson, Edward 1936–49
Wakeling, Gwen (Pathé) 1927–29,
1930–32
Wills, Mary (Goldwyn) 1949–52
Woulfe, Michael 1949–57

COMPOSERS AND MUSIC DIRECTORS

Bakaleinikoff, Constantin 1941–52
Eisler, Hanns 1944–47
Harline, Leigh 1943–50
Herrmann, Bernard 1941–42
Hollander, Frederick 1949–51

Lange, Arthur 1944–45
Shilkret, Nathaniel 1936–37
Steiner, Max 1930–35
Webb, Roy 1933–52

EDITORS

Amy, George 1950–53
Beetley, Samuel 1946–52
Berman, Henry 1936–41
Crone, George 1934–43
Dawson, Ralph 1945–46
Gerstad, Harry 1946–47
Gilmore, Stuart 1950–56
Gross, Roland 1942–55
Hamilton, William 1931–41
Hilton, Arthur 1937–39
Hively, George 1933–41
Knudtson, Frederic 1933–55
Ludwig, Otto 1952–54
Mandell, Daniel 1930–32, (Goldwyn)
1941–52

Marker, Harry 1937–54
Marquette, Desmond 1935–50
Marshek, Archie 1929–36
Milford, Gene 1943–45
Morley, James 1934–36
Nyby, Christian 1950–52
Robson, Mark 1941–43
Schmidt, Arthur 1934–36
Swink, Robert 1944–51
Todd, Sherman 1947–52
Weatherwax, Paul 1933–34
White, Merrill 1947–49
Williams, Elmo 1946–49
Wise, Robert 1934–43
Wrangell, Basil 1933–34

SCRIPTWRITERS

Bodeen, Dewitt 1942–44, 1947
Fields, Joseph 1931–39
Mainwaring, Daniel 1946–50
Mankiewicz, Herman J. 1940,
1944–48
Murfin, Jane 1929–36
Nichols, Dudley 1935–38, 1943–47
Offner, Mortimer 1934–38

Ornitz, Samuel 1932–33
Paxton, John 1944–47
Scott, Allan 1934–40
Trumbo, Dalton 1938–40
Twist, John 1933–43
Veiller, Anthony 1934–37
Yost, Dorothy 1934–38

The Academy Awards

In its comparatively short life as a major studio, RKO produced a number of interesting, individualistic pictures of high, and often enduring, quality. This is reflected in twelve Academy nominations for Best Picture in the nine-year period from 1933–42. It is all the more surprising, therefore, that only one RKO film, *Cimarron*, ever won the coveted award. The general level of the studio's technical excellence was also acknowledged with many nominations, but few wins. It was RKO's actresses who reaped the richest harvest for the studio, with numerous Academy nominations – and other awards. Only one director, John Ford, ever won an Oscar and actors didn't fare too well either. Nonetheless, *Citizen Kane*, with nine nominations but only a single award, remains recognized as one of the single most influential films ever made.

There are many examples in the history of the Academy Awards of an Oscar going to a new or relatively new face on the movie screen. Luise Rainer and, much later, Barbra Streisand and Audrey Hepburn were encouraged in this way – not that it did much for Rainer, whose career ground to a halt after two successive wins – and similarly the Academy voted the Best Picture award for 1930/31 to RKO for its epic Western, *Cimarron*, the first movie ever nominated from the new studio. The most successful Western of the early sound era, remembered even today for its spectacular land-rush sequence, *Cimarron* was the only Western to win the top prize until *Dances with Wolves* in 1990, just 60 years later.

This award gave a great boost to RKO at the time, since such established studios as Fox and Warner Bros. had yet to win *their* first Best Picture honours. Unfortunately, though, RKO was never again to win in this category, and, thereafter, performed relatively poorly in the annual Oscar stakes considering the orginality and quality of so many of its pictures. Indeed, from 1933 through 1942, 12 RKO productions were nominated for Best Picture. Orson Welles' first two features, the remarkable *Citizen Kane* (1941) and *The Magnificent Ambersons* (1942), for example, were fobbed off with only a single Oscar between them (for

Best Screenplay) though *Kane* at least was nominated in nine different categories. In fact, RKO fared better at the hands of the New York Film Critics who voted *Citizen Kane* their top picture of the year and presented Agnes Moorehead with their best actress award for her performance in *The Magnificent Ambersons*.

The studio's only other Oscar winners of note were *The Best Years of Our Lives* (1946), a Sam Goldwyn production merely distributed by RKO, while *The Informer* (1935) was a quite unexpected success. It won statuettes for director John Ford, actor Victor McLaglen, scriptwriter Dudley Nichols and composer Max Steiner. Though passed over by the Academy for the top award, again the New York Critics disagreed and selected *The Informer* as their top film of the year.

During the course of its relatively brief lifespan RKO did best with its star actresses, one of the few areas in which the studio was able to compete successfully. Ann Harding was nominated for her performance in *Holiday* (1930), and Irene Dunne for both *Cimarron* and *Love Affair* (1939). But RKO's two leading ladies of the 30s were Katharine Hepburn and Ginger Rogers, and this was reflected in the Oscar results. Katharine Hepburn's performance not only contributed to the Best Picture nominations of both *Little Women* (1933) and *Alice Adams*, but gained her the Best Actress award for the touching *Morning Glory* (1933). Similarly, the first two Fred Astaire-Ginger Rogers musicals, *The Gay Divorcee* (1934) and *Top Hat* (1935), were not only immensely popular at the box-office, but gained Best Picture nominations as well, as did *Stage Door* (1937), co-starring Hepburn and Miss Rogers, supported by Lucille Ball, Gail Patrick and Eve Arden, while Miss Rogers finally won an Oscar for her role as *Kitty Foyle* (1940).

Though Joan Fontaine failed to make much impression during her early years at RKO in the 30s, by the time she returned in 1941 to appear in *Suspicion* she was a major star. The combination of Miss Fontaine and Cary Grant directed by Alfred Hitchcock was an obvious winner, and she won both the Best Actress Oscar and the New York Critics Award for her performance. It was a good year for RKO, with *Citizen Kane* and *The Little Foxes* (a Goldwyn production released by RKO) capturing almost 20 nominations between them. Composer Bernard Herrmann, who had arrived at RKO with Orson Welles, was nominated for *Citizen Kane* and won for his inventive and memorable dramatic score for *All That Money Can Buy*.

Strong performances on the distaff side continued to feature in RKO productions with nominations for Ingrid Bergman in *The Bells Of St Mary's* (1945), for Rosalind Russell (*Sister Kenny*, 1946, and *Mourning Becomes Electra*, 1947), Irene Dunne in *I Remember Mama* (1948), Susan Hayward in *My Foolish Heart* (1949) and, going on into the 50s, Jane Wyman in *The Blue Veil* (1951) and Joan Crawford in *Sudden Fear* (1952).

The last RKO actress to win an Oscar was Loretta Young, after studio production chief Dore Schary convinced her that she could master a Swedish accent and would be just right for the part of *Katie For Congress*, later retitled *The Farmer's Daughter* (1947). Note that RKO won this, its last major award, in the year prior to Howard Hughes' takeover of the studio.

From 1931 when scriptwriter Howard Estabrook and art director Max Ree won Academy Awards for *Cimarron*, the quality of RKO's studio personnel was never in doubt. The music department was particularly strong, headed by the hard-working Max Steiner from 1929 through 1935, followed by Roy Webb. Ditto the design department under Van Nest Polglase. Both came together on the Astaire-Rogers musicals in the 30s which were regularly nominated for songs, scores, the art direction of Polglase and Carroll Clark, and the choreography of Hermes Pan, who won his only award for the 'Fun House' number in *A Damsel In Distress* (1937), with Astaire partnered by George Burns and Gracie Allen. Art director nominees in later years included Mark Lee Kirk, Perry Ferguson (for *Citizen Kane*) and Albert D'Agostino, while Constantin Bakaleinikoff and Arthur Lange were most often nominated for their scores. But despite many nominations the talented RKO technical personnel won few Oscars, though a special effects award went to Willis O'Brien for *Mighty Joe Young* in 1949.

For the virulently anti-Communist Hughes there was a special irony in the fact that the very last Oscar won by RKO, in 1956, for the script of the King Bros. production of *The Brave One* was awarded to one Robert Rich, in reality the blacklisted writer Dalton Trumbo.

United Artists, founded in 1919 by three famous stars and a distinguished director, was soon distributing many outstanding pictures. Joseph Schenck came to run UA in 1924 and attracted new stars and major producers. Though UA lost some top stars who failed to succeed in sound movies, this was counterbalanced by the signing of important new producers such as Walt Disney, Darryl F. Zanuck and Alexander Korda. Internal disputes caused the departure of Schenck, Zanuck, Disney – and Samuel Goldwyn; but in spite of this UA released many top-quality features in the 30s before hitting a serious decline in the 40s. A new management team headed by Arthur Krim and Robert Benjamin arrived in 1951 and restored confidence in the company. UA was taken over by the Transamerica Corporation in 1967, and sold again – to MGM – in 1981 and to Pathé as part of the MGM deal in 1990.

The rapid growth of Paramount and First National in the late 'teens, and rumours of a possible deal between these two movie giants early in 1919, posed a serious threat to the many independent stars and producers in Hollywood. Around this same time the idea of a new company controlled by the film-makers themselves was taking shape and was seen by the powerful producer-stars Mary Pickford, Douglas Fairbanks and Charlie Chaplin as the next logical step. Only in this way could they protect their own interests and maintain complete control over the production and distribution of their pictures.

Events moved ahead rapidly in 1919 and by April an agreement was worked out between Pickford, Fairbanks, Chaplin and leading director D. W. Griffith for setting up the new United Artists Corporation. (Western star William S. Hart was meant to join them, but withdrew at the last minute when he received a lucrative new offer from Paramount boss Adolph Zukor.) 'So, the lunatics have taken charge of the asylum', quipped Metro president Richard Rowland on hearing of the formation of the new company. This remark was typical of the sceptical reaction in Hollywood to the idea of a firm run by such a diverse group of artistic types not especially noted for their business sense. There is some confusion over who devised the original plan for the company. Former Paramount publicity chief B. P. Schulberg claimed that he had first suggested it to senior executive Hiram Abrams, who went on to take a top post in the new organization, while Schulberg was shut out.

UA was essentially a distribution company set up to give its founder members greater control over the marketing of their pictures while cutting the costs of distribution. Thus they could retain a larger share of the profits from their own productions, and also share in the profits generated by the new company.

The most pressing problem faced by UA in the early years was a severe shortage of product. Of the four founding partners, only Fairbanks was free to begin producing features for UA immediately. Both Pickford and Chaplin had to complete their First National contracts, while Griffith still owed one feature to Paramount-Artcraft and had just signed a new contract to direct and produce three features for First National. Ironically, he needed the money to meet his commitments to UA and build a new studio (at Mamaroneck, New York). It thus became necessary for the company to turn to other independents such as comedy producer Mack Sennett and actor-producer George Arliss in order to maintain even the barest minimum level of releases needed to sustain the distribution operation. Aiming at 12 features per year, UA released an annual average of 10 during 1920–27 and was struggling to break even throughout this period.

Though UA benefited from the expertise of Hiram Abrams as general manager and then president, who opened new exchanges in the US and abroad to fulfil the company's function as a distributor, it was not able to secure adequate financial backing on the production side. Each of the producers was faced with the problem of financing his/her own pictures. In fact, the four partners had three different studios between them. Mary Pickford and Douglas Fairbanks, who had become the world's most famous married couple in 1920, shared a studio on Santa Monica Boulevard, while Chaplin's was located at La Brea and Sunset Boulevard, and Griffith continued to operate on the East Coast. Griffith's production costs, however, when added to the studio overheads, were so high that by 1924 he was unable to survive as an independent producer. He was the first to fulfil his original commitment to deliver nine features to UA, but most of them lost money, and he left to sign with Zukor at Paramount.

Griffith's departure was a blow, but it was softened later that year when UA struck a new agreement with producer Joseph Schenck. He was persuaded to join UA as a new partner, and to take up the post of chairman of the board with authority to reorganize the company. His arrival came at an opportune time, just as UA was recording a deficit of over $250,000, its largest annual loss thus far. A firm hand was needed to run the company – wielded by someone who had the confidence of the three remaining partners and could also attract new producers of quality, and Schenck fitted the bill.

Schenck brought with him his actress-wife Norma Talmadge, and signed William S. Hart and Rudolph Valentino. In the event, Hart contributed only one picture, the memorable but unprofitable Western epic, *Tumbleweeds* (1925), and Valentino only starred in two features before his sudden death in 1926. Other new arrivals of note were Gloria Swanson, Buster Keaton and independent producer Samuel Goldwyn.

With all this talent lined up and Schenck at the helm, the outlook was bright but progress was slow, and UA continued to lose money. The number of releases did not begin to grow until 1927, but by 1928 the company had moved firmly into profit for the first time.

The years 1928 and 1929 were especially successful for UA, combining the last important group of pictures from the original partners with a useful selection of features from the other independents. Chaplin contributed *The Circus* (1928) while Fairbanks produced and starred in *The Gaucho* (1928) and *The Iron Mask* (1929); in 1929 Mary Pickford starred in the studio's first full talkie, *Coquette*, followed by the Pickford-Fairbanks co-starring, co-production of *The Taming Of The Shrew*. D. W. Griffith returned to UA to direct a few last features for Schenck's Art Cinema Company, but these were disappointing. However, Gloria Swanson starred as a memorable *Sadie Thompson*, Buster Keaton was *Steamboat Bill Jr* (both 1928), and Ronald Colman made his successful sound debut in Goldwyn's *Bulldog Drummond* (1929).

The coming of sound posed special problems for the company.

Three of the four original founders were reaching the end of their careers and only Chaplin would continue to produce and star in the occasional hit picture. Many of the other stars associated with UA, for instance Gloria Swanson, Norma Talmadge and Buster Keaton (who was signed by MGM), were similarly affected. Whereas in the 20s UA had distributed pictures from a wide range of actor-producers, by the early 30s virtually none of them were left. There had been a gradual change in the character of UA, more or less coinciding with the beginning of the talkie era. The company was more dependent than ever before on its big producers, Schenck and Goldwyn, and on a new group that included Howard Hughes, Walt Disney, who was just emerging as Hollywood's leading producer of cartoon shorts, Alexander Korda in Britain and Darryl F. Zanuck. Not surprisingly, this situation led to strains and conflicts between the original partners and the newer producers who were supplying the bulk of the pictures and therefore wished to play a greater role in the actual running of the company.

One of the most fascinating aspects of UA's history concerns the behaviour of those famous personalities who controlled the studio for many years, most notably Charlie Chaplin and Mary Pickford or, more precisely, Charlie Chaplin *versus* Mary Pickford. Chaplin is the one who has been most criticized over the years for his stubborn opposition to enlarging UA or changing the way it was run. In her autobiography Miss Pickford reflects that 'nothing in the world would induce me to live over the agonizing years I experienced with Charlie as a business partner'; Chaplin, on the other hand, was quite astonished at her 'legal and business acumen'. Chaplin retained a special hostility to the giant corporations which dominated the American film industry and was most outspoken in his opposition to possible mergers with MGM or Warner Bros., demonstrating the strongest attachment to the original idea of 'united artists' as a small but successful alternative distributor and a determination to preserve its special character. Undoubtedly a valid attitude in the 20s and early 30s when Chaplin can be credited with vetoing the more questionable plans for expansion devised by Schenck, it became less easy to justify by the late 40s, when the company was in serious trouble.

The fortunes of UA had again declined after 1935 when it lost Joseph Schenck. He had joined with Darryl Zanuck and William Goetz in 1933 to set up 20th Century Pictures, and this new independent company was soon supplying UA with a large proportion of its most successful movies. As a result, a plan was devised to reorganize UA and give a larger role to Zanuck (and Goldwyn), but the scheme fell through at the last moment and Schenck resigned. He joined Zanuck (and 20th Century) in a promising and lucrative venture, a merger with the ailing Fox studio to form the new 20th Century-Fox Film Corporation.

Schenck's departure marked the beginning of a seemingly endless series of management changes and disputes which continued over the following years. Al Lichtman lasted only three months as president, then Mary Pickford, as first vice-president, tried her hand at running the company; she was followed by A. H. Giannini with George Schaefer as general manager. In 1937 yet another scheme was devised whereby Goldwyn and Korda, who were providing the bulk of the UA pictures, could buy out the original partners, but they failed to raise the necessary amount of money in time.

Samuel Goldwyn, however, was still determined to play a larger role in the running of the company and insisted that his man, Murray Silverstone, be engaged as general manager in 1938. Giannini immediately left, followed by vice-president George Schaefer who was soon to make his name as the new president of RKO. Though changes were made in the way the company operated, Goldwyn remained dissatisfied. He sued to end his contract early in 1939, and the dispute dragged on for two long years before it was finally settled.

In spite of these problems and the loss of Disney (who signed with RKO in 1936), UA was able to attract a number of other leading producers who maintained the quality of its releases throughout this period. David O. Selznick had left MGM to set up his own independent company in 1935 and he immediately signed an eight-picture deal with UA. Similarly, Walter Wanger accepted an attractive offer to begin producing for UA in 1936, while producer Hal Roach arrived in 1938. In addition, there were a number of other producers, such as Edward Small and Herbert Wilcox in Britain, supplying UA with movies to fill out its release schedule.

As an indication of the high standard of UA productions, no less than eight were nominated for the Academy's Best Picture Award in 1939/40, with Selznick's production of *Rebecca* winning in 1940. Unfortunately, these pictures represented the final flowering of UA's peak years. Sam Goldwyn left the company early in 1941, following Disney and George Schaefer to RKO – the one major studio demonstrating the greatest willingness to accommodate independent producers. David Selznick failed to produce a single movie for UA during 1941–43 and his Vanguard Films, supposedly set up to develop projects for UA (with Dore Schary at the helm), was more active in co-producing with RKO (though Selznick and Vanguard did provide UA with two of its biggest 40s hits, *Since You Went Away*, 1944, and *Spellbound*, directed by Hitchcock in 1945).

Walter Wanger left UA in 1941, followed by Korda in 1942, and Selznick's 10-year association with the studio came to an acrimonious end in 1946. His dispute with the company over his latest production, *Duel In The Sun*, was but the last in a series of disagreements which he had had with his UA partners over the years. Though he had supplied many quality pictures, Selznick had never demonstrated much of a commitment to the company, as reflected most clearly in his apparent lack of interest in helping to run UA in the 40s when the opportunity had been offered to him.

It thus became necessary for UA to turn to a new group of producers in the 40s. A generally solid but undistinguished lot, the new arrivals included Sol Lesser, David Loew, Hunt Stromberg, Benedict Bogeaus, and Seymour Nebenzal, while Hal Roach turned to cheaply produced featurettes or 'streamliners' in place of the quality features he had been making in his early years at UA. The studio even distributed numerous cheap Westerns and Hopalong Cassidy movies for Paramount in order to fill out its schedule.

Profits had been declining ever since the mid-30s and, with its clear lack of popular or quality releases, UA became the only major studio to record a loss for one of the booming war years. That was in 1944, and by 1948 the company was recording annual losses as a matter of course. It was close to collapse in 1950 when a new management team headed by Paul McNutt was brought in, but made little progress in its efforts to turn the company around. Finally, in 1951, McNutt turned to a more experienced group headed by Arthur Krim and Robert Benjamin. They succeeded where McNutt, and others before him, had failed, because they recognized the need for a more radical change in company policy. Rather than merely serving as a distributor for the benefit of independent producers, henceforth UA would participate more fully in the financing of projects and would share in the profits of successful pictures. With financial backing of $3.5 million from Chicago financier Walter Heller and a $500,000 loan from 20th Century-Fox's president Spyros P. Skouras, who was reluctant to see UA collapse, the company gained a new lease of life. And UA's future was assured by a pair of smash hits – *The African Queen* (1951) and *High Noon* (1952) – which helped the company back into profit in 1951 and 1952.

According to the terms of the original agreement, Krim and Benjamin and their associates only owned 50% of the UA stock. In 1955, they were able to buy out Chaplin, and then Mary Pickford in 1956, and went public the following year with a first sale of shares to the general public. Under Krim and Benjamin UA developed a reputation for encouraging the best of Hollywood's independent producers, especially actor-producers John Wayne (with his Batjac Company), Burt Lancaster (Hecht-Hill-Lancaster) and Kirk Douglas (Bryna Productions), recalling UA's many actor-producers in the early days. As Robert Stanley noted, 'UA's policy of trusting talent to make their own films with a minimum of front-office interference encouraged directors like Otto Preminger, Billy Wilder, Joseph Mankiewicz and William Wyler to release their films under the UA banner.'

UA profits continued to grow throughout the 50s and early 60s, and the studio won more than its share of Oscars and other awards. Such continuing success meant that UA came to be closely identified with Krim and Benjamin and was able to preserve a remarkable continuity of management during a period when most of the other large studios were going through many disruptive changes. Even when UA was taken over in 1967 by Transamerica, a financial services and insurance conglomerate, Krim and Benjamin remained in charge.

Unfortunately, UA experienced a few bad years in the early 70s which strained relations between Transamerica and the UA management. Though the company rapidly recovered and continued to perform well, Transamerica imposed various constraints on the UA management which were a continuing source of irritation. In an attempt to regain their autonomy, Krim and Benjamin proposed to spin off UA from Transamerica. But when their plans were rejected, they resigned (in January 1978) and set up a new independent company, Orion Pictures.

A new management team headed by Andy Albeck and Steven Bach faced the daunting task of restoring the company's credibility. But though UA's prestige had suffered a severe blow it continued to do reasonably well, with profits during most of 1978–80 continuing at the same healthy level as 1977. Unfortunately, the company's new and relatively inexperienced bosses failed to control the escalating costs of Michael Cimino's epic Western, *Heaven's Gate* (1980), and UA was faced with the most expensive flop in its history. The disastrous failure of the picture thus confirmed all Transamerica's worst fears regarding the uncertainties of the movie business, and it decided to sell the company to Kirk Kerkorian and MGM in 1981 for $380 million.

In a series of management changes, Albeck and Bach had been replaced by Norbert Auerbach who was replaced in turn by David Begelman, transferred from his post as head of MGM. But Begelman, too, lasted less than a year before he was dismissed in 1982 – shortly before the publication of the book, 'Indecent Exposure', in which his involvement in a notorious embezzlement scandal (revealed by actor Cliff Robertson) at Columbia in the late 70s was examined in great detail. Clearly the MGM/UA partnership was not very successful, and in a complicated deal with TV mogul Ted Turner, the companies were sold and then repurchased in 1986.

In spite of continual changes in ownership and management, and the serious disruptions during 1985 and 1986, UA attempted yet another fresh start late in 1986 led by Tony Thomopoulos (chairman and chief operating officer), Robert Lawrence (president), and Dean Stolber (executive vice-president) – lone survivor of the 70s. But this too proved short-lived. In the summer of 1988 MGM/UA chairman Lee Rich resigned, followed by Thomopoulos, and owner Kirk Kerkorian resumed his deal making. Ironically, around this same time UA had the biggest hit in its history with *Rain Man*. The sale of UA to the Australian Qintex group in 1989 fell through, but was followed by a similar deal with Italian mogul Giancarlo Parretti's Pathé Communications who took over in 1990.

United Artists had struggled throughout the decade, and in spite of the success of *Rain Man*, by the late 80s had virtually reached the end of its life as a viable film company, surviving as little more than a famous name, and that too appears to have faded away as a result of the latest takeover. For, although Parretti's acquisition meant that Pathé was now the parent company of MGM/UA, in fact, the new studio was generally referred to as MGM/Pathé. In 1991, 72 years after its formation, United Artists appears to be finished, bringing to a close a fascinating chapter in the history of Hollywood.

United Artists Studio Chronology
1919 Formation of the company by Charles Chaplin, Mary Pickford, Douglas Fairbanks and director D. W. Griffith.

1924   Griffith leaves. Joseph Schenck brought in as a new partner and chairman of the board, with authority to reorganize the company.

1925   Producer Samuel Goldwyn joins the company.

1926   Schenck takes the post of president after the death of Hiram Abrams who had served as president since 1920.

1928   A profit of $1.6 million is recorded – the highest to date, and not to be surpassed until the 50s.

1931   Cartoon producer Walt Disney signs a distribution deal.

1933   Leading British producer Alexander Korda signed up.
Schenck joins with Darryl F. Zanuck to form 20th Century Pictures.

1935   Schenck resigns. He and Zanuck (and 20th) merge with Fox to form 20th Century-Fox.
David O. Selznick signs with the company.

1937   Disney pulls out to take up a better offer from RKO.

1940   The company wins its first Best Picture Oscar for Selznick's production of *Rebecca* directed by Alfred Hitchcock.
Goldwyn leaves and signs with RKO.

1946   Selznick leaves to set up his own distribution company.

1951   Arthur Krim and Robert Benjamin take over the management of UA and set about reorganizing the company.

1955   The Hecht-Hill-Lancaster production of *Marty* wins the Best Picture Oscar. It is the first of many wins over the next 23 years.

1967   The Transamerica Corporation, an insurance and financial services conglomerate, takes over the company.

1970   A record loss of $45 million is registered.

1973   The company agrees to serve as distributor for MGM in the US.

1978   Krim and Benjamin and their associates leave to form Orion Pictures, a new independent company releasing through Warner Bros.

1980   The $40 million *Heaven's Gate* flops at the box-office.

1981   A loss of $11 million in the first half of the year is recorded and Transamerica sells the company to Kirk Kerkorian and MGM. He sets up the new MGM/UA Entertainment Company.

1985/1986   TV and cable mogul Ted Turner buys both companies, and sells first UA and next MGM back to Kerkorian while retaining the film and TV libraries. The reorganized and slimmed down studio is renamed the MGM/UA Communications Company.

1988   UA wins the Oscar for Best Picture for a record twelfth time with *Rain Man*, the biggest hit in the company's history.

1990   Having lost much of its identity during the 80s, UA virtually reaches the end when Italian financier Giancarlo Parretti of Pathé buys MGM/UA and renames it MGM/Pathé.

The Releases

The range of UA pictures was limited by the fact that it distributed a relatively small number of features in comparison with the other major studios, and decisions regarding the type of picture were made by the various individual producers. Though the company suffered from a shortage of product, the numbers rose steadily from an average of only 10 features per year initially to 20 by the late 30s. The higher total in the 40s included a substantial number of B Westerns and comedies, but during the peak years of the 30s UA distributed a remarkably large selection of historical biopics, costumers and literary adaptations of quality, the kind of prestige productions favoured by the leading producers. The company's early interest in colour was reflected in *The Black Pirate* (1927) starring Douglas Fairbanks, and Sam Goldwyn's production of *Whoopee!* (1930), both filmed in two-strip Technicolor. David O. Selznick was UA's leading Technicolor producer in the 30s, but some of the most interesting examples came from Britain, for example Korda's *The Four Feathers* (1939) and *The Life And Death Of Colonel Blimp* (1943) from Michael Powell and Emeric Pressburger. UA was slow to increase its investment in colour and in the new technical processes in the 50s, but had a big success with the first 3-D feature, *Bwana Devil* (1952), and with Mike Todd's *Around The World In 80 Days* (1956) filmed in Todd-AO.

Since UA was not a production company, it never set out to distribute pictures of any particular type and the choice of subjects was made by the various independent producers. This could have been a problem early on, with both Chaplin and Fairbanks known for their comedies, Mary Pickford mixing comedy and serious roles, and only D. W. Griffith providing dramatic pictures. Though the others continued in the same vein, it was Douglas Fairbanks who broadened the range and appeal of UA features by switching from comedy roles to costumers and swashbucklers which were tremendously popular. He began with *The Mark Of Zorro* (1920), followed by *The Three Musketeers* (1921), and then *Robin Hood* (1922), the most elaborate, expensive and successful of all. He was the first UA star effectively to dominate a particular genre, and such was his success that the other Hollywood studios rushed to get in on the act. (Metro had Ramon Novarro as *The Prisoner Of Zenda*, 1922, and *Scaramouche*, 1923, while Fox starred Tom Mix as *Dick Turpin* in 1925 and John Barrymore made a memorable *Don Juan* at Warner Bros. in 1926, but none of them could match the inimitable Doug.)

With a variety of contributions from many different producers UA was able to maintain a balanced mixture of comedies, dramas and costumers during the 20s, with the occasional venture into fantasy (Fairbanks as *The Thief Of Bagdad*, 1924), Westerns (William S. Hart in *Tumbleweeds*, 1925), and thrillers (*The Bat*, 1926, produced by Roland West). But the main problem was the shortage of quality features. From 1922 on, the preparation and care lavished on their pictures by Doug and Mary meant that they each produced only one feature per year, while Chaplin averaged one every three years and D. W. Griffith left the company in 1924. Thus, UA released an average of only 10 movies per year in the period up to 1926. With Joe Schenck in charge the numbers rose during 1927–28, reaching an average of 15 per year in 1929–33. They rose again to the point where UA was distributing 20 features per year during 1934–41, boosted initially by the output of Zanuck's 20th Century and maintained through the 30s by Goldwyn, Selznick and Wanger as well as a large number of interesting British films from Alexander Korda and Herbert Wilcox, among others.

At the same time UA came to be identified most closely with the well-crafted, well-acted and prestigious literary adaptation which was popular in the 30s. This choice of picture represented a kind of common denominator, most often favoured by, and providing a link between, many of the company's leading producers. Thus, plays adapted to the screen ranged from *The Front Page, Street Scene* (both 1931), and *Rain* (1932), to *These Three* (1936, from Lillian Hellman's 'The Children's Hour'), *Dodsworth* (both 1936), *Dead End* (1937), *The Long Voyage Home* (1940) and *Major Barbara* (1941). The many well-known novels which served as the source for UA movies in the 30s included *Arrowsmith* (1931), *Nana* (1934), *Les Miserables, The Scarlet Pimpernel* and *The Call Of The Wild* (all 1935), *Little Lord Fauntleroy* (1936), *Stella Dallas* and *The Prisoner Of Zenda* (both 1937), *The Adventures Of Tom Sawyer* (1938), *Wuthering Heights* and *Of Mice And Men* (both 1939), and *Rebecca* (1940). In addition, UA appears to have had a special attraction to historical figures of many different epochs and nationalities ranging from Abraham Lincoln, Henry VIII, Cellini and P. T. Barnum, to Clive of India, Rembrandt, the Rothschilds, Cardinal Richelieu and Marco Polo. The only ladies similarly honoured were Catherine the Great played by Elisabeth Bergner, and Lady Hamilton, portrayed by Vivien Leigh opposite Olivier's Lord Nelson.

UA did not pretend to cover the same wide range of subjects as the larger Hollywood studios. There were no horror films, for example, though Korda attempted a pair of science-fiction adaptations from H. G. Wells, *Things To Come* (1936) and *The Man Who Could Work Miracles* (1937). There was one outstanding contribution to the early 30s gangster cycle, Howard Hughes' production of *Scarface* (1932), directed by Howard Hawks, and one equally memorable thriller, Fritz Lang's *You Only Live Once* (1937), a Walter Wanger production. The Topper pictures, inspired by a Thorne Smith novel, were a series of sophisticated ghost stories blending comedy and fantasy with engaging performances from Roland Young as a stuffy banker and Billie Burke as his wife – while Constance Bennett, Cary Grant and Joan Blondell played amiable ghosts in different entries in the series. In addition, Selznick signed Fredric March and borrowed Carole Lombard from Paramount to star in UA's most delightful 30s screwball comedy, *Nothing Sacred* (1937). Surprisingly, the number of musicals, at a time when the other studios were churning them out, was relatively small. Most successful were those starring Eddie Cantor and produced by Sam Goldwyn. Though there were few Westerns, UA played a role in the late 30s revival as the distributor of John Ford's *Stagecoach* (Walter Wanger, 1939), followed by *The Westerner* (Goldwyn, 1940) and Howard Hughes' *The Outlaw*, filmed in 1941 but not released till a few years later.

With the loss of many of the company's top producers in the 40s, there was an overall decline in the quality of UA releases, although the output continued to rise slightly. There were large numbers of B pictures, especially cheap comedies, Westerns and musicals, balanced by a relatively small number of prestige productions. The shortage of quality product was more acute than ever before, while the general mixture was not very different from that of other small studios and reflected the extent to which UA had lost something of its special character. (The company even purchased a package of features from Paramount, mainly 21 Hopalong Cassidy Westerns, which filled out its schedule, but with a delightful 1942 René Clair comedy, *I Married A Witch*, surprisingly included as well.)

Among the most memorable UA releases of the decade there were three outstanding thrillers from Alfred Hitchcock – *Rebecca* and *Foreign Correspondent* (both 1940) and *Spellbound* (1945), Ernst Lubitsch's last great comedy, *To Be Or Not To Be* (1942), and a pair of satires from Charlie Chaplin who finally shed his famous tramp image – to good effect in *The Great Dictator* (1940), but less successfully with *Monsieur Verdoux* (1947). Veteran Howard Hawks produced and directed a classic Western for UA in *Red River* (1948), while producer Stanley Kramer came up with two hard-hitting dramas, *Champion* and *Home Of The Brave* (both 1949). There were also several outstanding British productions in both black-and-white and colour from directors David Lean, Powell and Pressburger, and Laurence Olivier who also starred as *Henry V* (1945).

After Arthur Krim and Robert Benjamin took over in 1951 and began to make deals with a variety of independent producers, the general quality (and profitability) of UA features began to improve once again. But at the same time UA became more like a mainstream Hollywood company than ever before, not least because the others were endeavouring to cut back on their overheads by shedding contract stars and production studios, and began competing with UA to sign up the leading independents. Ironically, as UA grew and prospered in the course of the 50s, it came to look less like a small maverick company and more like an industry leader. Though the range of quality pictures matched those of the other companies at a time when colour and the larger and wider screen were becoming the norm, its continuing commitment to the small, black-and-white picture recalled the UA of old. The best-known examples included *High Noon* (1952), the Oscar-winning *Marty* (1955), *Twelve Angry Men* (1957), and *Witness For The Prosecution* (1957) and *Some Like It Hot* (1959), both directed by Billy Wilder; also the early features of Stanley Kubrick, and an especially memorable run of thrillers and gangsters films from *Gun Crazy* (1950) and *The Prowler* (1951) to *Kiss Me Deadly* and *Night Of The Hunter* (both 1955), as well as *Sweet Smell Of Success* and *Baby Face Nelson* released in 1957.

Colour and Widescreen

Not surprisingly, the first UA producer to begin filming in colour was Douglas Fairbanks. He realized that colour would enhance the look of his costume pictures, and the result was *The Black Pirate*, the first two-strip Technicolor feature to be widely distributed and gain a measure of popular success. Unfortunately, it was rather stodgily directed by Albert Parker, but the colour is lovely and the film includes the most famous and magical of all the Fairbanks stunts: at one point he plunges his dagger into a sail and makes a rapid descent, holding tight to the handle as the blade slices its way down to the deck below.

The next UA producer to become interested in colour was Sam Goldwyn. During the peak years of 1929 and 1930 Technicolor was used in many movie musicals and, not to be outdone by the other studios, Goldwyn decided to take on the added cost for introducing his new musical star, Eddie Cantor. Unimaginatively adapted from the Ziegfeld show of the same name, *Whoopee!* (1930) cost all of $1.3 million, but was a tremendous hit. It is best remembered for a few nice colour effects and the kaleidoscopic dance patterns devised by Busby Berkeley, here working in the cinema for the first time.

Far more interesting, however, was Goldwyn's next use of colour four years later in another Cantor vehicle, *Kid Millions* (1934). Though a few other producers had already experimented with introducing three-strip Technicolor sequences, the Goldwyn picture was special. Art director William Pogany was brought in to design a giant set with outsize props for the final, Technicolored reel set in an ice-cream factory. The result turned out to be a veritable masterpiece of pastel-coloured 'pop art' – long before the term was invented.

Three years later (1937), Goldwyn embarked on his first Technicolored feature, sparing no expense to hire a great assortment of talents including writer Ben Hecht and choreographer George Balanchine, with songs from the Gershwins and Gregg Toland behind the camera. But there was a notable lack of stars, and the cast of *The Goldwyn Follies*, headed by Adolphe Menjou, Andrea Leeds and Vera Zorina, could do little with the feeble script. The $2 million production was a major disappointment, as was Walter Wanger's sole venture into colour for UA around the same time, *Vogues Of 1938*. Blending a fashion theme with the story of a producer's struggles to mount his Broadway show, the picture cost $1.4 million to little effect other than the stunning selection of 30s fashions designed by Omar Kiam and Irene.

Yet another producer, David O. Selznick, came unstuck with his first Technicolored feature for UA. He surprisingly chose to remake from a rather old-fashioned Robert Hichens novel, *The Garden Of Allah*, with an international cast sporting an extraordinary multiplicity of accents – Marlene Dietrich's was German, Charles Boyer's heavily French, while Joseph Schildkraut favoured thick Russian-Jewish and the director in charge of it all was the Polish-born Richard Boleslawski. All in all, the completed film was more memorable for its beautifully subtle and low-keyed colour photography than for its plot or acting.

When he had first set up his independent production company with backing from Jock Whitney, among others, Selznick had agreed to take over the commitment of Pioneer Pictures to continue producing Technicolored features in the late 30s. Though *The Garden of Allah* (1936) was unsuccessful, he did better with *A Star Is Born* and *Nothing Sacred*, both released in 1937, and both demonstrating the importance of a strong cast and intelligent script – ingredients which tended to be neglected in many of the early colour films. Clearly, Technicolor alone could not attract the movie audiences.

After the completion of *The Goldwyn Follies* and Selznick's *The Adventures Of Tom Sawyer* late in 1937, UA's early involvement in colour filming in the USA came to an abrupt end. Rather, it was the company's British producers who supplied many excellent Technicolored features in the coming years, beginning with Alexander Korda. *The Four Feathers* (1939), starring Ralph Richardson and John Clements, was a witty and dramatic adventure film which stands as one of the very best colour productions of the 30s. Korda's young Indian star discovery, Sabu, appeared in both *The Thief Of Bagdad* (1940) and *The Jungle Book* (1942), but the best British colour movies of the 40s came from UA's short-lived agreement with the production-distribution-exhibition company J. Arthur Rank. These included the remarkable Powell-Pressburger production, *The Life And Death Of Colonel Blimp* (1943), their first in colour, followed by Laurence Olivier's entertaining and colourful adaptation of *Henry V* (1945), while *Blithe Spirit* (1945) was a delightful domestic comedy with a fantasy theme and the added bonus of a witty use of colour. (UA also distributed the overly long and tedious Gabriel Pascal film of Shaw's *Caesar And Cleopatra*, 1946, which did surprisingly well at the American box-office.)

UA's return to solvency in the early 50s was linked with a number of colour pictures which had been filmed abroad – *The African Queen* (1951) and *Moulin Rouge* (1952), both directed by John Huston, and Arch Oboler's *Bwana Devil* (1952). This cheaply produced movie, filmed on location in Africa in Ansco Colour and Natural Vision 3-D, was so successful, with rentals of $2.7 million, that it sparked off a vogue for 3-D movies in America.

In spite of the success of these films, UA was very slow to increase its investment in colour filming or in the various new processes, and only a small number of its pictures were photographed in CinemaScope in the 50s or in Panavision in the 60s. The company did back producer Mike Todd, who shot his epic production of *Around The World In 80 Days* (1956) in the newly developed Todd-AO process, but they remained wary of the high cost of 70mm filming. It was a struggle to merely break even on such expensive ventures as King Vidor's *Solomon And Sheba* (1959) filmed in Technirama and the Todd-AO production of *The Alamo* (1960), produced, directed by and starring John Wayne, and UA's luck really ran out with *The Greatest Story Ever Told* (1965), a Biblical epic that was a costly and disastrous flop. However, on a more positive note, three of the company's biggest hits of the early 60s were filmed in the new 70mm Panavision – Otto Preminger's *Exodus* (1960), the Robert Wise-Jerome Robbins-Mirisch Company production of *West Side Story* (1961) and Stanley Kramer's *It's A Mad, Mad, Mad, Mad World* (1963).

Widescreen and 3-D Releases 1952–69

Process	1952	1953	1954	1955	1956	1957	1958	1959	1960	1961	1962	1963	1964	1965	1966	1967	1968	1969
CinemaScope			1	3	9	2b	1	3b										
Technirama					1	1	3	2										
Panavision								1	3	3	7	7	5	7	7	5	5	8
Techniscope													2	3	1	5	3	1
SuperScope			1	1	1													
Large format (70mm)					1				2	1		1		2	1		1	
3-D	1	2	2															

b includes one Vista Vision

The Finances

United Artists struggled to break even in the early years.
Joseph Schenck was appointed chairman late in 1924,
and by 1928–29 the company was recording its best
ever profits. Though UA rarely fell into the red in the
30s, profits were generally quite small. Revenues grew
in the late 30s and on into the 40s but so did costs and
overheads, so that, during a period when virtually all
the other studios were chalking up record profits, those
of UA remained tiny. Once the company fell seriously
into the red in the late 40s, there appeared to be no way
out. Then, in 1951, Arthur Krim and Robert Benjamin
arrived. With substantial financial backing and a new
policy of direct investment in the productions of leading
independents, they succeeded in rescuing the situation.
UA's revenues and profits continued to grow throughout
the 50s and most of the 60s, attracting the interest of the
Transamerica Corporation which took over the company
in 1967. In spite of a poor performance during 1969 and
1970, the company did well in the 70s, but was hurt by
the departure of Krim and Benjamin in 1978 and the
failure of *Heaven's Gate* in 1980. Transamerica sold UA to
Kirk Kerkorian and MGM in 1981 and the company has
continued to struggle ever since, though it had one smash
hit with *Rain Man* in 1988.

United Artists made a promising start, achieving a modest hit with its
first release *His Majesty, The American*, starring Douglas Fairbanks, in
the autumn of 1919. It then did surprisingly well with D. W. Griffith's
darkly atmospheric *Broken Blossoms* (1919) which he had produced
extremely cheaply. Though it soon became evident that the company
did not have enough pictures to distribute, the general standard was
quite high and the big earners were spread throughout the 20s.

In 1921 the company broke even, benefiting from D. W. Griffith's biggest 20s hit, *Way Down East*, while the earnings of Fairbanks' *The Three Musketeers* and Mary Pickford as *Little Lord Fauntleroy*, released late in the year, carried over into 1922. A spectacular and expensive ($1.5 million) production of *Robin Hood*, starring Fairbanks in one of his favourite costume roles, helped UA to earn a small profit in 1923; but in 1924 and 1925 the company recorded losses – in spite of the success of Fairbanks again as *The Thief Of Bagdad* (1924) and the tremendous box-office appeal of *The Gold Rush* (1925), Charlie Chaplin's first starring feature for UA. On a more morbid note, the company profited from the death of Valentino in 1926 which greatly boosted revenues from the posthumous release of his last feature, *The Son Of The Sheik*, helping UA to move back into the black once again.

Joseph Schenck had joined the company late in 1924, and by 1926–27 his policies were having some effect with the appearance of the first features from Sam Goldwyn, Buster Keaton, Gloria Swanson, and his own Art Cinema Corporation. In addition Schenck initiated the United Artists Theater Circuit in 1926 – a move towards fighting back against the giant companies by acquiring first-run cinemas of its own or going into partnership when it could not buy them outright.

Though UA released more pictures in 1927 than ever before, the results were disappointing. There was only one feature from the original partners – *My Best Girl* – which proved once again that Mary Pickford's fans were not enthusiastic about her appearance in grown-up roles. (Most of Pickford's pictures were profitable and, though not as spectacularly successful as the Fairbanks and Chaplin productions, they also cost far less.) Most disappointing of all, the rentals from Buster Keaton's masterpiece, *The General*, failed to cover the costs of this, his most expensive feature. Yet at $500,000 it was hardly in the lavish Fairbanks class. In fact, Keaton's UA features brought in less at the box-office than his earlier Metro and MGM productions, suggesting that the company was still having problems in getting lucrative first-run showings for its features.

UA recorded the worst loss of its early history in 1927, but finally managed the big breakthrough in the following year. Income virtually doubled to just over $20 million and the profit was the highest thus far – $1.6 million – as a result of such hits as Chaplin's *The Circus*, Fairbanks in *The Gaucho* and Gloria Swanson giving one of her best-ever performances as *Sadie Thompson*. Clearly UA had finally turned the corner financially and, from this point on, though profits generally remained small, the company did stay in the black virtually every year till the late 40s.

With its high overheads and relatively small number of releases, UA had to struggle to stay in profit. Since it functioned mainly as a distributor, if a picture did poorly the company stood to lose money, and if it did really well most of the profits went to the original producer. The fact that UA continued reasonably successful year after year proved that it was possible to compete in Hollywood on a small scale with a large proportion of quality pictures, each handled individually rather than produced and distributed on an assembly-line basis.

Though UA producers took the largest share of any profits, they had problems too. Since the company did not provide financing (except in a few, exceptional cases), and merely loaned money to producers in the form of advances against the rental fees of pictures already in distribution, each producer was very much on his or her own, having to finance often quite expensive and risky productions. The Chaplin features and Fairbanks costumers tended to be costly, while Griffith was finally forced to give up his independence and leave UA because his pictures were not profitable enough to cover his costs.

From 1928 to 1937, UA experienced a cycle similar to, but less extreme than, that of the other leading Hollywood studios. Healthy profits during 1928–31 were followed by a decline in 1932 and 1933, but the company bounced back strongly and had two of its best years in 1934 and 1935 with profits well over the $1 million mark. This reflects the special contribution made by Darryl Zanuck's 20th Century Pictures. Thus, the loss of Zanuck in 1935 was a major blow, as was the departure of Disney in 1937. Chaplin, the lone survivor of the original group as actor-producer contributed two hits, but the most consistently successful producer by far was Sam Goldwyn who did equally well at the box-office with Eddie Cantor musicals such as *Whoopee!* (1930) and *The Kid From Spain* (1932) as with his more serious dramatic pictures, including *Dodsworth* (1936) and *Dead End* (1937), both directed by William Wyler.

Goldwyn's productions were generally less profitable in the late 30s, however, at about the same time that producer Alexander Korda was experiencing serious financial difficulties in England, while many of the pictures from Walter Wanger were more expensive and performed less well than expected. The net result was that, at a time when the US film industry was growing, UA was performing comparatively poorly from a financial standpoint, in spite of the outstanding quality of so many of its releases. Revenues were at a new peak level during 1937–39, but costs and overheads had grown rapidly which meant that profits were relatively small.

With the outbreak of war in Europe, UA's overseas earnings declined rapidly but, whereas most of the other Hollywood studios soon experienced a compensating growth and were able to take advantage of the boom in America's moviegoing, UA continued to do poorly. Its profits had been on a downward spiral ever since the peak years of 1934–35, reaching the dismally low level of $120,000 per year during 1941–42. Then, surprisingly, the company had a good year in 1943 when profits topped the $1 million mark, boosted by the unexpected success of *Lady Of Burlesque*, produced by Hunt Stromberg and starring Barbara Stanwyck, and the Noel Coward-David Lean stirringly patriotic tribute to the British navy, *In Which We Serve*, starring Coward himself.

The company's ups and downs continued throughout the rest of the decade. UA fell into the red in 1944 for the first time since 1932, then recovered during 1945–47 aided by the box-office success of Selznick's last UA production, *Spellbound* (1945) directed by Alfred Hitchcock, and the notorious Howard Hughes Western, *The Outlaw*.

The latter had been completed in 1941, but its release in 1943 had been complicated by a dispute with the Breen Office which administered the Production Code's censorship regulations and UA benefited from the first widespread showings of the film in 1946.

In the late 40s, however, UA was back in the red again, and this time it was really serious. The company was in terrible shape, with no solution in sight, when a new management team headed by Arthur Krim and Robert Benjamin took over in 1951 and set about reorganizing the company. With substantial financial backing behind them, they were in a good position to begin investing in new projects. They made a special effort to restore UA's credibility as an efficiently run company sympathetic to the needs of independent producers, and soon succeeded in attracting many independent film-makers of note.

The company moved back into profit surprisingly quickly, helped by three hits in a row in 1951–52 – *The African Queen* and *Moulin Rouge* from director John Huston and, in between, Stanley Kramer's production of *High Noon*. (Kramer had represented one of the few bright spots at UA around this time, providing the company with its only successes in 1949, *Home Of The Brave* and *Champion*, and in 1950 with *Cyrano De Bergerac*.) During the following years UA enjoyed a steady run of hits which continued on into the early 60s, while revenues and profits also grew year by year. The biggest contributions came from Burt Lancaster, producer-star of *Vera Cruz* (1954) and *Trapeze* (1956) and Oscar-winner for *Elmer Gantry* (1960), and Stanley Kramer, producer turned producer-director with *Not As A Stranger* (1955), *On The Beach* (1959) and *It's A Mad, Mad, Mad, Mad World* (1963). Otto Preminger had a surprise hit with *The Moon Is Blue* (1953), a modest and cheaply produced little black-and-white comedy which benefited from the notoriety surrounding its release without the Production Code seal of approval (the word 'virgin' was mentioned), and succeeded with his epic treatment of the founding of Israel in *Exodus* (1960). But UA's most spectacular success of the decade came from showman-producer Mike Todd who had the ingenious idea of assembling an all-star cast, mostly appearing in tiny cameo roles, for his *Around The World In 80 Days* (1956). It chalked up domestic rentals of $22 million which placed it among the very top hits of the 50s, in third spot behind MGM's *Ben-Hur* (1959), directed by William Wyler, and Cecil B. DeMille's *The Ten Commandments* (Paramount, 1956).

UA continued to do well throughout most of the 60s, too, with a combination of many profitable British productions and a series of hits from the tremendously successful Mirisch company. Top of the Mirisch hit list was *West Side Story* (1961), along with a pair of Billy Wilder films, *The Apartment* (1960) and *Irma La Douce* (1963) both starring Jack Lemmon and Shirley Maclaine. The British list was headed by the enormously lucrative James Bond series which continued on into the 70s and 80s, while *Tom Jones* (1963) was a surprise Oscar winner and smash hit.

In fact, UA had only one really bad year in the early 60s. It recorded a small loss in 1963 due to the escalating expense of the George

Stevens epic, *The Greatest Story Ever Told*, one of the few costume epics of the period to be filmed in the USA where the costs were substantially higher than in Europe. It ended up costing $20 million and earned back only a fraction of that amount. Thus, if inflation is taken into account, this picture could rival the notorious *Heaven's Gate* (1980) as the most disastrous flop in United Artists' history.

Attracted by UA's steady record of earnings over the years, the giant Transamerica Corporation took over the company in 1967 – in time to share in the movie industry crisis of the late 60s and early 70s. Like most of the other majors, UA had a number of expensive flops, including *Chitty Chitty Bang Bang* (1968) and Billy Wilder's *The Private Life of Sherlock Holmes* (1970), both costing about $10 million, and the $12 million *Battle Of Britain* (1969). All three were British productions, and thus had the immediate effect of drastically reducing UA's substantial investment in that country's movie industry.

In the 70s UA was boosted by three series in particular – the ever reliable James Bond, the Pink Panther movies produced and directed by Blake Edwards and starring Peter Sellers, and the Rocky pictures, written by and starring Sylvester Stallone who also directed the later entries. But the biggest individual hit was *One Flew Over The Cuckoo's Nest* (1975) with US rentals of about $60 million, hardly spectacular in the era of the Steven Spielberg-George Lucas mega-hits which gave a tremendous boost to the earnings of a number of other studios. With small but steady profits year after year, UA was obviously vulnerable to the disastrous failure of *Heaven's Gate* which pushed the company into the red in 1981 for the first time since 1970 and led Transmerica to unload the company to Kirk Kerkorian and MGM.

During more recent years United Artists has obviously been struggling. It has had few box office successes and in the late 80s even its two most dependable series, based on the exploits of James Bond and boxer Rocky (Balboa), finally began to show signs of running out of steam. The surprise was that the *Rocky* sequels had done so well for so long. As late as *Rocky IV* in 1985 UA had had a major hit, the third biggest movie that year behind *Back To The Future* and *Rambo: First Blood Part II*, also starring Sylvester Stallone. But *Rocky V* flopped in 1990, the same year that Cubby Broccoli announced his retirement, after 28 years and 16 films, as producer of the James Bond series. However, UA did have one last smash hit in *Rain Man* (1988), the biggest box office success in the company's history, but it came too late to save UA from being sold by owner Kerkorian.

Box Office Hits

TITLE	Cost	North American rentals
1914–31	(in $ million)	(in $ millions)
Whoopee! (Goldwyn) (1930)	(1.3)	2.7
The Gold Rush (Chaplin) (1925)	(0.7)	2.5

TITLE	Cost	North American rentals
1914–31 cont'd	(in $ million)	(in $ millions)
Way Down East (Griffith) (1920)	(1.0)	2.0
City Lights (Chaplin) (1931)	(1.5)	1.5
Stella Dallas (Goldwyn) (1926)	(0.5)	1.5
The Thief Of Bagdad (Fairbanks) (1924)	(1.8)	1.5
1932–40		
The Kid From Spain (Goldwyn) (1932)		2.6
Roman Scandals (Goldwyn) (1933)		2.4
Modern Times (Chaplin) (1936)	(1.5)	1.8
Dodsworth (Goldwyn) (1936)		1.6
Dead End (Goldwyn) (1937)	(1.0)	1.5
Rebecca (Selznick) (1940)	(1.3)	1.5
1941–50		
The Outlaw (Hughes) (1946)	(3.0)	5.1
Spellbound (Selznick) (1945)	(1.7)	4.9
Since You Went Away (Selznick) (1944)	(2.0)	4.9
Stage Door Canteen (Lesser) (1943)		4.4
Red River (Hawks) (1948)	(3.4)	4.0
1951–60		
Around The World In 80 Days (Todd)	(6.0)	22.0
Exodus (Preminger) (1960)	(4.1)	8.3
The Alamo (Wayne/Batjac) (1960)	(12.0)	7.9
Trapeze (Hecht-Lancaster) (1956)		7.3
The Apartment (Mirisch) (1960)	(3.0)	6.7
Not As A Stranger (Kramer) (1955)	(1.5)	6.2
1961–70		
Thunderball (Eon) (1965)	(5.5)	27.0
Goldfinger (Eon) (1964)	(3.0)	22.5
It's A Mad, Mad, Mad, Mad World (Kramer) (1963)	(9.0)	20.8
West Side Story (Mirisch/7 Arts) (1961	(7.0)	19.5
You Only Live Twice (Eon) (1967)	(9.5)	18.0
Tom Jones (Woodfall) (1963)	(1.1)	17.2
Midnight Cowboy (Hellman) (1969)	(3.2)	16.3
1971–80		
One Flew Over The Cuckoo's Nest (Zaentz) (1975)		59.2
Rocky (Chartoff-Winkler) (1976)	(1.5)	55.9
Rocky II (Chartoff-Winkler) (1979)		43.0
Fiddler On The Roof (Mirisch) (1971)		40.5
Apocalypse Now (Coppola) (1979)	(31.0)	37.3
1981–90		
Rain Man (Guber-Peters) (1988)	(30.0)	86.8
Rocky IV (Chartoff-Winkler) (1985)	(30.0)	76.0
Rocky III (Chartoff-Winkler) (1982)	(17.0)	66.3
War Games (Sherwood) (1983)		37.9
Octopussy (Eon) (1983)	(30.0)	34.0

The Stars

UA started out with three of the top stars of the silent era, co-founders of the company Charlie Chaplin, Douglas Fairbanks and Mary Pickford. They were joined by various producer-stars in the 20s, including Norma Talmadge and Gloria Swanson, as well as many others who did not last for long. In the 30s the leading UA producers had their own lists of contract players and a few major stars such as Eddie Cantor, Merle Oberon, Joel McCrea and Laurence Olivier, and were often able to borrow the additional big names they needed from the other, larger studios. In later years UA turned increasingly to the many independent producer-stars to provide quality pictures, among them James Cagney in the 40s, and Burt Lancaster and Kirk Douglas in the 50s. More recently, two artists of totally contrasting styles and interests – Woody Allen and Sylvester Stallone – have combined their starring performances in UA pictures with writing and directing as well.

Operating primarily as a distribution company, UA had no stars of its own. Though many top Hollywood players appeared in UA pictures at one time or another, they rarely stayed for long and relatively few are closely identified with UA in particular, apart from Pickford, Fairbanks and Chaplin in the 20s of course, then Eddie Cantor in the 30s, Burt Lancaster in the 50s and, most recently, Woody Allen in the 70s. Aside from the earliest period in the 20s when producer-stars were a UA specialty, the stars were generally under contract to independent producers releasing through UA, and the rapid turnover reflected a general lack of box-office success. But most of the producer-stars fared no better. Among those who spent just a year or two filming for UA in the 20s were George Arliss, Charles Ray, Max Linder, Alla Nazimova, William S. Hart, John Barrymore, also Rudolph Valentino and Buster Keaton who were handled by Joe Schenck. Only Norma Talmadge, Schenck's wife, and Gloria Swanson carried on a little longer than the others, but they were adversely affected by the coming of sound.

The three mainstays of the company throughout the 20s were the original superstar founders, Pickford, Fairbanks and Chaplin, but they, too, were hurt by the arrival of the talkies. For Mary and Doug it was impossible to maintain their own special screen image any longer – Mary best known for her little-girl roles and Doug as the acrobatic, swashbuckling hero. Chaplin alone found that by the careful preparation and spacing of his films, one every four or five years, he could still achieve some measure of success in later years.

Producer-director D. W. Griffith had his own group of stars in the early 20s, headed by Lillian Gish and Carol Dempster, but he never mastered the growing star system before his own career wound down. In contrast, producer Sam Goldwyn started out in the 20s with silent stars such as Vilma Banky and Ronald Colman, but only hit his stride in the 30s when he had an especially strong line-up of men under contract led by Eddie Cantor, Gary Cooper, Joel McCrea, Walter Brennan, and David Niven who was his one genuine discovery. Goldwyn was less successful with the ladies, however. Vilma Banky's career was cut short when the talkies arrived and Goldwyn spent a lot of money trying to turn the beautiful Anna Sten into a star before he was forced to admit defeat.

With a shortage of readily available talent, UA producers often shared or exchanged stars. Thus, Charles Boyer worked mainly for Walter Wanger in the 30s, but was loaned to Selznick for *The Garden of Allah* (1936), while Adolphe Menjou shuttled between Selznick, Goldwyn, Edward Small and Hal Roach in the late 30s. Merle Oberon was one of Alexander Korda's British star discoveries (and later his wife) who joined Goldwyn in the US where she and Laurence Olivier, another Korda player, appeared in Goldwyn's production of *Wuthering Heights* (1939).

Between them the leading UA producers in the 30s controlled a not inconsiderable assortment of star talent. David Selznick greatly strengthened his star list in the 40s by signing up Jennifer Jones (who would become the second Mrs Selznick), Joseph Cotten, Guy Madison and a teenaged Shirley Temple, then brought them all together – with Claudette Colbert and Monty Woolley – in his smash-hit, wartime, multi-star vehicle, *Since You Went Away* (1944). Selznick then paired his top star, Ingrid Bergman, with his biggest 40s discovery, Gregory Peck, in Hitchcock's *Spellbound* (1945). But a continuing source of irritation to UA was his success in loaning his stars to other studios at a substantial profit for himself, but with little benefit to his hard-pressed partners at UA.

With the decline of the star system and the new trend for major stars to go independent, UA found itself once again turning to producer-stars. First of this new breed was James Cagney in the 40s, while Burt Lancaster made the greatest contribution to UA in the 50s with his Hecht-Lancaster company (later Hecht-Hill-Lancaster).

More recently, many UA stars have been associated with a particular type of picture. The Jack Lemmon-Billy Wilder comedies began with *Some Like It Hot* (1959) and *The Apartment* (1960) and continued on into the 60s, while the tremendously popular James Bond series starred

Sean Connery in the 60s, then Roger Moore, with Timothy Dalton taking over in 1986. Clint Eastwood first made his name as the star of the Italian-produced Westerns of Sergio Leone, and Peter Sellers starred in numerous comedies for UA in the 60s and 70s of which the Pink Panther films, conceived by producer-director Blake Edwards, were the most successful. Woody Allen got his start as scriptwriter and co-star of *What's New Pussycat?* (1966), then went on to write, direct and star in his own comedies, while Sylvester Stallone was closely identified with his screen creation, Rocky Balboa.

STARS

Allen, Woody 1971–80
Ankers, Evelyn (Korda) 1936
Arliss, George 1921–22, (20th) 1933–34
Ayres, Lew 1951–53
Ball, Lucille 1933–34
Banky, Vilma (Goldwyn) 1925–29
Barrymore, John 1927–28
Bennett, Constance (20th) 1934
Bennett, Joan (Wanger) 1937–40
Bergman, Ingrid (Selznick) 1944–45
Brennan, Walter (Goldwyn) 1935–40
Brynner, Yul 1962–64, 1966
Burke, Billie 1938–39
Cagney, James (Williams Cagney) 1943–48
Cantor, Eddie (Goldwyn) 1930–35
Chaplin, Charlie 1924–52
Clift, Montgomery 1960–61
Colman, Ronald (Goldwyn) 1926–33
Cooper, Gary (Goldwyn) 1937–40
Cotten, Joseph (Selznick) 1944–45
Del Rio, Dolores (Carewe) 1928–29
Dempster, Carol (Griffith) 1920–24
Dix, Richard 1942
Fairbanks Sr, Douglas 1919–32
Fairbanks Jr, Douglas (Selznick) 1937–38
Gish, Lillian (Griffith) 1920–21
Goddard, Paulette (Chaplin) 1935, 1940
Grable, Betty (Goldwyn) 1930–32
Gray, Coleen 1952–53
Harlow, Jean (Hughes) 1929–30
Hart, William S. 1925
Hayden, Sterling 1956–58
Hopkins, Miriam (Goldwyn) 1935–36

Hunter, Tab (Small) 1953–54
Jones, Jennifer (Selznick) 1944–45
Jory, Victor (Sherman) 1943
Keaton, Buster (Schenck) 1926–27
Keyes, Evelyn 1951–53
La Marr, Barbara (Fairbanks) 1921
Lancaster, Burt 1954–55, 1957–62
March, Fredric 1934, (Selznick) 1937
Mature, Victor (Roach) 1939–40
McCrea, Joel (Goldwyn) 1935–37, 1957–58
Menjou, Adolph (Roach) 1939–41, 1956–57
Merkel, Una 1930
Mitchum, Robert 1955–56
Montgomery, George 1955–57
Niven, David (Goldwyn) 1938–39
Oberon, Merle (Korda) 1933–34, 1937–38. (Goldwyn) 1935–38
Peck, Gregory 1954, 1958–59
Pickford, Mary 1919–32
Poitier, Sidney 1961–63
Presley, Elvis 1961–62
Raft, George 1945–49
Roland, Gilbert 1927–29
Ryan, Robert 1956–59
Sabu (Korda) 1937–41
Sanders, George 1946
Scott, Randolph 1945
Stack, Robert 1952–53
Swanson, Gloria 1926–32
Talmadge, Norma (Schenck) 1927–30
Valentino, Rudolph 1925–26
Winters, Shelley 1955
Young, Loretta (20th) 1934–35
Young, Roland (Roach) 1937–40

The Directors

In the 20s and 30s UA was dominated and run by its stars and producers. The only director among the original founders, D.W. Griffith, was the first to leave the company. Directors who made the greatest contribution in the early years were Raoul Walsh, Henry King and Lewis Milestone. There were a few producer-directors, too, including Alexander Korda in Britain and the eccentric Howard Hughes who personally took charge of his two best-known productions, *Hell's Angels* (1930) and the notorious *The Outlaw* (1943). Famous directors like John Ford, William Wyler and Alfred Hitchcock were associated with UA for a time in the 30s and early 40s. But it was only under the new regime, after 1951, that a new breed of a producer-directors began to make their influence felt. These included established figures such as John Huston, Billy Wilder and Robert Wise, and successful British directors Tony Richardson, John Schlesinger and Ken Russell. In the 70s, writer-director-star Woody Allen was most closely identified with UA.

Many leading American directors worked on UA pictures at one time or another. Few, however, could be said to have played an important role in the company in the early years, aside from contributing their services to the occasional successful production. UA was mainly run by stars and producers, so it is not surprising to find directors occupying a subsidiary position. (Here it is useful to distinguish between the years prior to 1951, and the later period when Krim and Benjamin took over and studio policy changed in many important respects.)

Perhaps it is not mere coincidence that D. W. Griffith, the only director among the original founders, was the first to leave, due to the lack of profitability of his films. Yet his movie-star partners were flourishing – in spite of the fact that they often employed directors who were less than first rate.

In most cases the directors were hired by individual producers. Henry

King was employed by Goldwyn in the 20s and is best remembered for the silent version of *Stella Dallas* (1925), while Lewis Milestone worked on the successful comedy, *Two Arabian Knights* (1927) and the classic newspaper drama, *The Front Page* (1931) for Howard Hughes, and was hired by Joe Schenck to direct Joan Crawford in *Rain* (1932). There was also a handful of producer-directors, such as Herbert Wilcox and Alexander Korda in Britain, and Chaplin, who directed all his own pictures. Most eccentric among them was the multi-millionaire Howard Hughes who conducted a strange off-and-on relationship with UA over a period of 20 years before he bought RKO in 1948. He was an experienced pilot, and took charge of directing the World War I flying movie, *Hell's Angels* (assisted by dialogue director James Whale). The movie was fraught with problems, as was his second venture as a director, *The Outlaw* (1943), but this time at least the result was profitable.

Goldwyn's leading director at UA in the 30s was William Wyler who handled most of the prestige dramas, but the producer-dominated environment of the period was best exemplified by David O. Selznick's paternalistic attitude. He stuck to directors like John Cromwell and William Wellman whom he felt he could handle and refused to hire John Ford. Thus, *Stagecoach* (1939) was produced by Walter Wanger instead, and the same team of Ford, Wanger and John Wayne went on to do a memorable follow-up movie, *The Long Voyage Home* (1940). The inimitable Alfred Hitchcock made a major contribution to UA with *Rebecca* (1940) and *Spellbound* (1945) for Selznick, and *Foreign Correspondent* (1940) for Wanger, while producer-directors Ernst Lubitsch (with *To Be Or Not To Be*, 1942) and Howard Hawks (with *Red River*, 1948) provided two of the rare 40s productions of note.

These men were forerunners of the new breed of independent producer-directors who would become a staple ingredient of the rejuvenated UA in the 50s. It was particularly apparent that the company reached its lowest ebb in the 40s when leading directors were beginning to play a more important role in Hollywood generally. UA had no counterpart to Wilder at Paramount, Kazan and Mankiewicz at Fox, Minnelli at MGM or Huston at Warner Bros. The new policies of Krim and Benjamin in the 50s meant that UA was able to take advantage of the independent status of some of these men. For the first time in the history of UA, a large number of directors developed a continuing relationship with the company, among them such established figures as Huston, Wilder and Robert Wise, and relative newcomers Robert Aldrich, Stanley Kubrick and producer turned producer-director Stanley Kramer. In the 60s and 70s there was a mixture of leading English and American directors, reflecting the extensive UA investment in British film production. These included John Sturges, Blake Edwards, Norman Jewison and Billy Wilder whose UA pictures were most often produced by the highly successful Mirisch brothers, Walter, Marvin and Harold, but the influence of the company waned after the death of Harold in 1968. In Britain there was the American-born Richard Lester, as well as Ken Russell, and Oscar winners Tony Richardson (for *Tom Jones*, 1963) and John Schlesinger (for *Midnight Cowboy*, 1969). Most recently

Woody Allen and Sylvester Stallone have performed well as UA's leading writer-director-stars.

DIRECTORS

Aldrich, Robert 1953–56
Allen, Woody 1971–80
Archainbaud, George, 1947–48
Ashby, Hal 1976–79
Boleslawski, Richard (20th) 1935
Chaplin, Charles 1923–52
Cromwell, John (Selznick) 1936–39
Del Ruth, Roy 1934–35
De Toth, Andre 1944–48
Douglas, Gordon 1939–41
Dwan, Allan (Small) 1944–45
Fitzmaurice, George 1926–27, 1929–30
Florey, Robert 1948–50
Freeland, Thornton 1929–30, 1935–37
Garnett, Tay 1938–39
Green, Alfred 1947–49
Griffith, D.W. 1920–25, 1927–31
Hill, George Roy 1963–66
Hitchcock, Alfred (Selznick) 1939–40, 1944–45, (Wanger) 1940
Howard, William K. 1937
Huston, John 1951–54
Jewison, Norman (Mirisch) 1965–71; 1974–77
King, Henry 1925–30
Kramer, Stanley 1955–63
Kubrick, Stanley 1955–57
Lee, Roland 1934–36
Lester, Richard 1962–69
Lewis, Joseph H. 1957–58

Losey, Joseph 1951–52
Lubin, Arthur 1945, 1947–49, 1951
Lubitsch, Ernst 1941–42
Mann, Delbert (Hecht-Hill-Lancaster) 1954–58
Marin, Edwin L. 1942, 1946–47
Mayo, Archie 1938–40, 1946
McLeod, Norman Z. (Roach) 1937–39
Milestone, Lewis (Hughes) 1927–29, 1931–33
Neumann, Kurt 1942–43
Potter, H.C. 1948
Rawlins, John 1951–53
Robson, Mark (Kramer) 1949
Russell, Ken 1967–70
Santell, Alfred 1943–44
Selander, Lesley 1942–44
Sherman, Lowell 1933–34
Sirk, Douglas 1944–47
Stone, Andrew 1943–47
Sturges, John 1960–67
Sutherland, A. Edward 1931–32
Taylor, Sam 1927–31
Ulmer, Edgar 1946–47
Wellman, William (Selznick) 1937
West, Roland 1926–31
Wilder, Billy 1958–72
Wise, Robert 1957–62
Wood, Sam 1940
Wyler, William (Goldwyn) 1935–37, 1939–41

The Creative Personnel

In the 20s the UA producers employed many of the leading cameramen and art directors in Hollywood, and the general standard of production was high. Top cinematographers included Charles Rosher, George Barnes, Hendrick Sartov, Arthur Edeson and the veteran Billy Bitzer. The most famous of all was Gregg Toland, occasionally loaned out to other producers, but who spent virtually his entire career with Sam Goldwyn. UA was one of the first companies to recognize the importance of the art director.

Distinguished designers who worked on early UA productions included Wilfred Buckland, Danny Hall, Charles M. Kirk and, especially, William Cameron Menzies, the most active of all over two decades. Hal Kern, William Hornbeck and Robert Parrish were among the top editors who worked on UA productions, while Daniel Mandell was employed by Goldwyn, then later joined Billy Wilder on such pictures as *The Apartment* (1960). The French-born costume designer René Hubert was brought to Hollywood by Gloria Swanson, while the American-born (in spite of his name) Omar Kiam handled the Goldwyn costumes. Memorable scores came from the pens of Alfred Newman and Miklos Rozsa, but the most famous UA composer was Dimitri Tiomkin, best remembered for his Oscar-winning score and theme song for *High Noon* (1952).

Cameramen and Art Directors

The leading producers at UA, most notably Pickford, Fairbanks and Griffith, were among the first in Hollywood to recognize the important contribution which the best technicians could make toward raising the quality of their pictures. Thus, in spite of the fact that the company released a relatively small number of features in the early 20s, it played an influential role – comparable to the giant Paramount – in helping to raise the standards of production generally.

Griffith brought his regular cameraman, Billy Bitzer, to UA and continued to use him in tandem with the talented and younger Hendrick Sartov, while Charles M. Kirk served as his art director and is best remembered for his impressive exterior set designs depicting 18th-century Paris in *Orphans Of The Storm* (1922).

If Rollie Totheroh, Chaplin's cameraman for over 30 years, was reliable but undistinguished, at least his designer at UA was one of the best. Danny Hall's name is associated with the Universal horror cycle, but he provided memorable settings for many Chaplin features, ranging from the dance hall and lone snow-bound cabin teetering on the edge of the cliff in *The Gold Rush* (1925) to the imaginatively designed factory and giant machinery of *Modern Times* (1936).

Mary Pickford, too, had a favourite cameraman, Charles Rosher, who had first begun to work for her at Paramount/Artcraft in 1918. One of the most brilliant cinematographers of the silent era, Rosher combined great technical expertise with an artistic sensibility which meant that Pickford's pictures invariably looked stunning and were full of little imaginative touches – with dream sequences and double-exposure effects achieved within the camera. Between them, Rosher and George Barnes, Goldwyn's top cameraman in the 20s, dominated the very first Oscar ceremony, for 1927/28, with three nominations each, but Rosher won for the only non-UA production, Fox's *Sunrise*, filmed in collaboration with another UA cameraman, Karl Struss.

Unlike his UA partners, Douglas Fairbanks employed a number of different technicians during the 20s. After the success of his first swashbucklers, he became more ambitious, and for *Robin Hood* (1922) he assembled an outstanding team of art directors headed by Wilfred Buckland who had first made his name with DeMille. (This was Buckland's most important assignment of the 20s, assisted by Anton Grot, William Cameron Menzies, and Edward Langley who worked on most of the Fairbanks costumers.) Then, on *The Thief Of Bagdad* (1924), Menzies took over as the top art director for the first time, demonstrating a special flair for, and love of, fantasy. Both pictures were photographed by Arthur Edeson and stand up today as Fairbanks' most remarkable and accomplished of the period, raising the costume adventure movie to a new level of stylish visual achievement.

As an example of how UA producers occasionally shared personnel, around this same time Menzies designed the Spanish settings for the Mary Pickford–Ernst Lubitsch *Rosita* (1923), and he soon emerged as the leading art director at UA, designing films for Valentino, Norma Talmadge, Gloria Swanson, Joe Schenck, Griffith and Goldwyn. He worked on a large proportion of the best known UA productions of the silent era up to and including the changeover to sound during 1929–31.

Menzies returned to UA in the late 30s and was once again employed by a number of different producers during a kind of golden age of UA production and production design when men such as Goldwyn, Korda, Selznick and Wanger were at the peak of their prestige and hiring many of the top designers in Hollywood. These included Richard Day, Goldwyn's leading art director and double Oscar winner, also Alexander Golitzen and James Basevi whose many Goldwyn productions included a memorable collaboration on the visually impressive *The Hurricane* (1937). Alexander Toluboff was employed by Walter Wanger, Lyle Wheeler by David Selznick and Jack Schulze by producer Edward Small. In Britain Alexander Korda had one of the best designers in his brother, Vincent, and even Hal Roach, attempting to break away from comedies in the late 30s, hired Danny Hall and Nicholai Remisoff (who continued to design pictures for Hunt Stromberg in the 40s).

There were many outstanding cameramen, too, among them Hal Rosson, Lee Garmes, Rudolph Maté and Leon Shamroy. Though they tended to be employed haphazardly and often on a freelance basis, there were a couple of important exceptions, such as the outstanding French cinematographer, Georges Périnal, who gave a special visual quality to many of Korda's productions in the 30s. Similarly, Sam Goldwyn was fortunate in signing Gregg Toland in 1929. The most celebrated of UA cameramen – though some of his best work was done in the 40s after he and Goldwyn had left UA – Toland was equally at home with the sharp, low-keyed photography of a contemporary drama like *Dead End* which earned him an Oscar nomination in 1937, as with the romantic costume classic, *Wuthering Heights* (1939), which won him the only Oscar of his long and distinguished career.

Other Departments

UA producers employed many of the top technicians and creative personnel in Hollywood over the years. Leading editors included Hal Kern, employed by the demanding David Selznick, and Daniel Mandell, Goldwyn's favourite editor in the late 30s and 40s who was later to spend 10 years with Billy Wilder (and Mirisch), winning an Oscar for his contribution to *The Apartment* (1960). William Hornbeck, one of the most respected of editors, made his name as Korda's supervising editor in the 30s and came top of a recent poll of 100 leading editors questioned as to whose work they would choose as the most 'consistently outstanding'.

A number of UA's top editors swiftly graduated to directing. Stuart Heisler moved up from Goldwyn editor in the early 30s to second unit director on *The Hurricane* (1937), then director at Paramount in the 40s. Robert Parrish's work on *Body And Soul* (1947) provides a classic example of the value of a close working relationship between director (Robert Rossen), cameraman (James Wong Howe) and editor. Howe employed a few ex-combat cameramen to shoot additional hand-held footage, which Parrish (and co-editor Francis Lyon) then edited into the memorable 600-foot sequence seen in the final film. Not long after this Parrish switched to directing. More recently, Hal Ashby followed a similar route from Oscar-winning editor – for Norman Jewison in the 60s, including *In The Heat Of The Night* (1967) – to directing pictures himself for UA in the 70s.

Another creative technician who later became a leading director was Mitchell Leisen. He first established himself as a costumier of note in 1922–24, shared between Douglas Fairbanks (*Robin Hood*, 1922, *The Thief Of Bagdad*, 1924) and Mary Pickford, who wanted the most lavish costumes for *Dorothy Vernon Of Haddon Hall* (1924), one of the few period movies in which she attempted to break away from her little-girl image.

Around the same time, while filming *Madame Sans-Gêne* (Paramount, 1925) in France, Gloria Swanson discovered René Hubert. She persuaded him to return to Hollywood with her and continue working on her pictures. The leading costume designer at UA in the 30s, Omar Kiam, was employed primarily by Goldwyn but was loaned out to Selznick, Wanger, Pickford-Lasky and, especially, 20th Century, where he had some of his best opportunities to dress period films such as *Cardinal Richelieu*, *Les Miserables*, and the Maurice Chevalier-Merle Oberon musical *Folies Bergère* (all 1935 releases).

Music and musicals did not play an important role at UA during the studio era. The single dominating figure in this field at UA in the 30s was Alfred Newman, beginning his long and productive career. He worked mainly for Goldwyn, and for 20th Century where he caught the attention of Darryl Zanuck who eagerly invited him to 20th Century-Fox. Here there was more scope for his talent and he stayed on for the next 20 years. Korda's leading composer was the Hungarian-born Miklos Rozsa. Korda brought him to Hollywood in 1940 where *The Thief Of Bagdad* was being completed, and he stayed on to become one of the most sought-after Hollywood composers during the next 40 years. (He won his first Oscar for his haunting and evocative score for the Selznick-Hitchcock production of *Spellbound* in 1945).

The leading composer at UA in the 40s and early 50s, however, was the brilliant Dimitri Tiomkin. Though he provided memorable scores for numerous Stanley Kramer productions, he was mainly associated with UA's none-too-frequent, prestige Westerns, ranging from *The Westerner* (1940) and *Red River* (1948) to *The Alamo* and *The Unforgiven* (both 1960), and the last of his Kramer pictures – *High Noon* (1952). A double Oscar winner – for score and theme song, 'Do Not Forsake Me, Oh My Darlin'' – this was the movie that turned Tiomkin into a household name and started a new vogue for introducing theme songs into feature films.

CAMERAMEN

Andriot, Lucien 1944–50

Barnes, George (Goldwyn) 1926–31

Bitzer, Billy (Griffith) 1920–25, 1927–31

Cortez, Stanley 1943–44

Edeson, Arthur 1924–25

Garmes, Lee (Selznick) 1937–46

Glennon, Bert 1937–38, 1947

Greene, W. Howard (Selznick) 1936–37

Howe, James Wong (Selznick) 1937

June, Ray 1929–33

Laszlo, Ernest 1948–49

Lawton, Charles Jr 1944–45

Marley, J. Peverell (20th) 1933–35

Maté, Rudolph 1936–42

Mellor, William 1946, 1948–49
Mescall, John 1943–45, 1950
Metty, Russell 1945–46
Périnal, Georges (Korda) 1933–40
Planck, Robert 1929–30, 1932, 1934–36, 1938–39
Rosher, Charles (Pickford) 1919–28,

(20th) 1934
Rosson, Hal 1934–36
Sartov, Hendrick (Griffith) 1919–24
Shamroy, Leon 1936, 1938
Struss, Karl (Art Cinema) 1928–30, 1946–48
Toland, Gregg (Goldwyn) 1929–41

ART DIRECTORS

Basevi, James 1936–40, (Selznick) 1945
Borg, Karl Oscar 1926–27
Carrere, Edward 1957–59
D'Agostino, Albert 1928–29, 1933
Day, Richard (Goldwyn) 1930–38
Fegté, Ernst 1946–48
Golitzen, Alexander (Goldwyn) 1934–41
Goosson, Stephen 1929
Grot, Anton 1922–25
Hall, Charles D (Chaplin) 1925–31, 1935, (Roach) 1938–43
Harkrider (Goldwyn) 1930–33
Herzbrun, Bernard 1942–46
Juran, Nathan (Enterprise) 1947
Kirk, Charles M. (Griffith) 1921–25

Kirk, Mark-Lee 1944
Leisen, Mitchell (Fairbanks) 1922–24
Leven, Boris 1953
Menzies, William Cameron 1923–30, 1935–40
Oliver, Harry 1925–27, (Hughes) 1929–31
Pogany, William A. (Goldwyn) 1927–31
Polglase, Van Nest (Bogeaus) 1949–50
Remisoff, Nicolai (Roach) 1939–41, (Stromberg) 1944–47, 1951–54
Schulze, Jack (Pickford) 1925, 1927, (Reliance) 1934–36, (Small) 1938–42
Toluboff, Alexander (Wanger) 1936–39

COSTUME DESIGNERS

Anderson, Milo (Goldwyn) 1932
Banton, Travis (Selznick) 1938–39
Harkrider (Goldwyn) 1930, 1933
Hubert, René (Korda) 1935–38
Irene 1937–41
Kiam, Omar 1934–38

Leisen, Mitchell 1922–24
Plunkett, Walter (Selznick) 1938–39
Royer 1940–42
Saltern, Irene 1940–41
Wakeling, Gwen (20th) 1933–34

COMPOSERS/MUSIC DIRECTORS

Michelet, Michel 1944–50
Newman, Alfred 1931–38
Roemheld, Heinz 1946–48
Rozsa, Miklos (Korda) 1938–42

Steiner, Max (Selznick) 1936
Tiomkin, Dimitri 1940–44, 1948–50
Ward, Edward 1940–43

EDITORS

Bennett, Hugh (Goldwyn) 1931–32
Clancey, Margaret 1935–38
Crosland, Alan Jr 1954–55
Gerstad, Harry (Kramer) 1948–51

Harrison, Doane (Wilder) 1961–66
Heisler, Stuart (Goldwyn) 1924–25, 1929–34
Hornbeck, William (Korda) 1934–41

Kern, Hal (Selznick) 1935–45
Kern, Robert 1929–30
Knudtson, Frederic (Kramer) 1957–63
Lawrence, Viola 1927–30
Lovering, Otho (Wanger) 1937–40, 1945–46
Mandell, Daniel (Goldwyn) 1936–40, (Wilder) 1957–66
McLean, Barbara 1929–30, (20th) 1933–35
McNeil, Allen 1927–35
Newcom, James 1937–47
Nosler, Lloyd (Inspiration) 1929–30, (20th) 1933–35

Smith, James (Griffith) 1920–25, 1927–30, 1944–47
Spencer, Dorothy (Wanger) 1937–41
Sullivan, Frank 1949–50
Todd, Sherman 1934–40
Webster, Ferris 1960–65
White, Merrill (Wilcox) 1934–35
Whytock, Grant 1931–41, 1961–70
Winters, Ralph 1964–70
Wright, Maurice (20th) 1933–34
Ziegler, William (Roach) 1938–40, (Selznick) 1944–45

SCRIPTWRITERS

Biro, Lajos (Korda) 1932–39
Diamond, I. A. L. (Wilder) 1958–66, 1970–72
Foreman, Carl (Kramer) 1947–51
Hecht, Ben (Goldwyn) 1931–38, (Selznick) 1944–45
Hellman, Lillian (Goldwyn) 1935–37
Howard, Sidney 1929–31, 1936
Johnson, Nunnally (20th) 1933–34
Lawson, John Howard (Wanger) 1938–39

Maibaum, Richard (Eon) 1962–89
Meredyth, Bess (20th) 1934–35
Poe, James 1955–56
Rose, Reginald 1956–58
Sherwood, Robert 1931–39
Sullivan, C. Gardner 1925–29
Swerling, Jo 1938–40
Veiller, Anthony 1951–52, 1956–59
Wimperis, Arthur (Korda) 1932–38

The Academy Awards

UA achieved a few successes with the Academy in the early years, with nominations or awards for many of its leading stars and technical personnel. The company continued to earn many nominations, thus reflecting the generally outstanding quality of its productions in the 30s, but had few winners and fared better at the hands of the New York Film Critics. The first UA production to win the Oscar for Best Picture was *Rebecca* (1940), but the standard of production fell off in the 40s and there were no other major awards for the rest of the decade. A rapid recovery in the early 50s under a new management was reflected in UA's success with the Oscars which extended over a period of more than 20 years. The first, back-to-back, winners of the Best Picture were the small scale, black-and-white drama *Marty* (1955) and the epic adventure movie, *Around The World In 80 Days* (1956). Other top winners included *The Apartment* (1960), *West Side Story* (1961) and the British-produced *Tom Jones* (1963) in the 60s; *One Flew Over The Cuckoo's Nest* (1975), which swept the top five awards, and Woody Allen's most honoured picture, *Annie Hall* (1977), in the 70s. The company has done less well recently, but had one last big success with *Rain Man* in 1988.

Many of UA's quality productions gained recognition from the Academy in the 20s and early 30s. Nominations and awards were spread among the leading UA stars, producers and technical personnel. Chaplin was honoured for *The Circus* (1928), Gloria Swanson nominated for her performances in both *Sadie Thompson* (1928) and her first talkie, *The Trespasser* (1929) and Mary Pickford won for her first all-talking role as *Coquette* (1929).

Director Lewis Milestone gained UA's very first Oscar for *Two Arabian Knights* (1927) and a nomination for *The Front Page* (1931)

– both pictures produced by Howard Hughes. Finally, there were many nominations for leading cameramen George Barnes and Charles Rosher and art directors William Cameron Menzies and Richard Day.

A number of new UA producers began to make their mark beginning in 1933 when Alexander Korda had a tremendous and unexpected success with *The Private Life of Henry VIII*. It was the first British production to receive a nomination for Best Picture, with the top acting award going to Charles Laughton for his lively and entertaining performance in the title role. A pair of 20th Century productions, *The House of Rothschild* (1934) and *Les Miserables* (1935), were nominated for Best Picture, setting a pattern which continued throughout the rest of the 30s. The most outstanding UA movies regularly earned Oscar nominations – *Dodsworth* in 1936, *A Star Is Born* and *Dead End* in 1937, *Stagecoach*, *Wuthering Heights* and *Of Mice And Men* in 1939 – but the company failed to win a single major award from the Academy from 1934 through 1939. The only UA winners were confined to supporting actor (Walter Brennan in *Come And Get It*, 1936, and Thomas Mitchell in *Stagecoach*), the various technical categories and, especially, Walt Disney's cartoon shorts which took the Oscar for five years running, 1932–36.

When UA won the Best Picture Oscar in 1940 for the first time, for Selznick's production of *Rebecca* directed by Alfred Hitchcock, it marked the end of an era, rather than a new beginning, for it more or less coincided with the departure of many of the top producers. UA did poorly in the 40s, but revived in the early 50s, winning the Best Actor Oscar for three years running – Jose Ferrer as *Cyrano De Bergerac* (1950), Humphrey Bogart in *The African Queen* (1951) and Gary Cooper for *High Noon* (1952) and continued during 1955–67 with Ernest Borgnine as *Marty* (1955), David Niven in *Separate Tables* (1958), Burt Lancaster as *Elmer Gantry* (1960) and Maximilian Schell for *Judgment At Nuremburg* (1961); also Sidney Poitier, the first black actor to win this award, for *Lilies of the Field* (1963) followed by Walter Matthau for *The Fortune Cookie* (1966) and Rod Steiger for *In the Heat of the Night* (1967).

But the most convincing demonstration of UA's new status was its remarkable success with the coveted top award. From 1955 through 1977 UA won the Oscar for Best Picture 10 times. Even MGM at its peak only managed nine wins in over 30 years, 1928–59.

The first two winners could not have been more different, thus reflecting the diversity of UA's interests. The naturalistic, relatively cheaply-made black-and-white *Marty* (1955) was filmed mainly on location in and around New York City without a single major star.

In contrast, Mike Todd's epic production of *Around The World In 80 Days* (1956) was shot in colour and Todd-AO in many countries, with a multi-star cast. It was a bargain at about $6 million, though this was more than 15 times the cost of *Marty*. About the only thing the two pictures had in common was the fact that they were both based on well-crafted (Oscar-winning) scripts. And, indeed, if there is one aspect of movie-production which most characterized UA under Arthur Krim and Robert Benjamin, it was that partnership's attraction to strong, intelligent scripts. Not surprisingly, the company developed its best working relationships with many writer-directors – John Huston, Billy Wilder, Blake Edwards, Woody Allen. During the years 1955–78 UA pictures received 40 script nominations of which 15 were winners.

Billy Wilder won Oscars for scripting and directing *The Apartment* (1960), the first of UA's Best Picture winners in the 60s and the first of three from Mirisch, the most successful independent company producing movies for UA during this period. The other Mirisch winners were the hit musical, *West Side Story* (1961) and a thriller, *In The Heat Of The Night* (1967), which gained the best acting award for Rod Steiger. UA's important British connection was represented by the Woodfall production of *Tom Jones* (1963) directed by Tony Richardson, and producer-director John Schlesinger's contribution to *Midnight Cowboy* (1969). These two films completed UA's tally of five Best Picture winners in the 60s and, in both cases, earned directing and scripting awards as well.

The big breakthrough in the 70s came six years later with *One Flew Over The Cuckoo's Nest*. It was UA's top hit, the top Academy Award winner of the decade, and the first film since Columbia's *It Happened One Night* (1934) to sweep the board, taking Oscars for Best Picture, director (Milos Forman), actor (Jack Nicholson), actress and script. Between *Rocky*, and *Network* the following year, UA also did well, and yet again with *Annie Hall* in 1977 which almost matched the feat of *One Flew Over The Cuckoo's Nest*. But to do so would have meant three awards to writer-director-star Woody Allen; in the event, he won two and lost out to actor Richard Dreyfuss for the third.

UA generally had less success with its actresses. When Susan Hayward won the Best Actress Oscar in 1958 for *I Want To Live!*, she was the first UA winner in this category since Mary Pickford, but the company did markedly better in the 70s. Oscars went to Glenda Jackson for *Women In Love* (1970), Louise Fletcher for *One Flew Over The Cuckoo's Nest*, Faye Dunaway for *Network* (a UA/MGM co-production), Diane Keaton as *Annie Hall* and Jane Fonda for *Coming Home*, with additional nominations to Sissy Spacek (*Carrie*, 1976) and Meryl Streep (*The French Lieutenant's Woman*, 1981).

The company has been less successful during recent years. Although Francis Coppola's remarkable production, *Apocalypse Now*, won the top award at the 1979 Cannes Festival and was nominated for Best Picture and director, it only won Oscars for cinematography and editing, while Robert De Niro's stunning performance in *Raging Bull* (1980) gained UA its only major Oscar in the early 80s. However, the company did triumph in 1988 when Barry Levinson's downbeat drama, *Rain Man*, gained awards for Best Picture, director, actor (Dustin Hoffman) and original screenplay. This was the twelfth UA production to win the Best Picture award, a record unequalled by any other Hollywood studio.

UNIVERSAL

The true character of the studio was established by its founder Carl Laemmle, who aimed to turn out pictures in quantity, if not of the highest quality. Universal, one of the earliest major studios, maintained its position within the industry throughout the 20s, but was slow to adapt to sound. Ironically, just when it was releasing the most prestigious picture in its history, *All Quiet On The Western Front* in 1930, it was beginning to struggle. The story of the next 40 years is one of gradual recovery and growth. In the early 70s Universal clearly emerged as a top Hollywood company and one of the industry leaders, with a large number of impressive productions and spectacular hits to its credit, as well as substantial investment in TV production. This continued on into the 80s with such hits as E T. *The Extra-Terrestrial* (1982), *Back to the Future* (1985) and the Oscar-winning *Out Of Africa* (1985).

Carl Laemmle, the founder of Universal, opened his first nickelodeon in Chicago in 1906. Quick to recognize the possibilities in this rapidly expanding new industry, it was not long before he was running a chain of small cinemas. As the next logical step, he formed his own distribution company, the Laemmle Film Service, which turned out to be an extremely profitable enterprise. But Laemmle's remarkable success was threatened in 1908 by the formation of the Motion Picture Patents Company, a monopolistic outfit, generally known as the Trust, which was attempting to control the entire movie industry through its ownership of a number of key patents of motion picture cameras and projection equipment. Refusing to be intimidated, Laemmle decided to continue expanding and begin producing his own pictures. His new Independent Motion Picture Company, or IMP for short, was formed early in 1909 and was soon turning out one-reelers beginning with *Hiawatha* from the Longfellow poem. In 1910 he hired 'The Biograph Girl', Florence Lawrence, and publicized her real name, then went on to sign up 'The girl with the golden curls', Mary Pickford.

During the following years Laemmle continued to produce his own movie shorts while leading a successful battle against the Trust, whose fate was sealed early in 1912 when the Justice Department attacked its monopolistic practices. Soon after this Laemmle succeeded in organizing the merger of IMP with a group of smaller film companies including Bison, Powers, Nestor and others to form the Universal Film Company. The new company got off to a tremendous start when its first feature-length picture, *Traffic In Souls* (1913) directed by George Loane Tucker, was a big box-office hit. But in spite of this success Laemmle was reluctant to commit himself to feature production and continued to turn out mainly one- and two-reelers. Another early feature, *Neptune's Daughter* (1914) starred Australian swimming star Annette Kellerman whose life story was brought to the screen by MGM almost 40 years later in *Million Dollar Mermaid* (1952) with Esther Williams in the title role.

With small studios operating in New York, New Jersey and California, Laemmle finally decided that it would be more practical to build a single large, modern and fully-equipped studio. With this in mind he purchased a 230-acre site on the north side of the Hollywood Hills, renamed it Universal City, and opened the new studio with much fanfare early in 1915. He realized that he was taking a big risk with such a commitment to what was still a relatively backward and undeveloped area of California – 'I hope I didn't make a mistake coming out here', he is reported to have remarked.

As the name Universal City implies, the studio was more like a giant ranch, a small community spread over a vast tract of land with a useful variety of terrain and a large number of standing sets. Ideal for film-making, it was difficult, if not impossible, for the studio manager to supervise and keep track of all the different pictures which were shooting at any one time. On one of his frequent visits to the studio from his New York offices in 1919, Laemmle brought along his new private secretary, young Irving Thalberg, who was fascinated by the film-making activities. Thalberg spent his time observing and making notes and suggestions and was particularly concerned at how inefficiently the studio was being run. So impressed was Laemmle that he appointed Thalberg general manager of the studio about a year or so later, before Thalberg had reached his 21st birthday.

Thalberg's effectiveness as studio boss was reflected in the fact that the studio's profits and revenues rose steadily during his two-and-a-half years at the helm. However, he is probably best remembered for his confrontations with the studio's most brilliant but least disciplined talent, writer-director-actor Erich von Stroheim. His success in controlling Stroheim was symbolic of the growing power of the producer within the new Hollywood studio system, with a corresponding diminishment of the prestige and independence of the directors. In 1921 Thalberg actually halted filming on Stroheim's most lavish and remarkable production, *Foolish Wives*, a picture which, even in an incomplete state, brought Universal new status when it was released. Then the 'boy wonder', as he became known, dismissed Stroheim from his next production, *Merry-Go-Round*, in 1922 when it began to run behind schedule, and brought in Rupert Julian to complete it. But Thalberg had already left to join the Mayer Company before the release of his most successful project, *The Hunchback Of Notre Dame* in 1923.

During the middle and late 20s Universal continued to turn out large numbers of mainly undistinguished films while expanding its activities overseas. Of all the major Hollywood studios, it was the slowest to make the changeover to sound filming in 1929, at the same time that Carl Laemmle Jr was appointed by his father to take over as the new head of production.

Carl Jr got off to a good start with pictures like *Broadway* (1929), *King Of Jazz* (1930) and the Oscar-winning *All Quiet On The Western Front* (1930), but these expensive productions failed to boost the studio's profits. The company fell into the red in 1930 and continued to lose money throughout most of the decade, although releasing as many movies as ever (aside from the two worst years, 1930 and 1931). The output included shorts, early cartoons from Walter Lantz (who later created Woody Woodpecker), newsreels, serials, and B-Westerns, in addition to the wide range of features. Though some years were better than others and the memorable productions averaged no more than one or two per year, this pattern continued more or less unchanged up to 1946, in spite of various changes of management.

The failure of the studio's two most expensive productions of 1935 – *Showboat* and *Sutter's Gold* – led to the departure of Carl Laemmle, leaving Paramount's Adolph Zukor as the last active survivor of the original pioneer Hollywood producers. Laemmle sold his interest in the studio to a group of industrialists headed by John Cheever Cowdin in 1936, bringing to an end an impressive 24 years as head of Universal. The company was briefly run by R.H. Cochrane (president) and Charles R. Rogers (production chief) until early 1938 when a new team took over headed by Nate Blumberg, with Cliff Work in charge of the studio.

Finally Universal climbed out of the red in 1939, and profits continued to grow virtually every year up to 1946; but these were only moderate in relation to those of the top studios. Though the number of Universal releases was at a 20-year peak, most of them were routine programmers and reflected a shortage of top stars and directors. The studio's failure to take advantage of the boom in filmgoing is reflected in the list of the industry's top hits for the peak years, 1946 and 1947. Universal's top hits in 1946 were all thrillers – *The Dark Mirror* starring Olivia de Havilland tied for 45th place (with rentals of $2.75 million) and *The Killers* (directed by Robert Siodmak) and *Scarlet Street* (directed by Fritz Lang) tied at 49th. In 1947 Universal had its one smash hit of the decade, *The Egg And I* starring Claudette Colbert (rentals of $5.75 million putting it at eighth place); but its next-best earner for the year, *The Wistful Widow Of Wagon Gap* starring Abbott and Costello and Marjorie Main, could only manage a tie for 53rd.

In 1946 the studio merged with the small independent company International Pictures which had been formed by William Goetz and Leo Spitz in 1943. In a deal that echoed the merger of 20th Century and Fox just 11 years earlier, Goetz and Spitz took over the running of the studio in Hollywood, while Cowdin and Blumberg continued to head the company, renamed Universal-International, in New York.

In an effort to improve the average quality of its productions the company dropped its output of serials and B features, at the bottom end of the market, but this did little to improve the standard at the top. The other studios, too, were making important changes, so that at the end of the day Universal-International was relatively no better off than before. If anything, the film industry was more competitive than ever. An agreement with J. Arthur Rank to distribute many of the best British productions in the US added to the studio's prestige, but did little to boost its finances, though it did land the company with the Best Picture Oscar winner in 1948, Olivier's *Hamlet*. This, and other British pictures of 'quality' like *Great Expectations, Black Narcissus* and *Odd Man Out* (all released in 1947), appeared distinctly out of place alongside the bulk of Universal-International's own features. For the 'new look' company once again found itself depending on cheap series like Ma And Pa Kettle and Francis The Talking Mule, as well as a clutch of Audie Murphy Westerns – not, in truth very different from the Universal of old.

After two years in the red (1948 and 1949) the studio returned to profitability in the early 50s when important changes took place in the ownership of the company. Cowdin, Blumberg, Goetz and Spitz all left when Decca Records bought a controlling interest. With Milton Rackmil as president and Edward Muhl appointed studio manager, the company finally came up with the kind of formula required to boost it into the ranks of the Hollywood leaders. Major contributions came from a new group of producers (Aaron Rosenberg, Ross Hunter, Albert Zugsmith), directors (Douglas Sirk, Anthony Mann) and the strongest line-up of stars in the studio's history, many of them independents (James Stewart, Jane Wyman, Lana Turner), signed up on short-term deals.

During the 50s Universal was one of the first Hollywood studios to exploit the possibilities of combining TV and film production under one roof. The giant MCA – Music Corporation of America – agency (whose founder and chairman was Dr Jules Stein – also a renowned ophthalmologist), had become interested in Universal's studio facilities for the production of its TV programmes, and began a takeover in 1959 which it completed in 1962, when Universal and Decca were absorbed into the MCA conglomerate headed by Lew Wasserman.

Universal continued to do well in the 60s, and the true revitalization of the studio, which had begun over 20 years earlier, was finally confirmed in 1973 when it won its first Best Picture Oscar since *All Quiet On The Western Front* with a comedy-thriller, *The Sting*, starring Paul Newman and Robert Redford.

During the 80s Universal released a number of dramatic films of note such as *Melvin And Howard* (1980), *Missing* (1982), the Oscar-winning *Out Of Africa* (1985), *Field of Dreams* and *Born On The Fourth Of July* (both 1989). But it continued to benefit financially from the link with producer-director Steven Spielberg who had provided the studio with its top 70s hit in *Jaws* (1975) and repeated with *E.T. The Extra-Terrestrial* (1982) while serving as executive producer of the highly popular Back To The Future features.

After months of negotiating in 1990, Matsushita, Japan's largest electronics manufacturer, demonstrated that it could keep pace with arch rival Sony by purchasing MCA and Universal for the hefty sum of over $6 billion in cash and shares. This was the biggest US acquisition by a Japanese company thus far, and involved a purchase price almost twice that of Sony's takeover of Columbia one year earlier.

Universal Studio Chronology

1909   Carl Laemmle founds the IMP (Independent Motion Picture) Company to produce one-reelers.

1912   IMP is merged with a number of smaller companies to form Universal Film Manufacturing Company.

1913   Laemmle has his first big hit with the feature-length *Traffic In Souls*.

1915   The company moves into its new studio at Universal City in California.

1921   Production is halted on Erich von Stroheim's *Foolish Wives* by the young studio boss, Irving Thalberg.

1922   Release of *Foolish Wives* in incomplete form.

1923   The studio releases its first classic horror movie, *The Hunchback Of Notre Dame* with Lon Chaney.

1930   *All Quiet On The Western Front* wins the Best Picture Oscar.

1931   The studio releases *Dracula*, followed by *Frankenstein*.

1936   Carl Laemmle sells out his interest in Universal.

1946   Universal merges with International Pictures to become Universal-International, with William Goetz as production chief.

1952   Decca Records buys a controlling interest in the studio.

1962   MCA Inc., headed by Lew Wasserman, completes its takeover of Universal (and Decca) which thus becomes the film production subsidiary of this entertainment giant.

1972   Ned Tanen appointed as production chief.

1973   Universal wins the Best Picture Oscar for the second time with *The Sting*.

1975   The studio releases the spectacularly successful *Jaws*, Steven Spielberg's second feature as a Universal director.

1976   Ned Tanen promoted to president of Universal.

1982   The studio releases *E.T. The Extra-Terrestrial*.
        Departure of Ned Tanen; replaced by Frank Price.

1985   Universal wins the Oscar for Best Picture for *Out Of Africa* and has another huge Spielberg (as producer) hit with *Back To The Future*.

1986   Frank Price resigns.

1990   The Japanese electronics giant, Matsushita Electric Industrial Co. purchases MCA and Universal for about $6.6 billion.

The Releases

Throughout its early history Universal released large numbers of programmers in a variety of genres. Best remembered for its horror films, and weepies such as *Magnificent Obsession* and *Imitation Of Life*, first filmed in the 30s and remade 20 years later, the studio also produced many cheap musicals, Westerns and comedies. Universal began turning out a few horror movies and exotic adventure flicks (starring Maria Montez) in Technicolor in the 40s. They moved to increase their output of colour pictures in the 50s, but these were mainly B Westerns and adventure movies. At the same time the studio began to cut back on its large number of releases while trying both 3-D and CinemaScope in selected productions. In later years Universal improved its image with classier stars and pictures. Its most recent success with the fantasy movies of Steven Spielberg, such as *E.T. The Extra-Terrestrial* and the Back To The Future pictures, is in the true Universal tradition.

Comedies, Westerns, and dramatic pictures of all lengths and types were the staple items in Universal's output. Though most were routine productions of little special interest, the studio did attempt to turn out at least one or two films of note each year. *Traffic In Souls* (1913) was a lurid exposé of the white slave traffic, and during the following years the studio developed a special interest in topical social themes, Prison reform, birth control, drugs, alcoholism, capital punishment and the plight of orphaned children were all grist to the Universal movie mill. (Twenty years later Warner Bros. achieved distinction exploiting these subjects.) The studio's output grew significantly after its move into the new Universal City studios in California in 1915.

An eight-reel version of Jules Verne's *20,000 Leagues Under The Sea* (1916) was one of the studio's most ambitious early productions, filmed on location with some outstanding underwater photography. This movie also suggests an early interest in the fantasy and horror subjects which were to become a Universal trademark in later years; indeed, Herbert Brenon had directed a two-reel version of *Dr Jekyll And Mr Hyde* starring King Baggott as early as 1913. Anticipating the later Invisible Man pictures, the invisibility theme was explored in a couple of shorts in 1916, *Her Invisible Husband* and *Through Solid Walls*, while futuristic gadgetry of all sorts was a staple item in many of the studio's early serials.

World War I provided the subject for such pictures as *Treason* (1917), *The Kaiser, Beast Of Berlin* (1918) and, most notably, the nine-reel feature, *The Heart of Humanity* (1919) starring Dorothy Phillips and Erich von Stroheim. This, Stroheim's initial appearance in a Universal movie, was soon to be followed by his own first outstanding production as writer-director-star – *Blind Husbands* (1919). Here, and in the pictures which followed, like *Foolish Wives* (1922), he demonstrated a special talent for transforming the kind of social intrigues and domestic drama which the studio churned out year after year into something rather more perceptive and sophisticated. In a similar vein was Clarence Brown's memorable social drama *Smouldering Fires* (1924) starring Pauline Frederick. Tod Browning, in contrast, contributed more offbeat fare, such as the underworld drama *Outside The Law* (1921), starring Lon Chaney, and the adventure yarn *Under Two Flags* (1922). There was the occasional costume picture of note, for example *A Lady Of Quality* (1924) directed by Hobart Henley, but most of the Universal releases in the 20s were quickly forgotten.

In order to provide some variety of subject matter and plot, sports and show-biz themes were introduced into numerous movies. Football within a college-campus setting, boxing dramas and circus stories were popular and flappers, too, were all the rage in such pictures as *The Mad Whirl* (1925) directed by William Seiter, who also directed the best of the Reginald Denny comedies. The first entry in a successful new 'Jewish and Irish' comedy series, *The Cohens And The Kellys*, appeared in 1926 and continued on into the 30s.

Universal's most celebrated productions of the mid-20s, however, were *The Hunchback Of Notre Dame* (1923) and *The Phantom Of The Opera* (1925) and they marked the beginning of the studio's special identification with horror, fantasy and the macabre. The best of the horror films were often the product of a close collaboration between the studio's European immigrant directors, actors and designers. German-born director Paul Leni carried on the tradition with *The Cat And The Canary* (1927), *The Man Who Laughs* (1928) starring Conrad Veidt, and *The Last Warning* (1928), all designed by the outstanding, British-born art director Danny Hall.

The cycle really took off in 1931, however, with the release of *Dracula* starring Bela Lugosi, and was followed later in the year by *Frankenstein*. This was the most famous and successful of them all, and the first of a number of notable collaborations between a British team led by director James Whale, designer Hall, and a cast headed by Boris Karloff and Colin Clive. The same team was reassembled for an outstanding sequel, *The Bride Of Frankenstein*, which brought Universal's most memorable horror cycle to a close in 1935 along with *The Raven*, teaming Karloff and Lugosi, and *The Werewolf Of London*. Other entries included *The Old Dark House* (1932), Whale-Hall-Karloff again, joined by Charles Laughton; *Murders In The Rue Morgue* (1932) with Lugosi directed by Robert Florey; and Karloff as *The Mummy* (1932), directed by ace cameraman Karl Freund who had been behind the camera on *Dracula* and *Rue Morgue*. In 1933 Whale and Hall offered Claude Rains as *The Invisible Man*, while *The Black Cat* (1934), starring Karloff and Lugosi, was designed by Hall and was directed by Edgar Ulmer.

A kind of offbeat epilogue to the cycle was provided by *The Invisible Ray* and *Dracula's Daughter* in 1936. But it was not long before the monsters were back in business with a new and inferior series of movies which recycled many of the same themes and characters (the Invisible Man, Frankenstein's monster, Dracula, the Wolf Man, the Mummy) throughout the 40s. The characters were finally presented as foils for Abbott and Costello in a number of movies which only came to an end in 1955 with *Abbott And Costello Meet The Mummy*.

The studio had averaged well over 50 features per year throughout the 20s. However, the coming of sound, with the added costs involved and the technical difficulties experienced, meant a steady decline in the number of features released. From a peak of over 60 in 1927, the number had fallen by two-thirds by 1931, but there was a steady recovery during the rest of the 30s with an average of 30–40 in the middle years rising to a new peak of over 50 between 1940 and 1943.

With the arrival of the talkies in 1928 Universal had been firmly relegated to the position of a second-rate studio. It still continued to turn out a large number of pictures of all types including serials, shorts, cartoons (from Walter Lantz), and a twice-weekly newsreel (from 1931) in addition to the features, which balanced cheap comedies and dramas against Westerns and horror films. And since a number of talented people spent some time at the studio, there continued to be one or two films of note each year. These tended to be surprisingly different from year to year and depended on what talent was available.

In 1928 Paul Fejos directed a remarkably original and perceptive part-talkie, *Lonesome*, filmed on location in and around New York City, and he made the lavish musical *Broadway* the following year. *All Quiet On The Western Front*, a truly exceptional and unique achievement for the little Universal studio, dominated 1930, also the year of the memorable *King Of Jazz*, and a Western of note from William Wyler, *Hell's Heroes*. The following year belonged to *Dracula* and *Frankenstein*, while 1932 saw the release of the Kaufman-Hart comedy, *Once In A Lifetime*, *Law And Order* – a first-rate Western, and *The Mummy*. In 1933 Wyler directed John Barrymore in *Counsellor-At-Law* while other releases included the offbeat musical *Moonlight And Pretzels* and *The Invisible Man*. *The Black Cat* was released in 1934 as was John Stahl's melodrama, *Imitation Of Life*. Stahl followed with another tearjerker, *Magnificent Obsession*, in 1935, when the other noteworthy releases were a bitter-sweet comedy, *The Good Fairy*, from writer Preston Sturges and director Wyler, and *The Bride Of Frankenstein*. Universal's most celebrated screwball comedy, *My Man Godfrey*, appeared in 1936, as did a costly production of *Showboat* and the first Deanna Durbin musical, *Three Smart Girls*, marking the long overdue beginning of a musical revival at the studio. Universal's A-grade movies were quite a mixed bag, with only the horror movies providing a continuous theme.

This diverse mixture of subjects reflects the fact that for much of the time Universal went its own way and made only a limited effort to follow the trends established by the other, larger studios. Universal's attitude to the musical is perhaps indicative of the somewhat quirky way in which it operated. Having been slow to join the early rush into musicals in 1928–29, then badly burned by the costly *King Of Jazz*, the studio abandoned the genre for many years. It ignored the revival which began as early as 1933 (with Busby Berkeley at Warner Bros.) and saw new musical stars emerging at most of the other studios. Finally, in 1936, Universal discovered its own musical star in Deanna Durbin and slowly revived its interest in this genre. By the early 40s the studio had swung to the opposite extreme and was turning out cheap (and largely undistinguished) black-and-white musicals at an astonishing rate. During the peak period of 1940–45, it was releasing an average of 15 (often forgettable) musicals per year, more than any other Hollywood company, and was introducing songs or musical numbers into many dramatic pictures and Westerns as well.

By 1946, however, musicals were out yet again, in spite of the fact that MGM, Fox and other top studios continued to film them in colour until well into the 50s. A detailed breakdown for 1945, the last big musical year, shows that 20 of 47 Universal features were black-and-white musicals. Deanna Durbin did not appear in a single one, but was cast in a comedy and a thriller instead as the studio made an effort to broaden her appeal and establish her in more adult roles. But she was reaching the end of her movie career and the studio was changing. By 1946 Universal was not only cutting back on musicals and B Westerns but had eliminated serials entirely. The horror cycle was nearing its end, as was the Sherlock Holmes series starring Basil Rathbone and the Inner Sanctum murder mysteries with Lon Chaney Jr. In an attempt to upgrade its image under the new Universal-International banner, the studio dropped a large number of its contract stars such as Chaney Jr, and musical performers Gloria Jean, Peggy Ryan and Susanna Foster.

There was an increase in the output of quality thrillers, comedies, and Westerns in the 50s, and the studio released more pictures from independent producers as well as many of the best British productions from J. Arthur Rank, Gainsborough, Ealing and Two Cities. Similarly, Universal increased its investment in colour productions in the early 50s when the number of releases climbed back to an average of slightly over 30 per year, having fallen to the low 20s in 1947–49 from the peak levels of 1940–43.

The new-look Universal pursued its own individual style, but appeared strangely reminiscent of the Universal of old with its choice of a wide range of comedy and drama, along with adventure pictures and Audie Murphy Westerns, which were little better than cheap programmers, though filmed in colour. The studio maintained a line in quirky comedies – Abbott and Costello and Ma and Pa Kettle were joined by Francis the Talking Mule, part of an anthropomorphic animal comedy cycle which included such notable entries as James Stewart starring alongside an invisible giant white rabbit named *Harvey* (1950), and Ronald Reagan teamed with a chimp in *Bedtime For Bonzo* (1951). Finally, the studio's cycle of cheap but imaginative and entertaining fantasy and science-fiction movies, most often directed by Jack Arnold, corresponded to the horror cycles of earlier years.

Since Universal was turning out far fewer pictures than ever before, the proportion of noteworthy productions was correspondingly higher. Comedies and women's pictures of quality from director Douglas Sirk and producer Ross Hunter, and the tough James Stewart-Anthony Mann films led the way, and there were a number of special productions of interest: the war veteran's drama *Bright Victory* (1952); Kirk Douglas as the *Man Without A Star* (1955) directed by King Vidor; Cagney as Chaney in *Man Of A Thousand Faces* (1957); and a fast-moving thriller from Orson Welles, *Touch Of Evil* (1958).

The number of releases dropped yet again from 1959 on, but there was a marked improvement in quality. Since Universal was always known for its diversity as a studio, it easily made the transition to the post-studio era. While other companies – MGM for example – had trouble making the adjustment, Universal held its own during the 60s and emerged stronger than ever in the 70s. Successful releases ranged from Doris Day and Cary Grant comedies to musicals such as *Thoroughly Modern Millie* (1967) and *Sweet Charity* (1969); there were epics (*Spartacus*, 1960, *The War Lord*, 1965, *Anne Of The Thousand Days*, 1969); Westerns (*Shenandoah*, 1965, *Two Mules For Sister Sara*, 1970), and Hitchcockian-style thrillers. This pattern continued on through the 80s. The studio benefited from its connection with producer-director Steven Spielberg and his particular line of teen and pre-teen adventure and fantasy in *E.T. The Extra Terrestrial* and the three *Back to the Future* features. During recent years the company has been most readily identified with a trendy line in offbeat comedy, as represented by *Fletch* (1985), *Harry and the Hendersons* (1987), and *Twins* (1988), also *Parenthood* and *Uncle Buck* (both 1989), while the successful comedy-thrillers included *Dragnet* (1987) *Bird on a Wire* and *Kindergarten Cop* (both 1990).

Colour and Widescreen

The studio was quick to take advantage of the new two-strip Technicolor in 1925, noticeably with the masked-ball sequence in *The Phantom Of The Opera* which looked particularly effective in colour. But Universal did not repeat the experience until 1929 when colour had come to be regarded as a standard ingredient in the opulent musicals then being produced in Hollywood. Not to be outdone by the competition, the studio introduced Technicolor sequences into *Broadway* while its most ambitious musical, *King Of Jazz*, directed by John Murray Anderson, was filmed spectacularly in Technicolor in 1930.

As one of the smaller and least profitable of the majors, Universal was wary of the added cost of colour filming in the 30s and was slow to develop an interest in the new, improved three-strip Technicolor. In fact, the studio's first ventures into colour in 1942–43 can be seen as part of a more general trend which developed around that time. But whereas the other producers were filming mainly musicals and Westerns, Universal came up with its own colour formula, initially a series of exotic adventure movies starring Maria Montez (the first was *Arabian Nights* in 1942), and two horror pictures. The studio's $1.5 million remake of *The Phantom Of The Opera* (1943), starring Claude Rains, placed the emphasis more on spectacle than horror and won colour Oscars for photography and art direction. However, a follow-up production, *The Climax* (1944) which starred Boris Karloff, was less successful.

Universal continued to turn out a modest but regular number of colour films, averaging three to four titles per year throughout the rest of the 40s, but without much success. *Can't Help Singing* (1944) was Deanna Durbin's only musical in Technicolor, while Yvonne De Carlo replaced Montez as the studio's leading Technicolor star, combining Westerns such as *Frontier Gal* (1945) and *Calamity Jane And Sam Bass* (1949) with exotic roles in *Slave Girl* and *Song Of Scheherazade* (both 1947).

The studio more than doubled its output of colour films in the early 50s, making mainly routine Westerns and adventure movies featuring contract stars such as Rock Hudson, Audie Murphy, Jeff Chandler, Yvonne De Carlo and Julie Adams. *The World In His Arms* starring Gregory Peck and Ann Blyth, directed by Raoul Walsh and photographed by Russell Metty, and the Anthony Mann-James Stewart Western *Bend Of The River* (with Rock Hudson and Julie Adams in co-starring roles) were Universal's first colour hits in 1952. Though the studio continued to expand its production of colour features in the mid-50s, it resisted the introduction of the new special processes such as CinemaScope and VistaVision. (Universal, however, *did* join the other companies in the relatively brief experiment with 3-D filming in 1953–54, but most of its best-known examples e.g. *It Came From Outer Space*, 1953, and *The Creature From The Black Lagoon*, 1954, were shot in black-and-white.)

Late in 1956 Universal made a sudden and unexpected turnabout, at about the same time that 20th Century-Fox decided to allow black-and-white filming in CinemaScope (which had previously been an all-colour process). The results can be seen in the output of the studio's leading contract director, Douglas Sirk. Whereas he had only used CinemaScope twice prior to 1956, all four of his pictures released between December 1956 and September 1958 were in 'Scope, beginning with *Battle Hymn* photographed by Russell Metty.

Sirk also made effective use of black-and-white CinemaScope for *The Tarnished Angels* (1957) but dropped it for his last Universal production, the remake of *Imitation Of Life*, filmed in 1958 in Eastmancolor, since the studio's interest in CinemaScope was on the wane.

By late 1959 Universal had virtually given up anamorphic filming; having drastically cut down on its CinemaScope productions, it was also slow to switch to Panavision and Techniscope, only doing so in the late 60s. In addition, the studio distributed a number of early Technirama productions, the most famous of which was Stanley Kubrick's *Spartacus* (1960) with Oscar-winning photography by Russell Metty. The studio's one big 70mm hit was Ross Hunter's production of *Airport* (1970), filmed in Todd-AO.

Widescreen and 3-D Releases 1953–69

Process	1953	1954	1955	1956	1957	1958	1959	1960	1961	1962	1963	1964	1965	1966	1967	1968	1969
CinemaScope		2	6	4[b]	18	17	7	1									
Technirama					2			1	1								
Panavision						1	3	1	2	2	2		1	4	2	3	2
Techniscope													1	7	10	18	4
3-D	3	2	1														

b includes one VistaVision

note one large format (70mm) release in 1970

The Finances

The studio's financial history can be divided into three distinct periods: the years prior to 1939 when Universal was a relatively small company earning tiny profits (through most of the 20s) or making small losses (in the 30s). During the 40s and through to the 60s the studio generally became more successful, upgrading its image and earning steady profits throughout most of this period. But only during the most recent years, from the early 70s up to the present, has Universal emerged as one of the most profitable Hollywood studios for the first time in its long history. Beginning with *Airport* (1970), Universal has produced many of the top hits of the past 16 years, including *American Graffiti* and *The Sting* in 1973 and three of Steven Spielberg's most successful blockbusters: *Jaws* (1975), *E.T. The Extra-Terrestrial* (1982) and *Back To The Future* (1984).

Carl Laemmle's policy of turning out large numbers of cheaply produced pictures, aimed at small-town audiences, meant that the studio's profits remained slight (if steady) in relation to total revenues in the early years. In 1921 and 1922, for example, Universal's annual revenues averaged just under $17 million, only slightly behind Fox and Metro, but the studio's profits were substantially lower. A rare venture into high-cost filming, Stroheim's $1.1 million production of *Foolish Wives* was released early in 1922 and did well at the box-office, but not well enough to cover its substantial costs. The most prestigious of Universal movies, it did nothing to boost the studio's profitability and actually recorded a net loss of about $250,000.

Revenues grew slowly during the 20s, but profits failed to keep pace after 1926. Stroheim's last Universal production, *Merry-Go-Round* (completed by Rupert Julian) earned a tidy profit of almost $350,000, more than balancing the loss on *Foolish Wives* and contributing to the studio's profits in 1923, while later that year the release of *The Hunchback Of Notre Dame*, Universal's biggest hit of the decade, carried over into 1924. This was the beginning of the company's most profitable period, 1924–26, when profits averaged just under $2 million per year – with a major boost from the studio's second big Lon Chaney vehicle, *The Phantom Of The Opera* (1925). Universal would have to wait 14 years (till the early 40s) before it would again see profits of even this fairly modest size.

Since Universal turned out mainly routine programmers, lacked its own first-run cinemas and was slow to move into sound, it was vulnerable to the increasingly sophisticated and intense competition. Having existed on the fringes of the leading film companies for many years, Universal was overtaken by such upstarts as the expanding Warner Bros. and an important new arrival, RKO. Fox, too, shot ahead of Universal with a major investment in theatres and talkie production. Whereas the companies had been roughly similar in size in the early 20s, by 1929–30 Fox's revenues of over $40 million were almost twice those of Universal, with profits at a hefty $10 million while Universal was struggling merely to break even. The studio's profits had in fact been *falling* during the boom years of the late 20s, and it recorded a loss in 1930.

Universal had, however, been unlucky with two of its biggest pictures, released early in 1930 under the supervision of the new studio boss Carl Laemmle Jr. More of a prestige success than a commercial moneymaker, *All Quiet On The Western Front* cost $1.25 million to produce, and though it did fairly well at the box-office, it was banned in Germany and ended up earning only a small profit. However, the remarkable Technicolored musical *King Of Jazz* was a disaster for the studio. Costing all of $1.65 million, it was only released toward the end of the cycle of talkie musicals which had so glutted the market. Though it did not do too badly, all things considered, it dismally failed to recover its exceptional cost, and lost the company a massive $1 million.

The first major studio to be hit by the Depression, Universal was also the last to recover, recording annual losses throughout the 30s. Though these losses were generally small – the studio never had to cope with the huge deficits registered by many of the larger companies – the company was in financial difficulty through most of this period. Universal continued to concentrate on relatively cheap features, serials and Westerns and did best at the box-office with its cycle of low-cost horror movies in the early 30s and with the Deanna Durbin musicals later on. (*Frankenstein* in 1931 had cost only $250,000 to produce, and *Three Smart Girls* in 1936 had its budget *increased* to about $350,000 when studio executives suspected they might have a hit on their hands.) It has often been stated that Durbin's pictures alone saved the studio. There is little evidence to support this, but they certainly did help to keep the studio's losses at manageable levels during the difficult years after 1936 when Laemmle sold out his interest in Universal.

Having missed out entirely on the 1936–37 recovery in profits experienced by many of the other companies, Universal finally made its long-overdue return to profitability in 1939 – under a new management team which carried on successfully through the war years. The good news was that the company was back in the black. The bad news was that Universal, with its lack of film theatres and top stars, was limited in the extent to which it could take advantage of the wartime boom. Though the Abbott and Costello movies were most successful at the box-office, the studio had few big hits. Profits only managed to top the $4 million mark in 1946, near the end of the boom, and began to fall off by 1947 – in spite of the release of the studio's single biggest hit of the decade, *The Egg And I* starring Claudette Colbert.

After merging with International Pictures in 1946 to form Universal-International, the new company set out to upgrade its image with average budgets set at $1–1.5 million, the gradual phasing out of B features, more movies to be shot in colour, and agreements with a number of independent producers to supply the studio with pictures. But the company was faced with an extremely competitive and shrinking market, and profits continued to fall. After two years in the red (1948–49), chairman of the board J. Cheever Cowdin resigned in 1950. One important new development, however, was a percentage agreement with James Stewart which first took effect on two pictures in 1950, the Western *Winchester '73*, directed by Anthony Mann, and the comedy, *Harvey*. Both were relatively low-cost ($1 million) black-and-white movies which earned a good profit.

Late in 1951 the Decca Record Company bought a major shareholding in Universal and took control of the studio in 1952, leading to yet another change in management. Profits and revenues grew slowly, but steadily, from 1950 to 1956, and Universal brought home big hits with such pictures as *Bend Of The River* (1952) and *The Glenn Miller Story* (1954), both produced by Aaron Rosenberg, directed by Mann and starring Stewart, and *Magnificent Obsession* (1954) starring Jane Wyman and Rock Hudson, produced by Ross Hunter and directed by Douglas Sirk. All of these were filmed economically – *Magnificent Obsession*, for example, cost only $800,000 – and thus earned healthy profits.

Though profits fell off badly in 1957–58, the studio bounced back in 1959 and was able to maintain a reasonable level of profits of just under $5 million per year throughout the early 60s, aided by a regular flow of hit movies. *Imitation Of Life* (1959) starred Lana Turner and was directed by Sirk, and *Pillow Talk* (1959) was the first of the Doris Day comedies, followed by Blake Edwards' *Operation Petticoat* in 1960. That year, too, Stanley Kubrick's *Spartacus* cost all of $12 million, the studio's most expensive production to date; it did well enough at the box-office to break even, but failed to show a profit. Doris Day scored again in *Lover Come Back* (1961) and *That Touch Of Mink*, co-starring Cary Grant in 1962, also the year of *To Kill A Mockingbird*. Hitchcock's *The Birds*, and director Stanley Donen's Hitchcockian *Charade* starring Grant and Audrey Hepburn, were notable in 1963.

At the time of Universal's recovery in the 50s, the MCA talent agency, which had been responsible for negotiating James Stewart's 1950 percentage deal, was growing and prospering under the guidance of Jules Stein and Lew Wasserman. MCA not only expanded its agency activities, but – alongside Universal, one of the first Hollywood studios to become actively involved with television – ventured into TV production as well, with such successful shows as 'Alfred Hitchcock Presents.'

By the early 60s MCA had far outgrown its simple agency origins. With the threat of prosecution by the Department of Justice under the anti-trust laws, the company gave up its agency in 1962 and completed its takeover of Decca and Universal that had begun in 1959. These companies became subsidiaries of the newly expanded MCA conglomerate headed by Lew Wasserman, the first successful agent to take charge of major Hollywood studio. (Many others would follow in his footsteps in later years.)

The studio continued to do reasonably well under its new boss throughout most of the 60s, producing such hits as *Shenandoah* (1965) starring James Stewart, and *Thoroughly Modern Millie* (1967) with Julie Andrews. Like most of the other major studios Universal was hit hard by the slump in 1969, but was the first to recover, boosted by the biggest hit in the company's history up to that date, *Airport* (1970). The movie cost $10 million but brought in rentals of $44.5 million.

The company continued successful during the following years, starting slowly but spearheading the revival in filmgoing which took place during the 70s. This revival was led by such spectacularly successful young directors as George Lucas and Steven Spielberg. The big turning point came in 1973 with the unexpected success of Lucas' *American Graffiti*, a relatively modest, low-cost ($750,000) picture which brought in rentals of over $50 million, most of which was clear profit. It was followed later that same year by *The Sting* which cost $5.5 million, of which $1 million was split between the two stars, Paul Newman and Robert Redford, and brought in rentals of almost $80 million. Suddenly Universal had become the most profitable studio in Hollywood, confirmed in 1975 by the hugely successful *Jaws* directed by Steven Spielberg. Operating income grew from an average of less than $20 million per year from 1971 to 1973 (before profits from *The Sting* had started rolling in) to $68 million in 1974 and an impressive $110 million during 1975–77.

The flow of moneymaking hits continued with *Smokey And The Bandit* (1977, cost $4 million), *National Lampoon's Animal House* (1978, cost $2.7 million) and *The Jerk* (1979). Universal had its ups and downs during the late 70s and into the 80s, but even the downs were not too bad by the standards of the other, less profitable companies. Operating income peaked at $175 million in 1979 then fell back in 1980 and 1981. But the studio's weakest years – 1981 with an operating income of $72 million and 1984 at $62 million – were immediately followed by spectacular successes. The studio had a record operating income of $212 million in 1982, the year of Spielberg's *E.T. The Extra-Terrestrial* (which had cost only slightly over $10 million) and almost $150 million in 1985, mainly due to another Spielberg production, the $22 million *Back To The Future*, which became the top box-office hit of the year. But the company fell back in 1986 as both *Legal Eagles* and *Howard The Duck* proved to be expensive flops. And results in the late 80s were similarly uneven. The top hits included the two Back To The Future sequels and *Twins* (1988). The best recent year was 1989 when two surprise hits – Ron Howard's *Parenthood* and Oliver Stone's *Born On The Fourth Of July* – along with *Back To The Future 2* boosted Universal to the second spot (just behind Warners) in US market share.

Box Office Hits

TITLE	Cost	North American rentals
1914–31	(in $ million)	(in $ millions)
All Quiet On The Western Front (1930)	(1.3)	1.5
The Hunchback Of Notre Dame (1923)		1.5
1942–50		
The Egg And I (1947)		5.5
Hamlet (Rank/Two Cities) (GB) (1948)	(1.5)	3.3
Francis (1950)		2.9
The Dark Mirror (1946)		2.8
The Killers (1946)		2.5
Scarlet Street (1946)		2.5
Tap Roots (1948)		2.5
The Naked City (1948)		2.4
The Wistful Widow Of Wagon Gap (1947)		2.4
Ma And Pa Kettle (1949)	(0.2)	2.3
Winchester '73 (1950)	(0.9)	2.3
1951–60		
Spartacus (1960)	(12.0)	14.0
Operation Petticoat (1959)		9.3
The Glenn Miller Story (1954)		7.6
Pillow Talk (1959)		7.5
Imitation Of Life (1959)		6.5
To Hell And Back (1955)		6.0
Magnificent Obsession (1954)	(0.8)	5.2
Written On The Wind (1956)		4.3
1961–70		
Airport (1970)	(10.0)	44.5
Thoroughly Modern Millie (1967)		14.7
Lover Come Back (1962)		8.5
That Touch Of Mink (1962)		8.5
Shenandoah (1965)		7.8
To Kill A Mockingbird (1962)		7.2
Winning (1969)		6.6
Come September (1961)		6.5
Torn Curtain (1966)	(5.0)	6.5
Charade (1963)	(3.0)	6.2
Father Goose (1965)		6.0
The War Wagon (1967)		6.0
1971–80		
Jaws (1975)	(12.0)	133.4
The Sting (1973)	(5.5)	79.0
National Lampoon's Animal House (1978)	(2.7)	74.0
Smokey And The Bandit (1977)	(4.0)	61.0
American Graffiti (1973)	(0.7)	55.9
Jaws II (1978)	(20.0)	55.6
The Jerk (1979)		43.0
Coal Miner's Daughter (1980)		38.5
Smokey And The Bandit II (1980)		37.6
Earthquake (1974)	(7.0)	36.3
The Blues Brothers (1980)	(30.0)	32.2
The Deer Hunter (co-prod) (1978)	(13.0)	30.4
Airport 1975 (1974)	(4.0)	25.8
1941 (co-prod) (1979)	(27.0)	23.4

1981–90

E.T. The Extra-Terrestrial (1982)	(10.6)	228.4
Back To The Future (1985)	(22.0)	105.5
Back To The Future Part II (1989)	(40.0)	72.3
On Golden Pond (co-prod) (1981)	(9.5)	61.2
Twins (1988)	(17.0)	57.7
Parenthood (1989)	(20.0)	50.2
Back To The Future Part III (1990)		49.0
The Best Little Whorehouse in Texas (co-prod) (1982)	(35.0)	47.3
Out Of Africa (1985)	(30.0)	43.4
Bird On A Wire (1990)	(20.0)	38.4
Born On The Fourth Of July (1989)	(18.0)	36.8
Kindergarten Cop (1990)		34.0

The Stars

Though Universal had few major stars of its own, a large number passed through the studio at one time or another, often on loan from elsewhere. The studio's best-known names made a surprisingly diverse group: Lon Chaney, Boris Karloff and Bela Lugosi graced the early horror films, while Deanna Durbin and Donald O'Connor appeared in many musicals in the 30s and 40s. W. C. Fields, Abbott and Costello, and Marjorie Main were Universal's most popular comedy attractions, while Maria Montez appeared in a series of exotic 40s costumers. The studio's line-up of male stars in the 50s included James Stewart, Rock Hudson, Tony Curtis, Jeff Chandler and Audie Murphy, and Doris Day and Cary Grant arrived in 1959 to give a welcome boost to the studio near the end of their own movie careers.

Carl Laemmle played an important role in initiating the star system in 1910 when he had the idea of hiring Florence Lawrence, known as 'The Biograph Girl', and publicizing her true name for the first time. Increasing her salary from $25 to $200 per week, Laemmle launched her new career at IMP with an ingenious publicity gimmick: he planted a story that she had been killed in a streetcar accident, then claimed that the false story had been invented by the enemies of his IMP company.

Mary Pickford was next to inherit the title of 'The Biograph Girl' and the top Biograph salary of $100 per week which went with it. But she, too, was lured away by Laemmle toward the end of 1910 with the offer of $175 per week and turned out 34 one-reelers, mostly directed by Thomas Ince, in less than a year. Having worked with D.W. Griffith and his ace cameraman Billy Bitzer, Miss Pickford was dissatisfied with the standard of IMP productions: 'The photography was poor, and they did not light the pictures properly.' She soon left. But Laemmle continued to hire many more stars under his new Universal banner. Among those he had under contract, including some names which are all but forgotten today, were Herbert Rawlinson (1913–24), Hobart Bosworth (1915–16), Tyrone Power Sr (1916), Dorothy Phillips (1916–19), Louise

Lovely (1916–18), Jack Mulhall (1916–18), Mary Maclaren (1916–20) and Carmel Myers (1917–21).

Of special interest was the large number of actor-directors. King Baggott, one of Laemmle's first stars, emerged as a director of note in the 20s, and John Ford's elder brother, Francis, directed and starred in a number of two-reelers, action serials and features. (John began his movie career as a bit player and assistant on some of these pictures.) Lois Weber, the most important woman director of the early American cinema, occasionally co-starred with her husband Phillips Smalley, and specialized in serious dramatic themes from a feminine viewpoint – as in *Where Are My Children?* (1916) which treated the subject of birth control. Rupert Julian was another well-known actor-director, but the most celebrated of all was Erich von Stroheim who made his auspicious debut as star and director at Universal with *Blind Husbands* in 1919.

Ironically, the studio's three biggest star discoveries – the attractive Mae Murray with the bee-sting lips, romantic Rudolph Valentino who was paid $100 a week and the formidable Lon Chaney – all became famous after leaving Universal in 1919 and emerged as leading silent stars during the 20s. Chaney had appeared in a large number and variety of pictures, playing many different roles and even directing a few films, but there was little indication that he would one day become a top silent star. At least he returned to Universal for his two most celebrated roles, as *The Hunchback Of Notre Dame* (1923) and *The Phantom Of The Opera* (1925), in which he demonstrated his special qualities as a master of make-up and grotesque characterization on the screen. As the studio's first major star it is appropriate that he should have provided Universal with its first hits in that genre which would come to be most closely associated with the studio over the years, namely, the horror film.

Universal's first Western star, Harry Carey, made his name in a series of films with the studio's outstanding young director John Ford during 1917–21; and Hoot Gibson, too, got his start in a number of Ford pictures and continued at Universal up to 1930, earning $14,500 per week in the 20s. Between them they helped to establish the Western programmer as a staple ingredient in the studio's diet. The tradition was carried on through the 30s by Ken Maynard and Buck Jones, then Johnny Mack Brown (1937–43), and war hero Audie Murphy in the 50s.

During the 20s, the studio was generally forced to rely on stars of the second rank such as Norman Kerry, Laura La Plante and Reginald Denny, but with the coming of sound, Universal, like the other studios, gave an opportunity to many newcomers. Edward G. Robinson, Bette Davis and Jean Arthur all appeared in Universal pictures during 1929–31, but only emerged as stars after they left. The studio had more success with its expert horror stars, particularly Bela Lugosi (Dracula) and Boris Karloff (the Frankenstein monster), in the early 30s, and with the revival of the cycle from about 1939 on they were joined by Lionel Atwill, Lon Chaney Jr, and Basil Rathbone. Rathbone also starred in the studio's Sherlock Holmes series, with which he remains closely identified.

Like RKO, the studio turned out numerous 'women's pictures' of note during the early 30s with stars such as Gloria Stuart (1932–34), and the gifted Margaret Sullavan whose stay at Universal turned out to be all too brief. She first appeared in *Only Yesterday* (1933), followed by *Little Man What Now?* (1934) and *The Good Fairy* (1935), at a star salary which the studio could ill afford – $1200 a week – to keep her happy. But, as so often with Universal, its shortage of top stars forced it to rely on loans from other studios for a large number of A pictures. Claudette Colbert was borrowed from Paramount for *Imitation Of Life* (1934) and Irene Dunne from RKO for *Back Street* (1932), *Magnificent Obsession* (1935) with Robert Taylor (on loan from MGM), and the musical *Showboat*. Carole Lombard from Paramount and William Powell from MGM played the leads in the studio's famous screwball comedy of the 30s, *My Man Godfrey* (1936).

In the late 30s and on into the 40s, Universal's star roster presented a typically diverse mixture of talents, with stars both old and new. The most popular musical performer, Deanna Durbin, arrived in 1936 and by 1938 was earning $3,000 per week plus a bonus of $10,000 per film, and was clearly worth it to the hard-pressed studio. Buster Crabbe starred as Flash Gordon in three serials, and Universal acquired the services of two stars whose best years were behind them: Marlene Dietrich gave a suitably lively performance as Frenchie in *Destry Rides Again* (1939) at a reputed fee of less than $50,000, but the part helped to restore her drawing power and by 1941, when she earned $200,000, she was one of Universal's highest-paid actresses. Similarly, W.C. Fields proved that he still had a few good films left in him with *The Bank Dick* (1940) and *Never Give A Sucker An Even Break* (1941). His fee was $125,000 per picture with an additional $25,000 for the story. Maria Montez starred with Jon Hall and, occasionally, Sabu, in a series of exotic Technicolored fantasies beginning with *Arabian Nights* (1942). Yvonne De Carlo, more of an actress than Montez (which isn't saying much), took over from her as the studio's leading glamour queen in the mid-40s, mixing sultry roles with Westerns in colour.

The studio's youthful and high-spirited group of musical stars was led by Gloria Jean, Donald O'Connor and Peggy Ryan, along with Durbin who stayed on at Universal for more than a dozen years before she suddenly retired from the screen in 1948. Surprisingly enough, she never appeared on the list of top ten box-office stars, whereas the comedy team of Abbott and Costello was placed high on the list during 1941–44 and again during 1948–51, even reaching the number one spot in 1942. As the studio's leading stars of this era, their joint salaries came to almost $590,000 in 1941 and $790,000 the following year. Marjorie Main and Percy Kilbride were first teamed as Ma and Pa Kettle in supporting roles in *The Egg And I* (1947), the hit picture which briefly brought Claudette Colbert back to Universal. She left but 'the Kettles' stayed on to star in their own, popular comedy series. The tougher side of the studio was represented by Burt Lancaster, Dan Duryea and Ella Raines, who starred in many of the studio's best thrillers in the 40s.

The rapid star turnover at Universal was reflected in a continuing cycle of arrivals and departures. New arrivals included Ann Blyth, who joined in 1944, followed by Shelley Winters in 1947, Piper Laurie in

1949 and Julie Adams in 1951. But in the 50s the studio was stronger on the male side with James Stewart, Rock Hudson, Tony Curtis, Jeff Chandler, Joel McCrea, Van Heflin, John Gavin and Audie Murphy heading the line-up. The young female contract stars tended to lose out to better-known, established star ladies who were hired on short-term (two- or three-picture) deals. Thus, Barbara Stanwyck starred in *All I Desire* (1953), Jane Wyman co-starred with Hudson in *Magnificent Obsession* (1954) and *All That Heaven Allows* (1955), June Allyson with Stewart in *The Glenn Miller Story* (1954), Lana Turner with Gavin in *Imitation Of Life* (1959) and Susan Hayward with Gavin in *Back Street* (1961).

For the first time in its history Universal was employing many of the top stars in Hollywood, as reflected in the top ten list which included Claudette Colbert in 1947, Jane Wyman in 1954, and James Stewart in 1950, the year he was Oscar-nominated for *Harvey* and emerged as a major Western star with *Winchester '73*. (And he was back on the list during 1952–56, including his Universal years.) Most impressive of all was Rock Hudson, who first appeared on the list in the number one spot in 1957 and again in 1959, and never dropped below third place during 1960–64. He was joined at Universal in 1959 by Doris Day and Cary Grant, who also appeared on the list every year up to and including 1966. Miss Day was rated number one in 1960, 1962 and 1963, and the popularity of her lightweight, glossy comedies, often teamed with Hudson, contributed enormously to his popularity, too.

However, the last Universal star to feature prominently on the list was a bit player named Clint Eastwood who appeared in minor roles in many Universal movies during 1954–55. He returned in triumph 15 years later as a top star with his own production company, Malpaso, which operated out of Universal from 1970 to 1973. Eastwood was rated second in 1970–71 and first in 1972–73, when he starred in such films as *Two Mules For Sister Sara* (1970), *Joe Kidd* (1972) and *Magnum Force* (1973), and directed as well as starred in the thriller *Play Misty For Me* (1971), and *High Plains Drifter* (1973).

STARS

Abbott, Bud & Costello, Lou
  1940–55

Acord, Art 1925–27

Adams, Julia 1951–57

Albert, Eddie 1942

Allbritton, Louise 1942–46

Allyson, June 1957–58

Ames, Leon 1938–39

Andrews Sisters, The 1940–44

Ankers, Evelyn 1941–44

Arden, Eve 1938–39

Arlen, Richard 1939–41

Arnold, Edward 1935

Arthur, Jean 1931

Atwill, Lionel 1940–42, 1944–46

Auer, Mischa 1936–41

Ayres, Lew 1929–34

Bari, Lynn 1952–54

Barrie, Wendy 1936–38

Barrymore, Diana 1942–43

Bartholomew, Freddie 1938–39

Beery, Noah, Jr. 1932–38, 1943–45

Bellamy, Ralph 1941–42

Bey, Turhan 1941–45

Bickford, Charles 1940–41

Blyth, Ann 1944–52

Blythe, Betty 1932–33
Boles, John 1930–31
Brady, Scott 1949–52
Brendel, El 1938–39
Brennan, Walter 1929–30
Brent, George 1946–47
Brown, Johnny Mack 1937–43
Bruce, Virginia 1940–42
Burke, Billie 1943–44
Cameron, Rod 1944–47
Carey, Harry, Sr. 1916–21
Carey, MacDonald 1949–50
Carson, Jack 1939–40
Chandler, Jeff 1949–58
Chaney, Lon, Sr. 1915–18, 1921, 1923, 1925
Chaney, Lon, Jr. 1940–45
Coburn, Charles 1949–50
Conte, Richard 1950–52
Cooper, Jackie 1938–39
Cotten, Joseph 1942–43
Crabbe, Buster 1938–40
Crawford, Broderick 1940–42, 1946–47
Cummings, Robert 1938–40
Curtis, Tony 1949–56
Davis, Bette 1930–31
Day, Doris 1959–64
De Carlo, Yvonne 1945–50
Dee, Sandra 1958–65
Denny, Reginald 1922–29
Devine, Andy 1932–47
Dickinson, Angie 1963–64
Dietrich, Marlene 1939–40, 41–43
Donahue, Troy 1956–58
Douglas, Kirk (Bryna) 1959–61
Douglas, Melvyn 1932–33
Dunne, Irene 1935
Durbin, Deanna 1936–48
Duryea, Dan 1945–50, 1953–57
Eastwood, Clint 1954–55, (Malpaso) 1970–73
Errol, Leon 1940–41, 1942–44
Ewell, Tom 1950–52
Farrell, Glenda 1938
Fields, W.C. 1939–43
Fitzgerald, Barry 1943
Fontaine, Joan 1947–48
Foster, Preston 1938

Foster, Susanna 1943–45
Francis The Talking Mule 1949–56
Francis, Kay 1939–40
Gavin, John 1956–61
Gibson, Hoot 1915–30
Grant, Cary 1959–64
Graves, Ralph 1922
Grey, Virginia 1945–46, 1958–61, 1966–70
Hall, Jon 1942–47
Haymes, Dick 1948
Hayward, Susan 1946–48
Heflin, Van 1951–54
Hendrix, Wanda 1950
Hersholt, Jean 1917–18, 1925–28
Holt, Jack 1935–36
Horton, Edward Everett 1926
Hudson, Rock 1949–66
Jean, Gloria 1939–45
Jones, Allan 1940, 1942–45
Jones, Buck 1934–37
Karloff, Boris 1922, 1931–32, 1934–35, 1939, 1944, 1948–52
Keaton, Buster 1944–45
Kerry, Norman 1923, 1925–28
Keyes, Evelyn 1950
Lake, Arthur 1925–27
Lancaster, Burt 1946–48
La Plante, Laura 1923–30
Laurie, Piper 1949–56
Lindsay, Margaret 1932, 1939–40
Lowe, Edmund 1938–39
Lugosi, Bela 1931, 1935–36, 1939, 1941–42
Lukas, Paul 1933–34
Lund, John 1951–52
Lundigan, William 1937–39
Lynn, Diana 1950–52
MacMurray, Fred 1955–57
Main, Marjorie 1947–50, 1952–56
Malone, Dorothy 1956–57
March, Fredric 1947–48
Maynard, Ken 1929–34
McCrea, Joel 1950–54
McLaglen, Victor 1939–40
Merkel, Una 1939–41
Mix, Tom 1932–33
Montez, Maria 1940–47
Montgomery, Robert 1947–48

Moore, Constance 1937–40
Moran, Peggy 1939–42
Morris, Chester 1933–35
Murphy, Audie 1949–63
Murphy, George 1937–38
Murray, Mae 1917–19
O'Brien, Pat 1932
O'Connor, Donald 1941–44, 1947–50, 1953–54
O'Hara, Maureen 1949–53
O'Sullivan, Maureen 1932
Oakie, Jack 1944–45
Oberon, Merle 1945–46
Paige, Robert 1941–45
Peck, Gregory 1961–65
Pidgeon, Walter 1937
Pitts, ZaSu 1932–33
Powell, Dick 1940–41
Powell, William 1947–48
Prevost, Marie 1921–22
Price, Vincent 1939–40, 1947–50
Quinn, Anthony 1952–53
Raines, Ella 1943–47
Rains, Claude 1933–34
Rathbone, Basil 1939, 1941–46
Ray, Charles 1940–41

Raye, Martha 1940–41
Reagan, Ronald 1950
Ritz Brothers, The 1940–43
Romero, Cesar 1935–37
Rooney, Mickey 1932–34
Ryan, Peggy 1941–45
Sabu 1942–43, 1946–48
Scott, Randolph 1943
Sheridan, Ann 1950–52
Simmons, Jean 1958–60
Sondergaard, Gale 1941, 1943–46
Stack, Robert 1939–42
Stewart, James 1950, 1951–53
Stroheim, Erich von 1918–22
Stuart, Gloria 1932–34
Sullavan, Margaret 1933–35
Taylor, Rod 1962–63
Tobin, Genevieve 1930–31
Tone, Franchot 1944–45
Turner, Lana 1957–60
Valentino, Rudolph 1918–19
Veidt, Conrad 1927–29
Velez, Lupe 1930
Wayne, John 1936–37
Winters, Shelley 1947–53
Wray, Fay 1925–27, 1956–57

The Directors

The studio had relatively few directors of note, but a large number of minor talents spent a brief period there. During the silent era Rex Ingram, John Ford, Clarence Brown, Erich von Stroheim and William Wyler all got their start at Universal, but achieved their greatest successes after they left. The studio employed the first major woman director in the American cinema, Lois Weber (also a talented actress-writer). In later years Universal's leading directors were most closely identified with particular genres – 'women's pictures' (John Stahl, Douglas Sirk), horror (James Whale), musicals (Henry Koster), thrillers (Robert Siodmak, Alfred Hitchcock) and Westerns (Anthony Mann). During more recent years the studio's ace directors have included Don Siegel (thrillers and Westerns) and Steven Spielberg (adventure and fantasy).

Since Universal turned out a tremendous number of pictures throughout its history, many of them inexpensive to make, there were opportunities to employ a large number of directors and the studio could afford to take chances on relatively new or inexperienced men. Thus, John Ford recalls the casual way in which he was given his first film in 1917 – 'Well, they needed somebody to direct a cheap picture of no consequence with Harry Carey, whose contract was running out.' And William Wyler had a similar experience eight years later when he got his start as a director on a series of two-reel Westerns starring Jack Mower. He appreciated the freedom that the company allowed, to change the script and make other alterations, provided there was plenty of action and one stayed within the budget. 'The two-reelers were a training school for everybody, even girls', he recalled. 'Any young fellow who showed he was eager, ambitious and wanted to direct a Western could get it. The whole picture cost $2,000 and wasn't any great risk. Also, if a pretty girl came on the lot, they'd put her in a Western. That was her test. If she looked good on the screen, they'd sign her up.'

In fact, the list of directors who got their start at Universal during the silent era is a quite impressive one but, as was the case with the studio's star discoveries, they rarely stayed for long. Ford handled mainly Westerns before moving on to Fox in 1921 where he soon developed into one of the most important American directors. Wyler was exceptional in that he stayed on for nine years, working his way up to a high-ranking position before he realized that Universal had nothing more to offer him, and left to become the ace director for independent producer Sam Goldwyn. The studio's most celebrated directorial discovery, however, was Erich von Stroheim who managed to interest Carl Laemmle in 'The Pinnacle', his first project as director, writer and star. Retitled *Blind Husbands* (1919), the picture emerged as one of the most remarkable writer-director debuts in the history of the American cinema and immediately established Stroheim as the studio's leading director. His most memorable production at Universal was *Foolish Wives* (1922); but he left after a dispute over *Merry-Go-Round* (1923), moving on to Goldwyn and MGM (briefly), where a large number of Universal's discoveries ended up. Rex Ingram, for example, started out at Universal in 1916–17, then went to Metro where he directed ex-Universal bit player Valentino in the tremendously successful *The Four Horsemen Of The Apocalypse* (1921) before arriving at MGM in the mid-20s. Directors Robert Z. Leonard (at Universal 1915–19), Tod Browning (1918–23), Jack Conway (1916–17 and 1921–23) and Clarence Brown (1923–25) all got their first break at Universal but are best remembered for their later work at MGM.

The studio's two leading directorial talents during the 30s were John Stahl who specialized in women's pictures, including *Imitation Of Life* (1934), *Magnificent Obsession* (1935) and *When Tomorrow Comes* (1939), and James Whale, best remembered for such horror films as *Frankenstein* (1931) and *The Bride Of Frankenstein* (1935). Of special interest was the arrival of Henry Koster, who launched the studio's Deanna Durbin musicals in 1936 in partnership with producer Joe Pasternak. However, a large number of directors continued to pass through the studio during the 30s, including many newcomers who were given their first chance with B features. Aside from cameraman Karl Freund and Joseph H. Lewis, it was a rather undistinguished group that included Sidney Salkow, Lesley Selander, Kurt Neumann, Lew Landers (Louis Friedlander), Lewis Foster, S. Sylvan Simon and John Rawlins, none of whom stayed for long.

Following in the line of Stroheim, Ingram, Whale, Freund and Koster, Universal continued to be most successful with its British- or European-born directors. Robert Siodmak directed many of the studio's best thrillers in the 40s such as *Phantom Lady* (1944) and *The Killers* (1946), while Alfred Hitchcock's *Shadow Of A Doubt* (1943) was a remarkable movie, filmed entirely on location in Northern California. He would return to Universal in the 60s with *The Birds* (1963), *Marnie* (1964) and others. Anthony Mann teamed up with James Stewart mainly on Westerns in the 50s, but they had their biggest hit with *The Glenn Miller Story* (1954), while Jack Arnold specialized in science fiction and horror. But it was Douglas Sirk (born in Germany of Danish parents) who stands out as the studio's leading director in the 50s with a large number of successes including his Technicolor remakes of *Magnificent*

Obsession (1954) and *Imitation Of Life* (1959). In more recent years Don Siegel spent a useful period at Universal in the 60s and early 70s, directing a number of Clint Eastwood films, while Steven Spielberg graduated from TV movies to give the studio the two biggest hits in its history – *Jaws* (1975) and *E.T. The Extra-Terrestrial* (1982).

DIRECTORS

Arnold, Jack 1952–58
Bacon, Lloyd 1953
Barton, Charles 1945–52
Beebe, Ford L. 1936–45
Bell, Monta 1930–31
Boetticher, Budd 1951–53
Brown, Clarence 1923–25
Brown, Harry Joe 1930
Browning, Tod 1918–23, 1930–31
Buzzell, Edward 1933–34, 1936–37
Castle, William 1949, 1951
Cline, Edward 1939–45
Conway, Jack 1916–17, 1921–23
Crosland, Alan 1935
Cummings, Irving 1922, 1924
Dassin, Jules 1947
De Cordova, Frederick 1948–53
Dwan, Allan 1913–14
Edwards, Blake 1956–59
Enright, Ray 1942
Fejos, Paul 1928–29
Florey, Robert 1931
Ford, John 1916–21
Foster, Lewis R. 1936–37
Fregonese, Hugo 1950–52
Freund, Karl 1932–34
Garnett, Tay 1932–33
Gordon, Michael 1947–49
Hill, George Roy 1967–77
Hitchcock, Alfred 1941–42, 1962–76
Ingram, Rex 1916–17
Jewison, Norman 1962–64
Kenton, Erle C. 1941–46
Koster, Henry 1936–42
La Cava, Gregory 1941–42
Lamont, Charles 1939–56
Landers, Lew 1934–36, 1940
LeBorg, Reginald 1943–45
Lee, Rowland V. 1938–39
Leni, Paul 1927–28
Leonard, Robert Z. 1915–19

Lewis, Joseph H. 1937–38, 1942
Lubin, Arthur 1936–46, 1949–57
Mann, Anthony 1952–54
Mann, Delbert 1961–63
Marin, Edwin L. 1933–34
Maté, Rudolph 1952–53
McDonald, Frank 1938
Mulligan, Robert 1960–62
Neill, Roy William 1942–46
Neumann, Kurt 1932–35, 1951–52
Ophüls, Max 1947–48
Pevney, Joseph 1950–57
Pichel, Irving 1948–49
Rawlins, John 1938–46
Rogell, Albert 1926–27, 1939–41
Ruggles, Wesley 1927–29
Ryan, Frank 1943–46
Salkow, Sidney 1936–38
Santley, Joseph 1938–39
Schuster, Harold 1938–40
Sedgwick, Edward 1922–26, 1933–34
Seiter, William A. 1924–28, 1939–41, 1945–49
Selander, Lesley 1936–37
Sherman, George 1947–54
Siegel, Donald 1963–74
Simon, S. Sylvan 1937–38
Siodmak, Robert 1943–48
Sirk, Douglas 1950–58
Spielberg, Steven 1969–75
Stahl, John M. 1930–35, 1938–39
Stroheim, Erich von 1919–22
Sutherland, A. Edward 1940–41
Walker, Stuart 1934–35
Weber, Lois 1916–19
Whale, James 1931–39
Wyler, William 1925–34
Yarbrough, Jean 1943–46
Young, Harold 1937–39, 1941–43, 1945

The Creative Personnel

Universal was not primarily noted for its cameramen, yet could boast of some leading names such as William Daniels, Hal Mohr and for over 20 years Russell Metty. If cameramen took a back seat, it was largely due to the studio's large number of low-budget films which confined people of the calibre of Stanley Cortez to working on programmers. It was in the field of design that Universal really came into its own. The top art director for a long period was Charles D. 'Danny' Hall, and other notable and innovative designers included Ben Carré, and the Oscar-winning Herman Rosse. The studio's horror cycle lent itself to much imaginative work from the studio's art directors, and opened up special opportunities for unique contributions in special effects and make-up in which John P. Fulton, Jack Pierce and Bud Westmore distinguished themselves.

The studio was staffed by a solid core of professionals, many of whom stayed for long periods and ensured a high standard of technical expertise. A continuing studio operation, which encompassed both TV and film production from the 50s onwards, meant that important contract personnel remained active up to the early 70s. This situation embraced editing, costume design, and the music department which was developed by Charles Previn, grand-uncle of André.

Cameramen and Art Directors

Though the studio had only a few leading cameramen under contract, it more than made up for it with the quality of its art department. Striking set designs were a regular feature of Universal's occasional high-cost productions, beginning with Richard Day's impressive Monte Carlo settings for Stroheim's *Foolish Wives* in 1921. Charles D. 'Danny' Hall was the studio's top art director for many years, best remembered for his re-creation of medieval Paris in *The Hunchback Of Notre Dame* (1923) and interior sets for the Paris opera and masked-ball sequences in *The Phantom Of The Opera* (1925). (His collaborator, Ben Carré, was credited with the imaginative backstage and underground settings.)

The studio's horror-movie cycle provided Danny Hall with many of his best opportunities and he rose to the challenge in such pictures as *The Man Who Laughs* (1928), *Frankenstein* (1931) in collaboration with Herman Rosse, *The Black Cat* (1934), *The Bride Of Frankenstein* (1935) and many others. In marked contrast was *Broadway* (1929), one of Univeral's extravagant fantasy musicals of the early sound era. The filming of *Broadway* required a close working relationship between Hall and cameraman Hal Mohr who recalled the nightclub as the biggest interior set that had ever been built up to that time. 'We built the "Broadway" crane for that picture. Doc [Paul] Fejos [the director] and I designed it. It was really a great piece of engineering equipment with an arm 40 or 50 feet long ... With this thing you could swing around a full 360° in any position and rotate the camera platform at the same time. We made shots to exploit the abilities of this crane; it was pretty exciting.' It was used on many later productions, including *King Of Jazz* (1930) – an Oscar-winner for designer Herman Rosse – and *All Quiet On The Western Front* (1930), also designed by Hall. Here, the stark simplicity of Hall's designs succeeded admirably in evoking the young German soldiers' village and the World War I battlefield on the screen.

The studio's many other outstanding art directors included Ralph Berger (1934–39), John De Cuir (1938–49), Richard Riedel (1937–60), Jack Otterson (1936–47), multi-Oscar winner Alexander Golitzen (1942–74), and Robert Boyle, who has written about his work with Hitchcock at Universal in the 40s and again in the 60s: 'I find Hitch a catalyst to my own creative functioning. He is one of the few who really knows the materials of his craft and their effect – and he will use anything – in any combination – in any form, conventional or not – to make his statement, to tell his story.'

For the studio's cameramen, as for the art directors, the opportunities for making a creative contribution on a major production did not come all that often. Thus, cameraman Joe Valentine (1936–46) also appreciated the challenge of working with Hitchcock on *Saboteur* (1942), and especially on the location filming of *Shadow Of A Doubt* (1943). He, like Universal's other leading cameramen, including Milton Krasner (1936–48), Charles van Enger (1940–50) and Stanley Cortez (1937–43), spent most of his time assigned to the studio's many undistinguished programmers. (Cortez, for example, got *his* one big opportunity, and earned an Oscar nomination, on loan-out to RKO for Orson Welles' *The Magnificent Ambersons*, 1942.) 'Mostly the B pictures weren't that artistic in concept, so it was just good straighforward photography,' noted Hal Mohr, though he was generally more fortunate in his assignments – as were the studio's other Oscar winners, William Daniels (1947–58) and Russell Metty (1947–69). Metty, like Daniels, spanned the changeover from black-and-white to colour filming and handled many of the studio's prestige colour productions in the 50s, working closely with Douglas Sirk, in particular; but he was equally at home with the occasional black-and-white film of note, such as Orson Welles' nightmarish *Touch Of Evil* (1958) and, on loan-out to John Huston for *The Misfits* (UA) in 1960.

Other Departments

In general, the Universal technical personnel were hardworking professionals who handled large numbers of routine pictures each year and were rarely singled out for special recognition. For example, editors Milton Carruth (1929–66) and Ted Kent (1933–67) both spent their entire careers at the studio; they were joined by Russell Schoengarth in 1942 and these three men served as the core of Universal's editing department for a span of 40 years. They were virtually ignored by the Academy, with only Ted Kent receiving an Oscar nomination, near the end of his career. The studio's music department was more successful in gathering nominations and Oscars. It had developed under Charles Previn from 1936 and was bolstered by the arrival of Frank Skinner and Hans Salter in 1939 just as the studio began to increase its output of movie musicals. The star of the department for a brief period in the late 40s was Miklos Rozsa who provided suitably hard-boiled scores for such tough black-and-white pictures as *The Killers* (1946), *Brute Force* (1947), *A Double Life* and *The Naked City* (both 1948).

Similarly, the studio's main costume assignments were handled by a small and talented group who, between them, spanned the entire studio history from the 20s up to the 70s. Lucia 'Mother' Coulter began designing for Universal in the early silent days when the costumes were often provided on a fairly informal basis. She was one of the first to develop a proper wardrobe department. Soon after she left to join MGM in 1924, Vera West was hired as her replacement and stayed on for over 20 years, but was rarely given the kind of budget to produce something a bit special or spectacular as she did with *King Of Jazz* (1930), *Showboat* (1936) and *The Phantom Of The Opera* (1943) in Technicolor. Rosemary Odell arrived in 1945 followed by Bill Thomas, and they shared the assignments at Universal during the 50s. Thomas, however, took on the lion's share of the work, and is credited with over 100 titles including most of the Douglas Sirk pictures and *Spartacus* (1960). Finally, the most famous of Hollywood costumiers, Edith Head, arrived in 1968 (after 30 years at Paramount) and contributed to the new up-market Universal with her stylish designs for such pictures as *Airport* (1970), *Sweet Charity* (1969) and *The Sting* (1973).

Universal's particular interest in horror and science fiction meant that the studio made special demands on its make-up men and special-effects experts. The inventive Jack Pierce is credited with creating all of Universal's well-known horror figures, including the Frankenstein monster, Dracula, the Mummy and the Wolf Man, and headed the make-up department from 1936 to 1946. His successor was the equally imaginative Bud Westmore – one of a famous make-up family. He rose to the challenge of molding an authentically mobile mermaid's tail for Ann Blyth, co-star of *Mr Peabody And The Mermaid* (1948), and he created the remarkably convincing and frightening creature-monster for *The Creature From The Black Lagoon* (1954). As described by his brother Frank in 'The Westmores Of Hollywood', 'the basic suit for the monster was made of liquid rubber baked onto the statue of [stuntman] Ricou Browning ... He devised a scaled and jagged dorsal fin running all the way from the base of the skull down to the tailbone. The iguana-like head was separate from the suit, and it too had individually applied scales, while the monster's hands were unbelievable accomplishments of cosmetic engineering.' Bud's many other creations appeared in such 50s movies as *Tarantula* (1955), *The Mole People* (1956), and a particular favourite called *The Land Unknown* (1957) which featured 'strange, huge-headed extraterrestrial beings with their brains exposed.' Westmore spent 24 years in all at Universal.

The studio's master of special effects was John P. Fulton. His work on John Ford's *Air Mail* (1932) was impressive, but he is best remembered for his ingenious trick effects for *The Invisible Man* (1933) and its many sequels, as well as other horror and fantasy productions in the 30s and 40s. His successor in the 50s was Clifford Stine, who worked on the studio's many science-fiction ventures such as *Tarantula* and *The Incredible Shrinking Man* (1957), and was brought out of retirement in 1974 to work on the Oscar-winning special effects for Universal's spectacular disaster movie, *Earthquake*.

CAMERAMEN

Ballard, Lucien 1945–46	Krasner, Milton 1936–48
Barnes, George 1942	Maté, Rudolph 1940–41
Bredell, Woody 1937–46	McCord, Ted 1929–30, 1933–35
Brodine, Norbert 1933–36	Mellor, William 1947–48
Cortez, Stanley 1937–43, 1947–48	Mescall, John 1934–36
Daniels, William 1919–23, 1947–58	Metty, Russell 1947–69
De Vinna, Clyde 1923–24	Mohr, Hal 1929–30, 1939–48
Edeson, Arthur 1931–33	Planck, Robert 1935
Freund, Karl 1930–33	Planer, Franz 1947–49
Glennon, Bert 1920–21	Valentine, Joseph 1936–46
Greene, W. Howard 1942–47	Van Enger, Charles 1940–50
Ivano, Paul 1943–46	

ART DIRECTORS

Berger, Ralph 1934–39	Day, Richard 1921–23
Boyle, Robert 1941–43, 1947–56, 1961–64	DeCuir, John 1938–49
	Golitzen, Alexander 1942–74
Brown, Hilyard 1948–54	Goodman, John B. 1940–46
Bumstead, Henry 1961–78	Hall, Charles D. 1923–37
Clatworthy, Robert 1941–46, 1949–64	Harkrider, John W. 1934–37
	Herzbrun, Bernard 1946–54
D'Agostino, Albert 1934–36	Juran, Nathan 1948–52

Kirk, Charles M. 1927
Kuter, Leo E. 1925–26
Leven, Boris 1947–48
Lourié, Eugene 1943–47
Obzina, Martin 1939–46

Otterson, Jack 1936–47
Riedel, Richard 1937–60
Rosse, Herman 1930–32
Wright, Joseph C. 1927

COSTUME DESIGNERS

Adrian 1943
Banton, Travis 1945–48
Brymer 1933–37
Harkrider, John 1934–38
Head, Edith 1968–78

Odell, Rosemary 1945–67
Orry-Kelly 1947–50
Thomas, Bill 1949–60
West, Vera 1926–47
Wood, Yvonne 1945–51

COMPOSERS AND MUSIC DIRECTORS

Amfitheatrof, Daniele 1947–48
Gershenson, Joseph 1950–57
Green, Johnny 1947
Previn, Charles 1936–42
Rosen, Milton 1943–47
Rozsa, Miklos 1946–48

Salter, Hans J. 1939–47, 1950–52
Schwarzwald, Milton 1949–50
Skinner, Frank 1938–66
Ward, Edward 1943–45
Waxman, Franz 1935–36

EDITORS

Akst, Albert 1935
Allen, Fred 1929–30
Burton, Bernard 1933–41
Cahn, Philip 1933–46
Carruth, Milton 1929–66
Curtiss, Edward 1933–34, 1938–60
Curtiss, Ray 1925–29, 1934
Dawson, Ralph 1947–50
Goodkind, Saul 1940–47
Gross, Frank 1936–55
Havlick, Gene 1928–29
Hilton, Arthur 1940–47
Hornbeck, William (sup. ed.) 1960s

Kent, Ted 1933–67
Kolster, Clarence 1931–32
Landres, Paul 1937–47
Lawrence, Viola 1919–20
Ludwig, Otto 1939–50
Macrorie, Alma 1963–66
Mandell, Daniel 1924–29, 1933–35
Marker, Harry 1927–35
Schoengarth, Russell 1942–68
Stell, Aaron 1961–62
Todd, Sherman 1956–58
Wright, Maurice 1934–43

SCRIPTWRITERS

Brooks, Richard 1942–44, 1947
Bucknet, Robert 1948–51
Chase, Borden 1950–58
Cole, Lester 1937–39
Hoffman, Joseph 1949–54
Hurlbut, William 1933–35
Jackson, Felix 1938–45
Lehman, Gladys 1926–32
Manning, Bruce 1936–42

Millhauser, Bertram 1943–46
Siodmak, Curt 1939–45
Spigelgass, Leonard 1938–41
Stone, Peter 1963–68
Sturges, Preston 1934–35
Trumbo, Dalton 1960–62
Young, Waldemar 1917–19
Zuckerman, George 1950–57

The Academy Awards

Universal has not exactly led the field in the Oscar stakes. Indeed, it has only collected the Best Picture award three times in 60 years – for *All Quiet On The Western Front* (1930), *The Sting* (1973) and, most recently, *Out Of Africa* (1985). However, there have at least been many nominations and occasional winners in the minor, technical categories which brought well-deserved recognition to many of the studio's leading contract personnel. Cameramen Hal Mohr, William Daniels and Russell Metty, art directors Alexander Golitzen, John Goodman and Henry Bumstead, and composers Charles Previn and Miklos Rozsa were among Universal's Oscar winners over the years. Recently the studio has done somewhat better, reflecting its improved status, since the early 70s, as one of the top Hollywood film companies.

When *Out Of Africa* won the Academy Award for Best Picture in 1985 it was only the third time that Universal had carried off the top honour. With few first-ranking stars or directors under contract, the studio garnered a comparatively small number of nominations over the years in both major and minor categories, and must be judged the least successful of the major Hollywood studios in the annual Oscar stakes. However, it has done markedly better in the last dozen years or so, emerging in the early 70s as one of the leading studios for the first time in its history.

In fact, Universal originally got off to a good start. Though the studio failed to receive a single nomination in the first two Academy Award years, at the third ceremony (for 1929/30), it was the single most successful company. *All Quiet On The Western Front* deservedly won the Oscars for Best Picture and director Lewis Milestone, with nominations for the effective camerawork of Arthur Edeson and for the three scriptwriters. Though the remarkable contribution made by art director Charles D. Hall, who was responsible for the authentic look of the film, went unrecognized by the Academy, the studio won a third award for the art direction of Herman Rosse. His extraordinary designs for *King Of Jazz* were well worthy of the honour. (Unfortunately, Hall was never even nominated for his imaginative work at Universal in the 30s, probably because the kind of cheap horror films in which he specialized were not considered worthy of recognition at the time.) The studio had to wait 43 years for its next winner of the Best Picture Oscar – *The Sting* (1973). The studio's lack of success can be gauged from the fact that, in all the years prior to 1962, it gained only three additional Best Picture nominations – for *Imitation Of Life*, directed by John Stahl in 1934, and for the first two Deanna Durbin musicals, *Three Smart Girls* (1936) and *One Hundred Men And A Girl* (1937). The studio did reasonably during 1936–38 with a number of additional nominations going to the screwball comedy, *My Man Godfrey* (1936), and an Oscar won by Charles Previn and the studio music department for the score of *One Hundred Men And A Girl*.

Though Universal rarely *won* Oscars, at least the Academy Awards drew attention to the best of the studio's technical personnel. Thus, cameraman Joseph Valentine and art director Jack Otterson gained their first nominations in 1936–38; Charles Previn, Hans Salter and Frank Skinner each received a handful of nominations for their scores; sound man Bernard Brown was nominated every year from 1938 through 1945, eight nominations in all; and Walter Lantz's cartoon shorts gained seven nominations between 1933 and 1946. Total score: thirty-nine nominations, two winners.

Universal had its biggest success in the early 40s with a lavish Technicolor remake of *The Phantom Of The Opera* (1943) which earned Oscars for the stylish colour cinematography of Hal Mohr, and for an experienced design team headed by art directors Alexander Golitzen and John B. Goodman, and set decorators Russell Gausman and Ira Webb. The studio's standing was boosted later in the 40s when it released many high-quality British films in the USA (from producer J. Arthur Rank), including the multiple Oscar-winning *Hamlet* (1948) directed by and starring Laurence Olivier. (This was the first British film to win the Best Picture Oscar.) But Universal's own, occasional successes continued to come along in the various technical categories. Composer Miklos Rozsa earned an Oscar for his dramatic scoring of *A Double Life* (1947), and the Academy acknowledged the technical accomplishment of the filming of *The Naked City* (1948) by giving statuettes to cinematographer William Daniels and editor Paul Weatherwax. In 1960 an experienced group of Universal personnel won awards for their contribution to the studio's lavish production of *Spartacus*: cameraman Russell Metty, art director Alexander Golitzen with Eric Orbom, and costume designers Valles and Bill Thomas.

The closest that any Universal contract star ever came to winning an Oscar was in 1959 when Doris Day was nominated for her performance in *Pillow Talk*. Young Deanna Durbin was awarded a special juvenile statuette in 1938, and a handful of actors and actresses have won awards for Universal pictures during the postwar decades: Ronald Colman was voted Best Actor for *A Double Life*; Josephine Hull and Dorothy Malone were Best Supporting Actresses for *Harvey* (1950) and *Written*

On The Wind (1956) respectively; Peter Ustinov was Best Supporting Actor in *Spartacus* and Gregory Peck won Best Actor for *To Kill A Mockingbird* (1962) which was nominated for seven other Oscars including Best Picture, with further awards going to scriptwriter Horton Foote and art directors Golitzen and Henry Bumstead.

Universal's improved status from the mid-60s was reflected in the many productions which gained a large number of nominations. These included *Thoroughly Modern Millie* (1967); two British offerings from producer Hal B. Wallis, *Anne Of The Thousand Days* (1969) and *Mary, Queen Of Scots* (1971); *Earthquake* (1974), *Jaws* and *The Hindenburg* (both 1975) which gained recognition for their technical accomplishment – sound, editing and special effects. The best year of all was 1973 when *American Graffiti* gathered a number of nominations, including Best Picture, and the top award was won by *The Sting*, with six further Oscars going to that picture's director (George Roy Hill), scriptwriter (David S. Ward), art director (Henry Bumstead), editor (William Reynolds), composer (Marvin Hamlisch using themes from Scott Joplin) and costumer (Edith Head). This total was matched by another picture starring Robert Redford, *Out Of Africa*, just 12 years later. Once again the awards went to the director (Sydney Pollack) and the technicians, missing out the cast, but continuing Universal's long tradition of technical excellence. (From *King Of Jazz* to *Out Of Africa* the studio has enjoyed its greatest success in the art-direction category.)

The stars have not been entirely left out in recent years. Sissy Spacek captured the Best Actress award from the Academy and from the New York Film Critics in 1980 for *Coal Miner's Daughter*, and Mary Steenburgen carried off the same double in a supporting role the following year for *Melvin And Howard*, when Jonathan Demme also won the New York Film Critics award for directing the picture. Universal also had a share (through distribution in the USA) in the success of the EMI-produced *The Deer Hunter*, which was the top Oscar-winning picture in 1978 and, similarly, with the ITC production of *On Golden Pond* (1981) which earned sentimental Oscars for Henry Fonda (the first time he was so honoured) and Katharine Hepburn, another Oscar for screenplay, plus nominations for both best film and best director.

Universal's most recent Oscar success came in 1989 when the highly favoured *Born On The Fourth Of July* lost out for Best Picture and actor (Tom Cruise) but gained awards for editing and for director Oliver Stone (his second win in three years).

WARNER
BROS.

Incorporated in 1923, Warner Bros. began experimenting with sound in 1925, and two years later had great success with *The Jazz Singer*. Warners then became a major force in movie exhibition, too. When the Depression struck, Warners was forced to sell off assets and reduce costs; it began to specialize in cheaply made gangster pictures, dramas, comedies and musicals which gave the studio its special character in the 30s. Warners recovered strongly in the 40s under studio boss Jack Warner. In the 50s it ventured into 3-D, CinemaScope — and profitable programmes for TV. The studio was merged with Seven Arts Productions in 1967 and then taken over by the Kinney National Corporation in 1969. Warner Bros. has performed well during the 70s and 80s as the film-production arm of Warner Communications, a multi-media conglomerate involved in records, publishing, TV and video. In 1989 Warners merged with Time Inc. to form an even larger media giant known as Time Warner Inc.

During the peak years of the studio era Warner Bros. had a popular identity which rivalled that of the largest companies, MGM and Paramount. It was the studio that brought the talkies to Hollywood in the late 20s with *The Jazz Singer*, then went on to specialize in fast-talking and fast-moving gangster pictures and musicals in the 30s. Most fascinating of all is the story of how Warners was rapidly transformed from one of many small, struggling studios in Hollywood in the mid-20s into one of the giants of the industry.

In fact, the Warner brothers took a long time to reach Hollywood in the first place. Individually they had travelled widely and tried many different jobs ranging from soap salesman (Albert Warner) and cobbler (Harry) to carnival barker and ice-cream salesman (Sam), while Jack, the youngest, first earned his living as a boy soprano. But all four were together again in Youngstown, Ohio, around 1904 when Sam had the idea of starting up a nickelodeon. He served as the projectionist while Harry and Albert handled the finances and box-office takings, mother Rose played the piano and young Jack sang between the film shows. For a time the brothers took to the road as a travelling picture show, then operated a larger cinema, the Cascade, in Newcastle, Pennsylvania before branching out into distribution. They set up successful film exchanges in Western Pennsylvania and Norfolk, Virginia, but were closed down around 1909–1910 by the newly organized and powerful Motion Pictures Patents Company. They then tried producing a few pictures, but with little success, and they soon returned to distribution, extending their activities to the Far West for the first time.

In an effort to take advantage of the current popularity of war-related subjects (and anti-German sentiment) in 1917, the brothers bought the rights to a book by the ex-US ambassador to Germany and produced their first major feature, *My Four Years in Germany*. Filmed in upstate New York and released early in 1918, it was a big hit and provided a new incentive for them to increase production. The following year they opened their first, small studio in Hollywood, demonstrating that they were serious about producing movies on a more regular basis.

Initially, during 1920–22, they averaged only two or three features per year, but 1923 marked the real beginning of their new company, Warner Bros, Inc., with Harry as president, Albert the treasurer, and production responsibilities shared between Jack and Sam. Production quickly increased and the studio released 14 features in 1923, including the first of the Rin-Tin-Tin series.

Among the many new employees hired by the growing company in 1923 and 1924 were a number of young men who would soon develop into leading producers. Darryl F. Zanuck, a workaholic and ambitious scriptwriter started off providing stories for the Rin-Tin-Tin movies and turned out many other scripts as well under a variety of pseudonyms. He worked his way up to producer status, then studio manager and finally served as the company's production chief under studio boss Jack Warner. Hal Wallis was employed initially as an assistant in the publicity department, then turned to producing. He was placed in charge of the First National studio for a time when Warners took over that company in 1929, then served as a producer under Zanuck before he succeeded to the post of production chief after Zanuck resigned in 1933. When Warner Bros. hired leading director Ernst Lubitsch in 1923, they got his chief assistant, Henry Blanke, as a bonus. Lubitsch completed five features for the studio during 1923–26, including *The Marriage Circle* (1924) and *Lady Windermere's Fan* (1925), but when he left Blanke stayed on as a production supervisor and then became one of the studio's most dependable producers of quality pictures for over 25 years.

Under the supervision of Sam Warner and making use of the Vitagraph studio, newly acquired in 1925, the company soon began experimenting with sound filming with the modest aim of providing all Warner's features with full orchestral soundtracks – particularly useful in the small-town cinemas where many of the studio's pictures played, and in turning out musical shorts of high quality. However, the idea of full talking pictures was not immediately seen as a special attraction. According to Jack, when Sam Warner had remarked to Harry, '. . . but don't forget you can have actors talk, too', the immortal reply came back, 'Who the hell wants to hear actors talk?'.

The pace of events during these years was quite astonishing. It had taken almost 20 years in the movie business before the Warners had been able to establish their company, but now, only a little over two years later, they were expanding rapidly and taking the first steps toward revolutionizing the entire industry.

Early in 1926 a new company, the Vitaphone Corporation, was set up, in partnership with Western Electric, to exploit the Vitaphone sound-on-disc process for synchronized film-sound recording. When the first Vitaphone programme was premiered in August 1926 it included a number of musical shorts produced by Sam Warner, along with the feature *Don Juan* starring John Barrymore and backed by a full musical and sound-effects track. This film, and the following Vitaphone presentations which were unveiled in October 1926 and February 1927, were extremely successful.

The studio continued turning out Vitaphone features and shorts and constructed additional sound-proof stages in Hollywood where *The Jazz Singer* was filmed in 1927. When the picture opened in October it created a sensation. The event is generally regarded as the beginning of the sound era, though the picture was not a full talkie. Originally meant to include only synchronized songs, the impact on movie audiences of the additional fragments of dialogue, some of them adlibbed by the star, Al Jolson, made it clear that it was essential for Warners to take their experiments with sound further. For in spite of its tremendous success, *The Jazz Singer* was only one important stage in the transition to the 100% talkie.

The remarkable achievement of Warner Bros. during these years was slightly dampened by the sudden death of Sam Warner who had played such an important role in the company's remarkable beginnings. From this point on the control of the company was mainly divided between Harry, the president in charge of the New York office, and Jack, heading the Hollywood studio. This arrangement was not very different from the other family-run company, Columbia, where it was Harry (Cohn) who ran the studio and his brother Jack who took care of administrative and financial matters in New York. Though both companies had started out as shoestring outfits in the early 20s, Warners' spectacular growth meant that it became a major virtually over-night, while Columbia achieved the same result through 30 years of slow but steady growth. (Both dynasties ended in 1956 when the Warner brothers sold out their interest in the company, coinciding with the death of Jack Cohn at Columbia, while Harry Warner died in July 1958 just a few months after Harry Cohn.)

After the premiere of *The Jazz Singer*, the pace of events hardly slackened. In December the studio released its first all-talking short, *My Wife's Gone Away*, while a number of part-talkie features were already in production. Director Bryan Foy, who had been involved in filming many of the Vitaphone shorts, convinced Jack Warner to let him upgrade *Lights Of New York* to a one-hour feature. Completed at a total cost of less than $100,000 and ballyhooed as 'The First 100% All-Talking Picture' when it opened in July 1928, it proved to be yet another big money earner for the studio. Two months later *The Singing Fool* starring Al Jolson – the part-talking and singing follow-up to *The Jazz Singer* – registered as the biggest hit to date, and company profits climbed to peak levels.

Expanding rapidly in all directions simultaneously, Warners made its first major investment in movie theatres by taking over the important Stanley circuit in 1928 and gained a substantial stake in the First National company with its valuable 135-acre studio and back lot, its film exchanges, theatres and production personnel. Warners continued to develop its special interest in musicals by purchasing a number of leading music-publishing companies which would prove a ready source of songs and musical numbers. (Over 50 years later, a remarkable treasure trove of long-lost songs and unpublished scores of old Broadway musicals was discovered in a Warner Bros. warehouse in New Jersey; all material acquired by the company, put into storage, and forgotten till the early 80s.) The studio also made a special agreement with Herbert Kalmus, the head of the Technicolor Corporation. The studio planned to invest heavily in the production of two-strip Technicolor features, mainly musicals, beginning with *On With The Show* and followed by the smash hit *Gold Diggers Of Broadway* (both released in 1929), thus pioneering in the adoption of colour filming as it had done with sound.

Also in 1929, the company completed its takeover of First National, and the large, well-equipped studio at Burbank became the main Warners studio and the new home of Warner Bros.-First National Pictures. Founded in 1917 by a group of leading exhibitors, the First National Exhibitors Circuit had achieved a large degree of success by signing up many of the most bankable top stars such as Charlie Chaplin and Mary Pickford and constructed its Burbank studio in 1922. However, the company lost many of its leading actors and part of its theatre chain, and thus failed to hold its own in the extremely competitive movie industry of the middle and late 20s. For a brief period after the merger there continued to be separate lists of Warner Bros. and First National stars, directors and other personnel, but they were increasingly integrated during 1931–33 when the 'First National' designation lost any special meaning.

Having grown into a giant, vertically integrated company (producer-distributor-exhibitor) in only a few years, Warner Bros. hardly had a chance to enjoy its new position before it was confronted with the realities of the Depression which hit the industry in the early 30s, and was forced to deal with the problems faced by the other leading studios. The fall in its profits, for example, was as swift and spectacular as its previous growth. Though the company was deep in the red by 1931, it stubbornly resisted following the same path as Paramount, RKO and Fox – who had to file for reorganization in order to stave off bankruptcy – but sold off some assets and film theatres instead and cut back on wages and other costs. For example, Warners took part in the special, industry-wide plan by which all the studios cut their salaries simultaneously during an eight-week period early in 1933 but, when Warners was slow to restore them, Darryl F. Zanuck felt that he was in an impossible situation. He resigned and, soon afterwards, joined Joseph Schenck to form 20th Century Pictures. However, Zanuck had already played a major role in establishing the special Warners style and its new group of leading stars, and his influence continued to be felt long after he had left.

Hal Wallis replaced him as production chief for the next 10 years, assisted by a group of associate producers headed by Henry Blanke and Sam Bischoff, with Bryan Foy in charge of the B pictures. During this period the studio experience closely paralleled that of the rest of the industry – a steady recovery from 1932 to 1937 and an increase in the number of expensive, prestige productions, then, after a brief setback during 1938 and 1939, a move to take full advantage of the boom which developed in the 40s.

Hal Wallis resigned in 1944, apparently enraged at the fact that Jack Warner had stepped up to accept the Oscar for *Casablanca* which he, Wallis, had produced. (Steve Trilling was promoted from casting director to replace him.) Though profits were at peak levels, there were many other problems, which worsened once the war was over. The Warners' autocratic and paternalistic style of running the studio led to serious labour-relations disputes and a damaging strike, while many of the top stars, too, were beginning to rebel. In addition, the terms of the government's Consent Decree against monopolistic practices meant that the company was forced (along with several of the other major studios) to dispose of its extremely profitable chain of movie theatres in the early 50s.

The continuing decline of the movie industry, especially through the onset of television, meant that Warner Bros., along with most of the other companies, was confronted with problems it had never had to face before. The studio had some measure of success with 3-D and CinemaScope, but did best with its early ventures into TV production, opening up a whole new area of cheap but profitable filming which it has continued to exploit ever since. The company benefited from the fact that it was one of the first of the majors to begin making TV programmes in the mid-50s. The decision to go into TV production was made by Jack Warner himself who put his son-in-law, William T. Orr, in charge of the TV operation. The studio provided ABC-TV with three different series of hour-long programmes, screened in rotation under the catch-all title of 'Warner Bros. Presents' and derived from three of the company's feature-film properties – *Casablanca, King's Row* and *Cheyenne*.

Orr and Warners thus played an important role in establishing the kind of TV-series format which has remained fairly standard up to the present day: the careful building up of characters who are placed in dramatic situations and interesting or exotic locations, week after week. The success of its TV subsidiary clearly contributed to the survival of the struggling parent company. In addition, Warners sold the rights to 850 of its old features and over 1000 shorts for $21 million, and, around this time – 1956 – the two older brothers, Harry and Albert Warner, decided to retire. They sold their shares in the company to an investment group headed by Serge Seremenko and Charles Allen Jr. Jack Warner held on to his shares and stayed on as president, though his power was now much reduced.

In 1967 Warner Bros. was taken over by the Canadian-based Seven Arts Productions headed by Eliot Hyman who purchased Jack Warner's interest in the company. But the newly created Warner Bros.-Seven Arts Inc. only survived in this form for two years until the industry-wide slump of 1969 which hit the company hard. It was then taken over by the New York-based Kinney National Service Inc., a giant conglomerate headed by Stephen J. Ross.

With the movie studio (which reverted to its original name of Warner Bros.) and record companies (Atlantic and Warner/Reprise) as his cornerstones, Ross set out to turn the corporation into an entertainment and media giant as reflected in the new name, Warner Communications Inc, which he adopted in 1971. He acquired publishers like National Periodical Publications, and the Panavision company (best known for its cameras, lenses and other film-making equipment), and phased out a number of his non-media subsidiaries, while others were spun off into a separate firm, the National Kinney Corporation. Most important of all, Ross had acquired the services of Ted Ashley who was put in charge of Warner Bros. (He was one of a number of former talent agents who rose to power in Hollywood around this time.) Ashley succeeded in turning the company around in the early 70s with a series of top-grossing pictures which continued throughout most of the decade, along with a few prestige successes such as *All The President's Men* (1976).

In the late 70s the corporation expanded its investment in cable television and video. It also experienced an extraordinary phase with its Atari video game company, which brought in spectacular profits during 1980 and 1981 and recorded just as spectacular losses, in the order of hundreds of millions of dollars, in 1983. For a time this jeopardized the future of the corporation (and the film company). Warners bounced back to take the largest market share of any studio (18%) in 1985 with a number of hits including Steven Spielberg's *The Color Purple*. Although results were generally mixed during the late 80s, 1989 proved to be a memorable year in the history of the studio as it again led at the box office with such blockbusters as *Batman* and *Lethal Weapon 2* and was involved in a merger with Time Inc. (The original stock swap was disrupted by a rival offer to Time from Paramount and ended with Time making a friendly, but costly, takeover of Warners.) The new company name became Time Warner Inc. However, the outlook for the studio is a bit uncertain, due to the extremely large burden of debt which it carries into the 90s and vulnerability to the US business recession which developed late in 1990.

Warner Bros. Studio Chronology

1918   The four Warner brothers have their first feature film success with *My Four Years in Germany*.

1919   The brothers move to the West Coast and open their first, small studio in Hollywood on Sunset Boulevard.

1923   The formation of Warner Bros. Pictures Inc.

1925   Purchase of the Vitagraph company studio and exchanges, and first experiments with sound filming.

1926   The Vitaphone Corporation is formed as a subsidiary to develop sound pictures in partnership with Western Electric. Successful premiere of *Don Juan* with music track and sound effects along with a programme of Vitaphone shorts.

1927   Premiere of the first, tremendously popular part-talkie, *The Jazz Singer*, marking the beginning of the sound era.
Death of Sam Warner.

1928   Purchase of the Stanley Corporation of America, one of the largest theatre chains in the USA, followed soon after by purchase of a one-third interest in First National.

1929   The takeover of the giant First National company, including theatres, exchanges, stars and production personnel, is completed and their studios in Burbank become the new home of Warner Bros. Pictures. Profits hit a peak level of $14.5 million.

1932   The impact of the Depression causes record losses of $14.1 million.

1933   Darryl F. Zanuck resigns after almost four years as production chief under studio boss Jack Warner and is replaced by Hal Wallis.

1937   Oscar for Best Picture of the year for *The Life of Emile Zola* starring Paul Muni and Joseph Schildkraut.

1943   *Casablanca* wins the studio's second Best Picture Oscar.

1944   After ten years as production chief Hal Wallis resigns to become an independent producer.

1951   Divorcement of film theatres from production and distribution in accordance with the Government's Consent Decree.

1955   First successful ventures into TV production.

1956   Harry and Albert Warner sell out their interest, but Jack Warner stays on in a reduced capacity.

1958   Annual losses are recorded for the first time since 1934.

1964   Third Best Picture Oscar (plus seven other Oscars) for *My Fair Lady*, produced by Jack Warner.

1967   Merger between Warner Bros. and Seven Arts Productions. Jack Warner sells his interest.

1969   Takeover by the Kinney National Service Corporation, led by Stephen J. Ross with Ted Ashley appointed to head the film company.

1971   The new corporate name is Warner Communications Inc. However, the film, TV and records subsidiary reverts to its original name of Warner Bros.

1973   Release of the most spectacular hit of the decade, *The Exorcist*.

1978   First of the successful Superman movies.

1980   Robert A. Daly replaces Ted Ashley as Warner Bros. chairman and chief executive officer.

1983/84 The company successfully survives a financial crisis resulting from the tremendous losses experienced by the company's Atari video-games subsidiary which had contributed equally spectacular profits in 1981 and 1982. The company unloads Atari and other assets, shifting back to concentrate on movie and TV entertainment along with recording and publishing.

1984   The company's recovery is aided by *Gremlins*, Warners' biggest hit of the early 80s, directed by Joe Dante and produced by Steven Spielberg.

1989   Warner Communications is involved in a multibillion dollar merger with Time Inc. The new media giant is now known simply as Time Warner Inc.

The Releases

Warner Bros produced a wide range of generally undis-tinguished pictures in the early and middle 20s. Best remembered are the Rin-Tin-Tin actioners, John Barrymore costumers, and sophisticated marital comedies from director Ernst Lubitsch. Following the success of *The Jazz Singer* and *The Singing Fool*, however, the studio turned out large numbers of lightweight musicals, some of them filmed in the early two-strip Technicolor process. Added to the many First National features also distributed by Warners, the total reached a peak level in 1929 and 1930 but declined rapidly in the following years. The studio then turned instead to crime movies and topical social dramas 'ripped from today's headlines', along with fast moving comedies and more musicals. Recovering from the Depression in the late 30s, Warners began producing a few lavish costume movies each year in black-and-white – *Captain Blood, The Story Of Louis Pasteur* – and occasionally Technicolor, such as *The Adventures Of Robin Hood*. Quick to respond to the threat of war, the studio made many war-related films, beginning in 1938, and turned to *films noirs* in the postwar years. Warners finally increased its output of colour productions in the early 50s and ventured briefly into 3-D and CinemaScope with such successes as *House Of Wax* and the musical remake of *A Star Is Born*.

Lacking any major stars or directors, Warner Bros. started out producing a solid, if unimaginative, range of pictures in 1923 including dramas, comedies and actioners. The director Ernst Lubitsch introduced a more sophisticated type of comedy in 1924, while 'man's best friend' Rin-Tin-Tin emerged as the company's biggest star discovery, and his action-adventure movies (and Westerns) became a staple part of the Warner Bros. diet throughout the rest of the 20s. Top star John Barrymore was signed up and appeared in a memorable group of action and costume pictures beginning with *Beau Brummell* (1924) and *The Sea Beast*, a version of 'Moby Dick' filmed in 1925.

During the following years the studio continued to turn out mainly lightweight fare – romances, topical comedies featuring showgirls or flappers, and a sprinkling of tougher social dramas, thrillers and crime movies. Though the quality improved as Warners was able to afford better stars and directors, the talent continued to be spread rather thinly as the company was expanding in many directions simultaneously. The number of feature releases rose rapidly from 14 in 1923 to 43 in 1927, and when the changeover to sound in 1928 caused a fall in numbers, the gap was filled by the first of the First National pictures distributed by Warner Bros. There were more play adaptations – but then the studio had produced a lot of these in its silent days. The most important development was the new boom in the production of musicals. Having had its first big sound successes with *The Jazz Singer* (1927), followed by *Lights Of New York* and *The Singing Fool* (both in 1928), Warners rushed to turn out musicals in great numbers, a few of them filmed in the new, two-strip Technicolor, thus boosting the number of releases to peak levels in 1929 and 1930. With the full Warner Bros. and First National output added together the total came to some 80 pictures per year. This was a level which, clearly, could not be sustained for long. In fact, the cutback in 1931 reflected a drastic reduction in the number of musicals, and other features which incorporated songs, which had glutted the market and had alone accounted for a large proportion of the total.

A big shake-up took place at the studio at this time. The decline in profits and in the number of features coincided with a major turnover in stars. Many of the silent stars, including some inherited from First National, departed or retired, while an important group of new arrivals, many of them signed up from the theatre, helped to give the Warner Bros. movies a new look and what became a characteristic new style.

A genuine interest in the realities of life as it was being experienced during the Depression reflected the concerns of Harry Warner in particular, who was a strong supporter of Franklin Roosevelt; the signing of a tougher new breed of star, both male and female, and directors who were expert at handling fast-moving dialogue and action; the willingness of production chief Darryl Zanuck to take a chance on new and untried properties, trusting his own judgement as to what would make a good movie, rather than depending only on popular plays or novels – all these factors contributed to the new Warners. In addition, the studio's previous leaning toward city life and urban settings took on a special meaning in the 30s. Movies displayed a new emphasis on gangsters, crime and topical social dramas, newspaper pictures and related sports subjects – boxing especially, with its links with the criminal world and gamblers, also football and baseball. These were counter-balanced by numerous fast-moving comedies – and the musicals, so stunningly choreographed by Busby Berkeley.

In developing a very special character of its own, both on screen and off, the independent-minded studio went its own way. Economic pressures forced the studio to concentrate on cutting costs and even to ignoring the distinction usually made between A and B pictures.

According to Casey Robinson, one of the advantages of being a scriptwriter at Warners was that a larger proportion of the writer's contribution appeared on the screen – for Jack Warner was too tight-fisted to spend additional money on rewrites.

Thus, Warners came to be identified with a particularly hard-hitting, black-and-white picture of a type which overlapped the A and B categories. This makes it easier to generalize about a characteristic Warner Bros. style, which captured a more broad-based social flavour than, for example, the glossy, middle-class background to movies from MGM and Paramount.

In this respect it is revealing to note the running time of Warners' A pictures in the early 30s. Whereas B pictures were generally 75 minutes or less, so as to fit easily into the lower half of a double bill, Warners produced numerous As of this length featuring virtually all of its top stars. A short list, for example, could include George Arliss vehicles like *Alexander Hamilton* (1931) and *Voltaire* (1933); John Barrymore in *Moby Dick* (1930); a group of thrillers featuring Barbara Stanwyck, beginning with *Night Nurse* (1931), Edward G. Robinson as *The Hatchet Man* (1932), Bette Davis in *Fog Over Frisco* and Paul Muni in *Hi, Nellie!* (both 1934); and, of course, James Cagney, moving easily from con-man to taxi driver to trucker in such movies as *Blonde Crazy*, with Joan Blondell, *Taxi!* (both 1931) and *The St Louis Kid* (1934). All were filmed on the back lot, making use of the extensive range of standing sets and at a cost of less than $500,000 each.

As Nick Roddick has pointed out in his book, 'A New Deal In Entertainment', it is possible to trace a subtle change in tone from the bleak pessimism of the early 30s, best exemplified in *I Am A Fugitive From A Chain Gang* (1932), to a more general optimism and assertion of individualism combined with social themes in the Paul Muni biopics of the great scientist Louis Pasteur, the eminent writer Emile Zola and the Mexican leader Juarez, or given a more romantic flavour in the Errol Flynn movies such as *Captain Blood* (1935) and *The Adventures Of Robin Hood* (1938). To quote Roddick, 'The regaining of confidence was also reflected in a flood of pictures about a variety of institutions in which American individuals served the community. In *Here Comes The Navy* (1934), *Devil Dogs Of The Air* (1935), *Code Of The Secret Service* (1939), *The Fighting 69th* (1940) and *Dive Bomber* (1941), conflicts between high-spirited individualism and service to one's country were ironed out in military settings, while *Brother Rat* (1938), and *Brother Rat And A Baby* (1940) completed a cycle of college pictures which dealt with similar themes. And *Ceiling Zero* and *China Clipper* (both 1936) are the most typical of the flying pictures which re-affirmed a belief in American technology, know-how and the spirit of innovative adventure.'

There is a marked contrast between the early 30s and the later years when the company had recovered from the Depression and was determined to maintain its position as one of the handful of top studios. This meant a basic change in policy in restoring the standard distinction between A and B pictures in terms of running time and budgets, and with a select group of As allowed budgets of $1 million or more. The year 1935 was the turning point in this respect, with Warner Bros. back in profit for the first time since 1930 and the release of such important features as *A Midsummer Night's Dream* and *Oil For The Lamps Of China*, as well as *Captain Blood* featuring a pair of valuable new stars, Errol Flynn and Olivia de Havilland. In addition *The Story Of Louis Pasteur* was completed and the filming of *Anthony Adverse* begun.

During the following years a number of leading Warner stars were reaching their peak. They were all given their share of costume roles and other films which were relatively lavish by Warners' standards, including a few Technicolor productions. Thus Paul Muni was *Juarez* (1939) and Cagney starred in *Yankee Doodle Dandy* (1942); Errol Flynn appeared in *The Charge Of The Light Brigade* (1936) and *The Sea Hawk* (1940) among others; Bette Davis was the star of *Jezebel* (1938) and *All This And Heaven Too* (1940) and was cast opposite Flynn in *The Private Lives Of Elizabeth And Essex* (1939).

Of special interest was the studio's attitude to the threat of war in the late 30s and the war itself in the 40s. Emphasizing military preparedness with its many service pictures such as *Wings Of The Navy* (1938), starring George Brent, and *Espionage Agent* (1939), a thriller in opposition to the USA's isolationist policy, with Joel McCrea, the studio also starred Flynn in a quality remake of *The Dawn Patrol* (1938). But most explosive of all was the release early in 1939 of a quite compelling and effective exposé of the pro-Nazi German-American Bund, and the worldwide threat of Nazism, called *Confessions Of A Nazi Spy* with Edward G. Robinson. A picture in the true Warner Bros. tradition of topical and hard-hitting dramas, it had gone into production late in 1938 before the Bund trial was even concluded. It was followed by numerous war-related movies including *The Fighting 69th* (1940) and *Captains Of The Clouds* (1942) starring James Cagney, the smash hit *Sergeant York* with Gary Cooper (1941), *Across The Pacific* (1942), *Casablanca* and *Action In The North Atlantic* (both 1943) with Humphrey Bogart, while John Garfield starred in *Air Force* (1943) and *Pride Of The Marines* (1945), and Errol Flynn's many war pictures included *Burma Victory* (1945) directed by Raoul Walsh. Indeed, Warners outdid all the other studios in this field, and was noted for the ease and speed with which it switched its leading male stars from thrillers and actioners into war movies of all kinds.

At the same time the studio had been cutting back on production. Though the total of features had remained remarkably steady throughout the 30s at slightly over 50 titles per year, there was a decline in the early 40s as the company virtually gave up producing Bs. In fact, these had only been appearing for a few years under the supervision of producer Bryan Foy, son of the famous vaudeville entertainer Eddie Foy. He had been in charge of turning out about 26 programmers a year in

1936 and these had inevitably included large numbers of thrillers. The Torchy Blane series starred Glenda Farrell with Barton MacLane, and a juvenile variation, the Nancy Drew pictures, had Bonita Granville as the star, while Ronald Reagan was cast as a secret agent in a number of movies with an aerial background including such titles as *Code Of The Secret Service* (1939) and *Murder In The Air* (1940). In addition, Dick Foran starred in a dozen B Westerns, the studio's first venture into this area since the days of Rin-Tin-Tin, and a short-lived run starred John Wayne in 1932 and 1933. Finally, there were many cheap dramas and comedies, and remakes of earlier Warner pictures, as well as juvenile and sports movies to round out the Bs.

By 1943, and through to 1948, the studio was averaging only 20 feature releases per year, and though there was a slight recovery in the 50s, the total was still only about half of what it had been in the 30s. Slow to make the changeover to colour filming, the studio continued to have its biggest successes in black-and-white and made a major contribution to the development of 40s *film noir*. This was really only a variation on the type of low-keyed thrillers that the studio had been producing for many years. Humphrey Bogart, in particular, emerged as perhaps the leading *noir* star of the decade, beginning with *High Sierra* (1940) and *The Maltese Falcon* (1941), and was paired with Lauren Bacall (both on and off screen) in a memorable group of pictures beginning with *To Have And Have Not* (1944); new arrival Joan Crawford fitted in well at Warner Bros. with *Mildred Pierce* (1945) and *Possessed* (1947), and Cagney gave one last great performance as a psychotic gangster-loser in *White Heat* (1949). There were many black-and-white dramas of note ranging from Ronald Reagan in *King's Row* (1942) to *Humoresque* (1946) teaming Crawford with John Garfield, to Jane Wyman in *Johnny Belinda* (1948), and a last group of Bette Davis vehicles including *Now Voyager* (1942) and *Mr Skeffington* (1944).

Fredric March starred in *The Adventures of Mark Twain* (1944) while Bogart joined the veteran Walter Huston in *The Treasure Of The Sierra Madre* (1948). Director Raoul Walsh moved from *They Died With Their Boots On* (1941) to such postwar Westerns as *Pursued* (1947) and *Colorado Territory* (1948), and there were even some black-and-white musicals, including *Yankee Doodle Dandy* (1942), *Hollywood Canteen* (1944) and the Gershwin biopic *Rhapsody In Blue* (1945). It was the last, great era of black-and-white film-making, which continued up to the early 50s and in which Warner Bros. continued to play a major role with such notable productions as *A Streetcar Named Desire* starring Marlon Brando and Vivien Leigh, and Alfred Hitchcock's masterful *Strangers On A Train* (both released in 1951). But by this time the studio had lost many of its top stars and directors, and with the move into colour and CinemaScope its productions no longer looked recognizably like Warner Bros. pictures.

In addition, the studio finally gave up producing shorts in the mid-50s, one of the last studios to do so. Warner Bros. had first developed an interest in short films in the 20s when the early Vitaphone one- and two-reelers had played an important role in the introduction of sound. By 1930 Warners had turned out hundreds of (mainly musical) shorts, usually filmed in its east-coast studio in Brooklyn. When Sam Sax took over as studio production manager in 1931, there was a marked improvement in quality and many new young talents were borrowed from Broadway including Bob Hope, June Allyson, Phil Silvers, Dorothy Lamour and Betty Hutton, along with established names including Ruth Etting, Eddie Foy Jr, Jane Froman, Lillian Roth, and dancers Hal LeRoy and Bill 'Bojangles' Robinson. There was even a last group of comedies starring Fatty Arbuckle, who was attempting to make a comeback shortly before his death in 1933.

In 1935 the company expanded its production of shorts in Hollywood, many of them handled by Crane Wilbur, but Jean Negulesco and Don Siegel also directed shorts before graduating to features. Though the emphasis continued to be on musicals, the dramatic short subjects often featured new talent like Dane Clark, Nina Foch and Dorothy Malone, and as late as the 50s the studio was still having success with its long-running Joe McDoakes comedy series, travelogues and compilation shorts from Robert Youngson with their amazing mixture of film clips and newsreel extracts, including his When The Talkies Were Young series.

Though the studio won a few Academy nominations and Oscars for its shorts, the one area in which it truly excelled was the animated cartoon. Though Warners began releasing cartoons in 1930, it was only around 1936 that the studio began to find its own distinctive voice and break away from the influence of Disney. With the arrival of Tex Avery, Chuck Jones and Bob Clampett, followed by Frank Tashlin, a whole new style of fast-moving, free-wheeling animation was born in the Warner cartoon section, popularly known as 'Termite Terrace'. Breaking free from naturalistic conventions, and full of verbal as well as visual jokes, these shorts provided the perfect cartoon counterpart to the Warners features, and spotlighted a new group of stars headed by Bugs Bunny, Daffy Duck, Sylvester the Cat and the Road Runner, who lasted well into the 60s, long after the studio's human stars had departed.

Colour Productions

As part of its phenomenal growth in 1928, Warner Bros. turned its interest to the newly introduced two-strip Technicolor process. Having pioneered in the introduction of sound, the studio was prepared to do the same for colour and signed an agreement to produce 20 Technicolor features, about twice the total from all the other studios combined, at about the same time that it was absorbing First National. (Six of the 20 appeared under the First National banner.)

In fact, Technicolor was confined almost entirely to the early Warners sound musicals of 1929 and 1930. The first release, *On With The Show* (1929), could claim to be the first all-talking, all-singing, all-colour feature, while there were also a number of black-and-white movies which included Technicolor sequences, among them the operetta *The Desert Song* (1929), and the famous 1930 Al Jolson vehicle, *Mammy*. But the studio only enjoyed one really big Technicolor hit during this period,

Gold Diggers Of Broadway, in 1929, and few of the colour features made enough money to justify the added production problems and expense. Rapidly falling profits and the decline in popularity of the musical meant that the studio belatedly completed its contract with Technicolor with a pair of oddities, two horror movies directed by Michael Curtiz. *Dr. X* (1932) was followed by *The Mystery Of The Wax Museum* (1933) in which the most dramatic sequence, the fire which engulfs the museum with the grotesque distortions and destruction of the wax figures, gained an added impact through the use of colour.

Having been unsuccessful once, the studio was relatively slow to venture into colour in the mid-30s when the new three-strip Technicolor became available. Only after Walter Wanger's production of *The Trail Of The Lonesome Pine* (Paramount, 1936) proved to be a hit did Warners finally select a similar type of outdoor, forestry subject and setting for its first Technicolored feature, *God's Country And The Woman*. However, the picture is best remembered today for provoking a bitter dispute between Bette Davis and Jack Warner which ended up in the British law courts. As Warners' premier female star, it's not surprising that Miss Davis was assigned the lead in its first colour movie, but, rather than a major production, the project looked more like a quick attempt to cash in on the success of *The Trail Of The Lonesome Pine*, with colour used to boost the appeal of a weak story and script, as occurred in a number of other feeble 1936 productions like *The Dancing Pirate* (Pioneer/RKO) and *Wings Of The Morning* (Fox). Davis rejected the lead role of a 'female lumberjack' out of hand and was put on suspension, while filming proceeded with starlet Beverly Roberts instead. In fact, Miss Davis was one of many leading 30s stars who were hostile to the introduction of colour, often with good reason. As she recalled years later, 'They gave the colour to the terrible scripts as an added inducement to get the public in . . . My pictures brought the public in without the added expense.'

God's Country And The Woman was not a success and there was a gap of over a year before the studio released its second Technicolored feature, a Western drama about the California gold rush called *Gold Is Where You Find It* (1938), starring George Brent and Olivia de Havilland and directed by Michael Curtiz. This was quickly followed by *The Adventures Of Robin Hood* and two Westerns, making four 1938 releases in all, with a fifth, *Dodge City*, already in production. Thus, for a brief period before Fox began substantially to increase its production of colour features, Warners was the industry leader. Then, just as suddenly as it had boosted its investment in Technicolor, the studio virtually gave up the process from 1939 on. Certainly, profits were falling once again, recalling the studio's experience with two-strip Technicolor in 1930, and the Technicolor features had made little contribution to annual income, with the expensive *Robin Hood* failing to cover its high costs; but the extent of the cutback, at a time when other leading companies were increasing their investment in colour, was still a little surprising.

From this point on Warner Bros. only released one Technicolor picture per year up to the late 40s and thus failed to keep pace with the other industry leaders, Fox, Paramount and MGM, as well as some of the smaller studios. Of the eight colour pictures released by Warner Bros. between 1939 and 1946, six were directed by Michael Curtiz, the studio's leading contract director, who had first demonstrated his special abilities with colour as co-director on *The Adventures Of Robin Hood*, the picture which stands out as Warner Bros.' most enduring Technicolor contribution of the 30s. In this prime example of studio film-making at its best, Errol Flynn gave one of his most engaging and lively performances in the title role, backed by a strong supporting cast, and with fine contributions from many of the studio's leading technicians.

During the following years Curtiz directed Flynn in a variety of interesting, if not especially successful, colour productions. *Dodge City* was a sprawling, expensive Western which attempted to cram in virtually every Western theme imaginable – buffalo hunting, covered wagons, cattle drives and the opening up of the railroad; the corrupt saloon owner who runs the town is opposed by a crusading newspaper editor and his attractive lady assistant, while there is also a good-bad dance-hall girl and a sheriff who brings law and order. In addition, the picture featured one of the longest and most spectacular bar-room brawls ever seen on the screen. *The Private Lives Of Elizabeth And Essex* (1939) proved to be a mismatch with Bette Davis acting Flynn off the screen, while the last of the Curtiz–Flynn collaborations was the patriotic flying movie, *Dive Bomber* (1941).

Curtiz then directed Cagney in the air in *Captains Of The Clouds* (1942), Ronald Reagan in the extravagant Irving Berlin musical *This Is The Army* (1943), Cary Grant, miscast as Cole Porter in the musical biopic, *Night And Day* (1946), and William Powell in the movie adaptation of the smash-hit play *Life With Father* (1947). From this point on the Curtiz colour pictures become even less interesting as he was assigned to Doris Day musicals, a remake of *The Jazz Singer* starring Danny Thomas in 1953, and other forgettable efforts.

From 1949 the studio began releasing larger numbers of colour pictures for the first time, but most of them were undistinguished musicals and Westerns. Among the few films of special interest were the first colour efforts of Alfred Hitchcock: an extraordinary experiment with 10-minute takes and Technicolor in *Rope* (1948); an unusual costume drama, *Under Capricorn* (1949), set in Australia and starring Ingrid Bergman; a 3-D version of the play *Dial M For Murder* (1953), his first of several pictures with Grace Kelly. Then too, there were two colourful and entertaining swashbucklers starring the young and acrobatic Burt Lancaster: *The Flame And The Arrow* (1950) directed by Jacques Tourneur, and *The Crimson Pirate* (1952), directed by Robert Siodmak, but little else of note was made before the studio's first ventures into 3-D and CinemaScope in 1953 and 1954.

Widescreen and 3-D

Warner Bros. joined the rush into 3-D with four releases in 1953 and two others in production, and the studio had the biggest 3-D hit of all with *House Of Wax*, produced by Warners veteran Bryan Foy, directed by André de Toth and starring Vincent Price. The picture also introduced a new stereophonic sound process called WarnerPhonic and was one of the first to make use of the studio's version of the newly developed Eastman Color known as Warner Color. However, by the time the last of the 3-D movies, *Dial M For Murder*, was ready for release early in 1954, the fad was already over and it was mainly shown in a flat version.

By then the newest technical innovation sweeping Hollywood was CinemaScope, and again Warners was quick to respond and equally quick to drop it, virtually giving up the process by 1956 – the first company to do so, in a pattern which was by now becoming familiar and recalled the studio's early experiences with colour. Concentrated into this relatively brief period (1954 and 1955) were a number of top hits, expensive flops, and a few of the most imaginative of the early CinemaScope productions, handled by a select group of directors. William Wellman proved that CinemaScope could be effective within the enclosed space of an airplane in *The High And The Mighty* (1954), while George Cukor demonstrated a surprising fluidity in his use of the CinemaScope camera in the first musical version of *A Star Is Born* (1954) starring Judy Garland. Elia Kazan, too, was working in colour and CinemaScope for the first time with great assurance, imaginatively making use of asymmetrical compositions whenever possible, and determined 'to combat the shape', as he put it, in the filming of *East Of Eden* (from the best-selling novel by John Steinbeck) in 1954: 'I would put something big in the big in the foreground on one side, something black, that you couldn't see through, and put the action on the other side. The next time I'd have the action in a corner over there and have something blocking it here. I tried to make frames within the frame . . .' *East Of Eden*'s star, James Dean, played the lead in *Rebel Without A Cause* (1955) in which director Nicholas Ray also showed how an intimate dramatic picture could make good use of the new wide format.

By 1956 none of the studio's top colour pictures, such as *Giant, Moby Dick*, or John Ford's *The Searchers* was in CinemaScope. The look of the Ford film, however, was greatly enhanced by VistaVision (the only Warner Bros. production to use it), and Ford was one of the few Warner Bros. directors to make use of 70mm equipment in the 60s, for his production of *Cheyenne Autumn* (1964). The others were George Cukor with the opulent adaptation of *My Fair Lady* that same year and the British-made war movie *Battle of The Bulge* (1965), while the Broadway hit, *The Music Man* (1962), had been filmed in Technirama. (The company had briefly experimented with a 65mm process called Vitascope in 1930, but had dropped it after only two films, *Kismet* and *The Lash*.)

Widescreen and 3-D Releases 1953–69

Process	1953	1954	1955	1956	1957	1958	1959	1960	1961	1962	1963	1964	1965	1966	1967	1968	1969
CinemaScope	7	14	3^b	3	1	1											
Technirama					1		2		2								
Panavision									1		4	3	10	1	4	4	9
Techniscope														1	1	1	1
Large Format (70mm)												2	1				
3-D	4	2															

b includes 1 VistaVision

The Finances

Having earned good profits in its first years, Warner Bros. was able to raise substantial financial backing for expanding its distribution network, ownership of movie theatres and experiments with sound. These latter were extremely expensive and caused the company to fall into the red for a few years, but paid off handsomely in 1927–28 when Warners led the other studios in the changeover to the talkies. Profits boomed during 1928–30, boosted by such hits as *The Singing Fool* and *Gold Diggers Of Broadway*, and the studio grew rapidly, taking over First National and the Stanley theatre chain. But by 1930 audiences were declining and the company experienced terrible losses. The studio survived through its ability to turn out quality pictures extremely efficiently and inexpensively, and profits began to grow again in the late 30s. Though the company had less than its share of top hits, it did well during the war years, but less well in the 50s and 60s. As a subsidiary of Warner Communications, it has been one of the most consistently profitable movie companies in recent years with numerous big hits such as *The Exorcist* (1973), the Superman movies and, most recently, *Gremlins* (1984), and *Batman* (1989).

Officially founded in 1923, Warner Bros. got off to a good start and was already earning healthy profits by late 1924. Company president Harry Warner realized that in order for Warners to grow it was necessary to raise new and more secure financial backing. He managed to interest Waddil Catchings, of the leading Wall Street investment firm Goldman, Sachs, who saw the possibilities of developing Warners into a leading studio and was attracted to the opportunities offered by the movie industry. With Catchings' support and a $3 million revolving line of credit, the company was able to take over Vitagraph, expand its distribution network, purchase its first movie theatres and begin its first experiments with sound. All this activity took place within a relatively brief period of time in 1925. Clearly the Warner brothers was not afraid of taking risks; after many years attempting to establish themselves in the industry, this was a long-overdue opportunity.

Though revenues rose rapidly in 1925 and 1926, expenses had risen even faster, and the company recorded substantial losses, but such results were consistent with the phenomenon of a small but growing company. Even the success of the first Vitaphone screenings were not sufficient to bring the company back into profit, since the returns was limited by the small number of theatres equipped for projecting Vitaphone movies, and by this time Warners had invested well over $3 million in its sound experiments. (Expressed in calendar years, Warner Bros. found itself in the red from early in 1925 to the first months of 1927; the first quarterly profit for two years was announced in May of 1927.)

Unfortunately, over the years a myth has grown up that the studio was in serious financial trouble and suddenly had the idea of turning to sound as a means of rescue. This view has developed out of a total misreading of the data, since the losses were actually due to the cost of Warners' substantial investment in sound over a two-year period. (Of course, it is quite possible that if the sound experiment had failed, the company would have folded.)

By late 1927 Warner Bros. had turned the corner. *The Jazz Singer* which had only cost about $500,000 to produce brought in rentals of $3.5 million in the US alone, placing it among the handful of top hits of the decade and helping the company to earn a solid $2 million profit for the 1927/1928 fiscal year. Profits continued to grow while the company expanded its operations, enlarging and sound-proofing its Hollywood studio and taking over the Stanley theatre chain. Throughout 1928 revenues rolled in from the Vitaphone presentations and the highly profitable all-talking *Lights Of New York*, while *The Singing Fool* which had cost about $500,000 and brought in rentals of over $5 million could claim to be the single most profitable movie of the 20s. Though a no-expense-spared $2 million production of *Noah's Ark* flopped badly, the studio had another substantial hit with *Gold Diggers Of Broadway* in 1929 – at around the time it completed the takeover of the ailing First National studios.

In contrast to Warners' run of hits, First National's best years were long past. The company had done well from 1919 to 1924 when it had contracts with many leading producer-stars and shared in the profits of smash hits from Mary Pickford (*Daddy Longlegs*, 1919), Charlie Chaplin (*The Kid*, 1921) and Norma Talmadge (*Smilin' Thru*, 1922, *Secrets*, 1924). But revenues had levelled off after 1925 while profits fell, thus making the company vulnerable to a takeover at a time when other, healthier studios were growing and expanding.

In fact, Warner profits reached their peak of $14.5 million early in 1929, and though they continued at a high level for another year, the trend was down. Though the point is rarely made, it is important to understand the way in which the characteristic Warner Bros. style, of efficiently made, fast-moving contemporary dramas, gangster films and musicals, developed during a period when the company was falling into the red and budgets were particularly tight. The company was able to survive the worst years of the Depression through a combination of shrewd financial management and deals in Warners' stock between the film company and Renraw (Warner spelled backwards), the family holding company which had been created in 1923, together with the sale of unprofitable movie theatres and cost cutting in feature production.

During the worst year, 1931/32, losses rose to slightly over $14 million and, during the four worst years, totalled slightly over $30 million. By 1935–37 the studio was recovering strongly and was well on the way to paying off all its debts, although it had relatively few hits in the 30s. Having produced four of the top money-earning movies of the late 20s, the studio struggled to match that total throughout the 30s. It only registered a poor fifth in the box office stakes, behind MGM, Goldwyn/UA, Fox and Paramount, and managed to survive by keeping costs low and attempting to earn a small profit on each feature it produced. More than any other studio, it depended on efficient, assembly-line methods for turning out its pictures. Its directors and technicians had a reputation for working quickly and efficiently while maintaining high standards of production. The studio had few expensive stars under contract, and they were kept as busy as the rest of the contract personnel on a six-day week.

Thus, three of the most popular Warner Bros. musicals of 1933 – *42nd Street*, *Gold Diggers Of 1933* and *Footlight Parade* – all cost less than $500,000 each, as did *Little Caesar* (1930), *G-Men* (1935) and *The Story Of Louis Pasteur* (1936), while a studio-bound play like *Five Star Final* (1931) was brought in by the efficient Mervyn LeRoy at under $300,000, and *The Public Enemy* (1931) without any leading stars cost only $200,000. (At that time James Cagney was only earning $400 a week.)

Once the studio had recovered from the Depression in the mid-30s, it began to spend more on its A pictures. Warners typically turned out over 50 features per year within a total budget of about $25 million. However, since half were B movies accounting for only $5 million (and costing about $200,000 each), this meant that an average 'A' came in at about three times that amount, that is $600,000. But the studio was extremely unlucky with the vast majority of its most expensive pictures. Warner Bros. could do little better than break even with such ambitious productions as *Anthony Adverse* and *The Charge Of The Light Brigade* in 1936 and *The Prince And The Pauper* (1937) each of which cost over $1 million, while A *Midsummer Night's Dream* at $1.35 million may have managed a tiny profit to help the recovery along in 1935.

Income and profits rose strongly in 1936, but by the time the studio released the Oscar-winning *The Life Of Emile Zola*, which had cost only $700,000, in the summer of 1937, profits were declining once again. The studio received little comfort in the late 30s from its many high-cost pictures that included *Jezebel* and *Gold Is Where You Find It* (both 1938), *Juarez* and *The Private Lives Of Elizabeth And Essex* (both 1939) and *The Sea Hawk* (1940), all of which cost well over $1 million each. Biggest disappointment of all was the outstanding Errol Flynn vehicle, *The Adventures Of Robin Hood* (1938), which was filmed in Technicolor at a cost of almost $2 million but failed to earn a profit.

The situation improved tremendously in the 40s, however. Though the studio still had relatively few big hits, and did poorly in this respect compared with the other majors, it kept its overall costs low. A booming box-office meant that a larger proportion of its features were profitable than ever before, as were its cinemas, and all together they boosted the company profits to the highest levels so far. The studio did particularly well with its war-related pictures, such as *Sergeant York* (1941), which cost $1.6 million but was the studio's biggest hit of the decade aside from *This is The Army* (1943), the Irving Berlin musical for which the profits were donated to the Army Emergency Relief fund. Other hits included another patriotic musical, *Yankee Doodle Dandy* (1942) starring James Cagney, *Casablanca* (1943) which cost less than $1 million and earned three times that amount, and *Hollywood Canteen* (1944). Profits peaked during 1945–47 at over $20 million, aided by such additional hits as *Saratoga Trunk* (1945), the Cole Porter musical biopic *Night And Day* (1946) and the Technicolored, turn-of-the-century comedy, *Life With Father* (1947) starring William Powell and Irene Dunne.

Profits held up reasonably well until 1952 when the company was forced to sell off its movie theatres. The studio continued to have less than its share of top hits, and there were no longer large numbers of cheaply produced features and shorts contributing to the total earnings as in earlier years. Most successful at the box office was *Giant* (1956), followed by a pair of Technirama productions, *Sayonara* (1957) starring Marlon Brando, and *Auntie Mame* (1958) with Rosalind Russell. Warners also produced the biggest 3-D hit of the decade, *House Of Wax* (1953), and had been quick to move into CinemaScope in the mid-50s with distinctly mixed results. The hits included *The High And The Mighty* and the musical version of *A Star Is Born* (both 1954), also *Mr Roberts*, *Battle Cry* and *The Sea Chase* (all released in 1955); the studio was finding it profitable to continue fighting World War II on screen, while performing disastrously with its ventures into the ancient world. The estimated losses were $4 million on each of three features – *The Silver Chalice* (1954), which was Paul Newman's first and worst movie, *Land Of The Pharaohs* and *Helen Of Troy* (both 1955).

In the 60s, the few hits were also spread fairly evenly throughout the decade. These ranged from *The Music Man* (1962) and *Who's Afraid Of Virginia Woolf* (1966), to *Bonnie And Clyde* (1967), the studio's biggest success in the 60s, and *Bullitt* (1968) starring Steve McQueen. Such high-cost productions as *The Great Race* (1965) and *Camelot* (1967) merely broke even, while *My Fair Lady* (1964) was so expensive, with costs estimated at $17 million, and $5.5 million paid for the rights alone, that Warners fell into the red while filming it. (Though it won the top Oscar, it still lost money.)

It was not until *The Exorcist* in 1973 that the studio came up with its first really spectacular box-office success since *The Singing Fool* some 45 years earlier. Although the movie had gone far over budget and cost $10 million, rentals in the USA alone were nine times that amount.

As part of the newly renamed Warner Communications, the company continued to do well throughout the 70s, benefiting from its association with star-producer-director Clint Eastwood (*Dirty Harry*, 1971, and its three hit sequels, also *Every Which Way But Loose*, 1978, and its sequel, and *Heartbreak Ridge*, 1986); with Burt Reynolds (star of *Deliverance*, 1972, and *Hooper*, 1978); with Steven Spielberg, executive producer of *Gremlins* (1984) and *The Goonies* (1985), and producer-director of *The Color Purple* (1985). Warners also had a measure of success as distributor of the Superman pictures and with its own Police Academy series in the 80s. Most recently the studio had its best year in 1989 with *Batman*, *Lethal Weapon 2* and the Oscar-winning *Driving Miss Daisy* from the Zanuck company, then had a big hit with Kevin Costner as *Robin Hood: Prince of Thieves* in 1991.

Box Office Hits	Warner Bros and First National	
TITLE	*Cost*	*North American rentals*
1914–31	(in $ millions)	(in $ millions)
FIRST NATIONAL FILMS		
The Kid (1921) (Chaplin)	(0.5)	2.5
The Sea Hawk (1924) (F Lloyd)	(0.8)	2.0
Secrets (1924) (J Schenck/N Talmadge)		1.5
Daddy Long Legs (1919) (Pickford)		1.3
The Lost World (1925)		1.3
The Patent Leather Kid (1927)	(1.0)	1.2
Smilin' Through (1922) (J Schenck/N Talmadge)		1.0
WARNER BROS FILMS		
The Singing Fool (1928)	(0.5)	5.0
The Jazz Singer (1927)	(0.5)	3.5
Gold Diggers Of Broadway (1929)		2.3
1932–40		
42nd Street (1933)	(0.4)	2.3
Footlight Parade (1933)	(0.5)	1.8
A Midsummer Night's Dream (1935)	(1.4)	1.5
The Life Of Emile Zola (1937)	(0.7)	1.5
The Adventures of Robin Hood (1938)	(1.9)	1.5
The Old Maid (1939)		1.5
The Fighting 69th (1940)	(0.9)	1.5
Santa Fe Trail (1940)		1.5
1941–50		
This Is The Army (1943)		8.5
Sergeant York (1941)	(1.6)	6.1
Life With Father (1947)		5.1
Yankee Doodle Dandy (1942)		4.8
Saratoga Trunk (1945)		4.3
Hollywood Canteen (1944)		4.2
Johnny Belinda (1948)		4.1
Night And Day (1946)		4.0
Casablanca (1943)	(1.0)	3.7
1951–60		
Giant (1956)	(5.0)	12.0
Sayonara (1957)		10.5
Auntie Mame (1958)		9.1
Mister Roberts (1955)		8.5
Battle Cry (1955)		8.1

No Time For Sergeants (1958)		7.5
A Star Is Born (1954)	(5.0)	6.1
The High And The Mighty (1954)		6.1
The Sea Chase (1955)		6.0
The Nun's Story (1959)		5.8
Rio Bravo (1959)		5.8
Ocean's Eleven (1960)		5.5
East Of Eden (1955)		5.0
Pete Kelly's Blues (1955)		5.0
The Searchers (1956)		4.9
Moby Dick (1956)		4.8
House Of Wax (1953)		4.7
Dragnet (1954)		4.7
A Summer Place (1960)		4.7
Rebel Without A Cause (1956)		4.6

1961–70

Bonnie And Clyde (1967)	(3.0)	22.0
Bullitt (1968)	(5.5)	19.0
Who's Afraid Of Virginia Woolf? (1966)		14.5
Woodstock (1970)		14.5
Camelot (1967)	(15.0)	12.3
My Fair Lady (1964)	(17.0)	12.0
The Great Race (1965)	(10.0)	11.0
The Green Berets (1968)		9.7
The Fox (1967)		8.6
Wait Until Dark (1967)		7.8
Cool Hand Luke (1967)		7.2

1971–80

The Exorcist (1973)	(10.0)	88.5
Superman – The Movie (co-prod) (1978)	(40.0)	82.5
Every Which Way But Loose (1978)	(3.5)	51.8
Towering Inferno (co-prod) (1974)	(15.0)	50.0
Blazing Saddles (1974)		45.2
The Goodbye Girl (co-prod) (1977)	(3.3)	41.7
Any Which Way You Can (1980)		39.5
A Star Is Born (1976)	(6.0)	37.1
Hooper (1978)		34.9
Private Benjamin (1980)		34.0
Billy Jack (1971)	(1.0)	32.5
Oh, God! (1977)		31.4
The Shining (1980)	(18.0)	30.8
All The President's Men (1976)	(9.0)	30.0
What's Up Doc? (1972)	(4.0)	28.0
The Main Event (1979)		26.3
The Trial Of Billy Jack (1974)		24.0
The Enforcer (1976)	(4.0)	24.0
Deliverance (1972)		22.5
Dog Day Afternoon (1975)		22.5

1981–90

Batman (1989)	(50.)	150.5
Gremlins (1984)	(25.)	79.5
Lethal Weapon 2 (1989)	(30.)	79.5
Superman II (Co-prod) (1981)	(50.)	65.1
Driving Miss Daisy (co-prod) (1989)	(8.)	50.5
The Color Purple (1985)	(15.)	49.8
Presumed Innocent (1990)	(22.)	43.8
Arthur (co-prod) (1981)		42.0
Police Academy (co-prod) (1984)	(4.)	38.5
Superman III (co-prod) (1983)	(35.)	37.2

title	cost	North American rentals
1981–90	(in $ millions)	(in $ millions)
Sudden Impact (1983)		34.8
National Lampoon's Christmas Vacation (1989)	(27.)	34.8
Beetlejuice (co-prod) (1988)	(20.)	33.2
The Witches Of Eastwick (1987)	(35.)	31.8
Purple Rain (1984)		31.7
Chariots Of Fire (co-prod) (1981)	(6.)	30.6
Spies Like Us (1985)	(22.)	30.5
National Lampoon's Vacation (1983)		30.4
Risky Business (co-prod) (1983)		30.4
Tango & Cash (1989)	(55.)	30.1
Hard To Kill (1990)		30.0
The Goonies (1985)	(19.)	29.9
Lethal Weapon (1987)	(19.)	29.5

The Stars

The studio's earliest stars were Rin-Tin-Tin and John
Barrymore, but with the coming of sound Warners signed
up many new talents from the stage beginning with Al
Jolson, George Arliss and Joe E. Brown, and followed
by an impressive new group, among them James Cagney,
Edward G. Robinson, Bette Davis, Dick Powell and Paul
Muni, all of whom became staple figures at the studio
in the 30s. With its strong line-up of solid, down-to-
earth types the studio was a major force in developing
a new idea of stardom. Errol Flynn was signed in 1935,
along with Olivia de Havilland, while Humphrey Bogart
emerged as the studio's top star in the 40s. He was a
formidable presence in war and adventure dramas such as
Casablanca and *The Treasure Of The Sierra Madre*, but
was most often seen in *films noirs*. Talents in later years
included Doris Day, James Dean, Burt Lancaster and John
Wayne.

Warner Bros. made use of relatively minor actors in most of its early
pictures, along with a few better known names such as Henry B.
Walthall, Anna Q. Nilsson, Belle Bennett, and the freckle-faced juvenile
star Wesley Barry who made his first appearance in 1922. Once the
company began to expand, it acquired a new group of stars, all of whom
stayed on for a number of years and provided a core of leading performers
throughout the rest of the silent era. Louise Fazenda and Marie Prevost
were ex-Sennett girls who specialized in lightweight or comedy roles,
while Monte Blue and Irene Rich made their successful debuts at the
studio in *Brass*, a domestic drama directed by Sidney Franklin. But most
important of all was the German-shepherd dog Rin-Tin-Tin. Originally
known as Rinty, his outdoor adventure movies, kicking off with *Where
The North Begins*, quickly caught on and were tremendously popular at
the time. Well-made pictures in every sense, they were turned out at a
rate of three per year up to the early 30s. Many were originally scripted by
the young Darryl F. Zanuck, while production was efficiently organized

to ensure that the filming would go as smoothly as possible. This meant not just a number of stand-ins for the canine star, but a whole kennel full of dogs, each trained to do different tricks. 'Eventually we had 18 Rin-Tin-Tins,' noted Jack Warner in his autobiography, 'and we used them all. On the screen they all looked alike, but each animal was a specialist. One was used for attack scenes, another was trained to jump 12-foot walls, a third was a gentle house dog, and so on.'

John Barrymore arrived late in 1923 and made his biggest contribution to the studio when he starred in the first Vitaphone feature, *Don Juan* in 1926, but it was Al Jolson who held pride of place as Warner's first musical and talkie star. The success of *The Jazz Singer* (1927) and *The Singing Fool* (1928) was phenomenal, and Jolson was also a major stockholder in the studio. Though Warners had a head start over the other studios, the changeover from silents to sound was far from simple as far as the stars were concerned. With its takeover of First National in 1928–29, the company inherited the services of Richard Barthelmess, Billie Dove, Dorothy Mackaill and Loretta Young, among others, at about the same time that it was boosting the production of musicals. Thus, many of the First National leading ladies – like Alice White, Colleen Moore and Corinne Griffith – were thrust into musical roles whenever possible, along with such established Warners stars as Myrna Loy and Louise Fazenda.

There was a tremendous turnover in stars at the time, not least because the sudden increase in musicals brought in talents who quickly became superfluous once the boom was over. Just a short list of those who appeared in one or two Warner Bros. pictures at this time, most of them making their talkie debut, includes Fanny Brice, Sophie Tucker, Ethel Waters, Charlotte Greenwood, John Boles, Irene Bordoni and Texas Guinan, while famous showgirl Marilyn Miller appeared in three Warners musicals, and Joe E. Brown was one of the very few who survived and became a fixture at the studio in the 30s. Not only did a drastic reduction in musicals and in the total number of features provide a good excuse to get rid of many of the studio's last remaining silent stars and First National players, but Warners was already signing up the first of a new group of players who would help to transform the studio during the following years.

Thus, 1930 was a turning point, the year in which Edward G. Robinson, James Cagney and Joan Blondell arrived, and immediately set the studio on course for establishing a fresh, tougher identity. They represented a new breed of brash, street-wise personalities on screen and accurately reflected the new era, far removed from the romantic leads and flappers of the 20s. They were soon joined by Bette Davis and Barbara Stanwyck, followed by Glenda Farrell and Paul Muni, all solid, down-to-earth performers with stage experience who proved to be, in reality, the most reliable and hardest-working of Hollywood stars. The studio kept them busy, often giving them four or five films per year. Of course, there were a few classy sophisticates, too, among the new arrivals – Kay Francis, George Brent, Warren William – while musical talents Dick Powell and Ruby Keeler were paired for the first time in *42nd Street* late in 1932.

Glenda Farrell, there from 1932 to 1937, has recalled the generally good feeling which existed at the studio at this time. 'Warners never made you feel you were just a member of the cast. They might star you in one movie and give you a bit part in the next ... You were still well paid and you didn't get a star complex. We were a very close group – Cagney, Guy Kibbee, Hugh Herbert, Aline MacMahon, Dick Powell and Joan Blondell.'

The fact that this group was assembled within such a short space of time during a period when the studio was in some financial difficulty must be credited largely to production chief Darryl F. Zanuck. The powerful impact of the new leads was seen most clearly in four pictures released between 1930 and 1932. Edward G. Robinson signalled the evolution of a new type of movie gangster, men without any redeeming qualities, in 1930. As *Little Caesar* he gave an absolutely brilliant and powerful performance, filling every corner of a movie in which character was designed to take precedence over plot. No less astonishing was the cocky, fast-talking vitality of James Cagney as *The Public Enemy* (1931) in another classic gangster role, while Paul Muni gave the most moving performance of his early career as an innocent war veteran on the run from the law in the best of the first Warners social-protest films, *I Am A Fugitive From A Chain Gang* (1932). Finally, Bette Davis credits Zanuck with overriding the objections of director Michael Curtiz in offering her a first memorable part as the rich, vixenish Southern belle in *Cabin In The Cotton* (1932) – a spoilt, bad-girl role of a type with which she would become increasingly identified over the years, notably in *Jezebel* (1938).

In this early starring role Miss Davis dominated the picture, as she was to do so consistently throughout most of her career as a top star (one of the rare female top stars at Warners). Recognizing the qualities of these strong-minded, individualistic performers, Jack Warner rarely tried to pair them (and even more rarely succeeded) as was done so often at the other top studios.

In addition, Warners was a very self-contained studio, characterized by a kind of insularity which meant that it rarely borrowed or exchanged stars with the other studios. Thus Bette Davis had a real struggle to get Jack Warner to loan her to RKO for *Of Human Bondage* (1934) opposite Leslie Howard, and was convinced that the studio had sabotaged her chance of winning an Oscar. (She was not even nominated, but the movie made her name.) She was not loaned out again until 1941 when she played a memorable Regina in the Goldwyn production of *The Little Foxes* in exchange for Goldwyn's Gary Cooper who played *Sergeant York* for Warners.

There were no multi-star vehicles either, aside from a quite unexpectedly lavish and entertaining, if not entirely successful, version of Shakespeare's *A Midsummer Night's Dream* in 1935, starring James Cagney as Bottom and Joe E. Brown as Flute the bellows mender, along with Dick Powell, Anita Louise, Frank McHugh and new arrival Olivia de Havilland. The year 1935 was a 'big' one for the studio. Bette Davis finally won her first Oscar, for *Dangerous*, while Cagney, Powell and Brown made it on to the list of top box-office stars. Notable signings included Errol Flynn, soon to develop into a leading swashbuckler and costume star in the Barrymore-Fairbanks mould, the polished Claude Rains, and Humphrey Bogart who was cast in *The Petrified Forest* at the insistence of Leslie Howard. (Bogie had previously appeared briefly at the studio in 1932, but this time he was back to stay.)

A comparison of salaries in 1935 shows that Dick Powell earned slightly under $70,000, Warren William $95,000 and Kay Francis $115,000, topped by James Cagney at just under $150,000 and Joe E. Brown at $173,000. But by 1941, with the studio earning substantial profits once again, and in spite of the efforts of the Warners to keep salaries down, Cagney's earnings had increased to $360,000, compared with Errol Flynn's at $240,000, Bette Davis' $252,000 and Bogart, not yet in the top-star class, at just under $100,000.

In fact, Jack and Harry Warner were very paternalistic and dictatorial in handling their contract players, and paid the lowest salaries of all the leading studios in the 30s, leading to many long-running disputes. James Cagney, for example, walked out in 1932 after completing *Blonde Crazy* and only returned when his salary was raised from a paltry $450 to $1000 a week, more in keeping with his real value to the studio. But he baulked again the following year until he got another substantial raise, and even left Warners to go independent for a brief period in 1936 and 1937. Bette Davis' well-known dispute, however, was over the poor quality of her scripts, and her defiance led to a suspension and a court battle in 1936. Not surprisingly, it was another Warner star, Olivia de Havilland, who successfully contested the punitive provisions of her contract in the early 40s, at the cost of two years off the screen, but won what was to be a landmark court decision for actors in their contract wars against the studios.

The company continued to strengthen its contract list in the late 30s, adding a few ladies of note such as Ann Sheridan, Jane Wyman and Priscilla Lane, but it still continued to be weighted toward the men with such new additions as Wayne Morris, Ronald Reagan, John Garfield, and established movie tough-guy George Raft. At the same time the studio's stars began to rate more highly at the box-office than ever before. Though they generally appeared in the bottom half of the annual list of top ten stars, at least Bette Davis and Errol Flynn made the list for the first time in 1939 along with James Cagney, and both Cagney and Miss Davis continued to appear regularly during the early 40s. But it was Humphrey Bogart who emerged as the studio's top-rated actor of the decade with seven years on the list from 1943 to 1949.

A surprisingly late developer, Bogart had begun his movie career with other young hopefuls from the stage and appeared in the first features of both Spencer Tracy (*Up The River*, at Fox) and Bette Davis (*Bad Sister*, at Universal) in 1930. Generally type-cast as a gangster, his roles began to improve in the late 30s, but the big breakthrough came with two roles turned down by George Raft. In *High Sierra* (1940) he movingly portrayed the last days of a middle-aged gangster on the run, and he scored again the following year as the cynical private eye, Sam Spade, in *The Maltese Falcon* which also featured the inspired teaming of Peter Lorre and Sydney Greenstreet for the first of many Warners pictures together. In addition, Bogie's laid-back, anti-hero image made him more easy to cast than some of the other tough guys on the Warners back lot, which meant a succession of leading ladies of note including the street-wise but vulnerable young Ida Lupino and the delightful (and still beautiful) Mary Astor, who had first starred at Warner Bros. opposite John Barrymore almost 20 years earlier. Most memorable of all was his pairing with Ingrid Bergman, on loanout from Selznick, in *Casablanca* in 1942 which brought out the softer and more romantic side of his disillusioned, world-weary character and foreshadowed the later group of pictures with Lauren Bacall. Bogart and Bacall fell in love on the screen in *To Have And Have Not* (1944) and Miss Bacall became the last and most fondly remembered of his four wives. She was, however, a wasted asset for the studio which did not know what to do with her aside from casting her opposite Bogie.

In fact, Warner Bros. had continued to boast a strong list of contract players throughout the 40s, in spite of some departures. Paul Muni had left in 1939, followed by Pat O'Brien who had played second fiddle to Cagney in many pictures, most notably as the priest in *Angels With Dirty Faces* (1938). Another of the studio's most reliable second leads, George Brent, left in 1942 just as Paul Henreid arrived to step, more or less, into his shoes. But John Garfield was just coming into his own. A true original and a link between the older generation of Cagney and Bogart and such postwar stars as Brando and James Dean, he was most often cast as a rebellious and cynical young man and first hit his stride at Warners in *The Sea Wolf* (1941), effectively teamed with Ida Lupino and Edward G. Robinson (in one of his last Warner roles), *Pride Of The Marines* (1945), and *Humoresque* (1946) opposite Joan Crawford. Miss Crawford had left MGM in 1942 and found a new home at Warner Bros. the following year, along with a new and tougher persona more appropriate to the studio's world of 40s *film noir*. She was seen at her most expressive – and impressive – as the struggling career woman *Mildred Pierce* (1945) which perfectly suited her and won her an Oscar.

The studio was fortunate in that, in spite of the disputes and tensions, so many of its top names had stayed on for so long; but, by the late 40s, the writing was on the wall. Bogie left in 1948, followed by Bette Davis in 1949 along with a top pair of featured players – big Alan Hale who is best remembered as Errol Flynn's sidekick in innumerable actioners, and Jack Carson, who was to return a few years later to play his best known role as the vicious press agent in the 1954 remake of *A Star Is Born*. With the departure of Joan Crawford, Cagney and Flynn in 1951, an era came to an end.

A few established, independent stars appeared regularly in Warners pictures in the 50s. They included Burt Lancaster, Alan Ladd, Randolph Scott, Virginia Mayo and John Wayne, but the studio also attempted to groom a few younger newcomers for stardom. They began most auspiciously with a young, blonde musical discovery named Doris Day, who made her debut in *Romance On The High Seas* (1948), and was often teamed with singer Gordon MacRae, while others of note included Tab Hunter, Troy Donahue, Natalie Wood who co-starred in *Rebel Without A Cause* (1955), and Angie Dickinson who lit up the screen opposite John Wayne in *Rio Bravo* (1959). But most promising of them all was James Dean, who died tragically in 1955 after completing only three features. It was somehow appropriate that he should have flourished, albeit briefly, at the studio of Cagney, Garfield and Bogart and where a young Marlon Brando had first created a sensation as the star of *A Streetcar Named Desire* (1951). Most recently Burt Reynolds and, notably, Clint Eastwood, have most successfully carried on the macho tradition of the Warner Bros. men.

STARS

Albert, Eddie 1938–41
Alda, Robert 1945–48
Arden, Eve 1945–50
Arliss, George 1929–33
Astor, Mary 1933–35, 1941–42
Ayres, Lew 1947–48
Bacall, Lauren 1944–50
Baker, Carroll 1955–56
Bancroft, George 1938–39
Barrymore, John 1923–26, 1929–31
Barthelmess, Richard (FN) 1921–30, 1930–34
Bergman, Ingrid 1942–43
Blondell, Joan 1930–37
Blue, Monte 1923–29
Bogart, Humphrey 1932, 1935–48
Bolger, Ray 1949–53
Brent, George 1932–42
Bronson, Betty 1927–29
Brown, Joe E. 1929–36
Burton, Richard 1959–60
Cagney, James 1930–35, 1938–42, 1949–51
Canova, Judy 1935
Carson, Jack 1941–49
Chaney, Lon, Jr. 1952–53
Chapman, Marguerite 1941
Chatterton, Ruth 1932–33
Clark, Dane 1943–48
Coburn, Charles 1941–43
Cochran, Steve 1949–53
Compson, Betty 1929
Cooper, Gary 1940, 1949–51

Cortez, Ricardo 1933–34, 1935
Costello, Dolores 1925–31
Crawford, Joan 1944–51
Dahl, Arlene 1947
Daniels, Bebe 1931–33
Darwell, Jane 1934
Davies, Marion (Cosmopolitan) 1935–37
Davis, Bette 1931–49
Day, Doris 1948–54
Dean, James 1954–55
De Camp, Rosemary 1942–43, 1947–49, 1951–53
de Havilland, Olivia 1935–43
Del Rio, Dolores 1933–35
Dickinson, Angie 1958–60
Donahue, Troy 1959–64
Douglas, Kirk 1949–51
Dvorak, Ann 1932–35
Eastwood, Clint (Malpaso) 1976–87
Eilers, Sally 1928–29
Emerson, Faye 1941–45
Fairbanks, Douglas, Jr. 1929–33
Farrell, Glenda 1932–37
Fitzgerald, Geraldine 1939–43, 1945–46
Flynn, Errol 1935–51
Fonda, Henry 1937–38
Foster, Preston 1932–33
Francis, Kay 1932–39
Frederick, Pauline 1928–29
Garfield, John 1938–46
Granville, Bonita 1937–39

Greenstreet, Sydney 1941–49
Hall, James 1930
Harding, Ann 1943
Henreid, Paul 1942–46
Hopkins, Miriam 1939–40
Horton, Edward Everett 1928–29, 1935
Hunter, Ian 1935–38
Hunter, Tab 1954–58
Huston, Walter 1931, 1941–43
Jolson, Al 1927–30, 1933–35
Jory, Victor 1939
Karloff, Boris 1931, 1937
Karns, Roscoe 1932, 1935, 1940
Keeler, Ruby 1932–36
Kennedy, Arthur 1940–42
Ladd, Alan (Jaguar) 1954–57
Lancaster, Burt 1950–53
Lane, Priscilla 1937–40
Lee, Lila 1928–31
Leslie, Joan 1940–46
Lindsay, Margaret 1933–39
Lorre, Peter 1941–46
Louise, Anita 1934–38
Loy, Myrna 1926–30
Lukas, Paul 1943–44
Lundigan, William 1939–40
Lupino, Ida 1940–47
Lyon, Ben 1930–31
MacMahon, Aline 1931–35
MacRae, Gordon 1948–53
Malone, Dorothy 1945–49, 1954–55
Marvin, Lee 1955
Mayo, Virginia 1948–54
McAvoy, May 1927–28
McCrea, Joel 1948–49
Menjou, Adolphe 1933–34
Milland, Ray 1931–32
Morgan, Dennis 1939–52
Morris, Chester 1929–30
Morris, Wayne 1936–41, 1947–49
Muni, Paul 1932–39
Nagel, Conrad 1928–29
Neal, Patricia 1948–50
O'Brien, Pat 1933–40
Oland, Warner 1926–27
Paige, Janis 1944–50

Parker, Eleanor 1941–51
Payne, John 1938–39
Peck, Gregory 1950–51
Pitts, ZaSu 1929
Poitier, Sidney 1956–57
Powell, Dick 1932–39
Powell, William 1931–34
Prevost, Marie 1923–26
Quinn, Anthony 1940–41
Raft, George 1939–43
Rains, Claude 1935–44
Reagan, Ronald 1937–43, 1946–50, 1952
Rich, Irene 1923–28
Rin-Tin-Tin 1923–30
Robinson, Edward G. 1930–41
Rogers, Ginger 1932
Roman, Ruth 1949–51
Sakall, S.Z. 1943–51
Scott, Randolph 1950–57
Scott, Zachary 1944–50
Sheridan, Ann 1936–47
Sherman, Lowell 1929
Shirley, Anne 1932–33
Smith, Kent 1947, 1949–50
Sondergaard, Gale 1936–37
Sothern, Ann 1929–30
Stanwyck, Barbara 1931–35, 1944–45
Stevens, Craig 1941–48
Tearle, Conway 1929
Tobin, Genevieve 1933–36
Tracy, Lee 1932
Turner, Lana 1937–38
Veidt, Conrad 1941–42
Wayne, John 1932–33, (Wayne) 1952–55
Whitmore, James 1954–55
Wilde, Cornel 1940–41
William, Warren 1931–36
Wood, Natalie 1954–62
Woodward, Joanne 1966–68
Wyman, Jane 1936–50
Young, Gig 1941–43
Young, Loretta (FN) 1928–29, 1929–33

The Directors

Many of Hollywood's most efficient and versatile directors – especially those oriented toward the male-dominated genres of thrillers, gangster pictures and action-adventure movies – found a congenial home at Warner Bros. During 30 years with the studio Michael Curtiz handled a great variety of films, but is best remembered for his Errol Flynn actioners and his three Oscar winners, *Yankee Doodle Dandy*, *Casablanca* and *Mildred Pierce*. Musicals were most often assigned to Lloyd Bacon or the uniquely talented Busby Berkeley, and William Dieterle specialized in biopics starring Paul Muni or Edward G. Robinson. There were a few sympathetic actors' directors, too, notably Alfred E. Green and Edmund Goulding, who were given the Bette Davis vehicles or other women's pictures. Among the many men identified with the studio's tougher pictures were William A. Wellman, Mervyn LeRoy, and scriptwriter-turned-director John Huston, along with the experienced Raoul Walsh, and Howard Hawks who collaborated with top stars James Cagney and Humphrey Bogart, while Walsh also took over from Curtiz as Errol Flynn's favourite director in the 40s.

Though a relatively small company from 1923 to 1927, Warner Bros. was a growing enterprise and succeeded in establishing a strong list of efficient, craftsmen directors during this time. Many of them carried on into the 30s, making the transition from silents to sound and developing along with the studio. This group of skilled professionals appeared to be well suited to handling the kind of tightly scripted, fast-moving, crime movies, dramas, comedies and musicals most favoured by Warners.

William Beaudine, for example, who worked for Warners off and on from 1923 to 1939, was known for his ability with child actors and began by directing Wesley Barry comedies before graduating to other lightweight pictures, while Howard Bretherton (1926–34) specialized in cheap actioners and Rin-Tin-Tin movies. Archie Mayo and Ray Enright were two of the studio's most reliable and hardworking, if relatively anonymous, all-rounders who easily alternated between different genres, averaging a regular three of four movies per year. Alan Crosland made his name on the first Vitagraph features, *Don Juan* (1926) and *The Jazz Singer* (1927), but handled mainly routine thrillers in later years, while Roy Del Ruth graduated from small-scale silents starring Monte Blue and Louise Fazenda to popular musicals and James Cagney vehicles.

In fact, the contract list swelled for a brief period in the late 20s when the studio was releasing more pictures than ever before. A number of directors were inherited from First National but none of them stayed on for more than a year or two. (Most interesting of the group was Frank Lloyd who won an Oscar in 1929 for *The Divine Lady*, a First National picture distributed by Warners.)

Among the studio's many contract directors, four in particular stand out for quality. Most important of all was the legendary, Hungarian-born Michael Curtiz. Famous for his dictatorial behaviour and mangled English, he was an extremely skilled and efficient film-maker who was specially brought over from Germany in 1926 and turned out large numbers of movies of all types. Though the budgets got larger and he reduced his output in later years, he retained the mentality of the true contract director up to the very end. Curtiz reached his peak around 1935–45, a period which included his memorable collaboration with Errol Flynn on *Captain Blood* (1935), *The Adventures Of Robin Hood*, which he co-directed with William Keighley in 1938, and *The Sea Hawk* (1940), as well as the Cagney pictures *Angels With Dirty Faces* (1938) and *Yankee Doodle Dandy* (1942), and the Oscar-winners *Casablanca* (1943) and *Mildred Pierce* (1945).

Lloyd Bacon arrived at the studio the same year as Curtiz and was just as prolific and wide-ranging, but was best known for musicals such as *The Singing Fool* (1928) and *42nd Street* (1933) and an entertaining pair of comedy-thrillers starring Edward G. Robinson – *A Slight Case Of Murder* (1938) and *Brother Orchid* (1940). In contrast, Mervyn LeRoy was remembered for his tougher pictures including *Little Caesar* (1930), *I Am A Fugitive From A Chain Gang* (1932) – the best of the social dramas – and *They Won't Forget* (1937). Unlike Curtiz or Bacon, LeRoy aspired to join that small group of top-ranking directors who functioned as both producer and director, and he accepted a lucrative offer from MGM in 1938 where his films were more expensive, but not necessarily better, than those he had made at Warners. There was also William Keighley, less prolific, but who handled a variety of material. His Cagney vehicles of note included *G-Men* (1935), *Each Dawn I Die* (1939) and *The Fighting 69th* (1940), while he directed Errol Flynn in *The Prince And The Pauper* (1937) and *The Adventures of Robin Hood* (co-directed by Curtiz) and had a last comedy success in 1942 with *The Man Who Came To Dinner*.

There were a few other, more specialized directors at Warners in the 30s. Alfred E. Green was best known for his ability with performers and worked most often with leading ladies Barbara Stanwyck, Kay Francis, and Bette Davis who won the Best Actress Oscar for *Dangerous* (1935). William Wellman was more comfortable with tougher pictures like *The Public Enemy* and *Night Nurse* (both 1931). He fitted in well with the new Warners style in the early 30s and handled a few notable social dramas, too, including *Wild Boys Of The Road* (1933), before leaving to freelance in the 50s when his *The High And The Mighty* (1954) was a big hit. William Dieterle only emerged as a leading director in the late 30s, specializing in historical biopics of Pasteur, Zola, Reuter and others, starring either Paul Muni or Edward G. Robinson. But the studio's best-known name was that of the remarkable Busby Berkeley. Though officially known as a choreographer or director, his gifts lay in creating witty, unexpected and sometimes *risqué* special effects with large numbers of scantily clad show girls arranged in kaleidoscopic patterns, observed from a variety of angles or moving cameras. Berkeley made a tremendous impact with his first group of Warner Bros. musicals – the extremely popular *42nd Street*, followed by *Gold Diggers Of 1933* and *Footlight Parade* – all released in quick succession in 1933. But though the studio kept him busy throughout the rest of the decade, he never matched that initial success.

New arrivals in the late 30s included Edmund Goulding and Anatole Litvak, but most important of all was the veteran Raoul Walsh. A specialist in Westerns, thrillers and action pictures, he worked with all the studio's top male stars and made a big contribution in the 40s with his many gritty black-and-white productions in the true Warners tradition. He boosted Bogart to stardom in *High Sierra* (1940), directed Cagney in one of his last great gangster roles, as Cody Jarrett in *White Heat* (1949) and took over from Curtiz as Errol Flynn's favourite director on such films as *They Died With Their Boots On* (1941) and *Objective Burma* (1945). He soon became one of Jack Warner's favourites because he worked so quickly and kept within his generally tight budgets.

The only other 40s director in the Walsh class was Howard Hawks. One of the most durable and versatile of Hollywood independents, he was brilliant at matching his talents to the demands of the different studios. He had made 30s comedies at RKO and Columbia, for example, but returned periodically to direct action dramas for Warners. His biggest contribution came in the early 40s with the highly successful war pictures *Sergeant York* (1941) and *Air Force* (1943), followed by a pair of thrillers filmed back-to-back in 1944: *To Have And Have Not* and *The Big Sleep* teamed Lauren Bacall, Hawks' one great discovery, with Humphrey Bogart, and created a bit of screen magic.

The general insularity of the studio was reflected in the fact that, as with their stars, Warners preferred to stick with their own people as much as possible. (One of the few important 'outsiders', William Wyler, was almost sacked from the 1938 *Jezebel* for not keeping within the tight budget, and only Bette Davis' pleading and agreement to work long hours of overtime persuaded Jack Warner to change his mind.) Successful directors were encouraged to stay on for many years, while new directors were often promoted from among the other studio personnel. In the 40s Jean Negulesco advanced from shorts to features, while Irving Rapper graduated from assistant director and dialogue coach to full director status. But Don Siegel was so good at his job as the studio's montage and inserts expert that Jack Warner did not want him to switch to direction, though, of course, he finally did. Scriptwriters-turned-director were Vincent Sherman, Delmer Daves and, notably, John Huston. Having scripted *High Sierra* for Walsh and *Sergeant York* for Hawks, Huston naturally followed in the line of Warners' terse, male-oriented productions and developed an extremely good relationship with Bogart on *The Maltese Falcon* (1941), *The Treasure Of The Sierra Madre* and *Key Largo* (both 1948), which continued in the 50s after both had left the studio, most notably with *The African Queen* (UA, 1951).

Other new arrivals of note were David Butler who specialized in glossy musicals, and the inimitable producer-director Alfred Hitchcock who used Technicolor for the first time in *Rope* (1948) and *Under Capricorn* (1949), but was at his best in filming the tense, black-and-white thriller *Strangers On A Train* (1951). A surprisingly large number of ex-Warners directors returned to work for the studio again in the 50s, among them William Keighley, William Wellman, Roy del Ruth, Delmer Daves, Raoul Walsh (who had a big hit with *Battle Cry*, 1955), and Mervyn LeRoy (as co-director of *Mr Roberts*, 1955) while Don Siegel returned after almost 24 years and, in 1971, provided the first entry in an extremely violent and successful cop series with Clint Eastwood as *Dirty Harry*.

DIRECTORS

Adolfi, John G. 1928–33
Bacon, Lloyd 1926–43
Bare, Richard L. 1948–50, 1956–60
Beaudine, William 1923–25, (FN)
 1927–29, 1929–31, 1935–39
Bell, Monta 1924
Berkeley, Busby 1932–38
Bernhardt, Curtis 1940–42, 1945–47
Borzage, Frank 1934–37
Bretherton, Howard 1926–34
Butler, David 1943–44, 1946–56
Capra, Frank (FN) 1926–27, 1940–41
Clemens, William 1936–41
Cline, Edward 1929–30
Crosland, Alan 1925–31, 1933–35
Curtiz, Michael 1926–54
Daves, Delmer 1943–45, 1947–49,
 1958–64
De Cordova, Frederick 1945–48
del Ruth, Roy 1925–34, 1949–54
De Toth, André 1952–54
Dieterle, William 1930–39
Dillon, John Francis 1929–31
Douglas, Gordon 1951–61

Enright, Ray 1927–41
Farrow, John 1937–38
Florey, Robert 1933–35, 1941–42,
 1945–46
Godfrey, Peter 1944–50
Goulding, Edmund 1937–43
Green, Alfred E. 1929–36
Hawks, Howard 1931–32, 1941–45
Hitchcock, Alfred (Transatlantic)
 1948–49, 1950–53
Howard, William K. 1940–41
Humberstone, H. Bruce 1934
Huston, John 1941–48
Kazan, Elia 1954–57
Keighley, William 1932–42, 1950–53
Kubrick, Stanley 1971–87
Lederman, D. Ross 1927–29,
 1934–35, 1941–43
LeRoy, Mervyn (FN) 1927–29,
 1929–38, 1955–59
Litvak, Anatole 1937–41
Lloyd, Frank (FN) 1922–30, 1929–31
Lubitsch, Ernst 1923–26
Marin, Edwin L. 1950–51

Mayo, Archie 1927–37
McDonald, Frank 1935–38
McGann, William 1930–39
Milestone, Lewis 1925
Negulesco, Jean 1941–48
Neill, Roy William 1938–39
Nugent, Elliott 1932
Rapper, Irving 1941–47
St Clair, Malcolm 1924
Scorsese, Martin 1969–73
Seiter, William A. (FN) 1928–29,

1929–31
Sherman, Vincent 1939–50
Siegel, Donald 1945–48
Stahl, John (FN) 1920–26
Tuttle, Frank 1955–59
Vidor, King 1949–50
Walsh, Raoul 1939–51
Wellman, William A. 1930–33,
1953–58
Windust, Bretaigne 1948–51

The Creative Personnel

Warner Bros.' leading cameramen and art directors made a major contribution to developing the studio's characteristic black-and-white style in the 30s. A number of the best cameramen, including Sol Polito and Ernest Haller, were inherited when Warners took over First National, while the art department was headed by the prolific Robert Haas, the distinguished Carl Jules Weyl and the brilliant and imaginative Anton Grot who spent 20 years with the company. The studio excelled in other technical departments, too, and had its share of top special-effects experts, costume designers, led by the talented Orry-Kelly, writers such as Casey Robinson and Howard Koch, and composers, including the illustrious Erich Wolfgang Korngold and Max Steiner. But it was left to the song-writing team of Al Dubin and Harry Warren to capture the spirit of Warner Bros. in the 30s with such songs as 'We're In The Money' and 'My Forgotten Man' in *Gold Diggers Of 1933*, the Oscar-winning 'Lullaby Of Broadway' from *Gold Diggers Of 1935* and many, many others.

Cameramen and Art Directors

When Warner Bros. completed its takeover of First National in 1929, the studio inherited a number of new stars and directors, most of whom did not remain long with the new company. Many leading cameramen, however, stayed on and became fixtures. This is probably a unique example of a studio suddenly acquiring a staff of top cameramen which then served it remarkably well for over 20 years and played a major role in establishing the characteristic house style.

In many cases the careers of these cameramen reflect the development of the studio during these years. For example, best known of that group from First National was Sol Polito, who ranged from the early sound musicals and the best of Busby Berkeley (*42nd Street, Gold Diggers*

Of 1933) to the contemporary dramas and thrillers, especially those directed by LeRoy in the early 30s, including *I Am A Fugitive From A Chain Gang* (1932). In later years he worked mainly with Michael Curtiz, adopting a softer style on the historical adventure movies as in the superbly photographed *The Sea Hawk* (1940), while handling all the early Technicolor productions as well.

A comparable pattern can be seen in the work of his similarly Italian-born – but not First National – colleague, Tony Gaudio. He graduated from the low-keyed subjects of the early years, such as *Tiger Shark* (1932) and *Fog Over Frisco* (1934), to the biopics and costume dramas of later years. He won an Oscar for his contribution to *Anthony Adverse* (1936) and photographed many of the stylish Bette Davis movies in the early 40s, including *The Letter* (1941) for which he was Oscar-nominated.

In contrast, Ernest Haller took a longer time to establish himself after his arrival from First National. For him the big breakthrough came in 1938 when he was assigned to the relatively lavish *Jezebel*. He continued to shoot many Bette Davis movies in the following years, and worked well with other leading ladies of stature: Ingrid Bergman in *Saratoga Trunk* and Joan Crawford in *Mildred Pierce* (both 1945). Though most of Haller's Warner pictures were in black-and-white, he shared the Oscar for *Gone With The Wind* (MGM, 1939), a surprise choice by producer David Selznick for this most glossy of 30s productions. Haller left Warners in 1951 but was invited back to apply his skills to one of the most interesting of the early CinemaScope productions, *Rebel Without A Cause* (1955) and, appropriately enough, for the bizarre, black-and-white production of *Whatever Happened To Baby Jane?* (1962), co-starring the two ex-Warner stars, Bette Davis and Joan Crawford, too.

The third of the First National cameramen was Sidney Hickox, an action specialist who did some of his best work with Howard Hawks and Raoul Walsh in the 40s, and rounded out his Warner Bros. career with the highly successful *Battle Cry* (1955) in colour and CinemaScope. Then, too, there were two others from First National, Ted McCord, who returned to Warner Bros. in the mid-30s, and Arthur Edeson. Known as a master of atmospheric, black-and-white photography, Edeson hit his stride at Warners during 1939–42 when he worked on the war sequences of *Sergeant York* and *The Maltese Falcon* in 1941 and was nominated for his shooting of *Casablanca* the following year. Ted McCord, by contrast, was a late developer who spent many years on B actioners and Westerns and first made his name in the late 40s with *The Treasure Of The Sierra Madre* and *Johnny Belinda*, both released in 1948. McCord's work on *Sierra Madre* so impressed Elia Kazan that the director specially requested him for *East of Eden* in 1954, Kazan's first colour film and his first in CinemaScope, too.

All of these men spent 15–20 years or more at the studio but Hal Mohr's remarkable contribution was concentrated into a brief period in the late 20s and mid-30s. He was the first to cope with sound filming, on *The Jazz Singer* (1927), and worked on the disastrous $2 million epic, *Noah's Ark* (1929), but left before the filming of the dangerous flood sequence which caused a number of extras to be badly injured. He came back six years later to do a remarkable job on *A Midsummer Night's Dream* with its blend of fantasy, comedy and costume spectacle and was rewarded with the first Oscar given to a Warner Bros. cameraman.

Last of the studio's classic cinematographers was Harry Stradling Sr who arrived in the late 50s after all the others had left and took charge of many of the musicals and other notable productions. He earned four Oscar nominations during these years and greatly contributed to the quality of Warner Bros. pictures throughout his time there – and finally left in style after winning a statuette for his much-acclaimed 70mm filming of *My Fair Lady* in 1964.

With its emphasis on contemporary thrillers and drama, action pictures and comedies, mostly filmed quickly and relatively cheaply, the company required special qualities in its art directors, who played a major role in determining the distinctive 'look' of its features. Thus, the studio was fortunate in signing up the Polish-born Anton Grot, along with Robert Haas and John Hughes, its three most prolific and long-serving designers, quite early on. They all remained at Warners for about 20 years and accounted for a significant proportion of the studio's total output. Haas, for example, averaged seven films per year throughout most of the 30s, Hughes slightly fewer, and Grot was just as active and eclectic in the early years, but drastically reduced his work rate after 1935.

Grot had been at First National only briefly when the company was taken over by Warner Bros. and, soon after, late in 1928, he was given the opportunity to design their epic production of *Noah's Ark*. Most impressive of all was the giant temple set and the spectacular flood climax when the temple is destroyed and the people are swept along in the raging torrent. This was the first of 16 films on which Grot collaborated with director Michael Curtiz. His stylized, expressionistic designs for *Svengali* (1931), for example, were so striking that they made the photography appear exceptional and earned first Oscar nominations for himself and cameraman Barney McGill. His and the studio's turning point came in 1935 when he worked on three memorable films, *A Midsummer Night's Dream* and *Captain Blood*, followed by *Anthony Adverse*, and from this point on he concentrated on special productions including *The Life Of Emile Zola* (1937), *The Private Lives of Elizabeth And Essex* (1939) and *The Sea Hawk* (1940). Robert Haas similarly shared the more top-notch assignments in the late 30s. He designed *The Prince And The Pauper* (1937) and *Jezebel* (1938), followed by many other Bette Davis movies, while John Hughes handled many of the top action features ranging from *The Charge Of The Light Brigade* (1936) and the remake of *The Dawn Patrol* (1938) to *Sergeant York* (1941), along with a pair of Technicolored musicals, *This Is The Army* (1943) and *Night And Day* (1946).

Important changes had been taking place during 1935 and 1936. A general improvement in production standards (and budgets) coincided with the arrival of four new designers of note, all of whom stayed on till the late 40s. This meant that a leading art director could be available for virtually every Warner Bros. production. Most important of the new group was Carl Jules Weyl, yet another of those outstanding foreign-born designers who played such an important role in Hollywood. He worked on many Curtiz features in the 40s such as *Yankee Doodle Dandy* and the atmospheric back-lot creation of *Casablanca*, both filmed in 1942, but won his only Oscar for his stylish work on the Technicolored *The Adventures Of Robin Hood* (1938).

Hugh Reticker and Max Parker were assigned to large numbers of Bs and other black-and-white productions. Reticker ranged from *The Walking Dead* (1936) to *Humoresque* (1946), while Parker contributed his touch to such superior gangster pictures as *Each Dawn I Die* and *The Roaring Twenties* (both 1939). Ted Smith specialized in A Westerns in both colour and black-and-white, working with director Raoul Walsh in the 40s. And finally, there was Edward Carrere, who arrived in 1944 and worked on some of the last, classic black-and-white pictures of note – for example *The Fountainhead* and *White Heat* (both 1949) – provided a link with 50s CinemaScope (*Helen Of Troy*, 1955), and more recent productions including *Camelot*, for which he won an Oscar in 1967, and Sam Peckinpah's *The Wild Bunch* (1969).

Other Departments

As has previously been noted, there were two periods in particular when Warner Bros. acquired many of its leading personnel – 1928–29 when the company was expanding and adapting to sound, and 1935–36 with a selective shift into more expensive productions. Nathan Levinson, for example, was appointed head of the studio sound department in 1928, a post he held for over 20 years during which time he was nominated for Oscars 20 times, either on his own or in collaboration with special photographic-effects experts like Byron Haskin, another Warner Bros. veteran. Haskin, too, had started in the mid-20s as cameraman and director, then began to concentrate on special effects. The department had grown under Fred Jackman and by the late 30s, in the words of Haskin, 'was virtually a studio within a studio. We had our own designers, art directors and set-building facilities', along with a 'unit plan of organization' whereby each unit was under a capable special effects director. This system worked extremely well. One of the key personnel was young Don Siegel (long before his later career as a director of fast-moving crime and action pictures) who headed the inserts unit and provided memorable montage sequences for such pictures as *Confessions Of A Nazi Spy* in 1938 and *Casablanca* in 1942.

The arrival of sound called for new techniques and Leo F. Forbstein was appointed head of the music department and director of the Vitaphone orchestra. During the next 20 years he assembled a staff of top composers, song writers and arrangers. Lyricist Al Dubin teamed up with Joe Burke on a number of the early sound musicals beginning with *Gold Diggers Of Broadway* (1929), then was paired with Harry Warren. They soon emerged as one of the top composing teams of the decade, supplying songs for most of the Busby Berkeley musicals from

42nd Street on, and won an Oscar for 'Lullaby Of Broadway' included in *Gold Diggers Of 1935*.

New editors were also needed and the studio acquired three of the best in 1928. Ralph Dawson and George Amy stayed on for almost 20 years, and Owen Marks for over three decades. Between them they shared many of the top assignments and made an important contribution to developing the characteristically fast pace and economical style of the studio's product.

When Warner Bros. took over First National it had to choose between two talented Westmore brothers to head the newly expanded make-up department. In the event they opted for Perc (who had been at First National) and were not disappointed. Among his many accomplishments, he completely made over Bette Davis' face for her appearance as Queen Elizabeth and did a remarkable job transforming Paul Muni into Pasteur, Zola and Juarez.

The studio's most brilliant and prolific costume designer, Orry-Kelly, was hired in 1931 around the time that Warners was acquiring new leading ladies of the calibre of Bette Davis, Barbara Stanwyck and Kay Francis. Kelly excelled himself in dressing Miss Davis during her many years as reigning queen of the Warners lot, providing just the right touch to help define the various characters she created so effectively on the screen. He always strove for accuracy in period costume and the results were seen at their best in such pictures as *The Private Lives Of Elizabeth And Essex* (1939) and *Mr Skeffington* (1944). By contrast, for Kay Francis he aimed at contemporary high fashion at its most tasteful and original. Other designers at the studio, such as Earl Luick (in the early years) and the young Milo Anderson, were overshadowed by the formidable Mr Kelly. Anderson, however, was given good assignments in the late 30s, including such colour productions as *Gold Is Where You Find It* and *The Adventures Of Robin Hood* (both 1938), since Kelly's specialty was black-and-white. Anderson also dressed *Night And Day* and *Life With Father* (1947) after Kelly's departure. Leah Rhodes joined the department in the 40s, and was followed by Marjorie Best who carried on through the 50s.

By the mid-30s Hollywood was becoming more conscious of the importance of movie scores and the studio was quick to sign up an impressive new group of composers and orchestrators led by Erich Wolfgang Korngold, Max Steiner, Ray Heindorf and Adolf Deutsch. Korngold was quite new to the cinema. He was brought to the USA by director Max Reinhardt to score *A Midsummer Night's Dream* in 1935 and stayed on. Tremendously inventive and a master of musical techniques – he had been hailed as a boy genius in Vienna 25 years earlier – Korngold was extremely successful and influential (even influencing the experienced Max Steiner in his scoring of many of the lush Warners costume productions of the late 30s) and picking up Oscars for both *Anthony Adverse* (1936) and *The Adventures Of Robin Hood* (1938).

Among the studio's leading writers were Abem Finkel and Robert Buckner in the 30s; also Lenore Coffee, and the prolific Casey Robinson, who provided scripts for many Bette Davis movies, while Howard

Koch and the Epstein brothers won an Oscar for scripting *Casablanca* (1943).

CAMERAMEN

Barnes, George 1933–38
Bredell, Woody 1947–49
Burks, Robert 1937–44 (sp. effects), 1941–53
Edeson, Arthur (FN) 1924–27, 1934–49
Freund, Karl 1947–50
Garmes, Lee (FN) 1927–29, 1929–30
Gaudio, Tony 1929–43
Glennon, Bert 1941–46
Haller, Ernest (FN) 1926–30, 1930–51
Hickox, Sidney (FN) 1927–30, 1930–54
Howe, James Wong 1938–47
Marley, J. Peverell 1945–50
McCord, Ted (FN) 1924–29, 1936–57
McGill, Barney 1927–33
Mohr, Hal 1926–28, 1935–36
Musuraca, Nicholas 1925–26
Polito, Sol (FN) 1926–30, 1930–47
Rosher, Charles 1937–41
Sharp, Henry 1942–44
Stradling, Harry, Sr. 1955–64

ART DIRECTORS

Basevi, James 1953–54
Carré, Ben 1926–27
Carrere, Edward 1944–57, 1962–70
Grot, Anton (FN) 1928–30, 1931–48
Haas, Robert 1929–50
Hartley, Esdras 1923–24, 1928, 1931–40
Hughes, John J. 1933–49
Kuter, Leo E. 1943–64
Leven, Boris 1954–55
Okey, Jack (FN) 1924–30, 1931–34
Parker, Max 1928–31, 1935–47
Pogany, William A. 1933–34
Reticker, Hugh 1935–50
Smith, Ted 1936–49
Weyl, Carl Jules 1934–47

COSTUME DESIGNERS

Anderson, Milo 1933–52
Best, Marjorie 1948–60
Luick, Earl 1928–33
Mabry, Moss 1953–56
Newman, Bernard 1946–47
Orry-Kelly 1932–45
Rhodes, Leah 1941–50
Shoup, Howard 1935–41, 1952–67
Stevenson, Edward 1929–31
Travilla, William 1946–49

COMPOSERS AND MUSIC DIRECTORS

Buttolph, David 1948–51
Deutsch, Adolph 1937–46
Forbstein, Leo F. 1928–48
Friedhofer, Hugo 1945–47
Green, Johnny 1948–49
Harling, W. Franke 1936–37
Heindorf, Ray 1936–54
Hollander, Frederick 1942–47
Korngold, Erich Wolfgang 1935–47
Lava, William 1948–52
Roemheld, Heinz 1938–45
Silvers, Louis 1927–30
Steiner, Max 1936–65
Waxman, Franz 1943–47

EDITORS

Amy, George (FN) 1925–29, 1930–47
Blangsted, Folmar 1944–64
Crosland, Alan, Jr. 1944–52
Curtiss, Ray (FN) 1929, 1930–33
Dawson, Ralph 1927–45, 1953–54
Fehr, Rudi 1937–55
Gibbons, James 1930–43
Gross, Roland 1957–58
Holmes, William 1930–41
Killifer, Jack 1928–43
Kolster, Clarence 1922–27, 1933–58
Low, Warren 1932–44

Marks, Owen 1928–60
Morley, James 1932–33
Morra, Irene 1943–54
Morse, Terrell 1928–31, 1934–43
Nyby, Christian 1943–48
O'Steen, Sam 1955–67
Pratt, Thomas 1928–43
Richards, Frederick 1937–49
Richards, Thomas 1933–42
Stone, LeRoy (FN) 1928–29, 1930–31
Weisbart, David 1943–51
Ziegler, William 1951–67

SCRIPTWRITERS

Baldwin, Earl 1930–40
Buckner, Robert 1937–45
Busch, Niven 1931–34, 1938–39
Coffee, Lenore 1940–44
Coldeway, Anthony 1927–29, 1936–42
Daves, Delmer 1934–37
Diamond, I.A.L. 1946–49
Doyle, Laird 1934–37
Duff, Warren 1933–40
Epstein, Julius and Philip 1934–44
Finkel, Abem 1933–38
Gates, Harvey 1926–30
Gibney, Sheridan 1932–36
Hayward, Lillie 1929–37
Herbert, F. Hugh 1933–36
Holmes, Brown 1931–36
Hubbard, Lucien 1929–32

Huston, John 1937–41
Josephson, Julien 1928–31
Koch, Howard 1939–45
Kraly, Hans 1924–26
Krims, Milton 1936–40
Lord, Robert 1927–35
MacDougall, Ranald 1944–50
Macauley, Richard 1935–42
Maltz, Albert 1943–46
Miller, Seton I. 1934–40
Raine, Norman Reilly 1936–41
Robinson, Casey 1935–45
Rossen, Robert 1937–42
Thew, Harvey 1928–32
Turney, Catherine 1945–47
Wilbur, Crane 1936–40, 1950–53
Zanuck, Darryl F. 1924–28

The Academy Awards

Warner Bros. won a smaller number of Oscars than any other leading Hollywood studio, but had more success with the New York Film Critics Awards. The studio's characteristically lively and fast-moving black-and-white pictures in the early 30s generally failed to impress the Academy and its members, and the Warners stars and technicians tended to be neglected too. The turning point came in 1935 when Bette Davis won her first Oscar for *Dangerous*, followed by Paul Muni who was voted Best Actor for *The Story Of Louis Pasteur* the following year. Muni also contributed to the success of *The Life Of Emile Zola*, the Academy's Best Picture for 1937 (and the winner of the New York Critics' top award). In addition the studio gained many technical awards and nominations during the 1935–38 period. In 1943 the studio won the top Oscar for the second time with *Casablanca*, whose director Michael Curtiz, was honoured in his category. It was 21 years before Warner Bros. won its third Oscar for Best Picture with *My Fair Lady* (1964). This was the most honoured Warners picture of all with eight Oscars, including awards to actor Rex Harrison and director George Cukor. Over the years the studio has won a fair number of top awards from the New York Critics, including Best Picture Awards for *The Treasure Of The Sierra Madre* (1948), *A Streetcar Named Desire* (1951), *A Clockwork Orange* (1971) and *All The President's Men* (1976).

In general, Warner Bros. had little success with the Oscars, winning the Best Picture award just three times in 60 years. During the early years the studio appears to have suffered from a certain snobbism on the part of the Academy and its members who were not impressed by the kind of gritty, fast-moving thrillers, comedies and action movies which were the Warners specialty. The company's actors and technicians only began to gain the kind of recognition they deserved in the late 30s when the studio began to turn out more 'quality productions' but, even so, top stars like Edward G. Robinson, Olivia de Havilland and Errol Flynn were never nominated for any of their Warner Bros. pictures. The tremendously talented James Cagney had to wait till 1938 and *Angels With Dirty Faces* for his first nomination, while Humphrey Bogart was only nominated for *Casablanca* (1943). Both he and Olivia de Havilland won their Oscars shortly after leaving Warners. Veteran stage actor George Arliss won a statuette for his performance as *Disraeli* (1929), the studio's only major award before 1935.

Early on, the studio was most successful in the various writing categories. In 1930/31 alone, nominations included *Little Caesar* and *The Public Enemy*, with the remarkable early sound film from Howard Hawks, *The Dawn Patrol*, co-scripted by Hawks (uncredited) and John Monk Saunders, as the only winner. That same year *Svengali* earned nominations for the imaginative designs of Anton Grot and photography of Barney McGill, the only Warner Bros. picture to gain any sort of recognition for its visual qualities prior to 1935. *I Am A Fugitive From A Chain Gang* (1932), the most accomplished and memorable Warners production of the early 30s was at least nominated for Best Picture and actor (Paul Muni), but failed to win.

Beginning in 1935 Warner Bros. began to fare better. Bette Davis won a pair of statuettes for her performances in the otherwise unremarkable *Dangerous* (1935), and for the impressive *Jezebel* (1938), more typical of the studio's quality pictures in the late 30s. Similarly, Paul Muni was honoured for his first major costume role in *The Story Of Louis Pasteur* (1936), then contributed another outstanding historical performance the following year in *The Life Of Emile Zola* which helped the studio to win its first ever Oscar for Best Picture.

In addition, there were numerous nominations and awards in the minor and technical categories, giving long-overdue recognition to editor Ralph Dawson, cameramen Hal Mohr and Tony Gaudio and art director Carl Jules Weyl, each of whom won at least once. But the studio's leading designer, Anton Grot, never won an Oscar and neither did top black-and-white cameramen Sol Polito or James Wong Howe during their Warners years, though all were nominated at least twice. Composer Max Steiner, also nominated on numerous occasions, won only once at Warner Bros. for his appropriately romantic scoring of *Now Voyager* (1942), though he was also presented with the top music award at the 1948 Venice Film Festival for his outstanding dramatic score for *The Treasure Of The Sierra Madre*.

Surprisingly, Warner Bros. won the Best Actor award for three years in a row in the early 40s. Gary Cooper was the first for his performance as *Sergeant York*, with director Howard Hawks nominated for the only time in his long and distinguished career, followed by James Cagney whose long-overdue Oscar rewarded his portrayal of the renowned song-and-dance man George M. Cohan in *Yankee Doodle Dandy*, with a nomination for director Michael Curtiz, and Paul Lukas for his role in *Watch On The Rhine* (1943) which he had created on the Broadway stage two years earlier. Clearly 1943 was a good year for the studio with *Casablanca* winning the Best Picture, director (Michael Curtiz's only win after three previous nominations) and screenplay Oscars and a sweep of the three top New York Film Critics awards – for Paul Lukas again, with *Watch On The Rhine* as best picture, and actress Ida Lupino for *The Hard Way*.

The studio's last big Oscar success, and the most honoured picture in its history, was Jack Warner's lavish production of *My Fair Lady* which chalked up eight Oscars in 1964. Though mainly in the technical categories, they also included director George Cukor (who had been nominated for his sensitive handling of another Warners musical, *A Star Is Born* back in 1954), actor Rex Harrison, here re-creating his celebrated stage role as Professor Higgins, and Best Picture, along with the New York Critics and Golden Globe Awards.

Aside from *My Fair Lady*, during the years from 1945 up to the present Warners' relatively slender total of major Oscars was concentrated on the ladies, beginning with Joan Crawford, honoured for her typically dramatic, career-woman performance as *Mildred Pierce* (1945). In contrast, Jane Wyman won her Oscar for her sensitive playing of the deaf-and-dumb heroine of *Johnny Belinda* (1948), while Vivien Leigh won her second Oscar for her performance as Blanche in *A Streetcar Named Desire* (1951). Warner's only major Oscar in the 50s went to George Stevens for directing *Giant* in (1956).

In 1966 Elizabeth Taylor demonstrated to her detractors that she could really act, winning a well-deserved Oscar for her performance in one of the last major black-and-white movies of the 60s, *Who's Afraid Of Virginia Woolf*. Main Oscars in the 70s went to Jane Fonda for her astonishing performance as the prostitute Bree Daniels in the thriller *Klute* (1971), and to Ellen Burstyn for *Alice Doesn't Live Here Any More* (1974). In addition, the studio had a share in the Best Actor Oscar awarded to Richard Dreyfuss for *The Goodbye Girl* (1977), a WB/MGM co-production, and *Chariots Of Fire* (1981), the British-produced winner of the top Oscar distributed by Warner Bros. in the USA.

More recently the Best Picture award went to the Zanuck Co./Warner production *Driving Miss Daisy*, a surprise winner in 1989, with Jessica Tandy as best actress and the screenplay Oscar to author Alfred Uhry, while *Batman's* impressive sets, designed by Anton Furst, took the Oscar for art direction. In 1990 British actor Jeremy Irons was honoured for his performance in *Reversal Of Fortune* and Martin Scorsese's *GoodFellas*, a modern crime movie in the Warner Bros. tradition, was nominated for six awards, including Best Picture, but only Joe Pesci won for his supporting role.

PART 3

The Facts And The Figures

Much of the data which has been newly assembled for this book and which serves as the basis for discussion – and for many of the charts and tables – in Part 1 and throughout the individual studio chapters can be found here in Part 3. Most of the material falls into three general categories: career listings of leading stars, directors and technical personnel; feature-film release data; and financial and box-office figures – all relating to the eight major studios. For example, an outline of the studio career of the various categories of personnel appears on the master lists for each professional category, while each person is also included in the breakdown of employees of each studio. There are tables of total feature and colour releases by company and year, of early features in two-strip Technicolor, of films that reflect the transition from silents to talkies in 1928–29, and further tables showing the extent of 3-D, widescreen and 70mm filming in the 50s and 60s. Income and profits for the eight major studios (and a few of the closely related early companies) are presented for every year from the 20s through the 80s along with the box-office hits for each decade. In addition, there are tables of general film-industry and TV information, a selective bibliography and a comprehensive index.

Leading Hollywood Studio Personnel: By Profession

These listings of leading movie personnel present a guide to the studio careers of all the leading Hollywood stars, directors and technical personnel according to their feature-film credits, based on where and when they actually made their pictures (rather than contractual details) with special emphasis on their work for the eight leading companies during the peak studio era from the mid-20s to the mid-50s.

The main studios (and some minor ones) are indicated by standard abbreviations (see Key below) and the others are spelled out in full.

KEY to studio abbreviations:
AA = Allied Artists **AIP** = American International Pictures
Col = Columbia **FBO** = Film Booking Offices of America
FN = First National **Fox** = Fox/20th Century-Fox
MGM = Metro-Goldwyn-Mayer **Par** = Paramount **PDC** = Producers Distributing Corporation **PRC** = Producers Releasing Corporation
RKO = Radio-Keith-Orpheum/RKO Radio/RKO Pathé **20th** = 20th Century (before amalgamation with Fox) **UA** = United Artists
Univ = Universal **WB** = Warner Bros.

STARS

Abbott, Bud & Costello, Lou Univ 1940–55

Acord, Art Sameth/Madoc 1924, Truart 1925, Univ 1925–27, J. Charles Davis Prods 1928–29

Adams, Julia Lippert 1949–50, Univ 1951–57

Adorée, Renée Fox 1922, Mayer/Metro 1923, MGM 1924–30

Albert, Eddie WB 1938–41, Univ 1942, RKO 1943, Fox 1951, 1961–62, Par 1952–55

Alda, Robert WB 1945–48

Allbritton, Louise Univ 1942–46

Allyson, June MGM 1943–53, Univ 1957–58

Ameche, Don Fox 1936–44

Ames, Leon Fox 1936–39, Univ 1938–39, MGM 1945–50, Disney 1961–64

Andrews Sisters, The Univ 1940–44

Andrews, Dana Goldwyn/RKO 1940–43, 1949–51, Fox 1940–48, RKO 1956, Par 1964–65

Angeli, Pier MGM 1951–53, 1957

Ankers, Evelyn Korda/UA 1936, Fox 1937, Univ 1941–44

Arbuckle, Fatty Keystone 1913–16, Par 1917–21

Arden, Eve Univ 1938–39, MGM 1939–40, WB 1945–50

Arlen, Richard Par 1925–34, Col 1936–37, Univ 1939–41

Arliss, George UA 1921–22, WB 1929–33, 20th/UA 1933–34

Arnold, Edward MGM 1933–34, 1941–50, Par 1933–34, 1937, Univ 1935

Arthur, Jean Par 1928–31, Univ 1931, Col 1933–36, 1938–40, 1942–44

Astaire, Fred RKO 1933–38, MGM 1944–45, 1948–53

Astor, Mary Par 1923–24, FN 1924–28, Fox 1928–29, RKO 1930–32, WB 1933–35, 1941–42, Col 1936, MGM 1943–44, 1947–49

Atwill, Lionel MGM 1934–35, Fox 1938–40, Univ 1940–42, 1944–46

Auer, Mischa Univ 1936–41

Autry, Gene Republic 1935–42, 1946–47, Col 1947–53

Ayres, Lew Univ 1929–34, Fox 1934–35, Par 1936–37, MGM 1938–42, WB 1947–48, UA 1951–53

Bacall, Lauren WB 1944–50, Fox 1953–54

Baker, Carroll WB 1955–56

Ball, Lucille UA 1933–34, Col 1934, 1949–51, RKO 1935–42, MGM 1943–46,

Bancroft, Anne Fox 1952–54

Bancroft, George Par 1925–36, WB 1938–39

Bankhead, Tallulah Par 1931–32, Fox 1943–44

Banky, Vilma Goldwyn/UA 1925–29

Bara, Theda Fox 1915–19

Bari, Lynn Fox 1934–46, Univ 1952–54

Barrie, Wendy Par 1935, Univ 1936–38, RKO 1938–42

Barrymore, Diana Univ 1942–43

Barrymore, Ethel Fox & MGM (alternating) 1949–53

Barrymore, John Famous Players 1914–16, Par 1916–20, 1937–38, WB 1923–26, 1929–31, UA 1927–28, MGM 1932–33, 1936

Barrymore, Lionel Metro 1915–17, FN 1920–21, Par 1922, Chadwick 1924, MGM 1926–52

Barthelmess, Richard FN 1921–30, WB 1930–34

Bartholomew, Freddie MGM 1935–38, Univ 1938–39, RKO 1940, Col 1941

Baxter, Anne Fox 1940–52

Baxter, Warner Par 1921, 1924–27, Vitagraph 1922, FBO 1922–23, FN 1924, Fox 1928–39, Col 1943–49

Beery, Noah, Jr. Univ 1932–38, 1943–45

Beery, Wallace Par 1925–29, MGM 1930–48

Bel Geddes, Barbara RKO 1947–48, Fox 1950, Par 1959

Bellamy, Ralph Fox 1932, RKO 1933–34, Col 1934–39, Univ 1941–42

Bendix, William Par 1942–43, 1946–47, 1949, Fox 1943–46, RKO 1951–53

Bennett, Constance Pathé 1929–31, RKO 1932–33, 20th/UA 1934, Roach/MGM 1937–38

Bennett, Enid Par 1918–20, Metro 1923, MGM 1924

Bennett, Joan Fox 1930–33, 1941, 1942–45, Par 1934–36, Wanger/UA 1937–40

Benny, Jack MGM 1929, 1935, Par 1935–40

Bergman, Ingrid WB 1942–43, Selznick/UA 1944, RKO 1945–46

Bey, Turhan Univ 1941–45, Eagle-Lion 1947–49

Bickford, Charles MGM 1930, Col 1931–32, Par 1933, 1936–1937, Univ 1940–41, Fox 1943–45

Blaine, Vivian Fox 1942–46

Blair, Janet Col 1941–46, 1948

Blondell, Joan WB 1930–37, MGM

1956–57

Blue, Monte Par/Artcraft 1917–18, Par 1918–20, WB 1923–29

Blyth, Ann Univ 1944–52, MGM 1953–57

Blythe, Betty Vitagraph 1917–18, B.B. Prods 1922–23, Univ 1932–33, Fox 1933

Boardman, Eleanor Goldwyn 1922–24, MGM 1924–28, 1930–31

Bogart, Humphrey Fox 1930–31, WB 1932, 1935–48, Santana/Col 1948–51, Par 1955

Boland, Mary Par 1931–36, 1938–39, MGM 1939–40

Boles, John Univ 1930–31, Fox 1931–35

Bolger, Ray MGM 1935–39, RKO 1941, WB 1949–53

Booth, Shirley Wallis/Par 1952–53, 1958

Borgnine, Ernest Col 1951–53, UA 1954, MGM 1967–68

Bow, Clara Schulberg/Preferred 1925, Par 1925–31, Fox 1932–33

Boyd, William Par 1920–22, 1930–31, 1935–41, DeMille/PDC 1925–26, Pathé 1927–29

Bracken, Eddie Par 1940–46

Brady, Scott Eagle-Lion 1948, Univ 1949–52, Republic 1953, 1955–56, Fox 1956–58, Lyles/Par 1967

Brando, Marlon Col 1953–54

Bremer, Lucille MGM 1944–46

Brendel, El Par 1926–27, Fox 1929–33, 1936–38, Univ 1938–39

Brennan, Walter Pathé 1927, Univ 1929–30, Goldwyn/UA 1935–40, Republic 1950, Fox 1956–57

Brent, Evelyn Fox 1924, FBO 1924–26, Par 1926–30, 1936–37, Monogram 1942–48

Brent, George Fox 1930–31, WB 1932–42, RKO 1944–45, Univ 1946–47

Brian, Mary Par 1925–30, 1935–36

Britton, Barbara Par 1941–45, Col 1946–49

Bronson, Betty Par 1922–27, WB 1927–29

Brook, Clive FN 1924–25, Par 1926–32

Brooks, Louise Par 1925–28

Brown, Joe E. FBO 1928, Tiffany-Stahl 1929, WB 1929–36, RKO 1937, Col 1938–41, Republic 1942–43

Brown, Johnny Mack MGM 1927–31, Supreme 1935–36, Republic 1937, Univ 1937–43, Monogram 1943–52

Bruce, Virginia Par 1929–30, MGM 1931–32, 1935–36, 1938–39, Univ 1940–42

Brynner, Yul Fox 1956, MGM 1957–58, Col 1960, UA 1962–64, 1966

Burke, Billie Par 1917–21, RKO 1932–34, MGM 1934–35, 1937–40, UA 1938–39, Univ 1943–44

Burns, George & Allen, Gracie Par 1932–38

Burton, Richard Fox 1952–55, 1962, WB 1959–60

Bushman, Francis X. Metro 1915–19, MGM 1925, Sono-Art 1930

Cabot, Bruce RKO 1932–34, MGM 1936

Cagney, James WB 1930–35, 1938–42, 1949–51, Grand National 1936–37, Cagney/UA 1943–48

Calhern, Louis MGM 1949–56

Cameron, Rod Par 1940–43, Univ 1944–47, Republic 1951–52, 1954–55

Canova, Judy WB 1935, Par 1937, Republic 1940–43, 1951–55, Col 1944–46

Cantor, Eddie Goldwyn/UA 1930–35

Carey, Harry, Sr. Griffith/Biograph 1912–13, Univ 1916–21, FBO

1922–23, PDC 1924–25, Pathé 1926, 1928, MGM 1926–27

Carey, MacDonald Par 1942–50, Univ 1949–50, Fox 1951–52

Caron, Leslie MGM 1951–58

Carradine, John Par 1932–33, Fox 1937–43

Carroll, Madeleine Par 1935–36, 1938–41, Fox 1936

Carroll, Nancy Par 1928–33, Col 1934–35

Carson, Jack RKO 1937–38, Univ 1939–40, Par 1940, WB 1941–49

Caulfield, Joan Par 1945–49

Chadwick, Helene Pathé 1917, Goldwyn 1920–23, Col 1927–28

Chandler, Jeff Univ 1949–58

Chaney, Lon, Sr. Univ 1915–18, 1921, 1923, 1925, Par 1919, MGM 1924–30

Chaney, Lon, Jr. Univ 1940–45, WB 1952–53

Chaplin, Charlie Keystone 1914, Essanay 1915, Mutual 1916–17, Chaplin/FN 1918–22, Chaplin/UA 1924–52

Chapman, Marguerite WB 1941, Col 1942–48

Charisse, Cyd MGM 1946–58

Chatterton, Ruth Par 1928–31, WB 1932–33

Chevalier, Maurice Par 1929–33, MGM 1956–58

Clark, Dane WB 1943–48, Lippert 1951–54

Clark, Marguerite Famous Players 1914–16, Par 1916–1920

Clift, Montgomery Par 1949–51, UA 1960–61

Cobb, Lee J. Fox 1942–50, 1954–55, MGM 1957–58

Coburn, Charles MGM 1938–40, WB 1941–43, Univ 1949–50, Fox 1952–53

Cochran, Steve Col 1945, Goldwyn/RKO 1945–48, WB 1949–53

Colbert, Claudette Par 1928–35, 1937–39, 1941–43, RKO 1945

Collins, Joan Fox 1955, 1957–60

Colman, Ronald Goldwyn/FN 1924–25, Goldwyn/UA 1926–33, 20th/UA 1934–35, Par 1938–39, RKO 1940–41, MGM 1942–44

Compson, Betty Christie 1915–17, Par 1921–25, WB 1929, RKO 1931

Conte, Richard Fox 1943–49, Univ 1950–52, AA 1954–55, Col 1956–60

Conway, Tom MGM 1940–42, RKO 1942–46, Fox 1947–48

Coogan, Jackie Chaplin/FN 1919–20, FN 1921–23, Metro 1923, MGM 1924–27, Par 1930–31

Cooper, Gary Par 1927–40, 1942–44, Goldwyn/UA 1937–40, WB 1940, 1949–51, Goldwyn/RKO 1941–42, International 1944

Cooper, Jackie MGM 1932–36, Univ 1938–39

Cortez, Ricardo Par 1923–27, Tiffany 1928–29, RKO 1931–32, WB 1933–34, 1935, Fox 1939–41

Costello, Dolores WB 1925–31

Cotten, Joseph RKO 1940–42, Univ 1942–43, Selznick 1944–45, Fox 1952–53

Crabbe, Buster Par 1933–39, Univ 1938–40, PRC 1941–46, Col 1947, 1950–52

Crain, Jeanne Fox 1943–53

Crawford, Broderick Par 1938–39, Univ 1940–42, 1946–47, Col 1949–52

Crawford, Joan MGM 1925–42, WB 1944–51, Col 1955–57

Cregar, Laird Fox 1940–44

Cronyn, Hume MGM 1943–47

Crosby, Bing Par 1931–55, MGM 1956–57

Cummings, Constance Col 1931–32

Cummings, Robert Univ 1938–40

Curtis, Tony Univ 1949–56

Dahl, Arlene WB 1947, MGM 1948–51, Par 1952–53

Dailey, Dan MGM 1940–42, Fox
1947–54

Dana, Viola Metro 1916–24, Par
1924, FN 1924–25, FBO 1926–27

Daniels, Bebe Roach/Pathé 1915–18,
Par 1919–28, RKO 1929–30, WB
1931–33

Darnell, Linda Fox 1939–51, RKO
1952–54

Darwell, Jane Par 1930–32, WB
1934, Fox 1934–41, RKO
1942–43

Davies, Marion Select 1918–19, Par
1919–22, Cosmopolitan/MGM
1924–34, Cosmopolitan/WB
1935–37

Davis, Bette Univ 1930–31, WB
1931–49

Davis, Joan Fox 1936–41, Col
1943–44, RKO 1945–49

Day, Doris WB 1948–54, Univ
1959–64

Day, Laraine RKO 1938, 1943–49,
MGM 1939–42

Dean, James WB 1954–55

De Camp, Rosemary WB 1942–43,
1947–49, 1951–53

De Carlo, Yvonne Par 1942–44,
Univ 1945–50

Dee, Frances Par 1930–33,
1937–38, RKO 1933–34

Dee, Sandra MGM 1957–58, Univ
1958–65

De Haven, Gloria MGM 1940–50

de Havilland, Olivia WB 1935–43,
Par 1946

Del Rio, Dolores FN 1925–26,
Fox 1926–28, 1937, Carewe/UA
1928–29, RKO 1931–33, WB
1933–35

Dempster, Carol Griffith/Par
1918–19, 1925–26, Griffith/UA
1920–24

Denny, Reginald Univ 1922–29,
MGM 1930–31, RKO 1933–34,
Col 1936–37, Par 1937–39

Derek, John Col 1948–53,
Republic 1953–54, Fox 1954, Par
1956–59

Devine, Andy Univ 1932–47,
Republic 1947–48

Dickinson, Angie WB 1958–60,
Univ 1963–64, UA 1968–69

Dietrich, Marlene Par 1929–35,
1947, Univ 1939–40, 1941–43

Dix, Richard Goldwyn 1921–22,
Par 1923–29, 1940–41, RKO
1929–35, 1938, 1940, Col
1936–37, 1944–46, UA 1942

Donahue, Troy Univ 1956–58, WB
1959–64

Donlevy, Brian Fox 1936–38,
Par 1941–42, 1945–46, MGM
1947–48, Republic 1951–52,
Lyles/Par 1966–68

Douglas, Kirk RKO 1947, WB
1949–51, Par 1951, Bryna/Univ
1959–61

Douglas, Melvyn Univ 1932–33,
RKO 1934–35, Col 1936–1941,
MGM 1938–42

Douglas, Paul Fox 1948–51

Dove, Billie Par & Fox (alternating)
1924–25, FN 1926–31

Dressler, Marie MGM 1927–33

Drew, Ellen Par 1936–42, Col
1946–48

Dunn, James Fox 1931–35

Dunne, Irene RKO 1930–34,
1937–38, Univ 1935, 1941, Col
1936–37, 1944, MGM 1943

Durante, Jimmy MGM 1931–34,
1944–47

Durbin, Deanna Univ 1936–48

Duryea, Dan Goldwyn/RKO
1941–42, Univ 1945–50,
1953–57, RKO 1954

Dvorak, Ann MGM 1929–31, WB
1932–35

Eastwood, Clint Univ 1954–55,
Malpaso/Univ 1970–73,
Malpaso/WB 1976–87

Eddy, Nelson MGM 1933–41

Eilers, Sally WB 1928–29, MGM
1930–31, Fox 1931–33

Emerson, Faye WB 1941–45

Errol, Leon Par 1930–34,
RKO 1937–42, 1945, Univ

1940–41, 1942–44, Monogram
1945–50

Evans, Dale Republic 1943–51

Ewell, Tom Univ 1950–52, Fox
1955–56, 1961

Fairbanks, Douglas, Sr. Triangle
1915–16, Par 1917–19,
Fairbanks/UA 1919–32

Fairbanks, Douglas, Jr. Par 1923–25,
1939–40, FN 1929, WB 1929–33,
RKO 1937–38, Selznick/UA
1937–38

Farmer, Frances Par 1935–38, 1941

Farnum, William Fox 1915–23

Farrell, Charles Fox 1926–32

Farrell, Glenda WB 1932–37, Univ
1938, Col 1942–44

Faye, Alice Fox 1933–45

Ferguson, Elsie Par 1917–22

Ferrer, Mel MGM 1952–53

Fetchit, Stepin Tiffany-Stahl 1928,
Fox 1929, 1934–37

Fields, W.C. Par 1925–28, 1931–37,
Univ 1939–43

Fitzgerald, Barry RKO 1938–39,
Univ 1943, Par 1944–51

Fitzgerald, Geraldine WB 1939–43,
1945–46

Fleming, Rhonda Par 1948–51,
1957, RKO 1955–56

Flynn, Errol WB 1935–51

Foch, Nina Col 1943–49, MGM
1951–53, Par 1955

Fonda, Henry Fox 1935, 1938–43,
1958–59, Par 1935–36, WB
1937–38

Fontaine, Joan RKO 1936–38, Univ
1947–48, Par 1950–51, Fox
1958–61

Forbes, Ralph MGM 1927–28,
1933–34, 1936

Ford, Glenn Col 1939–43, 1945–50,
1953–54, MGM 1954–62

Ford, Harrison Par 1918–19,
1922, 1925, FN 1920–22,
Cosmopolitan/MGM 1924–25,
Metropolitan/PDC 1926–27,
DeMille/Pathé 1927

Foster, Preston Par 1929–31,

1939–40, WB 1932–33, RKO
1934–38, Univ 1938, Fox
1942–44, MGM 1945

Foster, Susanna Par 1939–42, Univ
1943–45

Francis The Talking Mule Univ
1949–56.

Francis, Anne Fox 1951–52, MGM
1954–57

Francis, Kay Par 1929–31, WB
1932–39, RKO 1939–40, Univ
1939–40, Monogram 1945–46

Frederick, Pauline Famous Players
1915–16, Par 1916–19, Goldwyn
1919–20, Robertson-Cole
1920–22, WB 1928–29

Freeman, Mona Par 1943–44,
1947–52

Gable, Clark MGM 1930–42,
1945–54, Par 1958–59

Garbo, Greta MGM 1926–41

Gardner, Ava MGM 1942–56

Garfield, John WB 1938–46

Garland, Judy MGM 1937–50

Garner, Peggy Ann Fox 1942–47

Garrett, Betty MGM 1948–49

Garson, Greer MGM 1939–54

Gavin, John Univ 1956–61

Gaynor, Janet Fox 1926–35

Gaynor, Mitzi Fox 1950–54, Par
1955–57

Gibson, Hoot Univ 1915–30, Allied
1931–33, Diversion 1935–36,
Monogram 1943–44

Gifford, Frances Par 1941–42,
MGM 1943–48

Gilbert, John Ince/Triangle 1915–17,
Paralta/Hodkinson 1918, Par
1920, Fox 1921–24, MGM
1924–33

Gilmore, Virginia Fox 1940–42

Gish, Dorothy Griffith/Biograph
1913–14, Griffith/Mutual 1914–15,
Griffith/Fine Arts 1915–17, Par
1918–21, Inspiration/FN 1922–23

Gish, Lillian Griffith/Biograph
1912–13, Griffith/Mutual
1914, Griffith Fine Arts
1915–17, Griffith Prods

1917–18, Griffith/Par-Artcraft 1918–19, Griffith/UA 1920–21, Inspiration/Metro 1923–24, MGM 1925–28

Goddard, Paulette Chaplin/UA 1935, 1940, Par 1939–48

Goudal, Jetta Par 1924–25, Cinema Corp-DeMille/PDC 1925–26

Grable, Betty Goldwyn/UA 1930–32, RKO 1933–36, Par 1937–39, Fox 1940–53

Grahame, Gloria MGM 1944–47, RKO 1948–49, Col 1953–54

Granger, Farley Goldwyn/RKO 1947–52, MGM 1952

Granger, Stewart MGM 1950–57

Grant, Cary Par 1931–36, Col & RKO (alternating) 1936–44, RKO 1946–48, Univ 1959–64

Granville, Bonita WB 1937–39, MGM 1940–41

Graves, Ralph Par 1919, Univ 1922, Fox 1926, Col 1927–32

Gray, Coleen Fox 1947–48, UA 1952–53, AA 1953–54

Grayson, Kathryn MGM 1941–53

Greene, Richard Fox 1937–40

Greenstreet, Sydney WB 1941–49

Greenwood, Charlotte Fox 1940–46

Greer, Jane RKO 1944–50, MGM 1952

Grey, Virginia MGM 1936–42, Republic 1942–45, Univ 1945–46, 1958–61, 1966–70

Griffith, Corinne Vitagraph 1916–22, Corinne Griffith/FN 1923–26, FN 1928–30

Hagen, Jean MGM 1949–53

Haines, William Goldwyn 1922–23, MGM 1924–31, Col 1925

Hale, Barbara RKO 1943–48, Col 1949–52

Hall, James Par 1926–30, Fox 1927, WB 1930

Hall, Jon Univ 1942–47

Hammerstein, Elaine Rapf 1917–18, Selznick 1919–23, Hoffman/Truart 1923, Col 1924–25

Harding, Ann Pathé 1929–30, 1931–35, WB 1943, MGM 1950–51

Hardwicke, Cedric RKO 1939–41, Fox 1943–45

Harlow, Jean Par 1928–29, UA 1929–30, MGM 1932–37

Harrison, Rex Fox 1946–48

Hart, William S. NY Motion Picture Co-Ince/Mutual 1914–15, Ince/Triangle 1915–17, Hart/Par 1917–24, Hart/UA 1925

Harvey, Laurence MGM & Wallis/Par (alternating) 1960–64

Hasso, Signe MGM 1942–45, Fox 1945

Haver, June Fox 1943–52

Havoc, June RKO 1941–42, Fox 1947–50, Par 1949

Hayden, Sterling Par 1940–41, 1946–51, Republic 1954–55, UA 1956–58

Hayes, Helen MGM 1933–35

Haymes, Dick Fox 1943–47, Univ 1948, Col 1952–53

Hayward, Susan Par 1939–42, Univ 1946–48, Fox 1949–55

Hayworth, Rita Fox 1935–36, Col 1937–48, 1951–53, 1956–59

Heflin, Van RKO 1936–37, MGM 1941–49, Univ 1951–54, Fox 1954, Col 1957–59, Par 1959–60

Hendrix, Wanda Par 1946–49, Univ 1950

Henie, Sonja Fox 1936–43

Henreid, Paul WB 1942–46

Hepburn, Audrey Par 1952–56

Hepburn, Katharine RKO 1932–37, MGM 1940–49

Hersholt, Jean Triangle 1916, Univ 1917–18, 1925–28, MGM 1931–35, Fox 1936–38, RKO 1939–41

Heston, Charlton Par 1950–56, MGM 1958–59

Hodiak, John MGM 1943–44, 1946–51, Fox 1944–45, Col 1953

Holden, William Col & Par (alternating) 1939–42, 1947–57

Holliday, Judy Col 1950–56

Holm, Celeste Fox 1946–50, MGM 1955–56

Holmes, Phillips Par 1928–32, MGM 1932–33

Holt, Jack Par 1917–26, 1928, Col 1927–41, Univ 1935–36, Republic 1948

Holt, Tim RKO 1938–52

Hope, Bob Par 1937–57

Hopkins, Miriam Par 1930–34, 1949–50, Goldwyn/UA 1935–36, WB 1939–40

Horne, Lena MGM 1942–49

Horton, Edward Everett Vitagraph 1922, Par 1923–25, 1932–33, 1937, Univ 1926, WB 1928–29, 1935

Hovick, Louise (Gypsy Rose Lee) Fox 1937–38

Hudson, Rock Univ 1949–66

Hunt, Marsha Par 1935–37, MGM 1939–45

Hunter, Ian WB 1935–38, MGM 1939–41

Hunter, Jeffrey Fox 1951–58

Hunter, Tab Small/UA 1953–54, WB 1954–58

Hussey, Ruth MGM 1937–42, Par 1949–51

Huston, Walter Par 1929, WB 1931, 1941–43, MGM 1932–33, Fox 1945

Hutton, Betty Par 1941–52

Jannings, Emil Par 1927–30

Jean, Gloria Univ 1939–45, Fox 1955

Johnson, Van MGM 1942–54

Jolson, Al WB 1927–30, 1933–35, Fox 1938–39

Jones, Allan MGM 1935–37, Par 1939, Univ 1940, 1942–45

Jones, Buck Fox 1918–27, Col 1930–34, 1937–38, Univ 1934–37, Monogram 1941–42

Jones, Jennifer Selznick 1944–45, 1948, Fox 1955–57

Jory, Victor Fox 1933–34, Col 1934–36, WB 1939, Sherman/UA 1943

Joy, Leatrice Goldwyn 1920–21, Par 1921–24, Cinema Corp-DeMille/PDC 1925–27, DeMille/Pathé 1927–28

Joyce, Alice Kalem 1910–15, Vitagraph 1916–21, Par 1925–26

Karloff, Boris Univ 1922, 1931–32, 1934–35, 1939, 1944, 1948–52, Robertson-Cole 1924–25, RKO 1930–31, 1944–46, WB 1931, 1937, Monogram 1939–40, Col 1940–41, AIP 1962–65

Karns, Roscoe Par 1927–28, 1932–38, WB 1932, 1935, 1940, Republic 1940–41, 1947, PRC 1945–46

Kaye, Danny Goldwyn/RKO 1943–48, Par 1953–55

Keaton, Buster Comicque/Par 1917–19, Schenck/Metro 1920–21, 1923–24, Schenck/FN 1921–22, MGM 1924–26, 1928–32, 1949, UA 1926–27, Fox 1939, Col 1939–41, Univ 1944–45, AIP 1965

Keel, Howard MGM 1950–55

Keeler, Ruby WB 1932–36

Kelly, Gene MGM 1942–57

Kelly, Grace Par 1954–55, MGM 1955–56

Kendall, Kay MGM 1955–58

Kennedy, Arthur WB 1940–42

Kerr, Deborah MGM 1947–53

Kerry, Norman Par 1920–22, Univ 1923, 1925–28, MGM 1927

Keyes, Evelyn Par 1937–39, Col 1940–50, Univ 1950, UA 1951–53

Kovacs, Ernie Col 1957–61

Ladd, Alan Par 1942–53, Warwick/Col 1953–54, Jaguar/WB 1954–57

Lake, Arthur Univ 1925–27, Col 1938–50

Lake, Veronica Par 1940–48

La Marr, Barbara Fairbanks/UA

1921, Metro 1922–23, Associated Pics/FN 1924–25

Lamarr, Hedy MGM 1939–43, Par 1949–51

Lamour, Dorothy Par 1936–47, 1951–52

Lancaster, Burt Univ 1946–48, WB 1950–53, Hecht-Lancaster/UA 1954–55, 1957–62, Par 1955–56

Landi, Elissa Fox 1930–33, Par 1934, MGM 1936

Lane, Priscilla WB 1937–40

Langdon, Harry Sennett/Pathé 1924–26, FN 1926–28, Roach/MGM 1929–30

Lansbury, Angela MGM 1944–49, 1951–52, 1961–62

Lanza, Mario MGM 1949–53

La Plante, Laura Fox 1921, Univ 1923–30

La Rocque, Rod Goldwyn 1918, Par 1923–25, DeMille/PDC 1925–26, DeMille/Pathé 1927–28, RKO 1939–40

Lassie MGM 1943–50

Laughton, Charles Par 1931–34, RKO 1939–42

Laurel, Stan & Hardy, Oliver Roach/Pathé 1927–28, Roach/MGM 1928–38, Fox 1941–44

Laurie, Piper Univ 1949–56

Lawford, Peter MGM 1942–52

Lee, Lila Par 1918–23, Regal/Hodkinson 1924, WB 1928–31

Leigh, Janet MGM 1947–53

Lemmon, Jack Col 1953–61, 1963

Leslie, Joan Fox 1940, WB 1940–46, Republic 1952–54

Lewis, Jerry Par 1949–65, Col 1966–68

Lindsay, Margaret Univ 1932, 1939–40, WB 1933–39, Col 1940–43

Lloyd, Harold Roach/Pathé 1915–23, Lloyd/Pathé 1924–25, Par 1926–32

Lombard, Carole Sennett/Pathé

1927–28, Pathé 1928–29, Par 1930–37, RKO 1939–40

Loren, Sophia Par 1957–60

Lorre, Peter Fox 1936–39, WB 1941–46, AIP 1962–63

Louise, Anita Tiffany 1930, RKO 1931, Fox 1934, WB 1934–38, Col 1940–47

Love, Bessie Triangle 1916–17, Vitagraph 1916–19, FN 1924–25, Par 1925, MGM 1928–30

Lowe, Edmund Fox 1924–27, 1929–32, 1934–35, FN 1928, Par 1932–33, MGM 1936, Univ 1938–39

Loy, Myrna WB 1926–30, Fox 1930–31, RKO 1932, MGM 1932–41

Lugosi, Bela Fox 1930, Univ 1931, 1935–36, 1939, 1941–42, Monogram 1941–44

Lukas, Paul Par 1928–32, Univ 1933–34, WB 1943–44, RKO 1944–45

Lund, John Par 1945–51, Univ 1951–52

Lundigan, William Univ 1937–39, WB 1939–40, MGM 1941–44, Fox 1949–53

Lupino, Ida Par 1933–36, WB 1940–47, RKO 1951–52

Lynn, Diana Par 1942–47, 1949–50, Univ 1950–52

Lyon, Ben FN 1923–27, WB 1930–31, Fox 1932, Republic 1935–36

MacDonald, Jeanette Par 1929–30, 1932, Fox 1930–31, MGM 1934–42

Mackaill, Dorothy FN 1925–30

MacLaine, Shirley Par 1955, 1958, MGM 1958

MacMahon, Aline WB 1931–35, MGM 1935, 1944–47

MacMurray, Fred Par 1934–44, Univ 1955–57, Disney 1960–62, 1966–67, 1971

MacRae, Gordon WB 1948–53

Macready, George Col 1944–47, 1949–50, Par 1948

Main, Marjorie Par 1932–34, MGM 1938–42, 1944, 1946, 1950–51, 1953–54, Univ 1947–50, 1952–56

Malden, Karl Fox 1944–50

Malone, Dorothy WB 1945–49, 1954–55, Col 1949–50, AA 1953–54, Univ 1956–57

Mansfield, Jayne Fox 1956–58

March, Fredric Par 1928–33, UA 1934, Selznick/UA 1937, Univ 1947–48

Marshall, Herbert Par 1932–33, MGM 1934, RKO 1936–37

Martin, Dean Par 1949–56

Martin, Mary Par 1939–43

Marvin, Lee Col 1952–54, 1965–66, Fox 1954, WB 1955, Par 1961–62

Marx Brothers, The Par 1929–33, MGM 1935–41

Mason, James Fox 1951, 1956–57, MGM 1957–58, Col 1964–69

Mature, Victor Roach/UA 1939–40, Fox 1941–42, 1946–48, 1950, 1953–54

Maxwell, Marilyn MGM 1942–47

Maynard, Ken Davis Distrib Co 1925, FN 1926–29, Univ 1929–34, Col 1935–36, Grand National 1937–38, Monogram 1943–44

Mayo, Virginia Goldwyn/RKO 1943–48, WB 1948–54

McAvoy, May Par 1921–23, MGM 1924, WB 1927–28

McCoy, Tim Par 1922–24, MGM 1926–29, Col 1931–35, Puritan 1936, Monogram 1938, 1941–42, PRC 1940

McCrea, Joel MGM 1929, 1949–50, RKO 1930–33, Goldwyn/UA 1935–37, Par 1941–45, WB 1948–49, Univ 1950–54, AA 1955–57, UA 1957–58

McDowall, Roddy Fox 1941–42, 1944, Monogram 1948–51, Fox 1962

McGuire, Dorothy RKO 1945–46, Fox 1946–50, MGM 1951

McLaglen, Victor Fox 1926–32, 1935–38, Par 1933–34, Univ 1939–40

Meighan, Thomas Lasky 1915–16, Par 1916–28, Fox 1931

Menjou, Adolphe Par 1921–29, MGM 1930–31, 1950–51, WB 1933–34, Fox 1936, RKO & Roach/UA (alternating) 1939–41, UA 1956–57

Merkel, Una UA 1930, Fox 1931, 1950–51, MGM 1932–39, Univ 1939–41

Milland, Ray MGM 1930–31, WB 1931–32, Par 1933–48, AIP 1961–63

Miller, Ann RKO 1937–38, Col 1941–45, MGM 1948–56

Minter, Mary Miles Par 1919–22

Miranda, Carmen Fox 1940–46

Mitchell, Thomas Col 1936–37, 1939, Fox 1942–45, MGM 1945–47

Mitchum, Robert RKO 1946–53, UA 1955–56

Mix, Tom Selig 1910–17, Fox 1917–28, FBO/RKO 1928–29, Univ 1932–33

Monroe, Marilyn Fox 1950–56

Montalban, Ricardo MGM 1947–53

Montez, Maria Univ 1940–47

Montgomery, George Republic 1938–39, Fox 1939–43, 1946, Col 1951–55, UA 1955–57, AA 1956–57

Montgomery, Robert MGM 1929–40, Univ 1947–48

Moore, Colleen Fine Arts/Triangle 1917, FN 1920–21, 1923–29

Moore, Constance Univ 1937–40, Par 1940–41, Republic 1944–46

Moore, Grace Col 1934–37

Moorehead, Agnes RKO 1940–43, MGM 1944–49, 1952–53, Fox 1954–55

Moran, Peggy Univ 1939–42

Moran, Polly MGM 1925–32

Moreno, Antonio Vitagraph
1915–16, Par 1923–24, MGM
1926, FN 1928

Morgan, Dennis MGM 1936–37, Par
1938, WB 1939–52

Morgan, Frank Par 1930, MGM
1933, 1935–49

Morley, Karen MGM 1931–33, Fox
1935, Par 1937, Col 1946–47

Morris, Chester WB 1929–30,
Univ 1933–35, MGM 1935–36,
Col 1936–37, 1941–48, RKO
1937–38, Par 1942–43

Morris, Wayne WB 1936–41,
1947–49, Col 1950, Monogram
1951–52, AA 1953–55

Muni, Paul Fox 1929, WB 1932–39,
Col 1944–45

Murphy, Audie Univ 1949–63

Murphy, George Col 1934–35,
Univ 1937–38, MGM 1937, 1940,
1946–51, RKO 1941–42, 1944

Murray, Mae Par 1916–17, 1920,
Univ 1917–19, Metro 1921–23,
MGM 1924–26

Nagel, Conrad Par 1920–23,
MGM 1924–27, 1929–30, 1932,
WB 1928–29, Grand National
1936–37

Naldi, Nita Par 1920–25, FN 1925

Neal, Patricia WB 1948–50, Fox
1951–52

Negri, Pola Union-UFA (Ger.)
1918–22, Par 1923–28

Newman, Paul MGM 1955–56, Fox
1957–61

Niven, David Goldwyn/UA
1938–39, Goldwyn/RKO 1947–48

Nolan, Lloyd Col 1935–36,
Par 1936–39, Fox 1940–45,
1965–67

Normand, Mabel Biograph 1911–12,
Keystone 1912–17, Sennett
1917–18, 1921–23, Goldwyn
1918–21

North, Sheree Fox 1955–58

Novak, Kim Col 1954–61

Novarro, Ramon Metro 1921–23,
MGM 1924–34

O'Brien, George Par 1923, Fox
1924–35, RKO 1936–40

O'Brien, Margaret MGM 1941–49

O'Brien, Pat Col 1932, 1940–42,
Univ 1932, WB 1933–40, RKO
1942–49

O'Brien, Virginia MGM 1940–47

O'Connor, Donald Par
1938–39, 1955–56, Univ
1941–44, 1947–50, 1953–54,
MGM 1952,

O'Hara, Maureen RKO 1939–43,
1945–46, Fox 1941–43, 1945–49,
Univ 1949–53

O'Sullivan, Maureen Fox 1930–31,
Univ 1932, MGM 1932–41

Oakie, Jack Par 1928–36, RKO
1936–38, Fox 1940–43, Univ
1944–45

Oberon, Merle Korda/UA 1933–34,
1937–38, Goldwyn/UA 1935–38,
Univ 1945–46, RKO 1947

Oland, Warner Fox 1915, 1932–37,
Pathé 1917, WB 1926–27, Par
1929–31

Oliver, Edna May Par 1923–25,
RKO 1930–33, MGM 1934–37

Paige, Janis WB 1944–50, MGM
1959–62

Paige, Robert Col 1938–39, Par
1939–40, Univ 1941–45

Parker, Eleanor WB 1941–51,
MGM 1951–55

Parks, Larry Col 1941–50

Patrick, Gail Par 1932–39, MGM
1940–41, Republic 1945–48

Payne, John WB 1938–39, Fox
1940–42, 1945–47, RKO
1954–56

Peck, Gregory Selznick 1945–47,
Fox 1947–49, 1951–52, WB
1950–51, GFD/UA (GB) 1954,
UA 1958–59, Univ 1961–65

Perkins, Anthony Par 1956–58

Peters, Jean Fox 1947–54

Pickford, Mary Griffith/Biograph
1909–12, IMP 1911,
Majestic 1911–12, Famous
Players 1913–16, Par

1916–18, FN 1919, UA
1919–32

Pidgeon, Walter FN 1929–31, Univ
1937, MGM 1937–56

Pitts, ZaSu Par 1917, 1922,
1927–28, 1930, 1934, Robertson-
Cole 1919–20, Goldwyn 1923,
WB 1929, RKO 1932, 1934, Univ
1932–33

Poitier, Sidney WB 1956–57, MGM
1956–57, Col 1958–60, UA
1961–63

Powell, Dick WB 1932–39, Par
1940, 1942–43, Univ 1940–41,
RKO 1944–45, 1952–55, MGM
1949–50

Powell, Eleanor MGM 1935–43

Powell, Jane MGM 1946–54

Powell, William Par 1924–31, WB
1931–34, MGM 1934–46, Univ
1947–48

Power, Tyrone Fox 1936–54, Col
1954–56

Presley, Elvis Par 1957–60,
1962–63, Fox 1960, UA
1961–62, MGM 1963, 1964,
1967–68

Preston, Robert Par 1938–42,
1947

Prevost, Marie Sennett 1917–19,
Univ 1921–22, WB 1923–26,
PDC 1926–27, Pathé 1927–28,
MGM 1930–31

Price, Vincent Univ 1939–40,
1947–50, Fox 1940–46, AIP
1960–66

Quinn, Anthony Par 1936–40,
1957–60, WB 1940–41, Fox
1942–44, 1964–65, RKO
1945–47, Col 1951, 1961–62,
Univ 1952–53

Raft, George Par 1931–38, WB
1939–43, RKO & UA (alternating)
1945–49

Rainer, Luise MGM 1935–38

Raines, Ella Univ 1943–47, Republic
1949–52

Rains, Claude Univ 1933–34, WB
1935–44, RKO 1949–50

Ralston, Vera Hruba Republic
1941–58

Rathbone, Basil MGM 1929–30,
1934–36, Fox 1939, Univ 1939,
1941–46, AIP 1962–63, 1965–66

Ray, Charles Ince 1916, Triangle
1917, Par 1918–20, Ray/FN
1920–22, Ince/Pathé 1924, MGM
1925–26, PDC 1926–27, Univ
1940–41, Fox 1941–42

Raye, Martha Par 1936–39, Univ
1940–41

Raymond, Gene Fox 1933–34, RKO
1935–37, 1940

Reagan, Ronald WB 1937–43,
1946–50, 1952, Univ 1950, Par
1951, RKO 1954–55

Reed, Donna MGM 1941–46, Col
1951–54, 1957–58

Reid, Wallace Lasky 1915–16, Par
1916–22

Remick, Lee Fox 1957–60

Rennie, Michael Fox 1950–57

Revier, Dorothy Goldstone
1923–24, Col 1925–30

Reynolds, Debbie MGM 1950–56

Rich, Irene WB 1923–28

Rin-Tin-Tin WB 1923–30

Ritter, Thelma Fox 1947–53, Par
1954–55

Ritz Brothers, The Fox 1936–39,
Univ 1940–43

Roberts, Theodore Lasky 1915–16,
Par 1916–26

Robertson, Cliff Col 1955, 1958–61

Robertson, Dale Fox 1949–54

Robinson, Edward G. WB 1930–41

Rogers, Charles 'Buddy' Par
1926–30

Rogers, Ginger Par 1930, Pathé
1931, WB 1932, RKO 1933–41,
RKO & Par (alternating) 1942–43,
Fox 1952

Rogers, Roy Republic 1937–51

Rogers, Will Goldwyn 1918–21,
Roach 1923–24, Fox 1929–35

Roland, Gilbert FN 1926–27,
UA 1927–29, Fox 1934–36,
Monogram 1946–47

Roman, Ruth WB 1949–51

Romero, Cesar Univ 1935–37, Fox 1937–49, Lippert 1951–52

Rooney, Mickey Univ 1932–34, MGM 1934–48

Ruggles, Charles Par 1929–37, 1939–40

Russell, Gail Par 1942–48, Republic 1948

Russell, Jane RKO 1950–54

Russell, Rosalind MGM 1934–39, 1941, Col 1942–46, 1949, RKO 1946–48

Rutherford, Ann Republic 1935–36, MGM 1937–42

Ryan, Peggy, Univ 1941–45

Ryan, Robert Par 1940, RKO 1943–44, 1946–52, Fox 1955–56, UA 1956–59

Sabu Korda/UA 1937–41, Univ 1942–43, 1946–48

Saint, Eva Marie MGM 1957–59, 1961, 1964–66

Sakall, S.Z. WB 1943–51, MGM 1951–53

Sanders, George Fox 1936–38, 1942–43, 1947–50, RKO 1939–41, UA 1946, MGM 1954–55

Scott, Lizabeth Par 1945–47, 1949–50

Scott, Randolph Par 1932–38, Fox 1938–41, Univ 1943, RKO 1944–45, UA 1945, Col 1949, Col & WB (alternating) 1950–57, Ranown/Col 1957–59

Scott, Zachary WB 1944–50, Fox 1951, Lippert 1952

Shearer, Norma MGM 1924–42

Sheridan, Ann Par 1934–35, WB 1936–47, Fox 1949–50, Univ 1950–52

Sherman, Lowell WB 1929, RKO 1930

Shirley, Anne Fox 1928–30, WB 1932–33, RKO 1934–44

Sidney, Sylvia Par 1930–35, 1938

Sills, Milton Goldwyn 1918–19, Par 1920–22, FN 1922–29, Fox 1930

Silvers, Phil Fox 1941–45

Simmons, Jean RKO 1952–53, Fox 1953–54, MGM 1956–57, Univ 1958–60

Simon, Simone Fox 1936–37, RKO 1941–42, 1944

Sinatra, Frank RKO 1943–44 MGM 1945–49, 1955–56

Skelton, Red MGM 1940–53

Skipworth, Alison Par 1932–34

Smith, Kent RKO 1942–49, WB 1947, 1949–50, MGM 1958

Sondergaard, Gale WB 1936–37, MGM 1938, Par 1939, Fox 1940, Univ 1941, 1943–46, Col 1942–43

Sothern, Ann WB 1929–30, Col 1934–36, MGM 1939–47

Stack, Robert Univ 1939–42, UA 1952–53

Stanwyck, Barbara Col 1929–32, WB 1931–35, 1944–45, RKO 1935–38, Par 1938–40, 1945–46, 1948–50, MGM 1950–52

Starke, Pauline Triangle 1917–18, Fox 1923–24, MGM 1926–27

Starrett, Charles Col 1935–52

Steiger, Rod Col 1954–56, RKO 1956–57

Stevens, Craig WB 1941–48

Stewart, Anita Vitagraph 1912–17, Mayer-Stewart/FN 1918–22, Cosmopolitan/Goldwyn 1923

Stewart, James MGM 1935–40, Fox 1949–50, Univ 1950, Par 1951–53 1953–54, Col 1958–60

Stockwell, Dean MGM 1945–47, 1949–50

Stone, Lewis FN 1924–27, MGM 1929–52

Stroheim, Erich von Griffith/Fine Arts 1916, Univ 1918–22, RKO 1931, Republic 1943–45

Stuart, Gloria Univ 1932–34, Fox 1935–39

Sullavan, Margaret Univ 1933–35, MGM 1938–40

Swanson, Gloria Essanay 1915, Keystone 1916–17, Sennett 1917,

Triangle 1918, Par 1918–26,
Swanson/UA 1926–32

Sweet, Blanche Griffith/Biograph
1909–14, Lasky 1915–16, Par
1916–17, Pathé 1919–20, FN
1923–25

Talmadge, Constance Vitagraph
1914–15, Griffith/Triangle
1915–16, Selznick/Select 1917–19,
Schenck/FN 1919–27

Talmadge, Norma, Vitagraph
1910–15, Triangle 1915–16,
Selznick/Select 1917–19,
Talmadge/FN 1922–26,
Schenck/UA 1927–30

Tamiroff, Akim MGM 1933–34, Par
1935–43

Taylor, Elizabeth MGM 1943–54

Taylor, Robert MGM 1934–43,
1946–58

Taylor, Rod MGM 1955–57.
1959–60, 1963–64, Univ 1962–63

Tearle, Conway Selznick/Select
1920–22, FN 1923–24, 1926,
WB 1929

Temple, Shirley Fox 1934–40, RKO
1946–48

Terry, Alice Vitagraph 1917–18,
Par 1919, Metro 1920–23, MGM
1924–27

Tierney, Gene Fox 1940–55

Tobin, Genevieve Univ 1930–31,
WB 1933–36

Tone, Franchot MGM 1933–39, Par
1943–44, Univ 1944–45

Totter, Audrey MGM 1944–47,
Col 1953

Tracy, Lee Fox 1929–30, WB 1932,
MGM 1933, Par 1934–35, RKO
1936–40

Tracy, Spencer Fox 1930–35, MGM
1935–53

Trevor, Claire Fox 1933–37, Col
1941–43, RKO 1944–46

Turner, Lana WB 1937–38, MGM
1938–55, Univ 1957–60

Twelvetrees, Helen Fox 1929,
1933–34, Pathé-RKO 1930–32

Valentino, Rudolph Univ 1918–19,

Metro 1920–21, Par 1921–25,
UA 1925–26

Vallee, Rudy Par 1942, RKO
1945–47, Fox 1948–49

Veidt, Conrad Univ 1927–29, MGM
1940–42, WB 1941–42

Velez, Lupe Univ 1930, MGM
1931–32, RKO 1939–43

Vera-Ellen Goldwyn/RKO 1944–45,
Fox 1946, MGM 1948–51

Wagner, Robert Fox 1950–59

Walker, Robert MGM 1943–47,
1950

Walsh, George Fox 1915–20,
Goldwyn 1923, Chadwick 1925,
Excellent 1926–27

Wayne, John Fox 1927–30, Col
1931, WB 1932–33, Monogram
1933–35, Republic 1935–36,
1938–42, Univ 1936–37, RKO &
Republic (alternating) 1943–51,
Wayne/WB 1952–55

Webb, Clifton Fox 1944–61

Weissmuller, Johnny MGM
1931–41, RKO 1942–47, Col
1948–55

Welles, Orson RKO 1940–42, Fox
1957–58

West, Mae Par 1932–37

White, Alice FN 1927–30

White, Pearl Powers 1910, Lubin
1911, Univ 1912–13, Pathé
1914–19, Fox 1920–22

Whitmore, James MGM 1949–53,
WB 1954–55

Widmark, Richard Fox 1947–54

Wilde, Cornel WB 1940–41, Fox
1941–43, 1945–48, Col 1944–45

Willes, Jean Col 1949–52, 1954–55,
AA 1955

William, Warren WB 1931–36,
Par 1936–37, MGM 1937, Col
1939–42

Williams, Esther MGM 1942–54

Winters, Shelley Col 1943–45, Univ
1947–53, MGM 1953, UA 1955

Withers, Jane Fox 1934–42,
Republic 1943–46

Wood, Nathalie Fox 1945–49, WB

1954–62

Woodward, Joanne Fox 1957–60, WB 1966–68

Wray, Fay Univ 1925–27, 1956–57, Par 1927–31, RKO 1933, Col 1933, 1936–37

Wright, Teresa Goldwyn/RKO 1941–42, 1946

Wyman, Jane WB 1936–50

Wynn, Keenan MGM 1942–55

Young, Clara Kimball Vitagraph 1912–15, Selznick/World Film 1915–16, Selznick/Select 1916–18, Equity 1919–22, Zierler/Metro 1922–23

Young, Gig WB 1941–43, MGM 1951–53

Young, Loretta FN 1928–29, WB 1929–33, 20th/UA 1934–35, Fox 1934–39, Col 1940–42, RKO 1945–48

Young, Robert MGM 1931–42, RKO 1945–47

Young, Roland MGM 1929–31, 1940–41, Par 1931–34, Roach/UA 1937–40, Fox 1939–40

DIRECTORS

Adolfi, John G. WB 1928–33

Aldrich, Robert UA 1953–56, Col 1955–56

Allen, Woody UA 1971–80, Orion 1982–90

Archainbaud, George FN 1924–26, Tiffany-Stahl 1927–29, Col 1929, 1952–53 RKO 1930–34, 1950, Fox 1935, Par 1936–40, UA 1943–48, Republic 1945

Arnold, Jack Univ 1952–58

Arzner, Dorothy Par 1927–32

Ashby, Hal UA 1976–79

Auer, John Republic 1937–43, 1947–55, RKO 1943–47

Bacon, Lloyd WB 1926–43, Fox 1944–49, 1951–53, Col 1949–50, Univ 1953, RKO 1953–54

Bare, Richard L. WB 1948–50, 1956–60

Barton, Charles Par 1934–38, Col 1939–44, Univ 1945–52

Beaudine, William WB 1923–25, 1929–31, 1935–39, FN 1927–29, Par 1932–34, Monogram & PRC (alternating) 1940–52, AA 1953–55

Beaumont, Harry MGM 1928–34, 1944–48

Beebe, Ford L. Mascot 1932–35, Univ 1936–45, Monogram 1947–52, AA 1953–55

Bell, Monta WB 1924, MGM 1924–28, Par 1929–31, Univ 1930–31

Berkeley, Busby WB 1932–38, MGM 1939–42

Bernhardt, Curtis WB 1940–42, 1945–47, MGM 1949, 1952–56

Blystone, John Fox 1924–36

Boetticher, Budd Col 1944–45, 1957–60, Eagle-Lion 1948, Monogram 1949–50, Univ 1951–53

Boleslawski, Richard MGM 1933–34, 1937, 20th/UA 1935

Borzage, Frank Par 1920–22, FN 1923–24, Fox 1925–32, WB 1934–37, MGM 1937–42, Republic 1946–48

Brabin, Charles FN 1926–28, MGM 1929–34

Brahm, John Col 1937–40, Fox 1941–44

Brannon, Fred C. Republic 1945–53

Bretherton, Howard WB 1926–34, Par 1935–36, Monogram & Republic (alternating) 1936–52

Brooks, Richard MGM 1950–58

Brown, Clarence Univ 1923–25, MGM 1926–52

Brown, Harry Joe Rayart 1925–27, FN 1927–29, Univ 1930, Par 1932–33

Browning, Tod Univ 1918–23, 1930–31, MGM 1925–29, 1932–34

Bucquet, Harold S. MGM 1938–45

Butler, David Fox 1927–38, WB

1943–44, 1946–56

Buzzell, Edward Col 1932–33, 1950, Univ 1933–34, 1936–37, MGM 1938–49

Capra, Frank FN 1926–27, Col 1927–39, WB 1940–41, Par 1949–51

Castle, William Col 1944–47, 1953–56, 1959–63, Univ 1949, 1951

Chaplin, Charles Keystone 1914, Essanay 1915, Mutual 1916–17, Chaplin/FN 1918–22, Chaplin/UA 1923–52

Clemens, William WB 1936–41, Par 1941–42, RKO 1943

Cline, Edward MGM 1924–25, FN 1928–29, WB 1929–30, Par 1931–32, 1935–36, Fox 1934–35, RKO 1937–39, Univ 1939–45, Monogram 1946–48

Conway, Jack Fine Arts/Triangle 1913–15, Univ 1916–1917, 1921–23, Fox 1924, MGM 1925–48

Corman, Roger AIP 1955–70

Cromwell, John Par 1929–32, RKO 1933–35, 1939–40, 1950–51, Selznick/UA 1936–39

Crosland, Alan WB 1925–31, 1933–35, Univ 1935

Cruze, James Par 1918–27

Cukor, George Par 1930–31, RKO 1932–33, MGM 1933–37, 1939–44, 1949–50, 1952–53

Cummings, Irving Univ 1922, 1924, FN 1925, Fox 1926, 1928–1931, 1933–36, 1938–43, 1945, Col 1932, 1943–44

Curtiz, Michael WB 1926–54, Par 1954–56

d'Arrast, Harry d'Abbadie Par 1927–28, 1930

Dassin, Jules MGM 1942–46, Univ 1947, Fox 1949–50

Daves, Delmer WB 1943–45, 1947–49, 1958–64, Fox 1950–53

De Cordova, Frederick WB 1945–48, Univ 1948–53

del Ruth, Roy WB 1925–34, 1949–54, UA 1934–35, Fox 1935–40, MGM 1936–37, 1941–44, AA 1947–48

DeMille, Cecil B. Lasky 1913–16, Par 1916–25, 1932–56, PDC/Pathé 1925–28, MGM 1929–31

de Mille, William Lasky 1915–16, Par 1916–25, PDC 1926–27, Pathé 1928, MGM 1929–30

De Toth, André Col 1943–44, UA 1944–48, 1955–59, WB 1952–54

Dieterle, William WB 1930–39, Fox 1933, RKO 1939, 1941–42, MGM 1942–44, Par 1948–53

Dillon, John Francis FN 1923–29, WB 1929–31, Fox 1932–33

Dmytryk, Edward Par 1939–40, Col 1941–42, 1952–54, RKO 1942–47, Fox 1954–55, 1957–59

Donen, Stanley MGM 1949–55, Fox 1966–69

Douglas, Gordon UA 1939–41, RKO 1943–48, Col 1948–50, WB 1951–61

Dwan, Allan American Film Co 1911–13, Univ 1913–14, Famous Players 1914–15, Triangle 1915–16, Par 1917–18, 1923–26, Associated Producers 1920–21, Fox 1926–27, 1929, 1931–32, 1935–40, FN 1928, Small/UA 1944–45, Republic 1946–53, RKO 1954–55, Fox 1957

Edwards, Blake Col 1951–56, Univ 1956–59

English, John Republic 1937–47, Col 1947–51

Enright, Ray WB 1927–41, Univ 1942

Farrow, John WB 1937–38, RKO 1939–40, Par 1942–49

Fejos, Paul Univ 1928–29

Fitzmaurice, George Par 1919–23, FN 1923–25, 1927–29, UA 1926–27, 1929–30, MGM 1931–32, 1936–38

Fleischer, Richard RKO 1946–51,

Fox 1955–61, 1966–69, Col 1971–72, De Laurentiis 1983–85

Fleming, Victor Par 1922–29, Fox 1930, MGM 1932–45

Florey, Robert Par 1928–29, 1935–40, Univ 1931, WB 1933–35, 1941–42, 1945–46, Col 1941, UA 1948–50

Ford, John Univ 1916–21, Fox 1921–31, 1933–35, 1938–41, RKO 1934–36, 1947–49

Forde, Eugene Fox 1932–47

Foster, Lewis R. Univ 1936–37, Par 1949–53

Foster, Norman Fox 1936–41, RKO 1943, 1948, Col 1949–50, MGM 1952, Disney 1955–62

Frank, Melvin (with **Norman Panama**) MGM 1950–52, Par 1954–59

Franklin, Sidney FN 1919–26, MGM 1926–37

Freeland, Thornton UA 1929–30, 1935–37

Fregonese, Hugo Univ 1950–52

Freund, Karl Univ 1932–34

Fuller, Samuel Lippert 1948–49, Fox 1951–57, RKO 1957–58, Col 1959–60

Garnett, Tay Pathé 1928–31, RKO 1932, Univ 1932–33, Fox 1936–37, UA 1938–39, MGM 1943–45, 1950, Par 1947–48

Gering, Marion Par 1931–36, Col 1936–38

Godfrey, Peter RKO 1941–42, WB 1944–50

Goldbeck, Willis MGM 1942–47

Gordon, Michael Col 1943, Univ 1947–49, Fox 1951

Goulding, Edmund MGM 1925–28, 1932–35, Par 1929–31, WB 1937–43, Fox 1946–58

Green, Alfred E. FN 1926, Fox 1927–29, WB 1929–36, Col 1936–37, 1942–46, UA 1947–49

Griffith, D.W. Biograph 1908–13, Reliance-Majestic/Mutual 1913–14, Fine Arts/Triangle 1915–16, Artcraft/Par 1917–19, FN 1919–20, UA 1920–25, 1927–31, Par 1926

Hall, Alexander Par 1932–37, Col 1938–42, 1944–47

Hathaway, Henry Par 1932–38, Fox 1940, 1942–56, 1958–60

Hawks, Howard Fox 1925–29, 1952–53, WB 1931–32, 1941–45, MGM 1932–33, Col 1938–39, RKO 1950–52

Hecht, Ben (with **Charles MacArthur**) Par 1934–36

Heisler, Stuart Par 1940–42

Hill, George Roy UA 1963–66, Univ 1967–77

Hill, George W. MGM 1925–32

Hiller, Arthur MGM 1963–66, Par 1970–71

Hitchcock, Alfred Selznick/UA 1940, RKO 1941, Univ 1941–42, 1962–76, Transatlantic/WB 1948–49, WB 1950–53, Par 1954–56

Howard, William K. Fox 1921, 1928–33, Par 1924–25, 1935–36, MGM 1934–35, UA 1937, WB 1940–41

Humberstone, H. Bruce Par 1932–33, WB 1934, Fox 1935–48

Huston, John WB 1941–48, MGM 1950–51, UA 1951–54, Fox 1957–58

Ingram, Rex Univ 1916–17, Metro 1920–23, MGM 1924–27

Jewison, Norman Univ 1962–64, Mirisch/UA 1965–71, UA 1974–77

Kane, Joseph Republic 1935–58

Kanin, Garson RKO 1938–41

Karlson, Phil Monogram 1944–47, Col 1948, 1951–58

Kazan, Elia Fox 1945, 1947–50, 1952–53, WB 1954–57

Keighley, William WB 1932–42, 1950–53

Kelly, Gene MGM 1949–58

Kenton, Erle C. Col 1928–31,

1935–37, Par 1933–34, RKO
1939–41, Univ 1941–46

King, Henry Inspiration/Metro
1923–24, UA 1925–30, Fox
1930–61

Koster, Henry Univ 1936–42, MGM
1944–47, Fox 1948–56

Kramer, Stanley UA 1955–63, Col
1965–67, 1970–73

Kubrick, Stanley UA 1955–57, WB
1971–87

La Cava, Gregory Par 1925–28,
Pathé 1929–30, RKO 1930–33,
1937–40, Univ 1941–42

Lachman, Harry Par 1932, Fox
1933–36, 1940–42, Col 1936–38

Lamont, Charles Chesterfield
1934–36, Grand National
1937–39, Univ 1939–56

Landers, Lew Univ 1934–36, 1940,
RKO 1936–39, 1947, Republic
1940–41, Col 1941–45, 1949–52,
PRC 1945–46

Lanfield, Sidney Fox 1930–33,
1935–39, Par 1942–47

Lang, Fritz MGM 1935–36,
Fox 1940–42, RKO 1951–52,
1955–56, Col 1953–54

Lang, Walter Col 1927, Worldwide
1930, Fox 1937–61

LeBorg, Reginald Univ 1943–45,
Monogram 1948–51, Lippert
1951–53

Lederman, D. Ross WB 1927–29,
1934–35, 1941–43, Col 1931–34,
1936–38, 1940, 1945–48

Lee, Rowland V. Fox 1922–27,
1932–34, Par 1928–31, FN 1931,
UA 1934–36, RKO 1937–38,
Univ 1938–39

Leeds, Herbert Fox 1938–48

Leisen, Mitchell Par 1933–51

Leni, Paul Univ 1927–28

Leonard, Robert Z. Univ 1915–19,
Metro 1921–24, MGM 1924–55

LeRoy, Mervyn FN 1927–29,
WB 1929–38, 1955–59, MGM
1939–45, 1948–54

Lester, Richard UA 1962–69

Levin, Henry Col 1944–51, Fox
1952–53

Lewis, Joseph H. Univ 1937–38,
1942, Col 1939–40, 1946–49,
Monogram 1940–41, MGM 1950,
1952–53, UA 1957–58

Litvak, Anatole WB 1937–41,
RKO 1945–47, Fox 1948, 1951,
1955–56

Lloyd, Frank Fox 1917–19,
1931–34, FN 1922–30, WB
1929–31, Par 1926–27, 1937–39,
MGM 1935, Col 1940–41

Losey, Joseph UA 1951–52

Lubin, Arthur Monogram
1934, Republic 1935, Univ
1936–46, 1949–57, UA 1945,
1947–49, 1951

Lubitsch, Ernst WB 1923–26, Par
1928–33, 1935–37, MGM 1934,
1939, UA 1941–42, Fox 1943–47

Lupino, Ida RKO 1950–53

MacFadden, Hamilton Fox 1930–34

Mamoulian, Rouben Par 1929–33,
Fox 1940–42

Mankiewicz, Joseph L. Fox 1945–51

Mann, Anthony Republic 1943–44,
RKO 1945–46, Eagle-Lion
1947–48, MGM 1949–51, Univ
1952–54

Mann, Daniel Par 1952–55,
1962–65, Col & MGM
(alternating) 1959–62

Mann, Delbert Hecht-
Hill–Lancaster/UA 1954–58, Univ
1961–63

Marin, Edwin L. Univ 1933–34,
MGM 1934–41, UA 1942,
1946–47, RKO 1944–45, Fox
1949, WB 1950–51

Marshall, George Fox 1920–21,
1926–27, 1934–38, Par 1942–50,
1952–54

Marton, Andrew MGM 1946,
1950–54

Maté, Rudolph Col 1947–48, Par
1950–51, Univ 1952–53

Mayo, Archie WB 1927–37, UA
1938–40, 1946, Fox 1940–44

Mazursky, Paul Fox 1974–80, Col 1982–84

McCarey, Leo Fox 1930, 1957–61, UA 1931, 1933, Par 1933–37, RKO 1939, 1942, 1945, 1948

McDonald, Frank WB 1935–38, Univ 1938, Republic 1939–47, Par 1943–44, Monogram 1950–52, AA 1953–55

McGann, William WB 1930–39

McLeod, Norman Z. Par 1930–36, 1947–51, Roach/UA 1937–39, MGM 1940–43, Goldwyn/RKO 1946–47

Milestone, Lewis WB 1925, UA 1927–29, 1931–33, Par 1935–36, RKO 1940–41, Fox 1943–45, 1951–52

Minnelli, Vincente MGM 1943–63

Mulligan, Robert Univ 1960–62

Murnau, F.W. Fox 1926–29

Nazarro, Ray Col 1945–52

Negulesco, Jean WB 1941–48, Fox 1948–58

Neilan, Marshall Par 1916–18, FN 1918–22, Metro 1922–23, MGM 1924–25

Neill, Roy William Fox 1925–27, Col 1930–36, WB 1938–39, Univ 1942–46

Neumann, Kurt Univ 1932–35, 1951–52, RKO 1936–37, 1945–47, Par 1938–40, UA 1942–43, AA 1948–49

Newman, Joseph M. Fox 1951–53

Niblo, Fred Par 1918–21, Metro 1923–24, MGM 1924–31

Nugent, Elliott WB 1932, RKO 1933–34, Par 1934–35, 1938–41, 1947

Ophüls, Max Univ 1947–48

Pevney, Joseph Univ 1950–57

Pichel, Irving RKO 1932–35, Republic 1936–37, Fox 1939–43, Par 1944–46, Univ 1948–49

Pollack, Sydney Col 1977–82

Potter, H.C. MGM 1939–40, RKO 1947–48, UA 1948

Preminger, Otto Fox 1936–37, 1942–50

Quine, Richard Col 1948, 1951–60

Rafelson, Bob BBS/Col 1968–72

Rapper, Irving WB 1941–47

Ratoff, Gregory Fox 1936–40, 1944–47, Col 1940–43

Rawlins, John Univ 1938–46, RKO 1947–48, UA 1951–53

Ray, Nicholas RKO 1948–49, 1951–52, Col 1948–49, Fox 1956

Reis, Irving RKO 1940–48, Fox 1949

Ritt, Martin Fox 1957–58, 1970–74

Roberts, Stephen Par 1932–33, RKO 1934–36

Robertson, John Stuart Vitagraph 1917–18, Par 1919–22, FN 1923–25, MGM 1927, 1929, RKO 1933–35

Robson, Mark RKO 1943–46, Kramer/UA 1949, Goldwyn/RKO 1949–50, Fox 1957–62

Rogell, Albert Rayart 1925, Univ 1926–27, 1939–41, FN 1927–29, Col 1929, 1933–38, Tiffany 1929–31, Pathé/RKO 1931, Republic 1942–46

Rossen, Robert Col 1947, 1949–51

Rowland, Roy MGM 1943–51, 1954–58

Ruben, J. Walter RKO 1931–34, MGM 1935–38

Ruggles, Wesley Vitagraph 1917–19, Metro 1920–21, Univ 1927–29, RKO 1931–32, Par 1932–39, Col 1940–41, MGM 1942–44

Russell, Ken UA 1967–70, MGM 1971–72

Ryan, Frank Univ 1943–46

St Clair, Malcolm WB 1924, Par 1925–28, Fox 1933, 1936–40, 1943–45, 1948

Sale, Richard Republic 1947–48, Fox 1950–53

Salkow, Sidney Univ 1936–38, Republic 1938–39, Col 1940–43, 1947, 1952–53

Sandrich, Mark RKO 1933–38, Par 1939–44

Santell, Alfred FN 1925–28, Fox 1929–33, Par 1938–42, UA 1943–44

Santley, Joseph Republic 1935–36, 1940–46, RKO 1936–38, Univ 1938–39

Saville, Victor MGM 1946–51

Schertzinger, Victor Fox 1925–27, Par 1928–30, 1940–41, RKO 1931, Col 1933–36

Schoedsack, Ernest Par 1925–31, RKO 1932–35, Col 1937

Schuster, Harold Fox 1937, 1941–43, Univ 1938–40, AA 1953–55

Scorsese, Martin WB 1969–73

Sears, Fred Col 1949–58

Seaton, George Fox 1945–50, Par 1952–61

Sedgwick, Edward Fox 1920–22, Univ 1922–26, 1933–34, MGM 1926–32

Seiter, William A. Univ 1924–28, 1939–41, 1945–49, FN 1928–29, WB 1929–31, RKO 1931–34, Par 1932, 1936, Fox 1936–38

Seitz, George MGM 1933–44

Selander, Lesley Univ 1936–37, Par 1937–41, UA 1942–44, Republic 1944–47, RKO 1948–52

Sherman, George Republic 1938–44, Col 1945–48, Univ 1947–54

Sherman, Lowell RKO 1930–31, UA 1933–34

Sherman, Vincent WB 1939–50

Sidney, George MGM 1941–54, Col 1956–63

Siegel, Donald WB 1945–48, RKO 1949, 1952, AA 1953–55, Univ 1963–74

Simon, S. Sylvan Univ 1937–38, MGM 1938–46, Col 1946–49

Siodmak, Robert Par 1941–42, Univ 1943–48

Sirk, Douglas UA 1944–47, Col 1948, Univ 1950–58

Sjöström, Victor Goldwyn 1923, MGM 1924–30

Spielberg, Steven Univ 1969–75

Springsteen, R.G. Republic 1945–56

Stahl, John M. Mayer/FN 1920–23, FN 1924–26, MGM 1926–27, Tiffany/Stahl 1927–30, Univ 1930–35, 1938–39, Fox 1942–49

Sternberg, Josef von Par 1927–35, Col 1935–36

Stevens, George RKO 1934–39, Col 1940–42, Par 1950–52

Stevenson, Robert RKO 1942–43, 1949–52, Disney 1957–76

Stiller, Mauritz MGM 1926, Par 1927–28

Stone, Andrew L. Par 1938–41, UA 1943–47, MGM 1955–62

Stroheim, Erich von Univ 1919–22, Goldwyn 1923–24, MGM 1924–25

Sturges, John Col 1946–49, MGM 1949–55, UA 1960–67

Sturges, Preston Par 1940–43, Hughes 1945–46, Fox 1948–49

Sutherland, A. Edward Par 1925–31, 1933, 1935–37, UA 1931–32, Univ 1940–41, RKO 1942

Tashlin, Frank RKO 1953–54, Fox & Par (alternating) 1955–62, Par 1963–64, MGM 1965–66

Taurog, Norman Tiffany 1929–30, Par 1930–36, Fox 1936–37, MGM 1938–51, Par 1952–56

Taylor, Sam Pathé 1923–25, UA 1927–31, Fox 1931–32

Tetzlaff, Ted RKO 1947–50

Thiele, Wilhelm MGM 1937–40, RKO 1943

Thorpe, Richard Pathé 1927–28, Chesterfield 1932–34, MGM 1935–63

Tourneur, Jacques MGM 1939–40, RKO 1942–49

Tuttle, Frank Par 1924–38, 1942–44, WB 1955–59

Ulmer, Edgar G. PRC 1942–46, UA 1946–47

Van Dyke, W.S. Fox 1924–25, MGM 1927–42

Vidor, Charles RKO 1935, Par 1936–37, Col 1939–41, 1943–48, MGM 1953–55

Vidor, King Robertson-Cole 1918–19, FN 1920–21, Associated Exhibitors 1921–22, Goldwyn 1923–24, MGM 1924–30, 1938–44, Par 1935–36, WB 1949–50

Walker, Hal Par 1945–52

Walker, Stuart Par 1931–33, Univ 1934–35

Wallace, Richard FN 1926–28, Par 1928–32, 1936–37, Col 1942–43, RKO 1943–44, 1947

Walsh, Raoul Fox 1915–20, 1926–32, 1955–56, 1958–61, Par 1925–26, 1935–36, 1938–39, WB 1939–51

Walters, Charles MGM 1947–64

Weber, Lois Univ 1916–19, Par 1920–21

Weis, Don MGM 1951–53

Welles, Orson RKO 1940–42

Wellman, William A. Fox 1923–24, Par 1926–30, 1938–41, WB 1930–33, 1953–58, MGM 1936, 1949–52, Selznick/UA 1937

Werker, Alfred L. Par 1928, 1934–35, Fox 1929–33, 1937–1939, 1941–42

West, Roland UA 1926–31

Whale, James Univ 1931–39

Wilcox, Fred M. MGM 1943–56

Wilder, Billy Par 1942–54, UA 1958–72

Windust, Bretaigne WB 1948–51

Wise, Robert RKO 1943–49, Fox 1950–53, 1964–68, MGM 1953–57, UA 1957–62

Witney, William Republic 1937–57

Wood, Sam Par 1919–26, MGM 1927–39, 1949, UA 1940, RKO 1940, 1944–45

Wyler, William Univ 1925–34, Goldwyn/UA 1935–37, 1939–41, Par 1949–55

Yarbrough, Jean Monogram

1941–42, 1949–51, Univ 1943–46

Young, Harold Par 1935–36, Univ 1937–39, 1941–43, 1945

Zinnemann, Fred MGM 1942–48, Col 1952–53

CAMERAMEN

Alton, John RKO 1940, Republic 1942–49, MGM 1949–52

Andriot, Lucien Pathé 1927–28, Fox 1928–31, 1936–44, RKO 1932, 1934–35, UA 1944–50

Arnold, John Metro 1917–24, MGM 1924–28, head of MGM camera dept 1929–56

August, Joseph Fox 1923–32, Col 1932–35, RKO 1935–41

Ballard, Lucien Par 1930, 1935, Col 1935–39, Fox 1942–44, 1951–55, Univ 1945–46, RKO 1947–48

Barnes, George Par 1919–21, Associated Exhibitors 1922–23, Metro 1924, MGM 1924–25, 1932, Goldwyn/UA 1926–31, WB 1933–38, Fox 1940–41, Univ 1942, RKO 1942–48

Bitzer, Billy Biograph 1898–1913, Reliance-Majestic/Mutual 1913–14, Fine Arts/Triangle 1915–16, Artcraft/Par 1917–19, FN 1919–20, UA 1920–25, 1927–31, Par 1926

Bredell, Woody Univ 1937–46, WB 1947–49

Brodine, Norbert Pathé/RKO 1929, MGM 1930–33, Univ 1933–36, Roach 1937–41, Fox 1943–49

Brown, Karl Par 1920–25

Burks, Robert WB 1937–44 (sp. effects), 1941–53

Clarke, Charles Fox 1928–33, 1938–61, MGM 1933–37

Cortez, Stanley Univ 1937–43, 1947–48, UA 1943–44

Daniels, William Univ 1919–23, 1947–58, MGM 1925–43

De Grasse, Robert RKO 1935–49

De Vinna, Clyde Univ 1923–24,

Goldwyn 1922, 1924–25, MGM 1924–42, Fox 1943–45

Edeson, Arthur UA 1924–25, FN 1924–27, Fox 1928–31, Univ 1931–33, WB 1934–49

Fapp, Daniel Par 1941–58

Fischbeck, Harry Par 1924–40

Folsey, George Par 1929–32, MGM 1933–59

Freund, Karl Univ 1930–33, MGM 1936–38, 1940–47, WB 1947–50

Garmes, Lee Par 1925–26, 1931–32, 1934–35, FN 1927–29, WB 1929–30, Fox 1932–34, Selznick/UA 1937–46

Gaudio, Tony WB 1929–43, Col 1945–46, Republic 1946–49

Glennon, Bert Univ 1920–21, Par 1922–28, 1932, RKO 1933, Fox 1934–36, 1939, UA 1937–38, 1947, WB 1941–46

Greene, W. Howard Selznick/UA 1936–37, Par 1940–41, Univ 1942–47

Griggs, Loyal Par 1951–62

Guffey, Burnett Col 1944–66

Haller, Ernest FN 1926–30, WB 1930–51

Harlan, Russell Par 1937–49

Hickox, Sidney FN 1927–30, WB 1930–54

Howe, James Wong Par 1922–26, Fox 1931–33, MGM 1933–36, Selznick/UA 1937, WB 1938–47

Ivano, Paul Monogram 1937–39, Univ 1943–46

June, Ray UA 1929–33, MGM 1933–53

Krasner, Milton Par 1933–34, Univ 1936–48, RKO 1945–46, 1949, Fox 1949–59, MGM 1959–66

Lang, Charles B. Par 1929–52

La Shelle, Joseph Fox 1943–54

Laszlo, Ernest Par 1944–47, UA 1948–49

Lawton, Charles, Jr. MGM 1936–43, UA 1944–45, Col 1945–62

Lindon, Lionel Par 1943–49, 1951–55

MacDonald, Joseph Fox 1941–59

MacWilliams, Glen Fox 1925–32, 1941–46

Marley, J. Peverell Par 1923–24, PDC 1926–27, Pathé 1927–29, MGM 1929–30, 20th/UA 1933–35, Fox 1934–44, WB 1945–50

Marsh, Oliver Goldwyn 1917–18, FN 1919–21, Metro 1922–23, MGM 1924–41

Maté, Rudolph Fox 1935–36, UA 1936–42, Univ 1940–41, RKO 1942, Col 1943–47

McCord, Ted FN 1924–29, Univ 1929–30, 1933–35, Col 1930, Pathé/RKO 1931–32, WB 1936–57

McGill, Barney WB 1927–33

Mellor, William Par 1934–42, UA 1946, 1948–49, Univ 1947–48, MGM 1950–54

Mescall, John Pathé/RKO 1927–30, Univ 1934–36, Fox 1938, Par 1941–42, UA 1943–45, 1950

Metty, Russell RKO 1934–44, UA 1945–46, Univ 1947–69

Miller, Arthur Pathé 1915–19, Par 1919–23, FN 1923–25, PDC 1925–27, Pathé/RKO 1928–32, Fox 1932–50

Milner, Victor Par 1925–44, RKO 1945

Mohr, Hal WB 1926–28, 1935–36, Univ 1929–30, 1939–48, Pathé/RKO 1931–32, Fox 1932–34

Musuraca, Nicholas WB 1925–26, FBO 1926–28, RKO 1928–54

Palmer, Ernest Fox 1925–50

Périnal, Georges Korda/UA 1933–40

Planck, Robert Art Cinema/UA 1929–30, 1932, Fox 1933, 1937–39, Monogram 1933–34, Univ 1935, UA 1934–36, 1938–39, MGM 1940–56

Planer, Franz Col 1938–45, 1949–50, Univ 1947–49

Polito, Sol FN 1926–30, WB 1930–47

Rennahan, Ray Par 1945–53

Rosher, Charles Par 1916–18, Pickford/FN 1919, Pickford/UA 1919–28, MGM 1930, 1934, 1942–54, RKO 1932–33, 20th/UA 1934, WB 1937–41

Rosson, Hal Par 1920–25, 1927–29, PDC 1926, Fox 1929, MGM 1930–34, 1936–53, UA 1934–36

Ruttenberg, Joseph RKO 1933, MGM 1934–63

Sartov, Hendrick Griffith/UA 1919–24, MGM 1925–28

Schneiderman, George Fox 1919–35

Seitz, John FN 1929–30, Fox 1931–36, MGM 1937–40, Par 1941–52

Shamroy, Leon Par 1933–37, UA 1936, 1938, Fox 1939–69

Sharp, Henry MGM 1926–30, Par 1932–40, 1944, WB 1942–44, Republic 1945–46, Monogram 1947, AA 1948

Stradling, Harry, Sr. RKO 1940–41, MGM 1942–49, WB 1955–64

Struss, Karl Par 1920–21, 1931–45, Art Cinema/UA 1928–30, UA 1946–48

Surtees, Robert MGM 1943–62

Tetzlaff, Ted First Division 1927–28, Col 1928–33, Par 1935–41

Toland, Gregg Goldwyn 1929–46

Tover, Leo RKO 1929–32, Par 1933–43, 1947–49

Valentine, Joseph Fox 1924–30, Univ 1936–46

Van Enger, Charles Fox 1929–30, Univ 1940–50

Walker, Joseph Col 1927–52

Wyckoff, Alvin Lasky 1914–16, Par 1916–26

ART DIRECTORS

Ames, Preston MGM 1936–70

Anderson, Roland Par 1932–69

Banks, Lionel Col 1934, 1937–44

Basevi, James MGM 1925–29, 1936, 1950–52, UA 1936–40, Fox 1941–47, Selznick 1945–46, Argosy/RKO 1948–50, WB 1953–54

Berger, Ralph Univ 1934–39, Par 1941–44, RKO 1944–51

Borg, Karl Oscar UA 1926–27

Boyle, Robert Univ 1941–43, 1947–56, 1961–64, RKO 1946–47, Col 1957–59

Brown, Hilyard Republic 1945–47, Univ 1948–54

Buckland, Wilfred Lasky 1914–16, Par 1916–20

Bumstead, Henry Par 1948–60, Univ 1961–78

Carfagno, Edward MGM 1943–70

Carré, Ben Gaumont (Fr.) 1907–11, Peerless/World Film Corp 1914–16, Par 1917–19, FN 1919–21, Pyramid/American Releasing 1922, Goldwyn 1924, MGM 1924–1926, 1939–44, WB 1926–27, Fox 1928–35

Carrere, Edward WB 1944–57, 1962–70, UA 1957–59

Cathcart, Daniel MGM 1936–58

Clark, Carroll Pathé 1930–31, RKO 1932–56, Disney 1956–68

Clatworthy, Robert Par 1938, 1947–48, Univ 1941–46, 1949–64

D'Agostino, Albert UA 1928–29, 1933, RKO 1933–34, 1940–58, Univ 1934–36, Par 1936–38

Darling, William Fox 1922–46

Davis, George Fox 1947–56, MGM 1959–70

Day, Richard Univ 1921–23, MGM 1924–29, Goldwyn/UA 1930–38, Fox 1939–47, Goldwyn/RKO 1949–51

DeCuir, John Univ 1938–49, Fox 1949–62

Douglas, Haldane Par 1941–47

Dreier, Hans UFA (Ger.) 1919–23, Par 1923–50

Duell, Randall MGM 1938–57

Fegté, Ernst Par 1925, 1933–45, Goldwyn/RKO 1944–45, Republic 1946, UA 1946–48

Ferguson, Perry RKO 1933–41, Goldwyn/RKO 1942–48

Ferrari, William MGM 1943–53, 1960–62

Fuller, Leland Fox 1943–61

Gibbons, Cedric MGM 1924–56

Gillespie, A. Arnold MGM 1924–63

Golitzen, Alexander Goldwyn/UA 1934–41, Univ 1942–1974

Goodman, John B. Par 1932–39, Univ 1940–46

Goosson, Stephen FN 1922–24, DeMille/Pathé 1927–29, UA 1929, Fox 1930, Col 1931–40, 1944–47, Goldwyn/RKO 1941, MGM 1943

Groesse, Paul MGM 1937–59

Grot, Anton Lubin 1913–16, Pathé 1916–20, UA 1922–25, DeMille/PDC 1925–28, FN 1928–30, WB 1931–48

Haas, Robert Par 1919–21, Henry King/Inspiration 1922–25, 1929–30, FN 1925–26, Fox 1927–28, WB 1929–50

Hall, Charles D. Univ 1923–37, Chaplin/UA 1925–31, 1936, Roach/UA 1938–43

Harkrider, John W. Goldwyn/UA 1930–33, Univ 1934–1937

Hartley, Esdras WB 1923–24, 1928, 1931–40

Hedrick, Earl Par 1932–57

Herman, Alfred RKO 1933–52

Herzbrun, Bernard Par 1926–37, Fox 1937–39, RKO 1939–42, UA 1942–46, Univ 1946–54

Hogsett, Albert Fox 1934–57

Hope, Frederic MGM 1926–37

Horning, William A. MGM 1934–59

Hotaling, Frank Republic 1944–54

Hughes, John J. Metro 1921–24, PDC 1926–27, FN 1925, 1929, WB 1933–49

Ihnen, Wiard Par 1919–20, 1928–34, 1936–38, FN 1923,
Pioneer/RKO 1935–36, Fox 1939–44, RKO 1945–46

Iribe, Paul Par 1921–24, DeMille/PDC 1925–26

Jenkins, George Goldwyn/RKO 1946–49

Jewell, Edward C. Pathé 1927–29, Col 1930, 1943–45, Chesterfield 1933–36, Crescent 1936–37, PRC 1945–46, Eagle-Lion 1947–49

Juran, Nathan Fox 1940–46, Enterprise/UA 1947, Univ 1948–52

Keller, Walter E. Par 1925–26, RKO 1942–54, Republic 1955–57

Kimball, Russell Republic 1942–45

Kirk, Charles M. Griffith/UA 1921–25, Par 1926, Univ 1927, Col 1928, Fox 1929–30, RKO 1933–37

Kirk, Mark-Lee Fox 1936–40, 1945–59, RKO 1940–43, UA 1944

Kuter, Leo E. Univ 1925–26, WB 1943–64

Leisen, Mitchell Par 1919–21, 1932–33, Fairbanks/UA 1922–24, PDC/Pathé 1925–28, MGM 1929–31

Leven, Boris Fox 1938–47, 1951–52, Univ 1947–48, UA 1953, WB 1954–55

Lonergan, Arthur MGM 1950–55, Par 1961–65

Lourié, Eugene Univ 1943–47

McCleary, Urie MGM 1937–68

Meehan, John Par 1935–50, Col 1951–53

Menzies, William Cameron Pathé 1917–18, Par 1919, Walsh/FN 1920–22, UA 1923–30, 1935–40, Fox 1931–33

Milton, Dave Monogram 1942–52, AA 1953–61

Obzina, Martin Univ 1939–46, Monogram 1951–52

Odell, Cary Col 1941–62

Odell, Robert A. Par 1930–40

Okey, Jack Tourneur/FN 1924, FN 1924–30, WB 1931–34, RKO 1943–53

Oliver, Harry UA 1925–27, Fox 1927–30, 1932, Hughes/UA 1930–31, Par 1933, MGM 1934, 1937, RKO 1935–37

Otterson, Jack Fox 1934–35, Univ 1936–47

Parker, Max PDC/Pathé 1925–27, WB 1928–31, 1936–47, Fox 1933–35

Pereira, Hal Par 1941–68

Peters, Hans Fox 1935–40, RKO 1943, MGM 1944–62

Peterson, Robert Col 1940–64

Pogany, William A. Goldwyn/UA 1927–31, WB 1933–34

Polglase, Van Nest Par 1919–28, MGM 1929–31, RKO 1932–42, Col 1943–46, Bogeaus/UA 1949–50, Bogeaus/RKO 1954–56

Pye, Merrill MGM 1925–68

Ransford, Maurice Fox 1940–61

Ree, Max MGM 1926, FN 1927–28, RKO 1929–31

Remisoff, Nicolai Roach/UA 1939–41, Col 1943, Stromberg/UA 1944–47, UA 1951–54

Reticker, Hugh WB 1935–50

Riedel, Richard Univ 1937–60

Rosse, Herman Univ 1930–32

Schulze, Jack FN 1921–26, Pickford/UA 1925, 1927, Fox 1929–32, Reliance/UA 1934–36, RKO 1937, Small/UA 1938–42

Scognamillo, Gabriel MGM 1934–42, 1949–53

Smith, Jack Martin MGM 1939–54, Fox 1954–73, American Film Theatre 1973–74

Smith, Ted WB 1936–49

Spencer, J. Russell Fox 1943–52

Sternad, Rudolph Fox 1936–40, Col 1940–53, Kramer 1948–63

Toluboff, Alexander MGM 1926–34, Wanger/Par 1935–36, Wanger UA 1936–39

Urban, Joseph Cosmopolitan/Par 1920–22, Cosmopolitan/Goldwyn 1923, Cosmopolitan/MGM 1924–25, Fox 1930–31

Usher, Robert Par 1933–44, UA 1946

Weyl, Carl Jules WB 1934–47

Wheeler, Lyle Selznick 1936–40, MGM 1942–44, Fox 1944–60, Preminger 1960–65

Wiley, Harrison Col 1928–30

Willis, Edwin B. Goldwyn 1919–24, MGM 1924–57

Wright, Joseph C. Metro 1923, Principal 1924, MGM 1925–26, 1934–39, Univ 1927, Col 1928, Fox 1929–33, 1939–53, 20th/UA 1933–34

COSTUME DESIGNERS

Adrian PDC/Pathé 1925–28, MGM 1928–42, Univ 1943

Anderson, Milo Goldwyn/UA 1932, WB 1933–52

Banton, Travis Par 1924–38, Selznick/UA 1938–39, Fox 1939–41, Col 1943–44, Univ 1945–48

Best, Marjorie WB 1948–60

Brymer Univ 1933–37

Cashin, Bonnie Fox 1943–49

Cassini, Oleg Fox 1942–50

Cox, David MGM 1927–30, Fox 1931–32

Dean, Kay MGM 1944–45

Dodson, Mary Kay Par 1944–51

Du Bois, Raoul Pene Par 1941–45

Greer, Howard Par 1923–27, RKO 1932–33, 1938

Harkrider, John Goldwyn/UA 1930, 1933, Univ 1934–38

Head, Edith Par 1927–67, Univ 1968–78

Herschel Fox 1936–43, MGM 1951–54

Hubert, René Par 1924–26, MGM 1927–31, Fox 1931–35, 1943–50, Korda/UA 1935–38

Irene UA 1937–41, Col 1941–42 MGM 1942–49

Jeakins, Dorothy Fox 1952–54

Kalloch, Robert Col 1932–40, MGM 1941–43

Kaufman, Rita Fox 1933–34

Keyes, Marion Herwood MGM 1944–46

Kiam, Omar UA 1934–38

King, Muriel RKO 1936, 1944

Lambert, William Fox 1933–36

Leisen, Mitchell Par 1919–21, UA 1922–24

LeMaire, Charles Fox 1943–59

Louis, Jean Col 1944–58

Luick, Earl WB 1928–33, Fox 1942–43

Mabry, Moss WB 1953–56, Fox 1963–68, Col 1965–66, 1968–73

Myron, Helen Fox 1935–40

Nelson, Kay Fox 1943–55

Newman, Bernard RKO 1934–36, WB 1946–47

Odell, Rosemary Univ 1945–67

Orry-Kelly WB 1932–45, Univ 1947–50

Palmer, Adele Republic 1938–56, Fox 1957–59

Plunkett, Walter RKO 1929–39, Selznick 1938–39, MGM 1947–65

Ree, Max FN 1927–29, RKO 1929–32

Renie RKO 1936–49, Fox 1950–54, 1957

Rhodes, Leah WB 1941–50

Rose, Helen Fox 1943, MGM 1943–67

Royer Fox 1933–39, UA 1940–42

Saltern, Irene Republic 1937–39, UA 1940–41

Sharaff, Irene MGM 1943–45, Goldwyn/RKO 1946–48

Shoup, Howard WB 1935–41, 1952–67, MGM 1942–46

Steele, Gile MGM 1938–44, Par 1946–49

Stevenson, Edward WB 1929–31, RKO 1936–49, Fox 1950–52

Taylor, Helen Wanger 1935–38

Thomas, Bill Univ 1949–60

Travilla, William Col 1941–43, WB 1946–49, Fox 1949–56

Tree, Dolly Fox 1929–32, MGM 1932–42

Valles MGM 1938–50

Visart, Natalie DeMille/Par 1934–39, 1942–44

Wachner, Sophie Goldwyn 1922–23, MGM 1924, Fox 1925–31

Wakeling, Gwen Pathé 1927–29, RKO 1930–32, 20th/UA 1933–34, Fox 1935–42, DeMille/Par 1947–49

West, Claire Par 1919–23

West, Vera Univ 1926–47

Wills, Mary Goldwyn/RKO 1949–52

Wood, Yvonne Fox 1943–45, Univ 1945–51

Woulfe, Michael RKO 1949–57

COMPOSERS AND MUSIC DIRECTORS

Amfitheatrof, Daniele MGM 1942–43, Univ 1947–48, Fox 1949

Antheil, George Republic 1946, Col 1949–50

Axt, William MGM 1925–29, 1932–39

Bakaleinikoff, Constantin RKO 1941–52

Bakaleinikoff, Mischa Col 1944–60

Bassman, George MGM 1943–47

Buttolph, David Fox 1935–47, WB 1948–51

Carbonara, Gerard Par 1936–43

Deutsch, Adolph WB 1937–46, MGM 1948–56

Dolan, Robert Emmett Par 1942–52

Duning, George Col 1945–61

Eisler, Hanns RKO 1944–47

Forbstein, Leo F. WB 1928–48

Friedhofer, Hugo Fox 1930–36,

1943–44, 1952, 1954–59, WB
1945–47

Gershenson, Joseph Univ 1950–57

Green, Johnny MGM 1942–48,
1949–58, Univ 1947, WB
1948–49

Harline, Leigh RKO 1943–50

Harling, W. Franke Par 1931–33,
WB 1936–37

Hayton, Lennie MGM 1942–53

Heindorf, Ray WB 1936–54

Herrmann, Bernard RKO 1941–42,
Fox 1944–47, 1951–56

Hollander, Frederick Par 1935–40,
Col 1941, WB 1942–47, RKO
1949–51

Kaper, Bronislau MGM 1935–62

Korngold, Erich Wolfgang WB
1935–47

Lange, Arthur Fox 1933–38,
1942–43, RKO 1944–45

Laszlo, Alexander Par 1944–45

Lava, Wiliam WB 1948–52

Lilley, Joseph J. Par 1943–57

Michelet, Michel UA 1944–50

Mockridge, Cyril J. Fox 1935–61

Newman, Alfred UA 1931–38, Fox
1938–59

Newman, Emil Fox 1941–47

Newman, Lionel Fox 1946–60

Previn, André MGM 1949–58

Previn, Charles Univ 1936–42

Raksin, David Fox 1942, 1944–49,
Col 1943, MGM 1950–52

Rapee, Erno Fox 1924–29, 1931

Roemheld, Heinz WB 1938–45, UA
1946–48, Col 1949–50

Rosen, Milton Univ 1943–47,
Fox 1948

Rozsa, Miklos Korda/UA (GB)
1938–40, (US) 1941–42, Par
1943–44, Univ 1946–48, MGM
1949–57

Salinger, Conrad MGM 1943–46,
1951–54

Salter, Hans J. Univ 1939–47,
1950–52

Schwarzwald, Milton Univ
1949–50

Shilkret, Nathaniel RKO 1936–37,
MGM 1943–46

Shuken, Leo Par 1937–44

Silvers, Louis WB 1927–30, MGM
1933, Col 1934–35, Fox 1936–40

Skiles, Marlin Col 1944–48

Skinner, Frank Univ 1938–66

Snell, David MGM 1937–48

Steiner, Max RKO 1930–35,
Selznick, UA 1936, WB 1936–65

Stoll, George MGM 1937–66

Stoloff, Morris Col 1936–53

Stothart, Herbert MGM 1933–50

Tiomkin, Dimitri MGM 1935, Col
1937–39, UA 1940–44, 1948–50,
Selznick 1947–48

Ward, Edward MGM 1935–40, UA
1940–43, Univ 1943–45

Waxman, Franz Univ 1935–36,
MGM 1936–42, WB 1943–47

Webb, Roy RKO 1933–52

Young, Victor Par 1936–37,
1940–49

EDITORS

Akst, Albert Univ 1935, MGM
1941–56

Allen, Fred FN 1928–29, Univ
1929–30, Fox 1935–43, Republic
& Eagle-Lion (alternating)
1944–49

Amy, George FN 1925–29, WB
1930–47, RKO 1950–53

Arzner, Dorothy Par 1921–26

Bauchens, Anne (De Mille) Par
1918–25, 1932–56, PDC/Pathé
1925–28, MGM 1929–31

Beetley, Samuel RKO 1946–52, Fox
1962–67

Bennett, Hugh FN 1926–29,
Goldwyn/UA 1931–32, Par
1933–41

Berman, Henry RKO 1936–41,
MGM 1962–70

Bischoff, Robert Fox 1933–35,
1939–42, Par 1936–38

Blangsted, Folmar Par 1929–35, WB
1944–64

Boemler, George MGM 1927–56, Fox 1961–62

Booth, Margaret FN 1924–25, MGM 1926–68 (supervising ed. 1939–68)

Bracht, Frank Par 1948–70

Bretherton, David Fox 1955–62

Bryant, Edwin Col 1951–63

Burton, Bernard Univ 1933–41

Cahn, Philip Univ 1933–46

Caldwell, Dwight Majestic 1933–35, Col 1936–41

Carruth, Milton Univ 1929–66

Clancey, Margaret Fox 1927–35, UA 1935–38

Clark, Al Col 1934–62

Clark, James B. Fox 1938–61

Colbert, Norman Fox 1938–46, Eagle-Lion 1947–50

Crone, George Sono-Art 1929–30, RKO 1934–43

Crosland, Alan, Jr. WB 1944–52, UA 1954–55

Curtiss, Edward Univ 1933–34, 1938–60

Curtiss, Ray Univ 1925–29, 1934, FN 1929, WB 1930–33, Par 1936–37, Fox 1943–44

Dawson, Ralph WB 1927–45, 1953–54, RKO 1945–46, Univ 1947–50

De Gaetano, Al Fox 1929–40, Eagle-Lion (supervising ed.) 1940s

De Maggio, Nick Fox 1935–53

Dietrich, Ralph Fox 1928–36

Dmytryk, Edward Par 1930–39

Douglas, Everett Par 1935–59

Dunning, John MGM 1947–60

Fantl, Dick Col 1936–50

Fazan, Adrienne MGM 1937–64

Fehr, Rudi WB 1937–55

Fowler, Hugh Fox 1952–62

Fritch, Robert Fox 1943–52

Gerstad, Harry RKO 1946–47, Kramer 1949–53

Gibbons, James WB 1930–43

Gilmore, Stuart Par 1937–45, RKO 1950–56, Fox 1957–59

Goodkind, Saul Univ 1940–47, Fox 1948

Gray, William MGM 1929–37

Gross, Frank Univ 1936–55

Gross, Roland RKO 1942–55, WB 1957–58

Hamilton, William FN 1923–26, MGM 1927–29, RKO 1931–41

Harrison, Doane FBO 1925–26, Pathé 1928–30, Par 1935–53, (supervising ed.) 1950s, Wilder/UA (supervising ed.) 1961–66

Havlick, Gene Univ 1928–29, Col 1929–57

Heisler, Stuart Goldwyn/UA 1924–25, 1929–34, FN 1927–29, Par 1935–36

Held, Tom MGM 1928–38

Hilton, Arthur Col 1933–36, RKO 1937–39, Univ 1940–47

Hively, George MGM 1926–32, 1943–45, RKO 1933–41

Hoagland, Ellsworth Par 1933–55

Holmes, William WB 1930–41

Hornbeck, William Sennett 1926–34, Korda/UA (GB) 1934–41, Capra 1943–47, Par 1949–53, Univ (supervising ed.) 1960s

Hull, Frank MGM 1924–26, 1933–49, Fox 1929–33

Johnson, Stanley Par 1951–52, 1960–63, Disney 1956–60

Jones, Harmon Fox 1944–50

Kent, Ted Univ 1933–67

Kern, Hal MGM 1933–34, Selznick/UA 1935–47, Par 1961–63

Kern, Robert Mayer/Metro/MGM 1923–25, Tiffany-Stahl 1928, UA 1929–30, MGM 1934–52

Killifer, Jack WB 1928–43

Knudtson, Frederic RKO 1933–55, Kramer/UA 1957–63

Kolster, Clarence WB 1922–27, 1933–58, Tiffany 1929–30, Univ 1931–32

Komer, Harry MGM 1938–56

Kress, Harold MGM 1939–63
Landres, Paul Univ 1937–47
Lawrence, Viola Univ 1919–20, UA 1927–30, Col 1931–60
Lewis, Ben MGM 1924–67
Loeffler, Louis Fox 1927–61
Lovering, Otho Par 1928–36, Wanger/UA 1937–40, UA 1945–46, Monogram/AA (supervising ed.) 1947–50, Ford/McLaglen 1962–66
Low, Warren WB 1932–44, Par (supervising ed.) 1946–70
Ludwig, Otto Univ 1939–50, RKO 1952–54
Lyon, William Col 1936–66
Macrorie, Alma Par 1937–62, Univ 1963–66
Mandell, Daniel Univ 1924–29, 1933–35, RKO 1930–32, Goldwyn/UA 1936–40, Goldwyn/RKO 1941–52, Wilder/UA 1957–66
Marker, Harry Univ 1927–35, RKO 1937–63
Marks, Owen WB 1928–60
Marquette, Desmond RKO 1935–50
Marshek, Archie FBO 1927–28, RKO 1929–36, Par 1937–67
McLean, Barbara UA 1929–30, 20th/UA 1933–35, Fox 1935–54
McNeil, Allen UA 1927–35, Fox 1935–43
McSweeney, John MGM 1952–68
Meyer, Otto Col 1933–45
Milford, Gene Chadwick/First Division 1927–28, Col 1929–40, RKO 1943–45
Morley, James PDC 1926, Pathé 1927–28, WB 1932–33, RKO 1934–36, Fox 1938
Morra, Irene Coogan/FN 1921–23, Coogan/MGM 1924, Fox 1928–38, WB 1943–54
Morse, Terrell WB 1928–31, 1934–43, Fox 1951–53
Murray, Jack Fox 1929–38, Ford/Argosy 1947–52, Ford 1953–61

Nelson, Charles Col 1942–67
Nervig, Conrad MGM 1926–54
Newcom, James MGM 1933–36, 1949–52, UA 1937–47
Nosler, Lloyd Mayer/Metro 1923–24, MGM 1924–26, Inspiration/UA 1929–30, 20th/UA 1933–35, Fox 1935–37
Nyby, Christian WB 1943–48, RKO 1950–52
O'Steen, Sam WB 1955–67
Pratt, Thomas WB 1928–43
Reynolds, William Par 1936–40, Fox 1947–60, 1965–70
Richards, Frederick WB 1937–49
Richards, Thomas WB 1933–42
Robson, Mark RKO 1941–43
Ruggiero, Gene MGM 1946–61
Santillo, Frank MGM 1956–66
Schmidt, Arthur RKO 1934–36, Par 1936–54, Lewis/Par 1961–65
Schoengarth, Russell Grand National 1936, Monogram 1937–40, Univ 1942–68
Schuster, Harold Fox 1929–35
Sewell, Blanche MGM 1925–49
Shea, William Par 1928–47
Simpson, Robert Fox 1937–69
Smith, Frederick MGM 1936–43
Smith, Howard Par 1944–62
Smith, James Griffith 1921–30, Par 1935–41, UA 1944–47
Spencer, Dorothy Wanger/Par 1936, Wanger/UA 1937–41, Fox 1943–63
Steinkamp, Fredric MGM 1959–67
Stell, Aaron Col 1943–54, Univ 1961–62, Pakula-Mulligan 1962–65
Stone, LeRoy FN 1924–25, 1928–29, WB 1930–31, Par 1935–49
Sullivan, Frank MGM 1925–47, UA 1949–50
Sweeney, James Col 1936–50
Swink, Robert RKO 1944–51, Par 1951–55
Thompson, Walter Fox 1937–43
Thoms, Jerome Col 1943–62

Todd, Sherman UA 1934–40, RKO 1947–52, Univ 1956–58

Tomasini, George Par 1947–58, Hitchcock 1957–64

Troffey, Alex Fox 1928–40

Vernon, Elmo MGM 1937–43

Warburton, Irvine MGM 1943–53, Disney 1956–72

Warren, Eda Par 1927–58

Weatherwax, Paul FN 1928, Fox 1929–30, RKO 1933–34, Par 1935–44

Webster, Ferris MGM 1939–59, UA 1960–65

Weisbart, David WB 1943–51

White, George MGM 1943–53

White, Merrill Par 1928–32, Wilcox (GB) 1934–40, RKO 1947–49, Fox 1951–53

Whytock, Grant Metro 1921–23, MGM 1924–30, UA 1931–41, 1961–70

Williams, Elmo Wilcox (GB) 1934–41, RKO 1946–49

Winters, Ralph MGM 1941–63, U 1964–70

Wise, Robert RKO 1934–43

Wrangell, Basil MGM 1925–33, 1935–37, RKO 1933–34

Wright, Maurice Col 1929–33, 20th/UA 1933–34, Univ 1934–4

Wynn, Hugh MGM 1924–35

Ziegler, William Roach 1935–40, Par 1941–43, Selznick/UA 1944–46, WB 1951–67

Box-Office Hits 1914–1990

The rental figure is the most readily available and reliable indicator of the box-office success of each film and the sum which can be set against the costs of production, distribution, advertising, etc, to determine whether the film was profitable or not. It reflects the size of the audience for each picture and adds up to about half the total box-office gross, with the other half going to the exhibitors. The standard figures, as shown here, are for North America only. Worldwide figures are not generally available for all pictures.

1914–1931
NORTH AMERICAN RENTALS
IN EXCESS OF $1.0 MILLION

	$MILLIONS
The Birth Of A Nation (1915, Epoch)	10.0
The Singing Fool (1928, WB)	5.0
The Four Horsemen Of The Apocalypse (1921, Metro)	4.5
Ben-Hur (1925, MGM)	4.0
The Covered Wagon (1923, Par)	3.5
The Big Parade (1925, MGM)	3.5
The Jazz Singer (1927, WB)	3.5
Sunny Side Up (1929, Fox)	3.3
The Broadway Melody (1929, MGM)	3.0
The Cock-Eyed World (1929, Fox)	2.7
Whoopee! (1930, Goldwyn/UA)	2.7
The Freshman (1925, Lloyd/Pathé)	2.6
The Kid (1921, Chaplin/FN)	2.5
The Ten Commandments (1923, Par)	2.5
The Gold Rush (1925, Chaplin/UA)	2.5
Gold Diggers Of Broadway (1929, WB)	2.3
Way Down East (1920, Griffith/UA)	2.0
The Sea Hawk (1924, FN)	2.0
What Price Glory? (1926, Fox)	2.0
Rio Rita (1929, RKO)	2.0
Min And Bill (1930, MGM)	2.0
Seventh Heaven (1927, Fox)	1.8
Street Angel (1928, Fox)	1.7
Common Clay (1930, Fox)	1.7
Girl Shy (1924, Lloyd/Pathé)	1.6
Palmy Days (1931, Goldwyn/UA)	1.6
The Sheik (1921, Par)	1.5

The Hunchback Of Notre Dame (1923, Univ)	1.5
Safety Last (1923, Lloyd/Pathé)	1.5
Secrets (1924, FN)	1.5
The Thief Of Bagdad (1924, Fairbanks/UA)	1.5
The Merry Widow (1925, MGM)	1.5
Beau Geste (1926, Par)	1.5
Stella Dallas (1926, Goldwyn/UA)	1.5
The King Of Kings (1927, DeMille/PDC)	1.5
Four Sons (1928, Fox)	1.5
All Quiet On The Western Front (1930, Univ)	1.5
Anna Christie (1930, MGM)	1.5
The Champ (1931, MGM)	1.5
City Lights (1931, Chaplin/UA)	1.5
Daddy Long Legs (1931, Fox)	1.5
Hot Water (1924, Lloyd/Pathé)	1.4
The Man Who Came Back (1931, Fox)	1.4
Daddy Long Legs (1919, Pickford/FN)	1.3
Blood And Sand (1922, Par)	1.3
The Lost World (1925, FN)	1.3
The Red Dance (1928, Fox)	1.3
In Old Arizona (1929, Fox)	1.3
Syncopation (1929, RKO)	1.3
Arrowsmith (1931, Goldwyn/UA)	1.3
A Connecticut Yankee (1931, Fox)	1.3
Dr Jekyll And Mr Hyde (1931, Par)	1.3
Merely Mary Ann (1931, Fox)	1.3
The Patent Leather Kid (1927, FN)	1.2
Song Of My Heart (1930, Fox)	1.2
Grandma's Boy (1922, Lloyd/Pathé)	1.1
East Lynne (1925, Fox)	1.1
Bad Girl (1931, Fox)	1.1
The Spoilers (1914, Selig)	1.0
Madame Dubarry (aka Passion) (1919, Union-UFA (Ger.))	1.0
The Miracle Man (1919, Par)	1.0
Robin Hood (1922, Fairbanks/UA)	1.0
Smilin' Through (1922, Talmadge/FN)	1.0
The Hollywood Revue of 1929 (1929, MGM)	1.0
Check And Double Check (1930, RKO)	1.0
Trader Horn (1930, MGM)	1.0
Cimarron (1931, RKO)	1.0

1932–1940
NORTH AMERICAN RENTALS
IN EXCESS OF $1.5 MILLION

	$MILLIONS
Gone With The Wind (1939, Selznick/MGM)	31.0
Snow White And The Seven Dwarfs (1937, Disney/RKO)	8.0
San Francisco (1936, MGM)	2.7
The Kid From Spain (1932, Goldwyn/UA)	2.6

Roman Scandals (1933, Goldwyn/UA)	2.4
Grand Hotel (1932, MGM)	2.3
42nd Street (1933, WB)	2.3
I'm No Angel (1933, Par)	2.3
Little Women (1933, RKO)	2.3
She Done Him Wrong (1933, Par)	2.2
Emma (1932, MGM)	2.0
Mutiny On The Bounty (1935, MGM)	2.0
The Great Ziegfeld (1936, MGM)	2.0
Saratoga (1937, MGM)	2.0
Footlight Parade (1933, WB)	1.8
State Fair (1933, Fox)	1.8
Modern Times (1936, Chaplin/UA)	1.8
The Crusades (1935, DeMille/Par)	1.7
Strike Me Pink (1936, Goldwyn/UA)	1.7
Dodsworth (1936, Goldwyn/UA)	1.6
The Trail Of The Lonesome Pine (1936, Wanger/Par)	1.6
Tarzan The Ape Man (1932, MGM)	1.5
Calvalcade (1933, Fox)	1.5
Dancing Lady (1933, MGM)	1.5
Queen Christina (1933, MGM)	1.5
Tugboat Annie (1933, MGM)	1.5
China Seas (1935, MGM)	1.5
David Copperfield (1935, MGM)	1.5
A Midsummer Night's Dream (1935, WB)	1.5
Top Hat (1935, RKO)	1.5
Camille (1936, MGM)	1.5
Libeled Lady (1936, MGM)	1.5
Dead End (1937, Goldwyn/UA)	1.5
The Good Earth (1937, MGM)	1.5
The Hurricane (1937, Goldwyn/UA)	1.5
The Life Of Emile Zola (1937, WB)	1.5
Lost Horizon (1937, Col)	1.5
Stella Dallas (1937, Goldwyn/UA)	1.5
Wells Fargo (1937, Par)	1.5
The Adventures Of Robin Hood (1938, WB)	1.5
Alexander's Ragtime Band (1938, Fox)	1.5
Boys' Town (1938, MGM)	1.5
The Goldwyn Follies (1938, Goldwyn/UA)	1.5
Happy Landing (1938, Fox)	1.5
In Old Chicago (1938, Fox)	1.5
Kentucky (1938, Fox)	1.5
Sweethearts (1938, MGM)	1.5
Test Pilot (1938, MGM)	1.5
You Can't Take It With You (1938, Col)	1.5
Babes In Arms (1939, MGM)	1.5
Drums Along The Mohawk (1939, Fox)	1.5
The Hunchback Of Notre Dame (1939, RKO)	1.5
Jesse James (1939, Fox)	1.5

Mr Smith Goes To Washington (1939, Col)	1.5
The Old Maid (1939, WB)	1.5
The Rains Came (1939, Fox)	1.5
The Wizard Of Oz (1939, MGM)	1.5
Arizona (1940, Col)	1.5
Buck Benny Rides Again (1940, Par)	1.5
The Fighting 69th (1940, WB)	1.5
Kitty Foyle (1940, RKO)	1.5
North West Mounted Police (1940, DeMille/Par)	1.5
Northwest Passage (1940, MGM)	1.5
Rebecca (1940, Selznick/UA)	1.5
Santa Fe Trail (1940, WB)	1.5
Strange Cargo (1940, MGM)	1.5
Strike Up The Band (1940, MGM)	1.5

1941–1950

NORTH AMERICAN RENTALS
IN EXCESS OF $4.0 MILLION

	$MILLIONS
The Best Years Of Our Lives (1946, Goldwyn/RKO)	10.4
Duel In The Sun (1946, Selznick)	10.0
Samson And Delilah (1949, Par)	9.0
This Is The Army (1943, WB)	8.5
The Bells Of St Mary's (1945, RKO)	8.5
The Jolson Story (1946, Col)	7.6
Going My Way (1944, Par)	6.5
For Whom The Bell Tolls (1943, Par)	6.3
Sergeant York (1941, WB)	6.1
Welcome Stranger (1947, Par)	6.1
Blue Skies (1946, Par)	5.7
Leave Her To Heaven (1945, Fox)	5.5
The Egg And I (1947, Univ)	5.5
Unconquered (1947, Par)	5.3
Meet Me In St Louis (1944, MGM)	5.2
The Yearling (1946, MGM)	5.2
The Outlaw (1946, UA)	5.1
Life With Father (1947, WB)	5.1
Mrs Miniver (1942, MGM)	5.0
The Song Of Bernadette (1943, Fox)	5.0
The Razor's Edge (1946, Fox)	5.0
Forever Amber (1947, Fox)	5.0
Green Dolphin Street (1947, MGM)	5.0
The Red Shoes (1948, Rank/Eagle-Lion)	5.0
Jolson Sings Again (1949, Col)	5.0
Since You Went Away (1944, Selznick/UA)	4.9
Spellbound (1945, Selznick/UA)	4.9
Yankee Doodle Dandy (1942, WB)	4.8
Notorious (1946, RKO)	4.8
King Solomon's Mines (1950, MGM)	4.8
Annie Get Your Gun (1950, MGM)	4.7

Battleground (1950, MGM)	4.7
The Green Years (1946, MGM)	4.6
Random Harvest (1942, MGM)	4.5
Anchors Aweigh (1945, MGM)	4.5
Road To Utopia (1945, Par)	4.5
Thrill Of A Romance (1945, MGM)	4.5
The Valley Of Decision (1945, MGM)	4.5
Easy To Wed (1946, MGM)	4.5
Till The Clouds Roll By (1946, MGM)	4.5
The Bachelor And The Bobby-Soxer (1947, RKO)	4.5
Road To Rio (1947, Par)	4.5
Easter Parade (1948, MGM)	4.5
The Paleface (1948, Par)	4.5
Stage Door Canteen (1943, UA)	4.4
The Harvey Girls (1945, MGM)	4.4
Two Years Before The Mast (1946, Par)	4.4
The Hucksters (1947, MGM)	4.4
Cheaper By The Dozen (1950, Fox)	4.4
Adventure (1945, MGM)	4.3
The Lost Weekend (1945, Par)	4.3
Saratoga Trunk (1945, WB)	4.3
Cinderella (1949, Disney/RKO)	4.3
Hollywood Canteen (1944, WB)	4.2
Thirty Seconds Over Tokyo (1944, MGM)	4.2
Weekend At The Waldorf (1945, MGM)	4.2
The Three Musketeers (1948, MGM)	4.2
Father Of The Bride (1950, MGM)	4.2
A Guy Named Joe (1944, MGM)	4.1
National Velvet (1945, MGM)	4.1
State Fair (1945, Fox)	4.1
Margie (1946, Fox)	4.1
Mother Wore Tights (1947, Fox)	4.1
Cass Timberlane (1948, MGM)	4.1
Homecoming (1948, MGM)	4.1
Joan Of Arc (1948, RKO)	4.1
Johnny Belinda (1948, WB)	4.1
I Was A Male Bride (1949, Fox)	4.1
The Snake Pit (1949, Fox)	4.1
Born Yesterday (1950, Col)	4.1
Reap The Wild Wind (1942, Par)	4.0
The Dolly Sisters (1945, Fox)	4.0
Holiday In Mexico (1946, MGM)	4.0
The Kid From Brooklyn (1946, Goldwyn/RKO)	4.0
Night And Day (1946, WB)	4.0
The Postman Always Rings Twice (1946, MGM)	4.0
Smoky (1946, Fox)	4.0
Ziegfeld Follies (1946, MGM)	4.0
The Emperor Waltz (1948, Par)	4.0
Red River (1948, Fox/UA)	4.0

Sands Of Iwo Jima (1949, Republic)	4.0
The Stratton Story (1949, MGM)	4.0

1951–1960
NORTH AMERICAN RENTALS
IN EXCESS OF $5.1 MILLION

	$MILLIONS
Ben-Hur (1959, MGM)	36.7
The Ten Commandments (1956, DeMille/Par)	34.2
Around The World In 80 Days (1956, Todd/UA)	22.0
The Robe (1953, Fox)	17.5
South Pacific (1958, Magna/Fox)	16.3
The Bridge On The River Kwai (1957, Spiegel/Col)	15.0
Spartacus (1960, Univ)	14.0
The Greatest Show On Earth (1952, DeMille/Par)	12.8
This Is Cinerama (1952, Cinerama)	12.5
From Here To Eternity (1953, Col)	12.2
White Christmas (1954, Par)	12.0
Giant (1956, WB)	12.0
Peyton Place (1957, Fox)	11.0
Quo Vadis? (1951, MGM)	10.5
Sayonara (1958, WB)	10.5
Cinerama Holiday (1955, Cinerama)	10.0
The Seven Wonders Of The World (1956, Cinerama)	9.3
Operation Petticoat (1960, Univ)	9.3
Auntie Mame (1958, WB)	9.1
Psycho (1960, Par)	9.1
The Caine Mutiny (1954, Kramer/Col)	8.7
Mr Roberts (1955, WB)	8.5
The King And I (1956, Fox)	8.5
Exodus (1960, UA)	8.5
Battle Cry (1955, WB)	8.1
The Shaggy Dog (1959, Buena Vista)	8.1
Shane (1953, Par)	8.0
20,000 Leagues Under The Sea (1954, Buena Vista)	8.0
The Alamo (1960, UA)	7.9
Swiss Family Robinson (1960, Buena Vista)	7.9
Cat On A Hot Tin Roof (1958, MGM)	7.8
The Glenn Miller Story (1954, Univ)	7.6
No Time For Sergeants (1958, WB)	7.5
Pillow Talk (1959, Univ)	7.5
How To Marry A Millionaire (1953, Fox)	7.3
Trapeze (1956, UA)	7.3
Oklahoma (1955, Magna)	7.1
Guys And Dolls (1955, Goldwyn/MGM)	6.9
Gigi (1957, MGM)	6.7
The Apartment (1960, UA)	6.7
The Snows Of Kilimanjaro (1952, Fox)	6.5
The Country Girl (1955, Par)	6.5

The Lady And The Tramp (1955, Buena Vista)	6.5
Search For Paradise (1957, Cinerama)	6.5
Imitation Of Life (1959, Univ)	6.5
Suddenly Last Summer (1960, Col)	6.4
Picnic (1955, Col)	6.3
War And Peace (1956, Par)	6.3
Not As A Stranger (1955, Kramer/UA)	6.2
The High And The Mighty (1954, WB)	6.1
A Star Is Born (1954, WB)	6.1
Hans Christian Andersen (1952, Goldwyn/RKO)	6.0
Ivanhoe (1952, MGM)	6.0
Peter Pan (1953, Disney/RKO)	6.0
The Sea Chase (1955, WB)	6.0
The Seven Year Itch (1955, Fox)	6.0
Strategic Air Command (1955, Par)	6.0
To Hell And Back (1955, Univ)	6.0
I'll Cry Tomorrow (1956, MGM)	6.0
Raintree County (1958, MGM)	6.0
The Vikings (1958, UA)	6.0
North By Northwest (1959, MGM)	6.0
Butterfield 8 (1960, MGM)	6.0
Old Yeller (1957, Buena Vista)	5.9
High Society (1956, MGM)	5.8
Rio Bravo (1959, WB)	5.8
The Nun's Story (1959, WB)	5.8
The Teahouse Of The August Moon (1957, MGM)	5.7
Seven Brides For Seven Brothers (1954, MGM)	5.6
Anatomy Of A Murder (1959, Col)	5.5
Ocean's Eleven (1960, WB)	5.5
Rear Window (1954, Par)	5.3
The Eddy Duchin Story (1955, Col)	5.3
Please Don't Eat The Daisies (1959, MGM)	5.3
Sleeping Beauty (1959, Buena Vista)	5.3
Showboat (1951, MGM)	5.2
Magnificent Obsession (1954, Univ)	5.2
The Blackboard Jungle (1955, MGM)	5.2
Solomon And Sheba (1959, UA)	5.2
From The Terrace (1960, Fox)	5.2
Gentlemen Prefer Blondes (1953, Fox)	5.1
Friendly Persuasion (1956, AA)	5.1
The Tall Men (1955, Fox)	5.0

1961–1970
NORTH AMERICAN RENTALS
IN EXCESS OF $8.6 MILLION

	$MILLIONS
The Sound Of Music (1965, Fox)	72.0
Love Story (1970, Par)	50.0
Airport (1970, Univ)	44.5
The Graduate (1967, Embassy)	43.1

Dr Zhivago (1965, MGM)	43.0
Mary Poppins (1964, Buena Vista)	31.0
M*A*S*H (1970, Fox)	30.0
Butch Cassidy And The Sundance Kid (1969, Fox)	29.2
Thunderball (1965, UA)	27.0
Patton (1970, Fox)	27.0
Cleopatra (1963, Fox)	26.0
Guess Who's Coming To Dinner? (1968, Col)	25.5
Funny Girl (1968, Col)	24.9
Goldfinger (1964, UA)	22.5
Bonnie And Clyde (1967, WB)	22.0
2001: A Space Odyssey (1968, MGM)	21.5
The Love Bug (1969, Buena Vista)	21.0
It's A Mad, Mad, Mad, Mad World (1963, UA)	20.8
The Dirty Dozen (1967, MGM)	20.1
Valley Of The Dolls (1967, Fox)	20.0
The Odd Couple (1968, Par)	20.0
West Side Story (1961, UA)	19.5
To Sir, With Love (1967, Col)	19.1
Bullitt (1968, WB)	19.0
You Only Live Twice (1967, UA)	18.0
The Longest Day (1962, Zanuck/Fox)	17.6
Tom Jones (1963, UA)	17.2
Easy Rider (1969, Col)	16.9
Oliver! (1968, Col)	16.8
Lawrence Of Arabia (1962, Col)	16.7
Midnight Cowboy (1969, UA)	16.3
Hawaii (1966, UA)	15.6
The Carpetbaggers (1964, Par)	15.5
The Bible – In The Beginning (1966, Fox)	15.0
Planet Of The Apes (1968, Fox)	15.0
Rosemary's Baby (1968, Par)	15.0
Hello, Dolly! (1970, Fox)	15.0
Little Big Man (1970, National General)	15.0
Thoroughly Modern Millie (1967, Univ)	14.7
Bob & Carol & Ted & Alice (1969, Col)	14.6
Who's Afraid Of Virginia Woolf? (1966, WB)	14.5
Romeo And Juliet (1968, Par)	14.5
Paint Your Wagon (1969, Par)	14.5
Woodstock (1970, WB)	14.5
True Grit (1969, Par)	14.3
Tora! Tora! Tora! (1970, Fox)	13.7
The Sand Pebbles (1967, Fox)	13.5
Ryan's Daughter (1970, MGM)	13.4
The Guns Of Navarone (1961, Col)	13.0
The Jungle Book (1967, Buena Vista)	13.0
A Man For All Seasons (1966, Col)	12.8
One Hundred And One Dalmatians (1961, Buena Vista)	12.5
Camelot (1967, WB)	12.3

Catch-22 (1970, Par)	12.3
How The West Was Won (1962, MGM)	12.2
Irma La Douce (1963, UA)	12.1
El Cid (1961, Bronston/AA)	12.0
My Fair Lady (1964, WB)	12.0
Cactus Flower (1969, Col)	11.9
Yours, Mine And Ours (1968, UA)	11.5
The Owl And The Pussycat (1970, Col)	11.5
The Parent Trap (1961, Buena Vista)	11.3
The Absent-Minded Professor (1961, Buena Vista)	11.1
The Great Race (1965, WB)	11.0
In The Heat Of The Night (1967, UA)	10.9
Goodbye Columbus (1969, Par)	10.5
Casino Royale (1967, Col)	10.2
Mutiny On The Bounty (1962, MGM)	9.8
The Russians Are Coming, The Russians Are Coming (1966, UA)	9.8
The Green Berets (1968, WB)	9.7
That Darn Cat (1965, Buena Vista)	9.5
Joe (1970, Cannon)	9.5
Cat Ballou (1965, Col)	9.3
Grand Prix (1967, MGM)	9.3
From Russia With Love (1964, UA)	9.2
Son Of Flubber (1963, Buena Vista)	9.1
Barefoot In The Park (1967, Par)	9.0
The Lion In Winter (1968, Embassy)	9.0
On Her Majesty's Secret Service (1969, UA)	9.0
Five Easy Pieces (1970, Col)	8.9
The Professionals (1966, Col)	8.8
The Fox (1968, WB)	8.6
Beneath The Planet Of The Apes (1970, Fox)	8.6

1971–1980
NORTH AMERICAN RENTALS

IN EXCESS OF $22.5 MILLION	$MILLIONS
Star Wars (1977, Fox)	185.1
The Empire Strikes Back (1980, Lucas/Fox)	134.2
Jaws (1975, Univ)	133.4
Grease (1978, Par)	96.3
The Exorcist (1973, WB)	88.5
The Godfather (1972, Par)	86.3
Superman – The Movie (1978, co-prod. Salkind/WB)	82.5
The Sting (1973, Univ)	79.0
Close Encounters Of The Third Kind (1977, Col)	77.0
Saturday Night Fever (1977, Par)	74.1
National Lampoon's Animal House (1978, Univ)	74.0
Kramer vs Kramer (1979, Col)	61.7
Smokey And The Bandit (1977, Univ)	61.1
One Flew Over The Cuckoo's Nest (1975, Fantasy/UA)	59.2

Stir Crazy (1980, Col)	58.4
Nine To Five (1980, Fox)	57.9
Star Trek (1979, Par)	56.0
American Graffiti (1973, Univ)	55.9
Rocky (1976, Chartoff-Winkler/UA)	55.9
Jaws II (1978, Univ)	55.6
Every Which Way But Loose (1978, WB)	51.8
Towering Inferno (1975, co-prod. Fox/WB)	50.0
Heaven Can Wait (1978, Par)	49.4
Blazing Saddles (1974, WB)	45.2
The Jerk (1979, Univ)	43.0
Rocky II (1979, Chartoff-Winkler/UA)	43.0
The Poseidon Adventure (1972, Fox)	42.0
The Goodbye Girl (1977, co-prod. WB/MGM)	41.7
Airplane! (1980, Par)	40.6
Fiddler On The Roof (1971, Mirisch/UA)	40.5
Alien (1979, Fox)	39.8
Any Which Way You Can (1980, WB)	39.5
Young Frankenstein (1975, Fox)	38.8
Coal Miner's Daughter (1980, Univ)	38.5
Smokey And The Bandit II (1980, Univ)	37.6
Apocalypse Now (1979, Omni-Zoetrope/UA)	37.3
A Star Is Born (1976, WB)	37.1
King Kong (1976, De Laurentiis/Par)	36.9
Earthquake (1974, Univ)	36.3
'10' (1978, Orion/WB)	36.0
The Amityville Horror (1979, AIP)	35.0
Hooper (1978, WB)	34.9
Private Benjamin (1980, WB)	34.0
Moonraker (1979, Eon/UA)	33.9
Billy Jack (1971, WB)	32.5
The Blues Brothers (1980, Univ)	32.2
The Muppet Movie (1979, ITC/AFD)	32.0
Oh, God! (1977, WB)	31.4
The Deep (1977, Col)	31.3
The Electric Horseman (1979, Col)	31.1
The Shining (1980, WB)	30.8
The Godfather, Part II (1974, Par)	30.7
The Deer Hunter (1978, co-prod. EMI/Univ)	30.4
All The President's Men (1976, WB)	30.0
Silver Streak (1976, Fox)	30.0
California Suite (1978, Col)	29.2
The Omen (1976, Fox)	28.5
The Blue Lagoon (1980, Col)	28.5
Up In Smoke (1978, Par)	28.3
What's Up Doc? (1972, WB)	28.0
Foul Play (1978, Par)	27.5
The French Connection (1971, Fox)	26.3
The Main Event (1979, WB)	26.3

The China Syndrome (1979, Col)	26.1
Airport 1975 (1974, Univ)	25.8
• The Return Of The Pink Panther	
(1975, Jewel/Pimlico/Mirisch/Geoffrey/UA)	25.4
The Black Hole (1979, Buena Vista)	25.4
The Way We Were (1973, Col)	25.0
✓ The Revenge Of The Pink Panther (1978, Jewel/UA)	25.0
The Bad News Bears (1976, Par)	24.9
Popeye (1980, co-prod. Par/Disney)	24.6
✓ The Spy Who Loved Me (1977, Eon/UA)	24.3
The Trial Of Billy Jack (1974, WB)	24.0
The Enforcer (1976, WB)	24.0
In Search Of Noah's Ark (1977, Sunn)	23.8
Urban Cowboy (1980, Par)	23.8
1941 (1979, co-prod. Col/Univ)	23.4
Ordinary People (1980, Par)	23.1
The Longest Yard (1974, Par)	23.0
Semi-Tough (1977, Merrick/UA)	22.8
The Rose (1979, Fox)	22.6
Deliverance (1972, WB)	22.5
Papillon (1973, AA)	22.5
Dog Day Afternoon (1975, WB)	22.5

1981–1990
NORTH AMERICAN RENTALS

IN EXCESS OF $34 MILLION	$MILLIONS
✓ E.T. The Extra-Terrestrial (1982, Univ)	228.4
Return Of The Jedi (1983, Lucas/Fox)	168.0
Batman (1989, Guber-Peters/WB)	150.5
Ghostbusters (1984, Col)	132.7
✓ Raiders Of The Lost Ark (1981, Lucas/Par)	115.6
✓ Indiana Jones And The Last Crusade (1989, Lucas/Par)	115.5
✓ Indiana Jones And The Temple Of Doom (1984, Lucas/Par)	109.0
Beverly Hills Cop (1984, Par)	108.0
Back To The Future (1985, Univ)	105.5
Home Alone (1990, JHughes/Fox)	100.0
✓ Tootsie (1982, Col)	94.9
Ghost (1990, Par)	94.0
✓ Rain Man (1988, Guber-Peters/UA)	86.8
✓ Pretty Woman (1990, Buena Vista)	81.9
✓ Three Men And A Baby (1987, Buena Vista)	81.4
✓ Who Framed Roger Rabbit (1988, Buena Vista)	81.2
Beverly Hills Cop II (1987, Par)	80.9
✓ Gremlins (1984, WB)	79.5
Lethal Weapon 2 (1989, WB)	79.5
Top Gun (1986, Par)	79.4
✓ Rambo: First Blood Part II (1985, Tri-Star)	78.9

Rocky IV (1985, UA)	76.0
Back To The Future Part II (1989, Univ)	72.3
Honey, I Shrunk The Kids (1989, Buena Vista)	72.0
Crocodile Dundee (1986, Par)	70.2
Fatal Attraction (1987, Jaffe-Lansing/Par)	70.0
Platoon (1986, Orion)	69.7
Look Who's Talking (1989, Tri-Star)	68.4
Die Hard 2 (1990, Fox)	66.5
Rocky III (1982, UA)	66.3
Superman II (1981, Spengler/WB)	65.1
Total Recall (1990, Carolco/Tri-Star)	65.0
Coming To America (1988, Par)	63.1
Teenage Mutant Turtles (1990, RChow/New Line)	62.0
On Golden Pond (1981, ITC/Univ)	61.2
Ghostbusters II (1989, Col)	60.5
Dances With Wolves (1990, Orion)	60.0
Dick Tracy (1990, Buena Vista)	59.5
The Hunt For Red October (1990, Par)	58.5
The Karate Kid Part II (1986, Col)	58.3
Good Morning, Vietnam (1987, Buena Vista)	58.2
Twins (1988, Univ)	57.7
Crocodile Dundee II (1988, Par)	57.3
Star Trek IV: The Voyage Home (1986, Par)	56.8
An Officer And A Gentleman (1982, Lorimar/Par)	55.2
Porky's (1982, Fox)	54.0
Big (1988, Fox)	52.0
Driving Miss Daisy (1989, Zanuck Co/WB)	50.5
Terms Of Endearment (1983, Par)	50.3
Parenthood (1989, Univ)	50.2
The Color Purple (1985, WB)	49.8
Back To The Future Part III (1990, Univ)	49.0
Dead Poets Society (1989, Buena Vista)	48.4
The Best Little Whorehouse In Texas (1982, RKO/Univ)	47.3
Presumed Innocent (1990, WB)	43.8
Aliens (1986, Fox)	43.7
Out Of Africa (1985, Univ)	43.4
The Karate Kid (1984, Col)	43.1
Arthur (1981, Orion/WB)	42.0
Back To School (1986, Orion)	41.9
When Harry Met Sally (1989, Col)	41.8
The War Of The Roses (1989, Fox)	41.4
Stripes (1981, Col)	40.9
Trading Places (1983, Par)	40.6
The Little Mermaid (1989, Buena Vista)	40.2
Another 48 HRS (1990, Par)	40.1
Star Trek: The Wrath Of Khan (1982, Par)	40.0
Cocoon (1985, Zanuck-Brown/Fox)	40.0
Steel Magnolias (1989, Tri-Star)	40.0
Days Of Thunder (1990, Par)	40.0

The Golden Child (1986, Par)	39.7
Star Trek III: The Search For Spock (1984, Par)	39.0
WarGames (1983, UA)	38.5
Police Academy (1984, Ladd/WB)	38.5
Bird On A Wire (1990, Univ)	38.4
Poltergeist (1982, MGM)	38.2
Annie (1982, Rastar/Col)	37.5
Superman III (1983, Spengler-Salkind/WB)	37.2
The Untouchables (1987, Par)	36.9
The Cannonball Run (1981, Fox)	36.8
Born On The Fourth Of July (1989, Univ)	36.8
The Jewel Of The Nile (1985, Fox)	36.5
Cocktail (1988, Buena Vista)	36.5
Flashdance (1983, Par)	36.2
Romancing The Stone (1984, Fox)	36.0
Die Hard (1988, Fox)	36.0
Turner & Hooch (1989, Buena Vista)	35.3
Sudden Impact (1983, WB)	34.8
National Lampoon's Christmas Vacation (1989, WB)	34.8
The Naked Gun (1988, Par)	34.4
Moonstruck (1987, MGM)	34.4
Splash (1984, Buena Vista)	34.1
Octopussy (1983, Broccoli/UA)	34.0
Footloose (1984, Par)	34.0
Kindergarten Cop (1990, Univ)	34.0

Notes

The rentals for North America (the USA and Canada), as shown here, represent about two-thirds of the worldwide box-office rentals: in the case of *Star Wars* (Fox, 1977), for instance, the worldwide gross up to the end of 1980 was $510 million, with total rentals of $250 million (half the gross) of which $185 million (two-thirds) came from North America alone.

The listings for 1914–31 and 1932–40 have been derived from the *Motion Picture Almanac* and information provided by the individual companies. Ever since the 40s the leading source for annual rental figures has been the trade publication *Variety* which publishes an annual, updated list in January of each year, from data provided by the film companies. These figures are estimates only and are occasionally revised, years later, as happened with *My Fair Lady* (WB, 1964), which was reduced from rentals of $32 million to $12 million 10 years after it was first released.

No attempt has been made here to adjust the figures to take account of inflation. Since the cinema has undergone many changes during the period covered by these lists, it would be extremely misleading to try to compare the rentals from a film today with one made 50 or 60 years ago. For example, it is not unusual for the advertising budget of a picture today to exceed the original negative cost. Furthermore, a successful film will generally be allowed a longer run at downtown cinemas than was the case 50 years ago, and similarly the blanket release of a new picture in 800 or 1000 cinemas simultaneously, backed by the extensive advertising, can give the kind of boost to a film's box-office takings that was undreamed of by the movie moguls of years gone by.

Releases - General Statistics

FEATURE FILMS RELEASED IN THE USA 1921-1990

Year	Columbia[1]	Fox	MGM	Paramount	RKO	United Artists	Universal	Warner Bros. (and First Nat.)[2]	MAJOR STUDIOS TOTAL[3]	US Produced
1921	3	65		60		11	55	54		
1922	2	66		60		11	56	48		
1923	7	51		52		12	60	61		
1924	9	46	34	56		8	50	65		
1925	21	42	43	72		9	51	78		
1926	11	51	43	62		8	57	84	449	
1927	25	50	51	78		11	66	98	510	501
1928	32	49	52	64		15	56	79	462	429
1929	22	53	52	68	35	17	41	81	393	379
1930	29	48	47	64	32	16	36	76	362	356
1931	31	48	46	62	47[a]	13	23	54	324	307
1932	29	40	39	65	46	14	30	55	318	300
1933	32	50	42	58	48	16	37	55	338	317
1934	43	52	43	55	46	20	44	58	361	350
1935	49	52	47	63	40	19	37	49	356	340
1936	52	57	45	68	39	17	28	56	362	348
1937	52	61	51	61	53	25	37	68	408	393
1938	53	56	46	50	43	16	46	52	362	346
1939	55	59	50	58	49	18	46	53	388	367
1940	51	49	48	48	53	20	49	45	363	348
1941	61	50	47	45	44	26	58	48	379	368
1942	59	51	49	44	39	26	56	34	358	346
1943	47	33	33	30	44	28	53	21	289	279
1944	51	26	30	32	31	20	53	19	270	262
1945	38	27	33	23	33	17	46	19	234	228
1946	51	32	25	22	40	20	42	20	252	239
1947	49	27	29	29	36	26	33	20	249	234
1948	39	45	24	25	31	26	35	23	248	225
1949	52	31	30	21	25	21	29	25	234	224
1950	59	32	38	23	32	18	33	28	263	242
1951	63	39	41	29	36	46	39	27	320	277
1952	48	37	38	24	32	34	39	26	278	252
1953	47	39	44	26	25	49	43	28	301	285
1954	35	29	24	17	16	52	32	20	225	197
1955	38	29	23	20	13	35	34	23	215	189
1956	40	32	24	17	20	48	33	23	237	210
1957	46	50	29	20	1	54	39	29	268	220
1958	38	42	29	25		44	35	24	237	174
1959	36	34	25	18		40	18	18	189	148
1960	35	49	18	22		23	20	17	184	119

Imported	INDEPENDENTS TOTAL	US Produced	Imported	TOTAL RELEASES	TOTAL US PRODUCED	Major Studios	Independents	TOTAL IMPORTED	Major Studios	Independents
				854						
				748						
				576						
				579						
				579						
	293			742						
9	233	177	56	743	678	501	177	65	9	56
33	372	212	160	834	641	429	212	193	33	160
14	314	183	131	707	562	379	183	145	14	131
6	283	153	80	595	509	356	153	86	6	80
17	298	194	104	622	501	307	194	121	17	104
18	367	189	178	685	489	300	189	196	18	178
21	306	190	116	644	507	317	190	137	21	116
11	301	130	171	662	480	350	130	182	11	171
16	410	185	225	766	525	340	185	241	16	225
14	373	174	199	735	522	348	174	213	14	199
15	370	145	225	778	538	393	145	240	15	225
16	407	109	298	769	455	346	109	314	16	298
21	373	116	257	761	483	367	116	278	21	257
15	310	129	181	673	477	348	129	196	15	181
11	219	124	95	598	492	368	124	106	11	95
12	175	142	33	533	488	346	142	45	12	33
10	138	118	20	427	397	279	118	30	10	20
8	172	139	33	442	401	262	139	41	8	33
6	143	122	21	377	350	228	122	27	6	21
13	215	139	76	467	378	239	139	89	13	76
15	238	135	103	487	369	234	135	118	15	103
23	211	141	70	459	366	225	141	93	23	70
10	245	132	113	479	356	224	132	123	10	113
21	359	141	218	622	383	242	141	239	21	218
43	334	114	220	654	391	277	114	263	43	220
26	185	72	113	463	324	252	72	139	26	113
16	233	59	174	534	344	285	59	190	16	174
28	202	56	146	427	253	197	56	174	28	146
26	177	65	112	392	254	189	65	138	26	112
27	242	62	180	479	272	210	62	207	27	180
48	265	80	185	533	300	220	80	233	48	185
63	270	67	203	507	241	174	67	266	63	203
41	250	39	211	439	187	148	39	252	41	211
65	203	35	168	387	154	119	35	233	65	168

(continued)

FEATURE FILMS RELEASED IN THE USA 1921-1990 (continued)

Year	Columbia[1]	Fox	MGM	Paramount	RKO	United Artists	Universal	Warner Bros. (and First Nat.)[2]	MAJOR STUDIOS TOTAL[3]	US Produced
1961	28	35	21	15		33	19	16	167	103
1962	30	25	21	17		36	18	15	162	102
1963	19	18	35	17		23	17	13	142	86
1964	19	18	30	16		18	25	18	144	86
1965	29	26	28	24		19	15	26	167	98
1966	29	21	24	22		18	23	12	149	93
1967	22	19	21	30		19	25	21	157	87
1968	20	21	27	33		23	30	23	177	98
1969	21	18	16	21		31	26	21	154	87
1970	29	15	23	15		39	16	16	153	73
1971	32	13	18	21		25	17	17	143	66
1972	26	25	24	14		22	16	18	145	74
1973	19	15	15	27		19	16	21	132	74
1974	19	20	5	25		26	12	22	129	58
1975	17	17	4	12		23	9	15	97	54
1976	15	20	4	19		23	12	15	108	58
1977	10½	14	3½	14½		10	14½	11	78	70
1978	12	8	5	14		13	22	17	91	60
1979	20	13	3	14		18	15	10	93	77
1980	14	16	6	15		16	18	17	102	76
1981	9	17	5	22		18	23	18	112	81
1982	14	16	9	20		11	18	17	103	50
1983	15	18	9	16		19	26	20	106	74
1984	17	18	5	13		15	21	27	116	84
1985	17	18	2	13		13	18	24	105	67
1986	20	18	10	16		7	13	18	102	107
1987	14	13	9	12		5	16	17	86	
1988	17	12	12	16		9	19	25	110	
1989	21	13	10	13		12	16	24	109	
1990	14	17	8	15		4	17	23	98	

Notes
1. Includes the following number of CBC releases:
   1921 - 3, 1922 - 2, 1923 - 3.
2. Includes the following number of First National releases:
   1921 - 50, 1922 - 43, 1923 - 50, 1925 - 52, 1926 - 52, 1927 - 55, 1928 -53,
   1929 - 45, 1930 - 37, 1931 - 30.
3. Total includes:
   In 1926 - FBO 62, PDC 39, Pathé 13. In 1927 - FBO 53, PDC 31, Pathé 47.
   In 1928 - FBO 62, Pathé 53. In 1929 - Pathé 24.
   In 1930 - Pathé 14.

FEATURE FILMS RELEASED IN THE USA 1921-1990 (continued)

Imported	INDEPENDENTS TOTAL	US Produced	Imported	TOTAL RELEASES	TOTAL US PRODUCED	Major Studios	Independents	TOTAL IMPORTED	Major Studios	Independents
64	295	28	267	462	131	103	28	331	64	267
60	265	45	220	427	147	102	45	280	60	220
56	278	35	243	420	121	86	35	299	56	243
58	358	55	303	502	141	86	55	361	58	303
69	285	55	230	452	153	98	55	299	69	230
56	302	63	239	451	156	93	63	295	56	239
70	305	91	214	462	178	87	91	284	70	214
79	277	82	195	454	180	98	82	274	79	195
84	55[b]	31[b]	24[b]	226[b]	118[b]	87[b]	31[b]	108[b]	84	24[b]
62	101	64	37	236	137	73	64	99	62	37
42	148	77	71	256	143	66	77	113	42	71
52	170	107	63	296	181	74	107	115	52	63
28	117	77	40	219	151	74	77	68	28	40
32	148	85	63	238	143	58	85	95	32	63
26	96	44	52	176	98	54	44	78	26	52
24	92	50	42	174	108	58	50	66	24	42
22	134	73	61	226	143	70	73	83	22	61
20	123	60	63	203	120	60	60	83	20	63
22	149	45	104	248	122	77	45	126	22	104
27	106	49	57	209	125	76	49	84	27	57
20	104	45	59	205	126	81	45	79	20	59
35	99	29	70	184	79	50	29	105	35	70
46	129	67	62	249	141	74	67	108	46	62
46	188	83	105	318	167	84	83	151	46	105
38	225	96	129	330	163	67	96	167	38	129
54	354	190	164	515	297	107	190	218	54	164

a. Includes 14 RKO-Pathé releases in 1931.
b. Independent films from 1969 onwards include only US-financed productions. Thus, the total is substantially down from previous year and does not match exactly with studio totals on facing page.
1/2 Half figures occur in cases of co-productions.
Sources: 1. *Film Daily Yearbook* - up to 1968; *The American Film Institute Catalog of Motion Pictures Produced in the US: Feature Films, 1921-30* (R.R. Bowker Co, NY, 1971); 3. *Variety, 'US Filming Here and Abroad (1969-86)'.*

THE TRANSITION TO SOUND: FEATURE-FILM RELEASES BY THE EIGHT MAJOR STUDIOS, 1928-1929

1928 Studios	All talking	Part talkie	Sound Effects and Background Music only	Silent	Total
Columbia	0	0	1	31	32
Fox	0	6	13	30	49
MGM	0	3	8	41	52
Paramount	0	4	7	53	64
United Artists	0	0	5	10	15
Universal	0	2	1	53	56
Warner Bros.	10	8	6	2	26
TOTAL	10	23	41	220	294
1929					
Columbia	12	4	1	5	22
Fox	31	6	15	0	52
MGM	23	6	12	11	52
Paramount	47	4	4	13	68
United Artists	9	4	3	0	16
Universal	16	15	1	9	41
Warner Bros.	28	11	0	0	39
TOTAL	166	50	36	38	290

FEATURES FILMED IN TWO-STRIP TECHNICOLOR, 1924-1933

Paramount	Total 3
1924 Wanderer Of The Wasteland	
1930 Follow Thru	
The Vagabond King	

United Artists	Total 2
1926 The Black Pirate (Fairbanks)	
1930 Whoopee! (Goldwyn)	

MGM	Total 3
1929 The Viking (Technicolor Corp.)	
The Mysterious Island	
1930 The Rogue Song	Total 1

Universal	
1930 King of Jazz	

RKO	
1931 Fanny Foley Herself	Total 2
The Runaround	

Warner Bros./First National	Total 20

Major Studios	Total 31

Warner Bros.	Total 14
1929 Gold Diggers Of Broadway	
On With The Show	
The Show Of Shows	
1930 Golden Dawn	
Hold Everything	
The Life Of The Party	
Song Of The West	
Sweet Kitty Bellairs	
Under A Texas Moon	
Viennese Nights	
1931 Fifty Million Frenchmen	
1932 Doctor X	
Manhattan Parade	
1933 The Mystery Of The Wax Museum	

First National	Total 6
1930 Bride Of The Regiment	
Bright Lights	
Sally	
Song Of The Flame	
1931 Kiss Me Again	
Woman Hungry	

Other Productions
1918 The Gulf Between (Technicolor Corp)
1922 Toll Of The Sea (Technicolor Corp./Metro)
1929 Mamba (Tiffany)

US FEATURE FILM RELEASES IN COLOUR, BY STUDIO, 1936-1968

Year	36	37	38	39	40	41	42	43	44	45	46	47	48	49
Columbia								1	1	3	2	3	7	1
Fox	1		1	5	5	6	6	7	7	7	7	8	6	6
MGM			1	1	2	3	0	5	5	5	7	4	12	10
Paramount	1	1	2	0	4	5	4	4	4	2	2	3	3	4
RKO*	1							0	1	2	0	2	2	1
United Artists		1												
Universal							1	2	5	3	2	4	3	5
Warner Bros.	1	0	4	2	0	1	1	1	1	1	2	2	4	9
Selznick (UA)**	1	2	1	1							1			
Goldwyn (RKO)***			1							2	1	1	1	
Korda/UA (GB)			2	1	2	0	1							
Total Colour Releases	5	4	12	10	13	15	13	20	26	24	24	27	38	36
Total Releases	362	408	362	388	363	379	358	289	262	236	252	249	248	234
Colour % Total	1	1	4	3	4	4	4	4	10	10	10	11	15	15

* RKO distributed two of the first films produced by Pioneer Pictures (*Becky Sharp* (1935) and *The Dancing Pirate* (1936); the last 6 RKO productions in 1957 were all distributed by Universal but are listed here as RKO and not included in the Universal total.

FEATURES FILMED IN 3D, 1952-1955

United Artists — Total 4
1952 Bwana Devil
1953 I, The Jury*
1954 Gog
 Southwest Passage

RKO — Total 5
1953 Devil's Canyon
 Louisiana Territory
 Second Chance
1954 Dangerous Mission
 The French Line

MGM — Total 2
1953 Arena
 Kiss Me Kate

Fox — Total 2
1953 Inferno
1954 Gorilla At Large

Columbia — Total 9
1953 Fort Ti
 Gun Fury
 Man In The Dark
 Miss Sadie Thompson
 The Nebraskan
 The Stranger Wore A Gun
1954 Drums of Tahiti
 Jesse James vs The Daltons
 The Mad Magician*

50	51	52	53	54	55	56	57	58	59	60	61	62	63	64	65	66	67	68
5	7	11	21	17	17	14	11	12	9	8	10	7	10	13	13	23	20	20
9	11	11	18	23	22	22	20	21	21	21	22	15	7	6	10	19	17	21
11	13	13	24	18	20	16	14	15	14	11	14	18	19	14	19	19	19	27
8	9	14	15	12	13	13	9	6	8	8	7	10	10	12	16	15	28	33
2	4	4	5	7	12	2	6											
1	3	5	6	10	10	20	6	9	8	7	7	10	14	12	13	16	19	23
11	13	15	24	21	19	17	16	16	11	4	14	8	10	18	13	22	24	30
8	8	12	16	15	19	12	9	11	12	9	11	9	7	7	10	11	21	23
		1							1									
55	68	86	129	123	132	116	91	90	84	68	85	77	77	82	94	125	148	177
263	320	278	301	225	215	237	267	237	189	184	167	162	142	144	167	149	157	177
21	21	32	43	55	61	49	34	38	44	37	51	48	54	57	56	84	94	100

**	1 Selznick film *Gone With the Wind* (1939) distributed by MGM
	1 Selznick film *Duel In The Sun* (1946) distributed by Selznick
***	1 Goldwyn film *The Goldwyn Follies* (1938) distributed by UA
	1 Goldwyn film *Porgy and Bess* (1959) distributed by Columbia

*Filmed in
black
and
white

Warner Bros.   Total 6

1953 The Charge At Feather River
      Hondo
      House Of Wax
      The Moonlighter
1954 Dial M For Murder
      Phantom Of The Rue Morgue

Paramount   Total 4

1953 Flight To Tangier
      Sangaree
      Those Redheads From Seattle
1954 Money From Home

Universal   Total 6

1953 The Glass Web*
      It Came From Outer Space*
      Wings Of The Hawk
1954 The Creature From
          The Black Lagoon*
      Taza, Son Of Cochise
1955 Revenge Of The Creature*

Grand Total   38

TOTAL MAJOR STUDIO RELEASES IN SPECIAL WIDESCREEN PROCESSES, 1953-1969

Widescreen Processes	1953	1954	1955	1956	1957
THE FIFTIES					
CinemaScope	4	34	72	56	63
RegalScope				3	17
SuperScope		2	10	4	1
Technirama					4
VistaVision		2	14	19	16
Total	4	38	96	83	101
Colour: CinemaScope	4	34	72	53	46
SuperScope		2	9	4	1
Technirama					4
VistaVision		2	12	15	10
Colour Total	4	38	93	72	61
B/W: CinemaScope				3	18
RegalScope				3	17
SuperScope			1		
VistaVision			2	4	6
B/W Total			3	10	41
THE SIXTIES					
Panavision: Colour					
Panavision: B/W					1
Panavision; Total					1
Techniscope					
Panavision/Techniscope Total					1
THE FIFTIES AND SIXTIES					
Grand Total	4	38	96	83	102
Colour Grand Total	4	38	93	73	61
Colour as % of Total Colour Releases	3	31	70	63	67
B/W Grand Total			3	10	41
Anamorphic Grand Total	4	36	82	64	86
Anamorphic as % of Total Releases	1	16	38	27	32
Large Format (70mm) Total*				3	1
Total Releases	301	225	215	237	268
Total Colour Releases	129	123	132	116	91

* Note: 2 last large format releases in 1970.

1958	1959	1960	1961	1962	1963	1964	1965	1966	1967	1968	1969
60	47	31	24	22	12	10	8	7	2		
8	4										
3	5	1	2	1	1						
14	11	3	1								
85	67	35	27	23	13	10	8	7	2		
45	40	32	31	25	8	7	8	7	2		
4	5	3	1	3		1					
8	8	2	2		1						
57	53	37	34	28	9	8	8	7	2	–	
17	16	10	4	5	3	4	3				
8	4										
6	3										
31	23	10	4	5	3	4	3		–		
2	11	17	17	19	26	18	32	37	38	51	44
1	3	4	2	5	6	4	11	2	1		
3	14	21	19	24	32	22	43	39	39	51	44
						8	9	16	24	29	9
3	14	21	19	24	32	30	52	55	63	80	53
88	81	56	46	47	45	40	60	62	65	80	53
57	60	45	41	39	36	33	49	60	64	55	53
62	71	66	47	51	47	40	52	48	43	32	34
31	21	11	5	8	9	7	11	2	1		
74	70	51	45	47	45	40	60	62	65	80	53
31	37	29	27	29	32	28	36	42	41	45	34
1	2	4	1	4	4	4	7	4	1	4	2*
237	189	184	167	162	142	144	167	149	157	177	154
90	84	68	85	77	77	82	94	125	148	177	154

WIDESCREEN AND 3-D RELEASES, 1952-1969

	1952	1953	1954	1955	1956	1957	1958
COLUMBIA							
Technirama							1
CinemaScope				8	8	3	5
Panavision							
Large format							
Techniscope							
3-D		5	4				
FOX							
CinemaScope		3	17	23	20	23	23
RegalScope (b/w)					3	17	8
Panavision							
Large format					2		1
3-D		1	1				
MGM							
CinemaScope		1	7	18	12	15	13
VistaVision					2		
Panavision						1	2
Technirama							1
Large format						1	
3-D		2					
PARAMOUNT							
VistaVision			2	14	15	15	14
Panavision							
Techniscope							
Technirama							
3-D		4	1				
UNITED ARTISTS							
CinemaScope				1	3	9	2[b]	1
SuperScope				1	1	1		
Technirama						1	1	3
Panavision							
Techniscope							
Large Format						1	
3-D	1	2	2				

1959	1960	1961	1962	1963	1964	1965	1966	1967–	1968	1969
	1	1	3							
5	3	2	2	5	1[c]	5	7	6	5	2
1	5		1			1	1	1	4	1
1					2	3				1
30	27	24	17	8	9	8	6	2		
4							3	8	9	10[c]
	1			1		3	1	1	1	1
2			2	2	1		1			
1										
9	11	7	10	12	10	14	12	10	15	9
1		1	2	1	1		1		2	
1										
9	3	1	3	2	2	6	5	4	8	5
		5			5	6	7	8	7	2
1		1	1		1				1	
3[b]										
2										
1	3	3	7	7	5	7	7	5	5	8
					2	3	1	5	3	1
	2	1		1		2	1		1	

(continued)

WIDESCREEN AND 3-D RELEASES, 1952-1969 (continued)

	1952	1953	1954	1955	1956	1957	1958
UNIVERSAL							
CinemaScope			2	6	4[b]	18	17
Panavision							1
Techniscope							
Technirama						2	
3-D		3	2	1			
WARNER BROS.							
CinemaScope			7	14	3[b]	3	1
Technirama						1	
Panavision							
Techniscope							
Large format							
3-D		4	2				
RKO							
SuperScope			1	9	3	1	
CinemaScope					2		
3-D		3	3				

a - includes 1 Technirama b - includes 1 VistaVision c - includes 1 Techniscope
d - includes 1 Warnerscope

1959	1960	1961	1962	1963	1964	1965	1966	1967	1968	1969
7 3	1 1 1	2	2	2		1 1	4 5	2 8	1 18	2 4
1^d 2	1		1 1	4	3 2	10 1	1 1	4 1	4 1	9^d 1

There was a marked contrast in the policies of the different studios with regard to widescreen pictures. As can be seen form the tables here and on the previous page, many of the different processes were related to particular periods and studios. It is also useful to distinguish between the numerous 35mm processes competing in the 50s and the changed situation in the 60s when Panavision emerged as the clear front runner.

FILMS SHOT IN LARGE FORMAT (mainly 70mm), 1956-1970

This chart presents a complete list of pictures from the major studios. Note that the majority of '70mm presentations' in the 60s, and virtually all releases in 70mm after 1970, have been blown up from 35mm negatives - in most cases from 35mm anamorphic Panavision originals, but also from releases (and re-releases) of VistaVision and Technirama films - as well as the misleadingly named Super Technirama 70 - which made use of a larger picture area than normal 35mm filming.

Film titles are followed by their date, name of Director/Producer, and process.

COLUMBIA

Porgy and Bess (1959) Otto Preminger/Sam Goldwyn (Todd-AO)

Lawrence of Arabia (1962) David Lean/Sam Spiegel (Super Panavision 70)

Lord Jim (1965) Richard Brooks (d/p) (Super Panavision 70)

MacKenna's Gold (1969) J. Lee Thompson/Carl Foreman (Super Panavision 70)

FOX

Carousel (1956) Henry King (d/p) ([1]CinemaScope 55)

The King and I (1956) Walter Lang/Charles Brackett ([1]CinemaScope 55)

South Pacific (1958) Joshua Logan/Buddy Adler [Magna] (Todd-AO)

Can-Can (1960) Walter Lang/Jack Cummings (Todd-AO)

Cleopatra (1963) Joseph L. Mankiewicz/Walter Wanger (Todd-AO)

The Agony and the Ecstasy (1965) Carol Reed (d/p) (Todd-AO)

The Sound of Music (1965) Robert Wise (d/p) (Todd-AO)

Those Magnificent Men In Their Flying Machines (1965) Ken Annakin/Stan Margulies (Todd-AO)

The Bible - In the Beginning (1966) John Huston/Dino De Laurentiis (Dimension 150)

Dr Dolittle (1967) Richard Fleischer/Arthur Jacobs (Todd-AO)

Star! (1968) Robert Wise/Saul Chaplin (Todd-AO)

Hello, Dolly! (1969) Gene Kelly/Ernest Lehman (Todd-AO)

Patton (1970) Franklin Schaffner/Frank McCarthy (Dimension 150)

MGM

Raintree County (1957) Edward Dmytryk/David Lewis ([2]Camera 65)

Ben Hur (1959) William Wyler/Sam Zimbalist ([2]Camera 65)

Mutiny On The Bounty (1962) Lewis Milestone/Aaron Rosenberg (Ultra Panavision 70)

The Wonderful World Of The Brothers Grimm (1962) Henry Levin/George Pal (Cinerama)

How The West Was Won (1963) Henry Hathaway - John Ford - George Marshall/Bernard Smith (Cinerama)

(MGM contd.)

Grand Prix (1966) John Frankenheimer/Edward Lewis ([3]Super Panavision 70)

Ice Station Zebra (1968) John Sturges/Martin Ransohoff ([3]Super Panavison 70)

2001: A Space Odyssey (1968) Stanley Kubrick (d/p) ([3]Super Panavision 70)

Ryan's Daughter (1970) David Lean/Anthony Havelock - Allan (Super Panavision 70)

PARAMOUNT

The Fall Of The Roman Empire (1964) Anthony Mann/Samuel Bronston (Ultra Panavision 70)

UNITED ARTISTS

Around The World In 80 Days (1956) Michael Anderson/Michael Todd (Todd-AO)

The Alamo (1960) John Wayne (d/p) (Todd-AO)

Exodus (1960) Otto Preminger (d/p) (Super Panavision 70)

West Side Story (1961) Robert Wise - Jerome Robbins/Wise (for Mirisch -7 Arts) (Ultra Panavision 70)

It's A Mad, Mad, Mad, Mad World (1963) Stanley Kramer (d/p) ([3]Ultra Panavision 70)

The Greatest Story Ever Told (1965) George Stevens (d/p) ([3]Ultra Panavision 70)

The Hallelujah Trail (1965) John Sturges (d/p for Mirisch) ([3]Ultra Panavision 70)

Khartoum (1966) Basil Dearden/Julian Blaustein ([3]Ultra Panavison 70)

Chitty Chitty Bang Bang (1968) Ken Hughes/Albert Broccoli (Super Panavision 70)

UNIVERSAL

Airport (1969) George Seaton/Ross Hunter (Todd-AO)

WARNER BROS.

Cheyenne Autumn (1964) John Ford/Bernard Smith (Super Panavision 70)

My Fair Lady (1964) George Cukor/Jack L. Warner (Super Panavision 70)

Battle Of The Bulge (1965) Ken Annakin/Milton Sperling, Philip Yordan, Sidney Harmon ([3]Ultra Panavison 70)

1. Fox experimented with a 55mm negative, but CinemaScope 55 was used for just two pictures; Fox adopted Todd-AO for most of its later, large-format productions.

2. The Camera 65 system made use of a 65mm negative, It was developed by MGM in partnership with the Panavision company and was used for two films in the late 50s. It was a forerunner of Super Panavision 70 which became the most widely used large format process in the early 60s.

3. The triple-camera Cinerama system was not used for filming after 1963, but many pictures filmed in Super or Ultra Panavision 70 continued to make use of the trade name 'Cinerama' and were road shown in Cinerama theatres on the giant curved screen as 'Cinerama presentations'

STUDIO REVENUES AND PROFITS, 1920-1990

All figures given in $ million

YEAR	COLUMBIA Film Revenues	Total Revenues	Profits	Operating Income	FOX AND 20TH CENTURY-FOX Film Revenues	Total Revenues	Profits	Operating Income	LOEW'S/MGM Film Revenues	Total Revenues	Profits	Operating Income (MGM PROFITS)	UNITED ARTISTS Film Revenues	Total Revenues	Film & TV Revenues	Profits	PARAMOUNT Film & TV Revenues	Film Revenues	Total Revenues	Profits	Operating Income
1920					12.6	15.5	1.4							3.7		(0.2)				5.2	
1921					13.7	17.6	1.7			18.1	1.8			4.9		(0.0)				4.7	
1922					12.7	18.5	2.7			19.6	2.3			7.3		(0.1)				4.1	
1923					11.2	17.0	1.8			19.6	2.4			8.1		0.1				4.2	
1924					9.9	17.8	2.0			42.9	2.9			6.6		(0.2)				5.4	
1925					11.8	22.1	2.6			56.3	4.7	2.0		9.3		(0.1)				5.7	
1926			0.1		14.3	22.7	3.1			62.2	6.4	3.1		13.7		0.1				5.6	
1927			0.2		17.0	22.5	3.1			79.6	6.7	2.9		11.3		(0.5)				8.1	
1928		1.4	0.3		22.6	66.5	6.0			99.3	8.6	5.3		20.6		1.6				8.7	
1929		2.4	0.6		30.8	83.2	9.5			116.2	10.9	6.8		19.7		1.3				15.5	
1930		2.4	1.0			102.0	10.3			129.5	14.9	9.9		17.1		0.4				18.4	
1931		4.4	1.0			85.8	(17.0)			120.5	12.2	6.3		20.6		0.9				(21.0)	
1932		11.4	0.6				(4.2)			107.0	8.0	3.0		10.8		(0.3)					
1933		10.5	0.7			24.3a	1.7			67.9	4.3	1.3		13.7		0.1			84.5		
1934		11.2	1.0			36.3a	1.3			79.2	8.6	4.1		23.1		1.1			90.2	0.8	
1935		14.4	1.8			42.4b	3.1			85.0	7.6			24.4		1.5			90.6	6.0	
1936		15.3	1.6			51.7b	7.7			94.8	10.6			23.8		0.9			102.8	6.0	
1937		19.1	1.3			56.2a	8.6			107.8	14.3			25.2		0.8			104.2	6.0	
1938		20.1	0.2			58.2a	7.3			108.9	9.9			25.1		0.3			100.9	2.9	
1939		19.4	0.0			53.8b	4.2			112.5	9.5			24.4		0.4			96.2	2.8	
1940		22.2	0.5			47.8b	(0.5)			121.9	8.7			22.5		0.2			96.0	6.3	
1941		21.6	0.6			49.6b	4.9			113.9	11.0			23.9		0.1			101.3	9.2	
1942		27.2	1.6			67.3a	10.6			119.5	11.8			22.8		0.1			123.3	13.1	
1943		32.4	1.8			154.3	10.9			138.8	13.4			28.3		1.0			140.9	14.5	
1944		37.1	2.0			172.6	12.5			145.1	14.5			24.1		(0.3)			153.2	14.7	
1945		36.0	1.9			178.2	12.7			154.2	12.9			34.4		0.6			158.2	15.4	

Year	1	2	3	4	5	6	7	8	9	10	11	12	13	14	15	16	17	18	19	20
1946		46.5	3.5			190.3	22.6			165.4	18.0			37.0	0.4				39.2	
1947		48.8	3.7			174.4	14.0			161.8	10.5			32.1	0.5				28.2	
1948		46.9	0.6			163.4	12.5			164.4	4.2			24.7	(0.5)			193.5	22.6	
1949		53.3	1.0			169.5	12.4			160.2	6.0			23.0	(0.2)			186.8	3.3	
1950		57.2	2.0			151.0	9.6			161.8	7.6			21.4	(1.0)			170.4	6.6	
1951		55.4	1.5			150.7	4.3			163.5	7.8			19.6	0.3			78.8c	5.5	
1952		59.1	0.8			99.8c	4.7			166.3	4.7			29.0	0.4			81.8	5.9	
1953		60.3	0.9			113.5	4.6			166.1	4.5			38.5	0.6			94.6	6.7	
1954		80.2	3.6			115.7	8.0			172.8	6.3			43.6	0.9			104.8	8.1	
1955		88.3	4.9			120.8	6.0			164.9	5.0			54.0	2.7			110.3	9.4	
1956		91.1	2.5			122.3	6.2			166.6	4.7			64.2	3.1			106.9	8.7	
1957		101.6	2.3			127.7	6.5			153.7	(0.5)			70.0	3.7			112.5	5.4	
1958		113.6	(5.0)			125.0	7.6		100.2	151.2	0.8			84.1	3.3			93.3	4.6	
1959		115.8	(2.4)			119.9	4.2		106.0	129.1c	7.7			95.1	4.1			108.0	4.4	
1960		118.6	2.1			118.4	(2.9)		96.1	129.3	9.6			108.5	4.0			101.8	7.0	
1961		130.3	(1.4)			117.4	(22.5)		97.8	139.3	12.7			126.8	3.8			111.9	5.9	
1962		134.6	2.7			96.4	(39.8)		117.8	135.9	2.6			124.6	9.3			126.2	3.4	
1963		141.1	2.6		74.1	102.9	9.1		107.4	132.6	(17.5)	26.8		181.4	12.8			114.4	5.9	
1964		145.3	3.2		73.0	115.0	0.6		114.5	170.0	7.4	31.9		195.0	13.6			102.7	6.6	
1965		140.6	2.0		102.5	162.6	11.8		139.7	160.7	7.8	32.0		170.6	19.5			113.9	6.2	
1966	70.5	174.7	2.9		132.2	227.3	12.5		134.7	184.7	10.2	26.6		197.8	15.3			127.6		
1967	85.5	209.8	6.5		130.6	195.5	15.4		132.0	226.0	14.0	39.2		249.0	16.2			124.5		
1968	113.7	243.2	9.4		123.9	233.3	15.0		98.5	209.8	9.4	60.1		268.0	(45.0)		61.0	140.0		
1969	131.1	206.2	5.9		84.8	184.8	(27.5)	(77.2)	111.1	191.3	(35.4)	36.4		211.0	1.0		73.0	215.9		7.6
1970	95.6	242.1	6.2		160.0	252.4	(76.4)	12.4	134.5	169.6	(8.2)	51.7		204.3	0.8		97.5	219.0		2.0
1971	137.9	233.3	(28.8)	7.3	143.2	226.8	9.7	8.1	138.8	169.3	7.8	116.5	97.2	315.0	14.0		128.0	224.0		20.1
1972	13.0	233.5	(3.4)	(61.5)	118.8	201.4	7.8	12.1	135.1	155.6	9.2	62.0	152.7	322.6	9.9		136.0	240.9		31.2
1973	100.0	205.4	(50.0)	24.9	152.6	253.5	10.7	12.9	100.7	159.6	2.1	63.9	164.0	288.6	11.5		94.0	278.7		38.7
1974	101.5	250.1	(2.3)	33.2	159.7	280.1	1.0	28.9	96.1	182.9	19.6	(21.3)	141.9	319.7	16.0		101.0	291.0		18.7
1975	111.3	325.5	11.5	28.3	210.8	342.7	22.7	17.1	110.7	193.0	29.4	65.8	187.4	377.7	26.6		139.0	277.5		29.9
1976	170.3	332.1	34.6	30.8	217.2	355.0	10.7	69.7	138.8	181.9	16.5	(23.0)	229.5	474.1	28.8		142.0	298.1		49.6
1977	152.2	390.5	68.8	80.1	321.5	501.5	50.8	91.1	193.2	299.4	23.2	(35.4)	318.5	416.8	26.6		120.0	360.3		36.2
1978	153.5	574.6	39.0	59.0	346.6	610.9	58.4	63.8	141.6	806.3	27.5		294.2	468.9	20.1		103.0	451.4		84.1
1979	263.1	613.3	44.9	59.5	316.4	658.0	57.3	55.2	256.5	723.0	41.9		381.0	424.8	(11.3)		175.0	469.6		116.4
1980	341.6	691.8	44.3	58.5	581.9	847.3	54.6		294.1	706.9	34.7						152.0	802.0		100.1
1981	a	686.6	a			371.0a	(16.9)	1.5	247.0	655.2	(58.8)					232.0	150.0	966.7		96.3
1982		a				567.5	(89.7)		255.4	526.4	17.9					384.0	287.0	1041.6		66.1
1983		849.5		90.6		776.5	(79.1)		355.4		(88.1)					551.0	427.0	1129.1		68.3
1984		884.7		121.1		745.0	30.4		427.6		(40.7)					603.0	392.0	1190.0		109.1
1985		1072.1		160.9		642.5	52.7		674.9		68.9					651.0	483.0	1276.0		69.1
1986		1373.8		235.4		568.3	55.6	51.8	526.4							719.0	354.0	1266.0		128.8
1987		1065.0		45.3		887.8	311.2									844.0	375.0	1063.0		297.3
1988		1615.7		147.6		821.3										1007.0	499.0	1145.0		251.8
1989						997.7										916.0	339.0	1849.5		255.0
1990																928.0	340.0	1862.2		210.0

Column 14 (1982–1990): MGM and UA now amalgamated. See figures under MGM.

STUDIO REVENUES AND PROFITS, 1920-1986

YEAR	UNIVERSAL CINEMA FILM REVENUES	UNIVERSAL FILM REVENUES	UNIVERSAL TOTAL REVENUES	UNIVERSAL PROFITS	UNIVERSAL FILM ENTERTAINMENT PROFITS	UNIVERSAL OPERATING INCOME	FIRST NATIONAL REVENUES	FIRST NATIONAL PROFITS	WARNER BROS. FILM REVENUES	WARNER BROS. TOTAL REVENUES	WARNER BROS. PROFITS	WARNER BROS. OPERATING INCOME	RKO RADIO REVENUES	RKO RADIO PROFITS	PATHÉ REVENUES	PATHÉ PROFITS	KEITH-ALBEE-ORPHEUM REVENUES	KEITH-ALBEE-ORPHEUM PROFITS	TOTAL STUDIO PROFITS ($ million)	TOTAL US CORPORATE PROFITS ($ billion)
1920			16.1	0.6			19.4	1.1		3.3	0.15									
1921			17.6	0.9			22.5	1.9		4.6	1.0									
1922			20.7	1.3			24.7	2.0		8.7	(1.3)									
1923			22.8	1.8			25.0	1.0		10.3	0.0									
1924			24.8	1.9			23.8	1.2			2.0									
1925			27.7	2.0			24.2	1.2		31.2	14.5						7.9	4.2		
1926			28.6	1.5						52.9	7.1				18.2	1.4	8.0	4.4		
1927			27.2	1.1							(7.9)				16.8	0.9	6.5	3.0		
1928			29.1	0.5							(14.1)		42.6		17.6	(2.2)	11.0	0.8		
1929			25.3	(1.8)							(6.3)		51.7	0.9	17.3	0.2				8.6
1930			20.5	(0.6)						84.5	(2.5)		71.4	1.7	18.2	0.5			54.5	2.9
1931			19.0	(1.2)						90.2	0.7		79.2	3.4	14.6	(1.0)e			52.1	(0.9)
1932			17.6	(1.0)						99.9	3.2		59.9	(5.7)					3.4	(2.7)
1933				(0.2)						102.2	5.9		44.0	(10.4)					(55.7)	0.4
1934			14.3	(0.7)						102.1	1.9		41.7	(4.4)					(4.9)	1.6
1935			17.4	(1.6)						100.3	1.7		45.5	(0.3)					9.0	2.6
1936			18.2	(1.0)						98.1	2.7		49.2	0.7					15.5	2.9
1937			20.2	(0.4)						114.9	5.4		52.9	2.5					30.9	5.3
1938			23.8	1.0						127.3	8.6		56.3	1.8					37.7	2.9
1939			27.6	2.2						136.1	8.2		51.4	0.2					22.3	5.6
1940			30.2	2.3						141.5	7.0		54.2	(1.0)					19.4	7.2
1941			39.1	3.0							9.9		53.3	0.5					19.1	10.1
1942			46.5	3.8									61.4	0.7					34.0	10.1
1943			51.6	3.4									78.8	7.0					49.5	11.1
1944			51.0	3.9									84.9	5.2					59.0	11.2
1945													96.1	6.0					63.3	9.0

Year										
1946		53.9	4.6		158.6	19.4	120.1	12.2	119.9	15.5
1947		65.0	3.2		164.6	22.1	123.1	5.1	87.3	20.2
1948		58.0	(3.2)		147.1	11.8	110.0	0.5	48.5	22.7
1949		56.7	(1.1)		135.0	10.3			33.6	18.7
1950		55.6	-1.4		126.9	10.5	46.6[c]	(5.8)	30.8	24.7
1951		65.2	2.3		116.7	9.4	57.7	0.3	31.1	21.3
1952		64.1	2.6		71.6	7.1	61.4	(10.2)	23.9	19.5
1953		70.5	3.8		68.9	2.9			22.8	20.2
1954		77.5	4.0		70.1	4.0			34.7	20.5
1955		77.6	4.0		75.7	4.8			36.0	26.4
1956		72.4	2.8		76.7	2.1			31.3	26.6
1957		56.7	(2.0)		71.2	3.4			23.2	25.5
1958		52.6	4.7		70.1	(1.0)			8.7	22.1
1959		58.4	6.3		87.1	9.4			32.1	28.0
1960		59.0	3.0		92.1	7.1			33.5	25.8
1961		72.8	4.4		88.4	7.2			31.4	25.8
1962		77.5	5.4		84.9	7.6			24.5	29.6
1963		80.6	5.3		92.4	5.7			27.9[a]	31.5
1964					73.3	(3.9)			38.5	36.7
1965					97.1	4.7			45.3[a]	44.3
1966	67.0	174.9	17.1		119.0	6.5				44.9
1967	96.9	175.0	14.6		137.8	3.0	102.0	9.1		46.2
1968	56.7	200.9	16.6	32.4	143.7	10.0	95.6	10.4		43.8
1969	61.9	220.0	13.5	15.0	142.9	(42.0)	64.2	(62.0)		37.0
1970	87.5	194.6	2.5	19.9	114.9		86.3	7.0		44.3
1971	205.0	204.6	13.3	20.2	124.3		144.3	14.8		54.6
1972	289.1	227.7	16.7	68.0	193.4		152.7	23.1		67.1
1973	213.4	387.5	20.9	124.0	209.5		275.3	31.1		74.5
1974	222.8	509.9	27.1	100.6			202.3	57.7		70.6
1975	318.7	506.9	59.2	107.4			221.7	41.7		92.2
1976	305.0	561.4	95.5	174.3			285.2	42.2		104.5
1977	397.7	724.4	90.2	133.9			353.2	58.0		121.5
1978	313.3	781.5	95.1	72.0			393.0	79.9		
1979	608.8	761.7	128.4	212.0	609.7		433.7	117.6		
1980	267.1	788.7	139.0	163.8	668.9		369.6	60.8		
1981	542.5	1014.8		61.9	755.2		439.9	24.7		
1982	348.6	927.0		145.7	693.5		388.6	101.8		
1983	207.7	888.9		89.0	877.8			109.4		
1984	314.8	1187.7		162.9	1090.0			150.4		
1985	283.9	1308.0			1200.0			160.2		
1986	194.8	1330.0			1250.0			172.2		
1987	248.6				1353.7			176.4		
1988					1571.0			203.0		
1989								312.0		
1990								370.0		

Notes

( ) A loss ie (1.8) = loss of $1.8 million.

a Columbia taken over by Coca-Cola: no figures available.

b Fox excludes income from film theatres between 1933 and 1943.

c Divestiture of film theatres.

d Fox half-year figures only, caused by switch to fiscal year.

e Estimate.

g On occasional years an exceptional loss by a studio distorts the total. These figures have been excluded as follows: 1961 & 1962, Fox; 1963, MGM; 1965 - no figures available for Paramount.

Film company profits and revenues prior to the 50s consist mainly of income from pictures released and cinemas. Studios which owned no cinemas, such as Columbia and Universal, thus appear even smaller compared with the giant companies.

MGM's profits for 1925-34 show the proportion of the Loew's total accounted for by films alone.

Gaps in rows of figures are most often caused by management changes, such as Coca-Cola's takeover of Columbia in 1982.

The profit figures here are 'net' after tax. When taken over by a conglomerate the film company no longer pays tax, which becomes the responsibility of the parent company. Instead it reports an operating income (or 'gross profits') which is generally much larger than, and should not be confused with, net profits.

GENERAL FILM INDUSTRY AND TV STATISTICS

NUMBERS OF US CINEMAS, 1923-1990 (in thousands)								
Year	Silent (4-wall Cinemas)	Sound (4-wall Cinemas)	Drive-ins Total	Cinemas Total	Screens	Average Weekly Attendence (millions)	Average Admission Price ($ and cents)	Price Including Admission Tax ($ and cents)
1921								
1922						40		
1923	15.0			15.0		43		
1924						46		
1925						48		
1926	19.5			19.5		50		
1927	21.6	0.0		21.7		57		
1928	22.2	0.1		22.3		65		
1929	22.5	0.8		23.3		75		
1930	14.1	8.9		23.0		80		
1931	8.9	13.1		22.0		70		
1932	4.8	13.9		18.7		55		
1933	4.1	14.4		18.6		50	0.23	
1934	2.5	14.4		16.9		50	0.23	
1935		15.3		15.3		55	0.24	
1936		15.9		15.9		55	0.25	
1937		18.2		10.2		60	0.23	
1938		18.2		18.2		60	0.23	
1939		17.8		17.8		60	0.23	
1940		19.0		19.0		65	0.24	
1941		19.6	0.1	19.8		68	0.24	
1942		20.3	0.1	20.4		77	0.25	0.27
1943		20.2	0.1	20.3		84	0.26	0.29
1944		20.3	0.1	20.4		84	0.27	0.32
1945		20.4	0.1	20.5		82	0.29	0.35
1946		18.7	0.3	19.0		82	0.33	0.40
1947		18.1	0.5	18.6		73	0.35	0.42
1948		17.6	0.8	18.4		66	0.37	0.44
1949		17.4	1.2	18.6		61	0.38	0.46
1950		16.9	2.2	19.1		55	0.40	0.48
1951		16.2	2.8	19.0		49	0.43	0.52
1952		15.3	3.3	18.6		43	0.46	0.56
1953		14.5	3.8	18.3		42	0.48	/0.58
1954		14.8	4.1	18.9		47	0.50	
1955		14.1	4.6	18.7		50	0.51	

	Silent (4-wall Cinemas)	Sound (4-wall Cinemas)	Drive-ins Total	Cinemas Total	Screens	Average Weekly Attendence (millions)	Average Admission Price ($ and cents)
	NUMBERS OF US CINEMAS, 1923-1990 (in thousands)						
Year							
1956		13.9	4.5	18.4		50	0.52
1957		13.7	4.5	18.2		41	0.53
1958		13.5	4.7	18.2		35	0.55
1959		13.2	4.8	18.0		32	0.58
1960		12.5	4.7	17.2		30	0.62
1961		12.0	4.7	16.7		27	0.67
1962		11.0	4.8	15.8		25	0.73
1963		10.3	4.5	14.9		22	0.82
1964		9.2	4.1	13.3		20	0.92
1965		9.2	4.2	13.4		20	1.01
1966		9.3	4.2	13.5		19	1.09
1967		9.5	3.7	13.2		18	1.20
1968		9.7	3.7	13.4		19	1.31
1969		9.8	3.7	13.5		18	1.42
1970		10.0	3.8	13.8		18	1.55
1971		10.3	3.8	14.1		16	1.65
1972		10.6	3.8	14.4		18	1.70
1973		10.9	3.8	14.7		17	1.77
1974		9.6	3.5	13.2	14.4	19	1.87
1975		9.9	3.5	13.4	15.0	20	2.05
1976		10.0	3.5	13.6	16.0	18	2.13
1977		10.0	3.5	13.6	16.5	20	2.23
1978		10.2	3.4	13.6	16.3	23	2.34
1979		10.3	3.3	13.6	16.9	22	2.52
1980		9.7	3.6	13.3	17.6	20	2.69
1981		11.4	3.3	14.7	18.0	21	2.78
1982			3.1		18.8	23	2.96
1983			2.9		18.9	23	3.15
1984		14.6	2.8	17.4	20.2	22	3.34
1985		15.1	2.8	17.9	21.1	20	3.51
1986		16.8	2.8	19.6	22.7	20	3.67
1987			2.5		23.6	21	3.91
1988			1.5		23.2	21	4.11
1989			1.1		23.1	22	4.45
1990			1.0		23.7	20	4.75

GENERAL FILM INDUSTRY AND TV STATISTICS

		BOX-OFFICE RECEIPTS, 1921-1990		
Year	Box-office Receipts ($ millions)	Receipts as a Percentage of Consumer Expenditure	Receipts as a Percentage of Recreation Expenditure	Receipts as a Percentage of Spectator Expenditure (including theatre and sports)
1921	301			
1922				
1923	336			
1924				
1925	367			
1926				
1927	526			
1928				
1929	720	0.94	16.6	78.9
1930	732	1.05	18.4	82.1
1931	719	1.18	21.8	84.2
1932	527	1.08	21.6	83.5
1933	482	1.05	21.9	84.1
1934	518	1.02	21.2	82.9
1935	556	0.99	21.1	82.7
1936	626	1.01	20.7	82.5
1937	676	1.01	20.0	82.6
1938	663	1.04	20.5	81.3
1939	659	0.98	19.1	80.3
1940	735	1.05	19.5	81.3
1941	809	1.00	19.1	81.3
1942	1022	1.15	21.9	84.9
1943	1275	1.29	25.7	87.6
1944	1341	1.24	24.7	85.8
1945	1450	1.21	23.6	84.6
1946	1692	1.18	19.8	81.9
1947	1594	0.99	17.2	79.6
1948	1506	0.87	15.5	78.5
1949	1451	0.82	14.5	77.5
1950	1376	0.72	12.3	77.3
1951	1310	0.64	11.3	76.3
1952	1246	0.57	10.3	75.3
1953	1187	0.52	9.3	74.0
1954	1228	0.52	9.4	73.4
1955	1326	0.52	9.4	73.6

Year	Box-office Receipts ($ millions)	Receipts as a Percentage of Consumer Expenditure	Receipts as a Percentage of Recreation Expenditure	Receipts as a Percentage of Spectator Expenditure (including theatre and sports)
			BOX-OFFICE RECEIPTS, 1921-1990	
1956	1394	0.52	9.3	73.4
1957	1126	0.40	7.3	68.0
1958	992	0.34	6.3	64.5
1959	958	0.31	5.6	61.0
1960	951	0.29	5.2	59.2
1961	921	0.27	4.7	56.7
1962	903	0.25	4.4	54.9
1963	904	0.24	4.1	53.4
1964	913	0.23	3.7	51.8
1965	927	0.21	3.5	51.2
1966	964	0.23	3.3	50.1
1967	989	0.22	3.2	48.8
1968	1045	0.20	3.1	46.7
1969	1099	0.19	3.0	48.6
1970	1167	0.19	2.9	48.0
1971	1170	0.18	2.7	47.7
1972	1644	0.22	3.0	47.0
1973	1524	0.20	3.5	50.8
1974	1909	0.28	4.1	54.0
1975	2115	0.26	3.8	53.2
1976	1994	0.27	4.1	53.6
1977	2376	0.29	3.9	45.1
1978	2811	0.30	3.1	48.4
1979	2946		3.0	46.9
1980	2750		2.7	43.6
1981	2966		2.3	40.1
1982	3453		2.7	45.8
1983	3766		2.4	41.8
1984	4156		2.3	41.0
1985	3749		2.0	38.5
1986	3778		1.9	38.2
1987	4252		1.9	37.2
1988	4458		1.7	35.3
1989	5033			
1990	5023			

GENERAL FILM STATISTICS, 1929-1989				
Year	Income Originating in Motion Picture industry	Total Employees (thousands)	Total Wages ($ millions)	Average Annual Earnings ($ thousands)
1921				
1922				
1923				
1924				
1925				
1926				
1927				
1928				
1929	440	153	308	2.0
1930	438	153		2.2
1931	36	147		2.2
1932	194	128		2.0
1933	210	124		1.9
1934	283	141		1.8
1935	329	155		1.9
1936	391	171		1.9
1937	437	184		2.0
1938	426	178		2.0
1939	434	179	339	1.9
1940	448	181		1.9
1941	513	191		2.0
1942	652	200	410	2.1
1943	830	211	459	2.1
1944	882	221	509	2.3
1945	929	222	552	2.5
1946	1128	236	679	2.9
1947	1045	234	649	2.8
1948	902	234	655	2.8
1949	885	235	659	2.8
1950	866	234	651	2.8
1951	877	233	668	2.9
1952	869	228	684	3.0
1953	849	221	678	3.1
1954	953	218	709	3.3
1955	979	216		3.8

Year	Income Originating in Motion Picture industry	Total Employees (thousands)	Total Wages ($ millions)	Average Annual Earnings ($ thousands)
		GENERAL FILM STATISTICS, 1929-1989		
1956	949	213		3.8
1957	899	203	·800	3.9
1958	828	188	795	4.0
1959	908	184	756	4.3
1960	894	184	789	3.9
1961	933	183	754	4.6
1962	890	174	833	4.6
1963	910	175	805	4.6
1964	1053	176	806	4.9
1965	1205	181	864	5.3
1966	1343	187	967	5.6
1967	1350	193	1039	5.7
1968	1535	194	1100	6.0
1969	1465	202	1172	6.3
1970	1551	210	1278	6.1
1971	1600	201	1274	6.4
1972	1600	199	1277	6.7
1973	1700	204	1343	7.0
1974	1700	203	1429	7.8
1975	1800	204	1575	8.1
1976	2400	205	1662	9.2
1977	2900	210	1887	10.2
1978		213	2133	11.5
1979		222	2449	13.0
1980		222	2879	13.9
1981		222	3076	15.4
1982		216	3418	16.7
1983		211	3604	18.1
1984		218	3985	20.0
1985		221	4416	21.3
1986		219	4862	22.6
1987		231	5141	26.0
1988		238	5980	27.0
1989		256	6445	

Year	Total Revenue of Networks and Stations ($ millions)	Television Households (millions)	Television Households as Percentage of Total Households	Colour Television Households (millions)	Colour Television Households as Percentage of Total Households
1921					
1922					
1923					
1924					
1925					
1926					
1927					
1928					
1929					
1930					
1931					
1932					
1933					
1934					
1935					
1936					
1937					
1938					
1939					
1940					
1941					
1942					
1943					
1944					
1945					
1946	0.5				
1947	1.9				
1948	8.7				
1949	34.3				
1950	106	3.9	9		
1951	236	10.3	24		
1952	324	15.3	34		
1953	433	20.4	45		

GENERAL TELEVISION STATISTICS, 1946-1986					
Year	Total Revenue of Networks and Stations ($ millions)	Television Households (millions)	Television Households as Percentage of Total Households	Colour Television Households (millions)	Colour Television Households as Percentage of Total Households
1954	593	26.0	56		
1955	745	30.7	65		
1956	897	34.9	72		
1957	943	38.9	79		
1958	1030	41.9	83		
1959	1335	44.0	86	0.4	
1960	1456	45.8	87	0.6	
1961	1514	47.2	89		
1962	1705	48.9	90		
1963	1836	50.3	91		
1964	2068	51.6	92	1.6	3
1965	2266	52.7	93	2.9	
1966	2558	53.9	93	5.2	10
1967	2634	55.1	94	11.3	20
1968	2916	56.7	95	13.7	24
1969	3236	58.3	95	18.7	32
1970	2809	59.6	95	23.4	39
1971	2750	60.9	96	27.6	45
1972	3180	62.4	96	32.8	53
1973	3460	65.6	96	38.4	60
1974	3800	66.8	97	45.0	67
1975	4094	68.5		48.5	71
1976	5200	69.6		51.2	74
1977	5889	71.2		54.9	77
1978	6913	72.9		56.9	78
1979	7875	74.5		60.3	81
1980	8808	76.3		63.4	83
1981	9815	77.8		66.3	
1982	10960	81.5		71.4	88
1983		83.3		73.9	89
1984		83.8		75.8	91
1985		84.9		77.7	91
1986		85.9		80.1	93

BIBLIOGRAPHY

GENERAL WORKS
Annual financial reports of the various film companies

Blum, Daniel, *A Pictorial History of the Silent Screen* (Spring Books, London, 1953)

Carr, Robert and Hayes, R.M., *Widescreen Movies* (McFarland, Jefferson, North Carolina, 1988)

Cawkwell, Tim and Smith, John (eds), *The World Encyclopedia of the Film* (November Books/Studio Vista, London, 1972)

Film Daily Yearbook (annual) (New York)

Halliwell's Film Guide, 6th edition (Grafton, London, 1987)

Katz, Ephraim, *The International Film Encyclopedia* (Macmillan, New York, 1980)

Limbacher, James, *Four Aspects of the Film* (privately published, 1968)

Lloyd, Ann (ed), *The Movie: The Illustrated History of the Cinema* (Orbis Publishing, London, 1980–82)

Manvell, Roger (ed), *The International Encyclopedia of Film* (Michael Joseph, London, 1972)

Moody's Manual of Investments: Industrial Securities (aka *Moody's Industrials*) (annual) (New York)

Motion Picture Almanac/International Motion Picture Almanac/ International Television Almanac (annuals) (Quigley Publications, New York)

Production Encyclopedia, 1948 edition (1943–47) (*The Hollywood Reporter*, Hollywood, Calif., 1991)

Quinlan, David, *Quinlan's Illustrated Directory of Film Stars* revised edition (Batsford, London, 1991)

Salt, Barry, *Film Style and Technology: History and Analysis* (Starword, London, 1983)

Shipman, David, *The Story of Cinema*, Vol. I (Hodder and Stoughton, London, 1982)

U.S. Department of Commerce, Survey of Current Business. Historical Statistics (monthly and annual), Washington, D.C.

Variety (weekly) (New York)

Walker, Alexander, *Hollywood, England* (Michael Joseph, London, 1974)

AMERICAN CINEMA
American Film Institute Catalog of Motion Pictures Produced in the US; Feature Films, 1921–30 (Bowker, New York, 1971)

Balio, Tino (ed), *The American Film Industry* revised edition (University of Wisconsin Press, Madison, 1985)

Basten, Fred E., *Glorious Technicolor: The Movies' Magic Rainbow* (Barnes and Co, New York, 1980)

Bordwell, David, Staiger, Janet and Thompson, Kristin, *The Classical Hollywood Cinema: Film Style and Mode of Production to 1960* (Routledge and Kegan Paul, London, 1985)

Brownlow, Kevin, *Hollywood, The Pioneers* (Collins, London, 1979)

Brownlow, Kevin, *The Parade's Gone By* (Secker & Warburg, London, 1968)

Brownlow, Kevin, *The War, The West and the Wilderness* (Secker & Warburg, London, 1979)

Cross, Robin, *The Big Book of B Movies, or How Low Was My Budget* (Frederick Muller, London, 1981)

Everson, William K., *American Silent Film* (Oxford University Press, New York, 1978)

Farber, Stephen and Green, Marc, *Hollywood Dynasties* (G.P. Putnam's Sons, New York, 1984)

Fernett, Gene, *American Film Studios: An Historical Encyclopaedia* (McFarland, Jefferson, North Carolina, 1988)

Friedrich, Otto, *City of Nets: A Portrait of Hollywood in the 1940s* (Harper and Row, New York, 1986)

Gabler, Neal, *An Empire of Their Own: How the Jews Invented Hollywood*, Crown, New York, 1988)

Gomery, Douglas, *The Hollywood Studio System* (BFI/Macmillan, London, 1986)

Gordon, David, 'Mickey Mouse is 50. And so is much of the rest of the American film industry,' in *The Economist*, 7 July 1973

Gordon, David, 'The Movie Majors' in *Sight & Sound*, Summer 1979

Hampton, Benjamin B., *History of the American Film Industry From Its Beginnings to 1931* (Dover, New York, 1970)

Haver, Ronald, *David O. Selznick's Hollywood* (Secker & Warburg, London, 1980)

Izod, John, *Hollywood and the Box Office* (Macmillan, London, 1988)

Jacobs, Lewis, *The Rise of the American Film* (Harcourt, Brace and Company, New York, 1939)

Kerr, Paul (ed), *The Hollywood Film Industry* (Routledge & Kegan Paul, London, 1986)

Maltin, Leonard, *The Great Movie Shorts* (Bonanza Books, New York, 1972)

Maltin, Leonard, *Of Mice and Magic: A History of American Animated Cartoons* (McGraw-Hill, New York, 1980)

Michael, Paul (ed), *The American Movies Reference Book: The Sound Era* (Prentice-Hall, Englewood Cliffs, N.J., 1969)

Miller, Don, *B Movies* (Curtis Books, New York, 1973)

Monaco, James, *American Film Now* revised and updated edition (New American Library, New York, 1984)

Pickard, Roy, *The Hollywood Studios* (Frederick Muller, London, 1978)

Pirie, David (ed), *Anatomy of the Movies* (Windward, London, 1981)

Ramsaye, Terry, *A Million and One Nights: A History of the Motion Picture* (Simon & Schuster, New York, 1926)

Rosten, Leo C., *Hollywood – The Movie Colony, The Movie Makers* (Harcourt, Brace and Company, New York, 1941)

Sacket, Susan, *The Hollywood Reporter Book of Box Office Hits* (Billboard Books, 1990)

Schatz, Thomas, *The Genius of the System: Hollywood Filmmaking in the Studio Era* (Simon & Schuster, New York, 1988)

Shale, Richard, *Academy Awards*, 2nd edition (Frederick Ungar, New York, 1982)

Sklar, Robert, *Movie-Made America, A Cultural History of American Movies* (Random House, New York, 1975)

Slide, Anthony, *The American Film Industry – A Historical Dictionary* (Greenwood Press, Westport. Conn., 1986)

Stanley, Robert H., *The Celluloid Empire: A History of the American Movie Industry* (Hastings House, New York, 1978)

Steinberg, Cobbett, *Reel Facts: The Movie Book of Records* (Vintage Books/Random House, New York, 1978)

Walker, Alexander, *The Shattered Silents* (Elm Tree/Hamish Hamilton, London, 1978)

Wanamaker, Marc, 'Historic Hollywood Movie Studios' in *American Cinematographer* (3 parts) March-May, 1976

Webb, Michael (ed) *Hollywood: Legend and Reality* (Little Brown & Co/Smithsonian, New York, 1986)

Wiley, Mason and Bona, Damien, *Inside Oscar: The Unofficial History of the Academy Awards* (Columbus, Bromley, Kent, 1986)

MOVIE PERSONNEL

Academy of Motion Picture Arts and Sciences, The, *Who Wrote the Movies, and What Else Did He Write? An Index of American Screenwriters and Their Works, 1936–69* (AMPAS, Los Angeles, 1970)

Albrecht, Donald, *Designing Dreams: Modern Architecture in the Movies* (Harper & Row, New York, 1986)

American Screenwriters, volumes 26 and 44, *Dictionary of Literary Biography*, (eds volume 26) Robert Mosberger, Stephen Lesser, and Randall Clark, (ed volume 44) Randall Clark (Bruccoli Clark/Gale Research, Detroit, 1984, 1986)

Ash, René L., *The Motion Picture Film Editor* (Scarecrow Press, Metuchen, N.J., 1974)

Bailey, Margaret J, *Those Glorious Glamour Years: Classic Hollywood Costume Design of the 1930s* (Lyle Stuart, New York, 1982)

Barsacq, Leon, and Stein, Elliott, *Caligari's Cabinet and Other Grand Illusions; A History of Film Design* (Little, Brown and Co., New York, 1976)

Chierichetti, David, *Hollywood Costume Design* (Studio Vista, London, 1976)

Corliss, Richard, *Talking Pictures: Screenwriters of Hollywood* (David & Charles, Newton Abbott, 1975)

Film Comment, Mar–April 1977 special section on 'The Film Editor'

Finler, Joel W., *The Movie Directors Story* (Octopus, London, 1985)

Focus on Film, No. 13, 'Great Cameramen' (1973)

French, Philip, *The Movie Moguls* (Weidenfeld & Nicolson, London, 1969)

Hambley, John and Downing, Patrick, *The Art of Hollywood: 50 Years of Art Direction* (Thames Television, London, 1979)

Heisner, Beverly, *Hollywood Art: Art Direction in the Days of the Great Studios* (McFarland, Jefferson, North Carolina, 1990)

Koszarski, Richard, 'The Men With the Movie Cameras', *Film Comment*, June 1972

Langman, Larry, *A Guide to American Screenwriters: The Sound Era 1929–1982* in two volumes (Garland Publishing, New York, 1984)

Leese, Elizabeth, *Costume Design in the Movies* (BCW Publishing, Bembridge, Isle of Wight, 1976)

Limbacher, James L., *Film Music: From Violins to Video* (Scarecrow Press, Metuchen, N.J., 1974)

Lyon, Christopher (ed), *Dictionary of Films and Filmmakers, Volume 2: Directors* (Macmillan, London, 1984)

Maeder, Edward (ed), *Hollywood and History: Costume Design in Film* (Thames & Hudson/LA County Museum of Art, 1987)

Maltin, Leonard, *The Art of the Cinematographer* (Dover, New York, 1978)

McCarty, Clifford, *Film Composers in America*: *A Checklist of Their Work* (Da Capo Press, New York, 1972)

Monaco, James, *Who's Who in American Film Now*, updated edition, 1975–86 (Zoetrope, New York, 1987)

Parrish, James Robert, and Pitts, Michael, *Film Directors: A Guide to Their American Films* (Scarecrow Press, Metuchen, N.J., 1974)

Quinlan, David, *The Illustrated Guide to Film Directors* (Batsford, London, 1983)

Truitt, Evelyn Mack, *Who Was Who On Screen*, 3rd edition (Bowker, New York, 1983)

Westmore, Frank, and Davidson, Muriel, *The Westmores of Hollywood* (W.H. Allen, London, 1976)

THE STUDIOS
Columbia

Capra, Frank, *The Name Above the Title: An Autobiography* (Macmillan, New York, 1971)

Hirschhorn, Clive, *The Columbia Story* (Pyramid Books, London, 1989)

Larkin, Rochelle, *Hail Columbia* (Arlington House, New Rochelle, New York, 1975)

McLintick, David, *Indecent Exposure* (William Morrow & Co, New York, 1982)

Okuda, Ted and Watz, Edward, *The Columbia Comedy Shorts: Two-Reel Hollywood Film Comedies, 1933–58* (McFarland, Jefferson, North Carolina, 1988)

Thomas, Bob, *King Cohn: The Life and Times of Harry Cohn* (G.P. Putnam, New York, 1967)

Fox

Allvine, Glendon, *The Greatest Fox of Them All* (Lyle Stuart, New York, 1969)

Curti, Carlo, *Skouras: King of the Fox Studios* (Holloway House, Los Angeles, 1967)

Dunne, John Gregory, *The Studio* (Farrar, Straus & Giroux, New York, 1969)

Gussow, Mel, *Don't Say Yes Until I Finish Talking: A Biography of Darryl F. Zanuck* (Doubleday, New York, 1971)

Harris, Marlys J, *The Zanucks of Hollywood: The Dark Legacy of an American Dynasty* (Virgin, London, 1990)

Mosley, Leonard, *Zanuck, The Rise and Fall of Hollywood's Last Tycoon* (Granada, London, 1974)

Silverman, Stephen M, *The Fox That Got Away: The Last Days of the Zanuck Dynasty at Twentieth Century-Fox* (Lyle Stuart, Secaucus, N. J., 1988)

Solomon, Aubrey, *Twentieth Century-Fox: A Corporate and Financial History* (Scarecrow Press, Metuchen, N. J., 1988)

Thomas, Tony and Solomon, Aubrey, *The Films of 20th Century-Fox* revised and enlarged edition (Citadel Press, Secaucus, N. J., 1985)

Upton Sinclair Presents William Fox (privately published, Los Angeles, 1933)

MGM

Bart, Peter, *Fade Out: The Calamitous Final Days of MGM* (William Morrow, New York, 1990)

BFI Dossier No. 1: MGM (BFI, London, 1980)

Crowther, Bosley, *Hollywood Rajah: The Life and Times of Louis B. Mayer* (Holt, Rinehart & Winston, New York, 1960)

Crowther, Bosley, *The Lion's Share: The Story of an Entertainment Empire* (Dutton, New York, 1957)

Eames, John Douglas, with Ronald Bergan, *The MGM Story: The Complete History of 65 Roaring Years*, revised and updated edition (Pyramid Books, London, 1990)

Fordin, Hugh, *The World of Entertainment: Hollywood's Greatest Musicals – The Freed Unit at MGM* (Doubleday, New York, 1975)

Marx, Samuel, *Mayer and Thalberg: The Make-Believe Saints* (Random House, New York, 1975)

Ross, Lillian, *Picture* (Rinehart, New York, 1952)

Schary, Dore, *Heyday: An Autobiography* (Little, Brown & Co., New York, 1979)

Thomas, Bob, *Thalberg: Life and Legend* (Doubleday, New York, 1969)

Paramount

DeMille, Cecil B., *Autobiography* (Prentice-Hall, Englewood Cliffs, N.J., 1959)

Eames, John Douglas, *The Paramount Story* (Octopus, London, 1985)

Irwin, Will, *The House That Shadows Built* (Doubleday, Garden City, New York, 1928)

Lasky, Jesse L. and Waldon, Don, *I Blow My Own Horn* (Doubleday, New York, 1957)

Schulberg, Budd, *Moving Pictures: Memories of a Hollywood Prince* (Stein & Day, New York, 1981)

Wallis, Hal and Higham, Charles, *Starmaker: The Autobiography of Hal Wallis* (Macmillan, New York, 1980)

Zukor, Adolph with Kramer, Dale, *The Public is Never Wrong: The Autobiography of Adolph Zukor* (G.P. Putnam's Sons, New York, 1953)

RKO

Dietrich, Noah and Thomas, Bob, *Howard: The Amazing Mr Hughes* (Fawcett, New York, 1972)

Jewell, Richard and Harbin, Vernon, *The RKO Story* (Arlington House, New York, 1982)

Lasky, Betty, *RKO: The Biggest Little Major of Them All* (Prentice Hall, Englewood Cliffs, N. J., 1984)

Maltin, Leonard, 'RKO Revisited' in *Film Fan Monthly* Nos 145, 146, 149, 151 and 153 (July 1973–March 1974)

Velvet Light Trap No. 10 (Fall, 1973). Special RKO Issue

United Artists

Bach, Steven, *Final Cut: Dreams and Disaster in the Making of Heaven's Gate* (Jonathan Cape, London, 1985)

Balio, Tino, *United Artists: The Company Built by the Stars* (University of Wisconsin Press, Madison, 1976)

Balio, Tino, *United Artists: The Company That Changed the Film Industry* (University of Wisconsin Press, Madison, 1987)

Behler, Rudy (ed), *Memo From David O. Selznick* (Viking, New York, 1972)

Berg, A. Scott, *Goldwyn – A Biography* (Knopf, New York, 1988)

Bergan, Ronald, *The United Artists Story* (Octopus, London, 1986)

Kulik, Karol, *Alexander Korda: The Man Who Could Work Miracles* (W.H. Allen, London, 1975)

Marx, Arthur, *Goldwyn: A Biography of the Man Behind the Myth* (W.W. Norton & Co., New York, 1976)

Robinson, David, *Chaplin: His Life and Art* (Collins, London, 1985)

Schickel, Richard, *D.W. Griffith* (Pavilion/Michael Joseph, London, 1984)

Thomas, Bob, *Selznick* (Doubleday, New York, 1970)

Universal

Brunas, Michael and John, and Weaver, Tom, *Universal Horrors* (McFarland, Jefferson, North Carolina, 1990)

Dettman, Bruce and Bedford, Michael, *The Horror Factory, The Horror Films of Universal, 1931–55* (Gordon Press, New York, 1976)

Drinkwater, John, *The Life and Adventures of Carl Laemmle* (Putnam, New York, 1931)

Edmonds, I.G., *Big U: Universal in the Silent Days* (A.S. Barnes, New York, 1977)

Fitzgerald, Michael G., *Universal Pictures: A Panoramic History* (Arlington House, New Rochelle, New York, 1977)

Hirschhorn, Clive, *The Universal Story* (Octopus, London, 1983)

Koszarski, Richard, *The Man You Loved to Hate: Erich von Stroheim and Hollywood* (Oxford University Press, New York, 1983)

Warner Bros.

Higham, Charles, *Warner Brothers* (Charles Scribner's Sons, New York, 1976)

Hirschhorn, Clive, *The Warner Bros. Story* (Octopus, London, 1979)

Roddick, Nick, *A New Deal in Entertainment: Warner Brothers in the 1930s* (British Film Institute, London, 1983)

Sennett, Ted, *Warner Brothers Presents, the Most Exciting Years: From The Jazz Singer to White Heat* (Arlington House, New Rochelle, New York, 1971)

Silke, James R., *Here's Looking at You Kid: 50 Years of Fighting, Working and Dreaming at Warner Bros.* (Little, Brown & Co., Boston, 1976)

Thomas, Bob, *Clown Prince of Hollywood: The Antic Life and Times of Jack L. Warner* (McGraw-Hill, New York, 1990)

Velvet Light Trap No. 1 and 15 (June 1971 and Fall 1975) Special issues devoted to Warner Bros.

Wallis, Hal, *Starmaker* (see Paramount)

Warner, Jack L. and Jennings, Dean, *My First Hundred Years in Hollywood* (Random House, New York, 1964)

INDEX

Abbott, Bud and Costello, Lou 360, 365, 367, 372, 376, 378, 379

Abbott and Costello Meet The Mummy (Universal, 1955) 365

Abbott, L.B, 'Bill' 182

Abe Lincoln In Illinois (RKO, 1940) 295

Abrams, Hiram 322, 323, 328

Absence of Malice (Columbia, 1980) 131

Academy of Motion Picture Arts and Sciences (AMPAS) 83, 84, 85
see also Oscars

Accused, The (Paramount, 1988) 286

Ace In The Hole (Paramount, 1951) 253, 274

Acord, Art 379

Across The Pacific (Warner Bros, 1942) 404

Action In The North Atlantic (Warner Bros, 1943) 404

Actors Equity 84

Adams, Julie 368, 379

Adam's Rib (Paramount, 1923) 58, 256

adaptations 87, 88

Adler, Buddy 119, 146, 147

Adolfi, John G. 427

Adoree, Renee 170, 217

Adrian (costume designer) 9, 82, 214, 226, 229, 231, 389

Adventure (MGM, 1945) 211

Adventures of Baron Munchausen, The (Columbia co-production, 1988) 121

Adventures of Marco Polo, The (UA, 1938) 57

Adventures of Mark Twain, The (Warner Bros, 1944) 405

Adventures of Robin Hood, The (Warner Bros, 1938) 35, 401, 403, 407, 408, 413, 414, 425, 432, 433

Adventures of Tom Sawyer, The (UA, 1938) 57, 330, 333

Advise and Consent (Columbia, 1963) 116

Affair In Trinidad (Columbia, 1952) 125

Affairs Of Anatol, The (Paramount, 1921) 246

African Queen, The (UA, 1951) 38, 326, 334, 338, 354, 427

Agony And The Ecstasy, The (Fox, 1965) 181

Ah, Wilderness (MGM, 1935) 198

Ahlschlager, Walter 20

Air Force (Warner Bros, 1943) 404, 426

Air Mail (Universal, 1932) 388

Airplane (Paramount, 1980) 260

Airport (Universal, 1970) 43, 369, 370, 373, 374, 387

Aitken, Henry 17

Akins, Zoe 282

Akst, Albert 231, 389

Aladdin And His Wonderful Lamp (Fox, 1917) 150

Alamo, The (UA, 1960) 90, 334, 340, 350

Albeck, Andy 327

Albert, Eddie 170, 268, 307, 379

Aldrich, Robert 74, 131, 345, 346

Alexander Hamilton (Warner Bros, 1931) 403

Alexander's Ragtime Band (Fox, 1938) 161, 163, 181, 182, 186

Alfie (Paramount, 1966) 286

Alice Adams (RKO, 1935) 289, 310, 318

Alice Doesn't Live Here Any More (Warner Bros, 1974) 438

Alice In Wonderland (RKO, 1951) 299

Alien (Fox, 1978) 24, 154

Alien (Fox, 1979) 164

Aliens (Fox, 1986) 154, 163, 164

Aliens III (Fox, 1991) 163

All About Eve (Fox, 1950) 89, 147, 175, 185, 186

All I Desire (Universal, 1953) 379

All Quiet On The Western Front (Universal, 1930) 28–9, 55, 87, 88, 357, 359, 365, 371, 374, 386, 390

All That Heaven Allows (Universal, 1956) 379

All That Jazz (Fox/Columbia, 1978) 187

All That Money Can Buy (RKO, 1941) 295, 314, 318

All The King's Men (Columbia, 1949) 33, 89, 107, 108, 115, 119, 126, 130, 133, 135, 138

All The President's Men (Warner Bros, 1976) 91, 399, 415, 436

All This And Heaven Too (Warner Bros, 1940) 404

Allbritton, Louise 379

Allen, Charles, Jr 398

Allen, Dede 79

Allen, Fred 17, 184, 389

Allen, Gracie 248, 266, 268, 273

Allen, Herbert, Jr 107

Allen, Woody 39, 75, 86, 91, 93, 341, 343, 344, 346, 353, 355

Allied Artists 16

Allyson, June 217, 379, 406

Aloma Of The South Seas (Paramount, 1941) 252

Altman, Robert 86, 286

Alton, John 220, 231, 315

Amadeus (Milos Forman, 1984) 91

Amarcord (Fellini, 1974) 86, 94

Ameche, Don 36, 96, 144, 152, 154, 155, 161, 167, 170, 187

American Cinematographer 8

American Graffiti (Universal, 1973) 62, 370, 373, 374, 392

American In Paris, An (MGM, 1951) 38, 86, 89, 195, 203, 209, 233, 234

American Madness (Columbia, 1932) 111, 129, 133

American Optical Company 42–3

American Romance, An (MGM, 1944) 202

Americanization Of Emily, The (MGM, 1964) 199

Ames, Leon 170, 217, 379

Ames, Preston 229, 230

Amfitheatrof, Daniele 184, 231, 389

Amos 'n' Andy (comedy team) 300

AMPAS (Academy of Motion Picture Arts and Sciences) 83, 84, 85; *see also* Oscars

Amy, George 316, 433, 435

Anastasia (Fox, 1956) 186

Anatomy Of A Murder (Columbia, 1959) 74, 90, 110, 116, 121, 130

Anchors Aweigh (MGM, 1945) 202, 211

Anderson, G.M. 'Bronco Billy' 67, 98

Anderson, John Murray 367

Anderson, Milo 351, 433, 434

Anderson, Roland 279, 281

Andrews, Dana 168, 170, 175, 268, 307

Andrews, Julie 170, 200, 373

Andrews Sisters, The 379

Andriot, Lucien 183, 315, 350

Andy Hardy series 196, 198, 234

Angel Face (RKO, 1952) 291, 297

Angeli, Pier 217

Angels With Dirty Faces (Warner Bros, 1938) 421, 425, 437

Anhalt, Edward 136

Animal Kingdom, The (1933) 21

Ankers, Evelyn 170, 343, 379

Anna And The King Of Siam (Fox, 1946) 180, 182

Anna Christie (MGM, 1930) 30, 207, 210

Anna Karenina (MGM, 1935) 208, 214, 234

Annabella (actress) 144, 154

Anne Of The Thousand Days (Universal, 1969) 367, 392

Annie (Columbia, 1982) 63, 122

Annie Get Your Gun (MGM, 1950) 209, 211

Annie Hall (UA, 1977) 86, 88, 91, 353, 355

Annie Oakley (RKO, 1935) 294

Another 48 HRS (Paramount, 1990) 259, 260

Anscocolor 38, 39, 203–4

Antheil, George 135

Anthony Adverse (Warner Bros, 1936) 56, 95, 404, 412, 430, 431, 433

Antonioni 200

Any Which Way You Can (Warner Bros, 1980) 415

Apartment, The (UA, 1960) 42, 88, 89, 90, 91, 95, 338, 340, 342, 347, 349, 353, 355

Apfel, Oscar 243

Apocalypse Now (UA, 1979) 87, 340, 355

Applause (Paramount, 1929) 248

Arabian Nights (Universal, 1942) 368, 378

Arbuckle, Fatty 14, 240, 246, 262, 263, 264, 268, 406

Archainbaud, George 131, 176, 274, 311, 346

Arden, Eve 217, 318, 379

Arena (MGM, 1953) 203

Arizona (Columbia, 1940) 118, 121

Arlen, Richard 105, 127, 247, 268, 379

Arliss, George 94, 322, 341, 343, 403, 417, 436

Arnaz, Desi 292, 303

Arnold, Edward 112, 217, 268, 379

Arnold, Jack 367, 383, 384

Arnold, John 226–7, 230

Arnow, Max 125–6

Around The World In 80 Days (UA, 1956) 40, 43, 59, 90, 158, 204, 329, 334, 338, 340, 353, 354

Arrowsmith (UA, 1931) 330

Arsenic And Old Lace (Warner Bros, 1941) 124

Art Cinema Company 323, 336

Arthur, Jean 106, 112, 123, 124, 126, 127, 130, 268, 377, 379

Arthur (Warner Bros, 1981) 415

Arzner, Dorothy 79, 112, 271, 273, 274, 276, 280, 282

Ashby, Hal 346, 349

Ashcroft, Peggy 96

Ashley, Ted 398–9, 400

Asphalt Jungle, The (MGM, 1950) 199

Astaire, Fred 56, 96, 98, 118, 124, 216, 217, 249, 253, 254, 288, 289, 292, 294, 298, 300, 301,

302, 304, 305–6, 307, 314, 319

Astor, Mary 95, 127, 170, 217, 268, 294, 305, 307, 421

Atari video games company 399, 400

Attenborough, Richard 93

attitudes, influence of cinema on 13–14

Atwill, Lionel 170, 217, 377, 379

audience figures 21–2, 31, 46–9, 208

Audioscopiks (3–D) 40

Auer, John 311

Auer, Mischa 379

Auerbach, Norbert 327

August, Joseph 132, 135, 178, 183, 315

Auntie Mame (Warner Bros, 1958) 413, 414

Autry, Gene 113, 115, 123, 127

Avengers, The (Columbia, 1930) 123

Avery, Tex 99, 192, 406

awards 85–7, 98, 234
see also Golden Globe awards;
New York
Film Critics awards; Oscars

Awful Truth, The (Columbia, 1937) 106, 110, 112, 118, 129, 134, 138, 285

Axelrod, George 184

Axt, William 231

Aylesworth, Merlin 288–9

Ayres, Lew 170, 217, 268, 343, 379

B films 28, 31–2, 58, 113, 118, 153, 191, 192, 247, 249, 331, 365, 367. 372, 386, 403, 404–5

Babes In Arms (MGM, 1939) 198, 201, 209, 210

Babes On Broadway (MGM, 1941) 209, 220

Baby Face Nelson (UA, 1957) 332

Bacall, Lauren 33, 169, 170, 407, 421, 426

Bach, Steven 327

Bachelor And The

Bobby-Soxer, The (RKO, 1947) 299

Bachelor Apartment (RKO, 1931) 294

Bachelor Mother (RKO, 1939) 289, 302, 310

Back Street, (Universal, 1932) 378; (Universal, 1961) 379

Back To Bataan (RKO, 1945) 296

Back To The Future (Universal, 1985) 62, 339, 361, 362, 363, 370, 373, 375

Back To The Future Part II (Universal, 1989) 62, 361, 363, 373, 375

Bacon, Lloyd 131, 176, 311, 384, 424, 425, 427

Bad And The Beautiful, The (MGM, 1952) 19, 227

Bad Girl (Fox, 1932) 185

Bad News Bears, The (Paramount, 1976) 260

Bad Sister (Universal, 1930) 420

Baggott, King 366, 377

Bakaleinikoff, Constantin 314, 316, 319

Bakaleinikoff, Mischa 134, 135

Balaban, Barney 237, 241, 242, 244, 258

Balanchine, George 333

Baldwin, Earl 435

Ball, Lucille 127, 218, 292, 303, 304, 306, 307, 315, 318, 343

Ballard, Lucien 133, 135, 183, 281, 315, 388

Bamba, La (Columbia, 1987) 122

Bancroft, Anne 41, 170

Bancroft, George 268

Bandit Of Sherwood Forest (Columbia, 1946) 114, 115, 118, 125

Bank Dick, The (Universal, 1940) 378

Bankhead, Tallulah 170, 268

Banks, Lionel 135, 138

Banky, Vilma 342, 343

Banton, Travis 82, 115, 135, 183, 265, 266, 276, 280, 281, 351, 389

Bara, Theda 142, 150, 159, 165–6

Barabbas (Columbia, 1962) 115

Bardelys the Magnificent (1926) 28

Bare, Richard L 427

Barefoot In The Park (Paramount, 1967) 260

Bari, Lynn 170, 379

Barker, Lex 295

Barnes, George 183, 230, 281, 312, 315, 347, 348, 350, 354, 388, 434

Barrie, Wendy 268, 307, 379

Barry, Wesley 417, 424

Barrymore, Diana 379

Barrymore, Ethel 95, 170, 217, 302

Barrymore, John 28, 112, 130, 217, 240, 263, 268, 272, 330, 341, 343, 365, 395, 399, 402, 403, 417, 418, 421

Barrymore, Lionel 88, 198, 214, 215, 217, 233, 268

Barthelmess, Richard 28, 54, 83, 248, 418

Bartholomew, Freddie 127, 198, 217, 307, 379

Barton, Charles 131, 274, 384

Basevi, James 180, 183, 228, 230, 315, 349, 351, 434

Bass, Saul 205

Bassman, George 231

Bat, The (UA, 1926) 330

Bates, Kathy 139

Batman, (Columbia, 1943) 113; (Warner Bros, 1989) 63, 397, 408, 412, 413, 436

Battle of Britain, The (UA, 1969) 62, 339

Battle Cry (Warner Bros, 1955) 413, 414, 427, 430

Battle Hymn (Universal, 1956) 368

Battle of Midway, The (1942) 92

Battle Of The Bulge (Warner Bros, 1965) 409

Battleground (MGM, 1949) 193, 199, 211

Bauchens, Anne 79, 231, 282

Baxter, Anne 168, 170
Baxter, Warner 127, 166, 167, 174, 185, 268
Beast Of Berlin (Universal, 1918) 366
Beatty, Warren 63, 93, 170, 258, 278, 286
Beau Brummell (Warner Bros, 1924) 28, 402
Beau Geste, (Paramount, 1926) 245, 247, 255, 257, 259, 272; (Paramount, 1939) 248
Beaudine, William 274, 424, 427
Beaumont, Harry 224
Becket (Paramount, 1964) 286
Becky Sharp (Pioneer/RKO, 1935) 35, 36, 156, 200, 251, 293, 298
Bedtime For Bonzo (Universal, 1951) 367
Beebe, Ford L. 384
Beery, Noah, Jr 379
Beery, Wallace 30, 197, 207, 214, 216, 217, 220, 234, 247, 268
Beetlejuice (Warner Bros, 1988) 414
Beetley, Samuel 184, 316
Begelman, David 107, 109, 120, 209, 327
Behind Office Doors (RKO, 1931) 294
Behind the Screen (1916) 19
Behind The Rising Sun (RKO, 1943) 296, 302
Behlmer, Henry 142
Behrman, S.N. 184, 232
Bel Geddes, Barbara 170, 268, 307
Bell, Book And Candle (Columbia, 1958) 126
Bell, Monta 224, 274, 384, 427
Bellamy, Ralph 112, 124, 127, 170, 307, 379
Belle Of The Nineties (Paramount, 1934) 247
Bells Are Ringing (MGM, 1959) 42, 204
Bells Of St Mary's, The (RKO, 1945) 57, 58, 292, 299, 302, 306, 318
Ben-Hur, (MGM, 1925) 34, 54, 150, 195, 197, 200,

206, 210, 226; (MGM, 1959) 19, 43, 45, 57, 58, 74, 89–90, 93, 189, 193, 195, 196, 204, 209, 211, 227, 233, 235, 338
Bend Of The River (Universal, 1952) 368, 372
Bendix, William 170, 250, 262, 267, 268, 307
Benjamin, Robert 321, 326, 328, 332, 335, 338, 344, 345, 354
Bennett, Belle 417
Bennett, Charles 282
Bennett, Constance 217, 294, 304, 307, 331
Bennett, Enid 217, 268
Bennett, Hugh 282, 351
Bennett, Joan 170, 268, 297, 343
Benny, Jack 217, 248, 268
Benton, Robert 93, 139
Berger, Ralph 281, 315, 386, 388
Bergman, Ingmar 86, 93, 94
Bergman, Ingrid 33, 60, 96, 186, 252, 294, 296, 306, 307, 318, 342, 343, 408, 421, 430
Bergner, Elisabeth 330
Berkeley, Busby 36, 145, 156, 181, 220, 223, 224, 332, 366, 402, 424, 426, 427, 429
Berlin, Irving 294
Berman, Henry 231, 316
Berman, Pandro S. 68, 234, 289, 292, 294, 305, 310
Bern, Paul 214, 264
Bernhardt, Curtis 224, 427
Bernhardt, Sarah 238
Bertolucci, Bernardo 108
Best Little Whorehouse in Texas, The (Universal, 1982) 375
Best, Marjorie 433, 434
Best Years Of Our Lives, The (Goldwyn/RKO, 1946) 58, 62, 89, 292, 299, 313, 318
Betty Boop series 249
Beverly Hills Cop (Para-mount, 1984) 63, 255, 261
Beverly Hills Cop II (Paramount, 1987) 63, 255, 261

Bey, Turhan 379
Beyond A Reasonable Doubt (RKO, 1956) 297
Beyond The Blue Horizon (Paramount, 1942) 252
Bible, The – In The Beginning (Fox, 1966) 162, 164
Biblical epics 38, 41, 203, 248; see also Ten Commandments, The
Bickford, Charles 127, 170, 217, 268, 379
Bicycle Thieves (1949) 93
Big Broadcast of 1937, The (Paramount, 1937) 257
Big Chill, The (Columbia, 1982) 122
Big Country, The (UA, 1958) 42
Big (Fox, 1988) 163, 164
Big Heat, The (Columbia, 1953) 130, 132
Big Parade, The (MGM, 1925) 28, 195, 206–7, 210, 222, 227
Big Sky The (RKO, 1952) 291
Big Sleep, The (Warner Bros, 1946) 33, 58, 426
Big Steal, The (RKO, 1949) 307
Big Trail, The (Fox, 1930) 152, 154
Billy Jack (Warner Bros, 1971) 415
Billy The Kid, (MGM, 1930) 197, 204; (MGM, 1941) 199
Binyon, Claude 282
Biograph Company 16, 18, 27, 45, 53, 65, 67, 376
biopics 153, 170, 294, 401, 403, 404, 405, 408, 412, 413, 424, 426, 436
Bird On A Wire (Universal, 1990) 375
Birds, The (Universal, 1963) 372, 382
Birdwell, Russell 24
Biro, Lajos 352
Birth Of A Nation, The (1914) 17, 23, 27, 45, 53, 57
Bischoff, Robert 184, 282
Bischoff, Samuel 291, 397
Bisset, Jacqueline 170

Bitter Tea Of General Yen, The (Columbia, 1932) 124, 129

Bitzer, Billy 281, 347, 348, 350, 376

Black Cat, The (Universal, 1934) 365, 386

Black, Karen 139

Black Narcissus (Universal, 1947) 37, 99, 360

Black Pirate, The (UA, 1926) 34, 329, 332

Black Swan, The (Fox, 1942) 145, 161, 167, 179

Blackboard Jungle, The (MGM, 1955) 199, 211

blacklisting 15, 89, 99, 125, 134

Blackton, J. Stuart 67

Blaine, Vivian 170

Blair, Janet 125, 127

Blair, Linda 96

Blangsted, Folmar 281, 437

Blanke, Henry 395, 397

Blazing Saddles (Warner Bros, 1974) 415

Blind Husbands (Universal, 1919) 366, 377, 383

Blithe Spirit (UA, 1945) 333

block booking by film companies 239

Blonde Crazy (Warner Bros, 1931) 403, 420

Blondell, Joan 30, 31, 217, 331, 403, 418, 419

Blondie series (Columbia) 111, 113

Blood And Sand, (Fox, 1941) 36, 145, 156, 175, 179; (Paramount, 1922) 54, 240, 256, 259, 280

Blood Ship, The (Columbia, 1927) 105

Blow-Up (MGM, 1967) 200

Blue Angel, The (Paramount, 1929) 249

Blue Bird, The (Fox, 1940) 56, 161, 181

Blue Dahlia, The (Paramount, 1946) 33

Blue Lagoon, The (Columbia, 1980) 122

Blue, Monte 268, 417, 425

Blue Skies (Paramount, 1946) 253, 259

Blue Veil, The (RKO, 1951) 299, 303, 318

Blues Brothers, The (Universal, 1980) 374

Bluhdorn, Charles 242, 244

Blumberg, Nate 360

Blystone, John 176

Blyth, Ann 217, 368, 378, 379, 388

Blythe, Betty 143, 170, 380

Boardman, Eleanor 218

Bob and Carol and Ted and Alice (Columbia, 1969) 62, 120, 121

Bodeen, Dewitt 316

Body And Soul (UA, 1947) 349

Boehm, Sydney 184, 282

Boemler, George 184, 231

Boers Bringing In Prisoners (1901) 27

Boetticher, Budd 131, 133, 384

Bogart, Humphrey 33, 38, 60, 95, 114, 119, 126, 127, 167, 170, 268, 354, 404, 405, 417, 420–1, 424, 426, 427, 437

Bogdanovich, Peter 39, 120, 121

Bogeaus, Benedict 325

Boggs, Francis 16

Bois, Curt 60

Boland, Mary 218, 268

Bolero (Paramount, 1934) 249

Boles, John 167, 170, 300, 380, 418

Boleslawski, Richard 224, 333, 346

Bolger, Ray 218, 307

Bombardier (RKO, 1943) 296

Bond, James series 210, 338, 339, 343

Bonnie And Clyde (Warner Bros, 1967) 39, 75, 90, 91, 413, 415

Boomerang (Fox, 1946) 153

Boorman, John 200

Booth, Margaret 79, 192, 229, 231, 235

Booth, Shirley 95, 268, 285

Border Incident (MGM, 1949) 199

Bordoni, Irene 418

Borg, Karl Oscar 351

Borgnine, Ernest 95, 127, 218, 354

Born On The Fourth Of July (Universal, 1989) 361, 373–4, 375, 392

Born To Love (RKO, 1931) 294

Born Yesterday (Columbia, 1950) 107, 115, 121, 126, 130, 138

Borzage, Frank 92, 132, 143, 151, 160, 166, 173–4, 176, 180, 185, 224, 273, 427

Bosustow, Steve 113

Bosworth, Hobart 105, 376

Boulle, Pierre 99

Bow, Clara 30, 170, 240, 247, 251, 262, 264, 265, 268, 272

Box Office Attractions Film Rental Company 142, 147, 159

Boy With Green Hair, The (RKO, 1948) 19, 298

Boyd, William 247, 268

Boyer, Charles 215, 333, 342

Boyle, Robert 135, 315, 386, 388

Boys Town (MGM, 1938) 210

Brabin, Charles 224

Bracht, Frank 282

Bracken, Eddie 252, 268

Brackett, Charles 184, 215, 282, 285

Brady, Alice 186

Brady, Scott 170, 268, 380

Brahm, John 131, 176

Brainstorm (MGM, 1983) 209

Brando, Marlon 94, 95, 110, 127, 139, 209, 254, 286, 405, 413, 421, 422

Brandt, Joe 104, 105–6, 108

Brass (Warner Bros, 1923) 417

Brave One, The (RKO, 1956) 99, 319

Bredell, Woody 388, 434

Breen Office (of censorship) 338

Bremer, Lucille 218

Brendel, El 167, 170, 180, 268, 380

Brennan, Walter 95, 155, 170, 186, 342, 343, 354, 380

Brenon, Herbert 142, 271, 272, 277, 366
Brent, Evelyn 170, 268
Brent, George 170, 307, 380, 404, 407, 418, 421
Bretherton, David 184
Bretherton, Howard 274, 424–5, 427
Brian, Mary 268
Brice, Fanny 418
Bride Of Frankenstein, The (Universal, 1935) 365, 366–7, 381, 386
Bridge On The River Kwai, The (Columbia, 1957) 53, 89, 93, 99, 107, 108, 110, 115, 121, 125, 129, 130, 134, 139
Brigadoon (MGM, 1954) 204
Brigham Young (Fox, 1940) 56, 161, 181
Bright Victory (Universal, 1952) 367
Bringing Up Baby (RKO, 1938) 56, 301, 310
Briskin, Samuel 105, 107, 289, 292
Brisson, Carl 249
British films 89, 90, 91, 93, 96, 98–9, 120, 234, 277, 286, 324, 325, 331, 333, 339, 354, 360, 366, 391
Britton, Barbara 127, 268
Broadway Danny Rose (Woody Allen 1984) 39
Broadway Melody of 1936 (MGM, 1936) 215
Broadway Melody The (MGM, 1929) 31, 34, 55, 85, 88, 191, 195, 197, 200, 207, 210, 227, 233
Broadway (Universal, 1929) 30, 34, 55, 359, 365, 367, 386
Broccoli, Cubby 339
Broderick, Helen 295
Brodine, Norbert 183, 230, 315, 388
Broken Arrow (Fox, 1950) 157, 179
Broken Blossoms (UA, 1919) 335
Bronson, Betty 268
Bronston, Samuel 42, 204, 254, 258
Brook, Clive 268

Brooks, James L. 286
Brooks, Louise 106, 173, 265, 268
Brooks, Mel 243
Brooks, Richard 115, 116, 193, 224
Brother Orchid (Warner Bros, 1940) 425
Brother Rat (Warner Bros, 1938) 403
Brother Rat And A Baby (Warner Bros, 1940) 403
Brothers Karamazov, The (MGM, 1958) 228
Brown, Bernard 391
Brown, Clarence 92, 197, 198, 199, 222, 223, 224, 234, 366, 382, 383, 384
Brown, David 63
Brown, Harry Joe 274, 384
Brown, Hilyard 388
Brown, Hiram 288, 289
Brown, Joe E. 127, 307, 417, 418, 419, 420
Brown, Johnny Mack 197, 218, 377, 380
Brown, Karl 277, 281
Brown Of Harvard (MGM, 1926) 197
Browning, Tod 191, 197, 224, 366, 383, 384
Brownlow, Kevin, Hollywood, The Pioneers 18
Bruce, Virginia 218, 268, 380
Bruckheimer, Jerry 63, 259
Brute Force (Universal, 1947) 387
Bryant, Edwin 136
Brymer (costume designer) 389
Brynner, Yul 127, 170, 186, 218, 343
Buccaneer, The, (Paramount, 1937) 248; (Paramount, 1958) 267
Buchman, Sidney 111, 132, 134, 136, 282
Buchwald, Art 64
Buck Benny Rides Again (Paramount, 1940) 259
Buckland, Wilfred 78, 276, 278, 279, 281, 347, 348
Buckner, Robert 389, 433, 435

Bucquet, Harold S. 224
Bugs Bunny 406
Bull, Clarence Sinclair 24
Bulldog Drummond (UA, 1929) 323
Bullitt (Warner Bros, 1968) 39, 413, 415
Bumstead, Henry 279, 281, 388, 390, 392
Burke, Billie 216, 246, 268, 307, 331, 343, 380
Burke, Edwin 184
Burke, Joe 432
Burks, Robert 254, 434
Burma Victory (Warner Bros, 1945) 404
Burns, George 96, 248, 266, 268, 273
Burstyn, Ellen 438
Burton, Bernard 389
Burton, Richard 96, 170
Bus Stop (Fox, 1956) 162, 169
Busch, Niven 435
Bushman, Francis X 218
Butch Cassidy And The Sundance Kid (Fox, 1969) 162, 164
Butler, David 174, 176, 427
Butler, Frank 283
Butler, Hugo 231
Butterfield 8 (MGM, 1960) 95, 211, 235
Buttolph, David 184, 434
Buzzell, Edward 132, 220, 221, 224, 384
Bwana Devil (UA, 1952) 40, 41, 329, 334
Byrd, Ralph 295

Cabin In The Cotton (Warner Bros, 1932) 419
cable TV 39
Cabot, Bruce 218, 307
Cactus Flower (Columbia, 1969) 121
Caesar And Cleopatra (UA, 1946) 333
Cagney, James 30, 31, 95, 341, 342, 343, 367, 403, 404, 405, 408, 412, 413, 417, 418, 419, 420, 421, 424, 436, 437
Cahn, Philip 389
Caine Mutiny, The (Columbia, 1954) 121
Calamity Jane And

Sam Bass (Universal, 1949) 368

Caldwell, Dwight 136

Calhern, Louis 218

California (MGM, 1927) 227

California Suite (Columbia, 1978) 63, 83, 96, 122

Call Northside 777 (Fox, 1948) 58, 175

Call Of The North, The (Paramount, 1914) 247

Call Of The Wild, The (UA, 1935) 330

Camelot (Warner Bros, 1967) 411, 413, 430

Cameo Kirby (Fox, 1923) 112

Camera 65 process 58, 204, 227

Cameramen and art directors 8, 66, 76–7, 78–9, 312–14; Columbia 132–3; Fox 178–81; MGM 226–9; Paramount 276–9, 281; RKO 312–14, 315; UA 347–9, 350–1; Universal 385–7, 388–9; Warner Bros 429–32, 436

Cameron, Rod 268, 380

Camille, (Fox, 1917) 150, 166; (MGM, 1937) 210, 213, 234

Can-Can (Fox, 1960) 158, 182

Cannes Film Festival 355

Cannonball Run, The (Fox, 1981) 164

Canova, Judy 127, 268

Can't Help Singing (Universal, 1944) 368

Cantor, Eddie 55, 331, 332, 337, 341, 342, 343

Canutt, Yakima 98

Capitol Theatre, New York 20

Capra, Frank 19, 56, 69, 88, 91, 92, 98, 103, 105, 106, 108, 110, 111, 112, 117, 118, 123, 124, 129–30, 131, 137–8, 274, 303, 427

Captain Blood (Warner Bros, 1935) 401, 403, 404, 425, 431

Captain From Castile (Fox, 1947) 157

Captain Kidd Jr (Famous Players-Lasky, 1919) 271

Captains Of The Clouds (Warner Bros 1942) 404, 408

Carbonara, Gerard 282

Cardiff, Jack 154–5

Cardinal Richelieu (UA, 1935) 350

Carefree (RKO, 1938) 56, 298

Carey, Harry, Sr. 218, 377, 380, 382

Carey, MacDonald 170, 268, 380

Carfagno, Edward 230, 235

Carmen (Fox, 1915) 166

Carney, Art 187

Carolco, (independent film company) 121

Caron, Leslie 216, 218

Carousel (Fox, 1956) 40, 158

Carpenter, Francis 150

Carpenter, John 99

Carpetbaggers, The (Paramount, 1964) 258, 260

Carradine, John 170, 268

Carre, Ben 78, 180, 183, 228, 230, 278, 281, 385, 386, 434

Carrere, Edward 351, 432, 434

Carrie (UA, 1976) 355

Carroll, Madeleine 170, 266, 268

Carroll, Nancy 127, 268

Carruth, Milton 387, 389

Carson, Jack 268, 306, 307, 380, 421

cartoons 35, 45, 57, 97, 99, 113, 192, 235, 249, 293, 298, 354, 365, 391, 406 Oscars for 99–100

Casablanca (Warner Bros, 1942) 58, 60–1, 88, 398, 399, 400, 404, 413, 414, 417, 421, 424, 425, 430, 432, 434, 436, 438

Cashin, Bonnie 182, 183

Cass Timberlane (MGM, 1947) 211

Cassini, Oleg 182, 183

Castle Rock (independent film company) 121

Castle, William 131, 384

Cat And The Canary, The (Universal, 1927) 366

Cat And The Fiddle, The (MGM, 1934) 198, 200

Cat Ballou (Columbia, 1965) 94, 95, 122

Cat On A Hot Tin Roof (MGM, 1958) 209, 211

Cat People, (RKO, 1942) 302

Catch-22 (Paramount; 1970) 260, 278

Catchings, Waddil 410

Cathcart, Daniel 230

Cattle Queen Of Montana (RKO, 1954) 40, 307

Caulfield, Joan 268

Cavalcade (Fox, 1933) 87, 88, 138, 144, 147, 161, 163, 174, 180, 185

CBC Film Sales Company 104–5, 110
 see also Columbia

CBS radio network 241, 248

CBS Televison 123

Ceiling Clipper (Warner Bros, 1936) 403

censorship 14, 163, 243, 338; *see also* blacklisting

Centaur Comedies 16

Centaur Film Company of New Jersey 16

Chad Hanna (Fox, 1940) 155

Chadwick, Helene 127

Chambers, John 181

Champ, The, (MGM, 1931) 210, 233; (MGM, 1979) 212

Champion (UA, 1949) 331, 338

Chan, Charlie 144, 152, 167

Chandler, Jeff 368, 376, 379, 380

Chandler, Raymond 284

Chaney, Lon, Jr 366, 378, 380

Chaney, Lon, Sr, 54, 197, 212, 218, 268, 361, 371, 377, 380

Chang (Paramount, 1927) 273

Chaplin, Charlie 17, 19, 28, 46, 54, 65–6, 75, 94, 97, 263, 322–4, 326, 327, 329, 330, 331, 336, 337, 341, 342, 343, 345, 346, 348, 353, 397, 411

Chaplin, Saul 229

Chaplin, Sydney 17

Chapman, Marguerite 127

Charade (Universal, 1963) 372, 374

Charge at Feather River, The (Warner Bros, 1953) 41

Charge Of The Light Brigade, The (Warner Bros, 1936) 404, 412, 431

Chariots Of Fire (Warner Bros, 1981) 91, 416, 438

Charisse, Cyd 216, 218

Charlie Chan Carries On (Fox, 1931) 152

Chase, Borden 389

Chase, Charley 113

Chatterton, Ruth 241, 268

Che! (Fox, 1969) 176

Cheaper By The Dozen (Fox, 1950) 163

Cheat, The (Paramount, 1915) 78, 276

Check and Double Check (RKO, 1931) 299

Cher 235

Chevalier, Maurice 198, 218, 241, 248, 249, 268, 268, 350

Cheyenne Autumn (Warner Bros, 1964) 409

Cheyenne (Warner Bros) 398

Chierichetti, David 8, 280

Children of A Lesser God (Paramount, 1986) 286

Children's Hour, The (1962) 74

China Clipper (Warner Bros, 1936) 403

China Seas (MGM, 1935) 208, 210

China Syndrome, The (Columbia, 1979) 122

Chinatown (Paramount, 1974) 90, 278, 279

Chinese Theatre, Hollywood 21

Chitty Chitty Bang Bang (UA, 1968) 339

chorus girls 125–6

Chrétien, Henri 41, 157

Christie, Julie 96

Christopher Strong (RKO, 1933) 294, 305

Cimarron (RKO, 1931) 88, 294, 299, 300, 305, 314, 317, 318, 319

Cimino, Michael 63, 93, 327

Cinderella (Disney, 1950) 299

Cinecolor 38, 253

cinema admission prices 21–2

cinema-building 20–1
  drive-ins 22, 40

CinemaScope 26, 38, 41–3, 49, 54, 58–9, 62, 99, 110, 114–15, 146–7, 149, 153, 157–9, 161–2, 179, 193, 203–4, 242, 250, 253, 293, 298–9, 334, 363, 368–9, 393, 398, 401, 405, 408–9, 432

Cinerama 40–1, 42, 58, 157, 196, 204–5

Circus, The (UA, 1928) 97, 323, 336, 353

Circus World (Paramount, 1964) 42, 254

Citizen Kane (RKO, 1941) 8, 77, 87, 92, 287, 288, 291, 292, 293, 296–7, 310, 312–13, 317–18

City Girl (Fox, 1930) 174, 180

City Gone Wild, The (Paramount, 1927) 247

City Lights (UA, 1931) 340

City Slickers (Columbia, 1990) 121

City Theatre, New York 20

Clair, René 331

Clampett, Bob 406

Clancey, Margaret 184, 351

Clark, Al 135, 136

Clark, Candy 96

Clark, Carroll 313–14, 315, 319

Clark, Dane 406

Clark, James B, 182, 184

Clark, Marguerite 240, 263, 268

Clarke, Arthur C, 200

Clarke, Charles 183, 230

Clarke, Harley 143

Clash By Night (RKO, 1952) 291, 297

Clatworthy, Robert 281, 388

Claws Of The Hun, The (Paramount, 1918) 246

Clemens, William 274, 311, 427

Clements, John 333

Cleopatra, (Fox, 1917) 166; (Fox, 1963) 43, 61, 74, 146, 158, 162, 164, 170, 176, 179, 181, 182; (Paramount, 1934) 248, 277

Clift, Montgomery 140, 268, 343

Climax, The (Universal, 1944) 368

Cline, Edward 176, 224, 274, 311, 384, 427

Clive, Colin 366

Clockwork Orange, A (Warner Bros, 1971) 86, 90, 91, 436

Close Encounters Of The Third Kind (Columbia, 1977) 62, 107, 109, 117, 120, 122, 131

Clyde, Andy 113

Coal Miner's Daughter (Universal, 1980) 374, 392

Cobb, Lee J, 168, 170, 218

Coburn, Charles 138, 170, 218, 220, 380

Coca-Cola Corporation 103, 107–8, 109, 120–1

Cochran, Steve 127, 307

Cochrane, R.H. 360

Cock-Eyed World, The (Fox, 1929) 28, 163, 174

Cocoanuts, The (Paramount, 1929) 241

Cocoon (Fox, 1985) 164, 187

Code Of The Secret Service (Warner Bros, 1939) 403, 405

Coffee, Lenore 232, 433, 435

Cohan, George M. 436

Cohen, Manny 241

Cohens And The Kellys, The (Universal, 1926) 366

Cohn, Harry 32, 68, 103–7, 108–9, 111, 112, 114, 115, 118, 123, 124, 125, 126, 130, 134, 137, 396

Cohn, Jack 103, 104, 108, 396

Cohn, Ralph 107

Colbert, Claudette 36–7, 112, 124, 138, 156, 241, 248, 249, 262, 265, 266, 268, 280, 285, 307, 342, 360, 372, 378, 379

Colbert, Norman 184

Coldeway, Anthony 435

Cole, Lester 389

Collins, Joan 169, 170

Colman, Ronald 30, 95, 218, 234, 247, 248, 257, 268, 307, 323, 342, 343, 391

Color Of Money, The (1986) 96

Color Purple, The (Warner Bros, 1985) 62, 86, 187, 412, 413

Colorado Territory (Warner Bros, 1948) 405

colour 7, 34–40, 49
    at Columbia 114–15; at Fox 145, 154–8; at MGM 200–3; at Paramount 245, 250–3, 278; at RKO 291, 293, 296, 297–9; at UA 298, 332–4; at Universal 367–9; at Warner Bros 405, 406–9

colourization process 15, 39

Columbia 7, 9, 19–20, 32, 33, 37–8, 47, 49, 50, 51, 52, 56, 103–39
    British films 120; cameramen and art directors 132–3; editors 135, 136; finances 117–23; history 68, 103–9, 396; Oscars 137–9;

sound 134; Westerns 113; writers 133, 134, 136

Coma (MGM, 1978) 212

Come And Get It (UA, 1936) 354

Come Back Little Sheba (Paramount, 1952) 285

Come September (Universal, 1961) 174

comedy 28, 111–13, 124, 129–30, 196–7, 330, 331, 364, 365–6, 367, 406

Coming Home (UA, 1978) 355

Coming to America (Paramount, 1988) 64, 257, 260, 261

Common Clay (Fox, 1930) 163

Compson, Betty 54, 268, 294, 300, 304, 307

Comstock, Daniel 34

Coney Island (Fox, 1943) 155

Confessions Of A Nazi Spy (Warner Bros, 1939) 404, 432

Connecticut Yankee, A (Fox, 1931) 163, 174

Connery, Sean 286, 343

Connolly, Walter 111

Conqueror, The, (Fox, 1917) 150; (RKO, 1956) 299

Conquerors, The (RKO, 1932) 300

Conquest (MGM, 1937) 215, 228

Conrad In Quest Of His Youth (Paramount, 1920) 272

Consent Decree (1948) 15, 22, 49, 107, 208, 242, 244, 255, 258, 303, 398, 400

Consolation Marriage (RKO, 1931) 294

Conte, Richard 127, 168, 170, 380

Conversation, The (Paramount, 1974) 90, 279, 286

Conway, Jack 176, 222, 224, 383, 384

Conway, Morgan 296

Conway, Tom 170, 218, 295, 307

Coogan, Jackie 218, 268

Cool Hand Luke (Warner Bros, 1967) 39, 415

Cooper, Gary 36, 57, 95, 124, 245, 247, 248, 250, 252, 262, 264, 266, 268, 272, 307, 342, 343, 354, 404, 419, 436

Cooper, Jackie 198, 218, 380

Cooper, Merian C, 40, 273, 288, 289, 292, 297, 298

Coppola, Francis Ford 45, 62, 75, 90, 93, 187, 242, 244, 279, 284, 286, 355

Coquette (UA, 1929) 323, 353

Cornered (RKO, 1945) 307

Cortez, Ricardo 170, 268, 307

Cortez, Stanley 313, 350, 385, 386, 388

Cosby, Bill 121

Costa-Gavras 93

Costner, Kevin 91, 93, 414

costs 52–64
    of colour 35–6; *see also* finances *under individual studios*

costume design 66, 79, 82, 98, 115, 132, 134–5, 178, 182, 183, 229, 265, 280, 315, 316, 333, 351, 433, 434

costume dramas 198, 293, 295, 401

Cotten, Joseph 170, 306, 307, 342, 343, 380

Coulter, Lucia 387

Counsellor-At-Law (Universal, 1933) 365

Count Of Monte Cristo, The, (Selig Polyscope, 1907) 16

Count Of Monte Cristo, The, (Paramount, 1913) 238

Country Girl, The, (Paramount, 1954) 253, 260, 267, 285–6

Cover Girl (Columbia, 1943) 110, 113, 114–15, 118, 124, 133, 134

Covered Wagon, The
(Paramount, 1923) 28,
54, 166, 240, 243, 246,
247, 250, 255, 256–7,
259, 272, 277, 280
Coward, Noel 337
Cowdin, John Cheever
360, 372
Cox, David 183, 231
Crabbe, Buster 127, 266,
269, 379, 380
Craig's Wife (Columbia,
1936) 112, 133
Crain, Jeanne 168, 170
Crash Dive (Fox, 1943) 182
Crawford, Broderick 114,
126, 127, 138, 269, 380
Crawford, Joan 24, 30, 33,
36–7, 95, 127, 196, 201,
213, 214, 215, 216, 217,
218, 229, 291, 318, 345,
405, 421, 430, 438
Creature From The Black
Lagoon, The (Universal,
1954) 368, 388
Cregar, Laird 168, 170
Cries and Whispers (Ingmar
Bergman, 1972) 86, 94
Crime And Punishment
(Columbia, 1935)
112, 133
Crime Does Not Pay
(shorts, MGM) 192
crime films *see film noir;*
gangster films; thrillers
Criminal Code, The
(Columbia, 1930) 92,
130, 132, 137
Crimson Pirate, The
(Warner Bros, 1952) 408
Crisp, Donald 95, 186, 271
Crocodile Dundee II
(Paramount, 1988) 260
Crocodile Dundee
(Paramount, 1986)
63, 260
Cromwell (Columbia,
1970) 120
Cromwell, John 274, 288,
290, 309, 310, 311,
345, 346
Crone, George 316
Cronyn, Hume 218
Crosby, Bing 95, 167, 218,
242, 245, 247, 249, 250,
252, 253, 254, 257, 258,
262, 266–7, 269, 285

Crosland, Alan, Jr. 351, 384,
425, 427, 435
Crossfire (RKO, 1947) 58,
291, 297, 303, 307
Crowd, The (MGM, 1927)
29, 191, 223
Crowther, Bosley 217
Cruise, Tom 257, 391
Crusades, The (Paramount,
1935) 55, 248, 259
Cruze, James 247,
256, 257, 272,
274, 277
Cucaracha, La (RKO, 1934)
35, 297–8
Cukor, George 19, 38, 106,
126, 129, 130, 131, 220,
221, 223, 224, 274, 288,
305, 309, 310, 311, 409,
436, 438
Culver City, California 17,
18, 190, 193
Cummings, Constance 127
Cummings, Irving 131, 151,
174, 176, 384
Cummings, Robert 380
Curtis, Tony 376, 379, 380
Curtiss, Edward 389
Curtiss, Ray 184, 282,
389, 435
Curtiz, Michael 8, 36, 60,
274, 407, 408, 419,
424, 425, 427, 430, 431,
436, 438
Cyrano de Bergerac (UA,
1950) 338, 354

d'Abbadie d'Arrast,
Harry 274
Daddy Long Legs, (First
National, 1919) 54,
411, 414; (Fox, 1931)
163, 166
Daffy Duck 406
D'Agostino, Albert
281, 313, 315, 319,
351, 388
Dahl, Arlene 218, 269
Dailey, Dan 168, 170, 218
Dalio, Marcel 60
Dalton, Timothy 343
Daly, Robert A, 400
Damsel In Distress, A
(RKO, 1937) 314, 319
Dana, Viola 110, 269
Dance Of Life (Paramount,
1929) 251

Dances With Wolves
(1990) 63, 91, 93, 317
Dancing Lady (MGM, 1933)
210, 305
Dancing Pirate, The
(Pioneer/RKO, 1936)
298, 407
Dangerous (Warner Bros,
1935) 94, 420, 426, 436
Daniels, Bebe 247, 269,
293, 300, 304, 307
Daniels, William 37, 201,
226, 230, 385, 386, 388,
390, 391
Dante, Joe 400
Dantine, Helmut 60
Dark Mirror, The
(Universal, 1946)
360, 374
Darling (Britain, 1965) 96
Darling Lili (Paramount,
1970) 62, 258
Darling, William 178,
179–80, 181, 183, 185
Darnell, Linda 156, 170,
175, 307
Darwell, Jane 95, 170,
269, 308
Dassin, Jules 176, 224, 384
Date With The Falcon, A
(RKO, 1942) 295
*Daughter Of The Gods,
The* (Fox, 1916) 150
Daves, Delmer 133, 175,
176, 427, 435
David And Bathsheba (Fox,
1951) 169
David Copperfield (MGM,
1935) 208, 210
Davies, Marion 19, 54,
193, 196, 197, 213, 214,
218, 269
Davis, Bette 24, 30, 37, 83,
94, 186, 306, 377, 380,
403, 404, 405, 407, 408,
417, 418, 419, 420, 421,
426, 430, 433, 436
Davis, George 181, 183,
187, 230
Davis, Joan 127, 170, 308
Davis, Martin S, 244
Davis, Marvin 146–7, 148,
159, 163
Dawley, J. Searle 271
Dawn, Jack 9, 230
Dawn Patrol, The, (Warner
Bros, 1931) 29, 92, 436;

(Warner Bros, 1938) 404, 431

Dawson, Ralph 316, 389, 433, 435, 436

Day, Doris 367, 372, 376, 379, 380, 390, 408, 417, 422

Day For Night (Truffaut, 1974) 94

Day, Laraine 218, 308

Day Of The Locust, The (Paramount, 1975) 278

Day, Richard 78, 98, 145, 178, 180, 181, 183, 186, 230, 315, 349, 351, 385, 388

Day, Robert 228

Day The Earth Stood Still, The (Fox, 1951) 154

Days Of Glory (RKO, 1944) 296, 302

Days Of Heaven (Paramount, 1978) 278

Days Of Thunder (Paramount, 1990) 64, 259, 261

De Carlo, Yvonne 268, 368, 378, 380

De Cordova, Frederick 384, 427

De Cuir, John 386

De Gaetano, Al 184

De Grasse, Robert 312, 315

De Haven, Gloria 217

De Havilland, Olivia 76, 94, 95, 186, 269, 285, 286, 296, 302, 360, 404, 407, 417, 419–21, 437

De Laurentiis 9

De Maggio, Nick 182, 184

de Mille, William 224, 272, 274

De Niro, Robert 268, 355

De Sica, Vittorio 93

De Toth, Andre 132, 346, 406, 427

De Vinna, Clyde 183, 226, 227, 230, 388

De Vito, Danny 187

Dead End (UA, 1937) 57, 330, 337, 340, 349, 354

Dean, James 94, 409, 417, 421, 422

Dean, Kay 231

Death Of A Salesman (Columbia, 1951) 138

Decca Record Company 360, 362, 372, 373

December 7th (1943) 92

DeCuir, John 181, 183, 187, 388

Dee, Frances 269, 308

Dee, Sandra 218, 380

Dee, The (Columbia, 1977) 122

Deer Hunter, The (EMI/Universal, 1978) 91, 374, 392

Del Rio, Dolores 170, 174, 304, 308, 343

del Ruth, Roy 176, 224, 346, 425, 427

Deliverance (Warner Bros, 1972) 414, 415

Demetrius And The Gladiators (Fox, 1954) 153

DeMille, Cecil B, 7, 17, 21, 27, 34, 36, 53, 54, 55, 58, 65, 69, 78, 83, 89, 119, 224, 239–4, 243, 244, 245, 247–8, 250, 253, 255–6, 257, 267, 271, 272, 274, 276, 277, 278

Demme, Jonathan 392

Dempster, Carol 269, 342, 343

Denny, Reginald 127, 218, 269, 308, 366, 377, 380

Depinet, Ned 291

Depression, effect on film industry 21, 26, 29, 31, 44, 47–8, 55, 75, 143, 152

Derek, John 126, 127, 170, 269

Desert Song, The (Warner Bros, 1929) 406

Desilu Productions 292, 303, 315

Desiree (Fox, 1954) 153

Desperadoes, The (Columbia, 1943) 114, 118

Destry Rides Again (Universal, 1939) 378

DeSylva, B,G, 'Buddy' 241, 243

Detective Story (Paramount, 1951) 253

Deutsch, Adolph 231, 433, 434

Devil Dogs Of The Air (Warner Bros, 1935) 403

Devil Is A Sissy, The (MGM, 1936) 198

Devine, Andy 380

Devotion (RKO, 1931) 294

Dial M For Murder (Warner Bros, 1953) 408, 409

Diamond, I.A.L. 184, 352, 435

Diary Of Anne Frank, The (Fox, 1959) 157

Dick Tracy series 296

Dick Turpin (Fox, 1925) 330

Dickinson, Angie 380, 422

Die Hard (Fox, 1988) 163, 164

Die Hard 2 (Fox, 1990) 63, 147, 163, 164

Dieterle, William 176, 224, 274, 309, 311, 424, 426, 427

Dietrich, Marlene 24, 35, 241, 249, 262, 265, 266, 269, 273, 280, 333, 378, 380

Dietrich, Ralph 184

Diller, Barry 147, 148, 241, 243

Dillon, John Francis 176, 427

Dimension-150 43

Diner (MGM, 1982) 200

Dinner At Eight (MGM, 1932) 214

directors, at Columbia 129–31; at MGM 221–5; at RKO 309–11; and contracts with studios 69, 74; foreign-language 93–4; Fox 143, 173–7; Oscars for 91–4; Paramount 271–5; role of 69–75; United Artists 344–6; Universal 360, 382–4; Warner Bros 401, 424–8

Directors Guild of America (DGA) 84, 86–7

Dirigible (Columbia, 1931) 110

Dirty Dozen, The (MGM, 1967) 209, 211

Dirty Harry (Warner Bros, 1971) 414, 427

Disney, Walt 9, 24–5, 35, 52, 97, 99, 113, 137, 290, 293, 321, 324, 325, 328, 337, 354

Disraeli (Warner Bros, 1929) 436

Dive Bomber (Warner Bros, 1941) 403, 408

Divine Lady, The (First National/Warner Bros, 1929) 425

Divorcee, The (MGM, 1930) 233

Dix, Richard 127, 247, 269, 300, 305, 308, 343

Dixie (Paramount, 1943) 252

Dmytryk, Edward 131, 176, 274, 276, 280, 282, 297, 302, 303, 310, 311

Docks Of New York, The (Paramount, 1928) 29, 277

documentaries 97, 98
    Oscars for 92, 99

Dodge City (Warner Bros, 1939) 36, 56, 407, 408

Dodson, Mary Kay 281

Dodsworth (UA, 1936) 330, 337, 340, 354

Dog Day Afternoon (Warner Bros, 1975) 90, 415

Dolan, Robert Emmett 282

Dolce Vita, La (1961) 94

Dolly Sisters, The (Fox, 1945) 161

Don Juan (Warner Bros, 1926) 28, 330, 395, 399, 418, 425

Donahue, Troy 380, 422

Donald Duck 25

Donat, Robert 96, 234

Donen, Stanley 115, 176, 223, 224, 372

Donlevy, Brian 170, 218, 269

Donovan Affair, The (Columbia, 1929) 123

Don't Change Your Husband (Paramount, 1918) 256

Dorothy Vernon Of Haddon Hall (UA, 1924) 350

Double Indemnity (Paramount, 1944) 267, 285

Double Life, A (Universal, 1948) 387, 391

Douglas, Everett 280, 282

Douglas, Gordon 131, 311, 346, 427

Douglas, Haldane 281

Douglas, Kirk 76, 267, 269, 307, 308, 326, 341, 343, 367, 380

Douglas, Melvyn 95, 96, 112, 124, 127, 215, 218, 308, 380

Douglas, Michael 187

Douglas, Paul 170

Dove, Billie 170, 250, 269, 418

Down Argentine Way (Fox, 1940) 156, 168, 181

Down To Earth (Columbia, 1947) 115

Doyle, Laird 435

Dr Cyclops (Paramount, 1940) 252

Dr Dolittle (Fox, 1967) 43, 158, 162, 182

Dr Jekyll And Mr Hyde (Paramount, 1920) 272; (Paramount, 1931) 92, 259, 285; (Universal, 1913) 366

Dr Kildare series 191, 196, 198

Dr No (UA, 1962) 119

Dr Strangelove (Columbia, 1963) 74, 87, 110, 116, 129

Dr X (Warner Bros, 1932) 34, 407

Dr Zhivago (MGM, 1965) 43, 205, 209, 211

Dracula (Universal, 1931) 31, 361, 366

Dracula's Daughter (UA, 1936) 365

Dragnet (Warner Bros, 1954) 415

Dreier, Hans 9, 78, 276, 279, 281

Dressler, Marie 94, 166, 196, 207, 214, 216, 218, 233, 235, 300

Drew, Ellen 127, 269

Dreyfuss, Richard 235, 355, 438

drive-in cinemas 22, 40

Driving Miss Daisy (Zanuck Co./Warner Bros, 1989) 91, 414, 415, 438

Drums Along The Mohawk (Fox, 1939) 36, 56, 153, 155, 156, 163

Du Bois, Raoul Pene 281

Dubarry, Woman of Passion (UA, 1930) 30

Dubin, Al 429, 432–3

Duel In The Sun (Selznick, 1946) 58, 68, 325

Duell, Randall 230

Duff, Warren 435

Dukakis, Olympia 235

Dunaway, Faye 235, 355

Duncan, Mary 174

Duning, George 135, 136

Dunn, James 167, 170

Dunn, Linwood 9

Dunne, Irene 94, 112, 125, 127, 134, 218, 247, 294, 301, 304, 305, 308, 318, 378, 380, 413

Dunne, Philip 184

Dunning, John 231

Durante, Jimmy 218

Durbin, Deanna 249, 366, 368, 371, 376, 378, 380, 383, 391

Duryea, Dan 308, 378, 380

Dvorak, Ann 218

Dwan, Allan 27, 65, 167, 173, 176, 180, 251, 271, 272, 274, 277, 307, 310, 311, 346, 384

E.T., The Extra-Terrestrial (Universal, 1982) 25, 62, 357, 361, 362, 363, 370, 373, 375, 385

Each Dawn I Die (Warner Bros, 1939) 425, 432

Ealing Films 366

Earthquake (Universal, 1974) 374, 388, 392

East Of Eden (Warner Bros, 1954) 38, 409, 415, 430

Easter Parade (MGM, 1948) 203, 211

Eastman Color 26, 38, 39, 157, 203, 368

Eastwood, Clint 343, 379, 380, 384, 414, 422, 427

Easy Rider (Columbia, 1969) 62, 120, 121

Easy To Wed (MGM, 1946) 211

Ebb Tide (Paramount, 1937) 252

Eddie Duchin Story, The (Columbia, 1955) 121

Eddy, Nelson 198, 215, 218, 249

Edens, Roger 229

Edeson, Arthur 183, 347, 348, 350, 388, 390, 430, 434

Edison company 26

Edison, Thomas 20, 65, 67

editors 79, 98, 135–6, 229, 280

Edouart, Farciot 82, 252, 276, 279–80

education and research 84

Educational Pictures Company 145

Edwards, Blake 131, 142, 200, 339, 343, 345, 355, 372, 384

Edwards, J. Gordon 142–3, 173

Edwards, Neely 104

Egg And I, The (Universal, 1947) 57, 360, 372, 374, 378

Egyptian, The (Fox, 1954) 153, 179

Eilers, Sally 170, 218

Eisler, Hanns 316

El Cid (1961) 42

Electric Horseman, The (Columbia, 1979) 122, 131

Elmer Gantry (UA, 1960) 90, 338, 354

Emma (MGM, 1932) 210

Emperor Waltz, The (Paramount, 1948) 259

Empire Strikes Back, The (Fox, 1980) 148, 163, 164

Enemy Mine (Fox, 1985) 163

Enforcer, The (Warner Bros, 1976) 415

English Army In The Battlefield (Edison, 1901) 26–7

English, John 131

Enright, Ray 384, 425, 427

Ephron, Henry and Phoebe 184

Epstein, Julius and Philip 434, 435

Errol, Leon 269, 295, 308, 380

Espionage Agent (Warner Bros, 1939) 404

Essanay Company 67

Estabrook, Howard 319

Etting, Ruth 406

Evans, Robert 242, 244

Everson, William 197

Every Which Way But Loose (Warner Bros, 1978) 414, 415

Ewell, Tom 170, 380

Exodus (UA, 1960) 74, 334, 338, 340

Exorcist, The (Warner Bros, 1973) 62, 90, 91, 400, 410, 413, 415

Fair Co-Ed, The (MGM, 1927) 197

Fair, Elinor 54

Fairbanks, Douglas, Jr 269, 298, 308, 343

Fairbanks, Douglas, Sr. 17, 27, 28, 34, 54, 83, 240, 246, 263, 269, 272, 322–3, 327, 329–30, 332, 335–6, 341, 342, 343, 347–8, 350

Falcon series (RKO) 295

Falcon's Brother, The (RKO, 1942) 295

Falkenburg, Jinx 125

Fall of Babylon, The (1919) 28

Fall Of The Roman Empire, The (Paramount, 1964) 254, 258

Family Affair, A (MGM, 1936) 198

family films 198

Famous Players Film Company 17, 20, 23, 45, 67, 237, 238–40, 243, 245, 262–3

Famous Players-Lasky Corporation 67, 240, 243, 271

   see also Paramount

fantasy 367, 378; *see also* science fiction

Fanti, Dick 136

Fapp, Daniel 278, 281

Farewell To Arms, A, (Paramount, 1932) 248, 277, 284; (Selznick, 1957) 68

Farmer, Frances 266, 269

Farmer's Daughter, The (Katie For Congress) (RKO, 1947) 318

Farnum, Dorothy 232

Farnum, Dustin 239, 247

Farnum, Joseph 235

Farnum, William 142, 150, 165, 166, 170

Farrar, Geraldine 263

Farrell, Charles 150, 165, 166, 170, 174

Farrell, Glenda 127, 380, 405, 418, 419

Farrow, John 274, 309, 427

fashion, influence of films on 24

Fat City (Columbia, 1972) 130

Fatal Attraction (Paramount, 1987) 241, 260

Father Goose (Universal, 1965) 374

Father Of The Bride (MGM, 1950) 211

Faye, Alice 36, 144, 152, 155, 161, 167, 170

Fazan, Adrienne 231

Fazenda, Louise 417, 418, 425

Feature Plays Company 243

Fegte, Ernst 279, 281, 315, 351

Fehr, Rudi 435

Fejos, Paul 29, 365, 384, 386

Feldman, Charles K. 33

Fellini, Federico 86, 93–4

Ferguson, Elsie 78, 263, 269, 278, 279

Ferguson, Perry 8, 77, 313, 315, 319

Ferrari, William 230

Ferrer, Jose 95, 354

Ferrer, Mel 218

Fetchit, Stepin 171

Fiddler On The Roof (UA, 1971) 340

Field Of Dreams (Universal, 1989) 361

Field, Sally 187

Fields, Joseph 316

Fields, Verna 79

Fields, W.C. 28, 245, 247, 248, 266, 269, 273, 376, 378, 380

Fiesta de Santa Barbara, La (MGM, 1936) 200

Fifty-five Days At Peking (1962) 42, 74

Fighting 69th, The (Warner Bros, 1940) 403, 404, 414, 425

Fighting Blade, The (First National, 1923) 28

Fighting Lady, The (1944) 92

Film Booking Offices of America (FBO) 287, 288, 292

film collections 84

film noir 133, 149, 153, 250, 267, 293, 296–7, 401, 405, 421
 see also thrillers

finances, Columbia 117–23; Fox 159–64, 371; MGM 206–11; Paramount 255–61; RKO 300–3; United Artists 335–40; Universal 370–6; Warner Bros 410–16

financial crisis (1969–70) 43

Finch, Peter 235

Finkel, Abem 433, 435

First National Exhibitors' Circuit 7, 18, 21, 28, 46–7, 54, 239, 240, 263, 322, 397–8, 399, 401, 402, 406, 410, 411, 418, 425, 429

First Yank Into Tokyo, The (RKO, 1945) 296

Fischbeck, Harry 277, 281

Fish Called Wanda, A (MGM, 1988) 9, 200, 212

Fisher, Carrie 59

Fitzgerald, Barry 95, 269, 285, 308, 380

Fitzmaurice, George 224, 272, 274, 277, 278, 346

Fitzpatrick's Traveltalks 192, 200

Five Easy Pieces (Columbia, 1970) 86, 120, 122, 139

Five Star Final (Warner Bros, 1931) 31, 412

Flame And The Arrow, The (Warner Bros, 1950) 33, 408

Flanagan, Edward 104

Flash Gordon films 377

Flashdance (Paramount, 1983) 259, 261

Flatliners (Columbia, 1990) 122

Fleischer, Dave 248

Fleischer, Max 248

Fleischer, Richard 131, 176, 291, 310, 311

Fleming, Rhonda 253, 269, 308

Fleming, Victor 92, 176, 223, 224, 234, 271, 272, 274, 277

Flesh And The Devil (MGM, 1927) 213, 223

Fletcher, Louise 355

Flight (Columbia, 1929) 110

Florey, Robert 86–7, 131, 241, 273, 274, 346, 365, 384, 427

Flowers and Trees (Disney, 1932) 35, 97, 137

Flying Down To Rio (RKO, 1933) 292, 298, 305

Flying Leathernecks (RKO, 1951) 299

Flynn, Errol 35, 36, 56, 403, 404, 408, 413, 417, 420, 421, 425, 437

Foch, Nina 127, 218, 269, 406

Fog Over Frisco (Warner Bros, 1934) 403, 430

Folies Bergère (UA, 1935) 350

Follow Thru (Paramount, 1930) 251

Folsey, George 227, 230, 281

Fonda, Henry 36, 96, 144, 145, 153, 154, 155, 156, 165, 167–8, 171, 175, 186, 248, 251, 269, 392

Fonda, Jane 355, 438

Fonda, Peter 62–3

Fontaine, Joan 94, 171, 252, 269, 306, 308, 318, 319, 380

Fontanne, Lynn 214

Fool There Was, A (Fox, 1915) 165

Foolish Wives (Universal, 1921) 23, 54, 78, 359, 361, 366, 370, 383, 385

Foote, Horton 392

Footlight Parade (Warner Bros, 1933) 412, 414, 426

Footloose (Paramount, 1984) 259, 261

For Me And My Gal (MGM, 1942) 209

For Pete's Sake (Columbia, 1974) 120

For Whom The Bell Tolls (Paramount, 1943) 252, 258, 259

Foran, Dick 405

Forbes, Ralph 218

Forbstein, Leo F. 60, 432, 434

Ford, Francis 378

Ford, Glenn 113, 114, 115, 118, 123, 124, 125, 127, 130, 218

Ford, Harrison 59, 218, 243, 268, 269

Ford, John, and Columbia 112, 115–16, 129; Fox 141, 143, 145, 150, 151, 153, 156, 160, 166, 167, 173, 174–5, 176; Oscars 91, 92, 185, 186, 254; and RKO 290, 301, 309, 310, 311, 317, 318; and technical advances 36, 37, 38, 41, 69, 74–5, 98; and UA 344, 345; and Universal, 377, 382–3, 384, 409; and Warner Bros 254, 409

Forde, Eugene 176

Foreign Correspondent (UA, 1940) 331, 345

foreign language films 93–4, 97

Foreman, Carl 99, 135, 137, 352

Forest Rangers, The (Paramount, 1942) 252

Forever Amber (Fox, 1947) 157, 161, 163, 182

Forman, Milos 91, 93, 355

Formula, The (MGM, 1980) 209

Fortune Cookie, The (UA, 1966) 39, 354

48 HRS (Paramount, 1982) 259

Forty-Second Street

(Warner Bros, 1933) 414, 426, 429, 433

Fosse, Bob 187

Foster, Jodie 286

Foster, Lewis R. 274, 383, 384

Foster, Norman 131, 176, 224, 311

Foster, Preston 171, 218, 269, 308, 380

Foster, Susanna 269, 366, 380

Foul Play (Paramount, 1978) 260

Fountainhead, The (Warner Bros, 1949) 432

Four Devils (Fox, 1928) 143, 174, 179

Four Feathers, The (UA, 1939) 36, 329, 333

Four Horsemen Of The Apocalypse, The (Metro, 1921) 45, 54, 190, 194, 210, 222, 383

Four Hours To Kill (Paramount, 1935) 248

Four Sons (Fox, 1928) 143, 160, 163, 174

Fowler, Hugh 184

Fox 7, 17, 21, 22, 24, 28, 29, 32, 36, 43, 44, 46–7, 49, 50, 52, 53–4, 56, 61–2, 68, 141–87, 289, 324, 328; cameramen and art directors 178–81; finances 159–64, 371; history 142–8; musicals 168; Oscars 158, 185–7; successes 55; Westerns 151–2, 153, 156, 166, 168

Fox Broadcasting (TV) 147

Fox Movietone 143, 147, 151–2 newsreels 145

Fox, The (Warner Bros, 1967) 415

Fox West Coast Theatres 143–4

Fox, William 17, 45, 46, 65, 66, 67, 141, 142–3, 147, 149–50, 159, 160–1, 192, 207, 238, 239

Foxes Of Harrow, The (Fox, 1947) 181

Foy, Bryan 31, 397, 398, 404–5, 406

Foy, Eddie, Jr 406

Francis, Anne 171, 218

Francis, Kay 265, 269, 306, 308, 380, 418, 420, 425, 433

Francis the Talking Mule 367, 380

Francis (Universal, 1950) 374

Frank, Melvin 224, 274, 275, 282

Frankenheimer, John 75

Frankenstein (Universal, 1931) 31, 361, 366, 371, 383, 386

Franklin, Chester 150

Franklin, Sidney 150, 222, 224, 234

Freaks (MGM, 1932) 191, 197

Frederick, Pauline 246, 269, 366

Free Soul, A (MGM, 1931) 233

Freed, Arthur 198, 201, 202, 208–9, 229, 234

Freeland, Thornton 346

Freeman, Mona 269

Freeman, Y. Frank 241, 244

Fregonese, Hugh 384

Freleng, Friz 99

French Connection, The (Fox, 1971) 62, 90, 94, 163, 164, 185, 187

French Lieutenant's Woman, The (UA, 1981) 355

French Line, The (RKO, 1954) 298, 299

Frenchman's Creek (Paramount, 1943) 252

Freund, Karl 227, 230, 365, 383, 384, 388, 434

Friedhofer, Hugo 182, 184, 434

Friedkin, William 62, 75, 90, 93, 187

Friendly Persuasion (1956) 99

Fritch, Robert 184

Frohman, Daniel 238

From Here To Eternity (Columbia, 1953) 107, 108, 115, 121, 130, 133, 139

Froman, Jane 406

Front Page, The (UA, 1931) 31, 330, 345, 353

Frontier Gal (Universal, 1945) 368

Fuller, Leland 181, 183

Fuller, Samuel 131, 175, 176, 311

Fulton, John P. 82, 276, 280, 385, 388

Funny Face (Paramount, 1957) 254

Funny Girl (Columbia, 1968) 63, 120, 121, 126, 139

Funny Lady (Columbia, 1975) 120

Furst, Anton 438

Furthman, Jules 111, 184, 272, 281

Fury (MGM, 1936) 92, 191

Fury Of The Jungle (Columbia, 1933) 111

Futureworld (MGM, 1974) 200

G-Men (Warner Bros, 1935) 412, 425

Gable, Clark 30, 31, 76, 112, 124, 197, 213, 214–15, 216, 218, 268

Gainsborough Studios 366

Gandhi (Columbia, 1982) 91, 93, 96, 107, 122, 139

Gang's All Here, The (Fox, 1943) 145, 156, 181

gangster films 30, 31, 393, 394

Garbo, Greta 24, 30, 37, 94, 98, 196, 199, 201, 207, 213–14, 215, 216, 218, 220, 222, 223, 233, 234

Garden Of Allah, The (UA, 1936) 35, 56, 333, 342

Gardner, Ava 157, 216, 218

Garfield, John 33, 404, 405, 420, 421

Garland, Judy 19, 35–6, 37, 98, 198, 201, 209, 213, 215, 216, 217, 218, 220, 234, 409

Garmes, Lee 78, 178, 183, 277, 278, 282, 349, 350, 432

Garner, Peggy Ann 168, 171

Garnett, Tay 176, 224, 274, 309, 311, 346, 384
Garralaga, Martin 60
Garrett, Betty 218
Garson, Greer 213, 215, 216, 218, 233, 234
Gates, Harvey 435
Gaucho, The (UA, 1928) 323, 336
Gaudio, Tony 135, 430, 434, 436
Gausman, Russell 390
Gavin, John 379, 380
Gay Divorcee, The (RKO, 1934) 305, 306, 318
Gaynor, Janet 35, 95, 143, 150, 160, 165, 166, 171, 174, 185
Gaynor, Mitzi 171, 269
General Died At Dawn, The (Paramount, 1936) 248
General Teleradio Corporation 291, 292, 303
General, The (UA, 1927) 336
Gentleman's Agreement (Fox, 1947) 89, 147, 175, 185, 186
Gentlemen Prefer Blondes (Fox, 1953) 157, 169, 175
Georgy Girl (Columbia, 1967) 120
Gerald McBoing Boing 113
Gering, Marion 131, 274
Gershenson, Joseph 389
Gershwin, Ira 333
Gershwin, George 294, 333
Gerstad, Harry 316, 351
Getting Straight (Columbia, 1970) 120
Ghost (Paramount, 1990) 63, 255, 259, 261, 286
Ghostbusters (Columbia, 1984) 107, 117, 120, 122
Ghostbusters II (Columbia, 1988) 117, 121, 122
Giannini, A. H. 324, 325
Giant (Warner Bros, 1956) 93, 409, 413, 414, 438
Gibbons, Cedric 8, 78, 82, 83, 97, 191, 202, 214, 226, 228–9, 230, 233, 279, 313
Gibbons, James 435
Gibney, Sheridan 435

Gibson, Hoot 377, 380
Gibson, Mel 200
Gielgud, John 96
Gifford, Frances 218, 269
Gigi (MGM, 1958) 38, 89, 93, 193, 209, 211, 223, 233, 234
Gilbert, John 28, 30, 171, 213, 214, 218, 269
Gilda (Columbia, 1946) 33, 58, 117, 118–19, 124, 125, 126, 133, 134, 135
Gilles, Geneviève 170
Gillespie, A. Arnold 82, 228, 230, 235
Gilliam, Terry 121
Gilmore, Stuart 184, 282, 316
Gilmore, Virginia 171
Ginsburg, Harry 241
Girl Can't Help It, The (Fox, 1956) 169
Girl In Every Port, A (Fox, 1928) 143, 173
Girl In Pink Tights, The (Fox, 1953) 169
Girl In The Red Velvet Swing, The (Fox, 1955) 169
Gish, Dorothy 269
Gish, Lillian 20, 29, 54, 98, 191, 197, 214, 216, 218, 222, 269, 342, 343
Glass Key, The (Paramount, 1935) 248
Gleason, James 294
Glenn Miller Story, The (Universal, 1954) 372, 374, 379, 383
Glennon, Bert 183, 281, 315, 350, 388, 434
Gliese, Rochus 180
Glorifying The American Girl (Paramount, 1929) 34, 251
Godard, Jean Luc 41
Goddard, Paulette 266, 269, 343
Goddess, The (Columbia, 1958) 116
Godfather, The (Paramount, 1972) 63, 90, 95, 242, 255, 258, 261, 278, 284, 286
Godfather, The, Part II (Paramount, 1974) 63,

90, 240, 242, 260, 277, 278, 283, 285
Godfather, The, Part III (Paramount, 1990) 63, 259
Godfrey, Bob 100
Godfrey, Peter 311, 427
God's Country And The Woman (Warner Bros, 1936) 35, 37, 407
Goetz, William 68, 144, 324, 360, 362
Going My Way (Paramount, 1944) 58, 88–9, 95, 242, 244, 259, 267, 273, 284, 285
Gold Diggers Of 1933 (Warner Bros, 1933) 412, 426, 429
Gold Diggers Of 1935 (Warner Bros, 1935) 429
Gold Diggers Of Broadway (Warner Bros, 1929) 31, 34, 396, 406–7, 410, 411, 414, 432
Gold Is Where You Find It (Warner Bros, 1938) 407, 412, 433
Gold Rush, The (UA, 1925) 336, 339, 348
Goldbeck, Willis 224
Goldberg, Whoopi 286
Golden Boy (Columbia, 1939) 106, 112, 124, 129
Golden Child, The (Paramount, 1986) 261
Golden Globe awards 86, 87, 90, 97, 438
Golden, Max 144
Goldfinger (UA, 1964) 340
Goldwyn Company 17, 18, 54, 190; see also MGM
Goldwyn Follies, The (UA, 1938) 35, 57, 333
Goldwyn, Samuel 38, 55, 57, 58, 68, 89, 98, 115, 190, 239–40, 243, 290, 318, 321, 323, 324–5, 328, 330, 332–3, 336, 337, 342
Golitzen, Alexander 349, 351, 386, 388, 390, 391, 392
Gomery, Douglas 302
Gone With The Wind (1939) 7, 17, 23, 35, 36, 45, 57, 68, 88, 89, 98,

195, 196, 197, 201–2, 208, 210, 223, 229, 233, 234–5, 287, 430

Good Earth, The (MGM, 1938) 57, 210, 227

Good Fairy, The (Universal, 1935) 365, 378

Good Morning, Vietnam (1988) 52

Goodbye Columbus (Paramount, 1969) 260

Goodbye Girl, The (MGM/Warner Bros, 1977) 212, 235, 415, 438

Goodbye Mr Chips (MGM, 1939) 96, 234

GoodFellas (Warner Bros, 1990) 438

Goodkind, Saul 184, 389

Goodman, John B. 279, 281, 388, 390, 391

Goodrich, Francis 232

Goonies, The (Warner Bros, 1985) 412, 414

Goosson, Stephen 132, 133, 138, 180, 183, 185–6, 230, 315, 351

Gordon, Michael 131, 176, 384

Gordon, Ruth 232

Gorilla At Large (Fox, 1954) 41

Gottschalk, Robert 43, 204

Goudal, Jetta 269

Goulding, Edmund 175, 176, 224, 274, 424, 426, 427

Government Girl (RKO, 1943) 296, 320

Grable, Betty 36, 141, 152, 155, 157, 165, 168, 169, 171, 249, 269, 306, 308, 343

Graduate, The (1967) 86

Grahame, Gloria 126, 127, 130, 218, 307, 308

Grainger, James 291

Grand Hotel (MGM, 1932) 88, 195, 208, 210, 214, 228, 234

Grand National studio 32

Grand Prix (MGM, 1966) 205, 211

Grande Illusion, La (1938) 93

Grandeur widescreen process 40, 154, 160

Granger, Farley 218, 308

Granger, Stewart 218

Grant, Cary 33, 76, 94, 112, 123, 124, 127, 130, 175, 262, 266, 269, 295, 296, 302, 304, 306, 308, 318, 331, 367, 372, 376, 379, 380, 408

Granville, Bonita 218, 405

Grapes Of Wrath, The (Fox, 1940) 96, 145, 153, 156, 167, 175, 182, 186

Grass (Paramount, 1926) 273

Graves, Ralph 110, 123, 127, 171, 268, 380

Gray, Coleen 171, 343

Gray, William 231

Grayson, Kathryn 218

Grease (Paramount, 1978) 25, 258, 260

Great Dictator, The (UA, 1940) 331

Great Expectations (Universal, 1947) 99, 360

Great McGinty, The (Paramount, 1940) 92, 285

Great Meadow, The (MGM, 1930) 204

Great Race, The (Warner Bros, 1965) 411, 413

Great Train Robbery, The (1903) 27, 65, 238

Great Ziegfeld, The (MGM, 1936) 88, 89, 95, 192, 196, 198, 210, 234

Greatest Show On Earth, The (Paramount, 1951) 7, 89, 253, 258, 260, 267, 271, 284, 286

Greatest Story Ever Told, The (UA, 1965) 43, 61, 74, 334, 338–9

Greed (MGM, 1924) 222, 251

Green, Alfred E. 130, 131, 176, 346, 424, 425–6, 427

Green Berets, The (Warner Bros, 1968) 415

Green Dolphin Street (MGM, 1947) 211

Green Grass of Wyoming (Fox, 1948) 157

Green, Johnny 230, 231, 389, 434

Green Years, The (MGM, 1946) 211

Greene, Richard 171

Greene, W. Howard 281, 350, 388

Greenstreet, Sydney 60, 421

Greenwich Village (Fox, 1944) 155

Greenwood, Charlotte 168, 171, 418

Greer, Howard 82, 280, 281, 316

Greer, Jane 218, 304, 307, 308

Gremlins (Warner Bros, 1984) 62, 400, 410, 413, 414

Grey, Virginia 218, 380

Grey, Zane 26

Griffith, Corinne 418

Griffith, D.W. 16, 17, 23, 27–8, 45, 53, 54, 65, 69, 77, 98, 257, 274, 322–3, 327–8, 329–30, 330, 335–6, 337, 342, 344, 346, 347–8, 376

Griffith Fine Arts Studio 17

Griffith, Raymond 247

Griggs, Loyal 281

Groesse, Paul 228, 230

Gross, Frank 389

Gross, Roland 316, 435

Grot, Anton 8, 78, 348, 351, 429, 431, 434, 436

Guardsman, The (MGM, 1931) 214

Guber, Peter 108, 109

Guess Who's Coming To Dinner? (Columbia, 1967) 121, 138

Guffey, Burnett 132, 133, 138

Guilaroff, Sydney 230

Guinan, Texas 418

Guinness, Alec 59, 96, 139

Gulf + Western conglomerate 50, 237, 242, 243, 244, 255, 258

Gulf Between, The (Technicolor Corporation, 1917) 34

Gun Crazy (UA, 1950) 332

Gunfight At The OK Corral (Paramount, 1957) 254

Gunfighter, The (Fox, 1950) 37, 169, 175

Gunga Din (RKO, 1939) 56, 289, 293, 295, 301

Guns of Navarone, The (Columbia, 1961) 121

Gunzburg, Milton 41

Guy Named Joe, A (MGM, 1943) 211

Guys And Dolls (MGM, 1956) 211

H.M. Pulham Esq. (MGM, 1941) 220

Haas, Robert 183, 278, 281, 429, 431, 434

Hackett, Albert 232

Hackett, James K. 238

Hackman, Gene 94, 187

Hagen, Jean 218

Haines, William 105, 127, 197, 218

Hal Roach studio 17

Hale, Alan 421

Hale, Barbara 127, 308

Hall, Alexander 130, 131, 273, 275

Hall, Charles B. 'Danny' 78, 347, 348, 349, 351, 366, 385–6, 388, 390

Hall, James 171, 269

Hall, Jon 378, 380

Hall Room Boys 104

Halleluiah (MGM, 1929) 191, 224

Haller, Ernest 429, 430, 434

Hamill, Mark 59

Hamilton, William 231, 316

Hamlet (Universal, 1948) 89, 96, 99, 360, 374, 391

Hamlisch, Marvin 392

Hammerstein, Elaine 105, 127

Hanna, William and Barbera, Joseph 192, 235

Hannah And Her Sisters (Woody Allen, 1986) 86

Hanover Square (Fox, 1944) 181

Hans Christian Andersen (RKO, 1952) 291, 299

Happy Days (Fox, 1929) 152, 154

Happy Go Lucky (Paramount, 1942) 252

Happy Landing (Fox, 1938) 161, 163

Hard To Kill (Warner Bros, 1990) 416

Hard Way, The (Warner Bros, 1943) 438

Harding, Ann 21, 218, 294, 304, 305, 308, 318

Hardwicke, Cedric 171, 308

Harkrider, John W. 351, 388, 389

Harlan County USA (1976) 100

Harlan, Russell 281

Harline, Leigh 316

Harling, W. Frank 282, 434

Harlow, Jean 30, 213, 214–15, 216–17, 218, 264, 269, 343

Harman, Hugh 192

Harris, Julie 138

Harrison, Doane 280, 282, 351

Harrison, Rex 171, 436, 438

Harry and Tonto (Fox, 1974) 187

Hart, William S. 166, 240, 246, 257, 262, 263, 264, 269, 322, 323, 330, 341, 343, 365

Hartley, Esdras 434

Harvey Girls, The (MGM, 1946) 202, 209, 211

Harvey, Laurence 218, 269

Harvey (Universal, 1950) 367, 372, 379, 391

Haskin, Byron 432

Hasso, Signe 171, 218

Hatchet Man, The (Warner Bros, 1932) 403

Hathaway, Henry 146, 153, 173, 175, 176, 247, 248, 274, 275

Haver, June 168, 171

Havlick, Gene 135, 136, 389

Havoc, June 269, 308

Hawks, Howard 17, 33, 41, 57, 74, 75, 92, 98, 112, 130, 131, 132, 138, 143, 173, 175, 176, 224, 291, 297, 310, 311, 331, 345, 424, 426, 427, 436

Hayakawa, Sessue 246

Hayden, Sterling 266, 269, 343

Hayes, Helen 95, 96, 214, 218, 233

Hayes, John Michael 282

Haymes, Dick 127, 168, 171, 380

Hays Code (of morality) 14, 163, 243

Hays, Will H. 14, 264

Hayton, Lennie 229, 231

Hayward, Lillie 435

Hayward, Susan 157, 171, 248, 266, 269, 318, 355, 379, 380

Hayworth, Rita 33, 37, 106, 110, 113, 114, 115, 118–19, 123, 124–5, 127, 133, 135, 154, 156, 171, 175

Head, Edith 82, 98, 265, 266, 276, 280, 281, 387, 389, 392

Hearst, William Randolph 54, 193, 291

Heart Of Humanity, The (Universal, 1919) 366

Heartbreak Ridge (Warner Bros, 1986) 414

Heaven Can Wait (Fox, 1943) 156; (Paramount, 1978) 258, 260

Heaven's Gate (UA, 1980) 63, 258, 327, 328, 335, 339

Hecht, Ben 16, 247, 275, 282, 333, 352

Hecht, Harold 33

Heckle and Jeckle 145

Hedrick, Earl 279, 281

Heflin, Van 127, 171, 199, 215, 218, 234, 269, 306, 308, 379, 380

Heindorf, Ray 433, 434

Heiress, The (Paramount, 1949) 285

Heisler, Stuart 275, 282, 349, 351

Held, Tom 231

Helen Of Troy (Warner Bros, 1955) 41, 74, 413, 432

Heller, Walter 326

Hellman, Lillian 330, 352

Hello Dolly! (Fox, 1969) 43, 158, 163, 164, 170, 181, 182

Hello Frisco, Hello (Fox, 1943) 155

Hello-Goodbye (Fox, 1970) 170

Hell's Angels (UA, 1930) 29, 344, 345, 365

Henabery, Joseph 272, 277

Hendrix, Wanda 269, 380

Henie, Sonja 144, 152, 161, 167, 171

Henley, Hobart 366

Henreid, Paul 60, 298, 421

Henry V (UA, 1945) 331, 333

Hepburn, Audrey 95, 242, 253, 254, 262, 267, 269, 317, 372

Hepburn, Katharine 37, 38, 56, 95, 139, 213, 215, 216, 218, 220, 288, 294, 295, 301, 304, 305, 306, 308, 318, 392

Her Invisible Husband (Universal, 1916) 366

Her Jungle Love (Paramount, 1938) 252

Herbert, F. Hugh 419, 435

Here Comes Mr Jordan (Columbia, 1941) 124, 130, 134, 138

Here Comes The Navy (Warner Bros, 1934) 403

Herman, Alfred 315

Herrick, Margaret 83

Herrmann, Bernard 8, 182, 184, 280–1, 312, 314, 316, 318

Herschel (costume designer) 182, 183, 231

Hersholt, Jean 171, 218, 295, 308, 380

Herzbrun, Bernard 183, 281, 315, 351, 388

Heston, Charlton 19, 218, 253, 262, 267, 269

Hi, Nellie! (Warner Bros, 1934) 403

Hiawatha (Universal, 1909) 358

Hickox, Sidney 430, 434

High And The Mighty, The (Warner Bros, 1954) 409, 413, 415, 426

High Noon (UA, 1952) 89, 326, 332, 338, 347, 350, 354

High Plains Drifter (Universal, 1973) 379

High Sierra (Warner Bros, 1940) 405, 420–1, 426, 427

High Society (MGM, 1956) 211, 254

High, Wide And Handsome (Paramount, 1937) 247

Hill, George Roy 346, 384, 392

Hill, George W. 224

Hill, The (MGM, 1965) 199

Hiller, Arthur 224, 275

Hilton, Arthur 137, 316, 389

Hindenburg, The (Universal, 1975) 392

Hirschfield, Alan 107, 109, 120, 146–7

His Girl Friday (Columbia, 1940) 112, 118, 130

His Majesty, The American (UA, 1919) 335

His Neighbour's Wife (Paramount, 1913) 238

Hitchcock, Alfred 37, 74, 92, 242, 253, 254, 258, 267, 271, 274, 275, 277, 280–1, 306, 309, 311, 318, 331, 344, 345, 346, 372, 382, 383, 384, 386, 408, 427

Hitler's Children (RKO, 1943) 296, 302

Hively, George 231, 316

Hoagland, Ellsworth 280, 282

Hodiak, John 127, 171, 218

Hodkinson, W.W. 239, 240, 243

Hoffenstein, Samuel 282

Hoffman, Dustin 63, 107, 120, 131, 139, 355

Hoffman, Joseph 389

Hogsett, Albert 183

Holden, William 112, 114, 123, 124, 125, 127, 266, 269, 285

Hole In The Wall, The (Paramount, 1929) 241

Holiday (Columbia, 1938) 106; (RKO, 1930) 318

Holiday in Mexico (MGM, 1946) 211

Hollander, Frederick 135, 282, 316, 434

Holliday, Judy 95, 114, 123, 124, 126, 127, 130, 138

Hollywood Canteen (Warner Bros, 1944) 405, 413, 414

Hollywood Cavalcade (Fox, 1939) 155

Hollywood Foreign Press Association 85, 86

Hollywood Hotel 16

Hollywood Revue Of 1929 (MGM, 1929) 197, 200, 201, 207, 210

Holm, Celeste 171, 218

Holmes, Brown 435

Holmes, Phillips 218, 269

Holmes, Sherlock 366, 378

Holmes, Stuart 142

Holmes, William 435

Holt, Jack 105, 110, 123, 127, 247, 250, 269, 380

Holt, Jennifer 123

Holt, Nat 290

Holt, Tim 123, 294, 304, 306, 308

Home Alone (Fox, 1990) 63, 147, 163, 164

Home In Indiana (Fox, 1944) 155

Home Of The Brave (UA, 1949) 331, 338

Homecoming (MGM, 1948) 211

Honor System, The (Fox, 1917) 150

Hooper (Warner Bros, 1978) 414, 415

Hopalong Cassidy series (Paramount) 247, 249, 326, 331

Hope, Bob 242, 245, 249, 250, 253, 262, 266–7, 269, 406

Hope, Frederic 230

Hopkins, Miriam 249, 269, 343

Hopper, Dennis 62–3, 120

Hornbeck, William 276, 282, 347, 349, 351, 389

Horne, Lena 216, 218

Horner, Harry 187

Horning, William A. 228, 230, 235

horror films 31, 34, 197, 252, 296, 331, 363, 364–6, 366–7, 367, 371, 377, 382, 383, 385, 391

Horsley brothers 16

Horton, Edward Everett 269, 380

House Of Rothschild, The (20th-Century/UA, 1934): 154, 354

House Of Wax (Warner Bros, 1953) 41, 401, 406, 413, 415

House On 92nd Street, The (Fox, 1945) 153, 175

Houseman, John 96, 187

Hovick, Louise (Gypsy Rose Lee) 171

How Green Was My Valley (Fox, 1941) 87, 88, 145, 161, 175, 179, 181, 182, 185, 186

How The West Was Won (MGM, 1962) 196, 204–5, 209, 211

How To Be Very Very Popular (Fox, 1955) 169

How To Marry A Millionaire (Fox, 1953) 41, 61, 146, 157, 164, 169

Howard, Leslie 21, 420, 421

Howard, Ron 374

Howard, Sidney 352

Howard The Duck (Universal, 1986) 63, 373

Howard, William K. 176, 224, 275, 346, 427

Howards of Virginia, The (Columbia, 1940) 112

Howe, James Wong 78, 99, 131, 178, 180, 183, 231, 256, 278, 279, 282, 349, 350, 432, 434

Hubbard, Lucien 435

Hubert, René 182, 183, 231, 281, 347, 350, 351

Hucksters, The (MGM, 1947) 211

Hud (Paramount, 1963) 95, 254, 277, 286

Hudson Hawk (Columbia, 1991) 121

Hudson, Rock 368, 372, 376, 379, 380

Hughes, Howard 47, 49, 287, 288, 290–1, 291, 292, 298, 300, 303, 319, 324, 331, 337, 344, 345, 354

Hughes, John J. 431, 434

Hull, Frank 184, 231

Hull, Josephine 391

Human Desire (Columbia, 1954) 130, 133

Humberstone, H. Bruce 174, 176, 275, 427

Humoresque (Warner Bros, 1946) 405, 421, 432

Hun Within, The (Paramount, 1918) 246

Hunchback Of Notre Dame, The, (RKO, 1939) 56, 289, 293, 295, 299, 300, 301–2, 306, 312, 313; (Universal, 1923) 359, 361, 366, 370, 374, 377, 386

Hunt For Red October, The (Paramount, 1990) 261

Hunt, Helen 114

Hunt, Marsha 218, 269

Hunter, Ian 218

Hunter, Jeffrey 171

Hunter, Ross 361, 367, 369, 372

Hunter, Tab 343, 422

Hurlbut, William 389

Hurrell, George 24

Hurricane, The (UA, 1938) 57, 349

Hussey, Ruth 218, 269

Hustler, The (Fox, 1961) 96, 157

Huston, John 38, 74, 92, 130–1, 176, 224, 334, 338, 344, 346, 355, 387, 424, 427, 435

Huston, Walter 130, 171, 218, 269, 406

Hutton, Betty 252, 253, 266, 269, 406

Hyman, Bernie 221

Hyman, Eliot 50, 398

I Am A Fugitive From A Chain Gang (Warner Bros, 1932) 87, 185, 403, 419, 425, 430, 436

I Married A Witch (Paramount, 1942) 331

I Remember Mama (RKO, 1948) 294, 318

I Want To Live! (UA, 1958) 355

I Wanted Wings (Paramount, 1941) 280

I Was A Communist For The FBI (Warner Bros, 1951) 99

I Was A Male War Bride (Fox, 1949) 161, 164, 175

Ice Follies Of 1939 (MGM, 1939) 201

Ice Station Zebra (MGM, 1968) 205

If I Were King (Paramount, 1938) 248

Ingster, Boris 296–7

Ihnen, Wiard 145, 157, 180, 181, 183, 278, 281, 315

I'll Cry Tomorrow (MGM, 1955) 211

I'll Take Manilla (MGM, 1941) 220

I'm No Angel (Paramount, 1933) 257, 259

Imitation Of Life, (Universal, 1934) 363, 365, 378, 383, 391; (Universal, 1959) 363, 368, 372, 374, 379, 384

In A Lonely Place (Columbia, 1950) 126

In Cold Blood (Columbia, 1967) 39, 116

In Name Only (RKO, 1939) 301, 306

In Old Arizona (Fox, 1929) 151, 163, 174, 185

In Old Chicago (Fox, 1937) 56, 161, 163, 180, 181–2, 186

In The Heat Of The Night (UA, 1967) 39, 86, 90, 349, 354, 355

In Which We Serve (UA, 1943) 337

Ince, Thomas 16, 17, 18, 190, 376

'Inceville', Hollywood 16

Incredible Shrinking Man, The (Universal, 1957) 388

independent directors/producers 63, 68–9, 129, 130, 175, 222, 290, 322–3, 341

Independent Motion Picture Company (IMP) 358, 361

Indiana Jones series (Paramount) 62, 254, 255, 259, 260

Inferno (Fox, 1953) 41

Informer, The (RKO, 1935) 84, 89, 289, 290, 301, 310, 313, 314, 318

Ingram, Rex 54, 69, 190, 191, 222, 224, 382, 383, 384

Inner Sanctum murder series (Universal) 366

International Pictures 360, 362

Intolerance (D.W. Griffith, 1916) 17, 27–8, 53, 77–8

Intruder In The Dust (MGM, 1949) 199

Invisible Man series (Universal) 364, 388

Invisible Man, The (Universal, 1933) 365, 388

Invisible Ray, The (Universal, 1936) 365

Irene (costume designer) 135, 227, 231, 333, 351

Iribe, Paul 279, 281

Irma La Douce (UA, 1963) 338

Iron Horse, The (Fox, 1924) 151, 166, 173, 257

Iron Mask, The (UA, 1929) 323

Irons, Jeremy 438

Irving G Thalberg Memorial Award 98, 234

Ishtar (Columbia, 1985) 63, 121

Ising, Rudolph 192

Island, The (Universal, 1980) 63

It Came From Outer Space (Universal, 1953) 368

It Happened One Night (Columbia, 1934) 87–8, 106, 108, 110, 111, 112, 118, 124, 129, 137, 138, 285, 355

It (Paramount, 1927) 264

It's A Mad, Mad, Mad, Mad World (UA, 1963) 334, 338, 340

It's A Wonderful Life (RKO, 1946) 303

Ivanhoe (MGM, 1952) 203, 211

Ivano, Paul 388

Jack And The Beanstalk (Fox, 1917) 150

Jack William Votion Productions 290

Jackman, Fred 432

Jackson, Felix 389

Jackson, Glenda 96, 355

Jacobs, Lewis 21

Jaffe, Leo 107

Jaffe, Stanley 243, 244

Jailhouse Rock (MGM, 1957) 40, 42, 204

James Bond series 210, 338, 339, 343

Jannings, Emil 244, 247, 264, 266, 269, 272, 284

Jarre, Maurice 135

Jaws (Universal, 1975) 62, 79, 91, 361, 362, 370, 373, 374, 385, 393

Jaws II (Universal, 1978) 63, 374

Jazz Singer, The, (Warner Bros, 1927) 55, 84, 97, 394–6, 399, 401–2, 411, 414, 418, 425, 430; (Warner Bros, 1953) 408

Jeakins, Dorothy 183

Jean, Gloria 171, 366, 378, 380

Jenkins, George 315

Jennings, Gordon 82, 276, 279–80

Jennings, Humphrey 98

Jennings, Talbot 232

Jergens, Adele 125

Jerk, The (Universal, 1979) 373, 374

Jesse James (Fox, 1939) 36, 153, 155, 163, 168

Jesse L. Lasky Feature Play Company 17, 67; *see also* Lasky

Jewel Of The Nile, The (Fox, 1985) 164, 187

Jewell, Edward C, 135

Jewison, Norman 235, 345, 346, 349, 384

Jezebel (Warner Bros, 1938) 404, 412, 419, 426, 430, 431, 436

Joan Of Arc (RKO, 1948) 294, 299

Joan Of Paris (RKO, 1942) 296

Joan The Woman (Famous Players-Lasky, 1916) 255

Joe Kidd (Universal, 1972) 379

Joe McDoakes series 406

John Stahl Productions 17

Johnny Angel (RKO, 1945) 307

Johnny Belinda (Warner Bros, 1948) 405, 414, 430, 438

Johnny Eager (MGM, 1942) 220, 234

Johnny O'Clock (Columbia, 1947) 133

Johnson, Ben 96

Johnson, Nunnally 144, 184, 352

Johnson, Joseph McMillan 281

Johnson, Van 218

Jolson, Al 45, 55, 171, 396, 406, 417, 418

Jolson Story, The (Columbia, 1946) 57, 107, 108, 110, 114, 115, 117, 118, 121, 125, 132, 134

Jolson Sings Again (Columbia, 1949) 107, 114, 117, 119, 121

Jones, Allan 218, 269, 380

Jones, Buck 113, 123, 127, 142, 150, 165, 166, 171, 377, 380

Jones, Chuck 99, 406

Jones, Harmon 184

Jones, Jennifer 171, 186, 342, 343

Jory, Victor 111, 127, 171, 343

Josephson, Julien 435

Journey Into Fear (RKO, 1942) 297

Joy, Leatrice 269

Joy Of Living (RKO, 1938) 301

Joyce, Alice 269

Juarez (Warner Bros, 1939) 56, 404, 412

Judgement At Nuremberg (UA, 1961) 95, 354

Judith of Bethulia (Biograph, 1913) 53
Julia (Fox, 1977) 94, 187
Julian, Rupert 359, 370, 377
Julius Caesar (MGM, 1953) 199
June, Ray 227, 230, 350
Jungle Book, The (UA, 1942) 333
Jungle Princess, The (Paramount, 1936) 249, 266
Jupiter's Darling (MGM, 1955) 209
Juran, Nathan 180, 181, 183, 351, 388
Just Imagine (Fox, 1931) 154, 180, 186
Justine (Fox, 1969) 179

Kahane, B.B. 289
Kaiser, The (Universal, 1918) 364
Kalem Company 16, 67
Kalloch, Robert 132, 134, 135, 231
Kalmus, Herbert 34, 396
Kanin, Garson 126, 136, 232, 309, 310, 311
Kaper, Bronislau 231
Karate Kid, The (Columbia, 1984) 107, 120, 122
Karate Kid: Part II, The (Columbia, 1986) 120, 122, 164
Karloff, Boris 127, 308, 364–5, 368, 376, 377, 380
Karlson, Phil 131
Karns, Roscoe 111–12, 269
Katie For Congress (The Farmer's Daughter) (RKO, 1947) 318
Katz, Lee 60
Katz, Sam 244
Kaufman, Rita 183
Kaufman, Victor 109
Kaye, Danny 37, 38, 242, 253, 269, 291, 293, 296, 298, 308
Kazan, Elia 33, 38, 74, 89, 92, 129, 139, 141, 146, 153, 173, 175, 176, 185, 186, 409, 427, 430
Keaton, Buster 28, 98, 113, 127, 171, 196, 213, 218,

246, 269, 323, 324, 336, 341, 343, 380
Keaton, Diane 200, 355
Keel, Howard 216, 218
Keeler, Ruby 419
Keene, Tom 294
Keighley, William 425, 427
Keller, Walter E. 281, 315
Kellerman, Annette 150, 358
Kellogg, Ray 182
Kelly, Gene 113, 115, 118, 176, 203, 216, 218, 223, 224
Kelly, George 112
Kelly, Grace 95, 216, 219, 262, 267, 269, 285–6, 408
Kendall, Kay 219
Kennedy, Joseph P. 288
Kent, Sidney 143–4, 145
Kent, Ted 387, 389
Kenton, Erle C, 131, 275, 311, 384
Kentucky (Fox, 1938) 36, 155, 163, 186
Kept Husbands (RKO, 1931) 294
Kerkorian, Kirk 51, 52, 194, 195, 209, 210, 327, 328, 335, 339
Kern, Hal 231, 282, 347, 349, 352
Kern, Jerome 294
Kern, Robert 231, 352
Kerr, Deborah 94, 140, 216, 219
Kerry, Norman 219, 269, 377, 380
Key Largo (Warner Bros, 1948) 427
Keyes, Evelyn 114, 125, 127, 269, 343, 380
Keyes, Marion Herwood 231
Keystone Comedies 16
Kiam, Omar 333, 347, 350, 351
Kibbee, Guy 295, 419
Kid From Brooklyn, The (Goldwyn/RKO, 1946) 296, 299
Kid From Spain, The (UA, 1932) 337, 340

Kid, Millions (UA, 1934) 332
Kid, The (First National, 1921) 54, 411, 414
Kilbride, Percy 378
Killers, The (Universal, 1946) 360, 374, 383, 387
Killifer, Jack 435
Kindergarten Cop (Universal, 1990) 375
Kinemacolor 34
Kinetoscope viewing machine 20, 26
King And I, The (Fox, 1956) 164
King, Henry 36, 83, 144, 146, 153, 154, 155, 157, 169, 173, 174, 175, 176, 344, 345, 346
King and I, The (Fox, 1956) 40, 158, 162, 179, 186
King of Jazz (Universal, 1930) 31, 55, 359, 365, 366, 367, 371, 386, 387, 391
King of Kings (MGM, 1961) 42, 204
King of Kings, The (Cecil B. DeMille, 1927) 21
King Kong, (Paramount, 1976) 261; (RKO, 1933) 21, 82, 287, 288, 289, 292, 297, 300, 301, 305, 310, 313, 314
King, Louis 157
King, Muriel 316
King Solomon's Mines (MGM, 1950) 203, 211, 227
King's Row (Warner Bros, 1942) 398, 405
Kingsley, Ben 96
Kingsley, Dorothy 232
Kinney National Service Corporation 393, 398, 400
Kinskey, Leonid 60
Kirk, Charles M, 135, 183, 281, 315, 347, 348, 351, 389
Kirk, Mark-Lee 180, 183, 313, 315, 319, 351
Kismet, (MGM, 1955) 199; (Warner Bros, 1930) 409
Kiss For Cinderella, A (Paramount, 1925) 272

miss Me Deadly (UA, 1955) 332

Kiss Me Kate (MGM, 1953) 203

Kiss Of Death (Fox, 1947) 175

Kitty Foyle (RKO, 1940) 299, 306, 318

Kleine, George 67

Klute (Warner Bros, 1971) 91, 438

Knights Of The Round Table (MGM, 1953) 203

Knock On Any Door (Columbia, 1948) 126

Knudtson, Frederic 316, 352

Koch, Howard 429, 434, 435

Koerner, Charles 291, 292, 302–3

Kolster, Clarence 388, 433

Kopple, Barbara 100

Korda, Alexander 35, 36, 321, 324, 325, 328, 330, 331, 333, 337, 342, 344, 345, 349, 354

Korda, Vincent 349

Korngold, Erich Wolfgang 230, 427, 431, 432

Koster, Henry 176, 224, 382, 383, 384

Kovacs, Ernie 127

Kraly, Hans 435

Kramer, Stanley 74, 119, 131, 133, 331, 334, 338, 345, 346

Kramer vs Kramer (Columbia, 1979) 87, 91, 103, 107, 109, 117, 120, 122, 137, 139

Krasna, Norman 111, 232, 291

Krasner, Milton 179, 183, 230, 281, 315, 386, 388

Kress, Harold 231

Krim, Arthur 321, 326, 328, 332, 335, 338, 344, 345, 354

Krims, Milton 435

Kubrick, Stanley 74, 86, 90, 116, 129, 205, 332, 345, 346, 369, 372, 427

Kurtz, Gary 59

Kuter, Leo E, 389, 434

Kyser, Kay 295

La Cava, Gregory 273, 275, 309, 310, 311, 384

La Marr, Barbara 343

La Plante, Laura 171, 294, 377, 380

La Rocque, Rod 269, 308

La Tour, Charles 60
labour relations 84, 398

Lachman, Harry 131, 176, 275

Ladd, Alan 33, 127, 250, 253, 262, 266, 267, 269, 421

Ladd, Alan, Jr 146, 147–8, 194, 195

Ladd Company 146

Ladies of Leisure (Columbia, 1929) 123

Lady For A Day (Columbia, 1933) 111, 129, 137–8

Lady From Shanghai, The (Columbia, 1948) 119, 124, 129, 133, 297

Lady In The Dark (Paramount, 1944) 252

Lady Of Burlesque (UA, 1943) 337

Lady Of Quality, A (Universal, 1924) 364

Lady Refuses, The (RKO, 1931) 294

Lady Windermere's Fan (Warner Bros, 1925) 396

Laemmle, Carl 17, 23, 45, 65, 66, 67, 75, 104, 142, 143, 239, 357, 358–9, 358–60, 361, 362, 370, 376, 383

Laemmle, Carl, Jr 359, 371

Laemmle Film Service 358

Lake, Arthur 127, 380

Lake, Veronica 24, 33, 250, 266, 267, 269

Lamarr, Hedy 215, 219, 220, 269

Lamb, Thomas 20

Lambert, William 183

Lamont, Charles 384

Lamour, Dorothy 37, 242, 245, 247, 249, 250, 252, 262, 266, 269, 406

Lancaster, Burt 33, 76, 139, 269, 326, 338, 341, 342, 343, 354, 378, 380, 408, 417, 421

Land Of The Pharaohs (Warner Bros, 1955) 41, 74, 413

Land Unknown, The (Universal, 1957) 388

Landers, Lew (Louis Friedlander) 131, 311, 383, 384

Landi, Elissa 171, 219, 269

Landres, Paul 389

Lane, Priscilla 420

Lanfield, Sidney 174, 176, 275

Lang, Charles B, 276, 277, 281

Lang, Fritz 36, 41, 92, 129, 130, 131, 145, 153, 156, 175, 176, 191, 224, 291, 293, 297, 307, 309, 310, 311, 331, 360

Lang, Walter 131, 174, 176

Langdon, Harry 113, 219

Lange, Arthur 184, 316, 319

Langley, Edward 348

Langtry, Lillie 238

Lansbury, Angela 219

Lansing, Sherry 147

Lantz, Walter 359, 365, 391

Lanza, Mario 219

Lash, The (Warner Bros, 1930) 409

LaShelle, Joseph 179, 183

Lasky Company 7, 245; *see also* Famous Players-Lasky

Lasky, Jesse 45, 53, 54, 57, 65, 83, 152, 237, 239–40, 241, 243, 244, 247, 256, 264, 278

Lasky, Jesse, Jr 282

Lassie 193, 202, 219

Lassie Come Home (MGM, 1943) 193, 202

Last Command, The (Paramount, 1928) 284

Last Days Of Pompeii, The (RKO, 1935) 295, 301

Last Emperor, The (Columbia, 1987) 91, 108, 139

Last Hurrah, The (Columbia, 1958) 116

Last Man On Earth, The
(Fox, 1924) 153–4
Last Picture Show, The
(Columbia, 1971) 39,
110, 116, 120
Last Warning, The
(Universal, 1928) 364
Laszlo, Alexander 282
Laszlo, Ernest 281, 350
Laughton, Charles 96, 247,
269, 273, 295, 304, 306,
308, 354, 365
Laura (Fox, 1944) 145, 175,
179, 182
Laurel, Stan and Hardy,
Oliver 28, 97, 171,
192, 219
Laurie, Piper 378–9, 380
Lava, William 434
Law And Order (Universal,
1932) 365
Lawford, Peter 219
Lawrence, Florence 75,
165, 358, 376
Lawrence Of Arabia
(Columbia, 1962) 90,
93, 103, 107, 109, 110,
115, 121, 129, 130, 134,
137, 139
Lawrence, Robert 327
Lawrence, Viola 135, 136,
352, 389
Lawson, John Howard
134, 352
Lawton, Charles, Jr 132,
133, 230, 350
Lean, David 93, 109, 115,
129, 130, 131, 139, 205,
331, 337
Leave Her To Heaven
(Fox, 1945) 57, 145, 155,
156, 161, 163
LeBaron, William 240, 241,
288, 292, 314
LeBeau, Madeleine 60
LeBorg, Reginald 384
Lederer, Charles 184, 232
Lederman, D. Ross 131, 427
Lee, Lila 269
Lee, Rowland V. 173, 176,
275, 311, 346, 384
Leeds, Andrea 333
Leeds, Herbert 176
Legal Eagles (Universal,
1986) 373
Lehman, Gladys 389
Leigh, Janet 219

Leigh, Vivien 331, 405, 438
Leisen, Mitchell 82, 228–9,
230, 250, 252, 265, 271,
273, 275, 279, 280, 281,
310, 350, 351
LeMaire, Charles 178,
182, 183
Lemmon, Jack 114, 126,
127, 286, 338, 342
Leni, Paul 364, 384
Lennart, Isobel 232
Leo, Eve 142, 149, 150
Leonard Part 6 (Columbia,
1987) 121
Leonard, Robert Z. 220, 222,
224, 226, 383, 384
Leone, Sergio 343
Leopard, The (1963) 42
LeRoy, Hal 406
LeRoy, Mervyn 220, 223,
224, 234, 412, 424, 425,
427, 430
Leslie, Joan 171
Lesser, Sol 144, 152, 290,
295, 325
Lester, Richard 345, 346
Lethal Weapon (Warner
Bros, 1987) 416
Lethal Weapon 2 (Warner
Bros, 1989) 63, 399,
414, 415
Let's Make Love (Fox,
1959) 162
Letter, The (Warner Bros,
1941) 430
Letter To Three Wives, A
(Fox, 1949) 175, 186
Letty Lynton (MGM,
1932) 230
Levant, Oscar 17
Leven, Boris 145, 180, 181,
183, 351, 388, 432
Levien, Sonya 184, 232 282
Levin, Henry 130, 131, 176
Levinson, Barry 200, 355
Levinson, Nathan 432
Lewin, Albert 221
Lewis, Ben 231
Lewis, Jerry 129, 242, 253,
262, 267, 268, 269
Lewis, Joseph H. 130, 131,
224, 346, 383, 384
Lewton, Val 296, 297,
302, 310
Libeled Lady (MGM,
1936) 210
Liberty Films 274

Lichtman, Al 324
*Life And Death Of Colonel
Blimp, The* (UA, 1943)
37, 329, 333
Life Of Emile Zola, The
(Warner Bros, 1937) 88,
399, 412, 414, 431, 436
Life With Father (Warner
Bros, 1947) 408, 413,
414, 433
Life's Shop Window (Fox,
1914) 53, 142, 149
Lights Of New York
(Warner Bros, 1928) 30,
396, 402, 411
Lilies of the Field (UA,
1963) 354
Lilley, Joseph J. 282
Linder, Max 341
Lindon, Lionel 278, 281
Lindsay, Margaret 129, 380
Little American, The
(Paramount, 1917) 246
Little Caesar (Warner Bros,
1930) 412, 419, 425, 436
Little Colonel, The (Fox,
1935) 154
Little Foxes, The
(Goldwyn/RKO, 1941)
313, 318, 419
Little Lord Fauntleroy,
(UA, 1921) 336; (UA,
1936) 330
Little Man What Now?
(Universal, 1934) 378
Little Minister, The (RKO,
1934) 301
Little Nellie Kelly (MGM,
1940) 209
Little Old New York (Fox,
1940) 56
Little Women, (RKO, 1933)
185, 299, 300, 301,
305, 310, 318; (MGM,
1949) 228
Litvak, Anatole 176, 311,
426, 427
Livadary, John 105,
134, 138
Lives Of A Bengal Lancer
(Paramount, 1934) 248
Lloyd, Frank 92, 112, 131
138, 150, 173, 174,
176, 185, 224, 275,
425, 427
Lloyd, Harold 17, 28, 83,
247, 263, 268, 272

Lloyds Of London (Fox, 1936) 144, 180
locations 27, 155–6
Loeffler, Louis 182, 184
Loew, David 325
Loew, Marcus 66, 68, 190–1, 195, 207, 240
Loew's Inc 21, 22, 46, 159, 160, 190, 194, 195
see also MGM
Logan, Jacqueline 105
Lolita (Stanley Kubrick, 1962) 74
Lombard, Carole 35, 37, 112, 130, 249, 265, 266, 269, 280, 306, 308, 331, 378
London After Midnight (MGM, 1927) 197
London Can Take It (GPO Film Unit, 1940) 98
'Lone Star' studio 17
Lonely Wives (RKO, 1931) 294
Lonergan, Arthur 230, 281
Lonesome (Universal, 1928) 29, 365
Long Grey Line, The (Columbia, 1955) 41
Long, Samuel 67
Long Voyage Home, The (UA, 1940) 330, 345
Longest Day, The (Fox, 1962) 162, 164
Longest Yard, The (Paramount, 1974) 260
Look Who's Talking (Tri-Star, 1989) 121, 122
Looking For Mr Goodbar (Paramount, 1977) 278
Loos, Anita 214, 232
Lord, Del 113
Lord Jim (Columbia, 1965) 115
Lord, Robert 435
Loren, Sophia 269
Lorimar-Telepictures 20
Lorre, Peter 60, 112, 152, 171, 421
Losey, Joseph 19, 298, 309, 310, 346
Lost Horizon, (Columbia, 1937) 56, 118, 121, 130, 133; (Columbia, 1973) 120

Lost Patrol, The (RKO, 1934) 301, 314
Lost Voyage, The (TV, 1953) 86–7
Lost Weekend, The (Paramount, 1945) 88, 89, 242, 258, 259, 274, 278, 284, 285
Lost World, The (First National, 1925) 82, 414
Louis B, Mayer Productions 190
see also Mayer, Louis B, MGM
Louis, Jean 132, 134–5
Louise, Anita 127, 129, 171, 308, 419
Louise, Ruth Harriet 24
Lourie, Eugene 389
Love Affair (RKO, 1939) 289, 301, 318
Love, Bessie 219, 270
Love Is A Many Splendored Thing (Fox, 1955) 153, 182
Love (MGM, 1927) 214
Love Parade, The (Paramount, 1929) 248
Love Story (Paramount, 1970) 61, 63, 242, 255, 258, 260
Lovejoy, Frank 99
Lovely, Louise 376–7
Lover Come Back (Universal, 1961) 372, 374
Lovering, Otho 282, 352
Loves Of Carmen, The (Columbia, 1948) 115, 125
Low, Warren 282, 435
Lowe, Edmund 166, 171, 219, 270, 380
Loy, Myrna 171, 199, 213, 215, 216, 217, 219, 220, 304–5, 308, 418
Lubin, Arthur 346, 384
Lubin Company 16, 65, 67
Lubin, Sigmund 67
Lubitsch, Ernst 36, 92, 156, 175, 176, 198, 215, 224, 241, 248, 249, 265, 271, 273, 275, 284, 285, 345, 346, 396, 401, 427
Lucas, George 25, 45, 59,

62, 63, 75, 146, 147, 254, 373
Lucas, Marcia 79
Ludwig, Otto 316, 389
Ludwig, William 232
Lugosi, Bela 171, 364–5, 376, 377, 380
Luick, Earl 183, 433, 434
Lukas, Paul 95, 270, 308, 380, 438
'Lullaby Of Broadway' from *Gold Diggers Of 1935* (Warner Bros, 1935) 429, 433
Lum and Abner comedies 290
Lumet, Sidney 75
Lund, John 270, 380
Lundigan, William 171, 219, 380
Lunt, Alfred 214
Lupino, Ida 270, 307, 308, 310, 311, 421, 438
Lust For Life (MGM, 1956) 204
Lusty Men, The (RKO, 1952) 291
Lynn, Diana 270, 380
Lyon, Ben 171
Lyon, Francis 349
Lyon, William 135, 136

Ma And Pa Kettle (Universal, 1949) 374
Ma and Pa Kettle series 367, 378
Mabry, Moss 135, 183, 434
Macao (RKO, 1952) 291, 307, 310
MacArthur, Charles 232, 275, 282
Macauley, Richard 435
McAvoy, May 219, 270
McCarey, Leo 58, 88, 92, 106, 129, 138, 176, 242, 247, 248, 250, 271, 273, 275, 285, 295, 309, 311
McCleary, Urie 228, 230
McCord, Ted 135, 315, 388, 430, 434
McCoy, Tim 113, 129, 197, 270
McCrea, Joel 219, 247, 270, 305, 308, 341, 342, 343, 379, 380, 404
McDaniel, Hattie 95, 285
McDonald, Frank 275, 384, 428

MacDonald, Jeanette 171, 198, 200, 215, 216, 219, 248, 249, 265, 270
MacDonald, Joseph 179, 183
MacDougall, Ranald 435
McDowall, Roddy 171
MacFadden, Hamilton 176
McGann, William 428
McGill, Barney 431, 434, 436
Macgowan, Kenneth 288
McGuire, Dorothy 168, 171, 219, 296, 308
McHugh, Frank 419
Mackaill, Dorothy 294, 418
MacKenna's Gold (Columbia, 1969) 120
McLaglen, Victor 150, 165, 166, 171, 173, 270, 318, 380
MacLaine, Shirley 95–6, 219, 268, 270, 286, 338
MacLane, Barton 405
Maclaren, Mary 377
McLaren, Norman 100
McLean, Barbara 79, 144, 178, 182, 184, 352
McLeod, Norman Z. 225, 273, 274, 275, 311, 346
MacMahon, Aline 219, 419
MacMurray, Fred 262, 265, 266, 267, 270, 380
McNeil, Allen 184, 352
McNutt, Paul 326
Macpherson, Jeanie 83, 282
McQueen, Steve 413
MacRae, Gordon 422
Macready, George 119, 126, 127, 270
Macrorie, Alma 280, 282, 389
McSweeney, John 231
MacWilliams, Glen 183
Mad Whirl, The (Universal, 1925) 364
Madame Butterfly (1915) 271
Madame Du Barry (Fox, 1917) 150
Madame Sans-Gêne (Paramount, 1925) 350
Madison, Guy 342
Magnani, Anna 95, 286
Magnascope 250
Magnificent Ambersons, The (RKO, 1942) 291,

295, 302, 306, 310, 312, 313, 317–18, 386
Magnificent Obsession, (Universal, 1935) 363, 365, 379, 384; (Universal, 1954) 363, 372, 374, 380, 384–5
Magnum Force (Universal, 1973) 379
Magoo, Mr 113
Mahin, John Lee 232
Maibaum, Richard 352
Main Event, The (Warner Bros, 1979) 415
Main, Marjorie 219, 220, 270, 360, 376, 378, 380
Mainwaring, Daniel 282, 316
Major Barbara (UA, 1941) 330
Make Mine Music (Disney/RKO, 1946) 296
Make Way For Tomorrow (Paramount, 1937) 248
make-up artists 82, 98, 181, 385, 387–8, 433
Malden, Karl 171
Male And Female (Paramount, 1919) 246, 279, 280
Malone, Dorothy 129, 380, 391, 406
Malpaso (Clint Eastwood's production company) 379
Maltese Falcon, The (Warner Bros, 1941) 92, 405, 421, 427, 430
Maltz, Albert 435
Mammy (Warner Bros, 1930) 406
Mamoulian, Rouben 35, 36, 92, 106, 112, 129, 156, 175, 176, 203, 241, 247, 248, 271, 273, 275, 298
Man Alive (RKO, 1945) 302
Man For All Seasons, A (Columbia, 1966) 96, 107, 109, 120, 121, 137, 139
Man Of A Thousand Faces (Universal, 1957) 367
Man To Remember, A (RKO, 1938) 310

Man Who Came Back, The (Fox, 1931) 163
Man Who Came To Dinner, The (Warner Bros, 1942) 425
Man Who Could Work Miracles, The (UA, 1937) 331
Man Who Knew Too Much, The (Paramount, 1956) 279
Man Who Laughs, The (Universal, 1928) 364, 386
Man Who Would Be King, The (Columbia, 1975) 131–2
Man Without A Star (Universal, 1955) 367
Mancuso, Frank 243, 244.
Mandell, Daniel 98, 316, 347, 349, 352, 389
Manhattan (Woody Allen, 1979) 39
Mankiewicz, Herman J. 8, 232, 282, 316
Mankiewicz, Joseph 274, 282, 326, 36, 38, 74, 89, 92, 130, 131, 141, 146, 153, 173, 175, 176, 185, 186, 191, 217
Mann, Anthony 38, 199, 224, 311, 361, 367, 368, 372, 382, 383, 384
Mann, Daniel 132, 225, 275
Mann, Delbert 75, 346, 380
Manning, Bruce 389
Mannix, Eddie 192, 201
Man's Castle (Columbia, 1933) 132
Mansfield, Jayne 169, 171
Mantrap (Paramount, 1926) 272
March, Fredric 30, 35, 138, 215, 241, 262, 270, 285, 331, 343, 380, 405
March of Time, The (documentary series) 98
Margie (Fox, 1946) 161, 164
Marie Antoinette (MGM, 1938) 57, 228
Marin, Edwin L. 176, 225, 311, 346, 384, 427

Marion, Frances 214, 232, 235, 282
Marion, Frank 67
Mark of Zorro, The (Fox, 1940) 167, 175, 330
Marker, Harry 316, 389
Marks, Owen 433, 435
Marley, J. Peverell 183, 230, 276, 281, 350, 434
Marnie (Universal, 1964) 383
Marquette, Desmond 316
Marriage Circle, The (Warner Bros, 1924) 396
Marsh, Oliver 226, 230
Marshall, George 176, 274, 275
Marshall, Herbert 219, 270, 308
Marshek, Archie 280, 282, 314, 316
Martin, Dean 242, 253, 262, 267, 268, 270
Martin, Mary 249, 252, 270
Martin, Vivian 246
Marton, Andrew 225
Marty (UA, 1955) 90, 95, 328, 332, 353, 354
Marvin, Lee 94, 95, 127, 171, 270
Marx Brothers 196, 215, 219, 241, 245, 248, 262, 266, 270, 273, 301
Mary Of Scotland (RKO, 1936) 294, 295, 313
Mary Pickford Motion Picture Company 263
    see also Pickford, Mary
Mary, Queen Of Scots (Universal, 1971) 392
Maryland (Fox, 1940) 155
Mascot Pictures 16
MASH (Fox, 1970) 62, 162, 164
Mason, James 127, 171, 219
Masquerader, The (1914) 19
Master Race, The (RKO, 1944) 296
Matchmaker, The (Paramount, 1958) 254
Mate, Rudolph 115, 131,

133, 138, 183, 275, 315, 349, 350, 384, 388
Mathis, June 232
Matlin, Marlee 286
Matsushita Corporation 9, 52, 361, 362
Matthau, Walter 354
Mature, Victor 168, 171, 343
Maxwell, Marilyn 219
Mayer, Edwin Justus 282
Mayer, Louis B, 17, 23–4, 30, 53, 54, 66, 68, 83, 84, 180, 189, 190–3, 195, 196, 197–8, 206, 213, 216–17, 221, 222, 223, 233
Mayes, Wendell 184
Maynard, Ken 129, 377, 380
Mayo, Archie 176, 346, 425, 428
Mayo, Virginia 308, 421
Mazursky, Paul 62, 120, 131, 176
MCA (Music Corporation of America) 9, 50, 52, 361, 362, 372–3
Meehan, John 135, 232, 281
Meet Me In St Louis (MGM, 1944) 38, 57, 89, 202, 207, 209, 211
Meighan, Thomas 54, 171, 246, 263, 265, 270, 272
Melford, George 271
Méliès (French film company) 67
Mellor, William 230, 278, 281, 351, 388
Melvin And Howard (Universal, 1980) 361, 392
Member Of The Wedding, The (Columbia, 1952) 130, 138
Men In Black (Columbia, 1934) 113
Menjou, Adolphe 171, 219, 270, 308, 333, 342, 343
Menzies, William Cameron 78, 183, 202, 278–9, 281, 347, 348–9, 351, 354
Mercury Productions (Orson Welles) 291, 297, 306

Meredith, Burgess 96
Meredyth, Bess 83, 206, 232, 233, 352
Merely Mary Ann (Fox, 1931) 163
Merkel, Una 171, 219, 343, 380
Merry Widow, The, (MGM, 1925) 195, 206, 207, 210, 222, 226; (MGM, 1934) 198, 228
Merry-Go-Round (Universal, 1923) 359, 370, 383
Merton of the Movies (1924) 19
Mescall, John 183, 281, 315, 351, 388
Metro Pictures 17, 18, 46, 68, 190, 194
    see also MGM
Metro-Goldwyn-Mayer *see* MGM
Metty, Russell 312, 315, 351, 368, 369, 385, 386–7, 388, 390, 391
Meyer, Otto 136
MGM 7, 8, 9, 17, 18, 19–20, 21, 23, 23–4, 28, 29, 30, 32, 43, 44, 46, 47, 49, 51, 52, 57, 189–235, 289, 292, 321, 327, 328; budgets 55; cameramen and art directors 78, 226–9; directors 221–5; diversification 194; history 68, 190–5, 207, 240; introduction of colour 200–3; introduction of sound 207; merged with United Artists 206, 209–10; musicals 197, 198–9, 208–9, 215–16, 234; Oscars 88, 89, 233–5; use of widescreen 203–5; Westerns 197, 199
MGM Grand Hotels 209
MGM/UA Entertainment Company 9, 194, 195
Michelet, Michel 351
Mickey Mouse 25, 97
Mickey's Orphans (Columbia, 1931) 137
Middle Of The Night (Columbia, 1959) 116

Midnight Cowboy (UA, 1969) 93, 340, 345, 355

Midsummer Night's Dream, A (Warner Bros, 1935) 56, 404, 412, 414, 419–20, 431, 433

Mighty Joe Young (RKO, 1949) 297, 319

Mighty Mouse 145

Mildred Pierce (Warner Bros, 1945) 33, 405, 421, 424, 425, 430, 438

Milestone, Lewis 74, 92, 175, 176, 275, 311, 344, 345, 346, 353, 390, 428

Milford, Gene 136, 316

Milland, Ray 95, 219, 248, 250, 252, 262, 265, 266, 270, 285

Miller, Ann 113, 125, 127, 219, 306, 308

Miller, Arthur 37, 178, 179, 183, 186, 277, 279, 281, 315

Miller, David 235

Miller, Marilyn 418

Miller, Patsy Ruth 294

Miller, Seton I, 435

Millhauser, Bertram 389

Million Dollar Mermaid (MGM, 1952) 150, 358

Mills, John 96

Milner, Victor 277, 281, 315

Min And Bill (MGM, 1930) 207, 210, 234

Minnelli, Vincente 37, 42, 93, 202, 203, 204, 221, 223, 225, 228, 234

Minter, Mary Miles 264, 270, 277

Mintz, Charles 113

Miracle Man, The (Paramount, 1919) 54, 259

Miracle Woman, The (Columbia, 1931) 111, 123–4

Miranda, Carmen 36, 152, 156, 168, 171

Mirisch company 334, 338, 345, 355

Miserables, Les (UA, 1935) 330, 350, 354

Misery (Columbia, 1990) 121, 122, 139

Misfits, The (UA, 1961) 170, 387

Miss Achilles Heel (MGM, 1941) 220

Miss Lulu Brett (Paramount, 1921) 272

Missing (Universal, 1982) 361

Mitchell, Thomas 127, 171, 219, 354

Mitchum, Robert 304, 307, 308, 343

Mix, Tom 142, 143, 150, 165, 166, 171, 308, 330, 380

Moby Dick, (Warner Bros, 1930) 403; (Warner Bros, 1956) 409, 415

Mockridge, Cyril 184

Modern Times (UA, 1936) 340, 348

Mogambo (MGM, 1953) 203

Mohr, Hal 178, 183, 315, 385, 386, 388, 390, 391, 430–1, 434, 436

Mole People, The (Universal, 1956) 388

Molly Maguires, The (Paramount, 1970) 62, 258, 278

Money From Home (Paramount, 1953) 253

Monkey Business (Fox, 1952) 175

Monogram 16, 32

Monroe, Marilyn 141, 146, 157, 162, 165, 169–70, 171, 175

Monsieur Hulot's Holiday (Jacques Tati, 1955) 93

Monsieur Verdoux (UA, 1947) 331

Monster, The (MGM, 1925) 197

Montalban, Ricardo 219

Montana Belle (RKO, 1952) 294

Monte Carlo Story, The (Titanus/UA, 1956) 40, 42

Montez, Maria 37, 252, 363, 368, 376, 378, 380

Montgomery, George 127, 171, 343

Montgomery, Robert 214, 215, 219, 380

Moon Is Blue, The (UA, 1953) 338

Moon Over Miami (Fox, 1941) 155

Moonfleet (1955) 41

Moonlight And Pretzels (Universal, 1933) 365

Moonstruck (MGM, 1988) 9, 200, 213, 236

Moore, Colleen 418

Moore, Constance 270, 380

Moore, Grace 113, 118, 124, 127

Moore, John 204

Moore, Roger 343

Moore, Victor 295

Moorehead, Agnes 171, 219, 306, 308, 318

Moran, Peggy 381

Moran, Polly 219

More The Merrier, The (Columbia, 1943) 112, 118, 126, 130, 138

More To Be Pitied Than Scorned (CBC, 1922) 104

Moreno, Antonio 219, 270

Morgan, Dennis 219, 270

Morgan, Frank 219, 270

Morgan, Helen 248

Morley, James 184, 316, 436

Morley, Karen 127, 171, 219, 270

Morning Glory (RKO, 1933) 301, 305, 318

Morra, Irene 184, 231, 435

Morris, Chester 127, 219, 270, 308, 380

Morris, Wayne 127, 420

Morse, Terrell 184, 435

Most Dangerous Game, The: (RKO, 1932) 305

Mother and the Law, The (1919) 28

Mother Wore Tights (Fox, 1947) 164

Motion Picture Almanac 21, 46

Motion Picture Association of America (MPAA) 14

Motion Picture Patents Company 18, 45, 67, 75, 142, 149, 239, 358, 394

Motion Picture Producers

and Distributors of
America (MPPDA)
14, 264
Motion Picture Production
Code 120, 338
Moulin Rouge (UA, 1952)
334, 338
Mourning Becomes Electra
(RKO, 1947) 303, 318
Movietone newsreels 160
Movietone sound
system 159
Moving Picture Weekly 23
Mower, Jack 383
MPPDA (Motion Picture
Producers and
Distributors of America)
14, 264
*Mr Belvedere Goes To
College* (Fox, 1949) 161
Mr Deeds Goes To Town
(Columbia, 1936) 89,
107, 112, 118, 124,
130, 138
Mr Lucky (RKO, 1943) 302
Mr Mom (Fox, 1983) 164
*Mr Peabody And The
Mermaid* (Universal,
1948) 388
Mr Roberts (Warner Bros,
1955) 90, 413, 414, 427
Mr Skeffington (Warner
Bros, 1944) 405, 433
*Mr Smith Goes To
Washington* (Columbia,
1939) 56, 108, 118, 121,
130, 134
Mrs Miniver (MGM,
1942) 88, 92, 195, 211,
234, 235
Mrs Soffel (MGM,
1984) 200
Muhl, Edward 361
Mulhall, Jack 377
Mulligan, Robert 384
multi-screen cinemas 22
Mummy, The (Universal,
1932) 365
Muni, Paul 30, 31, 127,
171, 399, 403, 404, 417,
418, 419, 421, 424, 427,
433, 436
Mura, Corinna 60
Murder By Death
(Columbia, 1976) 120
Murder In The Air (Warner
Bros, 1940) 405

Murder My Sweet (RKO,
1944) 297, 307
*Murders In The Rue
Morgue* (Universal,
1932) 365
Murdoch, Rupert 9, 147,
148, 163, 194
Murfin, Jane 232, 316
Murnau, F.W. 29, 143, 151,
173, 174, 176, 178–9,
180, 185
Murphy, Audie 360, 366,
368, 376, 377, 379, 381
Murphy, Eddie 63, 243,
259, 268
Murphy, George 127, 219,
308, 381
Murphy's Romance
(Columbia, 1985) 121
Murray, Jack 184
Murray, Mae 213, 219, 222,
270, 377, 381
music 98
    Columbia 134, 135;
    MGM 229–30;
    Paramount 280–1;
    RKO 314; UA 350,
    351; Universal 387,
    389; Warner Bros
    433–4, 434, 435;
    see also musicals
Music Box, The (1932) 97
Music Corporation of
America (MCA) 9, 50,
52, 361, 362, 372–3
music directors 82
Music Man, The (Warner
Bros, 1962) 409, 413
musicals 30–1, 32, 36,
37, 38, 55, 89, 113,
152–4, 252
    Columbia 110, 124;
    Fox 168; MGM
    194, 197, 198–9,
    208–9, 213–14,
    234; Paramount
    248–9, 251;
    RKO 288, 293, 294;
    United Artists 331,
    332–3; Universal
    366, 382; Warner
    Bros 402, 424
Musuraca, Nicholas 296–7,
312, 314, 315, 434
Mutiny On The Bounty,
(MGM, 1935) 88, 89,
192, 196, 197, 208, 210,

234; (MGM, 1962) 43,
61, 199, 204, 209, 211
Mutual-Triangle company
17
My Best Girl (UA,
1927) 336
My Darling Clementine
(Fox, 1946) 37, 168
My Fair Lady (Warner
Bros, 1964) 61, 87, 400,
409, 411, 413, 431,
436, 438
My Favorite Spy (RKO,
1942) 295
My Favorite Wife (RKO,
1940) 310
My Foolish Heart (RKO,
1949) 318
My Four Years In Germany
(Warner Bros, 1918)
395, 399
My Gal Sal (Fox, 1942)
155, 181
My Man Godfrey
(Universal, 1936) 365–6,
378, 391
My Name Is Julia Ross
(Columbia, 1945) 133
My Sister Eileen (Columbia,
1942) 118, 125, 138
My Wife's Gone Away
(Warner Bros, 1927) 396
Myers, Carmel 377
Myron, Helen 183
*Mystery Of The Wax
Museum, The* (Warner
Bros, 1933) 34, 407

Nagel, Conrad 219, 270
Naked City, The (Universal,
1948) 387, 391
Naked Gun, The
(Paramount, 1988) 261
Naldi, Nita 270
Nana (UA, 1934) 330
Nancy Drew series
(Warner Bros) 405
Napoleon's Barber (Fox,
1927) 151
Narrow Margin, The (RKO,
1952) 291
Nashville (Paramount, 1975)
86, 287
National Board of
Review 87
National Film Board of
Canada (NFBC) 100

National Lampoon's Animal House (Universal, 1978) 373, 374

National Lampoon's Christmas Vacation (Warner Bros, 1989) 414

National Lampoon's European Vacation (Warner Bros, 1985) 414

National Society of Film Critics 87

National Velvet (MGM, 1944) 202, 211

Natural, The (Tri-Star, 1984) 122

Naughty Marietta (MGM, 1935) 198, 215

Navy Comes Through, The (RKO, 1942) 296

Nazarro, Ray 131

Nazimova, Alla 341

Neal, Patricia 95, 171, 286

Neal, Tom 296

Nebenzal, Seymour 325

Negri, Pola 247, 265, 270

Negulesco, Jean 175, 176, 406, 426, 428

Neighbours (National Film Board of Canada) 100

Neilan, Marshall 222, 225, 240, 271, 275

Neill, Roy William 131, 176, 384, 428

Nelson, Charles 136

Nelson, Kay 182, 183

Neptune's Daughter (Universal, 1914) 358

Nervig, Conrad 231

Nestor/Christie studio 16

Network (MGM/UA, 1976) 212, 235, 355

Neumann, Kurt 274, 311, 346, 383, 384

Never Give A Sucker An Even Break (Universal, 1941) 378

New York Film Critics Awards 85–6, 87, 89, 90, 94, 138, 139, 186, 234, 285, 286, 318, 353, 392, 436, 438

New York Motion Picture Company 16

Newcom, James 231, 352

Newman, Alfred 82, 145, 178, 182, 184, 186, 347, 350, 351

Newman, Bernard 316, 434

Newman, Emil 184

Newman, Joseph M, 176

Newman, Lionel 184

Newman, Paul 96, 171, 219, 361, 373, 413

newsreels 26–7, 104, 192–3, 365

Next Voice You Hear, The (MGM, 1950) 193

Niagara (Fox, 1953) 169

Niblo, Fred 206, 222, 225, 233, 275

Nicholas and Alexandra (Columbia, 1971) 120

Nichols, Dudley 84, 184, 303, 316, 318

Nichols, Mike 93

Nicholson, Jack 200, 268, 355

nickelodeons 13, 20, 67, 142, 238, 358

Night And Day (Warner Bros, 1946) 408, 413, 414, 431, 433

Night Nurse (Warner Bros, 1931) 403, 426

Night Of The Hunter (UA, 1955) 332

Night Of The Iguana, The (MGM, 1964) 199

Nights of Cabiria (Fellini, 1957) 94

Nilsson, Anna Q, 277, 417

Nine To Five (Fox, 1980) 164

1941 (Columbia/Universal, 1979) 63

Ninotchka (MGM, 1939) 215, 234, 285

Niven, David 95, 308, 342, 343, 354

No Time For Sergeants (Warner Bros, 1958) 415

Noah's Ark (Warner Bros, 1929) 411, 430–1

Nob Hill (Fox, 1945) 155

Nocturne (RKO, 1946) 307

Nolan, J.J. 292

Nolan, Lloyd 127, 171, 270

None But The Lonely Heart (RKO, 1944) 302

Norma Rae (Fox, 1979) 187

Normand, Mabel 264

North of '36 (Paramount, 1924) 247, 250, 257

North By Northwest (MGM, 1959) 209, 211, 254

North, Edmund 187

North, Sheree 169, 171

North West Mounted Police (Paramount, 1940) 36, 79, 248, 252, 259

Northwest Passage (MGM, 1940) 36, 199, 202, 211

Nosler, Lloyd 184, 231, 352

Not As A Stranger (UA, 1955) 338, 340

Nothing Sacred (UA, 1937) 35, 56, 331, 333

Notorious Landlady, The (Columbia, 1962) 126

Notorious (RKO/Vanguard Films, 1946) 33, 296, 297, 299, 302, 306, 309

Novak, Kim 123, 126, 127

Novarro, Ramon 150, 198, 200, 206, 213, 219, 330

Now Voyager (Warner Bros, 1942) 405, 437

Nugent, Elliott 275, 311, 428

Nugent, Frank 136

Nun's Story, The (Warner Bros, 1959) 415

Nyby, Christian 316, 435

Nye, Ben 181

Oakie, Jack 171, 241, 249, 266, 270, 274, 308, 380

Oberon, Merle 308, 341, 342, 343, 350, 380

Objective Burma (Warner Bros, 1945) 426

Oboler, Arch 41, 334

O'Brien, Brian 42

O'Brien, George 150, 152, 165, 166, 171, 270, 294, 306, 308

O'Brien, Margaret 216, 219

O'Brien, Pat 31, 127, 302, 308, 381, 421

O'Brien, Virginia 219

O'Brien, Willis 82, 297, 313, 319

Obzina, Martin 389

Ocean's Eleven (Warner Bros, 1960) 415

Octopussy (UA, 1983) 340

Odd Couple, The (Paramount, 1968) 258, 260

Odd Man Out (Universal, 1947) 360

Odell, Cary 115, 133, 135, 138

Odell, Robert A. 281

Odell, Rosemary 387, 389

Odets, Clifford 112

Odlum, Floyd 289, 291, 292, 303

Of Human Bondage (RKO, 1934) 94, 306, 310, 419

Of Mice And Men (UA, 1939) 330, 354

Officer And A Gentlemen, An (Paramount, 1982) 260

Offner, Mortimer 316

Oh, God! (Warner Bros, 1977) 415

O'Hara, Maureen 37, 168, 171, 298, 306, 308, 381

Oil For The Lamps Of China (Warner Bros, 1935) 404

Okey, Jack 315, 434

Oklahoma (Magna, 1955) 38, 40, 42–3

Oland, Warner 144, 152, 167, 171, 270

Olcott, Sidney 271

Old Dark House, The (Universal, 1932) 365

Old Gringo (Columbia, 1988) 121

Old Ironsides (Paramount, 1926) 245, 247, 250, 259, 272

Old Maid, The (Warner Bros, 1939) 414

Old Wives For New (Paramount, 1918) 246, 256

Oliver! (Columbia, 1968) 90, 93, 107, 109, 120, 121, 139

Oliver, Edna May 219, 270, 294, 308

Oliver, Harry 180, 183, 230, 281, 315, 351

Olivier, Sir Laurence 89, 93, 96, 99, 331, 333, 341, 342, 343, 391

Omen, The (Fox, 1976) 164

On Dangerous Ground (RKO, 1952) 297

On Golden Pond (Universal, 1981) 96, 375, 392

On The Beach (UA, 1959) 338

On The Waterfront (Columbia, 1954) 107, 108, 110, 115, 130, 139

On With The Show (Warner Bros, 1929) 397, 406

Once In A Lifetime (Universal, 1932) 365

Once Upon A Honeymoon (RKO, 1942) 295

One Flew Over The Cuckoo's Nest (UA, 1975) 91, 339, 340, 353, 355

One Hour With You (Paramount, 1932) 284

One Hundred Men And A Girl (Universal, 1937) 391

One Night Of Love (Columbia, 1934) 113, 118

One Romantic Night (UA, 1930) 30

One-Eyed Jacks (Paramount, 1961) 254

O'Neal Tatum 96

O'Neil Thomas F 292

O'Neill, Eugene 30

O'Neill, James 238

Only Angels Have Wings (Columbia, 1939) 112, 130

Only Game In Town, The (Fox, 1969) 62, 163, 170

Only Yesterday (Universal, 1933) 378

Operation Petticoat (Universal, 1960) 372, 374

Ophuls, Max 93, 384

Orbom, Eric 391

Ordinary People (Paramount, 1980) 91, 93, 260, 268, 286

Orion Pictures 9, 45, 51, 327, 328

Ornitz, Samuel 316

Orphans Of The Storm (UA, 1922) 54, 348

Orr, William T 398

Orry-Kelly 61, 82, 389, 429, 433, 434

Oscar, The (1966) 83

Oscars 7, 28, 29, 33, 35, 37, 38, 42, 83–100, 111
for cinematography 179, 186, 202, 227, 277, 390, 391, 431; Columbia 137–9; for costume-design 98; craft awards 98–9; for editing 98; for foreign-language directors 93–4; Fox 157, 166, 185–7; honorary awards 97–8; MGM 233–5; for music 98; Paramount 237, 284–6; refused 84, 94, 97, 187; RKO 317–19; scientific/technical awards 79, 97; selection procedure 85; sentimental awards 94, 95–6, 392; for sound recording 97; for supporting categories 95, 98; UA 353–5; Universal 390–2; Warner Bros 436–8; for writers 99

O'Shaughnessy's Boy (MGM, 1935) 198

O'Steen, Sam 435

O'Sullivan, Maureen 171, 215, 219, 381

O'Toole, Peter 96

Otterson, Jack 183, 386, 389, 391

Our Blushing Brides (MGM, 1930) 228

Our Dancing Daughters (MGM, 1928) 214

Our Gang (shorts) 28, 192

Out Of Africa (Universal, 1985) 91, 357, 361, 362, 375, 390, 392

Out Of The Past (RKO, 1947) 307

Outlaw, The (UA, 1943) 331, 337–8, 340, 344, 345

Outside The Law
(Universal, 1921) 366
Over The Moon (UA,
1938) 35
Owl And The Pussycat,
The (Columbia, 1970)
120, 122
Oxbow Incident, The (Fox,
1943) 37, 145, 153,
156, 168

Pacino, Al 94, 268
Page, Joy 60
Paige, Janis 219
Paige, Robert 127, 270, 381
Paint Your Wagon
(Paramount, 1969) 62,
258, 261
Paisan (Rossellini, 1949) 93
Paleface, The (Paramount,
1948) 253, 261
Palmer, Adele 183
Palmer, Ernest 178,
179, 183
Pan, Hermes 298, 314, 319
Panama, Norman 274, 282
Panavision 26, 40, 42, 70,
158, 196, 204, 254, 334
Panic In The Streets (Fox,
1950) 175
Paper Chase, The (Fox,
1973) 187
Paper Moon (Peter
Bogdanovich, 1973) 39
Paradise cinema, Bronx 22
Paramount 7, 8, 21, 22,
28, 29, 32, 42, 44, 46,
47, 49, 51, 52, 53, 64,
237–86, 322
court case 64;
finances 254–64;
introduction of
colour 245, 250–3,
278; music 280–1;
musicals 247–8, 248;
Oscars 237, 284–6;
Westerns 245,
247–8, 256–7
Paramount cinema, New
York 20
Paramount News 249
Paramount On Parade
(Paramount, 1930) 251
Parenthood (Universal,
1989) 373, 375
Park, Nick 100
Parker, Albert 332

Parker, Dorothy 232
Parker, Eleanor 219
Parker, Max 183, 432, 434
Parks, Larry 113–14, 115,
118, 123, 125, 127
Parretti, Giancarlo 9, 52,
194, 195, 206, 327, 328
Parrish, Robert 136,
347, 349
Pascal, Gabriel 333
Passenger, The (MGM,
1974) 200
Pasternak, Joe 383
Patent Leather Kid, The
(First National, 1927)
28, 412
Pathe Communications
17, 34, 47, 52, 67, 194,
195, 206, 288, 292, 294,
301, 327
Pathe Weekly Bulletin, The
23
Paths of Glory (Stanley
Kubrick, 1957) 74
Patrick, Gail 219, 270, 318
Patton (Fox, 1970) 62, 97,
158, 164, 185, 187
Pavarotti, Luciano 209
Paxton, John 136, 316
Payne, John 168, 171, 253,
307, 308
Peck, Gregory 157, 165,
169, 171, 186, 296, 302,
342, 343, 368, 381, 392
Peckinpah, Sam 432
Penn, Arthur 75
Penner, Joe 249
Pennies From Heaven
(MGM, 1981) 200, 209
People's Vaudeville
Company 190
Pereira, Hal 279, 281
Perelman, S.J. 282
Périnal, Georges 349, 351
Perkins, Anthony 242,
267, 270
Pesci, Joe 438
Pete Kelly's Blues (Warner
Bros, 1955) 413
Pete Smith Specialties
(comedies) 192
Peter Pan, (Disney, 1953)
299; (Paramount, 1924)
272, 277
Peters, Hans 180, 183, 228,
230, 315
Peters, Jean 168, 171

Peters, Jon 108, 109
Peterson, Robert 133, 135
Petrified Forest, The
(Warner Bros, 1935) 420
Pevney, Joseph 384
Peyton Place (Fox, 1957)
153, 162, 164
Phantom Lady (Universal,
1944) 383
Phantom Of The Opera,
The (Universal, 1925) 34,
366, 367, 368, 371, 377,
386; (Universal, 1943)
387, 391
Phfft (Columbia, 1954) 126
Philadelphia Story, The
(MGM, 1940) 234
Phillips, Dorothy 366, 376
Phillips, Fred 126
Pichel, Irving 176, 275, 311
Pickford, Jack 246, 271
Pickford, Mary 17, 27, 46,
54, 65, 75, 78, 83, 165,
239, 240, 246, 262, 263,
270, 271, 272, 278,
322–4, 326, 327, 329,
341, 342, 343, 347–8,
350, 353, 355, 358, 376,
398, 411
Picnic (Columbia, 1955) 90,
110, 115, 121, 125
Pidgeon, Walter 213, 217,
221, 381
Pierce, Jack 385, 387
Pilgrimage (Fox, 1933) 174
Pillow Talk (Universal,
1959) 372, 374, 391
Pink Panther films 339, 343
Pinky (Fox, 1949) 161, 175
Pioneer Pictures 35, 181,
292, 293, 297–8, 333
Pirate, The (MGM, 1948)
203, 209
Pitts, ZaSu 270, 295,
308, 381
Place In The Sun, A
(Paramount, 1951) 86,
99, 253, 280
Plainsman, The (Paramount,
1936) 248, 257
Planck, Robert 183, 230,
351, 388
Planer, Franz 135,
388
Planet Of The Apes (Fox,
1967) 154, 162, 164,
179, 181

Platoon (Oliver Stone, 1986) 63, 86, 91

Play Misty For Me (Universal, 1971) 379

Please Don't Eat The Daisies (MGM, 1960) 211

Plough And The Stars, The (RKO, 1936) 295

Plunkett, Walter 201, 229, 231, 312, 314, 315, 316, 351

Plymouth Adventure (MGM, 1952) 209

Podesta, Rossana 41

Poe, James 352

Pogany, William A, 332, 351, 434

Point Blank (MGM, 1967) 200

Poitier, Sidney 90, 127, 219, 343, 354

Polanski, Roman 90

Polglase, Van Nest 8, 9, 78, 97, 135, 228, 230, 278, 281, 312, 313, 315, 319, 351

Police Academy series (Warner Bros) 413

Polito, Sol 429–30, 434, 436

Pollack, Sydney 93, 120, 129, 131, 392

Poltergeist (MGM, 1982) 62, 210, 213

Pony Express, The (Paramount, 1925) 247, 277

Poor Little Peppina (Lasky, 1915) 271

Poor Little Rich Girl (Paramount, 1917) 263, 272

Popeye (Paramount, 1980) 261

Popeye The Sailor 58, 249

Porgy And Bess (Columbia, 1959) 115

Porky's (Fox, 1982) 148, 164, 408, 413

Porter, Cole 294

Porter, Edwin S, 27, 65, 236

Poseidon Adventure, The (Fox, 1972) 163, 164, 182

Possessed (Warner Bros, 1947) 405

Postman Always Rings Twice, The (MGM, 1946) 33, 211

Potter, H.C. 225, 311, 346

Powell, Dick 219, 251, 270, 307, 308, 381, 417, 419, 420

Powell, Eleanor 198, 201, 215, 219, 221

Powell, Jane 216, 219

Powell, Michael 37, 99, 329, 331

Powell, William 30, 199, 213, 215, 219, 221, 247, 270, 378, 381, 408, 413

Power, Tyrone 127, 141, 144, 153, 155, 156, 161, 165, 167, 169, 171, 175

Power, Tyrone, Sr. 377

Pratt, Thomas 435

Predator (Fox, 1987) 164

Prelude To War (1942) 92

Preminger, Otto 74, 116, 130, 131, 153, 173, 175, 176, 291, 326, 338, 343

Presley, Elvis 42, 171, 204, 219, 242, 268, 270, 343

Pressburger, Emeric 99, 329, 331

Preston, Robert 248, 270

Presumed Innocent (Warner Bros, 1990) 413

Pretty Woman (1990) 63

Previn, Andre 229, 231

Previn, Charles 385, 387, 389, 390, 391

Prevost, Marie 219, 381, 417

Price, Frank 107, 109, 121, 362

Price, Vincent 171, 381, 406

Prickett, Oliver 60

Pride And Prejudice (MGM, 1940) 228

Pride Of The Clan, The (Paramount, 1916) 272

Pride Of The Marines (Warner Bros, 1945) 404, 421

Prime Of Miss Jean Brodie, The (Fox, 1969) 96, 186

Prince And The Pauper, The (Warner Bros, 1937) 56, 412, 425, 431

Prince Valiant (Fox, 1954) 153

Principal Artists Productions 290

Prisoner Of Zenda, The, (Paramount, 1913) 238; (Metro, 1922) 222, 330; (UA, 1937) 56, 68, 330

Prisoner Of Shark Island, The (Fox, 1936) 174

Private Benjamin (Warner Bros, 1980) 413

Private Life of Henry VIII, The (UA 1933) 96, 354

Private Life Of Sherlock Holmes, The (UA, 1970) 62, 339

Private Lives Of Elizabeth And Essex, The (Warner Bros, 1939) 56, 404, 408, 412, 431, 433

Prizmacolor 34

Prodigal, The (MGM, 1955) 199

Professionals, The (Columbia, 1966) 123

Prowler, The (UA, 1951) 332

Psycho (Paramount, 1960) 258, 262, 267, 280–1

Public Enemy, The (Warner Bros, 1931) 410, 417, 424, 434

Public Is Never Wrong, The (book) 239

publicity system 22–5, 165

Publix (theatre subsidiary of Paramount) 240, 245, 257

Purple Heart, The (Fox, 1944) 175

Purple Rain (Warner Bros, 1984) 414

Pursued (Warner Bros, 1947) 403

Puttnam, David 108, 109, 122

Pye, Merrill 230

Qualen, John 60

Quality Street (RKO, 1937) 56, 295, 301

Queen Christina (MGM, 1933) 210

Queen Elizabeth (Paramount, 1912) 238, 243

Queen of Sheba, The (Fox, 1921) 143

Quick Millions (Fox, 1931) 31
Quimby, Fred 192
Quine, Richard 131, 133
Quinn, Anthony 127, 171, 270, 308, 381
Quo Vadis? (MGM, 1951) 203, 208, 211

Racket, The, (Paramount, 1928) 247; (RKO, 1951) 307
Rackmil, Milton 360–1
radio 249
Radio City Music Hall, New York 20–1
Radio Corporation of America 287, 288
Radio-Keith-Orpheum Corporation (RKO) see RKO
Rafelson, Bob 86, 131, 139
Raft, George 248, 249, 266, 270, 307, 308, 343, 420
Raiders Of The Lost Ark (Paramount, 1981) 261
Rain Man (UA, 1988) 9, 91, 210, 327, 328, 335, 339, 340, 353, 355
Rain (UA, 1932) 330, 345
Raine, Norman Reilly 435
Rainer, Luise 94, 95, 219, 233, 234, 317
Raines, Ella 378, 381
Rains Came, The (Fox, 1939) 56, 163, 182
Rains, Claude 60, 308, 365, 368, 381, 420
Raintree Country (MGM, 1957) 40, 43, 204, 211
Raksin, David 135, 182, 184, 231
Ralston, Esther 294
Rambo: First Blood Part II (Tri-Star, 1985) 122, 339
Rambo III (Tri-Star, 1988) 122, 339
Ramona (Tri-Star, 1936) 144, 154, 155
Rancho Notorious (RKO, 1952) 291
Random Harvest (MGM, 1942) 211, 234
Rank, J. Arthur 333, 360, 366, 391
Ransford, Maurice 180, 181, 183

Ransom of Red Chief, The (1952) 17
Rapee, Erno 184
Rapf, Harry 83, 233
Raphaelson, Samson 184, 273–4, 282
Rapper, Irving 426–7, 428
Rasputin and The Empress (MGM, 1933) 214
Rathbone, Basil 152, 171, 219, 251, 366, 377, 381
Rathvon, N. Peter 291, 292
Ratoff, Gregory 131, 176
Raven, The (Universal, 1935) 367
Rawlins, John 311, 346, 383, 384
Rawlinson, Herbert 376
Ray, Charles 171, 219, 246, 270, 341, 381
Ray, Nicholas 38, 74, 126, 131, 176, 204, 291, 293, 297, 310, 311, 409
Raye, Martha 249, 270, 381
Raymond, Gene 171, 295, 308
Razor's Edge, The (Fox, 1946) 163, 181
RCA (Radio Corporation of America) 47, 288, 292
Reagan, Ronald 269, 307, 308, 367, 381, 405, 408, 420
Realife (widescreen process) 204
Reap The Wild Wind (Paramount, 1942) 252, 258, 259, 280
Rear Window (Paramount, 1954) 253, 258, 260, 267
Rebecca (UA, 1940) 88, 92, 325, 328, 330, 331, 340, 345, 353, 354
Rebecca of Sunnybrook Farm (Paramount, 1917) 263
Rebel Without A Cause (Warner Bros, 1955) 409, 415, 422, 430
Reckless Moment, The (Columbia, 1949) 133
Red Badge Of Courage, The (MGM, 1951) 193, 199
Red Dance, The (Fox, 1928) 163, 174, 180

Red Dust (MGM, 1932) 214
Red Hair (Paramount, 1927) 251
Red River (UA, 1948) 37, 331, 340, 345, 350
Red Shoes, The (1948) 37, 99
Red-Headed Woman (MGM, 1932) 214
Redford, Robert 93, 268, 286, 361, 373, 392
Redgrave, Vanessa 94, 187
Reds (Paramount, 1981) 93, 278, 286
Redskin (Paramount, 1928) 247, 251
Ree, Max 230, 315, 316, 319
Reed, Carol 93, 120, 139
Reed, Donna 127, 139, 217
RegalScope 40, 158
Regent Cinema, Harlem 20
Reid, Wallace 246, 262, 263, 264, 270
Reiner, Rob 121, 139
Reinhardt, Max 433
Reis, Irving 176, 311
Reisch, Walter 184, 232
Reitman, Ivan 120
Reliance-Majestic 53
Remick, Lee 170, 171
Remisoff, Nicolai 135, 349, 351
Renie (costume designer) 182, 183, 316
Rennahan, Ray 154–5, 201, 281
Rennie, Michael 171
Renoir, Jean 93, 98, 296
Report From The Aleutians (1943) 92
Republic studio 16, 32
Reticker, Hugh 432, 434
Return Of Frank James, The (Fox, 1940) 36, 145, 155, 156, 168
Return Of The Jedi (Fox, 1983) 148, 164
Reversal Of Fortune (Warner Bros, 1990) 438
Revier, Dorothy 123, 127
Rex studio 23
Reynolds, Burt 414, 422
Reynolds, Debbie 217, 219
Reynolds, William 182, 184, 282, 393

Rhapsody In Blue (Warner Bros, 1945) 405
Rhinestone (Fox, 1984) 163
Rhodes, Leah 433, 434
Rhythm On The Range (Paramount, 1936) 243
Rich, Irene 417
Rich, Lee 195, 327
Richards, Frederick 435
Richards, Thomas 435
Richardson, Ralph 333
Richardson, Tony 91, 93, 344, 345, 355
Riedel, Richard 387, 390
Rin-Tin-Tin series 393, 402, 417–18, 425
Rio Bravo (Warner Bros, 1959) 415, 422
Rio Rita (RKO, 1929) 34, 288, 293, 299, 300, 304, 314
Riper, Kay van 198
Riskin, Robert 111, 132, 134, 136
Risky Business (Warner Bros, 1983) 416
Ritt, Martin 75, 176
Ritter, Thelma 168, 171, 270
Ritz Brothers, The 171, 381
River Of No Return (Fox, 1954) 146
River, The, (Fox, 1928) 174
Rivkin, Allen 184, 232
RKO 7, 8, 9, 19, 21, 22, 32, 33, 42, 47, 49, 52, 56, 287–319
    art department 312, 313–14; colour 291, 293, 296, 297–9; directors 309–11; finances 300–3; history 288–92; music 314; musicals 288, 294; Oscars 317–19; and sound 323–4; Westerns 294
Roach, Hal 17, 28, 192, 325, 349
Road Runner cartoons 406
'Road' series 241–2, 249, 266
Road To Rio (Paramount, 1947) 259
Road To Singapore (Paramount, 1939) 266

Road To Utopia (Paramount, 1944) 259
Roaring Twenties, The (Warner Bros, 1939) 432
Robards, Jason 187
Robbins, Jerome 334
Robe, The (Fox, 1953) 40, 41, 58–9, 61, 147, 153, 157, 161, 164, 179, 187
Roberta (RKO, 1934) 305, 306
Roberts, Beverly 407
Roberts, Stephen 274, 311
Roberts, Theodore 270
Robertson, Cliff 128, 327
Robertson, Dale 172
Robertson, John Stuart 225, 272, 275, 311
Robin Hood: Prince of Thieves (Warner Bros, 1991) 414
Robin Hood (UA, 1922) 54, 330, 336, 348, 350
Robinson, Bill 'Bojangles' 406
Robinson, Casey 184, 282, 403, 429, 433, 435
Robinson, Edward G. 30, 31, 94, 124, 200, 220, 241, 297, 378, 403, 404, 417, 418, 419, 421, 424, 425, 426, 437
Robson, Mark 176, 289, 309, 310, 311, 312, 314, 316, 346
Robson, May 111
Rock, William 67
Rocky films 210, 339
Rocky (UA, 1976) 87, 91, 355
Rocky III (UA, 1982) 340
Rocky IV (UA, 1985) 339, 340
Roddick, Nick, *A New Deal In Entertainment* 403
Roemheld, Heinz 135, 351, 434
Rogell, Albert 131, 384
Rogell, Mark 311
Rogell, Sid 291
Rogers, Charles 'Buddy' 249, 270
Rogers, Charles R. 360
Rogers, Ginger 30, 56, 172, 249, 252, 270, 288, 289, 292, 295, 296, 300, 301,

302, 304, 305, 306, 308, 314, 318
Rogers, Will 143, 144, 161, 165, 166, 167, 172, 174
Rogue Song, The (MGM, 1930) 200
Roland, Gilbert 172, 343
Rolin Film Company 17
Roman Holiday (Paramount, 1953) 253
Roman Scandals (UA, 1933) 340
Romance On The High Seas (Warner Bros, 1948) 422
Romancing The Stone (Fox, 1984) 164, 187
Rome, Open City (Rossellini, 1946) 93
Romeo And Juliet, (MGM, 1936) 57; (Paramount, 1968) 258, 260, 286
Romero, Cesar 168, 172, 381
Ronde, La (Max Ophuls, 1951) 93
Room At The Top (1959) 89
Room Service (RKO, 1938) 301
Rooney, Mickey 96, 198, 201, 213, 216, 219, 220, 381
Roosevelt, Franklin D. 402
Rope (Warner Bros, 1948) 33, 408, 427
Rose, Helen 183, 229, 231
Rose, Jack 282
Rose, Reginald 352
Rose Tattoo, The (Paramount, 1955) 254, 277, 286
Rosemary's Baby (Paramount, 1968) 39, 258, 260, 279
Rosen, Milton 184, 389
Rosenberg, Aaron 361, 372
Rosher, Charles 78, 179, 202, 227, 230, 281, 315, 347, 348, 351, 354, 434
Rosita (UA, 1923) 348
Ross, Stephen J. 50, 398, 400
Rosse, Herman 385, 386, 389, 390–1
Rossellini, Roberto 93

Rossen, Robert 89, 129, 130, 131, 136, 138, 349, 435

Rosson, Harold (Hal) 183, 191, 227, 230, 277, 281, 349, 351

Roth, Joe 147, 148

Roth, Lillian 406

Rothafel, Sammy 'Roxy' 20–1

Rough Riders, The (Paramount, 1927) 247

Rowland, Richard 322

Rowland, Roy 223, 225

Roxy cinema, New York 20

Royer (costume designer) 182, 183, 351

Rozsa, Miklos 231, 235, 282, 347, 350, 351, 387, 389, 390, 391

Ruben, J. Walter 225, 311

Ruggiero, Gene 231

Ruggles, Charlie 248, 270

Ruggles, Wesley 131, 225, 273, 275, 311, 384

Ruggles Of Red Gap (Paramount, 1935) 247, 273

Rumba (Paramount, 1935) 249

Russell, Gail 270

Russell, Jane 175, 252, 294, 298, 304, 307, 308

Russell, Ken 225, 344, 345, 346

Russell, Rosalind 94, 112, 124, 125, 128, 130, 138, 217, 220, 294, 302, 308, 318, 413

Rutherford, Ann 198, 216, 219

Ruttenberg, Joseph 227, 230, 235, 315

Ryan, Frank 384

Ryan, Peggy 366, 378, 381

Ryan, Robert 172, 270, 304, 307, 308, 343

Ryan's Daughter (MGM, 1970) 43, 62, 196, 205, 209, 211

Saboteur (Universal, 1942) 386

Sabrina (Paramount, 1954) 253

Sabu 333, 343, 378, 381

Sadie Thompson (UA, 1928) 29, 323, 336, 353

Sagansky, Jeffrey 108

St Clair, Malcolm 176, 273, 275, 277, 428

Saint, Eva Marie 139, 219

St Louis Kid, The (Warner Bros, 1934) 403

Saint, The series 295

Sakall, S.Z. 60, 219

salaries 53, 76

Sale, Richard 176

Salinger, Conrad 229, 231

Salkow, Sidney 131, 383, 384

Salome (Fox, 1918) 166

Salter, Hans 387, 389, 391

Saltern, Irene 351

Samson And Delilah (Paramount, 1949) 58, 119, 250, 259

San Francisco (MGM, 1936) 196, 197, 208, 210

Sand (Fox, 1949) 157

Sand Pebbles, The (Fox, 1966) 162, 164, 181

Sanders, George 172, 219, 295, 308, 343

Sandrich, Mark 99, 274, 275, 310, 311

Santa Fe Trail (Warner Bros, 1940) 414

Santana (Bogart's independent film company) 128

Santell, Alfred 176, 275, 346

Santillo, Frank 231

Santley, Joseph 311, 384

Saratoga (MGM, 1937) 210, 215

Saratoga Trunk (Warner Bros, 1945) 413, 414, 430

Sarnoff, David 47, 288, 292

Sartov, Hendrick 230, 347, 348, 351

Saturday Night Fever (Paramount, 1978) 25, 258, 260

Satyricon (Fellini, 1970) 94

Saunders, John Monk 282, 436

Save The Tiger (Paramount, 1973) 284

Saville, Victor 225

Sax, Sam 406

Sayonara (Warner Bros, 1957) 413, 414

scandals 14, 107, 160, 264, 327

Scaramouche (Metro, 1923) 222, 330

Scarface, (UA, 1932) 331

Scarlet Pimpernel, The, (Fox, 1917) 150; (UA, 1935) 330

Scarlet Street (Universal, 1946) 360, 374

Schaefer, George 289–91, 292, 301, 302, 324–5

Schaffner, Franklin 75, 187

Schary, Dore 111, 193, 195, 199, 221, 224, 232, 291, 292, 303, 318, 325

Schell, Maximilian 95, 354

Schenck, Joseph 68, 83, 144, 145, 147, 161, 190, 321, 323, 324, 328, 330, 335, 336, 398

Schenck, Nicholas 190–1, 193, 195, 207

Schertzinger, Victor 131, 176, 275, 311

Schildkraut, Joseph 333, 399

Schlesinger, John 93, 344, 345, 355

Schmidt, Arthur 280, 282, 316

Schneider, Abe 107

Schneiderman, George 178, 183

Schnitzer, Joseph 288, 289

Schoedsack, Ernest B. 131, 273, 301, 310, 311

Schoengarth, Russell 387, 389

Schofield, Paul 96, 139

Schoonmaker, Thelma 79

Schulberg, B.P, 23, 68, 238, 240–1, 244, 246, 264, 322

Schulze, Jack 183, 315, 349, 351

Schuster, Harold 176, 184, 384

Schwartz, Arthur 115

Schwarzenegger, Arnold 121

Schwarzwald, Milton 389

science fiction 153–4, 200, 367, 383

Scognamillo,

Gabriel 228, 230

Scorsese, Martin 39, 75, 91, 120, 428, 438

Scott, Allan 316

Scott, George C, 94, 97, 187

Scott, Gordon 295

Scott, Lizabeth 269

Scott, Randolph 114, 115, 123, 126, 128, 172, 247, 252–3, 266, 270, 306, 308, 343, 380, 421

Scott, Zachary 172

Screen Actors Guild 84

Screen Directors Guild 84

Screen Gems (TV subsidiary) 107, 119

Screen Snapshots 104, 113

Screen Writers Guild 84

scriptwriters 8, 132, 134, 136, 222, 273–4

Scudda Hoo, Scudda Hay (Fox, 1947) 169

Sea Beast, The (Warner Bros, 1925) 402

Sea Chase, The (Warner Bros, 1955) 413, 415

Sea Hawk, The, (First National, 1924) 28, 414; (Warner Bros, 1940) 404, 412, 425, 430, 431

Sea Wolf, The (Warner Bros, 1941) 421

Searchers, The (Warner Bros, 1956) 254, 409, 415

Sears, Fred 131

Seaton, George 176, 184, 274, 275

Secrets (First National, 1924) 411, 414

Sedgwick, Edward 177, 225, 384

Seiderman, Maurice 9

Seiter, William A, 177, 311, 366, 384, 428

Seitz, George 105, 223, 225

Seitz, John 78, 183, 230, 276, 278, 281

Selander, Lesley 275, 311, 346, 383, 384

Selig Polyscope Company 16, 67

Selig, William 16, 18, 65, 67, 166

Sellers, Peter 94, 339, 343

Selter, William 275

Selzer, Eddie 99

Selznick, David 0, 17, 23, 35, 56–7, 58, 68, 192, 195, 201–2, 208, 223, 233, 241, 246, 288–9, 292, 298, 301, 305, 309, 325, 328, 329, 330, 333, 342, 345, 349, 430; Vanguard Films 290, 296, 325

Sennett, Mack 16, 28, 98, 322

Separate Tables (UA, 1958) 354

Seremenko, Serge 398

Sergeant York (Warner Bros, 1941) 57, 404, 413, 414, 419, 426, 427, 430, 431, 436

Sersen, Fred 181–2

Set-Up, The (RKO, 1949) 297

Seven Arts Productions 394, 398, 400

Seven Beauties (Lina Wertmuller, 1976) 94

Seven Brides For Seven Brothers (MGM, 1954) 211

Seven Days Leave (RKO, 1942) 295

Seven Year Itch, The (Fox, 1955) 61, 146, 161–2, 164, 169

Seventh Heaven (Fox, 1927) 55, 143, 150, 151, 160, 163, 166, 174, 180, 185

Seventh Sin, The (MGM, 1957) 223

Severed Head, A (Columbia, 1971) 120

Sewell, Blanche 231

Seymour, Dan 60

Shadow Of A Doubt (Universal, 1943) 383, 386

Shadow Of The Thin Man (MGM, 1941) 220

Shadow, The (Columbia, 1940) 113

Shaft (MGM, 1971) 200

Shall We Dance (RKO, 1937) 301

Shampoo (Columbia, 1975) 107, 120

Shamroy, Leon 145, 156, 157, 158, 178, 179, 183, 186, 281, 349, 351

Shane (Paramount, 1953) 253, 258, 260

Shanghai Express (Paramount, 1932) 277

Shanley, John Patrick 235

Sharaff, Irene 182, 229, 231, 316

Sharp, Henry 230, 281, 434

She Done Him Wrong (Paramount, 1933) 257, 259, 284

She (RKO, 1935) 301, 306

Shea, William 282

Shearer, Douglas 97, 204, 226, 230, 235

Shearer, Norma 37, 57, 196, 199, 201, 213, 215, 216, 219, 220, 233, 234

Sheehan, Winfield 142, 143, 147, 152, 154

Sheik, Son Of The (UA, 1926) 336

Sheik, The (Paramount, 1921) 54, 240, 255, 256, 259, 271

Shenandoah (Universal, 1965) 367, 373, 374

Shepherd Of The Hills (Paramount, 1941) 252

Sheridan, Ann 172, 269, 381, 420

Sherlock Holmes series (Universal) 366, 377

Sherman, George 131, 384

Sherman, Lowell 308, 311, 346

Sherman, Vincent 427, 428

Sherwood, Robert 352

Shilkret, Nathaniel 231, 33896

Shining, The (Warner Bros, 1980) 413

Shirley, Anne 172, 308

Shoeshine (Vittorio De Sica, 1947) 93

shorts 27–8, 99, 112–13, 145, 192, 200, 235, 248, 405–6
   see also cartoons

Shoup, Howard 231, 434

Show Boat (MGM, 1950) 209, 211

Show People (King Vidor, 1927) 19

Showboat (Universal, 1936) 359, 366, 378, 387

Shuken, Leo 282

Sidney, George 99, 131, 192, 202, 223, 225, 235

Sidney, Sylvia 96, 241, 251, 262, 270

Siegel, Don 99, 311, 382, 384, 406, 427, 428, 432

Sign Of The Cross, The (Paramount, 1932) 248

silent films 13–14, 75, 84 *see also* sound

Silent Movie 243

Sills, Milton 28, 172, 270

Silver Chalice, The (Warner Bros, 1954) 413

Silver Streak (Fox, 1976) 164

Silvers, Louis 135, 184, 231, 434

Silvers, Phil 172, 406

Silverstone, Murray 325

Simmons, Jean 172, 219, 308, 381

Simon, S. Sylvan 131, 225, 383, 384

Simon, S Sylvan 220

Simon, Simone 151, 172, 308

Simpson, Don 63, 259

Simpson, Robert 182, 184

Sin Of Madelon Claudet, The (MGM, 1932) 233

Sinatra, Frank 139, 216, 219, 306, 308

Sinbad The Sailor (RKO, 1947) 298, 314

Since You Went Away (UA, 1944) 325, 340, 342

Sinclair, Upton, *Upton Sinclair Presents William Fox* 160

Singin' in the Rain (MGM, 1952) 19

Singing Fool, The (Warner Bros, 1928) 45, 55, 397, 401, 402, 410, 411, 414, 418, 425

Sinner's Holiday (Warner Bros, 1930) 31

Siodmak, Curt 389

Siodmak, Robert 275, 296, 360, 382, 383, 384, 408

Sirk, Douglas 38, 131, 346, 361, 367, 368, 372, 382, 383–4, 387

Sister Kenny (RKO, 1946) 294, 302, 318

Six Of A Kind (Paramount, 1934) 273

Sjostrom, Victor 29, 191, 222, 225

Skelton, Red 219

Skiles, Marlin 135

Skinner, Frank 387, 389, 391

Skippy (Paramount, 1931) 284, 285

Skipworth, Alison 270

Skolsky, Sidney 83

Skouras, Spyros P. 145, 147, 162, 326

Slave Girl (Universal, 1947) 368

Slight Case Of Murder, A (Warner Bros, 1938) 425

Small, Edward 325, 349

Smalley, Phillips 377

Smart Woman (RKO, 1931) 294

Smilin' Thru (First National, 1922) 54, 411, 414

Smiling Lieutenant, The (Paramount, 1931) 249, 284

Smith, Albert 67

Smith, Frederick 231

Smith, Harold Jacob 99

Smith, Howard 282

Smith, Jack Martin 178, 181, 183, 187, 228, 230

Smith, James 282, 352

Smith, Kate 249

Smith, Kent 219, 308

Smith, Maggie 96, 186

Smith, Ted 432, 434

Smokey And The Bandit (Universal, 1977) 373, 374

Smokey And The Bandit II (Universal, 1980) 374

Smoky (Fox, 1946) 157, 161

Smouldering Fires (Universal, 1924) 366

Snake Pit, The (Fox, 1948) 161, 186

Snell, David 231

Snow White And The Seven Dwarfs (Disney, 1937) 35, 45, 57, 298, 299

Snows Of Kilimanjaro, The (Fox, 1952) 157, 164, 169

So This Is Love? (Columbia, 1928) 110

social themes, treatment of 89, 92–3, 145–6, 149, 153, 157, 175, 365, 401, 402–3

Sodom and Gomorrah (1962) 74

Solomon And Sheba (UA, 1959) 42, 334

Some Came Running (MGM, 1958) 42, 95, 204

Some Like It Hot (UA, 1959) 169–70, 332, 342

Son Of The Sheik, The (UA, 1926) 336

Sondergaard, Gale 95, 130, 172, 219, 270, 381

Song of Bernadette, The (Fox, 1943) 161, 163, 175, 180, 186

Song of Scheherazade (Universal, 1947) 368

Song To Remember, A (Columbia, 1945) 113, 115, 125

Song Without End (Columbia, 1960) 134

Sons And Lovers (Fox, 1960) 157

Sony Corporation 9, 52, 108, 109, 117, 123, 194, 361

Sony Pictures Entertainment (formerly Columbia) 108, 109

Sorrows Of Satan, The (Paramount, 1926) 257

Sothern, Ann 130, 219, 295

Soul Of Broadway, The (Fox, 1915) 150

Souls At Sea (Paramount, 1937) 248

sound 14–15, 18, 21, 26, 29, 75 at Columbia 134; at Fox 143, 150–2; at MGM 191–2, 207; at Paramount 241, 248–9; at

RKO 323–4; at UA 323–4; at Universal 365; at Warner Bros 395–6; and film music 82; and naturalism 29; stereo 157

Sound Of Music, The (Fox, 1965) 43, 61, 90, 93, 146, 147, 158, 159, 162, 170, 181–2, 185, 187

South Pacific (Fox, 1958) 43, 158, 162, 164, 179

Soylent Green (MGM, 1973) 200

Spacek, Sissy 355, 392

Spanish Main, The (RKO, 1945) 298, 302, 314

Spartacus (Universal, 1960) 42, 61, 74, 367, 369, 372, 374, 387, 391, 392

Spawn Of The North (Paramount, 1938) 248, 280

special effects 59, 82, 117, 181–2, 279–80, 313, 319, 385

Spellbound (UA, 1945) 325, 331, 337, 340, 342, 345, 350

Spencer, Dorothy 182, 184, 282, 352

Spencer, J. Russell 183

Spiegel, Sam 33, 59, 108, 109, 115, 119, 130

Spielberg, Steven 45, 62, 63, 64, 75, 86, 91, 109, 117, 120, 131, 187, 252, 361, 367, 370, 373, 384, 400, 414

Spies Like Us (Warner Bros, 1985) 414

Spigelglass, Leonard 389

Spiral Staircase, The (RKO/Vanguard) 296

Spitz, Leo 289, 292, 360

Spoor, George K. 67

Springtime In The Rockies (Fox, 1942) 155

Squaw Man, The (Paramount, 1914) 17, 53, 239, 243, 245, 247, 255–6

Stack, Robert 343, 380

Stage Door Canteen (UA, 1943) 340

Stage Door (RKO, 1937) 310, 318

Stage Struck (Paramount, 1925) 251

Stagecoach (UA, 1939) 156, 331, 345, 354

Stahl, John 156, 173, 175, 177, 225, 233, 365, 382, 383, 384, 391, 428

Stalag 17 (Paramount, 1953) 285

Stallings, Lawrence 232

Stallone, Sylvester 339, 341, 343, 346

Stanfill, Dennis C, 146, 147

Stanley Corporation of America (theatre chain) 399, 410, 411

Stanley and Livingstone (Fox, 1939) 56

Stanley, Robert 326

Stanwyck, Barbara 30, 37, 94, 110, 123–4, 128, 219, 250, 267, 270, 294, 304, 306, 307, 308, 337, 379, 403, 418, 425, 433

Star! (Fox, 1968) 43, 62, 158, 162, 170, 181

Star Is Born, A, (UA, 1937) 19, 35, 56, 68, 83, 92, 125, 333, 354; (Warner Bros, 1954) 19, 38, 83, 125, 401, 409, 413, 415, 421, 438; (Warner Bros, 1976) 415

star system 8–9, 23, 33–4, 66, 75–6, 112, 213, 214, 216–17, 264, 342

Star Trek: The Motion Picture (Paramount, 1979) 261

Star Trek II (Paramount, 1982) 260

Star Trek III (Paramount, 1983) 260

Star Trek IV (Paramount, 1986) 260

Star Trek series 257, 258

Star Wars (Fox, 1977) 25, 59, 62, 79, 146, 147, 154, 159, 163, 164, 187, 254

Star Wars trilogy (Fox) 25, 62

Stark Love (Paramount, 1926) 277

Stark, Ray 63, 120, 126

Starke, Pauline 172, 219

Starrett, Charles 113, 123, 124, 128

State Fair, (Fox, 1933) 161, 163, 166; (Fox, 1945) 161, 163

Steamboat Bill Jr (UA, 1928) 323

Steel Cavalry (MGM, 1941) 220

Steel, Dawn 108, 109

Steel Magnolias (Tri-Star, 1989) 121, 122

Steele, Gile 231, 281

Steenburgen, Mary 392

Steiger, Rod 90, 128, 308, 354, 355

Stein, Elliott 133

Stein, Jules 361, 372

Steiner, Max 60, 82, 229, 312, 314, 316, 318, 319, 351, 429, 433, 434, 436

Steinkamp, Fredric 231

Stell, Aaron 136, 389

Stella Dallas, (UA, 1925) 340, 345; (UA, 1937) 57, 330

Sten, Anna 342

Sternad, Rudolph 133, 135, 138, 180, 183

Sternberg, Josef von 29, 92, 112, 131, 240, 247, 249, 265, 271, 273, 275, 277, 284, 310

Stevens, George 38, 74, 75, 93, 129, 130, 131, 138, 242, 253, 258, 271, 274, 275, 295, 301, 309, 310, 311, 338–9, 438

Stevenson, Edward 183, 312, 315, 316, 434

Stevenson, Robert 311

Stewart, Donald Ogden 232

Stewart, James 76, 88, 94, 124, 128, 172, 215, 219, 234, 262, 267, 270, 361, 367, 368, 372, 373, 376, 379, 381, 383

Stiller, Mauritz 191, 222, 225, 275

Stine, Clifford 388

Sting, The (Universal, 1973) 63, 90, 361, 362, 370, 373, 374, 387, 390, 391, 392

Stir Crazy (Columbia, 1980) 122
Stockwell, Dean 219
Stolber, Dean 327
Stoll, George 231
Stoloff, Morris 134, 135, 138
Stone, Andrew L. 225, 275, 346
Stone, John 144, 152
Stone, LeRoy 282, 435
Stone, Lewis 219
Stone, Oliver 63, 86, 91, 93, 187, 374, 392
Stone, Peter 389
Stooges, The Three 113
stopmotion photography 82
Storaro, Vittorio 278
Story of Louis Pasteur, The (Warner Bros, 1936) 399, 402, 410, 433, 437
Story of Vernon and Irene Castle, The (RKO, 1939) 56, 289
Stossel, Ludvig 60
Stothart, Herbert 229, 231
Strada, La (1956) 93–4
Stradling, Harry, Jr 315
Stradling, Harry, Sr 230, 431, 434
Straight Way, The (Fox, 1916) 150
Strange Cargo (MGM, 1940) 211
Strange Love Of Martha Ivers, The (Paramount, 1946) 267
Stranger On The Third Floor, The (RKO, 1941) 296–7
Stranger, The (RKO, 1946) 296, 297
Strangers On A Train (Warner Bros, 1951) 405, 427
Strasberg, Lee 96
Strategic Air Command (Paramount, 1955) 254, 260, 267
Stratton Story, The (MGM, 1949) 211
Strawberry Blonde, The 114
Streep, Meryl 139, 355
Street Angel (Fox, 1928) 163, 166, 174, 185

Street Girl (RKO, 1929) 300
Street Scene (UA, 1931) 330
Streetcar Named Desire, A (Warner Bros, 1951) 33, 405, 422, 436, 438
Streisand, Barbra 120, 123, 126, 139, 170, 317
Strickling, Howard 24
Strike Up The Band (MGM, 1940) 209, 211
Stripes (Columbia, 1981) 122
Stroheim, Erich von 23, 29, 54, 69, 78, 191, 207, 223, 225, 226, 251, 257, 308, 359, 361, 366, 370, 377, 381, 382, 383, 384
Stromberg, Hunt 192, 221, 325, 337, 349
Struss, Karl 179, 276, 277, 281, 348, 351
Stuart, Gloria 172, 377, 381
studio system *see* star system
Sturges, John 131, 225, 345, 346
Sturges, Preston 19, 74, 92, 177, 224, 242, 250, 271, 274, 275, 282, 285, 365, 389
Submarine (Columbia, 1928) 105, 117, 123
Sudden Fear (RKO, 1952) 291, 318
Sudden Impact (Warner Bros, 1983) 416
Suddenly Last Summer (Columbia, 1959) 116, 121, 130
Suez (Fox, 1938) 56, 181–2
Sullavan, Margaret 215, 219, 234, 378, 381
Sullivan, C. Gardner 232, 282, 352
Sullivan, Frank 231, 352
Summer Holiday (MGM, 1948) 203, 209
Summer Place, A (Warner Bros, 1960) 415
Sunny Side Up (Fox, 1929) 55, 149, 152, 154, 160, 163, 174
Sunrise (Fox, 1927) 29, 143, 166, 174, 178–9, 180, 185, 348

Sunset Boulevard (Paramount, 1950) 19, 267, 274, 278, 280
SuperCinecolor 38
Superman series 398, 408, 412
Superman – The Movie (Warner Bros, 1978) 413
Superman II (Warner Bros, 1981) 413
Superman III (Warner Bros, 1983) 415
SuperScope 40, 42, 250, 293, 298–9
Suratt, Valeska 150
Surtees, Robert 227, 230, 235
Suspicion (RKO, 1941) 306, 309, 318
Sutherland, A. Edward 275, 311, 346, 384
Sutter's Gold (Universal, 1935) 359
Svengali (Warner Bros, 1931) 431, 436
Swanee River (Fox, 1939) 56, 155
Swanson, Gloria 29, 75, 240, 246, 247, 251, 262, 263, 264, 267, 270, 272, 277, 323, 324, 336, 341, 343, 347, 350, 353
Swarthout, Gladys 249
Sweeney, James 136
Sweet, Blanche 222, 270
Sweet Charity (Universal, 1969) 367, 387
Sweet Smell Of Success (UA, 1957) 332
Sweethearts (MGM, 1938) 155, 200, 210
Swerling, Jo 111, 136, 352
Swing Time (RKO, 1936) 314
Swink, Robert 282, 316
Swordsman, The (Columbia, 1947) 114
Sylbert, Richard 279
Sylvester the Cat 406
Sylvia Scarlett (RKO, 1936) 301
Syncopation (RKO, 1929) 299

takeovers and mergers 50–2
Tale Of Two Cities, A,

(Fox, 1917) 150; (MGM, 1935) 192

Tales of Manhattan (Fox, 1942) 181

Talk Of The Town, The (Columbia, 1942) 138

Tall Men, The (Fox, 1955) 162, 164

Tally, Thomas 16

Talmadge, Norma 30, 54, 75, 323, 324, 341, 343, 411

Taming Of The Shrew, The (UA, 1929) 323

Tamiroff, Akim 219, 270

Tandy, Jessica 96, 438

Tanen, Ned 243, 244, 362

Tango and Cash (Warner Bros, 1989) 416

Tap Roots (Universal, 1948) 374

Taradash, Daniel 136

Tarantula (Universal, 1955) 388

Tarnished Angels, The (Universal, 1957) 368

Tarzan films 215, 230, 290, 295

Tarzan The Ape Man (MGM, 1932) 210

Tarzan Triumphs (RKO, 1943) 296

Tarzan's Secret Treasure (MGM, 1941) 220

Tashlin, Frank 99, 136, 169, 177, 225, 274, 275, 283, 311, 406

Tati, Jacques 93

Taurog, Norman 92, 177, 220, 223, 225, 273, 274, 275, 285

Tavoulouris, Dean 279

Taxi! (Warner Bros, 1931) 403

Taxi Driver (Columbia, 1976) 87, 91, 120

Taylor, Elizabeth 95, 170, 202, 215, 216, 220, 235, 438

Taylor, Robert 192, 197, 215, 216, 220, 378

Taylor, Rod 220, 381

Taylor, Sam 177, 346

Taylor, William Desmond 264, 271

Teahouse Of The August

Moon, The (MGM, 1956) 211

Technicolor 7, 26, 34–8, 42, 56, 57, 110, 114, 154, 168, 181, 200–2, 245, 250, 251–2, 292, 297–8, 329, 332–3, 367–9, 406–8

Technicolor Corporation 34, 35, 42, 396

Technirama 40, 42, 58, 115, 204, 254, 334, 368–9, 409

Techniscope 254, 368–9

Teenage Rebel (Fox, 1956) 40, 157

television 15, 38, 49, 114, 393, 400
 awards 86–7; cable 39; co-productions 361, 372–3; and colour film 39; high-definition 15; subsidiaries of film companies 107, 398, 400

Temple, Shirley 98, 144, 152, 161, 165, 166, 167, 168, 172, 174, 249, 267, 307, 308, 342

Temptress, The (MGM, 1926) 222

Ten Commandments, The, (Paramount, 1923) 34, 54, 240, 243, 245, 246, 250, 256, 259, 279, 280; (Paramount, 1956) 7, 45, 244, 246, 256, 259, 262, 268, 272, 338

Ten Rillington Place (Columbia, 1971) 120

Tender Comrade (RKO, 1943) 296

Tennessee's Partner (RKO, 1955) 307

Terminator 2: Judgment Day (Tri-Star, 1991) 121, 122

Terms Of Endearment (Paramount, 1983) 91, 96, 260, 268, 286

Terry, Alice 213, 220, 270

Terry And The Pirates (Columbia, 1940) 113

Terry, Paul 145

Terrytoons (cartoons) 145

Tess Of The D'Urbervilles (MGM, 1924) 222

Tess Of The Storm Country (Famous Players, 1914) 239

Test Pilot (MGM, 1938) 210

Tetzlaff, Ted 135, 281, 310, 311

Texas Rangers, The (Paramount, 1936) 247

Texasville (Columbia, 1990) 122

Thalberg, Irving 54, 68, 83, 98, 189, 190–2, 195, 196, 206–7, 213, 214, 216, 221–2, 233, 289, 359, 361; Memorial Award 98, 234

Thalberg, Sylvia 214, 232

That Certain Thing (Columbia, 1927) 110

That Night In Rio (Fox, 1941) 156

That Touch Of Mink (Universal, 1962) 372, 374

That's Entertainment (MGM, 1974) 194, 212

Thau, Benny 192

theatre, relationship to Hollywood 30

theatre television 242

Theodora Goes Wild (Columbia, 1936) 112, 134

These Three (UA, 1936) 330

Thew, Harvey 436

They Died With Their Boots On (Warner Bros, 1941) 405, 426

They Knew What They Wanted (RKO, 1940) 306

They Live By Night (RKO, 1949) 297, 310

They Won't Forget (Warner Bros, 1937) 425

Thief Of Baghdad, The, (UA, 1924) 54, 330, 336, 340, 348, 350; (UA, 1940) 36, 333, 350

Thin Man, The (MGM, 1934) 199, 215

Thing From Another

World, The (RKO, 1951) 297

Things To Come (UA, 1936) 331

Thirty Seconds Over Tokyo (MGM, 1944) 211, 227

This Is Cinerama (1952) 40, 41

This Is The Army (Warner Bros, 1943) 408, 413, 414, 431

This Is The Life (Fox, 1917) 150

This Land Is Mine (RKO, 1944) 296

Thomas, Bill 387, 389, 391

Thomas, Danny 408

Thomas, Jeremy 108

Thomas, Lowell 40

Thomopoulos, Tony 327

Thompson, Walter 184

Thoms, Jerome 136

Thoroughbreds Don't Cry (MGM, 1937) 198

Thoroughly Modern Millie (Universal, 1967) 367, 373, 374, 391

Thorpe, Richard 224, 226

Thousand And One Nights, A (Columbia, 1945) 124, 125

Thousands Cheer (MGM, 1943) 201

Three Bad Men (Fox, 1926) 143, 151, 174

Three Coins In The Fountain (Fox, 1954) 153, 179, 187

Three Comrades (MGM, 1938) 235

Three Faces Of Eve, The (Fox, 1957) 186

Three Godfathers (MGM, 1948) 203

Three Little Pigs, The (Disney, 1933) 35

Three Live Ghosts (Paramount, 1921) 278

Three Musketeers, Ther (MGM, 1948) 203, 211; (UA, 1921) 330, 336

Three Ring Circus (Paramount, 1954) 253

Three Smart Girls (Universal, 1936) 366, 371, 391

3.10 to Yuma (Columbia, 1957) 115

Three Who Loved (RKO, 1931) 294

Thrill Of A Romance (MGM, 1945) 211

thrillers 32–3, 90–1, 113, 157, 197, 200, 248, 250, 258, 291, 296, 297, 332, 360, 382, 383, 405
 see also film noir; gangster films

Through Solid Walls (Universal, 1916) 366

Thunderball (UA, 1965) 340

Thunderbolt (Paramount, 1929) 247

Tibbett, Lawrence 200

Tierney, Gene 155, 156, 168, 172, 175

Tiger Shark (Warner Bros, 1932) 430

Till The Clouds Roll By (MGM, 1946) 209, 211

Time Warner Inc 52, 394, 399, 400

Tin Pan Alley (Fox, 1940) 186

Tiomkin, Dimitri 135, 231, 347, 350, 351

Titanic (Fox, 1953) 181

To Be Or Not To Be (UA, 1942) 331, 345

To Catch A Thief (Paramount, 1955) 254

To Each His Own (Paramount, 1946) 286

To Have And Have Not (Warner Bros, 1944) 405, 421, 426

To Hell And Back (Universal, 1955) 374

To Kill A Mockingbird (Universal, 1962) 372, 374, 392

To Sir, With Love (Columbia, 1967) 120, 121

To The Shores of Tripoli (Fox, 1942) 155

Toast Of New York, The (RKO, 1937) 295

Tobin, Genevieve 381

Todd, Mike 40, 42–3, 59, 329, 334, 338

Todd, Sherman 316, 352, 389

Todd-AO process 40, 42–3, 58–9, 115, 149, 158, 162, 179, 204, 329, 334

Toland, Gregg 8, 37, 92, 98, 296, 312–13, 315, 333, 347, 349, 351

Toler, Sidney 152

Toll of the Sea, The (Technicolor Corporation, 1922) 34

Toluboff, Alexander Wanger 230, 281, 349, 351

Tom and Jerry cartoons 192, 235

Tom Jones (UA, 1963) 90, 91, 93, 119, 338, 340, 345, 353, 355

Tom Sawyer (Famous Players-Lasky, 1917) 271

Tomasini, George 282

Tommy (Columbia, 1975) 120

Tone, Franchot 214, 220, 270, 381

Tonight And Every Night (Columbia, 1944) 126

Tootsie (Columbia, 1982) 63, 107, 117, 120, 122, 131

Top Gun (Paramount, 1986) 63, 255, 261

Top Hat (RKO, 1935) 289, 299, 314, 318

Topper series (UA) 331

Tora! Tora! Tora! (Fox, 1970) 62, 163, 164, 176, 181, 182

Torch Singer (Paramount, 1933) 249

Torch Song (MGM, 1953) 201

Torchy Blane series (Warner Bros) 405

Torn Curtain (Universal, 1966) 374

Torpedo Run (MGM, 1958) 204

Total Recall (Tri-Star, 1990) 121, 122

Totheroh, Rollie 348

Totter, Audrey 128, 220

Touch Of Class, A (1973) 96

Touch Of Evil (Universal, 1958) 367, 387

Touchstone (Disney) company 9, 45, 52

Tourneur, Jacques 192, 225, 310, 311, 408

Tourneur, Maurice 27, 65, 78, 180, 240, 272, 278

Tover, Leo 278, 281, 315

Towering Inferno (Fox/Warner Bros, 1975) 164, 413

Toy, The (Columbia, 1982) 122

Tracy, Dick, series 296

Tracy, Lee 172, 220, 270, 308

Tracy, Spencer 31, 36, 94, 167, 172, 202, 213, 215, 216, 220, 233, 234, 420

Trader Horn (MGM, 1930) 207, 210, 227

Trading Places (Paramount, 1983) 259, 260

Traffic In Souls (Universal 1913) 23, 53, 104, 358, 361, 365

Trail Of '98, The (MGM, 1927) 197

Trail Of The Lonesome Pine, The (Wanger/Paramount, 1936) 35, 155, 245, 251, 257, 259, 407

Transamerica Corporation 50, 321, 326–7, 328, 335, 339

Transatlantic (Fox, 1931) 180

Trapeze (UA, 1956) 338, 340

Travilla, William 135, 183, 434

Travolta, John 258, 268

Treason (Universal, 1917) 366

Treasure Of The Sierra Madre, The (Warner Bros, 1948) 405, 417, 427, 430, 436

Tree, Dolly 183, 231

Trent's Last Case (Fox, 1929) 173

Trespasser, The (UA, 1929) 353

Trevor, Claire 128, 172, 308

Tri-Star Pictures 9, 45, 51, 108, 109, 120–1

Trial Of Billy Jack, The (Warner Bros, 1974) 415

Triangle Film Corporation 17

Trilling, Steve 398

Troffey, Alex 184

Trotti, Lamar 184

Trouble With Harry, The (Paramount, 1955) 278

True Grit (Paramount, 1969) 260, 285

Truffaut, François 94

Trumbo, Dalton 99, 232, 310, 316, 319, 389

Trust, The *see* Motion Picture Patents Company

Tucker, George Loane 358

Tucker, Sophie 418

Tugboat Annie (MGM, 1933) 210

Tugend, Harry 184

Tumbleweeds (UA, 1925) 257, 323, 330

Turner, Kathleen 187

Turner, Lana 33, 198, 199, 215, 216, 220, 361, 372, 379, 381

Turner, Ted 39, 194, 195, 327, 328

Turney, Catherine 435

Turning Point, The (Fox, 1977) 187

Tuttle, Frank 273, 275, 428

Twelve Angry Men (UA, 1957) 89, 332

Twelve O'Clock High (Fox, 1949) 169, 175, 186

Twelvetrees, Helen 172, 294, 308

Twentieth Century (Columbia, 1934) 112, 130

Twentieth Century-Fox *see* Fox

Twentieth Century Pictures 9, 141, 144, 147, 324, 337, 398 *see also* Fox

20,000 Leagues Under the Sea (Universal, 1916) 363

Twins (Universal, 1988) 373, 375

Twist, John 316

Two Arabian Nights (UA, 1927) 345, 353

Two Cities (British production company) 366

Two Mules For Sister Sara (Universal, 1970) 367, 379

2001: A Space Odyssey (MGM, 1968) 62, 200, 205, 209, 211

Two Weeks In Another Town (MGM, 1962) 223

Two Years Before The Mast (Paramount, 1946) 259

Two-Faced Woman (MGM, 1941) 220

Tycoon (RKO, 1947) 298, 303

Typhoon (Paramount, 1940) 252

Uhry, Alfred 438

Ulmer, Edgar 346, 365

Uncommon Valor (Paramount, 1983) 261

Unconquered (Paramount, 1946) 248, 253, 259

Under Capricorn (Warner Bros, 1949) 33, 408, 427

Under Two Flags (Universal, 1922) 366

Underwater (RKO 1955) 298, 299

Underworld (Paramount, 1927) 247

Underworld USA (Columbia, 1961) 133

Unforgiven, The (UA, 1960) 350

Unholy Partners (MGM, 1941) 220

Union Pacific (Paramount, 1938) 248

unions *see* labour relations

United Artists 7, 9, 17, 32, 33, 44, 46, 47, 49, 50, 51, 52, 56–7, 239, 321–55
    finances 335–40; history.75, 322–8; and independents 66 and introduction of colour 298, 332–4; musicals 331, 332–3; Oscars 353–5; takeover of 194; Westerns 350

United Artists Theater Corporation 336

United States, domination of film industry 14, 45, 50, 67

Universal 7, 9, 17, 23, 32, 33, 37–8, 44, 46, 47, 49, 51, 52, 64, 357–92 finances 370–6; history 358–62; and introduction of colour 367–9; musicals 366, 382; Oscars 390–2 Westerns 363, 365, 366–7, 377, 382

Universal City, California 18, 358–9, 361, 365

Universal Weekly (newsreel) 104

Untouchables, The (Paramount, 1987) 262, 284

Up In Arms (RKO, 1944) 298

Up In Smoke (Paramount, 1978) 260

Up The River (Fox, 1930) 31, 420

Urban, Charles 16

Urban Cowboy (Paramount, 1980) 260

Urban, Joseph 183, 230, 308

Usher, Robert 279, 281

Ustinov, Peter 392

Vagabond King, The (Paramount, 1930) 251

Vagabond Lover, The (RKO, 1929) 300

Vajda, Ernest 232, 283

Valentine, Joseph 183, 386, 388, 391

Valentino, Rudolph 14, 28, 54, 190, 240, 256, 262, 263, 270, 271, 323, 336, 341, 343, 377, 381, 383

Vallee, Rudy 172, 252, 270, 300, 308

Valles (costume designer) 231, 391

Valley Of Decision, The (MGM, 1945) 211

Valley Of The Dolls (Fox, 1967) 162, 164, 181

Valley Of The Giants

(Warner Bros, 1937) 35

Van Dyke, W.S. 'Woody' 150, 177 220, 222, 225, 226

Van Enger, Charles 183, 386, 388

Van Upp, Virginia 115, 132, 134, 136

Vanguard Films 296, 325; see also Selznick, David O.

Vanishing American, The (Paramount, 1925) 247

vaudeville acts 27

Veidt, Conrad 60, 220, 366, 381

Veiller, Anthony 316, 352

Velez, Lupe 220, 295, 308, 381

Vengeance (Columbia, 1930) 123

Venice Film Festival 437

Vera Cruz (UA, 1954) 40, 338

Vera-Ellen 172, 220, 308

Verdict, The (Columbia, 1982) l48

Vernon, Elmo 231

Vertigo (Paramount, 1958) 254, 267, 279, 280

Victor/Victoria (MGM, 1982) 200

video 15, 22, 39, 51

Vidor, Charles 106, 114, 125, 130, 131, 225, 275, 311

Vidor, King 19, 29, 36, 69, 92, 191, 197, 202, 206–7, 220, 221, 222–3, 225, 234, 247, 264, 275, 334, 367, 428

Viertel, Salka 232

Vigil In The Night (RKO, 1939) 310

Vignola, Robert 272

Viking, The (Technicolor/MGM, 1928) 200

Vikings The (UA, 1958) 42

Virginian, The (Paramount, 1914) 247; (Paramount, 1929) 247, 272

Visart, Natalie 282

VistaVision 7, 40, 42, 49, 58–9, 99, 242, 244, 245, 250, 252–3, 368–9, 409

Vitagraph Company 16, 18, 67

Vitaphone Corporation 395, 399

Vitaphone sound-on-disc process 395–6, 411

Vitarama 40–1

Vogues of 1938 (UA, 1938) 35, 37, 333

Voltaire (Warner Bros, 1933) 403

Vukotic, Dusan 100

Wachner, Sophie 183, 231

Wadleigh, Mike 100

Wagner, Robert 172

Waikiki Wedding (Paramount, 1937) 257

Wait Until Dark (Warner Bros, 1967) 415

Wakeling, Gwen 115, 182, 183, 282, 316, 351

Walburn, Raymond 112

Wald, Jerry 291

Walk In The Sun, A (Fox, 1945) 145, 175

Walker, Alexander, "The Shattered Silents" 151–2

Walker, Hal 274, 275

Walker, Joe 105, 117, 125, 132, 135, 138

Walker, Robert 220

Walker, Stuart 275, 384

Walker, Vernon 9

Walking Dead, The (Warner Bros, 1936) 432

Wall Street (Fox, 1987) 187

Wallace, Richard 131, 275, 311

Waller, Fred 40–1

Wallis, Hal B. 23, 60, 68, 267–8, 395, 397, 399, 400

Walsh, George 150, 172

Walsh, Raoul 29, 83, 142, 143, 150, 151, 160, 166, 173, 174, 177, 180, 275, 344, 368, 404, 405, 424, 426, 427, 428, 432

Walters, Charles 223, 225

Walthall, Henry B. 417

Wanderer Of The Wasteland (Paramount, 1924) 34, 250–1

Wanger, Walter 35, 68, 215, 240, 251, 325, 330, 333, 337, 345, 349

War And Peace
(Paramount, 1956)
254, 260

war films 28–9, 92, 246,
247, 293, 295–6, 366,
394, 401, 404, 413, 426

War Game, The (Peter
Watkins, 1966) 100

War Games (UA,
1983) 340

War Lord, The (Universal,
1965) 367

*War Of The Roses,
The* (Fox, 1989) 163,
164, 187

War Wagon, The
(Universal, 1967) 374

Warburton, Irvine 231

Ward, David S. 392

Ward, Edward 231,
351, 389

Ward, Fannie 246

Warner, Albert 394,
398, 400

Warner Bros 7, 8, 9, 18,
20, 21, 22, 23, 28, 29,
30, 32, 34, 37, 46–7, 49,
50, 51, 52, 55, 56, 64,
393–438; finances 410–6;
history 68, 394–400; and
introduction of colour
405, 406–9; and
introduction of sound
395–6; musicals
402; Oscars 436–8;
social themes 402–3;
Westerns 405

Warner Bros Presents
(TV) 398

Warner Communications
Inc. 393, 398–9, 400,
410, 414

Warner, Harry 83, 394,
396, 398, 400, 402,
410, 420

Warner, Jack 68, 83, 393,
394, 395, 396, 397, 398,
399, 400, 403, 407, 418,
419, 420, 426, 427, 438

Warner, Sam 394, 395,
396, 399

WarnerPhonic (stereo
sound process) 409

Warren, Eda 282

Warren, Harry 429, 432–3

Wasserman, Lew 50, 361,
362, 372, 373

Watch On The Rhine
(Warner Bros, 1943) 438

Waters, Ethel 418

Watkins, Peter 100

Watt, Harry 98

Waxman, Franz 231, 280,
389, 434

Way Down East (UA,
1920) 54, 336, 340

Way Of All Flesh, The
(Paramount, 1927)
271, 283

Way We Were, The
(Columbia, 1973) 63,
120, 122, 131

Wayne, John 76, 128, 152,
154, 172, 268, 285,
296, 303, 304, 308, 326,
334, 345, 381, 405, 417,
421, 422

We Were Dancing (MGM,
1941) 220

Weatherwax, Paul 184,
282, 316, 391

Weaver, Sigourney 200

Webb, Clifton 168, 172

Webb, Ira 391

Webb, Roy 314, 316, 319

Weber, Lois 275, 377,
382, 384

Webster, Ferris 231, 352

Wedding March, The
(Paramount, 1928) 29,
251, 257

Wee Willie Winkie (Fox,
1937) 166, 174

Weekend At The Waldorf
(MGM, 1945) 211

Weekend In Havana (Fox,
1941) 156

Weingarten, Laurence
220, 234

Weis, Don 225

Weisbart, David 435

Weissmuller, Johnny 19,
128, 215, 220, 295,
306, 308

Welch, Raquel 170

Welcome Stranger
(Paramount, 1947) 259

Welles, Orson 8, 37, 74,
77, 92, 98, 119, 124,
129, 172, 224, 292, 295,
296–7, 298, 302, 308,
309, 310, 311; Mercury
Productions 291,
297, 306

Wellman, William 92, 150,
173, 177, 225, 241, 271,
273, 275, 345, 346, 409,
424, 426, 427, 428

Wells Fargo (Paramount,
1937) 247, 257, 259

We're In The Navy Now
(Paramount, 1926) 250

Werewolf Of London, The
(Universal, 1935) 367

Werker, Alfred L. 177, 275

Wertmuller, Lina 94

West, Billy 104

West, Claire 280, 282

West, Claudine 232

West, Mae 241, 245,
247, 248, 257, 262,
265–6, 270, 273, 277,
280, 284

West, Roland 330, 346

West Side Story (UA,
1961) 93, 334, 338, 340,
353, 355

West, Vera 82, 387, 389

Westerner, The (UA, 1940)
331, 350

Westerns 16, 17, 23, 27,
31, 32, 34, 36, 37, 123
        Columbia 113;
        Fox 151–2, 153,
        156, 166, 168;
        MGM 197, 199;
        and Oscars 91;
        Paramount 245,
        247–8, 256–7; RKO
        294; United Artists
        350; Universal
        363, 365, 366–7,
        377, 382; Warner
        Bros 405

Westmore, Bud 82,
385, 387–8

Westmore, Ern 82, 181

Westmore, Frank,
        *The Westmores Of
        Hollywood* 388

Westmore, Perc 60,
114, 433

Westworld (MGM,
1973) 200

Weyl, Carl Jules 60, 429,
432, 434, 436

Whale, James 31, 345, 366,
382, 383, 384

What Price Glory? (Fox,
1926) 28, 55, 143, 160,
163, 166, 174

What Price Hollywood? (George Cukor, 1932) 19

Whatever Happened To Baby Jane? (Warner Bros, 1962) 74, 430

What's New Pussycat? (UA, 1966) 343

What's Up Doc? (Warner Bros, 1972) 415

Wheeler, Lyle 178, 180, 181, 183, 187, 201, 230, 349

Wheeler and Woolsey (comedy team) 293, 300, 301

When Harry Met Sally (Columbia, 1989) 117, 121, 122

When Knighthood Was In Flower (Cosmopolitan, 1922) 54

When Tomorrow Comes (Universal, 1939) 383

Where Are My Children? (Universal, 1916) 377

Where The North Begins (Warner Bros, 1923) 417

Where The Sidewalk Ends (Fox, 1950) 175

While Paris Sleeps (Fox, 1932) 180

While The City Sleeps (RKO, 1956) 297

White, Alice 418

White Christmas (Paramount, 1954) 40, 42, 59, 242, 244, 253, 260

White, George 231

White Heat (Warner Bros, 1949) 405, 426, 432

White, Jules 112, 138

White, Merrill 184, 282, 316, 352

White, Pearl 172

White Shadows In The South Seas (MGM, 1929) 227

Whitmore, James 220

Whitney, Clare 142

Whitney, John Hay 297, 333

Who Framed Roger Rabbit (Disney/Buena Vista, 1988) 52, 62

Whole Town's Talking, The (Columbia, 1935) 112, 124, 129, 132

Whoopee! (UA, 1930) 55, 327, 330, 335, 339

Who's Afraid Of Virginia Woolf? (Warner Bros, 1966) 39, 413, 415, 438

Why Change Your Wife? (Paramount, 1920) 256

Whytock, Grant 231, 352

widescreen and 3-D 7, 116 at Columbia 115–16; at Fox 154, 157–8; at MGM 203–5; at Paramount 250, 253–4; at RKO 298–9; at United Artists 334; at Universal 368–9; at Warner Bros 407

Widmark, Richard 168, 172

Wilbur, Crane 406, 435

Wilcox, Fred M. 225

Wilcox, Harvey Henderson 16

Wilcox, Herbert 325, 330, 345

Wild Boys Of The Road (Warner Bros, 1933) 426

Wild Bunch, The (Warner Bros, 1969) 432

Wild Is The Wind (Paramount, 1957) 254

Wild North, The (MGM, 1952) 40, 203

Wild Party, The (Paramount, 1929) 264

Wilde, Cornel 113, 114, 115, 118, 125, 128, 172

Wilder, Billy 19, 38, 74, 89, 91, 92, 169, 215, 224, 242, 250, 253, 267, 271, 274, 275, 278, 283, 285, 326, 332, 338, 339, 344, 345, 346, 347, 349, 355

Wiles, Gordon 180

Wiley, Harrison 135

Will Success Spoil Rock Hunter? (Fox, 1957) 169

Willat, Irvin 273

Willes, Jean 127

William, Warren 127, 221, 271, 416, 418

Williams, Elmo 316

Williams, Esther 150, 214, 221, 358

Williams, Richard 100

Williams, Tennessee 130

Willis, Bruce 121

Willis, Edwin B 231

Willow (MGM, 1988) 214

Wills, Mary 316

Wilson, Carey 83, 206, 232, 233

Wilson, Dooley 60

Wilson, Lois 272

Wilson, Michael 99

Wilson (Fox, 1944) 145, 149, 155, 157, 175, 181, 182

Wimperis, Arthur 352

Winchester '73 (Universal, 1950) 37, 372, 374, 379

Wind, The (MGM, 1928) 29, 191, 197, 222

Windust, Bretaigne 428

Wings (Paramount, 1927) 29, 88, 241, 244, 245, 247, 257, 273, 279, 284

Wings Of The Morning (Fox, 1936) 35, 144, 154–5, 407

Wings Of The Navy (Warner Bros, 1938) 404

Winning (Universal, 1969) 374

Winters, Ralph 231, 352

Winters, Shelley 125–6, 128, 220, 343, 378, 381

Wise, Robert 38, 41, 74, 93, 176, 177, 181, 182, 187, 225, 297, 309, 310, 311, 312, 314, 316, 334, 344, 346

Wistful Widow Of Wagon Gap, The (Universal, 1947) 360, 374

Witches Of Eastwick, The (Warner Bros, 1987) 414

With A Song In My Heart (Fox, 1952) 182

Withers, Jane 167, 172

Witness For The Prosecution (UA, 1957) 89, 332

Wizard Of Oz, The (MGM, 1939) 9, 19, 35–6, 57, 195, 196, 200–1, 210, 229, 230, 375

Woman At The Window, The (RKO, 1944) 297

Woman Of Experience, A (RKO, 1931) 294

Woman Of The Year (MGM, 1941) 220

Women In Love (UA, 1970) 96, 355
women's pictures 156, 223, 293, 294, 305, 367, 377–8, 382, 383
Wonderful World Of The Brothers Grimm, The (MGM, 1962) 199
Wood, Natalie 172, 209, 422
Wood, Sam 221, 222, 272, 275, 311, 346
Wood, Yvonne 183, 389
Woods, Frank 83
Woodstock (Warner Bros, 1970) 100, 415
Woodward, Joanne 95, 170, 172, 186
Woody Woodpecker cartoons 359
Woolley, Monty 342
Work, Cliff 360
World In His Arms, The (Universal, 1952) 368
Woulfe, Michael 312, 315, 316
Wrangell, Basil 231, 316
Wray, Fay 128, 270, 305, 308, 381
Wright, Joseph C. 135, 180, 181, 183, 230, 389
Wright, Maurice 136, 352, 389
Wright, Teresa 308
Writers Guild of America 87
Written On The Wind (Universal, 1956) 374, 391–2
Wurtzel, Sol 32, 143, 144, 152
Wuthering Heights (UA, 1939) 89, 330, 349, 354
Wyckoff, Alvin 78, 276, 277, 281
Wyler, William 37, 74, 75, 89, 92, 93, 120, 235, 242, 253, 267, 271, 274,
275, 326, 344, 345, 346, 365, 382–3, 384, 426
Wyman, Jane 303, 318, 361, 372, 379, 405, 420, 438
Wynn, Hugh 231
Wynn, Keenan 220

Yablans, Frank 244
Yankee Doodle Dandy (Warner Bros, 1942) 235, 404, 405, 413, 414, 424, 425, 432, 436–7
Yarbrough, Jean 384
Year Of Living Dangerously, The (MGM, 1983) 200
Yearling, The (MGM, 1946) 202, 211
Yes, Giorgio (MGM, 1982) 209
Yolanda And The Thief (MGM, 1945) 209
Yost, Dorothy 316
You Can't Take It With You (Columbia, 1938) 56, 88, 108, 118, 121, 130, 137, 138
You Only Live Once (UA, 1937) 331
You Only Live Twice (UA, 1967) 340
You Were Never Lovelier (Columbia, 1942) 118
Young Dr Kildare (MGM, 1938) 198
Young Frankenstein (Fox, 1974) 164
Young, Gig 220
Young, Harold 275, 384
Young, Loretta 95, 124, 128, 144, 154, 155, 167, 172, 308, 318, 343, 418
Young Man With Ideas (MGM, 1952) 228–9
Young Mr Lincoln (Fox, 1939) 145, 156, 167
Young, Ned 99

Young People (Fox, 1940) 168
Young, Robert 220, 306–7, 308
Young, Roland 172, 220, 270, 331, 343
Young, Victor 276, 280, 282
Young, Waldemar 232, 283, 389
Youngson, Robert 406

Z (Costa-Gavras, 1969) 93
Zabriskie Point (MGM, 1969) 209
Zanuck, Darryl F., and 20th Century Pictures 328, 337, 398; at Warner Bros 396, 399, 402, 417, 419, 435; control of Fox 56, 66, 68, 144–9, 161, 167, 170, 174–5, 289, 350; interest in colour 152–3, 181; as producer 98, 162; and United Artists 321, 324
Zanuck, Richard 63, 66, 146, 147, 170
Zeffirelli, Franco 286
Zelig (Woody Allen, 1983) 39
Ziegfeld, Florenz 300
Ziegfeld Follies (MGM, 1946) 202, 209, 211
Ziegler, William 282, 352, 435
Zinnemann, Fred 38, 99, 129, 130, 131, 139, 192, 225, 235
Zoo In Budapest (Fox, 1933) 180
Zorina, Vera 333
Zuckerman, George 389
Zugsmith, Albert 361
Zukor, Adolph 20, 45–6, 65, 66, 67, 190, 237, 238–40, 241, 242, 243, 244, 256, 262–3, 322, 360

A Selected List of Non-Fiction Available from Mandarin

While every effort is made to keep prices low, it is sometimes necessary to increase prices at short notice. Mandarin Paperbacks reserves the right to show new retail prices on covers which may differ from those previously advertised in the text or elsewhere.

The prices shown below were correct at the time of going to press.

☐ 7493 0109 0	**The Warrior Queens**	Antonia Fraser	£4.99
☐ 7493 0108 2	**Mary Queen of Scots**	Antonia Fraser	£5.99
☐ 7493 0010 8	**Cromwell**	Antonia Fraser	£7.50
☐ 7493 0106 6	**The Weaker Vessel**	Antonia Fraser	£5.99
☐ 7493 0014 0	**The Demon Drink**	Jancis Robinson	£4.99
☐ 7493 0016 7	**Vietnam – The 10,000 Day War**	Michael Maclear	£3.99
☐ 7493 0061 2	**Voyager**	Yeager/Rutan	£3.99
☐ 7493 0113 9	**Peggy Ashcroft**	Michael Billington	£3.99
☐ 7493 0177 5	**The Troubles**	Mick O'Connor	£4.99
☐ 7493 0004 3	**South Africa**	Graham Leach	£3.99
☐ 7493 0254 2	**Families and How to Survive Them**	Creese/Skynner	£5.99
☐ 7493 0060 4	**The Fashion Conspiracy**	Nicolas Coleridge	£3.99
☐ 7493 0179 1	**The Tao of Pooh**	Benjamin Hoff	£2.99
☐ 7493 0000 0	**Moonwalk**	Michael Jackson	£2.99

All these books are available at your bookshop or newsagent, or can be ordered direct from the publisher. Just tick the titles you want and fill in the form below.

Mandarin Paperbacks, Cash Sales Department, PO Box 11, Falmouth, Cornwall TR10 9EN.

Please send cheque or postal order, no currency, for purchase price quoted and allow the following for postage and packing:

UK	80p for the first book, 20p for each additional book ordered to a maximum charge of £2.00.
BFPO	80p for the first book, 20p for each additional book.
Overseas including Eire	£1.50 for the first book, £1.00 for the second and 30p for each additional book thereafter.

NAME (Block letters) ....

ADDRESS ....

....

....